Formal and Practical Aspects of Autonomic Computing and Networking:

Specification, Development, and Verification

Phan Cong-Vinh
NTT University, Vietnam

Managing Director:	Lindsay Johnston
Senior Editorial Director:	Heather Probst
Book Production Manager:	Sean Woznicki
Development Manager:	Joel Gamon
Development Editor:	Joel Gamon
Acquisitions Editor:	Erika Gallagher
Typesetters:	Jennifer Romanchak
Print Coordinator:	Jamie Snavely
Cover Design:	Nick Newcomer

Published in the United States of America by
Information Science Reference (an imprint of IGI Global)
701 E. Chocolate Avenue
Hershey PA 17033
Tel: 717-533-8845
Fax: 717-533-8661
E-mail: cust@igi-global.com
Web site: http://www.igi-global.com

Library of Congress Cataloging-in-Publication Data

Formal and practical aspects of autonomic computing and networking: specification, development, and verification / Phan Cong-Vinh, editor.
    p. cm.
  Includes bibliographical references and index.
  Summary: "This book outlines the characteristics, novel approaches of specification, refinement, programming and verification associated with automated computing and networking"--Provided by publisher.
  ISBN 978-1-60960-845-3 (hardcover) -- ISBN 978-1-60960-846-0 (ebook) -- ISBN 978-1-60960-847-7 (print & perpetual access) 1. Autonomic computing. 2. Computer networks. 3. Formal methods (Computer science) I. Cong-Vinh, Phan.
  QA76.9.A97F67 2012
  004--dc23
                              2011025143

British Cataloguing in Publication Data
A Cataloguing in Publication record for this book is available from the British Library.

Table of Contents

Section 1
Formal and Practical Aspects of Autonomic Computing

Foreword

The overall goal of Autonomic Computing and Networking (ACN) is to provide a possible solution for modern computing and networking systems, which can manage themselves without direct human interventions. Tackling this huge challenge demands a rigorous interdisciplinary approach. The paradigm of ACN has widely attracted attention from researchers in the field of autonomics'. Unfortunately, there is no book specifically focused on formal specification and verification aspects of ACN.

Formal and Practical Aspects of Autonomic Computing and Networking: Specification, Development and Verification is one of the salient documents for disseminating research results related to formal specification and verification of ACN. It contains original, peer-reviewed chapters reporting on new developments of interest to both the autonomics and formal methods communities in all remarkable topics of ACN. The major technical contents of the book include the following: rigorous interdisciplinary approaches to software architectures for ACN, resource sharing in ACN, autonomic middleware, swarm intelligence in ACN, self-* in ACN, architectures and topologies for ACN, ACN and autonomic communications, bio-inspired ACN, ACN for cognitive networks, ACN for P2P, Grid, ad hoc and sensor networks, and ACN for multi-agent systems; calculi for reasoning about behavior in ACN; methods and tools for ACN design and ACN component design; applications of formal methods in ACN development; formalizing languages that enable ACN; validation and verification techniques for ACN.

Although the emphasis of this work is on formal specification, development and verification of autonomic computing and networking, it contains very much content that will be of interest to those outside this field. More precisely, the book includes a fine collection of chapters emphasizing the multidisciplinary character of investigations from the point of view of not only the autonomics field involved but also the formal methods.

This book will usefully serve as a technical guide and reference material for computer science and computer engineering researchers and scientists as well as designers and developers in computing and networking systems by providing them with state-of-the-art research results and future opportunities and trends. To the best of my knowledge, this is the first book that presents achievements and findings of ACN research covering the full spectrum of formalizing ACN. These make the book unique and, in more than one respect, a truly valuable source of information that may be considered a landmark in the progress of ACN. Congratulations to the authors who have contributed to the highest technical quality of the book!

M. Bakhouya
Aalto University, Finland

Preface

A new computing and networking paradigm is currently on the spot as one of the priority research areas, and its research activities are booming recently: autonomic computing and networking (ACN), which are inspired by the human autonomic nervous system. ACN are characterized by their self-* facets such as self-organization, self- configuration, self-healing, self-optimization, self-protection, and so on, whose context-awareness used to dynamically control computing and networking functions.

The overarching goal of ACN is to realize computing and networking systems, which can manage themselves without direct human interventions. Meeting this grand challenge of ACN requires a rigorous approach to ACN and the notion of self-*. To this end, taking advantage of formal methods, in this book, we establish formal and practical aspects of ACN through specifying, refining, programming, and verifying ACN and their self-*. All of these are to achieve foundations and practice of ACN.

From the above characteristics, novel approaches of specification, refinement, programming, and verification are arising in formal methods for ACN. Therefore, new methodologies, programming models, tools, and techniques are imperative to deal with the impact of ACN and their self-* mentioned above on emerging computing and networking systems.

This book is preferred to be a reference material for readers who already have a basic understanding of ACN and are now ready to know how to specify, develop, and verify ACN using rigorous approaches. Hence, the book includes both theoretical contributions and reports on applications. For keeping a reasonable trade-off between theoretical and practical issues, a careful selection of the chapters was completed, on the one hand, to cover a broad spectrum of formal and practical aspects, and on the other hand, to achieve as much as possible a self-contained book.

Formal and practical aspects will be presented in a straightforward fashion by discussing the necessary components in detail and briefly touching on the more advanced components. Therefore, specification, development, and verification demonstrating how to use the formal methods for ACN will be described by sound judgments and reasonable justifications.

This book, with chapters contributed by prominent researchers from academia and industry, will serve as a technical guide and reference material for researchers, scientists, professionals, and students in computer science and computer engineering as well as developers and practitioners in computing and networking systems design by providing them with state-of-the-art research findings and future opportunities and trends. These contributions include formal approaches and applications in ACN. In particular, the book covers existing and emerging research issues in the formal methods for ACN.

The book has 13 chapters organized into two sections. The first section contains six chapters addressing formal and practical aspects of autonomic computing. The second section consists of seven chapters presenting formal and practical aspects of autonomic networking.

SECTION 1: FORMAL AND PRACTICAL ASPECTS
OF AUTONOMIC COMPUTING

This section includes Chapters 1-6 and covers various topics on formal and practical aspects of autonomic computing.

Chapter 1, by R. Calinescu et al., discusses ways in which rigorous mathematical techniques, termed formal methods, can be employed to improve the predictability and dependability of autonomic computing. Model checking, formal specification, and quantitative verification are presented in the contexts of conflict detection in autonomic computing policies, and of implementation of goal and utility-function policies in autonomic IT systems, respectively.

Chapter 2, by E. Vassev, presents ASSL (Autonomic System Specification Language), an initiative for self-management of complex systems whereby the problem of formal specification, validation, and code generation of autonomic systems is approached within a framework. Being a formal method dedicated to autonomic computing, ASSL helps developers with problem formation, system design, system analysis and evaluation, and system implementation. As part of the framework's proof-of-concept strategy, ASSL has been used to make a variety of existing and prospective systems autonomic.

Chapter 3, by A. Manzalini et al., presents the main concepts of an autonomic communications toolkit designed and developed in the EU project CASCADAS for creating and supervising service networking ecosystems, structured as ensembles of distributed and cooperating autonomic components. Moreover, it describes several use-cases developed for its validation and demonstration and reports the experimental results to assess the toolkit performances.

Chapter 4, by C. Anagnostopoulos et al., discusses the application of particle swarm intelligence in autonomic computing and networking. Basic concepts and definitions of particle swarm intelligence are mapped to autonomic computing, and contextual information exploration (detection, discovery, and exploitation) is investigated in autonomous dynamic environments.

Chapter 5, by H. S. Venkatarama et al., discusses simulation environments to implement approaches to automate the tuning of MaxClients parameter of Apache web server using fuzzy controllers. These are illustrations of the self-optimizing characteristic of an autonomic computing system.

Chapter 6, by L. Ferariu et al., discusses the features of genetic programming based identification approaches. In the context of complex identification problems, genetic programming brings some important benefits which basically refer to its inherent capacity of self-organizing the models, without restrictive working hypothesis.

SECTION 2: FORMAL AND PRACTICAL ASPECTS
OF AUTONOMIC NETWORKING

This section consists of Chapters 7–13, with a focus on formal and practical aspects of autonomic networking and communications.

Chapter 7, by P.C. Vinh, is a reference material for readers who already have a basic understanding of the mobile environments (MEs) for their applications and are now ready to know how to specify and verify formally aspect-oriented self-configuring P2P networking (ASPN) in MEs using categorical language, assured that their computing needs are handled correctly and efficiently. ASPN in MEs is presented in a straightforward fashion by discussing in detail the necessary components and briefly touching on the more advanced components. Several explanatory notes and examples are represented throughout the chapter as a moderation of the formal descriptions. Significant properties of ASPN in MEs, which emerge from the specification, create the firm criteria for verification.

Chapter 8, by S. Hallé et al., discusses self-configuration from a mathematical logic point of view. In contrast with imperative means of generating configurations, characterized by scripts and templates, the use of declarative languages such as propositional or first-order logic is argued. In that setting, device configurations become models of particular logical formulae, which can be generated using constraint solvers without any rigid scripting or user intervention.

Chapter 9, by C.S. Sahin et al., presents a topology control mechanism based on genetic algorithms (GAs) within a mobile ad hoc network (MANET). Formal and practical aspects of convergence properties of the force-based genetic algorithm, called FGA, are discussed. Within this framework, FGA is used as a decentralized topology control mechanism among active running software agents to achieve a uniform spread of autonomous mobile nodes over an unknown geographical terrain. FGA can be treated as a dynamical system in order to provide formalism to study its convergence trajectory in the space of possible populations.

Chapter 10, by V. Vlassov et al., introduces Niche, a general-purpose distributed component management system used to develop, deploy, and execute self-managing distributed applications. Niche consists of both a component-based programming model as well as a distributed runtime environment. It is especially designed for complex distributed applications that run and manage themselves in dynamic and volatile environments.

Chapter 11, by G. Rétvári et al., presents a practical guideline for building truly autonomic systems. This idea is demonstrated by an example of building advanced self-adaptive routing mechanisms on top of Open Shortest Path First (OSPF) routing protocol.

Chapter 12, by J. Antoniou, addresses enhanced Session Management (SM) for multiparty communications, i.e. how to set up and modify a multi-party session that may respond to context changes and adapt to satisfy the users of a service group. By using the users' situation information, i.e. environment and network context, the chapter illustrates ways to provide more accurate sessions for mobile communities.

Chapter 13, by U. Mir, provides an overview of using multiagent systems over cognitive radio networks for dynamic spectrum sharing. In this work, avoiding unnecessary spectrum wastage problem requires performing the sharing and allocation functions opportunistically. In accordance to developing spectrum sharing solutions where the cognitive radio nodes can work collectively, a comprehensive study of utilizing multiagent systems over cognitive radio networks is discussed.

This book has the following remarkable features:

- Provides a comprehensive reference on formal and practical aspects of ACN.
- Presents state-of-the-art formal and practical aspects of ACN.
- Formally specifies, develops and verifies ACN.
- Includes illustrative figures facilitating easy reading.
- Discusses emerging trends and open research problems in the formal methods for ACN.

Being an Editor devoted to this book, I am advised by an Editorial Advisory Board (EAB) that currently consists of Dr. Costin Badica (University of Craiova, Romania), Dr. Radu Calinescu (Aston University, UK), Prof. Chin-Chen Chang (Feng Chia University, Taiwan), Prof. Mieso Denko (University of Guelph, Canada), Prof. Petre Dini (Cisco Systems, USA / Concordia University, Canada), Prof.

Alois Ferscha (Johannes Kepler University Linz, Austria), Prof. Jianhua Ma (Hosei University, Japan), Prof. Jong Hyuk Park (Seoul National University of Technology, R.O.Korea), Dr. Emil Vassev (University College Dublin, Ireland), Prof. Fatos Xhafa (Universitat Politècnica de Catalunya, Spain) and Prof. Huibiao Zhu (East China Normal University, China). These members are appointed to the EAB as needed to review the manuscripts submitted for possible publication.

We owe our deepest gratitude to Dr. Nguyen Manh Hung – Rector, Dr. Nguyen Vinh Khanh – Vice Rector, and Ms. Nguyen Mai Lan – Personnel Director of NTT University at Ho Chi Minh City in Vietnam for their useful support of this project, especially to all the authors for their valuable contribution to this book and their great efforts. All of them are extremely professional and cooperative. We wish to express our thanks to IGI Global especially Joel A. Gamon for their support and guidance during the preparation of this book. A special thanks also goes to our families and friends for their constant encouragement, patience, and understanding throughout this project.

The book serves as a comprehensive and essential reference on ACN and is intended as a textbook for senior undergraduate and graduate-level courses. It can also be used as a supplementary textbook for undergraduate courses. The book is a useful resource for the students and researchers to learn ACN. In addition, it will be valuable to professionals from both the academia and industry and generally serves instant appeal to the people who would like to contribute to ACN technologies.

We highly welcome and greatly appreciate your feedback and hope you enjoy reading the book.

Phan Cong-Vinh
NTT University, Vietnam

Section 1
Formal and Practical Aspects of Autonomic Computing

Chapter 1
Formal Methods for the Development and Verification of Autonomic IT Systems

Radu Calinescu
Aston University, UK

Shinji Kikuchi
Fujitsu Laboratories Limited, Japan

Marta Kwiatkowska
Oxford University Computing Laboratory, UK

ABSTRACT

This chapter explores ways in which rigorous mathematical techniques, termed formal methods, can be employed to improve the predictability and dependability of autonomic computing. Model checking, formal specification, and quantitative verification are presented in the contexts of conflict detection in autonomic computing policies, and of implementation of goal and utility-function policies in autonomic IT systems, respectively. Each of these techniques is illustrated using a detailed case study, and analysed to establish its merits and limitations. The analysis is then used as a basis for discussing the challenges and opportunities of this endeavour to transition the development of autonomic IT systems from the current practice of using ad-hoc methods and heuristic towards a more principled approach.

INTRODUCTION

The development of IT systems with self-managing capabilities – termed *autonomic computing* – is a relatively young area of research (Kephart & Chess, 2003; Murch, 2004). Now past the period of initial hype characteristic of any major new paradigm in computer science, autonomic computing looks set to become an established approach to addressing the continual increase in the scale and complexity of today's IT systems. There are numerous indicators of this trend, including the

DOI: 10.4018/978-1-60960-845-3.ch001

emergence of generic development platforms for autonomic computing (Calinescu, 2009a; Garlan, Schmerl, & Cheng, 2009; Twidle, Dulay, Lupu, & Sloman, 2009; Vassev & Mokhov, 2009) and the use of autonomic IT systems across a wide range of application domains (Huebscher & McCann, 2008; Parashar & Hariri, 2006).

While this healthy pace of progress is well in line with the ambitious plan put forward by the autonomic computing manifesto (IBM Corporation, 2001), one concern remains. The vast majority of autonomic IT systems – whether under test in research labs or deployed in production – implement the high-level objectives that guide their operation using heuristics derived from and validated through a combination of experimentation, simulation and testing. As it is well known from more established areas of computer science, this is insufficient for developing IT systems that are highly predictable and dependable. Yet, autonomic IT systems are required to excel in precisely these characteristics (Dai, 2005; Sterritt, 2003; Sterritt & Bustard, 2003).

This chapter proposes that the major problem identified above is addressed by using rigorous mathematical techniques termed formal methods (Boca, Bowen, & Siddiqi, 2009). Building on the authors' previous work in the area (Calinescu & Kwiatkowska, 2009a, 2009b; Kikuchi, Tsuchiya, Adachi, & Katsuyama, 2007), the chapter explores ways in which formal methods can help overcome the discrepancy between what autonomic IT systems can deliver in terms of predictability and dependability, and what is expected of them. The next three sections look in turn at several aspects of autonomic computing that can benefit from the use of existing or enhanced techniques from the area of formal methods.

First, next section describes the use of model checking (E. M. Clarke, Grumberg, & Peled, 2000) to detect policy conflicts in autonomic computing systems. Given the potentially significant damage that conflicting policies can cause to autonomic systems, it is critical to ensure that policies express-

ing different system objectives do not interfere with each other. This section explains why model checking represents a better-suited technique for conflict detection than alternative approaches such as testing or simulation.

This is followed by two sections that present formal approaches to implementing two important classes of autonomic computing policies: goal policies and utility-function policies. Goal policies describe constraints that an autonomic system needs to observe at all times. Together, these constraints provide a formal specification (Abrial, 1996; Woodcock & Davies, 1996) for the system, and a technique termed model synthesis (Jackson, 2006) can be employed to update the system configuration in response to changes in its environment in ways that comply with this specification. This approach is presented in detail in the chapter. Utility-function policies provide a quantitative measure of the degree to which an autonomic system achieves its high-level objective, and request that the system configuration is adjusted automatically so that maximum utility is obtained in the presence of changes in the system state, workload and environment. The chapter describes the use of quantitative verification (Kwiatkowska, 2007) to implement this type of autonomic computing policy.

The final section concludes the chapter with a brief summary, and discusses the directions in which the field of formal methods for autonomic computing is headed. This discussion includes overviews of two emerging platforms that aim to employ formal techniques for the end-to-end development of autonomic IT systems. One development platform involves the model-driven, automatic generation of many of the components of an autonomic IT system starting from a quantitative model that defines the behaviour of its components. The other platform requires that the development process starts with the definition of a formal specification of the autonomic system, and generates its parts in a series of automated development steps.

The intended readership for the chapter includes engineers, scientists, practitioners and researchers interested in transitioning from the current practice of using ad-hoc methods and heuristics in their autonomic computing work towards a principled, rigorous approach to autonomic IT system development.

Conflict Detection in Autonomic Computing Policies

Autonomic systems are defined as systems that "manage themselves according to an administrator's goals" (Kephart & Chess, 2003). The effectiveness of the self-management depends on the quality of the autonomic computing policies used to express these goals. Poorly-defined policies lead to ineffective self-management; conflicting policies can be downright damaging to the autonomic system. This explains the significant research effort dedicated to detecting policy conflicts in all types of policy-based management systems, including autonomic IT systems.

This section describes how a formal technique termed *model checking* can be used to detect conflicts in autonomic computing policies. Note that this approach uses model checking to verify the correctness of self-management policies specified by the administrator of an autonomic IT system rather than to specify or implement such policies. We start by introducing model checking and explaining why it is better suited for detecting conflicts in autonomic computing policies than heuristic-based testing approaches. We then describe an approach to model checking autonomic computing policies, and illustrate its application to a case study from the area of data-centre resource management. We conclude with a summary of related work.

Background

Model checking (E. M. Clarke et al., 2000) represents a formal technique for verifying whether a system satisfies its specification. The technique involves building a mathematically-based model of the system behaviour, and checking that system properties specified formally in a temporal logic hold within this model. For each refuted property, the technique yields a counterexample consisting of an execution path for which the property does not hold. The result is based on an exhaustive analysis of the state space of the considered model - a characteristic that sets model checking apart from complementary techniques such as testing and simulation. Sophisticated algorithms have been devised over the past two decades to make possible the verification of ever larger systems without individually examining every single state of their model. Software tools that implement these algorithms are called model checkers, and are available both commercially and as free, open-source applications.

The system model most commonly used in model checking is termed a Kripke structure (E. M. Clarke et al., 2000). It consists of a state transition graph $M=(S,S_0,R,L)$, where S represents the finite set of states in which the system can exist, $S_0 \subseteq S$ is the set of the initial states, $R \subseteq S \times S$ is a relation that defines all possible transitions between states, and $L:S \longrightarrow 2^{AP}$ is a labelling function that labels each state with the set of atomic propositions that are true in that state.

Commonly used temporal logics include linear temporal logic (LTL) (E. Clarke & Lerda, 2007) and computation tree logic (CTL) (E. M. Clarke, Emerson, & Sistla, 1986). The approach to verifying autonomic computing policies described in this section uses LTL, which is a logic that adds the temporal operators in Table 1 and calculation

Table 1. Temporal operators in LTL

Syntax	Semantics
$\circ \varphi$	φ is true in the next states.
$[]\varphi$	φ is true in all reachable states.
$\Diamond \varphi$	φ is true in some reachable states.
$\psi U \varphi$	φ is true in some reachable states. ψ is true at every preceding state on the path.
$\psi R \varphi$	φ is always true, or φ is true until ψ becomes true.

for them to first-order logic. An LTL formula such as ϕ and Ψ in this table is a combination of atomic propositions, logical operators (i.e., ψ, $\neg$, and $\vee$) and the LTL temporal operators $\circ$, $[]$, $\Diamond$, U and R. Given a Kripke structure $M=(S,S_0,R,L)$, and an LTL formula ϕ, the notation $M| = \phi$ is used to state that the system model M satisfies the LTL formula ϕ. For example, if $a \in AP$ is an atomic proposition, $M| = [](\Diamond a)$ states that a is eventually true on the every path from each state $s \in S$.

Numerous model checkers have been developed in recent years, and employed in application domains ranging from circuit design and security protocol analysis to mission-critical system verification. Some of the most effective and widely used model checkers include NuSMV (Cimatti, Clarke, Giunchiglia, & Roveri, 1999), UPPAAL (Bengtsson, Larsen, Larsson, Pettersson, & Yi, 1995) and SPIN (Holzmann, 2003). The model checker used to illustrate the verification of autonomic computing policies in this section is SPIN, a tool developed at Bell Labs, and winner of a 2001 ACM System Software Award. SPIN can be downloaded freely from http://spinroot.com.

Model Checking Autonomic Computing Policies

Description of the Approach

Our approach to verifying autonomic computing policies requires that two types of information are available for the autonomic system:

- A structural model that specifies the system parameters that need to be monitored or controlled for the considered application, and their value domains. Consider, for example, an autonomic computing application that self-configures the number of servers allocated to services running within a data centre. In this example, the monitored system parameters to include in the structural model are the total number of servers in the data centre and the workloads of the services. The controlled parameters (i.e., the parameters adjusted by the self-managing system) are the numbers of servers allocated to individual services; these parameters and their value domains (i.e., the range of values they are allowed to take) have to be included in the structural model. Note that the information provided by the structural model defines the possible states of the system.

- A performance model that defines the relationships between the system parameters defined in the structural model, and between these parameters and any internal parameters that the system may have. For instance, for the data-centre autonomic application described above, the performance model will include the relationship between the number of servers allocated to a service and the maximum workload that the service can handle without violating its service-level agreement. We assume that these properties are obtained using a method such as benchmarking. Note that the information provided by the performance model specifies properties associated with different states of the system.

The sets of autonomic computing policies that can be verified using the method described in this section comprise two classes of policies:

- Action policies (also termed operation rules), i.e., "if condition then action"-style rules defining the actions the system can take to change its configurations and the set of conditions under which these actions may be taken. Note that these policies specify the possible transitions between system states.
- Goal policies, which express invariants that the system should fulfil at all times, or "final state" conditions that the system must comply with after the operation rules are executed.

The system information and the set of policies presented so far are used to derive a Kripke structure and a set of LTL formulas that must be satisfied by this structure in order to ensure that the autonomic computing policies are conflict free. The steps involved in building this Kripke structure $M = (S, S_0, R, L)$ and the LTL formulas are depicted in Figure 1 and detailed below:

1. The set of system states S and the set of initial system states $S_0 \subseteq S$ are derived from the structural model of the autonomic system.
2. The labelling function $L : S \rightarrow 2^{AP}$ is extracted from the performance model for the system. As illustrated by the case study presented later in this section, the atomic propositions correspond to key parameter values associated with specific system states.
3. The state transition relation $R \subseteq S \times S$ is defined by the operation rules (i.e., by the action policies) for the system.
4. Finally, system constraints specified by a goal policy correspond to LTL formulas ϕ that model M must always satisfy: $M \models \Box \phi$. Likewise, the final-state conditions ex-

Figure 1. Model checking autonomic computing policies

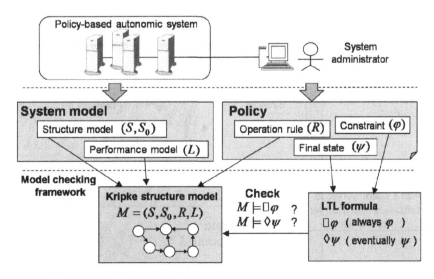

pressed by goal policies correspond to LTL formulas ψ that model M must "eventually" satisfy: $M \models \Diamond \psi$.

The assertions $M \models \Box \phi$ and $M \models \Diamond \psi$ obtained in step 4 are verified using a standard LTL model checker. If these assertions are true, then the policy set is conflict free, i.e., its action policies take the system from any initial state to a valid final state, transitioning only through intermediate states that satisfy the invariants specified by the constraint goal policies. If one or more assertions are not true, the policy set contains conflicts. The counterexample generated by the model checker for each such assertion can be used to identify reachable states that do not comply with the system invariants and/or unreachable final states, and thus represent a starting point for resolving the policy conflict.

Case Study

To illustrate the application of model checking to conflict detection in autonomic computing poli-

cies, we consider a case study involving the on-demand resource allocation within the autonomic data centre in Figure 2. This data centre handles user requests using a standard two-tier architecture: a web server, front-end tier and an application tier. Load balancers are deployed in each tier to distribute its workload among the servers running within that tier. Other than this "primary system" that is actively handling user requests, the data centre comprises a "spare system" that contains spare, standby servers.

As the data-centre workload increases, the primary system can be reinforced by adding standby servers to one or both of its tiers. Conversely, if the request rate reduces, active servers can be removed from the two tiers of the primary system and placed into the spare system, thus reducing the operational cost for the data centre without impacting its performance. An appropriate set of policies is necessary to ensure that the autonomic data centre provides the required level of service with minimal cost, by appropriately adding or removing servers from the primary system based on the rate of user requests

Figure 2. Running example setup: On-demand data centre

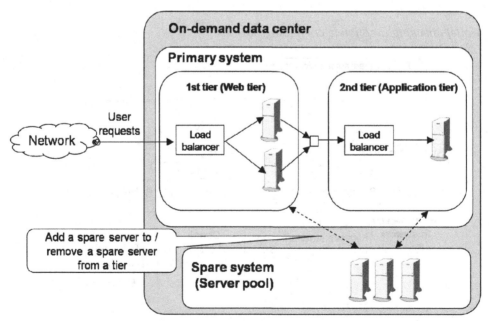

and on the capacity of the servers. A set of autonomic computing policies that aims to achieve this objective is proposed later in this section, and model checking is used to verify its correctness.

Structural Model and Performance Model

We start by defining the structural and performance model for the system below.

1. **Structural model.** The monitored and controlled data-centre parameters relevant for this case study are:
   The request rate $x > 0$ that the system should accommodate;
     - The number of spare servers A_i allocated to tier i, $1 \leq i \leq 2$.

   We will assume that $0 \leq x \leq 300$ requests/second; and that in the initial state $A_1 = A_2 = 0$.

2. **Performance model.** The data-centre comprises two sets of "internal" parameters (i.e., parameters that are neither monitored nor controlled, but are calculated based on the parameters defined in the structural model):
     - The total number of servers $N_i > 0$ in tier i of the primary system, $1 \leq i \leq 2$;
     - The processing time $T_i > 0$ required to handle a user request in tier i, $1 \leq i \leq 2$.

The set of relationships between all the system parameters comprise:

- The relationship between the total number of servers and the number of spare servers in the two tiers:
  $N_1 = 2 + A_1$ and $N_2 = 1 + A_2$.
- The relationship between the tier-one average processing time T^1, the request rate x and the number of servers in the first tier N^1. This is derived assuming an M/M/1 queuing model for this tier: $T_1 = \dfrac{\alpha}{1 - \alpha \cdot \frac{x}{N_1}}$,

where $\alpha > 0$ represents the service rate of a single server.

- The relationship between the tier-two average processing time T_2, the request rate x and the number of servers in the second tier N_2. This is assumed to be proportional to the ratio x/N_2: $T_2 = \beta \cdot \dfrac{x}{N_2} + \gamma$, where β and y are two positive constants.

Autonomic Computing Policies

The set of autonomic computing policies for the data centre comprise the policies described below.

1. **Action policies.** Two operation rules express the conditions in which the system configuration is modified:
     - **ADD Rule:** If $T_1 + T_2 \geq 0.6s$, then add a spare server to tier 1 if $T_1 \geq T_2$ or add a spare server to tier 2 if $T_1 < T_2$.
     - **REMOVE Rule:** If $T_1 + T_2 < 0.25s$ and $A_1 + A_2 > 0$, randomly select a spare server that is in use, remove it from the primary system and return it to the spare system.
2. **Goal policies.** The invariant and "final state" conditions that the system must achieve are:
     - **INVARIANT:** At all times, $A_1 + A_2 \leq 3$.
     - **FINAL STATE:** After applying the operation rules, the average processing time should eventually be at most 1s, i.e., $T_1 + T_2 \leq 1.0s$.

Policy Verification

To verify the correctness of this policy set, we need to construct the Kripke structure and to derive the LTL formulas associated with the structural and performance system models, and with the set of autonomic computing policies. This process is described below.

1. Constructing a Kripke structure $M = (S, S_0, R, L)$ for the autonomic data centre. Each combination of values that can be taken by the monitored and controlled parameters of the system corresponds to a different state $s \in S$. For our data centre, the only monitored parameter is x, and the controlled parameters are A_1 and A_2, so the set of states is, $S \equiv \{(x, A_1, A_2) \mid 0 \leq x \leq 300, A_1 \geq 0, A_2 \geq 0\}$.

Since initially $A_1 = A_2 = 0$, the set of initial states $S_0 \subseteq S$ is given by, $S_0 \equiv \{(x, 0, 0) \mid 0 \leq x \leq 300\}$.

In order to define the set of atomic propositions AP for the Kripke structure, we first take into account the fact that each state $s \in S$ represents a certain configuration for the system. Therefore, we start by including in AP atomic propositions representing the values of the configuration parameters for the system. To do so, we use the notation $[X = a]$ as an atomic proposition stating that the value of the parameter X is a. In addition, we need to determine the truth values for the conditions representing the invariants and final states defined by the goal policies for the system. In our running example, the invariant $(A_1 + A_2 \leq 3)$ and the condition for final state $(T_1 + T_2 \leq 1.0_s)$ have the generic form $X + Y \leq a$, where X and Y are variables and a is a constant. Therefore, we also include within AP atomic propositions of the form $[X + Y \leq a]$. As a result, the complete set of atomic propositions AP used to define the labelling function $L: S \rightarrow 2^{AP}$ consists of all atomic propositions,

$$AP = \{[X = a] \mid X \in \{x, A_1, A_2, T_1, T_2, N_1, N_2\}, a \geq 0\}$$
$$\cup \{[X + Y \leq a] \mid X, Y \in \{x, A_1, A_2, T_1, T_2, N_1, N_2\}, a \geq 0\}.$$

For example, given the state $s = (150, 1, 1)$ in which the system is receiving user requests at 150 transactions/second and one spare server is deployed to each tier, several of the atomic propositions that hold in state s are $[x = 150]$, $[A_1 = 1]$, $[A_2 = 1]$ and $[A_1 + A_2 \leq 2]$. Therefore, $L(s)$

contains these propositions, as well as all other propositions in AP that are true in state s. Finally, the possible state transitions R are derived from the action policies. The ADD Rule enables all transitions between encoded by the pairs of states in the sets,

$$R_1 \equiv \{(s_j, s_k) \mid T_1(s_j) + T_2(s_j) \geq 0.6, T_1(s_j) \geq T_2(s_j), x(s_j) = x(s_k),$$
$$A_1(s_k) = A_1(s_j) + 1, A_2(s_k) = A_2(s_j)\}$$
$$R_2 \equiv \{(s_j, s_k) \mid T_1(s_j) + T_2(s_j) \geq 0.6, T_1(s_j) < T_2(s_j), x(s_j) = x(s_k),$$
$$A_1(s_k) = A_1(s_j), A_2(s_k) = A_2(s_j) + 1\}$$

and the REMOVE Rule enables the transitions between associated with the state pairs in,

$$R_3 \equiv \{(s_j, s_k) \mid T_1(s_j) + T_2(s_j) \leq 0.25, A_1(s_j) > 0, x(s_j) = x(s_k),$$
$$A_1(s_k) = A_1(s_j) - 1, A_2(s_k) = A_2(s_j)\}$$
$$R_4 \equiv \{(s_j, s_k) \mid T_1(s_j) + T_2(s_j) \leq 0.25, A_2(s_j) > 0, x(s_j) = x(s_k),$$
$$A_1(s_k) = A_1(s_j), A_2(s_k) = A_2(s_j) - 1\}$$

Additionally, the variation in the request rate x is encoded by transition relation,

$$R_5 \equiv \{(s_j, s_k) \mid x(s_j)$$
$$\neq x(s_k), A_1(s_k)$$
$$= A_1(s_j), A_2(s_k) = A_2(s_j)\}.$$

The complete state transition relation for the Kripke structure is given by the union,

$$R \equiv R_1 \cup R_2 \cup R_3 \cup R_4 \cup R_5.$$

2. Deriving the LTL properties to be verified. The translation of the two goal policies into LTL formulas is straightforward. Thus, the INVARIANT "always $A_1 + A_2 \leq 3$" maps to the formula $\Box[A_1 + A_2 \leq 3]$ and the FINAL STATE goal that "eventually $T_1 + T_2 \leq 1.0s$ can be represented by the formula $\Diamond[T_1 + T_2 \leq 1.0]$.

The LTL properties derived so far were verified using the SPIN model checker (Holzmann, 2003). Version 4.2.6 of SPIN was run on a Red Hat Enterprise Linux, 3GHz Pentium-4 PC with 1 GByte of memory. To improve the efficiency of SPIN, we took advantage of its implementation of the state compression algorithm and of the partial-order reduction algorithm. The verification of the LTL properties was carried out for two system models characterised by different server performance parameters:

- Model A: $\alpha = 0.012$, $\beta = 0.001$, $\gamma = 0.15$;
- Model B: $\alpha = 0.01$, $\beta = 0.002$, $\gamma = 0.02$.

The purpose of choosing these two models was to demonstrate that the validity of autonomic computing policies depends on the scenario – or system model – to which they are applied.

When the verification of the LTL properties was performed for model A, SPIN found no invalid states, thus confirming that the policy set is conflict free in this scenario. More precisely, the "ADD Rule" and "REMOVE Rule" action policies are guaranteed to lead the system to suitable final states without causing any constraint violations: the autonomic data centre can cope with any request rate in the range 0 to 300 transactions/second.

In contrast, when the policy set was checked for system model B, SPIN detected a possible constraint violation. The counterexample trace generated by SPIN is depicted in Figure 3. This counterexample shows that the system can reach state $s_6 = (295, 2, 2)$ that violates the constraint $A_1 + A_2 \leq 3$ by starting from the initial state $s_0 = (199, 0, 0)$ and transitioning through the intermediate states in the sequence $\langle s_1, s_2, s_3, s_4, s_5 \rangle$. This demonstrates that managing the allocation of spare servers to primary-system tiers by means of the "ADD Rule" and "REMOVE Rule" action policies can result in a violation of the INVARIANT goal policy in the scenario encoded by system model B.

An important lesson to learn from this case study is that a set of autonomic computing policies that is valid for one scenario can exhibit conflicts when the autonomic system operates in a different scenario. Model checking provides the unique capability to verify autonomic computing policies

Figure 3. Counterexample trace for model B

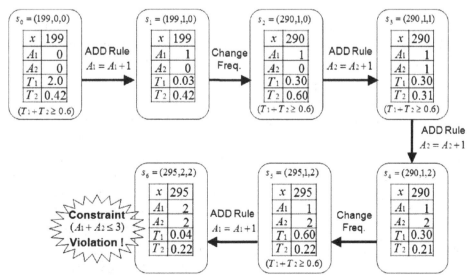

exhaustively and for the precise scenario in which the self-managing system operates.

Finally, note that a simple calculation applied to the invalid state s_6 from the counterexample in Figure 3 shows that if one spare server were removed from the second tier and added to the first tier, both goal policies would be achieved for system model B. However, the "REMOVE Rule" action policy precludes the removal of spare servers from any tiers when $T_1 + T_2 \geq 0.25$. This observation spawned by the analysis of the counterexample generated by the model checker represents of first step towards identifying the root cause of the policy conflict and resolving it.

Performance Evaluation

Performance statistics for the case study are shown in Table 2, which lists the number of verified states, the verification time, and the memory used for the analysis of each model. The results in this table show that the verification time is reasonably small for both models. Note that for Model B (for which a policy conflict was identified), the number of states and verification time were much smaller than for Model A. This is because the state-space exploration stopped for Model B when the conflict was identified.

To examine the effect the domain size of a system parameter has on performance, we performed the validation of the policy set for Model A when increasing the maximum number of transactions the system should accommodate from 100 to 500 transactions/second, in steps of 100 transactions/second. To ensure that the state space is searched exhaustively, we also changed the

Table 2. Statistics for the case study

Model	States	Time(sec)	Memory(Mb)
Model A	939463	6.98	204.5
Model B	40317	1.46	164.2

property to be checked so as not to cause any policy violations. Figure 4 shows the relation between the maximum number of transactions and the size of the state space verified in this experiment, and Figure 5 shows the dependence of the computational time and memory usage on the number of states. As expected, the number of states increases dramatically as the maximum number of transactions increases. At the same time, the computational time and memory usage also increase as the number of states increases.

These experimental results indicate that in order to be feasible, the proposed approach for conflict detection in autonomic computing policies has to be applied to small average-sized models. Obtaining such models requires that the number of parameters included in the model and their value ranges are carefully chosen. Model abstraction algorithms such as (Wang, Hachtel & Somenzi, 2006) can alternatively (or additionally) be employed to reduce the size of the state space further.

Related Work

There has been a lot of research on policy validity checking of policy-based management systems. For example, the policy inconsistency detection method for firewalls is proposed by Al- Shaer and Hamed (Al-Shaer & Hamed, 2003), but this type of analysis is concerned with static policy, so policy-based systems that change status dynamically by defined policy are beyond its scope. Another method uses event calculus (EC) (Kowalski & Sergot, 1986) framework for policy verification in (Bandara, Lupu, & Russo, 2003) (Charalambides et al., 2005). In this method, the situation in which an inconsistency occurs is identified by abductive inference on EC, which adds the notion of time to the framework of the first order predicate logic. However, in this method, all of the inference rules needed to identify inconsistencies must be described previously, but it is very difficult to describe all possible inconsistencies before they are

Figure 4. Max number of transactions and number of states

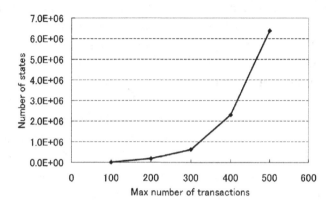

detected. Other than the above papers, while there has been research on policy conflict detection and resolution (Dunlop, Indulska, & Raymond, 2002), there has been little research on policy verification and validation that considers the relation between the policy and the system to which the policy is applied, which we do in our research.

Implementation of Goal Policies

As explained in the previous sections, goal policies represent high-level descriptions of the constraints, invariants and success states that an autonomic system is required to comply with or achieve. Often

specified using Boolean logic or first-order logic expressions, goal policies do not prescribe how the system objectives they define should or can be achieved. Instead, the configuration-change procedure required to implement goal policies (and thus to achieve the system objectives) has to be synthesised by the autonomic system.

This part of the chapter shows how a combination of related formal techniques, namely *formal specification* and *model synthesis*, can be employed to implement goal autonomic computing policies. Note that the implementation of such goal policies adds self-management capabilities

Figure 5. Number of states and resource consumption

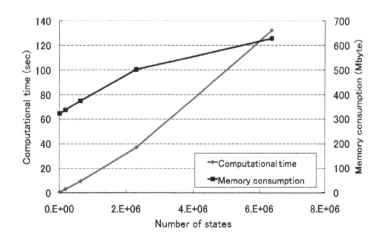

such as self-configuration and self-optimisation to IT systems.

The section starts with a brief description of the two formal techniques mentioned above. This is followed by a detailed presentation of our formal method for the implementation of goal policies. The section concludes with a summary of related work.

Background

Formal specification is a technique for the development of IT systems that consists of expressing the requirements of a system using mathematical notation drawn from set theory and first-order logic. By starting from a set of requirements defined in a formal specification language like Z (Woodcock & Davies, 1996) or B (Abrial, 1996), developers of high-integrity IT systems can reason formally about their designs, develop code that matches these requirements closely, and generate effective assertions and unit tests for their code. Furthermore, tool-supported formal specification frameworks such as Alloy (Jackson, 2006) and B-Method (Schneider, 2001) enable developers to start from an abstract specification of a system and derive a compliant model or a concrete realisation of it in a number of (semi)automatic, refinement steps.

Our method for the implementation of goal autonomic computing policies is based on the refinement process described above. The method uses as input an Alloy-encoded formal specification derived from a set of goal policies, and employs the Alloy Analyzer tool (Alloy, 2010) to synthesise a model of the system that satisfies all these constraints. The synthesised model corresponds to a system configuration that fulfils the Alloy specification, and which can be extracted and used to implement the original goal policies.

Before describing the method in more detail, we provide a brief overview of Alloy specifications and the Alloy Analyzer tool. An Alloy specification (Jackson, 2006) is a formal description of the constraints and behaviour of a system that is expressed in a declarative language based on first-order logic. In addition to the standard first-order logic operators (e.g., $\land$, $\lor$, $\neg$ and $\rightarrow$)the Alloy language supports the constructs and operations in Table 3.

Alloy Analyzer (Alloy, 2010) is a free, open-source tool that supports two analysis operations (Table 3): model finding (or synthesis) and assertion evaluation. Given a formal specification expressed in the Alloy declarative language, model finding consists of synthesising a model that satisfies all fact declarations. Assertion evaluation involves establishing whether an assertion holds at all times for a given Alloy specification. Note that the two operations are equivalent because identifying a scenario in which an assertion does not hold is equivalent to finding a model that satisfies all fact declarations and the negation of the considered assertion.

Several characteristics of the Alloy specification language and of the Alloy Analyzer tool make the Alloy platform particularly suitable for the implementation of goal autonomic computing policies using the method detailed later in this section:

- **Expressiveness:** The specification language supports the definition of the complex structural constraints and relationships encountered in autonomic IT systems.
- **Ability to represent state transitions:** The pred Alloy construct can be used to specify the operations associated with changes in the autonomic system configuration.
- **Effectiveness:** The search for a model in model finding operations explores the entire state space of the system. This exploration is conducted very efficiently, as it is based on translating Alloy specifications into a 3-SAT conjunctive normal formula (CNF) and using a powerful SAT solver such as

Table 3. Alloy constructs and operations; the examples are adapted from (Jackson, 2006)

Type	Keyword	Description	Example		
Signature	sig	Formal definition of system components and their relations	sig Man{wife: lone Woman}		
			(Entity **Man** has a field **wife** of type **Woman** and multiplicity **lone** - each **Man** is associated with no more than one **Woman** as **wife**.)		
Fact	fact	Constraint that always holds	fact{some m:Man|no m.wife} (There are some **Man** entities without a **wife**.)		
Predicate	pred	Parameterised constraint	pred spouse(p:Man,q:Woman) {q in p.wife} (If **q** is **p**'s wife, predicate **spouse(p,q)** is true)		
Function	Fun	Expression that returns a value	fun husband(q:Woman): set Man {q.(~wife)} (Function that returns a **Man** entity whose **wife** field is q)		
Assertion	assert	Assumption to be checked	assert A1{no q:Woman|#q.(~wife)>1} (There is no **Woman** entity that is the **wife** of more than one **Man**.)		
Model finding operation	run	Find a model that satisfies all fact declarations	run husband		
Assertion evaluation operation	check	Establish whether an assertion holds or not under the given facts	check A1		

SAT4J (Lens, 2010 or miniSat (Niklas & Niklas, 2003) to determine its satisfiability, and thus the existence of a model that satisfies the original specification.

Synthesis of Configuration-Change Procedures from Goal Autonomic Computing Policies

Description of the Approach

Our method for synthesizing a configuration procedure for an autonomic IT system starting from its goal policies is depicted in Figure 6. This method comprises four steps:

1. Structural and performance system models similar to those described in Section 2.2 are derived in this step. The system characteristics defined by the two system models are:
    - The types and numbers of system components;
    - The relationships between these components (e.g., "Server A is connected to Switch B" or "Application software C is available for operating system D");
    - The types and values of the component parameters that are relevant for the intended autonomic functionality (e.g., "Server A has a parameter called memorySize, and its value is 4GByte" or "Web server E has a parameter termed maxConnections, whose value is 300").

We assume this information can be derived from monitoring the running system, e.g., by means of discovery tools such as Tivoli Application Dependency Discovery Manager (IBM-Tivoli, 2010). The structural and performance system models need to be encoded in a well-defined, which for our realisation of the method is a customized XML format used to integrate system and management information called Resource Control eXtensible Markup Language (RCXML) and introduced in (Katsuno et al., 2007). Note that RCXML is capable of representing the various types of relations between the components of a

Figure 6. Synthesis of configuration-change procedures from goal policies

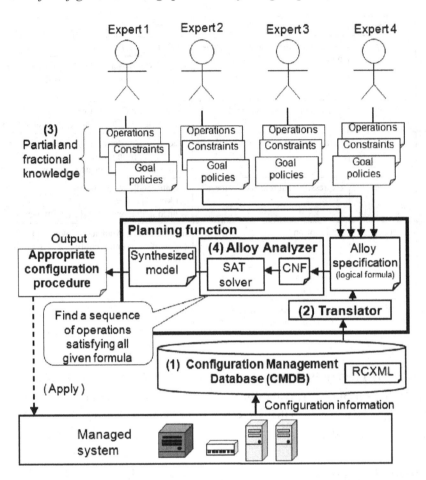

system. Therefore, we use it to specify a system consisting of various types of components, and then translate it into the states of a model that encodes the configuration of the system. Details about RCXML are provided when we present the case study used to illustrate the application of the method later in this section. However, note that any equivalent format can be used for the representation of this information, as long as the model transformation technique employed in the second step of the method is adjusted to cope with that equivalent format.

2. The system information obtained in step one is translated into Alloy sig declarations that define the system components and

their parameters, and fact declarations that specify the "facts" that hold in the initial system state (i.e., prior to executing any configuration change procedures synthesized by our method). The result is a partial Alloy specification that is augmented to a full specification in the next step of the method. In our realisation of the method, we use a Java translator that automates the generation of the Alloy sig and fact declarations from the RCXML representation of the structural and performance system models.

3. In this step, expert system management knowledge is acquired from domain experts in different aspects of the autonomic system, and is encoded in Alloy. For a typical IT sys-

tem, the domain experts from Figure 6 may include network experts, database experts, operating systems experts and/or application experts. The system management knowledge that each of these experts contributes with consists of constraints, descriptions of system configuration operations with pre- and post-conditions, and goal autonomic computing policies. All of these are encoded in the Alloy declarative language, either by these experts if they have experience with Alloy or, more likely, by the developer of the autonomic capabilities for the system. Thus, constraints are expressed as fact Alloy declarations encoding the relationships that must be maintained in all states. Next, the operations and their pre-/post-conditions are expressed as a combination of pred and fact Alloy constructs, or in some cases, merely as fact declarations. All of these Alloy definitions complete the partial Alloy specification from step two, producing the Alloy specification required to synthesize the configuration-change procedure.

4. In the final step of the method, the Alloy Analyzer tool is employed to identify a model that satisfies the specification built in the previous steps of the method. This model is produced as a sequence of value assignments to variables from the operation definitions in the specifications. As a result, the model maps directly to a sequence of state transitions satisfying all given fact declarations, or to a synthesized configuration procedure that takes the system from the initial/current state to a state satisfying its goal policies without violating any constraints.

Case Study

The case study used to illustrate the application of the method involves synthesising the procedure for system configuration changes in an IT system that employs Xen virtual machines (Barham et al., 2003) to run a three-tier software application. The system comprises three physical servers (Server_A, Server_B and Server_C), an OS-image storage device (OS_image) and a switch (Switch_S1) that can be used to organise any subset of the other components into a VLAN. The software application consists of an Apache web server, an Interstage application server (Fujitsu, 2010) and a MySQL database server that are each running within their own Linux virtual machines (VMs).

Figure 7 depicts the initial state of the system, in which Server_A, Server_B and OS_image are connected to Switch_S1, and belong to the same VLAN segment V1, while Server_C is not connected to the network. The three components of the software application are deployed as follows: Apache on the VM Guest_OS_A1 running on Server_A; Interstage on the VM Guest_OS_A2 which is also running on Server_A; and MySQL on Guest_OS_B1 running on Server_B.

To avoid overcommitting physical server resources, we quantify the capacity of the physical servers and the amount of resources necessary to run each VM. Thus, the CPU, memory and hard-disk (HDD) resources of each physical server are assigned a "size" parameter that can take values in the range 0 to 32. A size of one unit for any of these resource types corresponds to the capacity of that resource type for the entry-level VM offered by the Amazon EC2 service (Amazon-EC2, 2010), namely a 1.0-1.2 GHz Intel Xeon/AMD Opteron VM with 1.7 GB memory and 160 GB of local instance storage. Similarly, each guest OS (i.e., virtual machine) is assigned a "size" parameter, and the system is considered to be in a valid state if no physical server is running a set of VMs whose combined size exceeds the size of any server resource. For instance, the overall size of the two VMs running on Server_A from the system in Figure 7 is $8 + 2 = 10$, which is less than the sizes of the CPU (i.e., 12), memory (i.e., 12) and storage (i.e., 16) available on this server.

Figure 7. Xen-based architecture running a three-tier software application

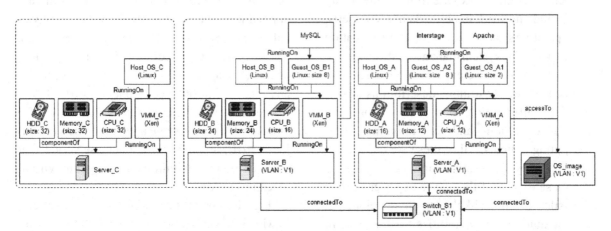

The remainder of this section describes how the four steps of the method for the synthesis of a configuration-change procedure are carried out for the autonomic IT system from our case study. The high-level objective of this autonomic system is to consolidate the virtual machines running the three-tier software application on as few servers as possible, so the synthesised configuration-procedure will involve migrating VMs across physical servers, and re-organising the VLAN and the access to the OS_image storage device.

1. In the first step of the method, RCXML-encoded structural and performance system models are derived from the information provided by the annotations in Figure 7. A fragment of the RCXML representation of the structural and performance model is shown in Figure 8. This fragment defines the physical configuration of Server_A, with its three physical components (CPU, memory and hard disk) and their relationships with the Server_A element (represented by means of "componentOf" links), and their performance as the "size" parameters. A fragment of the structural model is also shown in Figure 9, where "Link" XML elements with attributes such as "connectedTo" or "runningOn" represent relationships between other system components. The fact that some

components belong to the VLAN segment V1 is specified by the "VLANs" connections between these components and the element representing VLAN V1.

2. In the second step of the method, the RCXML system models are translated into a partial Alloy specification that consists of sig and fact declarations associated with the elements of these models. A fragment of the Alloy declarations for the system from our case study are shown in Figure 10. Notice how the sig State {...} declaration specifies the components of servers (i.e., CPU, memory and hard disk) as well as the other relationships between the elements of the IT system. Additionally, a fact declaration is generated that defines the initial configuration of the system; the use of the prefix first indicates that all parameter values correspond to the initial state of the system. Note that in our realisation of the method, the generation of this partial Alloy specification is fully automated by means of a Java translator that takes as input the RCXML-encoded models and uses a series of XPath queries to produce the required Alloy declarations. This technique and the Java tool are described in more detail in (Kikuchi & Tsuchiya, 2010).

3. We will split the description of this step of the method into three parts that correspond to the specification and translation into Alloy of three elements of the autonomic system: operations, constraints (or invariants) and goal policies.

Operations

We consider that the following operations are available:

- Connection - we can establish a physical network connection between any server and network device (e.g. a switch) with an Ethernet cable.
- Access configuration - We can modify some configuration files of servers in order to allow one server or piece of software to access another one.
- VLAN configuration - We can change VLAN configurations of servers or network devices in order to make them belong to some VLAN segments.
- Migration - We can move a virtual OS from one VMM to another by using the migration function of virtual machines under the condition where both physical servers accommodating these VMM can access the same OS_image storage.

These operations are fully defined by their pre- and post-conditions, as illustrated by the Alloy specification in Figure 11. In these Alloy definitions of the four operations, s and s' represent the system state before and after the execution of the operation, respectively. For example, the Alloy predicate for connect specifies several conditions that hold when a component src is connected to a component dst:

- no connectedTo relation exists from src to dst before executing the operation;
- no connectedTo relation exists from dst to src before executing the operation;

Figure 8. System configuration definition in RCXML

```
<Component>
  <Hardwares>
    <Servers>
      <Server id="Server_A">
        <Configuration>
          <CPU id="CPU_A" size="12" />
          <Memory id="Memory_A" size="12" />
          <HardDisk id="HDD_A" size="16" />
          <Link id="svrA_link1" src="CPU_A"
                dest="Server_A" type="componentOf" />
          <Link id="svrA_link2" src="Memory_A"
                dest="Server_A" type="componentOf" />
          <Link id="svrA_link3" src="HDD_A"
                dest="Server_A" type="componentOf" />
        </Configuration>
      </Server>
      ...
    </Servers>
    ...
  </Hardware>
</Componens>
```

Figure 9. Relation definition between components written in RCXML

```
<Links>
  <Link id="ctl1" src="Server_A" dest="Switch_S1" type="connectedTo" />
  <Link id="ctl2" src="Server_B" dest="Switch_S1" type="connectedTo" />
  <Link id="ctl3" src="OS_image" dest="Switch_S1" type="connectedTo" />
  ...
  <Link id="osl1" src="Host_OS_A"  dest="VMM_A" type="runningOn" />
  <Link id="osl2" src="Guest_OS_A1" dest="VMM_A" type="runningOn" />
  ...
  <Link id="acl1" src="VMM_A" dest="OS_image" type="accessTo" />
  <Link id="acl2" src="VMM_B" dest="OS_image" type="accessTo" />
  ...
  <Link id="btl1" src="Server_A" dest="V1" type="VLANs"/>
  <Link id="btl2" src="Server_B" dest="V1" type="VLANs"/>
  <Link id="btl3" src="Switch_S1" dest="V1" type="VLANs"/>
  <Link id="btl4" src="OS_image" dest="V1" type="VLANs"/>
  ...
</Links>
```

Figure 10. System configurations translated from RCXML to Alloy

```
/***  System state definition  ***/

sig State  {                              .
  size      : (CPU->Int)+(Memory->Int)+(HardDisk->Int)+(OS->Int),
  connectedTo: (Server -> NetworkDevice) + (NetworkDevice -> Server)
               +(NetworkDevice ->NetworkDevice),
  componentOf: (CPU + Memory + HardDisk) -> Server ,
  accessTo  : (Program + OS + Server) -> (Program + OS + Server) ,
  runningOn : (Program + OS ) -> (Program + OS + Server) ,
  ...
}

/*** Initial state configuration ***/
fact {
  first.size = (CPU_A -> Int[12]) + (CPU_B -> Int[16]) + (CPU_C -> Int[32])
             + (Memory_A -> Int[12]) + (Memory_B -> Int[24])+ ...
  first.componentOf = (CPU_A -> Server_A) + (Memory_A -> Server_A) + ...
  first.accessTo = (VMM_A -> OS_image) + (VMM_B -> OS_image)
  first.runningOn = (Host_OS_A -> VMM_A) + (Guest_OS_A1 -> VMM_A) + ...
  ...
}
```

- the connectedTo set of relations after the connect operation is the union of connectedTo before the operation and the set containing the newly established connection, i.e., {(src ⟶ dst)}.

The rest of the operations are defined in the same manner. For instance, the pre-conditions for the migrate operation require that src and dst are Xen VMs, and that OS_image is accessible to both.

Note that we need to define explicitly not only all changes effected by each operation, but also the fact that any unchanged parameters or relationship preserve their values. This so-called frame conditions (Reiter, 1991) are required to preclude the synthesis of impossible configuration changes in the last step of the method. In our Alloy

Figure 11. Operation definitions in Alloy

```
/*** Operation Definitions ***/

/* Connection operation: Connect src and dst */
pred connect[s,s':State, src,dst: Objects] {
  (not ((src->dst) in s.connectedTo)) &&
  (not ((dst->src) in s.connectedTo)) &&
  s'.connectedTo = s.connectedTo + (src->dst)&&
  s'.changes = connectedTo_c }

/* Access config operation: make src access to dst */
pred addaccessTo [s,s':State, src,dst: Objects]{
  not ((src->dst) in s.accessTo)) &&
  s'.accessTo = s.accessTo + (src -> dst) &&
  s'.changes = accessTo_c }

/* VLAN config operation: make src join dst */
pred joinVlan [s,s':State, src,dst: Objects]{
  s'.VLANs = s.VLANs + (src -> dst) &&
  s'.changes = VLANs_c }

/* Migration operation: migrate vm from src to dst */
pred migrate[s, s':State, vm,src,dst: Objects]{
  (Xen in (src.(s.name) & dst.(s.name)) ) &&
  (OS_image in (src.(s.accessTo) & dst.(s.accessTo)) ) &&
  ((vm->src) in s.runningOn) &&
  s'.runningOn = s.runningOn ++ (vm->dst) &&
  s'.changes = runningOn_c}
```

specification, the frame conditions are encoded by the frame_condition predicate in Figure 12. This predicate ensures that only parameters whose flags are set in an auxiliary variable s'.changes can be modified by any operation. To take advantage of this construct, each definition of an operation marks as changed all parameters that it rightfully modifies. For instance, a connect operation records the fact that it only changes the connectedTo parameter by including the expression s'.changes = connectedTo_c at the end of its code.

The system state transitions (i.e., it's possible configuration changes) associated with these operations can then be defined by integrating the operation knowledge encoded by the Alloy predicates in Figure 11 and the frame conditions in Figure 12. The resulting Alloy fact – depicted in Figure 13 – holds for components x, y, and z and for states s and s' if and only if the system transition from state s to state s' is valid.

Constraints

We further assume that three constraints were defined for the system: the network management expert defined an accessibility constraint and a VLAN constraint; and the VM management expert defined a capacity constraint. The three constraints, which must be complied with at all times, are presented below:

- **Accessibility constraint:** two network components can access each other only if they are connected via network links;
- **VLAN constraint:** two network components can access each other only if they belong to the same VLAN segment, or neither of them belongs to any VLAN segment;
- **Capacity constraint:** the total size of the guest operation systems (i.e., VMs) on a physical server must not exceed the size of any server resource.

Figure 12. Frame conditions

```
/*** Frame conditions ***/
pred frame_condition [s,s':State]{
  (s.connectedTo = s'.connectedTo || connectedTo_c in s'.changes) &&
  (s.componentOf = s'.componentOf || componentOf_c in s'.changes) &&
  (s.accessTo = s'.accessTo      || accessTo_c in s'.changes) &&
  ...
}
```

Figure 13. Definitions of state transitions with operation knowledge and frame conditions

```
/*** State Transition Definitions ***/
fact StateTransition { all s: State, s': ord/next[s] |
((some disj x,y:(s.Server + s.NetworkDevice)     | connect[s,s',x,y])    ||
 (some disj x,y:(s.Program + s.OS + s.Server)     | addaccessTo[s,s',x,y])||
 (some x: (s.Server + s.NetworkDevice)|some y: s.VLAN| joinVlan[s,s',x,y])  ||
 (some x: s.OS | some disj y,z: s.Program          | migrate[s,s',x,y,z]) )
   && frame_condition [s,s'] }
```

The Alloy fact declarations equivalent to these constraints are shown in Figure 14. For example, the accessibility constraint is defined by the fact declaration mentioning that if there is an accessTo relation between some components x and y in a state s, then y should be reachable from x through a set of runningOn and connectedTo relations and the inverse relations of them in the state. In the Alloy code, a reflexive transitive closure of a relation and its inverse are represented using the '*' operator and '~' operator, respectively. The concatenation of different types of relation is specified using the '.' operator.

Goal Policies

The goal policies for the system represent the last piece of information supplied by the system experts/administrators. In our case study, there is only one goal policy. This policy requires the consolidation of the three software components of the application running on the system (i.e., Apache, Interstage and MySQL) on the same physical server, in order to minimise operation costs. This goal policy can be encoded as the Alloy

fact construct in Figure 15, where the '^' operator represents the closure of relations without any reflexive relation. This fact declaration states the existence of a state s in which Apache, Interstage and MySQL are all running on the same server x.

In the final step of the method, the Alloy specification derived in the previous steps was supplied to the Alloy Analyzer tool. The experiment was carried out on a 64-bit Red Hat Enterprise Linux PC with an Intel Xeon 3GHz CPU and 2 GB memory, and Alloy Analyzer was configured to use miniSat (Niklas & Niklas, 2003) as its SAT solver engine.

In its search for a model satisfying the specification, Alloy Analyzer incrementally searches the state space within the range from 0 operations to a user-specified upper limit for the number of operations. In this manner, Alloy Analyzer finds a model representing a configuration procedure that can achieve the goal policies with the smallest number of configuration steps between 0 and the upper limit, assuming that such a model exists. If no model exists that satisfies the specification and has no more operations than the upper limit for the search, then the experiment is inconclusive: a

Figure 14. Declarative constraints

```
/*** Declarative constraints (invariants) ***/

/* Constraint 1: If x accesses to y, x and y should be connected */
fact {all s: State | all disj x,y: (s.Program + s.OS + s.Server) |
  (x->y) in s.accessTo => y in x.*(s.runningOn).
                    *(s.connectedTo + ~(s.connectedTo)). *(~(s.runningOn))}

/* Constraint 2: If x accesses to y, x's and y's server should belong to the
                 same VLAN */
fact {all s: State | all disj x,y: (s.Program +s.OS + s.Server) |
  (x->y) in s.accessTo => (no (x+y).*(s.runningOn).(s.VLANs)) ||
           y in x.*(s.runningOn).(s.VLANs).~(s.VLANs).*(~(s.runningOn))}

/* Constraint 3: Total OSs size should be under than components' capacity */
fact {all s: State | all x: s.Server | all c: x.(~(s.componentOf)) |
  c.(s.size) >= (sum y: x.^(~(s.runningOn)) | (y & s.OS).(s.size) )}
```

Figure 15. Goal policy

```
/*** Goal policy ***/

fact { some s: State | one x: s.Server |
  x in Apache.^(s.runningOn) &&
  x in Interstage.^(s.runningOn) &&
  x in MySQL.^(s.runningOn) }
```

larger model may exist, or the operations, conditions and goals specified by the domain experts may be conflicting.

For our case study, Alloy Analyzer took 200 seconds to synthesise a model that corresponds to the configuration-change procedure shown in Figure 16 and described below:

1. Connect Server_C with Switch_S1.
2. Incorporate Server_C into VLAN V1.
3. Establish access from Server_C to OS_image.
4. Move Guest_OS_B1 to VMM_C.
5. Move Guest_OS_A2 to VMM_C.
6. Move Guest_OS_A1 to VMM_C.

This synthesised procedure reveals several facts. First, due to the capacity constraint, the three pieces of software need to be consolidated on Server_C. However, in order to move VMMs to Server_C, it should be able to access OS_image. In addition, accessing OS_image requires

that Server_C and OS_image belong to the same VLAN segment and that a physical connection is established between them. Therefore, steps 1 to 3 are required to prepare the system for the VM migrations to Server_C.

Performance Evaluation

To evaluate the performance of our method for the implementation of goal policies, we changed the upper bound for the number of configuration steps and modified the initial configuration in the case study as described below. Then, we executed the synthesis of the procedure and evaluated the computational time and the number of clauses in the 3-SAT formula used internally by the Alloy Analyzer tool.

*   **Experiment 1:** We increased the number of configuration steps to be searched from 0 to 11, for a scenario in which the system

Figure 16. Procedure synthesis result

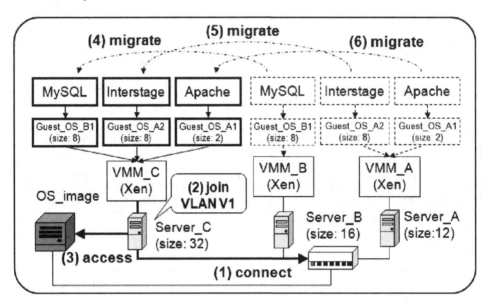

had the same architecture as in the original case study and started in the new initial state.

- **Experiment 2:** In addition to the changes from Experiment 1, we also increased the number of spare servers with the same configuration as Server_C from 1 to 5. As each spare server is represented by six components in the Alloy specification (i.e., the server itself, hard disk, memory, CPU, virtual machine, and its host OS), the number of such components for the experiment ranged from 26 to 50 in steps of six. The number of configuration steps in a sequence was fixed at six.

Figure 17 and Figure 18 plot the results for the two experiments. The results show that when the number of configuration steps to be synthesised or the number of components in an experiment increases, the computational time and the number of 3-SAT clauses also increase. The exception is the fluctuating computational time in Figure 17, which we found to be associated with early-terminated state searches due to the identification of instances satisfying the given conditions well before an exhaustive state search was conducted.

Note that the computational times to synthesise the configuration-change procedure comprises two parts: (1) the time for constructing the 3-SAT clauses from Alloy descriptions by the Alloy Analyzer; and (2) the time for the SAT solver (i.e., miniSat in our case) to find a model satisfying these 3-SAT formulas. Figure 19 shows the dependence between these computational times and the number of 3-SAT clauses in the experiments. These results show that it takes a larger amount of time for the SAT solver to find a model (represented by the solid lines) compared to the time required for the construction of the 3-SAT clauses (represented by the dotted lines) when there are many clauses. However, the times for constructing formulas and the number of 3-SAT clauses have almost linear relationships. This led us to the conclusion that 3-SAT clauses are derived in a naive way within the Alloy Analyzer. It is, however, a known fact that the number of 3-SAT clauses can be drastically reduced by customizing

Figure 17. Number of steps and 3-SAT clauses and computational time for Experiment 1

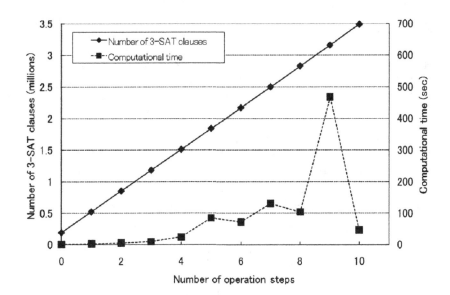

the CNF construction algorithm as described in (Nakamura, Naruse, Takagi, & Takagi, 2007). This improvement can be applied to reduce the computational times taken by the implementation of goal autonomic computing policies using the method presented in this section.

Related Work

The configuration of complex IT systems is widely regarded as one of the key challenges in system management (Brown, Keller, & Hellerstein, 2005). As such, multiple research projects

Figure 18. Number of components, 3-SAT clauses and computational time for Experment 2

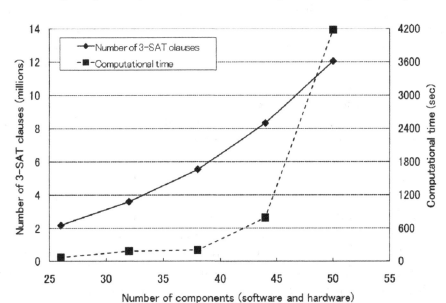

Figure 19. Relation between time for constructing SAT formulas and solving SAT

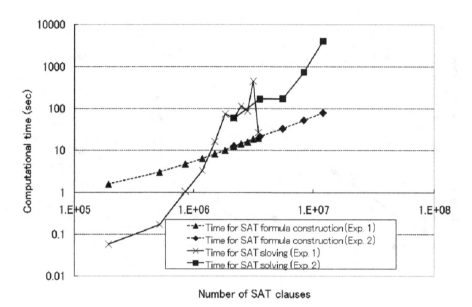

Number of SAT clauses

have investigated system configuration procedure planning, including Plaint (Arshad, Heimbigner, & Wolf, 2003) (Arshad, 2004) and LPG (Gerevini & Serina, 2002). Most of these techniques rely on procedural knowledge containing information about the pre- and post-conditions of each operation. They synthesize a procedure just by connecting operations in accordance with the procedural knowledge. However, various experts managing their systems have different areas of expertise about not only the procedure for configuration changes, but also the declarative constraints that should be kept in their system. Therefore, we believe that using only procedural knowledge to design configuration procedure for today's IT systems is insufficient, and that knowledge describing discrete conditions independent from the procedural knowledge is strongly required. In order to incorporate conditions independent from procedural knowledge into a configuration planning method, several approaches such as SPiCE (Eilam, Kalantar, Konstantinou, & Pacifici, 2004) (El Maghraoui, Meghranjani, Eilam, Kalantar, & Konstantinou, 2006) by IBM have been pro-

posed. They, however, require programming to define these constraints and cannot express these constraints in a declarative way. We suppose that system management knowledge can be added, removed or modified in system management life-cycles because of various reasons such as changes in the system management policy, emersions of new components and disposition of knowledge about obsolete components. Therefore, it is very disadvantageous to embed that knowledge in the procedural program code, because it is difficult to modify the embedded knowledge scattered in a planning algorithm. For these reasons, some researchers have started to realize the importance of using discrete and declarative constraints for system management (Microsoft Research, 2008), although most of their research is in the early stage and concerns the propositions of concept or architecture, in contrast with our approach that is based on a logical and mathematical foundation.

A couple of existing projects apply Alloy to system configuration (Narain, 2005) (Warren, Sun, Krishnamohan, & Weerasinghe, 2006). These approaches aim at finding static correct configurations at a specific point of time or detecting possible constraint violations. They are therefore completely different from our approach, which synthesizes a procedure for dynamically changing a system configuration using discrete knowledge.

Implementation of Utility-Function Policies

A utility function represents a measure of the degree to which a system satisfies its high-level objectives. Utility functions are typically defined as non-negative-valued expressions that depend on system parameters such as throughput, dependability or running costs. Utility-function autonomic computing policies specify a utility function whose value needs to be maximised through continually adjusting the configurable parameters of the system in line with changes in its workload, environment, etc.

This section describes an approach to implementing utility-function policies that is based on a formal technique termed *quantitative verification*. Through the implementation of these utility-function policies, autonomic IT systems provide self-optimisation functionality. We start by introducing quantitative verification next, then present our approach to implementing utility-function policies. The section concludes with a brief overview of related work.

Background

Quantitative verification is a mathematically-based technique for establishing the correctness, performance and reliability of systems that exhibit stochastic behaviour (Kwiatkowska, 2007). Given a precise mathematical model of a real-world system, and formal specifications of quantitative properties of this system, an exhaustive analysis of these properties is performed. Example properties include the probability that a fault occurs within a specified time period, and the expected

power consumption of an IT system under a given workload.

The most common system models used by quantitative verification are Markov models such as continuous- and discrete-time Markov chains (CTMCs and DTMCs), and Markov decision processes (MDPs). The approach for the implementation of utility-function policies described in this section works for autonomic systems whose components can be modelled using any of these types of Markov models. Because the case study used to illustrate the approach involves the quantitative verification of a continuous-time Markov chain (CTMC), we will introduce only this type of Markov model. A detailed description of DTMCs and MDPs in the context of quantitative verification is available from (Kwiatkowska, Norman, & Parker, 2007).

A CTMC is a tuple $CTMC = (S, s_0, \mathbf{R}, L)$, where S represents a finite set of states, $s_0 \in S$ is the initial state, $\mathbf{R} : S \times S \rightarrow R_{\geq 0}$ is a transition rate matrix, and $L:S \rightarrow 2^{AP}$ is a labelling function that associates a subset of the atomic propositions AP with each CTMC state. Given two states $s_1, s_2 \in S$, the probability of the transition between s_1 and s_2 being enabled within $t>0$ time units is $1 - e^{-\mathbf{R}(s_1,s_2) \blacklozenge t}$. The use of exponentially distributed delays between state transitions makes CTMCs effective at modelling real-world system characteristics such as component failures and repairs, and request inter-arrival and service rates.

The quantitative properties to be verified are expressed in probabilistic temporal logics such as Continuous Stochastic Logic (CSL) (Aziz et al., 2000; Baier, Haverkort, Hermanns, & Katoen, 2003) for CTMC models (Table 4). For example, given a state $s \in S$ and an atomic proposition $a \in AP$, $s \vDash P_{\geq p}[\text{true} U^{[0,t]} a]$ specifies that the probability of satisfying the atomic proposition a after at most $t>0$ time units after starting in state s is greater than or equal to p.

Table 4. CSL operators; the first two operators are used to build path formulas, and the last couple of operators build state formulas. A CSL formula is a state formula.

Operator	Syntax	Semantics
Next	$X\phi$	State formula ϕ *is true in the next state*
(Time0bounded) Until	$\Phi_1 U^I \phi_2$	State formula ϕ_2 is true at some moment in the time interval $I \subset R_{\geq 0}$ and Φ_1 is true at every preceding moment
Probabilistic operator	$P \bowtie p[\psi]$	Path formula ψ is true with probability $\bowtie p$, where $\bowtie \in \{<,>,\leq,\geq\}$ and $p \in [0,1]$.
Steady-state operator	$S \bowtie p[\phi]$	In the long run, state formula ϕ *is true with probability* is true with probability $\bowtie p$, where $\bowtie \in \{<,>,\leq,\geq\}$ and $p \in [0,1]$.

Probabilistic model checkers are software tools that can be used to establish quantitative system properties that can be expressed in CSL or in a similar probabilistic temporal logic. The probabilistic model checker PRISM (Kwiatkowska, Norman, & Parker, 2005b) that our approach uses to implement utility-function policies can handle probabilistic models including CTMCs, DTMCs and MDPs. These models are specified in the high-level PRISM modelling language. They consist of sets of modules that correspond to the components of the system, and whose parallel composition represents the model of the overall system. Each module is defined as a set of guarded commands that describe the possible changes in the values of a set of a variables associated with the module. A generic command from a CTMC model has the form

[label] guard -> rate: action.

This command specifies that the transitions in the value of the module variables given by action is enabled with the given rate whenever the Boolean expression guard is true *and* all transitions with the same label from other modules are also enabled.

Implementation of Utility-Function Policies Using Quantitative Verification

Description of the Approach

An autonomic IT system comprises parameters that are monitored by its MAPE loop and parameters whose values are adjusted by the MAPE loop in response to changes in the values of the monitored parameters. We shall call the first set of parameters state parameters, and the set of parameters that are modified by the MAPE loop configuration parameters. The state parameter changes induced by adjustments in the configuration parameter values represent the behaviour of the system, and a model that describes this relationship between the configuration and state parameters of a system is termed a behavioural model or operational model.

Given an autonomic IT system with the state parameters $s_i \in S_i$, $1 \leq i \leq n$ and the configuration parameters $c_i \in C_i$, $1 \leq i \leq m$, our approach can be used to implement utility-function policies based on a utility function of the form

$$utility : S_1 \times S_2 \times \cdots \times S_n \times C_1 \times C_2 \times \cdots \times C_m \rightarrow R$$

(1)

if a PRISM CTMC, DTMC or MDP operational model for the system is available. PRISM operational models for a wide range of application domains are available from (Kwiatkowska et al., 2005b; Kwiatkowska, Norman, & Parker, 2005a; Prism, 2010), and can be used directly or as templates for building operational models for new types of IT systems.

One class of utility functions that is particularly flexible and straightforward to use with our approach is the class of multi-objective utility functions defined analytically as linear combinations of several system objectives:

$$utility\left(s_1, s_2, \ldots, s_n, c_1, c_2, \ldots, c_m\right) = \sum_{i=1}^{r} w_i objective_i \; ,$$

(2)

where the weights $w_i \in R, 1 \leq i \leq R$, are used to specify the trade-offs between the $r \geq 1$ system objectives. Each objective function $objective_i, 1 \leq i \leq R$, is an analytical expression of system parameters and formally specified quantitative properties to be analysed using PRISM.

To implement a utility-function policy based on the utility given by Equation. (2), our realisation of the MAPE autonomic computing loop employs PRISM to analyse the quantitative properties used to define the system objectives $objective_i, 1 \leq i \leq R$. This analysis is performed each time when a change in the monitored system parameters triggers the execution of the MAPE loop, and consists of establishing the value of these quantitative properties for a set of possible values for the configurable system parameters c_i, $1 \leq i \leq m$. For systems whose configuration parameters can take a finite set of discrete values, all possible configurations can be analysed in this way, and new, optimal values for the configuration parameters are obtained as seen in Equation 3:

This is the scenario encountered in the case study presented later in this section. For systems that comprise configuration parameters that can take a continuous range of values, the same analysis is performed for a finite set of possible configurations $C_1^0 \quad C_2^0 ::: \quad C_m^0$ $C'_1 \times C'_2 \times \cdots \times C'_m \subseteq C_1 \times C_2 \times \cdots \times C_m$. While this precludes the calculation of the optimal configuration parameters, an effective suboptimal solution can be obtained for many real-world autonomic systems if the analysed set of configurations is chosen carefully – this scenario is presented and validated in our related work (Calinescu & Kwiatkowska, 2009b).

Several characteristics make the probabilistic model checker PRISM particularly suitable for the implementation of utility-function policies as described above. First, PRISM supports the concept of experiments, i.e., the analysis of quantitative properties for a range of values for the model parameters. Therefore, a single PRISM operation is sufficient to analyse a quantitative property associated with a system objective from (2) for all configurations examined during an execution of the MAPE loop. Furthermore, PRISM provides a command-line interface that the MAPE loop uses to run the quantitative verification automatically, as a background process. Finally, an extensive, independent performance analysis of a broad selection of probabilistic model checkers (Jansen et al., 2008) ranked PRISM as the best tool for the quantitative analysis of large models such as the ones encountered in the work described in this section.

Case Study

To illustrate the approach to implementing utility-function policies described so far, we will use a

Equation 3.

$$\left(c'_1, c'_2, \ldots, c'_m\right) = \underset{\left(x_1, x_2, \ldots, x_m\right) \in C_1 \times C_2 \times \cdots \times C_m}{\arg \max} utility\left(s_1, s_2, \ldots, s_n, x_1, x_2, \ldots, x_m\right)$$

case study that involves the adaptive allocation of servers within a data centre. Given a data centre comprising a set of clusters, the objective of this application is to dynamically adjust the allocation of the data-centre servers to clusters in line with changes in (a) the data-centre and cluster parameters; and (b) the user-specified data-centre objectives. The parameters of this system are

- $N \geq 1$, the number of clusters in the data-centre;
- $totalServers \geq 1$, the number of servers in the data-centre;
- $priority_i > 0$, the priority of cluster i, $1 \leq i \leq N$;
- $requiredServers_i \geq 1$, the number of servers that cluster i needs in order to handle its workload, $1 \leq i \leq N$;
- $allocatedServers_i \geq 0$, the number of servers allocated to cluster i, $1 \leq i \leq N$;
- $targetAvailability_i \in [0,1]$, the user-specified steady-state probability that cluster i has at least $requiredServers_i$ operational servers, $1 \leq i \leq N$.

Note that the configuration parameters of the system are $allocatedServers_i$, $1 \leq i \leq N$. All other parameters described above are state parameters. Also known, and assumed to be constant, are the cluster topology and the failure and repair rates of the cluster components (i.e., servers, switches and backbone).

We will use an existing PRISM Markov chain that models the behaviour of a cluster with these characteristics. This is a continuous-time Markov chain taken from (Prism, 2010) and shown in Figure 20. The original purpose of this CTMC was to perform off-line analysis of quantitative properties of the cluster.

The utility function for our case study, as seen in, Equation 4, is a linear combination of $N+1$ system objectives. The first N of these objectives use a CSL formula to express the requirement that each of the N clusters achieves its target availability, and the last objective encodes the requirement that as few data-centre servers as possible are allocated to the N clusters at any point in time: where $operationalServers_i$, $1 \leq i \leq N$, represents the number of operational servers in the i th cluster. Notice that the weights used for the first N system objectives are the priorities of the N clusters. The weight for the last objective is a small positive constant $\varepsilon \ll 1$; this makes the MAPE loop select the system configuration with the fewest allocated servers when several configurations exist that yield identical utility with respect to the first N system objectives.

The optimal configuration for the data centre is determined by the MAPE loop each time when there is a change in one of the state parameters of the system. Each such iteration of the MAPE loop involves performing a series of PRISM experiments to analyse the CSL-encoded property in eq. (3) for the N data-centre clusters. In performing these experiments, the parameters of the CTMC model that correspond to state parameters of the system (i.e., $totalServers$, $requiredServers_i$, and $targetAvailability_i$, $1 \leq i \leq N$) are fixed so as to match the parameter values obtained from monitoring the system and from the user-specified target availabilities. In contrast, the configuration parameters are assigned each possible value,

Equation 4.

$$utility = \sum_{i=1}^{N} priority_i \bullet (S_{\geq targetAvailability_i}[operationalServers_i \geq requiredServers_i] ? 1 : 0) - \varepsilon \sum_{i=1}^{N} allocatedServers_i$$

Figure 20. Cluster topology and Markov chain for the case study

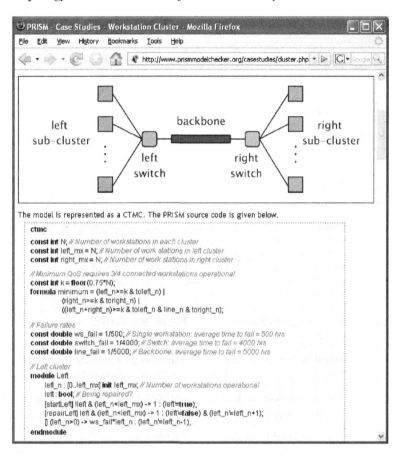

namely $allocatedServers_i = requiredServers_i,$ $requiredServers_i + 1, \cdots, totalServers,$ $1 \le i \le N$

Figure 21 depicts the result of the PRISM experiments carried out for a data centre with $N = 3$ clusters and $totalServers = 25$ when $requiredServers_1 = 5$, $requiredServers_2 = 7$, $requiredServers_3 = 10$. These experiments can be used, for instance, to establish the number of servers that should be allocated to each cluster in order to achieve two-nines or three-nines availability for that cluster.

Carrying out background PRISM experiments such as those illustrated in Figure 21 enables the MAPE loop to identify the optimal system utility and the configuration that yields it. This configuration is then used to ensure that the autonomic data centre achieves maximum utility in its new state.

We implemented an autonomic data-centre simulator, and we used it to simulate a data centre comprising $N=3$ clusters with different priorities: a "GOLD" cluster, a "SILVER" cluster and a "BRONZE" cluster. Figure 22 shows a typical set of experi-mental results that were obtained over a four-week period in simulated time. During this time period, the clusters were subjected to variable workloads by varying the values of the $requiredServers_i$ state parameters, $1 \le i \le 3$. Each such change triggered the execution of the utility-function policy (3), and thus the self-adjustment of the configuration parameters $allocatedServers_i$, $1 \le i \le 3$, based on the results of the quantitative analysis performed using PRISM experiments. With all possible data-centre configurations analysed by the PRISM experiments, the selection of the optimal configuration took up

Figure 21. PRISM experiments that analyse the expected availability of clusters with 5, 7 and 10 required servers, respectively

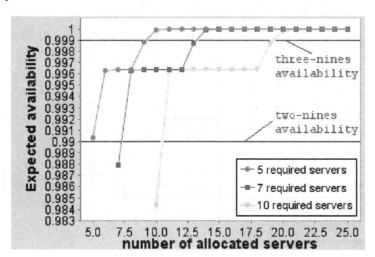

to 14 seconds with the experiments carried out on a 3.14GHz Intel Core-2 Duo CPU desktop PC. This response time is acceptable for this case study since under a quarter of a minute represents a small delay compared to the time required to provision a server when it is allocated to a new cluster. In another case study presented in (Calinescu & Kwiatkowska, 2009b), we demonstrate that sub-second response time can be achieved for a real-world autonomic system.

As indicated by the experimental results in Figure 22, implementing the utility-function policy ensures that sufficient servers to achieve the target availability are allocated to the highest priority cluster (i.e., "GOLD") at all times. During time intervals when all three clusters require large numbers of servers, this impacts the ability of the lower priority clusters (i.e., "BRONZE" and, sometimes, "SILVER") to realise their target availabilities. Whenever this happens, the two clusters of lower priority are allocated only their required numbers of servers, which represent the minimum values for the *allocatedServers$_2$* and *allocatedServers$_3$* configuration parameters that are considered by the MAPE loop.

Related Work

The use of runtime quantitative verification for the implementation of utility-function policies in autonomic IT systems was originally proposed in our preliminary work in (Calinescu & Kwiatkowska, 2009b, 2009a; Calinescu, 2009a). We are not aware of any other approaches to using techniques from the formal methods domain to support self- adaptation in autonomic systems.

Utility-function policies for autonomic computing were first advocated in (Walsh, Tesauro, Kephart, & Das, 2004), and have subsequently been used in a significant number of autonomic computing applications, including (White et al., 2004; Kephart & Walsh, 2004; Das et al., 2006; Kusic, Kephart, Hanson, Kandasamy, & Jiang, 2008; Calinescu, 2009a; Werkman, Schoonhoven, Jonge, & Matthijssen, 2010). The implementation of the utility-function policies in these applications often involves solving an integer or mixed-integer programming problem, e.g., (White et al., 2004; Das et al., 2006). Despite the availability of effective solvers for such problems, the solutions they produce cannot guarantee optimality. Using

Figure 22. Autonomic data-centre simulation results for a four-week period in simulated time

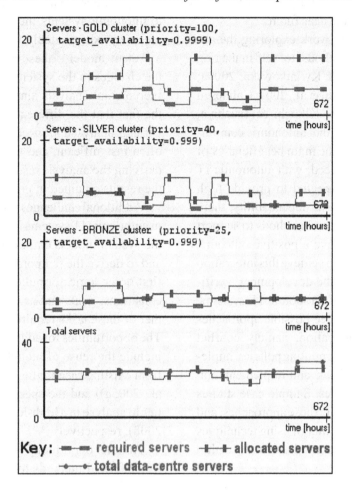

quantitative verification techniques overcomes this limitation.

In other applications, the autonomic systems are characterised by non-linear dependencies between their parameters. The implementation of utility-function policies on these systems can no longer be reduced to solving an integer/mixed-integer programming problem, and the typical approach in this case is to use heuristics such as (Kusic et al., 2008). This represents another scenario in which the approach described in this section supports the effective implementation of utility-function policies.

CONCLUSION

Formal methods and their supporting tools have come a long way in recent years. Examples of significant advances in the area include the advent of quantitative verification (Kwiatkowska, 2007) and of "lightweight" formal methods (Jackson, 2006), as well as the release of effective, open-source model checkers (Holzmann, 2003; Cimatti et al., 1999; Kwiatkowska et al., 2005a) and model finders (Alloy, 2010). The strong commitment to formal methods by the academic research community, and the growing interest that commercial organisations are taking in contributing to this research are indicators that the field will continue to develop rapidly in the near future.

Based on our recent work exploring the application of formal methods to self-managing IT systems (Calinescu & Kwiatkowska, 2009a; Calinescu, 2009a; Kikuchi et al., 2007; Calinescu & Kwiatkowska, 2009b; Kikuchi & Tsuchiya, 2010), we firmly believe that autonomic computing will become one of the main beneficiaries of these developments. Indeed, with autonomic IT systems increasingly expected to provide high levels of predictability and dependability, there is no doubt that using formal methods to support their operation would have a positive outcome. The key question is how to achieve this integration of formal methods into the development, verification and operation of autonomic IT systems. Our chapter looked at three possible approaches to achieving this integration, namely conflict detection in autonomic computing policies, implementation of goal policies, and implementation of utility-function policies. Sample case studies were presented to illustrate these approaches, and to demonstrate the feasibility of using techniques from various areas of formal methods within autonomic IT systems.

While the sample successful case studies presented in the chapter are based on real-world IT systems, it is clear that these applications of formal methods cannot readily benefit any type or size of autonomic IT system. The most significant challenge encountered in this work has been and will remain the state-space explosion (E. M. Clarke et al., 2000) – the often exponential increase in the number of model states with the increase of the system size, and a known limitation of model checking and model synthesis alike. Significant effort will be required to overcome this limitation and improve the scalability of the two techniques, especially when they are employed within a running autonomic system. One opportunity for achieving a substantial improvement that we would like to suggest is based on the concept of incremental analysis of updated models (Langville

& Meyer, 2006). When formal methods are applied to autonomic systems, the same system properties are analysed repeatedly for different variants of a system model – these variants correspond to the changes in the system parameters over time. Incremental analysis aims to take advantage of the fact that the differences between the model variants analysed in successive analysis steps are often insignificant, and to speed the process by deriving the analysis results for most steps from the results obtained in previous analysis steps.

Additional challenges in using formal methods in autonomic IT systems include the need to build the system models employed by these methods, and to derive the temporallogic properties or the first-order logic formulas encoding the system constrains, goals and/or utility. Carrying out either of these tasks requires significant expertise. The opportunities for addressing these challenges include the reuse of models or model templates from existing case studies (e.g., (Kwiatkowska et al., 2005a)) and the specification of the properties to analyse in a high-level language (Grunske, 2008), respectively.

Another opportunity to extend the applicability of formal methods to autonomic computing involves the use of formal techniques for the end-to-end development of autonomic IT systems. Two development platforms that fit this description have been proposed recently (Calinescu & Kwiatkowska, 2009a; Vassev & Hinchey, 2009a). The tool for the development of self-* systems presented in (Calinescu & Kwiatkowska, 2009a) employs a combination of formal software development techniques including model transformation, model-driven code generation and dynamic software reconfiguration (Calinescu, 2009a, 2009b) to add autonomic capabilities to systems whose components can be modelled as Markov chains. Given a PRISM-encoded Markov model of the form described in the previous section, the tool automates or aids (a) the development of the artifacts necessary to build the self-* system; and (b) their integration into a fully-operational self-* solution. The alternative development platform described in (Vassev & Hinchey, 2009a) is a framework that supports autonomic-system specification, validation and code generation. This platform comprises a formal notation and tool support for the definition and validation of autonomic system specifications, and includes generators that translate valid specifications into Java code that implements these specifications (Vassev & Mokhov, 2009; Vassev & Hinchey, 2009b).

Both platforms mentioned above speed up the development of autonomic systems compared to implementing equivalent systems manually. At the same time, they allow developers with limited expertise in formal methods to take advantage of the benefits offered by these techniques. We therefore envisage that this emerging trend to integrate formal methods within domain-independent platforms for the development of autonomic systems will grow to become one of the key areas of autonomic computing research in the future.

ACKNOWLEDGMENT

This work was partly supported by the UK Engineering and Physical Sciences Research Council grants EP/F001096/1 and EP/H042644/1. Shinji Kikuchi would like to thank to Dr. Tsuneo Katsuyama, Motomitsu Adachi and Satoshi Tsuchiya at Fujitsu Laboratories Limited for their support of this research and for their many insightful comments.

REFERENCES

Abrial, J.-R. (1996). *The B-Book: Assigning programs to meanings.* Cambridge University Press. doi:10.1017/CBO9780511624162

Al-Shaer, E., & Hamed, H. (2003, March). Firewall policy advisor for anomaly discovery and rule editing. In *Proceedings of IFIP/IEEE Eighth International Symposium on Integrated Network Management* (pp. 17-30).

Alloy. (2010). *Alloy Analyzer 4.* Massachusetts Institute of Technology. Retrieved from http://alloy.mit.edu/alloy4/

Amazon-EC. (2010). *Amazon elastic compute cloud.* Retrieved from http://aws.amazon.com/ec2/

Arshad, N. (2004). Automated dynamic reconfiguration using AI planning. In *Proceedings of 19th International Conference on Automated Software Engineering* (pp. 402-405).

Arshad, N., Heimbigner, D., & Wolf, A. (2003). Deployment and dynamic reconfiguration planning for distributed software systems. In *Proceedings of 15th IEEE International Confer-ence on Automated Software Engineering* (pp. 39-46).

Aziz, A. (2000). Model checking continuous-time Markov chains. *ACM Transactions on Computational Logic*, *1*(1), 162–170. doi:10.1145/343369.343402

Baier, C., Haverkort, B., Hermanns, H., & Katoen, J.-P. (2003). Model-checking algorithms for continuous-time Markov chains. *IEEE Transactions on Software Engineering*, *29*(6), 524–541. doi:10.1109/TSE.2003.1205180

Bandara, A., Lupu, E., & Russo, A. (2003). Using event calculus to formalise policy specification and analysis. In *Proceedings of 4th IEEE International Workshop on Policies for Distributed Systems and Networks* (pp. 26-39).

Barham, P., Dragovic, B., Fraser, K., Hand, S., Harris, T., Ho, A., et al. (2003). Xen and the art of virtualization. In *Proceedings of the Nineteenth ACM Symposium on Operating Systems Principles* (pp. 164-177). New York, NY: ACM.

Bengtsson, J., Larsen, K. G., Larsson, F., Pettersson, P., & Yi, W. (1995, octobre). Uppaal – A tool suite for automatic verification of real-time systems. In *Proc. of Workshop on Verification and Control of Hybrid Systems III* (pp. 232-243). Springer-Verlag.

Boca, P. P., Bowen, J. P., & Siddiqi, J. I. (2009). *Formal methods: State of the art and new directions*. Springer.

Brown, A., Keller, A., & Hellerstein, J. (2005). A model of configuration complexity and its application to a change management system. In *Proceedings of 9th IFIP/IEEE International Symposium on Integrated Network Management (IM 2005)* (pp. 631-644).

Calinescu, R. (2009a). General-purpose autonomic computing. In Denko, M. (Eds.), *Autonomic computing and networking* (pp. 3–30). Springer. doi:10.1007/978-0-387-89828-5_1

Calinescu, R. (2009b). Reconfigurable service-oriented architecture for autonomic computing. *International Journal on Advances in Intelligent Systems, 2*(1), 38–57.

Calinescu, R., & Kwiatkowska, M. (2009a). CADS*: Computer-aided development of self-* systems. In M. Chechik & M. Wirsing (Eds.), *Fundamental approaches to software engineering (FASE 2009)* (vol. 5503, pp. 421-424). Springer.

Calinescu, R., & Kwiatkowska, M. (2009b). Using quantitative analysis to implement autonomic IT systems. In *Proceedings of the 31st International Conference on Software Engineering (ICSE'09)* (pp. 100-110).

Charalambides, M., Flegkas, P., Pavlou, G., Bandara, A., Lupu, E., Russo, A., et al. (2005). Policy coflict analysis for quality of service management. In *Proceedings of Sixth IEEE International Workshop on Policies for Distributed Systems and Networks* (pp. 99-108).

Cimatti, A., Clarke, E., Giunchiglia, F., & Roveri, M. (1999). NuSMV: A new symbolic model verifier. In N. Halbwachs & D. Peled (Eds.), *Proceedings Eleventh Conference on Computer-Aided Verification (CAV'99)* (pp. 495-499). Springer.

Clarke, E., & Lerda, F. (2007). Model checking: Software and beyond. *Journal of Universal Computer Science, 13*(5), 639–649.

Clarke, E. M., Emerson, E. A., & Sistla, A. P. (1986). Automatic verification of finite-state con-current systems using temporal logic specifications. *ACM Trans. Program. Lang. Syst., 8*(2), 244–263. doi:10.1145/5397.5399

Clarke, E. M., Grumberg, O., & Peled, D. A. (2000). *Model checking*. MIT Press.

Corporation, I. B. M. (2001). *Autonomic computing: IBM's perspective on the state of information technology*. Retrieved from http://www.research.ibm.com/autonomic/manifesto/autonomic_computing.pdf

Dai, Y.-S. (2005). Autonomic computing and reliability improvement. In *Proceedings of the Eighth IEEE International Symposium on Object-Oriented Real-Time Distributed Computing (ISORC'05)* (pp. 204-206).

Das, R., et al. (2006). Towards commercialization of utility-based resource allocation. In *Proc. 3rd IEEE Intl. Conf. Autonomic Computing* (pp. 287-290).

Dunlop, N., Indulska, J., & Raymond, K. (2002). Dynamic conflict detection in policy-based management systems. In *Proceedings of Sixth International Enterprise Distributed Object Computing Conference (EDOC'02)* (pp. 15-26).

Eilam, T., Kalantar, M., Konstantinou, A., & Pacici, G. (2004). *Model-based automation of service deployment in a constrained environment*. IBM Research Report.

El Maghraoui, K., Meghranjani, A., Eilam, T., Kalantar, M., & Konstantinou, A. V. (2006). Model driven provisioning: bridging the gap between declarative object models and procedural provisioning tools. In *Middleware '06: Proceedings of the ACM/IFIP/USENIX 2006 International Conference on Middleware* (pp. 404-423). New York, NY: Springer-Verlag New York, Inc.

Fujitsu. (2010). *Fujitsu interstage*. Retrieved from http://www.fujitsu.com/interstage/

Garlan, D., Schmerl, B., & Cheng, S.-W. (2009). Software architecture-based self-adaptation. In Denko, M. (Eds.), *Autonomic computing and networking* (pp. 31–55). Springer. doi:10.1007/978-0-387-89828-5_2

Gerevini, A., & Serina, I. (2002). LPG: A planner based on planning graphs with action costs. In *Proceedings of the Sixth International Conference on Artificial Intelligence Planning and Scheduling (AIPS'02)*.

Grunske, L. (2008). Specification patterns for probabilistic quality properties. In *Proceedings 30th International Conference on Software Engineering (ICSE 2008)* (pp. 31-40). ACM.

Holzmann, G. J. (2003). *The SPIN model checker*. Addison-Wesley.

Huebscher, M. C., & McCann, J. A. (2008). A survey of autonomic computing – Degrees, models, and applications. *ACM Computing Surveys, 40*(3), 1–28. doi:10.1145/1380584.1380585

IBM-Tivoli. (2010). *Tivoli application dependency discovery manager*. Retrieved from http://www-01.ibm.com/software/tivoli/products/taddm/

Jackson, D. (2006). *Software abstractions: Logic, language, and analysis*. MIT Press.

Jansen, D. (2008). How fast and fat is your probabilistic model checker? An experimental comparison. In Yorav, K. (Ed.), *Hardware and software: Verification and testing (Vol. 4489*, pp. 69–85). Springer. doi:10.1007/978-3-540-77966-7_9

Katsuno, A. (2007). TRIOLE organic computing architecture. *Fujitsu Scientific and Technical Journal, 43*, 412–419.

Kephart, J. O., & Chess, D. M. (2003). The vision of autonomic computing. *IEEE Computer Journal, 36*(1), 41–50.

Kephart, J. O., & Walsh, W. E. (2004). An artificial intelligence perspective on autonomic computing policies. In *Proc. 5th IEEE Intl. Workshop on Policies for Distributed Systems and Networks*.

Kikuchi, S., & Tsuchiya, S. (2010). Configuration procedure synthesis for complex systems using model finder. In *Proceedings of the 15th IEEE International Conference on Complex Computer Systems*. Oxford, UK.

Kikuchi, S., Tsuchiya, S., Adachi, M., & Katsuyama, T. (2007). Policy verification and validation framework based on model checking approach. In *Proceedings of the 4th IEEE International Conference on Autonomic Computing*. Jacksonville, Florida.

Kowalski, R., & Sergot, M. (1986). A logic-based calculus of events. *New Gen. Comput., 4*(1), 67–95. doi:10.1007/BF03037383

Kusic, D., Kephart, J., Hanson, J., Kandasamy, N., & Jiang, G. (2008). Power and performance management of virtualized computing environments via lookahead control. In *Proc. IEEE International Conference on Autonomic Computing* (pp. 3-12).

Kwiatkowska, M. (2007). Quantitative verification: Models, techniques and tools. In *Proc. 6th Joint Meeting of the European Software Engineering Conference and the ACM SIGSOFT Symposium on the Foundations of Software Engineering (ESEC/FSE'07)* (pp. 449-458). ACM Press.

Kwiatkowska, M., Norman, G., & Parker, D. (2005a). Probabilistic model checking in practice: Case studies with PRISM. *ACM SIGMETRICS Performance Evaluation Review, 32*(4), 16–21. doi:10.1145/1059816.1059820

Kwiatkowska, M., Norman, G., & Parker, D. (2005b). Quantitative analysis with the probabilistic model checker PRISM. *Electronic Notes in Theoretical Computer Science, 153*(2), 5–31. doi:10.1016/j.entcs.2005.10.030

Kwiatkowska, M., Norman, G., & Parker, D. (2007). Stochastic model checking. In M. Bernardo & J. Hillston (Eds.), *Formal methods for the design of computer, communication and software systems: Performance evaluation (SMF'07)* (vol. 4486, p. 220-270). Springer.

Langville, A. N., & Meyer, C. D. (2006). Updating Markov chains with an eye on Google's PageRank. *SIAM Journal on Matrix Analysis and Applications, 27*(4), 968–987. doi:10.1137/040619028

Lens. (2010). *SAT4J*. Lens Computer Science Research Centre. Retrieved from http://www.sat4j.org/

Microsoft Research. (2008). *The rise and rise of the declarative datacentre*. (Technical Report, MSR-TR-2008-61).

Murch, R. (2004). *Autonomic computing*. IBM Press.

Nakamura, K., Naruse, T., Takagi, K., & Takagi, N. (2007). Efficient translation of logic circuits to CNF formulae with BDD for accaralating SAT-based formal verification. *IPSJ Technical Report SLDM, 2007*(27), 107-112. Retrieved from http://ci.nii.ac.jp/naid/110006250247/en/

Narain, S. (2005). Network configuration management via model nding. In *LISA '05: Proceedings of the 19th conference on Large Installation System Administration Conference*. Berkeley, CA: USENIX Association.

Niklas, E., & Niklas, S. (2003). An extensible SAT-solver. In E. Giunchiglia & A. Tacchella (Eds.), *SAT* (vol. 2919, pp. 502-518). Springer. Retrieved from http://dblp.uni-trier.de/db/conf/sat/sat2003.html

Parashar, M., & Hariri, S. (2006). *Autonomic computing: Concepts, infrastructure & applications*. CRC Press.

PRISM. (2010). Prism case study repository. Retrieved from http://www.prismmodelchecker.org/casestudies

Reiter, R. (1991). *The frame problem in the situation calculus: a simple solution (sometimes) and a completeness result for goal regression*. Artificial Intelligence and the Mathematical Theory of Computation.

Schneider, S. (2001). *The B-method*. Palgrave Macmillan.

Sterritt, R. (2003). Autonomic computing: The natural fusion of soft computing and hard computing. In *Proceedings of the IEEE International Conference on Systems, Man and Cybernetics* (vol. 5, pp. 4754{4759).

Sterritt, R., & Bustard, D. (2003). Autonomic computing: A means of achieving dependability? In *Proceedings of the 10th IEEE International Conference and Workshop on the Engineering of Computer-Based Systems (ECBS'03)*.

Twidle, K., Dulay, N., Lupu, E., & Sloman, M. (2009). Ponder2: A policy system for autonomous pervasive environments. In *Proceedings of the Fifth International Conference on Autonomic and Autonomous Systems (ICAS'09)*.

Vassev, E., & Hinchey, M. (2009a). ASSL: A software engineering approach to autonomic computing. *Computer*, *42*(6), 90–93. doi:10.1109/MC.2009.174

Vassev, E., & Hinchey, M. (2009b). Modeling the image-processing behavior of the NASA Voyager mission with ASSL. In *Proceedings of the Third IEEE International Conference on Space Mission Challenges for Information Technology* (pp. 246-253).

Vassev, E., & Mokhov, S. A. (2009). An ASSL-generated architecture for autonomic systems. In *Proceedings of the 2009 C3S2E Conference* (pp. 121-126). ACM Press.

Walsh, W. E., Tesauro, G., Kephart, J. O., & Das, R. (2004). Utility functions in autonomic systems. In *Proceedings of the 1st International Conference on Autonomic Computing* (pp. 70-77). New York, USA.

Wang, C., Hachtel, G. D., & Somenzi, F. (2006). *Abstraction refinement for large scale model checking (Series on Integrated Circuits and Systems)*. Secaucus, NJ: Springer-Verlag, Inc.

Warren, I., Sun, J., Krishnamohan, S., & Weerasinghe, T. (2006). An automated formal approach to managing dynamic reconfiguration. In *Proceedings of 21st IEEE/ACM International Conference on Automated Software* (pp. 37-46).

Werkman, E., van Schoonhoven, B., de Jonge, M., & Matthijssen, E. (2010). Development of autonomic management solutions for the military application domain. In *Proc. 15th IEEE International Conference on Engineering of Complex Computer Systems*.

White, S. R., et al. (2004). An architectural approach to autonomic computing. In *Proc. 1st IEEE International Conference on Autonomic Computing* (pp. 2-9). IEEE Computer Society.

Woodcock, J., & Davies, J. (1996). *Using Z. Specification, refinement and proof*. Prentice Hall.

Chapter 2
Theoretical and Practical Aspects of Developing Autonomic Systems with ASSL

Emil Vassev
Lero at University College Dublin, Ireland

ABSTRACT

ASSL (Autonomic System Specification Language) is an initiative for self-management of complex systems whereby the problem of formal specification, validation, and code generation of autonomic systems is approached within a framework. Being a formal method dedicated to autonomic computing, ASSL helps developers with problem formation, system design, system analysis and evaluation, and system implementation. The framework provides a powerful formal notation and suitable mature tool support that allow ASSL specifications to be edited and validated and Java code to be generated from any valid specification. As part of the framework's proof-of-concept strategy, ASSL has been used to make a variety of existing and prospective systems autonomic. This entry presents the ASSL formal specification model and tools. Moreover, two case studies are presented to reveal practical aspects of using ASSL for the development of prototypes of prospective space exploration systems incorporating autonomic features.

1. INTRODUCTION

It is widely recognized that high software complexity is a source of software failures that may have a disastrous effect, especially in safety-critical systems. This makes complexity one of the biggest challenges software producers are facing today. To respond to this threat, many initiatives such as Autonomic Computing (AC) (IBM Corporation, 2006), (Horn, 2001), (Kephart & Chess, 2003) have been started to deal with complexity in contemporary software systems. AC has emerged as a paradigm and research field tackling the development of complex large-scale systems by transforming them into special self-managing autonomic systems (ASs). Conceptually, ASs are intrinsically intended to reduce complexity through automation by applying principles of self-regulation from biology. In 2001, IBM Research introduced the term autonomic computing to draw

DOI: 10.4018/978-1-60960-845-3.ch002

an analogy between the computer systems and the human body's Autonomic Nervous System (Horn, 2001). The idea behind this is that computer systems must manage themselves, as the human body does, or they risk being crushed under their own complexity.

Although AC has recently inspired a tremendous number of initiatives for self-management of complex systems (note that company like IBM, Microsoft, Oracle and HP started AC-based programs), it still is not pervasive across the IT industry. The problem is that ASs cannot be developed successfully with the traditional software-development approaches, because these pay scant attention to many of the features of an AS and the very complexity inherent in many systems that lend themselves well to AC can often cause difficulty in designing that same ASs. Therefore, in order to avoid the threat of exploding complexity, we need to reconsider fundamentally the way we build AC software. However, although it is clear that new development approaches are needed to make AC take hold throughout the industry, the vast majority of IT companies is reluctant to invest in such development approaches. This is due mainly to the fact that traditional software development techniques (e.g., object-oriented programming) have proven their efficiency in practice as reliable approaches that guarantee low risk and high rate of return of investments.

This entry presents an approach towards building ASs with the Autonomic System Specification Language (ASSL) (Vassev, 2008), (Vassev, 2009), (Vassev & Hinchey, 2009), a formal method dedicated to AC. Conceptually, ASSL have been intended to help developers make the real transition to an "autonomic culture" by connecting AC with formal methods. Despite being a subject of controversy for decades, over the last decade (Bowen & Hinchey, 2004), formal methods have regained confidence and have proven to be

extremely useful in the development of reliable software for safety-critical systems such as modern avionics systems and nuclear plants (Amey, 2002), (Beveniste et al., 2003), where software failures easily emerge to safety hazards. The provided high level of abstraction and the formal treatment of the problems have motivated this success. ASSL builds on this by adding an AC domain-specific formal notation and tools for AS specification, validation, and code generation.

This entry presents ASSL from two perspectives – theoretical and practical. The entry introduces first both the ASSL specification model and tools as a theoretical background needed for understanding the following section where two case studies are presented. These case studies describe practical experience of using ASSL in the development of autonomic features for AC prototypes of space exploration missions based on swarm intelligence and prospective autonomic Voyager-like missions.

2. ASSL

Initially developed at Concordia University, Montreal, Canada, the Autonomic System Specification Language (ASSL) (Vassev, 2008), (Vassev, 2009), (Vassev & Hinchey, 2009) is a domain-specific formal tool whereby the problem of *formal specification*, *validation*, and *code generation* of ASs is approached within a framework. Being a formal method dedicated to AC, ASSL helps AC researchers with problem formation, system design, system analysis and evaluation, and system implementation. The framework provides a powerful formal notation and suitable mature tool support that allow ASSL specifications to be edited and validated and Java code to be generated from any valid specification.

2.1. Specification Model

The ASSL formal notation is defined through formalization tiers. Over these tiers, ASSL provides a multi-tier specification model that is designed to be scalable and to expose a judicious selection and configuration of infrastructure elements and mechanisms needed by an AS. ASSL defines ASs with special self-managing policies, interaction protocols (IPs), and autonomic elements (AEs), where the ASSL tiers and their sub-tiers describe different aspects of the AS under consideration. Table 1 presents the ASSL specification model. As shown, it decomposes an AS in two directions — (1) into levels of functional abstraction; and (2) into functionally related sub-tiers. The first decomposition presents the system from three different perspectives (three major tiers) (Vassev, 2008), (Vassev, 2009):

1. **General and global AS perspective:** defines the general *system rules* (providing AC behavior), *architecture*, and global *actions*, *events*, and *metrics* applied in these rules;
2. **Interaction protocol perspective:** defines the means of communication between AEs within an AS;
3. **Unit-level perspective:** defines interacting sets of individual computing elements (AEs) with their own AC behavior rules, actions, events, metrics, etc.

The second decomposition presents the major tiers (AS, ASIP, and AE – cf. Table 1) as composed of functionally related sub-tiers, where new AS properties emerge at each sub-tier. This allows for different approaches to AS specification. For example, we may start with a global perspective of the system by specifying the AS service-level objectives and self-management policies and by digging down to find the needed metrics at the very detail level of AE sub-tiers. Alternatively, we may start working at the detail level of AE

Table 1. ASSL multi-tier specification model

AS	AS Service-lever Objectives	
	AS Self-management Policies	
	AS Architecture	
	AS Actions	
	AS Events	
	AS Metrics	
ASIP	AS Messages	
	AS Channels	
	AS Functions	
AE	AE Service-level Objectives	
	AE Self-management Polocies	
	AE Friends	
	AEIP	AE Messages
		AE Channels
		AE Functions
		AE Managed Elements
	AE Recovery Protocols	
	AE Behavior Models	
	AE Outcomes	
	AE Actions	
	AE Events	
	AE Metrics	

sub-tiers and build our AS bottom-up. Finally, we can work on both abstract and detail level sides by constantly synchronizing their specification.

2.2. ASSL Tiers

The AS Tier specifies an AS in terms of service-level objectives (AS SLOs), self-management policies, architecture topology, actions, events, and metrics (cf. Table 1). The AS SLOs are a high-level form of behavioral specification that helps developers establish system objectives such as performance. The self-management policies could be any of (but not restricted to) the four so-called self-CHOP policies defined by the AC IBM blueprint (IBM Corporation, 2006): self-configuring, self-healing, self-optimizing, and self-protecting.

These policies are driven by events and trigger the execution of actions driving an AS in critical situations. The metrics constitute a set of parameters and observables controllable by an AS. With the ASIP Tier, the ASSL framework helps developers specify an AS-level interaction protocol as a public communication interface expressed with special communication channels, communication functions, and communication messages. At the AE Tier, the ASSL formal model exposes specification constructs for the specification of the system's AEs. Note that AEs are considered to be analogous to software agents able to manage their own behavior and their relationships with other AEs.

Note that ASSL targets only the AC features of a system and helps developers clearly distinguish the AC features from the system-service features. This is possible, because with ASSL we model and generate special AC wrappers in the form of ASs that embed the components of non-AC systems (Vassev, 2008), (Vassev, 2009), (Vassev & Hinchey, 2009). The latter are considered as managed elements, controlled by the AS in question. Conceptually, a managed element can be any software or hardware system (or sub-system) providing services. Managed elements are specified per AE (cf. Table 1) where the emphasis is on the interface needed to control a managed element. It is important also to mention that the ASSL tiers and sub-tiers are intended to specify different aspects of an AS, but it is not necessary to employ all of them in order to model such a system. For a simple AS, we need to specify (1) the AEs providing self-managing behavior intended to control the managed elements associated with an AE; and (2) the communication interface. Here, self-management policies must be specified to provide such self-managing behavior at the level of AS (the AS Tier) and at the level of AE (AE Tier). The following subsections briefly present some of the ASSL sub-tiers.

2.2.1. Self-Management Policies

The self-management behavior of an ASSL-developed AS is specified with the self-management policies. These policies are specified with special ASSL constructs termed *fluents* and *mappings* (Vassev, 2008), (Vassev, 2009). A fluent is a state where an AS enters with fluent-activating events and exits with fluent-terminating events. A mapping connects fluents with particular actions to be undertaken. Usually, an ASSL specification is built around self-management policies, which make that specification AC-driven. Self-management policies are driven by events and actions determined deterministically. The following ASSL code (Exhibit 1) presents a sample specification of a self-healing policy.

2.2.2. ASSL Events

ASSL aims at event-driven autonomic behavior. Hence, to specify self-management policies, we need to specify appropriate events (cf. Section 2.2.1). Here, we rely on the reach set of event types exposed by ASSL (Vassev, 2008), (Vassev, 2009). To specify ASSL events, one may use logical expressions over SLOs, or may relate events with metrics (cf. Section 2.2.3), other events, actions, time, and messages. Moreover, ASSL allows for the specification of special conditions that must be stated before an event is prompted.

2.2.3. ASSL Metrics

For an AS, one of the most important success factors is the ability to sense the environment and react to sensed events. Here, together with the rich set of events, ASSL imposes metrics that help to determine dynamic information about external and internal points of interest. Although four different types of metrics are allowed (Vassev, 2008), (Vassev, 2009), the most important type is

Exhibit 1.

```
ASSELF_MANAGEMENT {
  SELF_HEALING {
    FLUENT inLosingSpacecraft {
      INITIATED_BY { EVENTS.spaceCraftLost }
      TERMINATED_BY { EVENTS.earthNotified }
    }
    MAPPING {
      CONDITIONS { inLosingSpacecraft }
      DO_ACTIONS { ACTIONS.notifyEarth }
    }
  }
} // ASSELF_MANAGEMENT
```

the so-called *resource metrics*, which is intended to gather information about special managed element's quantities.

2.2.4. Managed Elements

An AE typically controls *managed elements*. In an ASSL-developed AS, a managed element is specified with a set of special interface functions intended to provide control functionality over that managed element. Note that ASSL can specify and generate interfaces controlling a managed element (generated as a stub), but not the real implementation of these interfaces. This is just fine for prototyping, however when deploying an AS prototype the generated interfaces must be manually programmed to deal with the controlled system (or sub-system).

2.2.5. Interaction Protocols

ASSL interaction protocols provide a means of communication interface expressed with messages that can be exchanged among AEs via communication channels and communication functions. Thus, by specifying an ASSL interaction protocol we develop an embedded messaging system needed to connect the AEs of an AS.

In a basic communication process ongoing in such a system, an AE relies on a communication function to receive a message over an incoming communication channel, changes its internal state and sends some new messages over an outgoing channel (Vassev, 2008), (Vassev, 2009).

2.3 ASSL Notation

ASSL is a declarative specification language for ASs with well-defined semantics (Vassev, 2008) (Vassev, 2009). The language provides a powerful formal notation that enriches the underlying logic with modern programming language concepts and constructs such as inheritance, modularity, type system, and high abstract expressiveness. As a formal language, ASSL defines a neutral (i.e., implementation-independent) representation for ASs described as a set of interacting AEs. Exhibit 2 is a generic meta-grammar in Extended Backus-Naur Form (BNF) (Knuth, 1964) presenting the syntax rules for specifying ASSL tiers. Note that this meta-grammar is an abstraction of the ASSL grammar, which cannot be presented here due to the complex structure of the ASSL specification model (cf. Section 2.1), where each tier has its own syntax and semantic rules. The interested reader is advised to refer to (Vassev, 2008) or

Exhibit 2.

```
GroupTier → FINAL? ASSLGroupTierId{Tier+}Tier → FINAL? ASSLTierId
TierName?{Data* TierClause+}TierClause → FINAL? ASSLClauseId ClauseName?{Data*}
Data → TypeDecl* | VarDecl* | CllctnDecl* | Statement*TypeDecl → CustTypeIden-
tifierVarDecl → Type VarIdentifierCllcntDecl → Type CustCllctnIdentifierType →
CustType | PredefTypeStatement → Assign-Stmnt | Loop | If-Then-Else | Cllctn-
StmntLoop → Foreach-Stmnt | DoWhile-Stmnt | WhileDo-Stmnt
```

(Vassev, 2009) for the complete ASSL grammar expressed in BNF and for the formal semantics of the ASSL language.

As shown in the grammar above, an ASSL tier is syntactically specified with an ASSL *tier identifier*, an optional *name* and a *content block* bordered by curly braces. Moreover, we distinguish two syntactical types of tier: *single tiers (Tier)* and *group tiers (GroupTier)*, where the latter comprise a set of single tiers. Each single tier has an optional *name (TierName)* and comprises a set of special *tier clauses (TierClause)* and optional *data (Data)*. The latter is a set of *data declarations* and *statements*. Data declarations could be: (1) *type declarations*; (2) *variable declarations*; and (3) *collection declarations*. Statements could be: (1) *loop statements*; (2) *assignment statements*; (3) *if-then-else statements*; and (4) *collection statements*. Statements can comprise *Boolean* and *numeric expressions*. In addition, although not shown in the grammar above, note that identifiers participating in ASSL expressions are either simple, consisting of a single identifier, or qualified, consisting of a sequence of identifiers separated by "." tokens.

2.4. ASSL Toolset

The ASSL Toolset helps developers edit and validate ASSL specifications and generate Java code (Vassev, 2008), (Vassev, 2009), i.e., the ASSL toolset provides powerful tools needed to formally

process an ASSL specification and automatically generate the corresponding implementation. The following subsections briefly present some of the ASSL framework's tools.

2.4.1. Consistency Checker

The Consistency Checker (cf. Figure 1) is a framework mechanism for verifying ASSL specifications by performing *exhaustive traversing*. In general, the Consistency Checker performs two kinds of consistency-checking operations: (1) light - checks for *type consistency, ambiguous definitions*, etc.; and (2) heavy - checks whether the specification model conforms to special *correctness properties*. The ASSL correctness properties are special ASSL semantic definitions (Vassev, 2008), (Vassev, 2009) defining tier-specific rules that make it possible to reason about the properties of the specifications created with ASSL. They are expressed in First-Order Linear Temporal Logic (FOLTL)[1] (Clarke et al., 2002), (Baier & Katoen, 2008), which allows for the formalization of rules related to system evolution over time. An example of a semantic rule defined for the AS/AE Self-management Policies Tier (cf. Table 1) is related to *policy initiation* (Vassev, 2008), (Vassev, 2009):

Every policy is triggered by a finite non-empty set of fluents, and performs actions associated with these fluents".

Figure 1. Consistency checking with ASSL

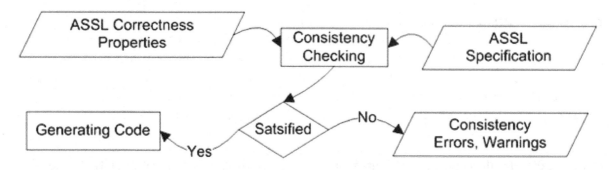

$$\forall \pi \in \Pi \cdot ((\mathbf{F} \not\equiv \varnothing \wedge A \not\equiv \varnothing) \Longrightarrow (\forall f \epsilon\ \mathbf{F} \cdot \exists a \in A \cdot (\text{trigger}(f, \pi) \Longrightarrow \text{perform}(a))))$$

where:

Π is the universe of self-management policies in the AS;
$\mathbf{F}$ is a finite set of fluents specified by the policy π;
A is a finite set of actions mapped to the fluents specified by the policy π.

Although, the ASSL correctness properties are expressed in FOLTL, in its first release the ASSL framework does not incorporate an FOLTL engine, and thus, the consistency checking mechanism implements the correctness properties as Java statements. Here, the FOLTL operators $\forall$ (forall) and $\exists$ (exists) work over sets of ASSL *tier instances* (ASSL-specified tiers or sub-tiers). In addition, these operators are translated by taking their first argument as a logical atom that contains a single unbound tier variable. Ideally, this atom has a relatively small number of ground tier instances, so the combinatorial explosion generally produced by these statements is controlled.

It is important to mention that the consistency checking mechanism generates consistency errors or warnings (cf. Figure 1). Warnings are specific situations, where the specification does not contradict the correctness properties, but rather introduces uncertainty as to how the code generator will handle it.

2.4.2. Model Checker

Although the Consistency Checker tool takes care of syntax and consistency errors, it still cannot handle logical errors and thus, cannot assert *safety* (e.g., freedom from deadlock) or *liveness* properties (Vassev et al., 2009). Thus, to ensure the correctness of the ASSL specifications, and that of the generated ASs, at the time of writing, there was ongoing research on model checking with ASSL:

- A part of this research is on a model-checking mechanism that takes an ASSL specification as input and produces as output a *finite state-transition system* (called *ASSL State Graph* (ASG) or *state machine*) such that a specific *correctness property* in question is satisfied if and only if the original ASSL specification satisfies that property (Vassev et al., 2009).
- Another research direction is towards mapping ASSL specifications to special *service logic graphs*, which support the so-called *reverse model checking* (Bakera et al., 2009).

Figure 2 depicts the first approach to model checking in ASSL. As shown, the Model Checker tool builds the ASG for the AS in question by using its ASSL specification to derive the system states and associates with each derived state special *atomic propositions* (defined in FOLTL) true in that state (Vassev et al., 2009). Note that in the case that a correctness property is not satisfied, the ASSL framework returns a *counterexample*. The latter is an execution path of the ASG for which the desired correctness property is not true. Moreover, the so-called *state explosion problem* (Clarke et al., 2002), (Baier & Katoen, 2008) is considered when the size of the state machine (or ASG) must be reduced in order to perform efficient model checking (Vassev et al., 2009).

The notion of state in ASSL is related to tiers. The *ASSL Operational Semantics* (Vassev, 2008), (Vassev, 2009) considers a state-transition model where tier instances can be in different *tier states*, e.g., AE/AS SLO can be evaluated as *satisfied* or *not satisfied* (Vassev, 2008), (Vassev, 2009). Formally, an ASG can be presented as a tuple **(S; Op; R; S_0 ; AP; L)** (Baier & Katoen, 2008) where: **S** is the set of all possible ASSL tier states; **Op** is the set of special ASSL state-transition operations (Vassev, 2008), (Vassev, 2009); $\mathbf{R} \subseteq \mathbf{S} \times \mathbf{Op} \times \mathbf{S}$ are the possible transitions; $\mathbf{S_0} \subseteq \mathbf{S}$ is a set of initial tier states; **AP** is a set of atomic propositions; $L:S \rightarrow 2^{AP}$ is a labeling function relating a set $\mathbf{L(s)} \in 2^{AP}$ of atomic propositions to any state s, i.e., a set of atomic propositions true in that state.

An ASSL-developed AS transits from a state to another when a particular tier instance evolves from a tier state to another tier state. Note that

due to the complex specification model exposed by ASSL (cf. Section 2.1), each sub-tier instance forms a distinct state machine (called basic machine) nested in the state machine of its host tier instance (recall that sub-tiers are nested in tiers – cf. Table 1). Here, the *AE state machine* is a Cartesian product of the state machines of its sub-tiers. It is important to mention that by taking the Cartesian product of a set of basic sub-tier machines, we form a *product machine* consisting of *product states*. The latter are tuples of *concurrent* basic sub-tier states. Moreover, the states in the state machine of the whole *AS product machine* is obtained by the Cartesian product of all the *AE product machines*. An example of model checking with ASSL is presented in Section 3.2.

2.4.3. Test Case Generator

To detect errors introduced not only with the ASSL specifications, but also with the supplementary coding (after the automatic code generation), the automatic verification provided by the ASSL tools is about to be augmented by appropriate test case generator tool (Vassev et al., 2010). This tool automates the generation of test cases for self-management policies in ways that support incremental testing and provide immediate visual feedback. ASSL-developed ASs are driven by self-management policies (cf. Section 2.2.1) and to test properly such ASs, the test case generator

Figure 2. Model checking with ASSL

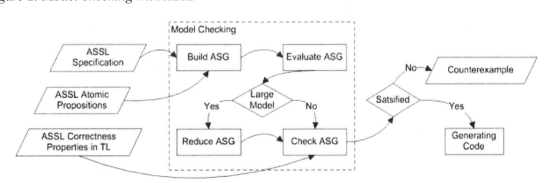

tool considers all implemented self-management policies. Two techniques for test case generation have been used: one using *random selection* and another using a *change-impact analysis approach* (Vassev et al., 2010). Conceptually, the test case generator tool accepts as input an ASSL specification comprising sets of policies *Π* that need to be tested and generates a set of tests *T* as tuples *T {Pex, A {I, R}}* comprising an execution path *Pex* and test attributes *A*. The latter is a tuple comprising needed inputs *I* and optional ASSL replacement constructs *R*. The latter are automatically or semi-automatically determined and generated as special stubs to ensure the execution of *Pex*.

As shown in Figure 3, the tool consists of four major components: policy extractor, change-impact analyzer, test suit generator, and test suit reducer. The key notion of the tool is to synthesize two or more execution paths of same fluent (cf. Section 2.2.1) in such a way that the test-coverage targets (e.g., certain policies, rules, or conditions) are covered by the synthesized execution paths. The change-impact analysis component can then determine for each execution path the needed test attributes *A* such as inputs *I* and optional replacement constructs *R* in the form of *ASSL events, ASSL actions,* and *tier clauses* (cf. Section 2.3) needed to be employed by an execution path in order to ensure the same. Based on the determined test attributes and execution paths, the tool generates tests *T*. Often the number of generated tests is large and it is not feasible for developers to manually inspect the tests' responses. To mitigate this issue, the final step of the test case generator reduces the number of generated tests by selecting tests based on policy structural coverage.

2.4.4. Code Generator

The ASSL framework is a comprehensive development environment that delivers a powerful combination of ASSL notation and ASSL tools. The latter allow specifications written in the ASSL notation to be processed and to generate Java applications of the same. Code generation is the most complex activity taking place in the ASSL framework. In general, it is about mapping formally validated ASSL specifications to Java classes by applying the ASSL Operational Semantics (Vassev, 2008), (Vassev, 2009). Thus, an operational Java application skeleton is generated for each valid ASSL specification. The former is generated as a fully operational multithreaded event-driven application with embedded messaging. The automatically generated code offers some major advantages over the analytic approach to implementation. The greatest advantage is that with the generated code we can be certain that our ASSL constructs are properly mapped to correctly generated Java classes. Some other advantages are:

- A logically consistent construction of Java classes is generated;
- The classes in the generated application are linked properly;
- The AS threads are started in the proper order;
- A messaging system is generated for the ASSL interaction protocols, including event-driven notification, distinct messages, channels, and communication functions;
- A proper type mapping is applied to generate code with appropriate data types;

Figure 3. Operational view of the ASSL test generator

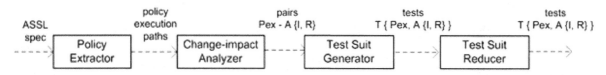

- Appropriate descriptive comments are generated.

Figure 4 depicts the process of code generation where the ASSL framework's components collaborate on producing Java classes from ASSL specification structures. Note that here the labeled Exhibits present different components (e.g., ASSL scanner) in the ASSL toolset and the labeled arrows are data flow arrows.

3. DEVELOPING SELF-MANAGING SYSTEMS WITH ASSL

As part of the ASSL framework validation and in the course of multiple research projects, ASSL has been used to specify autonomic properties and generate prototype models for the NASA ANTS concept mission (Vassev et al., 2008a), (Vassev et al., 2008b), (Vassev & Hinchey, 2009b), (Vassev & Hinchey, 2008) and NASA Voyager mission (Vassev & Hinchey, 2009c). Both ASSL specifications and generated prototype models have been used to investigate hypotheses about the design and implementation of intelligent swarm-based systems and possible future Voyager-like missions incorporating the principles of AC.

3.1. Modeling the NASA ANTS Mission

3.1.1. The ANTS Mission

The Autonomous Nano-Technology Swarm (ANTS) concept sub-mission PAM (Prospecting Asteroids Mission) is a novel approach to asteroid belt resource exploration (Truszkowski et al., 2004), (Rouff et al., 2005). ANTS necessitates extremely high levels of autonomy, minimal communication requirements with Earth, and a set of very small explorers with a few consumables (Truszkowski et al., 2004), (Rouff et al., 2005). These explorers forming the swarm are pico-class,

low-power, and low-weight spacecraft, yet capable of operating as fully autonomous and adaptable agents. The units in a swarm are able to interact with each other and self-organize based on the emergent behavior of simple interactions.

Figure 5 depicts the ANTS concept mission. A transport spacecraft launched from Earth toward the asteroid belt carries a laboratory that assembles the tiny spacecraft. Once it reaches a certain point in space, where gravity forces are balanced, termed a Lagrangian, the transport ship releases the assembled swarm, which will head for the asteroid belt. Each spacecraft is equipped with a solar sail, thus it relies primarily on power from the sun, using only tiny thrusters to navigate independently. Moreover, each spacecraft also has onboard computation, artificial intelligence, and heuristics systems for control at the individual and team levels.

As Figure 5 shows, there are three classes of spacecraft — *rulers*, *messengers*, and *workers*. They form teams that explore particular asteroids in an ant-colony analogy. ANTS exhibits self-organization since there is no external force directing its behavior and no single spacecraft unit has a global view of the intended macroscopic behavior. In general, a swarm consists of several sub-swarms, which are temporal groups organized to perform a particular task. Each swarm group has a *group leader* (ruler), one or more *messengers*, and a number of *workers* carrying a *specialized instrument*. The messengers are needed to connect the team members when they cannot connect directly, due to a long distance or a barrier.

3.1.2. Modeling Self-Healing Behavior with ASSL

ASSL has been successfully used for modeling ANTS self-management policies such as *self-configuring* (Vassev et al., 2008b), *self-healing* (Vassev & Hinchey, 2009b), *self-scheduling* (Vassev et al., 2008a), and *emergent self-adapting* (Vassev & Hinchey, 2008). In addition, a speci-

Figure 4. The code-generation process in ASSL

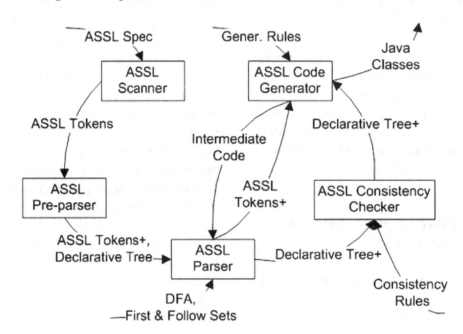

fication model for the *ANTS safety requirements* was proposed in (Vassev et al., 2008b). In this subsection, a self-healing behavior model for ANTS is presented.

In ANTS, self-healing is about recovering from failures, including those caused by damage due to a crash or an outside force. In our scenario, we assume that each worker sends, on a regular basis, *heartbeat messages* to the ruler. The latter can use those messages to determine when a worker is not able to continue its operation, due to crash or malfunction in its communication device. Moreover, a worker sends a *notification message* to the ruler if its instrument started malfunctioning or it got broken, due to a crash with an asteroid or another spacecraft. Thus, a ruler is notified in two ways for a worker loss:

- A heartbeat message from the worker has not been received;
- A message from the worker, notifying of a broken instrument, has been received.

Once the loss of an operational unit has been detected, the ruler checks if the number of workers is below the critical minimum, and if so, it requests a replacement from another ruler. If such a replacement is not possible it may notify the ground control on Earth and may request a replacement or further instructions.

Conceptually, an ASSL specification of the ANTS self-healing behavior requires a specification at the AS Tier for the global ANTS behavior and at the AE Tier for the self-healing behavior of every *ANT_Worker*, *ANT_Ruler* and *ANT_Messenger*. Here, only the ASSL specification of the *ANT_Worker* is presented. The interested reader is advised to refer to (Vassev, 2008) or (Vassev, 2009) for the specification of the self-healing behavior at the AS Tier and for that of the *ANT_Ruler* AE.

Figures 6, 7, 8, and 9 present a partial specification of the self-healing policy for ANTS workers (the *ANT_Worker* AE). In order to specify the self-healing autonomic property of a worker, we use the *SELF_HEALING* self-management policy (cf. Figure 6). The self-healing policy is specified as a set of *fluents* and *mappings*, where the latter

Figure 5. ANTS Mission Concept (Truszkowski et al., 2004)

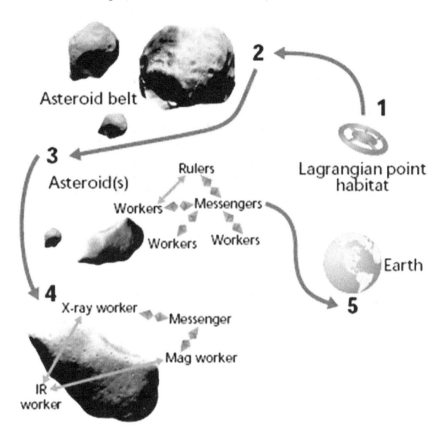

map the *fluents* to *actions*. Moreover, we specify the necessary *actions* (cf. Figure 8), *events* and *metrics* (cf. Figure 9), and the *AE interaction protocol* (cf. Figure 7). The latter comprises the messages that can be exchanged among the worker and its ruler, the communication functions, and a communication channel, all needed by the self-healing policy.

In addition, at the AEIP tier, we specify a managed element called *worker*, which provides a *getDistanceToNearestObject* interface function that is needed by the metric *distanceToNearestObject* to measure distance. Note that the *ANT_Ruler* is listed as a friend of the *ANT_Worker*, (cf. *FRIENDS {...}* clause in Figure 6) and thus, it can use the *ANT_Worker*'s private (AE-level, i.e., defined within the AE Tier) messages and channels (specified at the AE's AEIP sub-tier)[2]. The

following elements reveal some details of the self-healing policy specification.

inCollision

This fluent takes place when the worker crashes into an asteroid or into another spacecraft, but it is still able to perform self-checking operations. The fluent is initiated by a *collisionHappen* event that is prompted immediately after a collision with another object. Moreover, this fluent terminates when the *instrumentChecked* event happens (cf. Figure 6), i.e., when the worker has performed an instrument-checking operation. Further, this fluent is mapped to the *checkANTInstrument* action (cf. Figure 8). The *checkANTInstrument* action uses a special *IMPL[3]* action to perform a check operation on the worker's instrument. In case the instrument

Theoretical and Practical Aspects of Developing Autonomic Systems with ASSL

Figure 6. ANT_Worker self-healing specification: Self-healing policy

```
1.  AE ANT_Worker {
2.    AE SELF_MANAGEMENT {
3.      SELF_HEALING {
4.        FLUENT inCollision {
5.          INITIATED_BY { EVENTS.collisionHappen }
6.          TERMINATED_BY { EVENTS.instrumentChecked }
7.        }
8.        FLUENT inInstrumentBroken {
9.          INITIATED_BY { EVENTS.instrumentBroken }
10.         TERMINATED_BY { EVENTS.isMsgInstrumentBrokenSent }
11.       }
12.       FLUENT inHeartbeatNotification {
13.         INITIATED_BY { EVENTS.timeToSendHeartbeatMsg }
14.         TERMINATED_BY { EVENTS.isMsgHeartbeatSent }
15.       }
16.       MAPPING { // if collision then check if the instrument is still operational
17.         CONDITIONS { inCollision }
18.         DO_ACTIONS { ACTIONS.checkANTInstrument }
19.       }
20.       MAPPING { // if the instrument is broken then notify the group leader
21.         CONDITIONS { inInstrumentBroken }
22.         DO_ACTIONS { ACTIONS.notifyForBrokenInstrument }
23.       }
24.       MAPPING { // time to send a heartbeat message has come
25.         CONDITIONS { inHeartbeatNotification }
26.         DO_ACTIONS { ACTIONS.notifyForHeartbeat }
27.       }
28.     }
29.   } // AE SELF_MANAGEMENT

30.   FRIENDS {
31.     AELIST { AES.ANT_Ruler }
32.   }
```

is not operational, an *instrumentBroken* event is prompted (cf. line 79 in Figure 8).

inInstrumentBroken

This fluent (cf. line 8 in Figure 6) is triggered when the instrumentBroken event is prompted (see the specification of the *checkANTInstrument* action), and terminates with the *isMsgInstrumentBrokenSent* event (cf. line 97 in Figure 8). This event occurs when the *instrumentBrokenMsg* message, notifying of a broken instrument, is sent to the ruler (the *notifyForBrokenInstrument* action calls the function that sends this message). This message is specified in the *AEIP.MESSAGES* section (cf. line 35 in Figure 7) together with an *HBW_link* channel and the *sendInstrumentBrokenMsg* function. The former is the ASSL specification of the

communication link used for communication between the worker and its ruler.

inHeartbeatNotification

This fluent (cf. line 12 in Figure 6) is triggered when the *timeToSendHeartbeatMsg* event is fired. This event is a timed event, i.e., it is fired repeatedly after a particular amount of time has elapsed (in this case 1 minute). The fluent terminates with an *isMsgHeartbeatSent* event, which is fired when the heartbeat message is sent to the ruler. Moreover, this fluent is mapped to the *notifyForHeartbeat* action. This action uses the *sendHeartbeatMsg* AEIP function to send the *heartbeatMsg* message, over the *HBW_link* channel, to the ruler (cf. the AEIP specification section in Figure 7). Note that this action can be performed only if the self-healing

Figure 7. ANT_Worker self-healing specification: AEIP

```
33.    AEIP {
34.        MESSAGES {
35.            FINAL MESSAGE instrumentBrokenMsg {
36.                SENDER { AES.ANT_Worker }
37.                RECEIVER { AES.ANT_Ruler }
38.                MSG_TYPE { TEXT }
39.                BODY { "broken instrument" }
40.            }
41.            FINAL MESSAGE heartbeatMsg {
42.                SENDER { AES.ANT_Worker }
43.                RECEIVER { AES.ANT_Ruler }
44.                MSG_TYPE { TEXT }
45.                BODY { "alive" }
46.            }
47.        }
48.        CHANNELS {
49.            CHANNEL HBW_link {
50.                ACCEPTS { AEIP.MESSAGES.instrumentBrokenMsg , AEIP.MESSAGES.heartbeatMsg }
51.                ACCESS { SEQUENTIAL }
52.                DIRECTION { INOUT }
53.            }
54.        }
55.        FUNCTIONS {
56.            FUNCTION sendInstrumentBrokenMsg {
57.                DOES { AEIP.MESSAGES.instrumentBrokenMsg >> AEIP.CHANNELS.HBW_link }
58.            }
59.            FUNCTION sendHeartbeatMsg {
60.                DOES { AEIP.MESSAGES.heartbeatMsg >> AEIP.CHANNELS.HBW_link }
61.            }
62.        }
63.        MANAGED_ELEMENTS {
64.            MANAGED_ELEMENT worker {
65.                INTERFACE_FUNCTION getDistanceToNearestObject { RETURNS { DECIMAL } }
66.            }
67.        }
68.    } // AEIP
```

policy is currently operating in the *inHeartbeat-Notification* fluent (cf. the *GUARDS* clause of the *notifyForHeartbeat* action in Figure 8).

distanceToNearestObject

This metric is to measure the distance to the nearest object - an asteroid or a spacecraft unit. A special threshold class is specified to define a minimum value acceptable by the metric. The *collisionHappen* event is fired when this metric has changed its value and the threshold class is not held anymore, i.e., the distance goes below the bare minimum, which is considered as a collision (cf. the *GUARDS* clause in the *collisionHappen* event). In addition, the metric source (*METRIC_SOURCE* clause) is attached to the *getDistanceToNearestObject* interface function of the *worker managed element* (cf. line 112 in Figure 9). The latter specifies the interface needed by the metric to get that distance (cf. line 65 in Figure 7).

This specification model for ANTS was successfully validated with the ASSL consistency checker and the AS implementation was successfully generated (Vassev, 2008), (Vassev, 2009), (Vassev & Hinchey, 2009b). Moreover, this specification model was further used as a base for runtime self-management behavior experiments and testing (Vassev & Hinchey, 2009b). There, in order to explore all possible aspects of the self-healing behavior, three different versions of the ANTS self-healing model were developed: (1) the original one (presented here); (2) a version simulating a loss of a worker's instrument; and (3) a version simulating a worker loss. Note that all experiments demonstrated that the generated code (for all the three versions of the ANTS self-healing model) followed correctly the specified self-healing policy by reacting to the occurred self-healing events and thus, providing appropriate self-healing behavior.

Figure 8. ANT_Worker self-healing specification: Actions

```
69.    ACTIONS {
70.       ACTION IMPL checkInstrument {
71.          RETURNS { BOOLEAN }
72.          ENSURES { EVENTS.instrumentChecked }
73.       }
74.       ACTION checkANTInstrument {
75.          GUARDS { AESELF_MANAGEMENT.SELF_HEALING.inCollision }
76.          VARS { BOOLEAN canOperate }
77.          DOES { canOperate = CALL ACTIONS.checkInstrument }
78.          TRIGGERS {
79.             IF (not canOperate) THEN EVENTS.instrumentBroken END }
80.       }
81.       ACTION notifyForBrokenInstrument {
82.          GUARDS { AESELF_MANAGEMENT.SELF_HEALING.inInstrumentBroken }
83.          ENSURES { EVENTS.isMsgInstrumentBrokenSent }
84.          DOES { CALL AEIP.FUNCTIONS.sendInstrumentBrokenMsg }
85.       }
86.       ACTION notifyForHeartbeat {
87.          GUARDS { AESELF_MANAGEMENT.SELF_HEALING.inHeartbeatNotification }
88.          ENSURES { EVENTS.isMsgHeartbeatSent }
89.          DOES { CALL AEIP.FUNCTIONS.sendHeartbeatMsg }
90.       }
91.    } // ACTIONS
```

3.2. Modeling the NASA Voyager Mission

The NASA Voyager Mission (The Planetary Society, 2009) was designed for exploration of the Solar System. The mission started in 1977, when the twin spacecraft Voyager I and Voyager II were launched (cf. Figure 10). The original mission objectives were to explore the outer planets of the Solar System. As the Voyagers flew across the Solar System, they took pictures of planets and their satellites and performed close-up studies of Jupiter, Saturn, Uranus, and Neptune.

In the course of this research (Vassev & Hinchey, 2009c), we explored the image-processing system implemented on board the Voyager spacecraft (The Planetary Society, 2009). In order to take pictures, Voyager II carries two television cameras on board – one for wide-angle images and one for narrow-angle images, where each camera records images with a resolution of 800x800 pixels. Both cameras can record images in black-and-white only, but each camera is equipped with a set of color filters, which helps in the reconstruction of images be as fully-colored ones. To transmit pictures to Earth, Voyager II uses its 12-foot dish antenna (The Planetary Society, 2009) to send streams of pixels. It uses the same microwave frequencies used for radar. However, due to the long distance and to fundamental laws of physics, the strength of the radio signal is diminished proportionally and it reaches antennas on Earth with a strength 20 billion times weaker (Browne, 1989). To counter this, the signals are received by a network of enormous antennas located in Australia, Japan, California, and Spain. Next, all the faint signals received from Voyager II are combined and processed by the Voyager Mission base on Earth to reduce electronic noise, blend, and filter the composed pictures.

3.2.1. Voyager Image-Processing Behavior Algorithm

An autonomous-specific behavior is observed in the Voyager spacecraft when a picture must be taken and sent to Earth. The following elements describe the algorithm we applied to specify the image-processing behavior observed in the Voyager mission with ASSL.

Figure 9. ANT_Worker Self-healing Specification: Events & Metrics

```
92.    EVENTS { // these events are used in the fluents? specification
93.      EVENT collisionHappen {
94.        GUARDS { not METRICS.distanceToNearestObject }
95.        ACTIVATION { CHANGED { METRICS.distanceToNearestObject } }
96.      }
97.      EVENT isMsgInstrumentBrokenSent {
98.        ACTIVATION { SENT { AEIP.MESSAGES.instrumentBrokenMsg } }
99.      }
100.     EVENT instrumentBroken { }
101.     EVENT instrumentChecked { }
102.     EVENT timeToSendHeartbeatMsg {
103.       ACTIVATION { PERIOD { 1 min } }
104.     }
105.     EVENT isMsgHeartbeatSent {
106.       ACTIVATION { SENT { AEIP.MESSAGES.heartbeatMsg } }
107.     }
108.   } // EVENTS

109.   METRICS {
110.     METRIC distanceToNearestObject {
111.       METRIC_TYPE { RESOURCE }
112.       METRIC_SOURCE { AEIP.MANAGED_ELEMENTS.worker.getDistanceToNearestObject }
113.       DESCRIPTION { "measures the distance to the nearest space object" }
114.       MEASURE_UNIT { "KM" }
115.       VALUE { 100 }
116.       THRESHOLD_CLASS { DECIMAL [0.001 ~ ) }
117.     }
118.   } // METRICS

119. } // AE ANT_Worker
```

1. The Voyager II spacecraft:
   - uses its cameras to monitor space objects and decide when it is time to take a picture;
   - takes a picture with its wide-image camera or with its narrow-image camera;
   - notifies the antennas on Earth with "image session start" messages that an image transmission is about to start;
   - applies each color filter and sends the stream of pixels for each filter to Earth;
   - notifies antennas on Earth for the end of each session with "image session end" messages.
2. The antennas on Earth:
   - are prompted to receive the image by the "image session start" messages (one per applied filter);
   - receive image pixels;
   - are prompted to terminate the image sessions by "image session end" messages;
   - send the collected images to the Voyager Mission base on Earth.
3. The Voyager Mission base on Earth receives the image messages from the antennas.

3.2.2. Specifying Voyager Mission with ASSL

In order to specify the algorithm described in Section 3.2.1, we applied the ASSL multi-tier specification model and specified the Voyager II Mission at the three main ASSL tiers – AS (autonomic system) tier, ASIP (autonomic system specification protocol) tier, and AE (autonomic element) tier (cf. Section 2.1). Hence, in our specification, we specified the Voyager II spacecraft and the antennas on Earth as AEs that follow their encoded autonomic behavior and exchange predefined ASSL messages over predefined ASSL communication channels. The Voyager mission's

Figure 10. ASSL IMAGE_PROCESSING policy at Voyager AE

```
POLICY IMAGE_PROCESSING {
    ....
    FLUENT inProcessingPicturePixels {
        INITIATED_BY { EVENTS.pictureTaken }
        TERMINATED_BY { EVENTS.pictureProcessed }
    }
    ....
    MAPPING {
        CONDITIONS { inProcessingPicturePixels }
        DO_ACTIONS { ACTIONS.processPicture }
    }
}

ACTION processPicture {
    ....
    DOES {
        ....
        call AEIP.FUNCTIONS.sendBeginSessionMsgs
        ....
    }
}
```

autonomic behavior is specified at both AS and AE tiers as a self-management policy called *IMAGE_PROCESSING*. Thus, the global autonomic behavior of the Voyager II Mission is determined by the specification of that policy at each AE and at the global AS tier. Due to space limitations, the entire specification cannot be presented in this entry (the ASSL specification is rather long - over 1100 lines of ASSL code). A report (Vassev & Hinchey, 2009d) issued at Lero (The Irish Software Engineering Research Center) contains both the complete specification and evaluation results.

AS Tier Specification

At this tier, we specified the global AS-level autonomic behavior of the Voyager Mission. This behavior is encoded in the specification of an *IMAGE_PROCESSING* self-management policy. At this tier, that policy specifies an image-receiving

process taking place at the four antennas on Earth (located in Australia, Japan, California, and Spain). In fact, as specified at the AS Tier, this policy forms the autonomic image-processing behavior of the Voyager Mission base on Earth. Here, we specified four "*inProcessingImage_*" fluents (one per antenna), which are initiated by events prompted when an image has been received, and terminated by events prompted when the received image has been processed. Further, all the four fluents are mapped to a *processImage* action. Exhibit 3 shows a fluent specification together with its mapping:

Here, the specification of the events that initiate and terminate that fluent is the following (Exhibit 4):

Note that the *processImage* action is an *IMPL* action (Vassev, 2008), (Vassev, 2009), i.e., it is a kind of abstract action that does not specify any statements to be performed. The ASSL framework considers the IMPL actions as "*to be manually*

Exhibit 3.

```
FLUENT inProcessingImage_AntSpain  {
  INITIATED_BY { EVENTS.imageAnt SpainReceived }
  TERMINATED_BY { EVENTS.imageAnt SpainProcessed }
}
MAPPING {
  CONDITIONS { inProcessingImage _AntAustralia}
  DO_ACTIONS { ACTIONS. processImage ("Antenna_Australia") }
}
```

Exhibit 4.

```
EVENT imageAntS painReceived {
   ACTIVATION { RECEIVED { ASIP.MESS AGES.msgImag eAntSpain }
   }
}
EVENT imageAnt SpainProcessed { }
```

Exhibit 5.

```
ACTION IMPL processImage {
   PARAMETERS { string antennaName }
   GUARDS {
      ASSELF_MANAGEMENT. OTHER_POLICIES. IMAGE_PROCESSING .inProcessingImage_
AntAustralia
      OR
      ASSELF_MANAGEMENT. OTHER_POLICIES. IMAGE_PROCESSING .inProcessingI mage_
AntJapan
      ...
   }
   TRIGGERS {
      IF antennaName = "Antenna_Australia" THENEVENTS.imageAntAust raliaPro-
cessed
      END ELSE ...
   }
}
```

implemented" after code generation. Exhibit 5 is a partial specification of that action:

Here, the *processImage* action is specified to accept a single parameter. The latter allows that action to process images from all four antennas. Moreover, there is a special *GUARDS* clause that is specified to prevent execution of the action when none of the four fluents is initiated. The action triggers an *imageAnt*[antenna name]*Processed* event if the action is performed with no exceptions.

ASIP Tier Specification

At this tier, we specified the AS-level communication protocol – the autonomic system interaction protocol (ASIP) (cf. Section 2.1). This communication protocol is specified to be used by the four antennas when these communicate with the Voyager Mission base on Earth. Here, at this tier we specified four image messages (one per antenna), a communication channel that is used to communicate these messages, and communication functions (e.g., *sendImageMsg* and *receiveImageMsg*) to send and receive these messages over that communication channel. Note that the communication functions accept a parameter that allows same communication functions to send or receive messages to and from different antennas. Please refer to (Vassev & Hinchey, 2009d) for the ASSL specification of the Voyager ASIP.

AE Tier Specification

At this tier, we specified five AEs. The Voyager II spacecraft and all four antennas on Earth (the antennas located in Australia, Japan, California, and Spain), are specified as AEs. Note that here, we specified the *IMAGE_PROCESSING* self-management policy at the level of single AE and thus, this policy is realized over all AEs specified for the Voyager Mission. The following elements present important details of this specification. Please, refer to (Vassev & Hinchey, 2009d) for the complete specification.

AE Voyager

The most complex AE is the one specified for the Voyager II spacecraft. To express the *IMAGE_PROCESSING* self-management policy for this AE, we specified two fluents: *inTakingPicture* and *inProcessingPicturePixels*. The following ASSL listing (Exhibit 6) presents that self-management policy with both fluents and mapping sections.

Here, the *inTakingPicture* fluent is initiated by a *timeToTakePicture* event and terminated by a *pictureTaken* event. This event also initiates the *inProcessingPicturePixels* fluent, which is terminated by the *pictureProcessed* event. Both fluents are mapped to the actions *takePicture* and *processPicture* respectively.

In addition, we specified an AEIP (autonomic element interaction protocol) (cf. Section 2.1), which is used by the Voyager AE to communicate with the four antenna AEs and to monitor and control the two cameras (wide-image camera and narrow-image camera) on board. Thus, with this AEIP we specified:

Exhibit 6.

```
AESELF_MANAGEMENT {
  OTHER_POLICIES {
    POLICY IMAGE_PROCESSING {
      FLUENT inTak ingPicture {
        INITIATED_BY { EVENTS.timeTo TakePicture }
        TERMINATED_BY { EVENTS.pic tureTaken }
      }
      FLUENT inProcessing PicturePixels {
        INITIATED_BY { EVENTS.pi ctureTaken }
        TERMINATED_BY { EVENTS.pic tureProcessed }
      }
      MAPPING {
        CONDITIONS { intake ngPicture }
        DO_ACTIONS { ACTIONS.t akePicture }
      }
      MAPPING {
        CONDITIONS { inProcessing PicturePixels }
        DO_ACTIONS { ACTIONS.proc essPicture }
      }
    }
  }
} // AESELF_MANAGEMENT
```

- ASSL messages needed to send an image pixel and messages that notify the antenna AEs that an image-receiving session is about to begin or end.
- A private communication channel.
- Three communication functions that send the AEIP messages over the AEIP communication channel.
- Two special managed elements (termed *wideAngleCamera* and *narrowAngleCamera*) to specify interface functions needed by the Voyager AE to monitor and control both cameras. Through their interface functions, both managed elements are used by the actions mapped to the fluents *inTakingPicture* and *inProcessingPicturePixels* to take pictures, apply filters, and detect interesting space objects.

The following specification sample (Exhibit 7) shows a partial specification of one of these managed elements.

Moreover, an *interestingObjects* metric is specified to count all detected interesting objects, which the Voyager AE takes pictures of. The source of this metric is specified as one of the managed element interface functions (*countInterestingObjects*); i.e., the metric gets updated by that interface function.

Note that the *timeToTakePicture* event (it activates the *inTakingPicture* fluent) is prompted by a change in this metric's value. Here, in order to simulate this condition, we also activate this event every 60 seconds on a periodic basis.

The four antenna AEs are specified as *friends* (at the *FRIENDS* sub-tier) of the Voyager AE. According to the ASSL semantics (Vassev, 2008), (Vassev, 2009) friends can share private interaction protocols. Thus, the antenna AEs can use the messages and channels specified by the AEIP of the Voyager AE.

Antenna AEs

We specified the four antennas receiving signals from the Voyager II spacecraft as AEs, i.e., we specified AEs termed *Antenna_Australia*, *Antenna_Japan*, *Antenna_California*, and *Antenna_Spain*. Here, the *IMAGE_PROCESSING* self-management policy for these AEs is speci-

Exhibit 7.

```
MANAGED_ ELEMENT wideAng leCamera {
  INTERFACE_ FUNCTION takePic ture { }
  ...
  INTERFACE_ FUNCTION countInter estingObjects {
    RETURNS { integer }
  }
}
```

Exhibit 8.

```
METRIC interes tingObjects {
  METRIC TYPE { RESOURCE }
  METRIC_ SOURCE { AEIP.MANAGED _ELEMENTS.wideA ngleCamera.coun tInterestin-
gObjects }
  THRESHOLD_CLASS { integer [ 0~) }
}
```

Exhibit 9.

```
EVENT timeTo TakePicture {
  ACTIVATION { CHANGED { METRICS.interest ingObjects } OR PERIOD { 60 SEC } }
}
```

fied with a few pairs of *inStartingImageSession - inCollectingImagePixels* fluents. A pair of such fluents is specified per image filter and determines states of the antenna AE when an image-receiving session is starting and when the antenna AE is collecting the image pixels.

Because the Voyager AE processes the images by applying different filters and sends each filtered image separately, we specified for each applied filter different fluents in the antenna AEs (cf. (Vassev & Hinchey, 2009d) for the complete *IMAGE_PROCESSING* specification at the antenna AEs). This allows an antenna AE to process a collection of multiple filtered images simultaneously. Note that according to the ASSL formal semantics, a fluent cannot be re-initiated while it is initiated, thus preventing the same fluent be initiated simultaneously twice or more times (Vassev, 2008), (Vassev, 2009). Here, these fluents are initiated and terminated by AE events specified to be prompted by the Voyager AE's messages notifying that an image-receiving session begins or ends. The following partial specification (Exhibit 10) shows two of the *IMAGE_PROCESSING* fluents. These fluents are mapped to AE actions that collect the image pixels per filtered image.

In addition, an *inSendingImage* fluent is specified. This fluent activates when the antenna AE is done with the image collection work, i.e., all the filtered images (for all the applied filters) have been collected. The fluent is mapped to a *sendImage* action that sends the filtered images as one image to the Voyager Mission base on Earth. The following listing (Exhibit 11) presents two of the events used to initiate those fluents.

Note that the *greenImageSessionIsAboutTo-Start* event is prompted when the Voyager's *msgGreenSessionBeginSpn* message has been sent, and the *imageSessionStartedBlue* event is prompted when the Voyager AE's *msgBlueSessionBeginSpn* message has been received by the antenna. Moreover, each antenna AE specifies communication functions that allow the AE to receive the Voyager AE's messages (Vassev & Hinchey, 2009d). These communication functions are called by the AE actions.

Testing the Self-Managing Behavior

Due to specific features, common to all the Java applications generated with ASSL, at runtime, the ASSL-developed Voyager prototype produces log records that show important state-transition operations ongoing in the system (Vassev, 2008), (Vassev, 2009). Here, we used those records to trace and evaluate the behavior of the generated prototype model. In order to perform this exercise, we compiled the generated Java code with Java 1.6.0 first, and then we ran the compiled code. First, it started all system threads as it is partially shown in the following log records. Note that starting all system threads first is a standard running procedure applied to all prototype models generated with the ASSL framework.

Log Records "Starting System Threads"

Here records 1 through to 19 show the start-up process of the *ANTENNA_CALIFORNIA* autonomic element. Similar log records notified us that all the threads in all generated AEs started successfully.

Exhibit 10.

```
FLUENT inStartingGre enImageSession {
  INITIATED_BY { EVENTS.greenIm ageSessionIsA boutToStart },
  TERMINATED_BY { EVENTS.imageSess ionStartedGreen }
}
FLUENT inCollecting ImagePixelsBlue {
  INITIATED_BY { EVENTS.imageSessio StartedBlue }
  TERMINATED_BY { EVENTS.imageSess ionEndedBlue }
}
```

After starting up all the threads, the system ran in idle mode for 60 seconds, when the *TIME-TOTAKEPICTURE* timed event occurred (cf. record 99). This event is specified in the Voyager AE to run on regular basis every 60 seconds (cf. Section 3.2.2.3) and it triggers a series of system transitions following the specified autonomic behavior. The following log records demonstrate that the runtime image-processing behavior followed correctly the ASSL specification of the *IMAGE_PROCESSING* policy.

Log Records "Voyager Autonomic Behavior"

Here, records 99 through to 103 show the initiation and termination of the voyager's *INTAKINGPIC-TURE* fluent. This resulted in the execution of the *TAKEPICTURE* action (cf. record 101), which triggered the *PICTURETAKEN* event (cf. record 102). The latter consecutively initiated the *INPRO-CESSINGPICTUREPIXELS* fluent. Records 104 through to 109 and record 115 show the initiation and termination of that fluent. The *INPRO-*

CESSINGPICTUREPIXELS fluent prompted the execution of the *PROCESSPICTURE* action (cf. record 108), which executed the *PROCESSFIL-TEREDPICTURE* action three times (cf. records 105 through to 107). Each time, this action was called to apply a different filter color (blue, red, or green) and sent the filtered image to the antennas on Earth. Note that this action also uses the Voyager AE's AEIP-specified functions (Vassev & Hinchey, 2009d) *sendBeginSessionMsgs* and *sendEndSessionMsgs* to send begin-session and end-session messages for each applied filter to the antennas on Earth.

Subsequently, these messages prompted three [color]*ImageSessionIsAboutToStart* events for each antenna, one per a filter color (cf. record 110 for the *BLUEIMAGESESSIONISABOUTTO-START* event). Next these events initiated in the antenna AEs three *inStarting*[color]*ImageSession* fluents, one per filter color (cf. record 113 for the *INSTARTINGBLUEIMAGESESSION* fluent). Each of these fluents prompted the execution of

Exhibit 11.

```
EVENT greenImag eSessionIsAbou tToStart {
  ACTIVATION { SENT { AES.Voyag er.AEIP.MESSAGES .msgGreenSession BeginAus } }
}
EVENT imageSess ionStartedBlue {
  ACTIVATION { RECEIVED { AES.Voyager .AEIP.MESSA GES.msgBlue SessionB eginAus
} }
}
```

the *STARTIMAGECOLLECTSESSION* action (cf. records 116). Note that this action was executed twelve times (one time for each applied filter per antenna) and it prompted the operation of receiving the begin-session messages. Subsequently, the antennas received these messages and corresponding events were prompted to terminate *inStarting*[color]*ImageSession* fluents and initiate fluents to collect the image pixels.

For each antenna AE, the pixel-collection fluent prompted the execution of a special pixel-collection action (Vassev & Hinchey, 2009d). Thus, that action was executed for each antenna three times, one per a filter color. Internally, this action received image messages specified at the ASIP tier (cf. Section 3.2.2.2) including special end-session messages that terminated the image-transmission sessions (per filter color and per antenna). Next, every received end-session message terminated the current active fluent for the current antenna AE. In addition, the last end-session message, for every antenna, initiated another fluent (termed *inSendingImage* – cf. (Vassev & Hinchey, 2009d)) that prompted the execution of a special action (termed *sendImage*; cf. (Vassev & Hinchey, 2009d)). The latter prepared the collected image and sent it to the Voyager Mission base on Earth. Further, this operation prompted a particular event at each antenna that terminated the *inSendingImage* fluent.

Further, the system continued repeating the same steps on a regular basis due to the *TIMETO-TAKEPICTURE* timed event (cf. record 99), which occurs every 60 seconds (cf. the *timeToTakePicture* ASSL specification in Section 3.2.2.3). It is important to mention that the run-time behavior of the generated prototype model for the Voyager II mission strictly followed that specified with the ASSL *IMAGE_PROCESSING* self-management policy.

Model-Checking Self-Managing Behavior

This subsection demonstrates how the ASSL model checking mechanism (cf. Section 2.4.2) performs formal verification to check *liveness properties* of the ASSL-developed AS prototype of the NASA Voyager Mission. Here, a sample from the ASSL specification of the Voyager image-processing behavior (cf. Section 3.2.2 is used to demonstrate how a liveness property such as "*a picture taken by the Voyager spacecraft will eventually result in sending a message to antennas on Earth*" can be checked with the ASSL Model Checker tool.

Figure 10 presents a partial ASSL specification of the *IMAGE_PROCESSING* self-management policy of the Voyager AE. Here the *pictureTaken* event will be prompted when a picture has been taken. This event initiates the *inProcessingPicturePixels* fluent. The same fluent is mapped to a *processPicture* action, which will be executed once the fluent gets initiated. As it is specified, the *processPicture* action prompts the execution of the *sendBeginSessionMsgs* communication function (cf. Figure 10), which puts a special message *x* on a special communication channel (message *x* is sent over that channel). Note that the specification of both the *pictureTaken* event and the *sendBeginSessionMsgs* function is not presented here.

Product Machine

As it has been already mentioned in Section 2.4.2, the ASSL model checking mechanism builds the ASG (ASSL State Graph) from the ASSL specification. Figure 11, presents a partial ASG of the sub-tiers of the Voyager AE.

Here each sub-tier instance forms a distinct state machine (basic machine) within the AE state machine and the AE state machine is a Cartesian product of the state machines of its sub-tiers (cf. Section 2.4.2). It is important to mention that by taking the Cartesian product of a set of basic sub-tier machines, we form a product machine consisting of product states. The latter are tuples of concurrent basic sub-tier states. Moreover, in the AE product machine, the ASSL state-transition operations are considered product transitions that move from one product state to another. Note that the states in the state machine of the whole AS product machine can be obtained by the Cartesian product of all the AE product machines. Thus, by considering the sub-tier state machines we construct the Voyager AE product machine (cf. Figure 12). Note that this is again a simplified model where not all the possible product states are shown. Figure 12 presents the AE product states as large circles embedding the sub-tier states (depicted as smaller circles). Here, the following aliases are used:

- *e* states for Event state machine;
- *f* states for Fluent state machine;
- *a* states for Action state machine;
- *y* states for communication function state machine;
- *x* states for Message state machine.

Moreover, white circles present "idle" state and gray circles present the corresponding "active" state of the sub-tier state machine in question (such as prompted for events, initiated for fluents, etc.; cf. Figure 11).

Therefore, the formal presentation $(\mathbf{S}; \mathbf{Op}; \mathbf{R}; \mathbf{S}_0; \mathbf{AP}; \mathbf{L})$ of the Voyager AE ASG is (cf. Section 2.4.2):

$$\mathbf{S} = \{\mathbf{S}_1; \mathbf{S}_2; \mathbf{S}_3; \mathbf{S}_4; \mathbf{S}_5; \mathbf{S}_7; \mathbf{S}_8\}$$

Op = {Event; FluentIn; EventOver; ActionMap; Function; MsgSent}

$$\mathbf{R} = \{(\mathbf{S}_1; \mathbf{S}_2; \text{Event}); (\mathbf{S}_2; \mathbf{S}_3; \text{FluentIn}); (\mathbf{S}_3; \mathbf{S}_4; \text{EventOver}); (\mathbf{S}_4; \mathbf{S}_5; \text{ActionMap}); (\mathbf{S}_5; \mathbf{S}_6; \text{Function}); (\mathbf{S}_6; \mathbf{S}_7; \text{MsgSent})\}$$

$$\mathbf{S}_0 = \mathbf{S}_1 (\text{initial state})$$

- **AP** ={event **pictureTaken** occurs, event **pictureTaken** terminates, action **processPicture** starts, fluent **inProcessingPicturePixels** initiates, function **sendBeginSessionMsgs** starts, sends message **x**}

Here,

$$\mathbf{L}(\mathbf{S}_1) = \{\text{event } \textbf{pictureTaken} \text{ occurs}\}$$

$$\mathbf{L}(\mathbf{S}_2) = \{\text{fluent } \textbf{inProcessingPicturePixels} \text{ initiates}\}$$

$$\mathbf{L}(\mathbf{S}_3) = \{\text{event } \textbf{pictureTaken} \text{ terminates}\}$$

$$\mathbf{L}(\mathbf{S}_4) = \{\text{action } \textbf{processPicture} \text{ starts}\}$$

$$\mathbf{L}(\mathbf{S}_5) = \{\text{function } \textbf{sendBeginSessionMsgs} \text{ starts}\}$$

$$\mathbf{L}(\mathbf{S}_6) = \{\text{sends message } \textbf{x}\}$$

Moreover, the following correctness properties are considered for model checking:

- If an event occurs eventually a fluent initiates.
- If an event occurs next eventually it terminates.
- If a fluent initiates next actions start.
- If an action starts eventually a function starts.
- If a function starts eventually it sends a message.

Figure 11. State machines of the Voyager AE sub-tiers

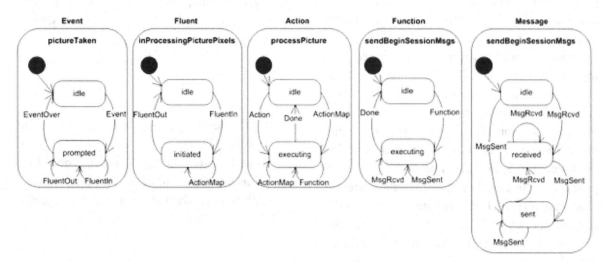

The ASSL model-checking mechanism uses the correctness properties to check if these are held over product states considering the atomic propositions **AP** true for that state. Thus, the ASSL framework is able to trace the state path shown in Figure 12 and to validate the liveness property stated above. Note that in this example, it is intentionally presented a *limited set* of atomic propositions and a *limited set* of correctness properties. Moreover, the Voyager AE product machine presents only product states relevant to this model-checking case study.

4. CONCLUSION

This entry has presented theoretical and practical aspects of ASSL (Autonomic System Specification Language), which is a powerful formal specifica-

tion framework for specification and code generation of ASs (autonomic systems). The extremely high complexity of the ASs necessitates the ASSL multi-tier specification model presented in this entry. This model decomposes an AS in two directions: (1) into levels of functional abstraction; and (2) into functionally related sub-tiers. Both tiers and sub-tiers in ASSL are complex specification constructs, each necessitating its own syntactical and semantic rules and providing abstractions of different aspects of the AS under consideration.

The ASSL framework exposes a reach set of tools that assist developers in the development of ASs. Tools for *consistency* and *model checking* allow for automatic formal validation that aids in the construction of correct ASs. In addition, the ASSL toolset allows for automatic implementation where an operational Java application can be automatically generated per any valid ASSL

Figure 12. Partial Voyager AE product machine

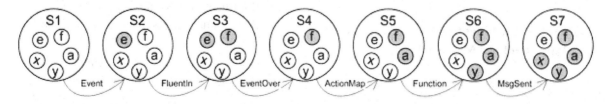

specification. Finally, to detect errors introduced not only with the ASSL specifications, but also with the supplementary coding, a special test generator tool is provided.

In this entry, to demonstrate the theoretical concepts and flavor of the ASSL approach, two case study examples have been presented. In the first one, an ASSL-developed self-healing model for the NASA ANTS (Autonomous Nano-Technology Swarm) systems has demonstrated how ASSL may be applied to the development of autonomic features for swarm-based systems. In addition, the second case study example has shown how ASSL may be used to develop AS prototypes of future Voyager-like systems.

In conclusion, it should be noted that ASSL provides the IT community with an extremely needed and powerful framework for AS specification, validation and implementation. Overall, ASSL is sufficiently generic and adaptable to accommodate most of the AS development aspects.

REFERENCES

Amey, P. (2002). *Correctness by construction: Better can also be cheaper*. CrossTalk Magazine.

Baier, C., & Katoen, J.-P. (2008). *Principles of model checking*. MIT Press.

Bakera, M., Wagner, C., Margaria, T., Vassev, E., Hinchey, M., & Steffen, B. (2009). Component-oriented behavior extraction for autonomic system design. In *Proceedings of the First NASA Formal Methods Symposium - NFM2009* (pp. 66–75). USA: NASA.

Benveniste, A., Caspi, P., Edwards, S., Halbwachs, N., Le Guernic, P., & De Simone, R. (2003). The synchronous languages twelve years later. *Proceedings of the IEEE, 91*(1), 64–83. doi:10.1109/JPROC.2002.805826

Bowen, J. P., & Hinchey, M. G. (2004). Formal methods. In A. B. Tucker, Jr. (Ed.), *Computer science handbook*, 2nd ed. (Section XI, Software Engineering, Chapter 106, pp. 106-1–106-25). Chapman & Hall / CRC, ACM.

Browne, W. M. (1989, August 26). Technical "magic" converts a puny signal into pictures. *NY Times*.

Clarke, E. M., Grumberg, O., & Peled, D. A. (2002). *Model checking*. MIT Press.

Corporation, I. B. M. (2006). *An architectural blueprint for autonomic computing*. White paper, 4 ed. IBM Corporation.

Horn, P. (2001, October). *Autonomic computing: IBM's perspective on the state of information technology*. Technical report. IBM T. J. Watson Laboratory.

Kephart, J. O., & Chess, D. M. (2003). The vision of autonomic computing. *IEEE Computer, 36*(1), 41–50.

Knuth, D. E. (1964). Backus normal form vs. Backus Naur form. *Communications of the ACM, 7*(12), 735–773. doi:10.1145/355588.365140

Rouff, C. A., Hinchey, M. G., Rash, J. L., & Truszkowski, W. F. (2005). Towards a hybrid formal method for swarm-based exploration missions. In *Proceedings of 29th Annual IEEE/NASA Software Engineering Workshop - SEW 2005* (pp. 253-264). IEEE Computer Society.

The Planetary Society. (2009). *Space topics: Voyager – The story of the mission*. Retrieved February 7, 2010, from http://planetary.org/ explore/ topics/ space_missions/ voyager/ objectives.html

Truszkowski, W., Hinchey, M., Rash, J., & Rouff, C. (2004). NASA's swarm missions: The challenge of building autonomous software. *IT Professional, 6*(5), 47–52. IEEE Computer Society. doi:10.1109/MITP.2004.66

Vassev, E. (2009). *ASSL: Autonomic system specification language - A framework for specification and code generation of autonomic systems.* Germany: LAP Lambert Academic Publishing.

Vassev, E., & Hinchey, M. (2008). ASSL specification of emergent self-adapting for NASA swarm-based exploration missions. In *Proceedings of the 2nd IEEE International Conference on Self-Adaptive and Self-Organizing Systems Workshops - SASOW 2008* (pp. 13–18). IEEE Computer Society.

Vassev, E., & Hinchey, M. (2009a). ASSL: A software engineering approach to autonomic computing. *IEEE Computer, 42*(6), 106–109.

Vassev, E., & Hinchey, M. (2009b). ASSL specification and code generation of self-healing behavior for NASA swarm-based systems. In *Proceedings of the 6th IEEE International Workshop on Engineering of Autonomic and Autonomous Systems - EASe'09* (pp. 77–86). IEEE Computer Society.

Vassev, E., & Hinchey, M. (2009c). Modeling the image-processing behavior of the NASA voyager mission with ASSL. In *Proceedings of the 3rd IEEE International Conference on Space Mission Challenges for Information Technology - SMC-IT'09* (pp. 246–253). IEEE Computer Society.

Vassev, E., & Hinchey, M. (2009d). *ASSL specification model for the mage-processing behavior in the NASA Voyager mission.* Technical Report, Lero - The Irish Software Engineering Research Center.

Vassev, E., Hinchey, M., & Nixon, P. (2010). Automated test case generation for ASSL self-managing policies. In *Proceedings of the 4th IEEE International Symposium on Theoretical Aspects of Software Engineering- TASE2010.* IEEE Computer Society.

Vassev, E., Hinchey, M., & Paquet, J. (2008a). Towards an ASSL specification model for NASA swarm-based exploration missions. In *Proceedings of the 23rd Annual ACM Symposium on Applied Computing - SAC 2008* (pp. 1652–1657). ACM.

Vassev, E., Hinchey, M., & Paquet, J. (2008b). A self-scheduling model for NASA swarm-based exploration missions using ASSL. In *Proceedings of the 5th IEEE International Workshop on Engineering of Autonomic and Autonomous Systems - EASe'08* (pp. 54–64). IEEE Computer Society.

Vassev, E., Hinchey, M., & Quigley, A. (2009). Model checking for autonomic systems specified with ASSL. In *Proceedings of the First NASA Formal Methods Symposium – NFM2009* (pp. 16–25). USA: NASA.

Vassev, E. I. (2008, November). *Towards a framework for specification and code generation of autonomic systems.* Ph.D. Thesis, Department of Computer Science and Software Engineering. Concordia University, Montreal, Canada.

ENDNOTES

[1] In general, FOLTL can be seen as a quantified version of linear temporal logic. FOLTL is obtained by taking propositional linear temporal logic and adding a first order language to it.

[2] This is an ASSL semantic rule (Vassev, 2008), (Vassev, 2009).

[3] The *IMPL* ASSL modifier states for "further implementation", which means that the ASSL framework will generate an empty routine and its content should be implemented manually (Vassev, 2008), (Vassev, 2009).

Chapter 3
Specification, Development, and Verification of CASCADAS Autonomic Computing and Networking Toolkit

Antonio Manzalini
Telecom Italia, Italy

Nermin Brgulja
University of Kassel, Germany

Roberto Minerva
Telecom Italia, Italy & Institut TELECOM SudParis, France

Corrado Moiso
Telecom Italia, Italy

ABSTRACT

Increasing complexity, heterogeneity, and dynamism of current networks (telecommunications, ICT, and Internet) are making current computational and communication infrastructures brittle, inefficient, and almost unmanageable. As a matter of fact, computing and storage are progressively embedded in all sorts of nodes and devices that are interconnected through a variety of (wireless and wired) technologies in Networks of Networks (NoNs). Dynamicity, pervasivity, and interconnectivity of future NoNs will increase the complexity of their management, control, and optimization more and more, and will open new challenges for service delivery in such environments. Autonomic communications principles and technologies can provide effective computing and networking solutions overcome these bottlenecks and to foster such challenging evolution. This chapter presents the main concepts of an autonomic communications toolkit designed and developed in the EU project CASCADAS for creating and supervising service networking ecosystems, structured as ensembles of distributed and cooperating autonomic components. Moreover, it describes several use-cases developed for its validation and demonstration and reports the experimental results to assess the toolkit performances. A brief overview of future research directions concludes the chapter.

DOI: 10.4018/978-1-60960-845-3.ch003

INTRODUCTION

Today's networks are becoming increasingly ubiquitous, complex and heterogeneous: computing and storage resources are embedded in different types of nodes and devices that are interconnected through a variety of wired and wireless networks and protocols. People, smart objects, machines and the surrounding space (e.g., sensors, RFID tags, etc.) are creating a highly decentralized cyber environment that augment physical space and it is highly pervasive. On one side, increasing dynamicity, pervasivity and interconnectivity of Networks of Networks (NoNs) promise to improve robustness of the system, but at the same time it increases the complexity of management, control and optimization and the fragility of current protocols in coping with such highly dynamic and scale-free environments. The development of self-managing computing and communications infrastructures - referred to as Autonomic Computing and Networking (ACN) - can provide effective solutions overcome these bottlenecks and to foster such challenging evolution. As a matter of fact, this is an avenue of considerable research and industrial interest (Parashar & Hariri, 2005).

The scope of this chapter is presenting the vision and the main concepts of the CAN model and toolkit developed in the EU project CASCADAS (Manzalini & Zambonelli, 2006; Manzalini & Zambonelli, 2009; Deussen & Baumgarten, 2009). In particular, the main goal of the project has been defining, developing and experimentally validating the novel architectural paradigm of service networking eco-systems for future Telecommunications-ICT and Internet. Architecture of CASCADAS eco-systems is based on a pervasive environment of distributed autonomic components named Autonomic Communication Elements (ACE). ACEs represent an engineering effort aimed at providing a component-model through which heterogeneous basic services can be designed and developed in accordance with requirements drawn from self-* properties.

More advanced services can be created through collections of ACEs that share locally available services and resources to enable autonomous organization, thus realizing a global eco-system autonomic behavior. ACEs organization is supported by a collaborative framework that allows the discovery in a distributed setting. Both the component-model and the framework are included in a software development kit, the ACE Toolkit (Benko & Brgulja, 2008), through which ACEs can be designed, developed and deployed. The Toolkit also contains related plug-and-play libraries for exploiting self-management, self-organization, security, and knowledge network capabilities. It is running on laptops, PDAs, mobile devices (for instance, all devices using Android software platform) and it is available as an open source project.

The chapter is organized as follows. Next section describes scenarios of future networks and the main limitations of current evolution, and it argues how ACN technologies and solutions could be a valuable approach for addressing the challenges for managing these environments and for delivering services on them. Then, this chapter reports a brief summary of the state-of-art of technologies and solutions related to ACN. The following sections describe the vision and the main concepts of an ACN Toolkit designed and developed in the CASCADAS Project, present several use cases adopted for its validation and demonstration, and report some experimental results to assess its performances. Finally, the chapter concludes with some recommendations for future work.

SCENARIOS AND MOTIVATIONS

Future pervasive distribution of digital devices (e.g., laptops, mobile phone, digital camera, music players, RFID, sensors, smart cards) will create a large distributed computational and networking environment that will foster a profound and ubiquitous integration of data and services into everyday objects and the living ambient. These environments will be dynamic (e.g. due to mobility and dynamicity), secure, situation and social status aware. Users' Personal Area Network together with surrounding people and smart objects, will be integrated with "global" communities to share the local experience with the global circle of friends and vice versa.

In this vision, Users, Enterprises, Providers as well as machines and "smart things" will produce, consume and elaborate large amounts of data. Users will constantly be one peer of many networks: for instance, the Personal Network, the local network, the global network, and the Enterprise network. In those networks, Users can have different identities and can play different roles (e.g., prosumers). The communication capabilities offered to users and smart objects will be ubiquitous, in order to be always best connected, according to the context in which they are acting. This means that the concept of Users' View on networked resources will assume an increasing importance. Users will want the network(s) to easily adapt to their requirements without requiring "too much" effort. Users' devices, smart objects/things, network nodes, servers, etc. must be handled as a highly decentralized common pool of abstract (network, processing and storage) resources (up to the edge) dynamically interconnected by "NoNs".

The NoNs will be highly distributed and ubiquitous, where intelligence is moving towards the devices at the edge. Resources will belong to more administrative domains, so the aggregation of resources should be carried out in a dynamic and cooperative way. The features provided by the resources must be virtualized, and equipped with mechanisms for their negotiation and allocation, also in a multiplexing way. As a consequence, pools of shared and virtualized resources has to be properly managed and optimized in order to make the best use of them according to the needs of the competing entities requesting services. In particular, these pools of resources have to be managed in order to avoid the "Tragedy of Commons", i.e.,

the egoistic usage of publicly available resources for maximize the individual benefits disregarding the community needs (Hardin, 1968).

Limitations of Current Evolution of Internet

Internet is the "natural" candidate to become the essential foundation for the development of future networked infrastructure able to accommodate for the requirements of pervasive computing and the integration of any "smart thing" of future NoNs.

Unfortunately current Internet and some evolution trends are not suitable to address the evolution towards pervasive and dynamic NoNs. Internet is not "symmetric" anymore because servers are more capable and "important" than clients. In fact, most of the companies providing applications on the Web are pushing the client-server approach to service delivery to such an extent that servers are now "inside" the network, and end-users devices, mainly relegated to the role of enriched GUI (Graphical User Interface). This trend will challenge the "end to end argument" (Clark & Wroclawski, 2005), one of the pillars of the Internet, and it hampers the design of open architectures that permit different players to build solutions based on different communications and computing paradigms. In order to exploit the increasing communication and computing characteristics of users' devices and their pervasive distribution in the environments, it is necessary, instead, to adopt architectures which establish symmetric relationships and interactions among all the entities involved in a NoNs. An example is the (peer to peer) "overlays" that try to solve decentralization, addressing and optimization problems, but they do so in a limited context and even aggravate the problems of the underlying Internet infrastructure (e.g., congestion, over-utilization of international costly links). Finally, the Internet is showing signs of "Ossification". For instance: it is difficult to adopt IPV6 (essential for addressing people, machines and objects), the choice of the data route is not optimized by existing protocols (e.g., Border Gateway Protocol), the network is not able to automatically distribute loads and it is prone to DDoS (Distributed Denial of Service) attacks, etc. In fact, Internet evolution is determined not only by technological progress but mainly from business contrapositions (tussles) that impede a smooth technical evolution and the realization of new business models (Clark & Wroclawski, 2005). An example is Identity Management: the concept of "customer ownership" is prevailing over a distributed and user-empowered management of Identity. The runtime characteristics of tussles require the adoption of new technical design principles, more flexible and self-adaptive, to allow choices, variations at runtime, so to accommodate "unexpected" tussles rather than preclude them.

Network Providers tend to bring intelligence in the network centralizing functions and creating complex platforms (e.g., IP Multimedia Subsystem – IMS (Poikselka & Mayer, 2009), and Service Delivery Platform – SDP (Kimbler & Taylor, 2008)), which concentrate the intelligence within single administrative domains and are not designed to scale to pervasive scenarios. In fact, service logic and orchestrated service components are mainly deployed on servers residing in the network infrastructure. Traditional service frameworks exhibit a number of limitations with regard to the characteristics required by future scenarios of pervasive and adaptable services dealing also with user-generated content and services. (1) It is quite difficult to integrate/combine functions belonging to different service providers/network operators without costly replications, due to lack of adoption of open and/or standard interfaces to access them. This introduces serious constraints and complexities in the process of creating and deploying new services, in particular in the presence of multiple stakeholders (including users themselves) wishing to contribute novel services and data. (2) It is also complicated to adapt services and functions to run on heterogeneous platforms and devices: the vertical layering makes it difficult to adapt low-level mechanisms to different devices and the lack of open and standard interfaces heavily constrains modularity and reuse. (3) Similar problems arise also for sharing functions across different platforms, and for load-balancing and fault-tolerance.

Coping with a huge number of small devices requesting granular services and data would create an insurmountable load on communication and processing resources. Therefore, a "redistribution" of the software stack shall be envisioned, beyond the client-server paradigm: computations that are now executed on the server should be performed on edge devices (Manzalini, Minerva & Moiso, 2009). This requires a more distributed, and autonomous infrastructure, able to dynamically react to performance changes, or fault events, and to optimize the use of computing and communication resources.

In conclusion, there is therefore the need to evolve Internet and future networks infrastructures to support and develop a pervasive and decentralized computing world. In this chapter, it is argued that ACN is a promising approach to achieve this global goal, by properly applying autonomic principles and control-loops at all OSI layers and the CASCADAS ACE Toolkit is a valuable first step to achieve this goal.

STATE OF ART

A wide number of researches is addressing from different perspectives the challenges posed by novel future network scenarios. Accordingly, in different areas, and along different directions, several research works and prototypes are trying to overcome the limitations of current computing/processing and networking/communication frameworks, as pointed out in the section Scenarios and Motivations.

Concerning traditional service frameworks adopted by Service and Network Providers, such as IMS/SDP-based network intelligence solutions or Web Services–based service-oriented architectures, all of them are typically characterized by a number of specialized mechanisms/protocols/services dealing with the various aspects of the business process. For example: use of specific servers for service logic execution, specialized mechanisms for services configuration and management, specific and/or proprietary protocols for the interaction of services with each other. There is the need to develop decentralized service framework, able to deal with evolving and pervasive contexts, and capable of achieving a dynamic and, possibly, optimized, resource allocations in order to adapt them according to traffic load and to available resources.

On the other hand, the ossification of Internet discussed in the previous section is creating several tussles. There is the need to re-think the networking paradigm in order to make it a viable and robust solution for the pervasive computing world. The focus should be on the improvement of the networks capabilities, the ability to better support the overlay networks, and the provision to them of reliable and useful network services. This does not mean to give up with the end-to-end principle, in fact it should hold also in the future networks, but the number of general network services should increase in order to improve the security, identity, data management and communication capabilities.

Future communications will engage any internetworking and combination of "people, machine and smart things". Service and network environments will be more and more complex and heterogeneous and the task of ensuring end-to-end performances, whilst optimizing cross-layer resource utilization, will be more and more challenging. There is common agreement on the need to manage, control and optimize future networks in a holistic way, by considering Users' devices, smart objects/things, network nodes, servers, etc. as a highly decentralized common pool of shared abstract (network, processing and storage)

resources (up to the edge) dynamically interconnected by dynamic NoNs.

Starting from these challenges, state of art on autonomic computing and networking models and technologies can be rooted mainly to architectures and component models, offering the basic building blocks with which to create applications, services and introducing functions for self-management of resource. Also programming model and a set of software engineering principles with which to program and structure applications based on the above component models should be addressed, but this is outside the scope of this chapter.

Autonomic Systems

The need to account for highly dynamic scenarios of usage calls for the integration, into the service framework, of mechanisms to enable autonomic composition and configuration. With this regard, several prototypical service frameworks aimed at enforcing autonomic and adaptable behaviors have been proposed in the past few years.

IBM, as part of its autonomic computing initiative (Kephart & Chess, 2003), has outlined the need for current service providers to enforce adaptability, self-configuration, self-optimization, and self-healing, via service (and server) architectures revolving around feedback loops and advanced adaptation/optimization techniques. Driven by such a vision, a variety of architectural frameworks based on "self-regulating" autonomic components have been recently proposed both by IBM (White & Hanson, 2004) and by independent research centers (Liu, 2004; Farha & Kim, 2005; Chen & Iyer, 2007), also with reference to the management of large data centers, Xu & Zhao 2007). The common underlying idea is to couple service components with software components called "autonomic manager" in charge of regulating the functional and non-functional activities of components.

Most of these approaches are typically conceived with centralized or cluster-based server architectures in mind and mostly account for the need of reducing management costs via self-management and self-configuration (Zambonelli, 2006) rather than for the need of providing innovative user-centric services, and definitely not account for the emerging vision of service ecosystems dealing with user-generated content and services.

Multi-Agent Environments

A very similar endeavor - though with a different target scenario – also characterizes several researches in the area of multiagent systems (Valckenaers & Sauter, 2007). Multi-Agent Systems researches aim at identifying suitable models and tools to enable the definition of adaptive applications based on autonomous software agents, capable of dynamically interacting with each other and with the computational environment in which they situate, so to achieve global application goals (typically concerned with scenarios related to the orchestration of distributed resources and or with the coordination of organizational activities). Although possibly conceived according to a different architectural model, agents represent de facto sorts of autonomic components which are capable of self-regulating their activities in accord to some specific individual goal and (by cooperating and coordinating with each other) in accord to some global application goal. However, it is worth emphasizing that that Multi-Agent Systems does not imply an autonomic behavior per-se. They are the most diffuse and promising software framework to engineer systems able to show emerging autonomic properties.

At the level of internal structure Belief Desire Intention (BDI) agent systems, as implemented in agent programming systems like Jadex, JACK or Jason (Bordini & Dastani, 2005) or in the context of the Cortex project (Biegel & Cahill, 2004), propose the use of intelligent agents to deal with autonomic and context-aware components. At the core of this model there is a rule-based engine taking actions on the basis of the component internal state that is explicitly represented by means of facts and rules (Klein & Schmid, 2008; Li & Powley, 2009).

At the level of multiagent systems and their interactions, agents are mostly supposed to get to know each other via specific agent-discovery services, and are supposed to be able to interact according to "social models", e.g., agent negotiations. This is definitely an important step towards the creation of "agent ecosystems" inspired by some social or economic metaphors. For instance, the ADELFE methodology (Bernon & Gleizes, 2002) proposes building complex multiagent systems in accord to the AMAS (Adaptive Multi-Agent System) theory (George, Edmonds & Glize, 2004). This focuses on the design of cooperative social interactions between agents, in which each agent possesses the ability of self-organizing its social interactions depending on the individual task it has to solve. However, the identification of suitable models and engineering methods for such sorts of agent ecosystems, and to exploit them for the realization of course service ecosystem, is only at the beginning. More on this will be analyzed later on.

In any case, both most of the proposed approaches for autonomic computing based on autonomic components and most multiagent systems proposal still requires the existence of solid shared middleware substrate to facilitate discovery and interactions between components.

Autonomic Service Eco-Systems

Overall, and without excluding the possibility of integrating, within an eco-system, specific components capable of internal self-regulating features whenever needed, more lightweight approaches, less dependent from the existence of complex middleware services. Even is some recent methodologies and approaches have tried to more explicitly focus on sorts of socio-inspired or ecosystem-inspired approaches, using them as they are simply not feasible.

In Autonomia framework (Dong & Hariri, 2003), the autonomic behavior of the system and the individual applications is handled by the so called mobile agents. The applications and services are composed of software components and system resources and managed by the mobile agents. Each mobile agent is responsible for monitoring a particular behavior of the system and reacting to the changes accordingly. Autonomia's architecture is composed by three modules: Autonomic Middleware Service, the Application Delegated Manager and the Application Management Editor, each of them concerned with the provision of components representing services registered in the repository, mapping these components to resources available locally as well as remotely, and bringing together such components to extent of assembling applications respectively. In Autonomia framework, the autonomic behavior of the system is implemented in the behavior of its mobile agents which from the implementation point of view means it is hardcoded.

A slightly different approach is provided by the AutoMate framework (Parashar & Liu, 2006). Its architecture contains three layers (system, component and application layer) and three engines (trust and access control, deductive and context awareness engine) all populated by a multitude of agents. The applications and services in AutoMate are composed out of Autonomic Components which reside in the component Layer and which are dynamically composed to applications and services. The components are mapped to the system resources and are controlled by the agents. Similar to Autonomia, the autonomic behavior in the AutoMate framework is handled by the agents and is implemented in form of first order logic rules. Agents continuously process these rules and policies among themselves and perform the desired actions. The autonomic behavior specification is specified at the controller agents and is distributed over the entire system.

In (Jennings & Van der Meer, 2007), the authors have presented the FOCALE architecture for developing autonomic network management. For modeling the autonomic behavior of the network, they propose the idea of mapping business level system constraints down to low level process constraints in an approach called policy continuum (Van der Meer & Davy, 2006). This policy based approach for specifying autonomic system behavior allows network administrators to specify business level policies for network management (using natural language) like for example different internet connection bandwidth rates for different users, Service Level Agreements (SLA), QoS policies etc. The high level policies, which define the system autonomic behavior, can be specified by the network designer or administrator using natural language and are translated by the FOCALE framework to the device level policies.

In conclusion, looking at the wide number of the proposed systems and their diversity, it is possible to see that all of them meets - at least partially - some of the requirements we highlighted for the future networks scenarios. However, on the one hand, there are no proposals addressing all of them at a satisfactory level; on the other hand, none of the above approaches seems to address the problem of globally re-thinking the whole system towards models and architectures specifically conceived for the an "ecosystem-based" approach, i.e., by uniformly modeling all components and resources involved as components of an ecosystems.

The CASCADAS project tried to identify, develop, and evaluate a general-purpose architecture for autonomic computing and networking. Beside the fact that CASCADAS rely on an internal and quite heavyweight architecture for individual components, one of the key ideas in CASCADAS is to exploit P2P overlay networks interconnecting autonomic components and dynamic semantic-based discovery mechanisms to realize any needed form nature-inspired structures of self-organization and self-aggregation of components. That is, to realize via nature-inspired mechanisms flexible, self-adaptable and self-managing, services. A very interesting feature of CASCADAS is that even contextual data, rather than playing the role of something endogenous whose digestion is solely a matter of individual components and their internals, become primary citizens in the overall framework (Baumgarten & Bicocchi, 2007). The same as service components self-organize and self-aggregate with each other, even pieces of contextual information can, in CASCADAS, self-organize and self-compose in accord to the same mechanisms, and the mechanisms for components to access contextual data is uniform to that for accessing other components.

Standardization Initiatives

The development of standards on ACN can foster the exploitation of real solutions with significant impact on Telecommunications, ICT and Future Internet markets; as a matter of fact standards can enable competition, enlarge, or open, markets by facilitating interoperability, accelerating technology take-up, and also ensuring products' dependability. In this direction, among the initiatives aiming at pre-standardization, the Autonomic Communication Forum (ACF) is targeting to provide a set of pre-standards for the definition and assessment autonomic network and service management. In ETSI the Autonomic Network Engineering for the Self-Managing Future Internet (AFI) Industry Specification Group has been recently created: the objective of AFI is to develop standard specifications for Autonomic Network Engineering for the Self-Managing Future Internet. Future initiatives may aim at bringing Autonomic Computing and Networking also in ITU and IETF, for example creating a "BoF" (Birds of a Feather) in the latter body, to raise wider awareness about the topics. Then, the longer term ambition might be to assess the need for, and if necessary to establish, special interest or working groups on relevant aspects.

CASCADAS ACE TOOLKIT DESIGN AND DEVELOPMENT

Within the CASCADAS project, a novel agent-based abstraction for the construction of situation-aware and dynamically adaptable services has been developed, known as the Autonomic Communication Element (ACE). ACE represent an engineering effort aimed at providing a component-model through which heterogeneous basic services can be designed and developed in accordance with requirements drawn from self-* properties. More sophisticated services, up to the scale of complex network services or effective autonomic systems, can be built through collections of ACEs that share locally available services to enable autonomous organization. ACEs behave on the basis of high-level plans that are created by the programmer at design time and modified at runtime, in the way specified by the programmer and in accordance to the evolution of the local context. ACEs organization is supported by a collaborative framework that allows the discovery in a distributed setting through the services they share. Both the component-model and the framework are included in the ACE Toolkit through which ACEs can be designed, developed and deployed. The ACE Toolkit has been entirely implemented in Java and is available open source (CASCADAS, 2009).

Autonomic Communication Element Model

ACEs are agent-based abstractions that facilitate the conception of networked systems as service-centric eco-systems. They behave similarly to the eco-systems found in real nature, where large amounts of heterogeneous entities autonomously enter and leave the environments, interact dynamically among each other, adapting their interactions to the way the surrounding conditions evolve. The ACE framework provides an environment that enables this paradigm. Its design was conceived around the consideration of scalability, heterogeneity, portability and reusability aspects. Once created and brought to life, ACEs can autonomously enter, execute in, and leave the environment. They are capable of autonomously adapting their execution process to reach an operative state, and dynamically organize and reorganize among each other to prosper in the system without any external human intervention.

In order to tackle the challenges and requirements of autonomic communication scenarios and to fulfill the previously highlighted scientific aspects, the ACE model was created under consideration of the following design principles (Figure 1).

ACE model is based on two complementary mechanisms relying on the control loop paradigm. The internal control-loop exploits the self-awareness encompassing reflection (self-model), self-control, planning and reasoning. The external control-loop produces the self-organization features: for instance, emergent capabilities through very simple cooperative behavior (biological, social metaphors), self-adaptation to the context, etc.

Explicit Behavior Definition

When programming an autonomic element, the developer is typically required to provide the high-level policies that define the element's original behavior (Parashar & Hariri, 2005). Within the ACE Toolkit, such policies are specified through a number of states, along with the transitions that lead the ACE execution process from one state to another, in a way similar to Finite State Machines (FSMs). In terms of ACEs, these policies are called *plans*. They represent structured behavioral directions an ACE is required to follow, and the overall ACE behavior can be specified within one or more plans that can execute concurrently or sequentially. The totality of plans specifies the overall behavior for an ACE, and is enclosed in the ACE's *self-model*.

In terms of plans it can be distinguished between the ACE's "normal behavior", which is its behavior when no events undermining the ordinary execution occur, and the "special cases" which might occur during the plan execution process and which could affect the regular ACE execution process. If such occurrences are foreseen, the

Figure 1. Autonomic communication element model

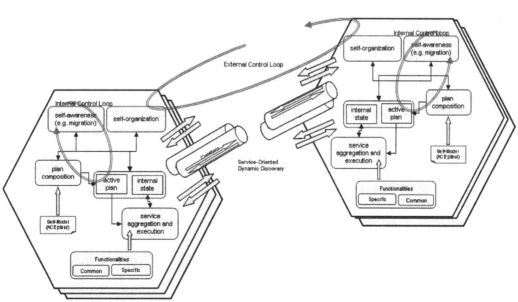

ACE behavior can be enhanced with Modification Rules, through which the ACE developer can specify the circumstances under which the original behavior can be relinquished, along with the new behavioral directions to follow. Modification rules essentially allow ACE behavior to be "deviated" from the original one when the ordinary execution is undermined in a way foreseen at design time.

The ACE behavior is specified explicitly, with the help of a definition language. Within the ACE architecture, this definition is located in a dedicated layer over the implementation logic of the ACE, forming a general object upon which the component can enforce reasoning activity, independently of both the application and the implementation issues. This degree of isolation, along with the explicit nature of the behavioral description, enables a higher degree of runtime control over the ACE.

With the term Behavioral Reusability we indicate the possibility to isolate part of the behavior specification within the self-model of one ACE and share it as a sort of behavioral pattern among ACEs of similar nature. In ACEs, this feature is achieved through Common Behaviors. Common Behaviors are composed by a self-contained set of states and transitions that are made available among a set of ACEs requiring their usage. The rationale behind this feature is to ease the development of self-models by giving the possibility to reuse already existing plans. However, their use also opens a much wider range of possibilities in terms of dynamic adaptation and extensibility. For instance, consider an ACE-based eco-system where ACEs share common behaviors among each other. As the number of ACEs grows, so does the number of common behaviors potentially available, and the result might be a sort of distributed behavior repository. This asset might reveal to be very useful in the economy of the system and promises to ease and speed-up the ACE development process.

Service-Oriented Dynamic Discovery

ACEs need to be proactive in finding the right configuration when they are injected in a system that consists of a collection of ACEs. In the vision of service eco-systems, sophisticated services are built through combination of basic services (Manzalini & Zambonelli, 2006), and therefore depend on a mechanism that quickly queries the presence of required services. This is achieved by equipping ACEs with a service discovery mechanism through which ACEs can scout for other ACEs that are offering required services. The management of discovered services is left to the ACE programmer, who specifies in the self-model what to do with discovered services and which ones to use.

Service discovery itself is realized through a protocol named GN/GA, which stands for Goal Needed/Goal Achievable. In a distributed setting, the GN/GA protocol is supported by one or more registries where ACEs register in order to join a service discovery overlay network. The register manages and provides only the information about the existence of an ACE, but the entire discovery process is left to the ACEs themselves. The service discovery is completely autonomous and self-organized which in particular means that every ACE knows which services it offers, as well as which other services it requires in order to execute.

Stipulated Group Communication

Group communication is fundamental in the interaction model of elements that aim at enabling the design of truly distributed systems. Consequently, it has paramount importance in the ACE framework. The motivations that might bring two or more ACEs to communicate are heterogeneous in nature, and interacting ACEs might be totally unknown to each other. Therefore, the communication should ideally provide some model for explicit agreement and fast identification of roles within the communication logic itself.

When designing the communication mechanism, we took inspiration from the use of SLA; while on the one hand these provide a mean for specifying the terms and conditions without space for ambiguities, on the other hand they hardly suit the needs of lightweight components such as ACEs that, when on mobile devices, might communicate on a non-regular basis. The result of this influence is a contract-based communication that foresees the establishment of a communication contract between the interacting parties. Contracts are essentially channels, which can be bilateral, when created between two ACEs, or multilateral, when created for a larger group of ACEs. Contract establishment needs explicit acceptance from all parties and, once established, contracts provide bidirectional channels through which connected parties can reliably exchange messages. The message exchange can also be "exclusive" within a multilateral contract in that it might target specific destinations only within a bigger group. The use of contract-based communication enables the fast identification of involved parties mentioned above by enforcing a role-based paradigm through which each of the parties is assigned a role. This, in turn, facilitates advanced optional features such as, for instance, contract supervision and provision of security features.

Decoupled and Modular Service Definition

Within a service eco-system, ACEs find their reason of existence in the provision of functionalities. Functionalities can be regarded as the smallest unit for service provision and are typically concerned with basic capabilities such as interfacing hardware or software resources like for example providing access to a storage space or a database, basic hardware control functionalities like for example turning a PC on/off etc. Functionalities can be combined with other functionalities to form services that are defined in our context as an aggregated set of functionalities. Services can be combined with other functionalities and/ or services in order to enlarge their dynamism, complexity and overall usefulness. Services are built proactively by ACEs on the basis of formerly discovered services and existing local functionalities, which need to be enhanced or complemented in a way specified within the self-model. Once a service has been created, the ACE becomes the owner of the new service and in turn executes it or offers it to other ACEs depending on self-model specifications.

Functionalities are defined, by the programmer, at design time in an explicit semantic way similar to the one used for the self-model. Using an explicit definition implies a clear separation from an actual implementation. More precisely, the functionality definition acts as an interface between the self-model, and thus the entity that uses the functionality, and the application code, that is the entity that realizes the functionality. This decoupling brings evident advantages to the system logic when updates, extensions or changes are necessary for the functionality. Furthermore, this modular structure makes it easy to define functionalities with a high degree of granularity.

Mobility and Replication

Mobility answers to eventual requests for higher levels of dynamism and long-term optimization ACEs might need in specific situations. Consider for instance a scenario where an ACE running on a mobile device requires to process large amount of data which will obviously create a significant increase in required workload and will cause suboptimal service provisioning. For that reason ACE can autonomously decide (as specified in the self-model) to move to another physical location from where the service can be appropriately provided. The mobility and replication features seems especially useful in cloud computing and promises to increase performance and optimize the resource usage of a cloud. The ACE framework supports mobility and replication through

Figure 2. ACE organs and their relations

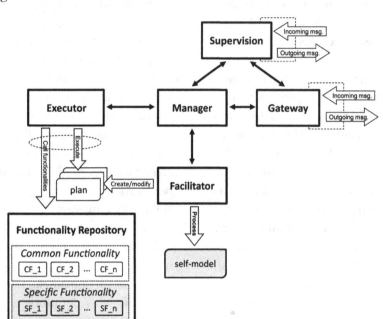

ACE migration and cloning. The process for the former operation is transparent to the current communication commitments, whereas contracts and connections to other ACEs are moved alongside with the ACE in a seamless way.

ACE Functional Architecture

From the very general idea of autonomic services living in an eco-system environment, over the basic ACE concept, up to its specification and implementation, the ACE personifies the idea of a biologically inspired computing entity. Having this vision in mind, the ACE structure has been modeled based on a living organism as a set of interoperating modules called organs, where each organ is responsible for a particular aspect, providing a specific vital functionality, and all organs together form ACE as a self-contained system. In means of organs, an ACE consists of Facilitator, Executor, Functionality Repository, Manager, Gateway, and Supervision organs. Furthermore every ACE has a self-model which defines the ACE autonomic behavior and upon which plans are created (see Figure 2).

In a very simplified view, ACE consists of the common and the specific part. Common part (blocks with white background in Figure 2) is available in each and every ACE. It consists of the organs, each taking care of a particular vital function, and a set of so called common functionalities which are essential to every ACE like the service discovery functionality for example. The specific part (blocks with grey background in Figure 2) on the other hand is ACE specific and varies from ACE to ACE. It consists of the self-model which contains the ACE behavior specification and a set of ACE-specific functionalities implemented in form of standard Java classes. From the implementation point of view, ACE developers are required to implement only the specific part. In the remainder of this section we proceed with the detailed description of ACE architecture.

The autonomic ACE behavior is defined by the developer within the self-model of an ACE and is carried out by the Facilitator organ. Facilitator is responsible for creating and adapting ACE plans on the basis of the self-model specification. During the ACE initialization phase, the Facilitator

Figure 3. ACE self-model and plans

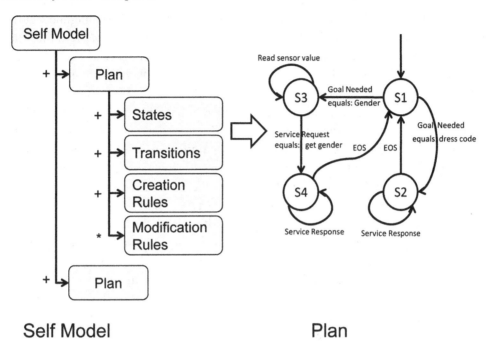

loads and analyses the self-model, and creates the initial plan once the ACE has been started. From there on, it continuously evaluates the need for further plan creations and/or modifications. The new plans, and respectively the modified ones, are forwarded to the Executor for realization. Facilitator maintains an exact copy of all active plans and continuously observes and evaluates their execution process based on specifications provided within the ACE self-model. Based on the outcome of the evaluation process it creates new and/or modifies the existing plans. The plans are then submitted to the Executor for execution.

The ACE autonomic behavior is specified within the self-model. The entire ACE logic, in particular all possible ACE Plans as well as the corresponding rules for their creation and modification are defined here. From the implementation point of view, the self-model is defined as an XML structure which has to be provided for every ACE either as a file or a DOM object. It is loaded by the Facilitator during the ACE initiation phase and is continuously evaluated during the entire ACE lifetime. As the outcome of the self-model

reasoning process, new plans are created or existing plans are modified. In terms of an ACE, the plan specifies the sequence of actions which has to be taken in order to achieve certain goal. ACE plan contains states and transitions where a state defines the current status of the plan execution process and transition defines the action to be performed. Figure 3 shows the relation between the self-model and the ACE plan. More detailed description on ACE autonomic behavior definition is provided in the later part of this chapter.

Executor organ takes care of executing the currently active plans which have been provided by the Facilitator. A plan typically refers to incoming events and to common and specific functionalities residing in the Functionality Repository. The main role of the Executor is to ensure efficient and correct plan realization. It ensures that the transition conditions are properly evaluated and the desired actions specified within a plan transition are invoked by the Functionality Repository. The Executor can execute multiple plans in parallel.

A Plan is an extended Finite State Machine (FSM), consisting of states and transition, where transitions have triggers, guard conditions and actions assigned and states are described by desirability levels (see Figure 7). Trigger of a transition is usually an incoming event. In case no trigger has been specified, the transition will be triggered automatically. When a transition gets triggered, first its guard condition is evaluated. In case of a positive evaluation result, the transition is selected for execution. Guard conditions can be simple logical or mathematical expressions (e.g. referring to the sender or content of the trigger message) or any complex custom comparator logic that is specified by the ACE developer. After a transition has been selected for execution, its action is invoked. In other words, an invocation request is sent to the Functionality Repository where the desired functionality will be invoked with parameters specified within the transition's action. The plan execution process will than move from the transition's source to the destination state. State desirability level is an indicator for desired or respectively undesired plan execution. In case the plan execution process ends up in a state with low desirability level, this will indicate an unwanted processing outcome or an error in plan execution. The executor will inform all other parties (e.g. Facilitator and Supervision) about the desirability level of the current state. The state desirability levels are used to check if the plan execution process performs well or not in order to take appropriate actions upon.

The Functionality Repository is responsible for maintaining, managing and controlling ACE functionalities. It maintains a registry of all deployed functionalities, both common as well as the specific ones, and performs calls (invokes them) when requested by the Executor. On the code level, functionalities are realized as Java classes and methods and the Functionality Repository is the one who translates the high-level plan actions, which are specified within the plan and are invoked by the Executor, into real low

level commands. It is further responsible for functionality thread handling and security permissions. From that point of view, the Functionality Repository can be seen as a container and a sandbox in one. Furthermore Functionality repository provides advanced features like for example operational timeouts which ensures smooth ACE operation. For example, by employing operational timeouts it can be guaranteed that calling a specific functionality will finish in a certain time or otherwise be reported as a failure.

At ACE start-up phase, the Functionality Repository loads the functionalities and checks their consistency. The successfully loaded functionalities will be available throughout the lifetime of the ACE. As shown in Figure 4, ACE Functionalities are modeled on three layers: Event layer (input/output events), Black-box layer (input and output parameters), and the Underlying call layer (real method calls and their parameter list). They are plugged into the Functionality Repository using an XML descriptor describing the three model layers. The functionality model was designed to be open but flexible. In simple cases, to transform a pre-existing external library into an ACE functionality is not more complex than providing a functionality descriptor for it. This in particular makes the ACE open to legacy technologies.

Figure 4 shows call flow of a functionality invocation request. The call is initiated by an event sent by the Executor, containing the input parameters and a reference to the execution environment. Based on the functionality Black-box description, the Repository extracts the required input parameters from the event. According to the Underlying call layer that is specified within the functionality descriptor, all necessary Java classes are instantiated, method calls are performed, return values are collected and the specified output events are sent. Our choice of functionality modeling enhances ACE self-reflection and self-awareness, and avoids limitations of the classical approaches like for example sending multiple events (return values) to different parties.

Figure 4. Functionality model and call-flow

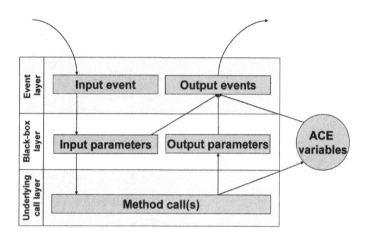

Gateway organ is in charge of providing ACE with the possibility to communicate with the external world which in terms of ACE means communication with other ACEs. Every ACE can per se communicate with every other ACE. The Gateway provides two communication mechanisms:

- Event-based session-less communication mechanism supporting the ACE discovery protocol. (It is used for ACE discovery purposes.)
- Point-to-point session-capable communication mechanism supporting complex interactions among ACEs. (It is used to access ACE's services.)

Event-based session-less communication of the ACE relies on publish-subscribe mechanism for transmission and routing of events, where some ACEs subscribe to events of interest and some other ACEs publish events. A suitable routing structure in form of an overlay network takes care of delivering the events to the proper subscribers. REDS (Reconfigurable Dispatching System) middleware (Cugola & Picco, 2006) which is a framework to build publish-subscribe applications for large, dynamic networks, has been chosen to implement such mechanism. REDS

has been chosen mainly because, in contrast to the vast majority of other approaches, it allows online reconfiguration of brokers, i.e., the broker network topology can change dynamically without disrupting the global event dispatching service. This is particularly useful in dynamic autonomic scenarios, like P2P and pervasive computing settings where nodes and devices can come and go at any time (Acosta & Avresky, 2005). This event-based communication mechanism is mainly used to support the GN/GA ACE discovery protocol which will be later described in more detail.

Point-to-point session-capable communication allows ACEs to directly communicate among each other while using dedicated communication channels. Once the desired ACEs has been successfully discovered, it is possible to establish a direct communication link among them in order to use their services (call their functionalities). The concept that that has been developed here is termed contractual connection. ACEs negotiate and set up contracts to send events among each other in a coordinated and regulated way. A contract is associated with a set of connections between participants, who can address each other with the help of roles. In general a contract forms an N-tuple of address and role name pairs, (where N is the number of ACEs involved) associated with additional information that are part of the underly-

Figure 5. ACE lifecycle state diagram

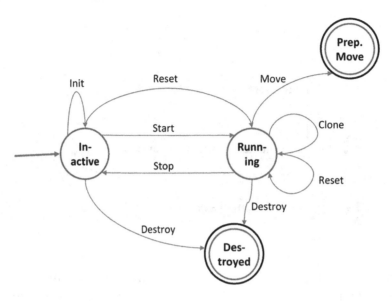

ing agreement. This communication scheme has been chosen as it clearly separates the role of an ACE within a collaborative collective, from its identity, facilitating the runtime discovery and binding of ACEs in a self-organizing fashion. It improves the robustness of a collective of ACEs through ensuring consistency, as ACE guarantee that a contract is unusable once it is invalidated (e.g. one of the ACEs leaves the contract for an unexpected reason). The collective is banned from further interaction, requiring a repair or set up a new contract. Gateway organ manages and continuously evaluates all contracts that an ACE holds. Events that are to be transmitted over a contractual connection are subjected to an evaluation by this organ. Once it checks that a contract

Figure 6. Definition of the self-model structure

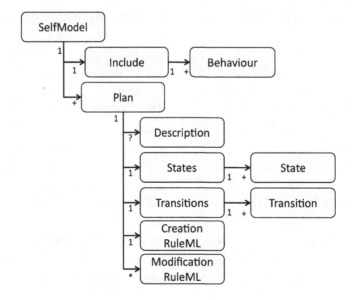

Figure 7. Self-model structure: states and transitions

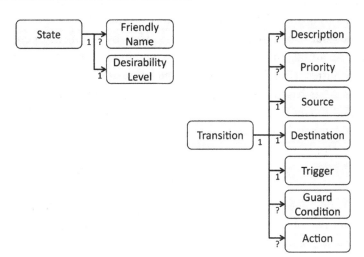

is valid and in place, ACE addresses are resolved based on the given role names and the message is sent. Using contracts it is also possible to implement arbitrary Service Level Agreements (SLA) between cooperating ACE.

Manager organ is responsible for handling the execution of the ACE lifecycle process and the internal ACE communication. ACE lifecycle management comprises scheduling, controlling, and executing any operation that influences the lifecycle of an ACE. The lifecycle begins when an ACE instance is created. As depicted in Figure 5, it comprises four states: inactive, running, prepared to move, and destroyed, which can be changed if a life cycle action takes place. With respect to this, any ACE must be in one of these states at all times. Manager actively controls all ACE organs when a lifecycle action has been issued and performs the requested lifecycle operation like for example start/stop the ACE execution or move ACE to the proposed new location. For the fact that the ACE lifecycle management supports cloning and moving across different execution environments, ACEs are flexible in choosing the most appropriate physical location that suits their current needs.

Manager is responsible for providing and maintaining communication among the ACE organs which is called intra-ACE-communication. It is an event-based, publish-subscribe type of communication which is implemented and carried out by a so called event bus. Event bus is part of the manager and all ACE organs are directly linked to it. They can publish their events to the event bus as well as subscribe for receiving events of a certain type. Using a bus to relay commands and disseminate information facilitates provides decoupling of the organ design decisions and runtime logic, and enables observation of the ACE's internal behavior for supervision (Deussen & Hoefig, 2007). It also integrates well with the state-machine approach for behavioral specification, and prepares the ground for future more sophisticated features, like activity recording or transactional rollbacks.

Supervision refers to the ongoing observation of ACEs and the issuing of corrective measures upon detection of hazardous situations. The **supervision organ** allows the monitoring of specific internal characteristics from which the cooperativeness of the ACE can be assessed. Its logic is triggered by the reception of specific supervision events from an external supervision service provider (Ferrari & Manzalini, 2009). This, on the other hand, implies that an external service needs to be setup in order to take advantage of the supervision functionalities. If such a service does not exist within an ACE-based system, the organ simply remains idle. On the contrary, when such service does exist, the supervision focuses on the observation of the contractual compliance of collaborating ACEs in the two aspects of analysis of network performance (e.g. packet delay for a contractual connection) and adherence to stated behavior. To these extents, two objects have been identified as good monitoring points, the internal event bus and the gateway. Observation of these objects allows monitoring internal and external interactions.

ACE Autonomic Behavior Specification

From the autonomic system point of view, the autonomic behavior specifies the way the system behaves, both under the normal and the special conditions, and defines the actions which need to be performed in order for the system to autonomously operate in an environment (Parashar & Hariri, 2005; Dobson & Denazis, 2006). Thus, we can state that the autonomic behavior consists of two integral parts: one that defines the "regular" component behavior and another that defines how this "regular" behavior needs to be modified when special conditions occurred.

In the CASCADAS framework, the behavior of an ACE is specified in an explicit way through a number of plans, each containing a number of states and transitions, within the ACE self-model. Specifying behavioral directions of an ACE is a task left to the human programmer, so that every aspect can be covered within an arbitrary level of accuracy on the basis of the priorities considered by the programmer. The definition of the ACE behavior, within the self-model, has to be specified in a XML based formal language which has been

purposely created for this task. Figure 6 shows its basic structure.

The root element opens one or more plans which in turn are composed by a block of *states* and *transitions* each of them carrying the entire set of states and transitions which might be used for this plan. Along with these, each plan also specifies the way the states and transitions need to be assembled into a state machine (*Creation-RuleML*) and eventually modified (*Modification-RuleML*) when special conditions occur. Plan creation and modification rules follow the standard RuleML syntax and are defined trough a specification of a number of rules.

Sometimes there might be also a common behavior or multiple behaviors, developer would like to share among multiple ACEs. In that case it is advantageous to isolate this autonomic behavior (e.g. in a separate file) and reuse it in other ACEs when needed. From their structure these behaviors follow exactly the same structure of the self-model and can be imported into the ACE's self-model within the *include* element. These imported common behaviors can be started either on ACE start-up or on demand from the self-model.

As presented in Figure 7, states have univocal identifiers and are defined within plans though a unique ID, friendly name and the desirability level. The friendly name aims at describing the state with a meaningful and user understandable name while the desirability level helps assessing the stability of the execution process. A low desirability level identifies a state the ACE would have probably wanted to avoid within the sphere of ordinary execution but which nevertheless can be entered. The recent state desirability level is continuously monitored by the ACE.

Transitions are defined by a number of elements, aimed at univocally defining terms and conditions for the transition to take place. The description is again dedicated to the programmer in order to provide him the possibility to describe the transition in a meaningful way. Source is the state from which the transition will start and destination is the state where the execution process will end as the result of successful transition execution. Priority allows developer to specify the order in which the transitions leading from the same state will be evaluated. Priorities do not add any significant feature to the definition, but allow handling complex cases while keeping the complexity low. A transition provides two levels of filtering. The first level filtering is implied by specifying the transition trigger which in terms of ACEs is usually an event. More exactly, trigger should specify the type of event upon which the transition should be eventually triggered. Trigger could be also set to "*@auto*" which defines a transition that should be evaluated/triggered immediately without requiring arrival of an event. The second level filtering can be optionally specified through the guarding conditions. This allows developers to cover cases where more than one transition can take place from the same source state while triggered by the same type of event. Guarding conditions allows checking events and their parameter values using first order logic expressions. When an incoming event satisfies both level of filtering, the action defined within the transition will be executed and the plan execution process will move towards the transition destination state. The action typically specifies the local functionality to be invoked.

Creation and modification rules specify when states and transitions defined as described above need to be created and modified within a plan. States and transitions for the normal ACE behavior are created within the block of creation rules, while the ones concerned with modification of the original states and transitions are enclosed in the block of modification rules. Our choice of the plan format - extended FSM - is more advanced than a sequence of actions which was common in earlier autonomic systems (Koehler & Gantenbein, 2003). This abstraction has been chosen because it is well-known, easy to understand, and has the descriptive power we needed.

Optimized Inter-ACE Communication

The CASCADAS approach takes the perspective that services are provided by large ensembles of relatively simple entities realized as ACEs, which interact for creating composed services or for organizing distributed algorithms. The functional composition of ACEs can be done by using clustering algorithms. A possible example is a novel protocol, called GN/GA (Goal Needed/Goal Achievable), defined and adopted in CASCADAS. It can be used as a decentralized mechanism for discovering services offered by ACEs. Figure 8 describes the basic flow of GN/GA protocol:

- **Goal Needed (GN):** this message is sent by an ACE to look for services offered by other ACEs; it contains a (semantic) description of the functionalities the ACE needs to achieve its goals;
- **Goal Achievable (GA):** this message is sent by an ACE to state the task(s) it is able to provide; it transports also a semantic task/service description.

In order to scale properly, this protocol must avoid flooding GN requests. This is achieved, for instance, by applying some locality rules and propagating the messages through overlays implemented, for instance, by the underlying communication middleware (i.e., REDS). For establishing a durable cooperation relation between two ACEs, a contract (e.g., representing a new link in the overlay) needs to be set up. Such a contract is basically an association between unique role names and ACE addresses together with a unique identification number. For the time being basic contracts are currently static: they are simply established or cancelled, but no negotiation of contractual content takes place. For example, if an ACE A wants to establish a connection to an ACE providing a needed service, e.g., the access to a repository of images, it initially has to find ACEs that are able to offer the required task,

Figure 8. Flow of the GN/GA protocol

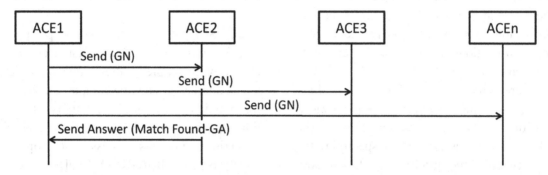

e.g., by sending a GN message. Eventually, when one or more ACEs able to fulfill the required task answer, e.g., with GA messages containing their addresses, ACE A can select one of them, and create a contract to it. Contracts may also be used to establish efficient and secure interactions among ACEs.

Although the details of the communication model can vary, the maximum "distance" over which two ACEs can communicate effectively is assumed to be small compared with the size of the entire system and each ACE usually communicates only with a few nearby neighbors. In order to achieve these requirements, interactions among ACEs are usually performed through overlay networks, whose links are set-up through clustering mechanisms and maintained/optimized by means of self-organization algorithms.

In fact, there could be the need to optimize the overlay networks, by incrementing the links between ACEs with similar properties (e.g., ACEs offering the same service type). Self-organization algorithms (Saffre & Tateson, 2008; Di Marzo Serugendo & Foukia, 2004) can be used for this purpose. For instance in the *passive clustering* (1) each of the ACEs interconnected through an overlay may randomly decide to assume the role of match-maker and initiate a procedure; (2) the match-maker randomly selects two of its own neighbors in the overlay and, if they have the same type, instructs them to link together; (3) if the two chosen nodes were not already directly

connected a new link is established between them, and (4) if the number of links must be constant, the match-maker deletes the link with one of its two selected neighbors. An alternative algorithm, named *on-demand clustering*, distinguishes between the initiator of a rewiring procedure and the match-maker; when an ACE randomly decides to assume the role of initiator, it selects one of its neighbors to act as the match-maker, which attempts to connect one of its neighbors to the initiator.

Variants of self-organization algorithms are the self-differentiation algorithms that can be used to define decentralized decision algorithms. Self-differentiation algorithms rely on the interactions through an overlay, in order to process and, possibly, modify, the state of two neighbors. Analogously to self-organization algorithms, each ACE in the overlay may randomly assume the role of "match-maker" and initiate the self-differentiation procedure: it randomly selects two of its neighbors, process their states, and instruct how to change them; in some cases, the match-maker may select only one neighbor, process its state with the one of the selected neighbor, and provide instruction on how to modify them.

Overlay networks can be used for disseminating information among ACEs through gossiping protocols (Jelasity, Montresor & Babaoglu, 2005), which are based on iterative information exchange: during each protocol step, a node exchanges to (a small subset of) its neighbors a small amount of data. Algorithms based on gossiping are inspired by the interactions in biological systems, such as those related to the spread of viruses and diseases or the synchronization of blinking of fireflies. Self-aggregation algorithms are an example of these algorithms: during each step of these algorithms, a node combines the data received from its neighbors during the previous step, with its local state, updates its state and forwards the combined information to (some of) its neighbors. It was theoretically proven, and confirmed through simulations, that these algorithms converge. For instance, gossip-based data aggregation, when applied on small-world or random graph topologies, converges at an exponential rate, whose exponent depends on the characteristics of overlay (Kowalczyk & Vlassis, 2005); moreover, convergence speed is highly related to the speed of information propagation, and the higher the link randomization in an overlay, the faster the convergence. In some practical situation, determining when the algorithm can terminate was solved through some local conditions, e.g., the algorithm is stopped after a predefined number of cycles, depending on the required accuracy (Friedman & Gavidia, 2007). Termination is not an issue, when gossiping algorithms are used to propagate information on the state of dynamically changing systems (e.g., traffic load, number of available nodes) across all the elements, so that each of them can have an approximated knowledge of its surrounding sub-system.

Due to the characteristics of these interaction mechanisms, systems structured as an ensemble of distributed ACEs are naturally scalable, resilient to faults, and adaptable to changes in environment. They can be adopted, for instance, to implement decentralized decision algorithms, in case global control is not feasible and global stable information is available. These algorithms can be implemented as a set of ACEs cooperating through a self-organized overlay network: even if each ACE performs autonomously according to simple rules, their cooperation, e.g., through self-

differentiation algorithms and gossiping protocols, determines the emergence of a global behavior.

An example is the decentralized supervision method for distributed systems described in the next section.

USE CASE AND DEMONSTRATIONS

The ACE Toolkit has been validated through the development of innovative distributed applications and has been demonstrated in several public events, including ICT2008 Conference and Exhibition (Lyon, November 23rd-25th, 2008).

One of the scenarios adopted for the experimental validation of the Toolkit is the service named Personal Behavioral Advertisement (PBA), a non-trivial example of both a pervasive computing system and a wide-area network application with near real-time constraints (Di Ferdinando & Rosi, 2009). PBA considers a crowded venue with a number of public screens, used to advertise the venue itself as well as commercial advertisements. Examples of such advertising screens can be seen in public spaces, such as museums, airports, metro and train stations, etc. In these venues, it is realistic to assume the presence of infrastructures (i.e., wireless networks, RFID receptors) that provide pervasive services (e.g., downloadable maps or events program for the venue, web navigation). End-users are assumed to be equipped with personal mobile devices (e.g., smart phones, netbooks, PDAs) through which the above services might be accessed, and publicly accessible information on user's profiles might be provided to the services.

Usually, advertising screens display information cyclically in a way independent of the context (i.e., independent of who is actually close to that screen). A smart service can exploit availability of the pervasive infrastructures, and the presence of pervasive devices, to gather information on users so as to adapt the contents to be shown on the basis of the peculiar interests of people detected.

Figure 9. Personal behavioral advertisement scenario

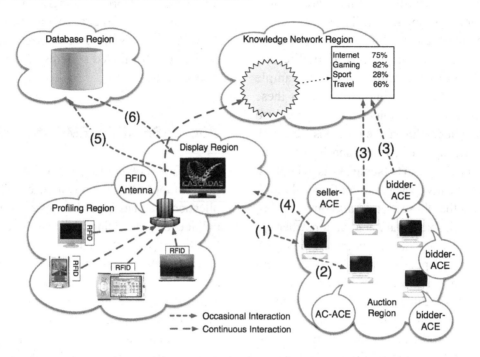

In the presence of a large number of screens and parties interested in buying time slots on them, an auction-based allocation paradigm could be adopted whereby advertisers compete in a context-aware fashion to acquire the rights of advertising on a specific screen at a specific time.

The PBA platform developed by means of the ACE Toolkit is populated by a number of originally disjoint ACEs, which self-organize in Regions according to the offered services (Figure 9). Each Region provides different services, made available to other regions so as to enhance on demand cooperation, achieved through inter-region aggregations that fosters a system-wide self-organization, optimized to offer the PBA service.

The Profiling Region makes available services for obtaining user information. It is composed by a collection of ACEs interacting with badges equipped with RFID tags via RFID antennas positioned by the screen in such a way to

detect the presence (and gather information) of people appearing and disappearing from the screen range. This activity is carried out on a continuous basis. Information so gathered is exchanged with the *Knowledge Network Region*, composed by a number of aggregated ACEs that seamlessly provide, as a single ACE, a situation-aware information service in full respect of the self-similar principles (Castelli, Mamei & Zambonelli, 2008).

The Display Region offers displaying capabilities for showing the advertisement. Allocation of the actual content to be shown takes place by invoking the slot allocation service provided by Auction Region (interaction (1) in Figure 9). The allocation of advertisement slots is performed through an iterative English auction, where advertisers compete to acquire the rights to expose own products in the slot of time under auction. The slot under auction offered by a seller-ACE, representing a display owner, is advertised by an Auction Centre ACE (interaction (2)) to bidder-

ACEs, representing the advertisers. The decisions of bidder-ACEs on whether to submit a bid or not make use the querying services offered by the Knowledge Network Region (interaction (3)): a bid is submitted if the trends of interests reported in the result of the query show sensitive relevance with the range of products the advertiser is aiming at displaying. Upon auction termination, communication of the auction winner is returned back to the Display Region (interaction (4)), and is used by the ACEs controlling the displays to select the right advertisement to show. The selection is offered as a service by the Database Region, which contains an advertisement database repository where advertisements are tagged based on owner and dominant relevance of interests (interaction (5), and (6)).

The possibility to execute ACEs also on small devices was exploited in order to directly deploy on mobile devices running Android environment ACEs which have to provide to the Knowledge Network the relevant data publicly available in end-users' profile and their changes.

Auction Region has been enriched with self-healing capabilities to handle failures of ACEs implementing sellers and the Auction Centre. They are achieved through a supervision service structured as an ensemble of ACEs offering basic autonomic supervision features, which dynamically self-organize to form MAPE-like control loops according to the structure of the system under supervision and its changes (Deussen & Baumgarten, 2009).

Another scenario used to validate the ACE Toolkit was the design of a framework for the management of highly distributed and dynamic systems. An example of such systems is a decentralized server farm created by interconnecting computing nodes, including both servers, clusters, and, also, users' devices, through a geographical-wide network (e.g., the Internet), in order to form a cloud of computing resources interconnected though an overlay network (Manzalini, Minerva & Moiso, 2009).

These distributed server farms can dynamically change their configurations, because the computing resources can join and leave the cloud in an unplanned way. Due to their characteristics, these clouds of computing resources cannot be supervised by a centralized system, but it is necessary to adopt highly distributed solutions, leveraging on self-* algorithms and gossiping protocols. The ACE Toolkit was adopted to design such a decentralized management framework: each computing resource has been equipped with an ACE in charge of its supervision (Figure 10).

These supervising ACEs interwork and cooperate in order to execute distributed supervision algorithms for the management of the whole cloud. They self-adapt their behavior, and the one of the controlled resource, according to local "supervision" logic defined in terms of self-model plans: it processes the internal state of the ACE and the one of the controlled resource, and exchange relevant information (e.g., on load, or faults) and cooperate with the supervising ACEs controlling the resources which are directly linked through the overlay network. This overlay, which is maintained and optimized though self-organization algorithms executed by the supervising ACEs, is used for transporting among the supervising ACEs data relevant for the distributed supervision of the whole cloud, by means of gossiping protocols. In this way, the supervision overlay guarantees the scalability, by keeping the locality of the interactions, and avoiding information flooding.

This distributed supervision framework was adopted in order to implement supervision algorithms for handling with fault recovery, load balancing and power savings (Ferrari & Manzalini, 2009). The performance of the algorithm in large systems involving thousands of nodes was evaluated through simulations, which showed that a global "quasi-optimal" (w.r.t. a hypothetical centralized solution) supervision behavior emerges from the local supervision logic executed by the ACEs and the local interaction among them.

Figure 10. Supervision of distributed server farms through cooperating ACEs

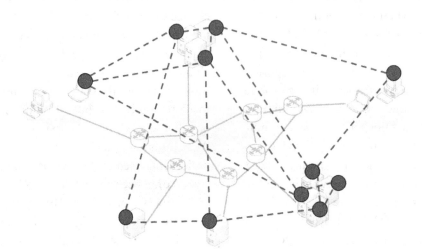

● ACEs supervising resources and executing distributed supervision algorithms

- - - - Links of the (self-organized) overlay network

CASCADAS ACE TOOLKIT EXPERIMENTAL VALIDATION

In our experimental evaluation we have analyzed the performance of the ACE Toolkit from the perspective of a distributed system. For this purpose several experiments have been performed aiming at measuring: threads, memory usage, and communication delay of ACE applications. Evaluating the ACE Toolkit performance and resource consumption from the distributed system perspective was important because ACEs are created to operate in such environments.

The first set of experiments analyses the thread consumption of ACE based applications. Figure 11 presents thread use over time of the different organs composing the ACEs in the Personal Behavioral Advertisement application. One can see that, after a bootstrap phase, the number of threads involved in the application remains stable for most of the organs. The only elements deviating from this pattern are timers associated to various tasks in the application. These elements add up in the wait state, until the associated time-periods expire

freeing the thread. This creates the saw-tooth plot in Figure 11.

From a complementary perspective, Figure 12 illustrates how the CPU time is divided among the kinds of thread in the system. From the pie chart one can see that the DIET infrastructure (Hoile & Wang, 2002), on which the ACE architecture executes, accounts for almost one third of the total CPU time. Since the application being considered is based on a number of ACEs interacting in a communication intensive service, the combination of the Gateway organs and REDS infrastructure accounts for another third of the total CPU time. The actual execution of the plan (Executor) and of internal communication (Bus) accounts for the remaining third of the operations. The fair balance of operation within the ACE architectures hints to a correct division of responsibilities among ACE organs.

The second set of experiments analyses the memory consumption of ACE based applications. For this purpose a new experiment has been created in which 100 ACEs are created and started one after another. Each time a new ACE has been

Figure 11. Thread classification

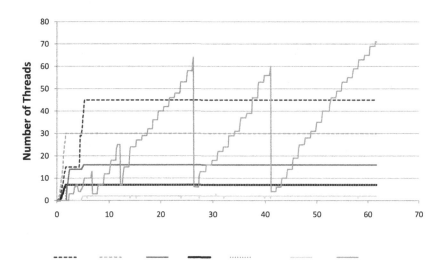

Figure 12. CPU consumption per thread class

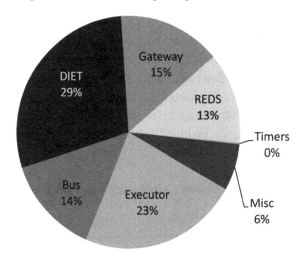

created and started, the memory that is allocated for the application has been measured. Different Java garbage collectors (Sun Microsystems, 2003) have been utilized and the results have been compared accordingly. Figure 13 depicts the memory allocation patterns when using the garbage collectors ParallelOldGC, ParallelGC, SerialGC whereas the Figure 14 presents the memory allocation pattern when using IncGC.

While the ParallelOldGC, ParallelGC, SerialGC garbage collectors exhibit a similar behavior suggesting a constant amount of allocated memory, the incremental garbage collector (IncGC), shows a memory consumption curve that linearly increases with the amount of ACEs. The oscillatory trend of all garbage collectors is due to the fact that they are not permanently cleaning up the memory but are only running periodically with a certain time delay between each execution. In conclusion of our experiment we can say that the memory consumption of ACE based applications in detail depends on the used garbage collector. Nevertheless, the results show that the amount of allocated memory grows only linearly with the number of ACEs within the application.

In the third set of experiments, the delays in inter-ACE communication in a distributed test-bed have been measured. Communication characteristics have been tested experimentally through executions on a test-bed composed by machines distributed over a LAN. The experiment was performed in the following way: In the initial setting, two ACEs find each other and start communicating through a simple request-response protocol. To this extent, a request message is sent every 500ms, with the source ACE recording the

Figure 13. Memory consumption using ParallelOldGC, ParallelGC, and SerialGC garbage collectors

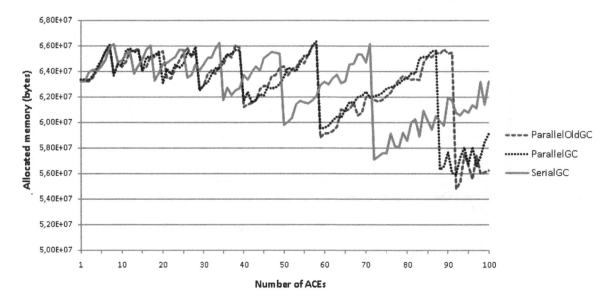

transmission time. Once the message is received, a reply message is sent back to the source where the reception time is recorded to measure the communication round-trip time. Every two minutes, a new ACE joins the system. This is quickly found by other ACEs, via the GN/GA protocol, and suddenly involved in the request-response process. The communication delay is calculated as the difference between the transmission time of the request message and the reception time of the reply message. The timings are recorded at ACE application level and to be more precise, the time delay recorded includes the actual network delay and the time needed for the packet to be processed

Figure 14. Memory consumption using incremental garbage collector IncGC

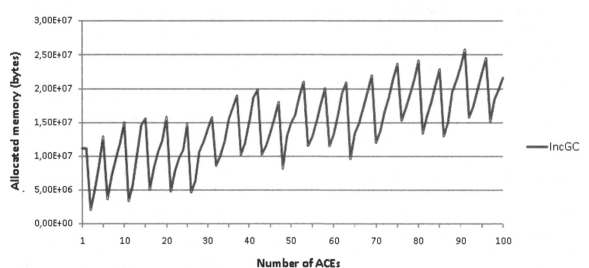

(at both source and destination). Nevertheless, considering the fact that the message processing at the ACE level means simply sending the same message back to its source, the time required for message processing will impact the recorded timings on a lesser extent.

As presented in the Figure 15, the communication delay increases linearly with the number of ACEs. The delay variations can be mainly imputed to variations in the message processing times. The quasi-linear increase of communication delays with the number of ACEs shows a linear scalability in ACE distributed applications. In conclusion of these experiments, it is possible to see that the ACE architecture is rather scalable along many dimensions (memory, threads, communication delay) in distributed setting. This supports the applicability of the ACE model in rather large autonomic communication scenarios.

FUTURE RESEARCH DIRECTIONS

The ACE Toolkit is a service networking environment composed by a run time execution environment enhanced with related plug-and-play libraries for exploiting self-management, self-organization, security, and knowledge network capabilities. The ACE Toolkit is running on laptop, PDA, mobile devices, such as Android-equipped mobile devices, and is available as an open source project (CASCADAS, 2009). Experimental assessment showed that the ACE Toolkit is stable and scalable in terms of memory, threads and communication delay. However, the ACE Toolkit has also opened several research questions which need to be answered in the future and which we will describe here.

First research challenge which has been identified is the need for advanced conceptual solution for specifying autonomic behavior at different levels of an autonomic system. In autonomic component-based systems, like the one that has been developed in CASCADAS project, autonomic applications are constructed from autonomic elements that manage their internal behavior and their relationships with other autonomic elements in accordance with policies specified by the programmer. As a result, self-managing behaviors at system and application level emerge from the self-managing behaviors of constituent autonomic elements and their interactions. Further research

Figure 15. Average inter-ACE communication delay

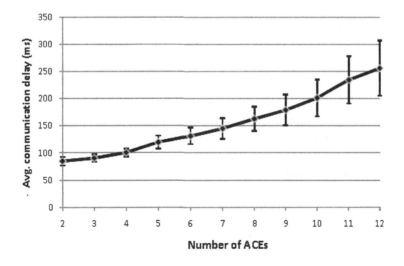

is required and solutions need to be provided in order to meet and integrate top-down goals, for instance achieved according to orchestration or choreography mechanisms, with bottom-up emergence of behavioral patterns in complex distributed ecosystems of autonomic components. Novel concepts and solutions should be designed in which local as well as global autonomic behaviors can be specified, implemented and controlled in a robust and predictable manner.

Providing effective solutions for autonomic behavior self-optimization is seen as another research challenge of an autonomic system. In autonomic computing, self-optimization is considered the ability of a computing component to seek ways to improve its operation, identifying and seizing opportunities to make itself more efficient in performance or cost (Kephart & Chess, 2003). Looking at the individual steps of the goal-achievement-process that is specified in the autonomic behavior, it is evident that one and the same goal can be achieved through different sets of individual steps which consequently may show difference in performance. From that perspective, advanced concepts need to be researched and solutions must be proposed which enable autonomic behavior self-optimization at different levels of autonomic systems.

New challenges also derive from innovative application scenarios. One of the most interesting concerns the management and the governance of future networks. In these networks, processing, storage and communication resources, e.g., provided by mobile devices and by surrounding space (e.g., by means of sensors, RFID tags, etc.) will be highly pervasive, and will enable the creation highly decentralized cyber environments of resources interconnected by dynamically configuring Networks of Networks. As communications will be extended to cover any combination of "people, machines and things", future Networks of Networks will be more and more complex and heterogeneous, with the challenging task of ensuring reliable services and guarantee the re-

quired end-to-end quality of service. Autonomic computing and networking toolkit could be the enabling technologies to implement a "Decentralized Cognitive Plane" (DCP), for cross-layer, cross-node and cross-network domain self-management, self-control and self-optimization of these Networks of Networks. For instance, the DCP could be structured as an ensemble of distributed and cooperating autonomic components (e.g., ACEs) in charge of monitoring and effecting the network at different layers. DCP components have to run data gathering, mining, reasoning and machine learning algorithms/techniques to extract useful information, and organize it in semantic knowledge networks, on what is happening in the network and in the distributed services running on it. Eventually, DCP is in charge of enacting specific autonomic behaviour on the basis of the collected data to assure self-management/control and optimization (Manzalini & Deussen, 2010).

Distributed autonomic component toolkits, such as CASCADAS one, could also be adopted in order to deal with the creation and the governance of service ecosystems in Network of Networks. In fact in these context, individuals will take up a more active and central role in the provision of contents and services. Distributed autonomic component platforms will be able to exploit the distributed presence of resources to be dynamically pooled and composed, leading to the development of a new form of service ecosystems, where several Players (from SME to LE, from network operators/service providers to Individuals) interact to produce, combine and consume services (Deussen, Hoefig & Manzalini, 2008). This evolution will yield a variety of challenges for the evolution of the autonomic component toolkits in both service delivery and service management, requiring solutions able to master complexity, dependability, and behavioral stability in complex and dynamic systems in the absence of a centralized control point.

CONCLUSION

In the future, computing and storage resources will become pervasively embedded in a variety of nodes and devices that are interconnected through diverse types of networks and protocols. In this vision, people, smart objects, machines and the surrounding space (sensors, RFID tags, etc.) create a highly decentralized cyber environment based on Networks of Networks. Dynamicity and pervasivity will increase the complexity of management, control and optimization of resources and will open new challenges for service delivery in such environments. Autonomic communications principles and technologies can provide effective computing and networking solutions to overcome limitations and to foster this challenging evolution.

In this direction, the chapter presented the vision and the main concepts of the autonomic communication toolkit developed and demonstrated in the EU project CASCADAS. Architectural vision considers ecosystems of applications built on the communication and networking services provided by a distributed ensemble of ACEs. ACEs are abstracting resources, functions and basic core services and interact with each other to provide more complex services thus realizing ecosystems characterized by a global autonomic behavior, robustness, reliability and scalability. The here presented and experimentally evaluated the ACE Toolkit has been successfully deployed to laptops, PDAs and mobile devices with Android software platforms and is available as the open source project (CASCADAS, 2009).

The lesson learnt from the development and experimental validation of the ACE Toolkit mainly addressed the feasibility of autonomic component-ware pervasive architectures robust and scalable in many dimensions (e.g. memory, threads, communication delay). Starting from this experience an interesting research avenue is to implement a "Decentralized Cognitive Plane", for cross-layer, cross-node and cross-network domain self-management, self-control and self-

optimization of future Networks of Networks, and to development a functional framework for deal with the creation and the governance of service ecosystems.

ACKNOWLEDGMENT

The authors would like to acknowledge the European Commission for funding the Integrated Project CASCADAS "Component-ware for Autonomic, Situation-aware Communications, And Dynamically Adaptable Services" (FET Proactive Initiative, IST-2004-2.3.4 Situated and Autonomic Communications) within the 6th IST Framework Program. Authors would like also to thank Rico Kusber, Antonio Di Ferdinando, Mario Giacometto, Borbala Benko, Edzard Hoefig, Franco Zambonelli and Marco Mamei for their support to the Project achievements.

REFERENCES

Acosta, J. R., & Avresky, D. R. (2005). Dynamic network reconfiguration in presence of multiple node and link failures using autonomous agents. In *International Conference on Collaborative Computing: Networking, Applications and Worksharing* (pp. 10-20). Washington, DC: IEEE Computer Society.

Baumgarten, M., Bicocchi, N., Kusber, R., Mulvenna, M., & Zambonelli, F. (2007). Self-organizing knowledge networks for pervasive situation-aware services. In *IEEE International Conference on Systems, Man and Cybernetics* (pp. 1-6). New York, NY: IEEE Computer Society.

Benko, B., Brgulja, N., Hoefig, E., & Kusber, R. (2008). Adaptive services in a distributed environment. In *8th International Workshop on Applications and Services in Wireless Networks* (pp. 66-75). Washington, DC: IEEE Computer Society.

Bernon, C., Gleizes, M. P., Peyruqueou, S., & Picard, G. (2002). ADELFE: A methodology for adaptive multi-agent systems engineering. In *3rd International Workshop Engineering Societies in the Agents World* (pp. 156-169). Heidelberg, Germany: Springer.

Biegel, G., & Cahill, V. (2004). A framework for developing mobile, context-aware applications. In *2nd International Conference on Pervasive Computing and Communications* (pp. 361-365). Washington, DC: IEEE Computer Society.

Bordini, R., Dastani, M., Dix, J., & Seghrouchni, A. (2005). *Multi-agent programming: Languages, platforms and applications.* Heidelberg, Germany: Springer.

CASCADAS. (2009). *ACE toolkit repository.* Retrieved April 27, 2010, from http://sourceforge.net/projects/acetoolkit/

Castelli, G., Mamei, M., & Zambonelli, F. (2008). Engineering contextual knowledge for pervasive autonomic services. *International Journal of Information and Software Technology, 50,* 36–50. doi:10.1016/j.infsof.2007.10.009

Chen, Y., Iyer, S., Liu, X., Milojicic, D., & Sahai, A. (2007). SLA decomposition: Translating service level objectives to system level thresholds. In *4th International Conference on Autonomic Computing* (pp. 3). Washington, DC: IEEE Computer Society.

Clark, D., Wroclawski, J., Sollins, K., & Braden, R. (2005). Tussle in cyberspace: Defining tomorrow's Internet. *IEEE/ACM Transactions on Networking, 13*(3), 462–475. doi:10.1109/TNET.2005.850224

Cugola, G., & Picco, G. P. (2006). REDS: A reconfigurable dispatching system. In *6th International Workshop on Software Engineering and Middleware* (pp. 9-16). New York, NY: ACM.

Deussen, P. H., Baumgarten, M., Mulvenna, M., Manzalini, A., & Moiso, C. (2009). Autonomic re-configuration of pervasive supervision services - The CASCADAS approach. In *1st International Conference on Emerging Network Intelligence* (pp. 33-38). IARIA.

Deussen, P. H., & Hoefig, E. (2007). Self-organizing service supervision. In *2nd International Conference on Bio-Inspired Models of Network, Information and Computing Systems* (pp. 245-246). Washington, DC: IEEE Computer Society.

Deussen, P. H., Hoefig, E., & Manzalini, A. (2008). An ecological perspective on future service environments. In *2nd IEEE International Conference on Self-Adaptive and Self-Organizing Systems Workshops* (pp. 37-42). Washington, DC: IEEE Computer Society.

Di Ferdinando, A., Rosi, A., Lent, R., Manzalini, A., & Zambonelli, F. (2009). MyAds: A system for adaptive pervasive advertisements. *Pervasive and Mobile Computing, 5*(5), 385–401. doi:10.1016/j.pmcj.2009.06.006

Di Marzo Serugendo, G., Foukia, N., Hassas, S., & Karageorgos, A. (2004). Self-organization: Paradigms and applications. In Carbonell, J. G., & Siekmann, J. (Eds.), *Engineering self-organizing systems: Nature-inspired approaches to software engineering* (pp. 1–19). Heidelberg, Germany: Springer.

Dobson, S., Denazis, S., Fernández, A., Gaiti, D., Gelenbe, E., & Massacci, F. (2006). A survey of autonomic communications. *ACM Transactions on Autonomous and Adaptive Systems, 1*(2), 223–259. doi:10.1145/1186778.1186782

Dong, X., Hariri, S., Xue, L., Chen, H., Zhang, M., Pavuluri, S., & Rao, S. (2003). Autonomia: An autonomic computing environment. In *IEEE International Conference on Performance, Computing, and Communications* (pp. 61-68). Washington, DC: IEEE Computer Society.

Farha, R., Kim, M., Leon-Garcia, A., & Won-Ki Hong, J. (2005). Towards an autonomic service architecture. In *5th IEEE International Workshop on IP Operations and Management* (pp. 58-67). Heidelberg, Germany: Springer.

Ferrari, L., Manzalini, A., Moiso, C., & Deussen, P. H. (2009). Highly distributed supervision for autonomic networks and services. In *5th Advanced International Conference on Telecommunications* (pp. 111-116). Washington, DC: IEEE Computer Society.

Friedman, R., Gavidia, D., Rodrigues, L., Viana, A. C., & Voulgaris, S. (2007). Gossiping on MANETs: The beauty and the beast. *SIGOPS Operative System Review, 41*(5), 67–74. doi:10.1145/1317379.1317390

George, J. P., Edmonds, B., & Glize, P. (2004). Making self-organizing adaptive multi-agent systems work. In Bergenti, F., Gleizes, M.-P., & Zambonelli, F. (Eds.), *Methodologies and software engineering for agent systems* (pp. 321–340). Heidelberg, Germany: Springer. doi:10.1007/1-4020-8058-1_20

Hardin, G. (1968). The tragedy of the commons. *Science Magazine, 162*, 1243–1248.

Hoile, C., Wang, F., Bonsma, E., & Marrow, P. (2002). Core specification and experiments in DIET: A decentralised ecosystem-inspired mobile agent system. In *1st International Conference on Autonomous Agents and Multi-Agent Systems* (pp. 623-630). New York, NY: ACM.

Jelasity, M., Montresor, A., & Babaoglu, O. (2005). Gossip-based aggregation in large dynamic networks. *ACM Transactions on Computer Systems, 23*(3), 219–252. doi:10.1145/1082469.1082470

Jennings, B., Van der Meer, S., Balasubramaniam, S., Botvich, D., Foghlu, M. O., Donnelly, W., & Strassner, J. (2007). Towards autonomic management of communications network. *IEEE Communications Magazine, 45*(10), 112–121. doi:10.1109/MCOM.2007.4342833

Kephart, J., & Chess, D. M. (2003). The vision of autonomic computing. *IEEE Computer, 36*(1), 41–50.

Kimbler, K., & Taylor, M. (2008). *SDP 2.0 – Service delivery platforms in the Web 2.0 era*. The Moriana Group. Retrieved April 27, 2010, from http://www.morianagroup.com

Klein, C., Schmid, R., Leuxner, C., Sitou, W., & Spanfelner, B. (2008). A survey of context adaptation in autonomic computing. In *4th International Conference on Autonomic and Autonomous Systems* (pp. 106-111). Washington, DC: IEEE Computer Society.

Koehler, J., Gantenbein, D., Giblin, C., & Hauser, R. (2003). *On autonomic computing architectures (Tec. Rep. RZ 3487 #99302)*. Zurich, Switzerland: IBM Zurich Research Laboratory, Computer Science.

Kowalczyk, W., & Vlassis, N. (2005). Newscast EM. *Advances in Neural Information Processing Systems, 17*, 713–720.

Li, J., Powley, W., Martin, P., Wilson, K., & Craddock, C. (2009). A sensor-based approach to symptom recognition for autonomic systems. In *5th International Conference on Autonomic and Autonomous Systems* (pp. 45-50). Washington, DC: IEEE Computer Society.

Liu, H. (2004). Component-based programming model for autonomic applications. In *1st International Conference on Autonomic Computing* (pp. 10-17). Washington, DC: IEEE Computer Society.

Manzalini, A., Deussen, P. H., Nechifor, S., Mamei, M., Minerva, R., & Moiso, C. (2010). Self-optimized cognitive network of networks. *The Computer Journal, 54*(2). doi:.doi:10.1093/comjnl/bxq032

Manzalini, A., Minerva, R., & Moiso, C. (2009). Exploiting P2P solutions in telecommunication service delivery platforms. In N. Antonopoulos, G. Exarchakos, M. Li, & A. Liotta (Eds.), *Handbook of research on P2P and Grid systems for service-oriented computing: Models, methodologies, and applications* (pp. 937-955). Hershey, PA: IGI Global.

Manzalini, A., & Zambonelli, F. (2006). Towards autonomic and situation-aware communication services: The CASCADAS vision. In *IEEE Workshop on Distributed Intelligent Systems: Collective Intelligence and its Applications* (pp. 383-388). Washington, DC: IEEE Computer Society.

Manzalini, A., Zambonelli, F., Baresi, L., & Di Ferdinando, A. (2009). The CASCADAS framework for autonomic communications. In Vasilakos, A., Parashar, M., Karnouskos, S., & Pedrycz, W. (Eds.), *Autonomic communication* (pp. 147–168). Heidelberg, Germany: Springer.

Parashar, M., & Hariri, S. (2005). Autonomic computing: An overview. In Banâtre, J.-P., Fradet, P., Giavitto, J.-L., & Michel, O. (Eds.), *Unconventional programming paradigms* (pp. 257–269). Heidelberg, Germany: Springer. doi:10.1007/11527800_20

Parashar, M., Liu, H., Li, Z., Matossian, V., Schmidt, C., Zhang, G., & Hariri, S. (2006). AutoMate: Enabling autonomic applications on the grid. *Cluster Computing, 9*(2), 161–174. doi:10.1007/s10586-006-7561-5

Poikselka, M., & Mayer, G. (2009). *The IMS: IP multimedia concepts and services*. London, UK: Wiley.

Saffre, F., Tateson, R., Halloy, J., Shackleton, M., & Deneubourg, J. L. (2008). Aggregation dynamics in overlay networks and their implications for self-organized distributed applications. *The Computer Journal, 52*(4), 397–412. doi:10.1093/comjnl/bxn017

Sun Microsystems. (2003). *Tuning garbage collection with the 5.0 Java Virtual machine documentation, Web resource*. Sun Developer Network. Retrieved April 27, 2010, from http://java.sun.com/docs/hotspot/gc5.0/gc_tuning_5.html

Valckenaers, P., Sauter, J., Sierra, C., & Rodriguez-Aguilar, J. A. (2007). Applications and environments for multi-agent systems. *Journal of Autonomous Agents and Multi-Agent Systems, 14*(1), 61–85. doi:10.1007/s10458-006-9002-5

Van der Meer, S., Davy, A., Davy, S., Carroll, R., Jennings, B., & Strassner, J. (2006). Autonomic networking: Prototype implementation of the policy continuum. In *1st International Conference on Broadband Convergence Networks* (pp. 163-172). Washington, DC: IEEE Computer Society.

White, S. R., Hanson, J. E., Whalley, I., Chess, D. M., & Kephart, J. O. (2004). An architectural approach to autonomic computing. In *1st International Conference on Autonomic Computing* (pp. 2-9). Washington, DC: IEEE Computer Society.

Xu, J., Zhao, M., Fortes, J., Carpenter, R., & Yousif, M. (2007). On the use of fuzzy modeling in virtualized data center management. In *4th International Conference on Autonomic Computing* (pp. 25). Washington, DC: IEEE Computer Society.

Zambonelli, F. (2006). Self-management and the many facets of nonself. *IEEE Intelligent Systems, 21*(2), 50–56.

Chapter 4
Swarm Intelligence in Autonomic Computing:
The Particle Swarm Optimization Case

Christos Anagnostopoulos
University of Athens, Greece

Stathes Hadjiefthymiades
University of Athens, Greece

ABSTRACT

Autonomic computing has become increasingly popular during recent years. Many mobile autonomic and context-aware applications exhibit self-organization in dynamic environments adopted from multi-agent, or swarm, research. The basic paradigm behind swarm systems is that tasks can be more efficiently dispatched through the use of multiple, simple autonomous agents instead of a single, sophisticated one. Such systems are much more adaptive, scalable, and robust than those based on a single, highly capable, agent. A swarm system can generally be defined as a decentralized group (swarm) of autonomous agents (particles) that are simple, with limited processing capabilities. Particles must cooperate intelligently to achieve common tasks.

INTRODUCTION

One of the scientific areas of autonomic computing is the investigation of mechanisms that exploit the collaborative behavior of the agents in order to deal with the information discovery. Specifically, in discovering contextual information an agent (e.g., mobile node) needs to explore, locate and track the source that generates the required contextual information – context (e.g., environmental parameters like temperature, humidity, situations like fire outbreak) for the executing context-aware, mobile application (e.g., the control of a group of robots). On the other hand, Swarm Intelligence (SI) (including Ant Colony Optimization, Particle Swarm Optimization, and Stochastic Diffusion

DOI: 10.4018/978-1-60960-845-3.ch004

Search) introduces a powerful new paradigm for building fully distributed systems in which overall system functionality is attained by the interaction of individual agents with each other and with their environment. Such agents coordinate using decentralized control and self-organization. Swarm systems are intrinsically highly parallel and exhibit high levels of robustness and reliability.

In this chapter, we discuss the application of Particle Swarm Intelligence in autonomic computing and networking. We map the basic concepts and definitions of particle swarm intelligence to autonomic computing and investigate the contextual information exploration (detection, discovery and exploitation) in autonomous dynamic environments. Specifically we focus on those scenarios where autonomous nodes with autonomic and context aware applications are autonomously adjusting their knowledge, policies and learning models in trying to (even physically) locate up-to-date contextual information, captured by other nodes. We also establish the concept of contextual information quality (an ageing framework deprecates contextual information thus leading to low quality) and how the nodes autonomously attempt to discover context in a collaborative manner. Nodes with low quality context cannot capture such information by themselves but are in need for "fresh" context in order to feed their application. In addition, we discuss the introduction of particle swarm optimization process in contextual information discovery and we report the performance of the reported algorithms in this area through simulations. Finally, we report a set of exercises for experimenting on the discussed algorithms focusing on better understanding of the swarm intelligence framework in autonomic computing.

Swarm Intelligence

Swarm Intelligence (SI) introduces a powerful new paradigm for building fully distributed systems in which overall system functionality is attained

by the interaction of individual agents with each other and with their environment. Such agents coordinate using decentralized control and self-organization. Swarm systems are intrinsically highly parallel and exhibit high levels of robustness and reliability:

- A SI-driven distributed system does not have hierarchical command and control structure and thus no-single failure point or vulnerability. Agents are often very simple and the overall swarm is intrinsically fault-tolerant since it consists of a number of identical units operating (sensing context) and cooperating (sharing context) in parallel. In contrast, a conventional complex distributed system requires considerable design effort to achieve fault tolerance.

- The key central concept in a swarm system is the simplicity of the agents -an agent can be a mobile phone carrying sensors. Simply increasing the number of agents assigned to a task (e.g., sensing context) does not necessarily improve the system's performance (i.e., efficiency and reliability). Agents collaborate by exchanging useful information in order to obtain the required context.

- In a totally distributed environment agents collaborate for discovering context with certain validity (e.g., related to time and/ or space constraints). Context periodically turns obsolete and has to be regularly determined and discovered. Moreover, the resources of simple agents are limited in terms of

  A. **Memory:** agents remember the history of their operation up to a certain extent,

  B. **Sensing Capabilities:** for agents moving around, the sensing radius can be small enough relatively to the coverage area once possible neighboring agents can provide analogous local information, and

C. **Communication Resources:** communication among agents is intended solely to convey information on the swarm.

The above-mentioned points lead us to examine the adoption of the SI paradigm in context discovery.

INTRODUCTION TO THE PARTICLE SWARM OPTIMIZATION

The Particle Swarm Optimization (PSO) is based on the swarm's intelligent behavior observed in flocks of birds, swarms of bees, or human social behavior, from which the idea is taken (Kennedy & Eberhart, 2001). The main strength of PSO is its fast convergence to optimal solutions, which compares favorably with many global optimization algorithms (e.g., Genetic Algorithms and Simulated Annealing). The PSO model consists of a swarm of N particles, which are initialized with a population of random candidate solutions (particles). They move iteratively through a d-dimension problem space R^d to search new optima. Let f: $R^d{\rightarrow}R$ be a *fitness* function that takes a particle's solution in R^d and maps it to a single decision metric. Each particle indexed by i has a position represented by a vector $\mathbf{x}_i \in R^d$ and a velocity represented by a vector $\mathbf{v}_i \in R^d$, $i=1, \ldots,$ N. Each particle "remembers" its own *best* position so far in vector $\mathbf{x}_i^{\#} = [x_{ij}^{\#}]$. The best position vector among the swarm so far is then stored in a vector $\mathbf{x}^* = [x_j^*]$. During the iteration (time) t, the velocity update is performed as in Equation (1). The new position is then determined by the sum of the previous position and the new velocity in Equation (2).

$$u_{ij}(t + 1) = wu_{ij}(t) + c_1r_1(x_{ij}^{\#}(t) - x_{ij}(t)) +$$
$$c_2r_2(x_j^*(t) - x_{ij}(t)) \qquad (1)$$

$$x_{ij}(t + 1) = x_{ij}(t) + u_{ij}(t + 1) \qquad (2)$$

w is an *inertia* factor. The r_1, r_2 random numbers are used to maintain the diversity of the population and are uniformly distributed in the interval $[0, 1]$ for the jth dimension of the ith particle. c_1 and c_2 are positive constants called *self-recognition* and *social* component, respectively. They interpret how much the particle is directed towards good positions. That is, c_1 and c_2 indicate how much the particle's private knowledge and swarm's knowledge on the best solution is affected, respectively.

The time interval between velocity updates is often taken to be unit, thus, omitted (the Equation (2) is dimensionality inconsistent). From Equation (1), a particle decides where to move at the next time considering its own experience, which is the memory of its best past position and the experience of the most successful particle in the swarm (or in a neighboring part of swarm). The inertia w regulates the trade-off between the *global* (wide-ranging) and *local* (nearby) exploration abilities of the swarm. A large inertia weight facilitates global exploration, i.e., searching new areas, while a small value facilitates local exploration, i.e., fine-tuning the current search area –exploitation (Engelbrecht, 2007).

The Particle Swarm Optimization Algorithm

The PSO algorithm is presented in Algorithm 1. The end criterion (line 2) may be the maximum number of iterations, the number of iterations without improvement, or the minimum objective function error between the obtained objective function and the best fitness value w.r.t. a pre-fixed anticipated threshold. Particles are started at random positions with zero initial velocities and search in parallel. What is needed is some attraction, if not to the absolutely best position known, at least towards a position close to the particle where the fitness is better than the fitness a particle has currently determined. All particles exploit at least one good position already found by some particle(s) in the swarm (line 7). Hence, particles adjust their own position and velocity based on this good position (line 9). Often, the position that is exploited is the best position yet found by any particle (line 5). In this case, all particles know the currently best position found and are attracted to this position. This, obviously, requires communication between particles and some sort of collective memory to the current global best (gbest). The $\mathbf{x}^*$ vector in Equation (1) represents the gbest position of the swarm (line 5).

Alternatively, a particle i can experience an attraction back to the best place yet found by it. The *personal best* (*pbest*) position for particle i results in its independent exploration without any input of the other particles. The *pbest* position for the ith particle is $\mathbf{x}_i^{\#}$ (line 7).

Balancing Between Global and Local Best Solutions

An idea for triggering a particle to direct to an attracted area is to balance the movement between the *gbest* and *pbest* positions by defining a *local* neighborhood around it. All N_i particles within an actual physical distance form the *neighborhood* of the ith particle. Each particle in N_i shares its fitness value with all other particles in that neighborhood. Hence, neighboring particles experience

Algorithm 1. The PSO algorithm

1	**Initialize** randomly the positions and zero velocities.
2	**While** (the *end criterion* is not met) **Do**
3	$t \leftarrow t + 1$;
4	**Calculate** the fitness value f of each particle;
5	$\mathbf{x}^* = \arg min^N_{i=1} \{f(\mathbf{x}^*(t-1)), f(\mathbf{x}_1(t)), \ldots, f(\mathbf{x}_i(t)), \ldots, f(\mathbf{x}_N(t))\}$;
6	**For** $i = 1$: N
7	$\mathbf{x}_i^{\#}(t) = \arg min^N_{i=1} \{f(\mathbf{x}_i^{\#}(t-1)), f(\mathbf{x}_i(t))\}$;
8	**For** $j = 1$:d
9	**Update** the jth dimension of $\mathbf{v}_i$ and $\mathbf{x}_i$ w.r.t. (1), (2); **Next**j
10 11	**Next**i **End While**

an attraction to the *local best* (*lbest*). The problem with *lbest* (not so critical as in *gbest*) is that, neighborhoods need to be calculated frequently and, thus, the computational cost for this operation has to be considered. The particles adjust their current velocity based on current *pbest* and prior knowledge derived from *gbest* and *lbest*. Based on *gbest*, particles have to communicate with the whole swarm for locating and maintaining information on the global best solution. In this case the best particle acts as an attractor pulling all the particles towards it. Eventually, all particles will converge to this position. Based on *lbest*, particles are required to check for any better solution appeared in adjacent particles.

In order to avoid the inherent communication cost in context discovery due to the information exchange among particles for estimating *gbest* and the premature convergence obtained from *gbest*, we relate the social component c_2 in (Deneubourg et al., 1990) to the *lbest* approach, i.e., the $\mathbf{x}^*$ vector in (Deneubourg et al., 1990) represents the *lbest* position of a given particle. c_2 indicates the willingness of a particle to be attracted by any probable neighbor. We also adopt random relative weights for combining *lbest* and *pbest*. The continuous movement toward a position of better fitness (w.r.t. *pbest*) biases the selection of particles with even better fitness than the existing one. The discovery process, which is based on *pbest*, dramatically improves the average fitness of the positions explored. Evidently, this may result in exploration stopping at a local optimum. But, with a number of different local neighborhoods in use, there is a very good probability that the whole swarm will not get so trapped, and that any trapped particle will escape, especially if the *lbest* approach is also simultaneously in use. We adopt both approaches together with r_1, r_2 factors to set the relative influences of each.

MAPPING AUTONOMIC CONTEXT DISCOVERY TO PARTICLE SWARM INTELLIGENCE

We firstly define the notions of *context* and *quality of context* and then map the parameters of context discovery into PSO.

Contextual Information Representation and Quality

Context refers to the current values of specific parameters that represent the activity / situation of an entity and environmental state (Agnosto-poulos et al., 2007). Let $\mathbf{Y} = [Y_1, ..., Y_m]$ be a *m*-dimensional vector of parameters, which assumes values y_l in the domain $\text{Dom}(Y_l)$, $l = 1, ..., m$. A parameter Y_l is considered instantiated if at time t some y_l value is assigned to Y_l. Hence, *context* **y** is the instantiated **Y**, i.e., $\mathbf{y} = [y_1, ..., y_m]$. For each instantiated Y_l, a function

$$v: Y_l \times T \to [0, a), a > 0,$$

is defined denoting whether the value y_l is valid at time t after the Y_l instantiation; T is the time index and a is a real positive number. The value y_l is valid at time t for a context-aware application that is executed on node i if $v(y_l, t) < \theta_{il}$ for a given threshold $\theta_{il} \in (0, a)$, which is application specific. A value of θ_{il} close to a means that y_l is not valid for the *i*th node. v can be any increasing function F with time t, i.e., $v = F(t)$. For simplicity reasons we can assume that F is the identity function (i.e., $v = t$). The value a is set w.r.t. application specification. For instance, in the case of context discovery, a is the maximum time from the sensing time of Y_l in which its value is not deprecated. A value of θ_{il} close to 0 means that y_l is of high importance. The indicator v increases over time from the sensing time of y_l. Hence, a value of v denotes the freshness of y_l, i.e., y_l refers to either an up-to-date (fresh) or obsolete measure. It should be noted that, v refers only to

the temporal validity of a value. Evidently, other validity functions can be defined referring to quality indicators like spatial scope (value is usable within certain geographical boundaries), the source credibility, the reliability of the measurement, and other objective or subjective indicators (Agnostopoulos et al, 2007b).

We introduce the quality of context indicator

$$g: \mathbf{Y} \times T \to [0, a)$$

for context **y** at time t denoting whether the values of the parameters of **y** are valid or not with respect to a certain threshold. The value of g is the minimum indicator of the values, that is

$$g(\mathbf{y}, t) = \min_{l=1}^{m}\{v(y_l, t)\} \text{ with threshold } \theta_{iy} = \min_{l=1}^{m}\{\theta_{il}\}.$$

A value of θ_{iy} close to a denotes invalid context, i.e., obsolete context, while a value of θ_{iy} close to 0 denotes fresh context. Context **y** turns obsolete once some parameter turns also obsolete.

Each node i attempts to maximize the time period Δt in which $g(\mathbf{y}, t + \Delta t) < \theta_{iy}$ for some t. That is, each node attempts to maintain fresh context as much time as possible. It is worth noting that a node i evaluates the quality of **y** differently from a node j, i.e., $g_i(\mathbf{y}, t) \neq g_j(\mathbf{y}, t)$. This means that, **y** may be of value for node i but not for node j at the same time. Without loss of generality we assume that all nodes evaluate the quality of context with the same θ_{iy}. That is, all nodes assess context with the same criteria / quality indicators. This does not imply that all nodes obtain context of the same quality. Instead, all nodes are interested in the same quality of context. This does not undermine the generality of the problem. In fact, if there are groups of nodes that assess context differently then groups of nodes will be formed and, consequently, each group will assess context with the same θ_{iy}.

Mapping Autonomic Context Discovery to Particle Swarm Optimization

The problem: Let us assume discrete time and consider a square terrain of dimension L. Consider a group of N mobile nodes that maps to a swarm of particles and a set of M mobile sources (i.e., sensors that sense context) that correspond to the possible solutions in PSO. Each source regularly generates fresh context meaning that each source measures context with a given frequency-sensing rate q. Each sensed value is time stamped at the source. Every node needs to move to an area with at least a source that carries fresh context. Alternatively, a node attempts to locate areas where other nodes carry fresh context or context of better quality than the context currently available in them. In addition, a node does not know the existence of a source in a certain area and the swarm does not even know the number of sources. This evidently denotes that the nodes continue searching until all sources are located or all nodes carries fresh context. However, the nodes have to adopt a mechanism in order to maintain context as fresh as possible as long as the validity fades over time.

The context discovery is considered as a 2-dimensional problem space in PSO ($d = 2$). It refers to the 2D location information (longitude and latitude) of the sources / nodes that carry fresh context. We assume that all nodes are capable of detecting any neighboring node in a region with given transmission range equal to R. The physical presence of a node in a neighborhood can be detected thus such node is assumed to be located in the corresponding neighborhood. Moreover, a node i moves towards to a neighboring node j, which carries fresher context than node i.

The target: The value of $g_i(\mathbf{y}, t)$ denotes the willingness of node i to seek for fresh, or at least of better quality (more up-to-date) context than the existing context. The quality of context indicator $g_i(\mathbf{y}, t)$ resembles the fitness function f in PSO. A node i attempts to:

- Minimize the value of $g_i(\mathbf{y}, t)$ at time t, and,
- Maximize the duration in which it maintains fresh context, i.e., $g_i(\mathbf{y}, t) < \theta_y$.

It should be noted that $g_i(\mathbf{y}, t)$ depends on time once the indicators for each parameter increase over time (w.r.t. sensing time). This means that a node i has to regularly update its fitness by dynamically adjusting its decision regarding the next movement w.r.t. *pbest* and *lbest*.

Let us calculate the *pbest* and *lbest* so that node i decides in which direction to move. Let N_i be the indices of the neighboring nodes of node i at time t. The $\mathbf{x}_i^{\#}$ vector at time t is the position $\mathbf{x}_j$ of the neighbor j, which carries fresher context $\mathbf{y}$ than that of node i and the freshest context among all neighbors of node i, i.e.,

$$\mathbf{x}_i^{\#} = \mathbf{x}_j : j = \mathrm{arg}min_{l \in \{Ni\}} \{g_l(\mathbf{y}, t) \text{ and } (g_i(\mathbf{y}, t) > g_l(\mathbf{y}, t))\}.$$

$\mathbf{x}_i^{\#}$ is currently the best position found at time t to which the node i adjust its next movement at time $t + 1$ assuming the *pbest* fitness value $g_i^{\#}(\mathbf{y}) = g_j(\mathbf{y}, t)$. The vector $(\mathbf{x}_i^{\#} - \mathbf{x}_i)$ refers to the self-recognition vector for node i that is attracted by the node j.

Furthermore, the node i can exploit its past knowledge. Based on *pbest* the node i locates the current best node j and moves towards it with a factor $r_1 c_1$. In addition, node i exploits the *average fitness* of all neighbors at time t that is

$$g_{N_i}(\mathbf{y}, t) = \frac{1}{|N_i|} \sum_{i=1..k} g_i(\mathbf{y}, t), k \in N_i - \{i\}$$

The average fitness $g_{Ni}(\mathbf{y}, t)$ refers to a *local fitness of the neighborhood* of node i. Node i can obtain a clear view of its neighborhood meaning that: if $g_{Ni}(\mathbf{y}, t) < \theta_{iy}$ (i.e., fresh context) then the node i might not decide to move far away from this neighborhood hoping that it will probably be within an area where nodes carry fresh context.

Similarly to $g_i^\#(\mathbf{y})$, we define the *lbest* $g_i^*(\mathbf{y})$ indicator that is an estimate for the freshness of $\mathbf{y}$ at time t obtained by the neighborhood of node i. If it holds true that $g_{Ni}(\mathbf{y}, t) < g_i^*(\mathbf{y})$ then the *lbest*$\mathbf{x}_i^*$ is the current $\mathbf{x}_i$ of node i at time t and the *lbest* fitness value $g_i^*(\mathbf{y})$ equals to $g_{Ni}(\mathbf{y}, t)$. However, it may hold true that $g_{Ni}(\mathbf{y}, t) > g_i(\mathbf{y}, t)$ but this does not imply that there might not be a neighboring node j that carries more fresh context than node i. In this case, the *lbest* position is not updated contrary to the *pbest* position. Instead, the node i adjusts its next movement by combining a movement towards the current *pbest*$\mathbf{x}_i^\#$ and previous *lbest*$\mathbf{x}_i^*$.

Based on the $g_i^*(\mathbf{y})$ and $g_i^\#(\mathbf{y})$ indicators, the node i self-controls its decision on the next movement at time $t + 1$. The vector $(\mathbf{x}_i^* - \mathbf{x}_i)$ refers to the social vector component for node i denoting the attraction of node i to its neighborhood. Moreover, $g_i^*(\mathbf{y})$ increases over time thus node i has to regularly update and check *lbest*. That is because as long as a previous neighborhood has maintained fresh context as a whole, at the next time the *lbest* position may not refer to the same neighborhood even with the same value of $g_{Ni}(\mathbf{y}, t)$. The node i simply stores the previously visited *lbest* position assigned to $g_i^*(\mathbf{y})$. Hence, the node i has the option to move towards to a previous visited position as a last resort.

Table 1 depicts the mapping between context discovery and PSO. It should be noted that the fitness function f in PSO depends only on the solution vector $\mathbf{x}_i$ and is not time dependent. The same holds true for the *pbest* and *lbest* positions in PSO. In context discovery the corresponding fitness $g_i(\mathbf{y}, t)$ depends on time t as long as the invalidity of $\mathbf{y}$ increases over time. Furthermore, the $g_i^\#(\mathbf{y})$ and $g_i^*(\mathbf{y})$ indicators increase over time as well.

PSO-BASED AUTONOMIC CONTEXT DISCOVERY

We refer a PSO-based context discovery algorithm in which nodes dynamically search for areas where better quality of context is obtained. In other words nodes attempt to find, locate and / or follow neighboring nodes (targets) that carry context of high value. The dynamic behavior of a mobile system means that the system changes state in a repeated manner. In our case the changes occur frequently, that is, both the location of a leader and the value of the optimum (context validity) vary[1] (Hu & Eberhart, 2001).

We also report several strategies for in order to:

- experiment with the required time for finding and maintaining high quality context,
- reduce the inherent network load that is used to automatically detecting and tracking various changes of the context validity and
- effectively respond to a wide variety of changes in context validity.

Table 1. Mapping between context discovery & PSO

Particle swarm intelligence concepts	Autonomic computing concepts
swarm of N particles	group of N mobile nodes
particle i	node i
problem space	context $\mathbf{y}$
global optimum solution $\mathbf{x}_i$	source positioned at $\mathbf{x}_i$
local optimum solution $\mathbf{x}_i$	node with fresh context positioned at $\mathbf{x}_i$
number of optima	number of sources M
fitness f	quality of context $g_i(\mathbf{y}, t)$
pbest$\mathbf{x}_i^\#$	position of neighboring node j that maximizes $g_j(\mathbf{y}, t)$
lbest$\mathbf{x}_i^*$	position of node i whose neighborhood maximizes $g_{Ni}(\mathbf{y}, t)$

The network load derives from the inter-communication among nodes. In addition, several constraints that refer to the temporal validity of context are taken into account. Therefore, the best solution for context discovery is time dependent (context turns obsolete over time).

The discussed behaviors of a node indicate the intention of a node in discovering and maintaining fresh context based on its mobility and other characteristics explained below. Specifically, a node transits between three states in order to discover context. In each state, the node decides on certain actions. A state k_i of node i can be *Obsolete* (O), *Partially satisfied* (P), or *Satisfied* (S) as depicted in Figure 1. Specifically,

- In state O, a node either carries obsolete context or is in need of context, i.e., $g_i(\mathbf{y}, t) > \theta_y$.
- In the S state, a node carries fresh context i.e., $g_i(\mathbf{y}, t) < \theta_y$. If context $\mathbf{y}$ turns obsolete then node i transits into O.
- In the P state, a node chooses to carry less obsolete context than the existing context as long as this is the current best solution it achieves (local optimum). This means

that the node i has found a neighbor j with fresher context i.e., $g_i(\mathbf{y}, t) > g_j(\mathbf{y}, t) > \theta_y$. The node i escapes from the P state once another node k, which carries more fresh context, is located i.e., $g_i(\mathbf{y}, t) > \theta_y > g_k(\mathbf{y}, t)$. We assume that all nodes adopt the same threshold for assessing the quality of context ($\theta_{iy} = \theta_y = \theta$, $i = 1, ..., N$).

Autonomic Context Exploration

A node i in state O initiates a foraging process for context acting as follows: The node i moves randomly ($\mathbf{v}_i \sim U(\mathbf{v}_{min}, \mathbf{v}_{max})$) in the swarm and intercommunicates with neighbors till to be attracted by a neighbor j. The node j is then called *leader*. The leader j either carries objectively fresh context i.e., $g_j(\mathbf{y}, t) < \theta_y$ or carries context that is more fresh than the context carried by node i i.e., $g_i(\mathbf{y}, t) > g_j(\mathbf{y}, t) > \theta_y$ (see obsolete state in Figure 1). In the former case, the node i transits directly to state S. In the latter case, the node j does not carry context of the exact quality that node i expects but such context is preferable than that of node i. Hence, node i can either follow node j hoping that it approaches areas (neighborhoods) with more fresh

Figure 1. States of a node in context discovery

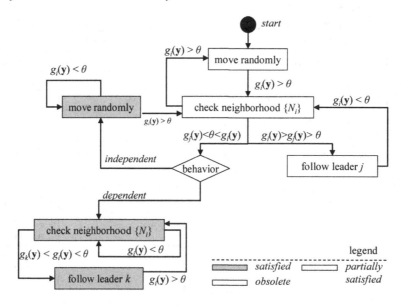

context -thus transiting to P state- or, alternatively, ignores such opportunity and continues moving at random -thus remaining at state O. In state P, node i settles with lower quality of context. This does not imply that node i stops communicating with other neighbors while moving. Instead, it continues exchanging information related to context quality with the purpose of locating another leader with more fresh context. The P state is an intermediary state between the O and S states (see partially satisfied state in Figure 1). The node is moving among neighborhoods carrying context of better quality and continues exploring areas. This policy reflects the idea of exploring the solution space even if a solution has already been reached (possibly a local optimum).

Node i attempts to retain fresh context for as long as possible. However, the $v(y_l, t)$ indicator for a sensed parameter Y_l increases over time t until that value turns obsolete after some Δt, i.e., $v(y_l, t + \Delta t) > \theta_l$. Hence, Y_l has to be regularly determined / sensed, with frequency at least $1/\Delta t$. In order for the node i to obtain up-to-date context $\mathbf{y}$, it follows leaders or sources that regularly generate objectively fresh context.

It should be noted that a localization system is needed in order to determine the solutions $\mathbf{x}_i^{\#}$ and $\mathbf{x}_i^*$, and the way node i is directed to its leader. Specifically, a node i carried by an agent (possibly a human) is directed to its leader once a GIS application displays directional information of the leader obtained, for instance, by a compass-based mechanism (Anjum & Mouchtaris, 2007) (or other techniques, e.g., the time-of-flight technique that adopts radio frequency and ultrasound signal to determine the distance between nodes [Savvides et al., 2001]). Moreover, a non-human node i (e.g., a robot) can "blindly" follow its leader by adjusting its direction / velocity through small improvement steps w.r.t. the signal quality (Matthias & Hanspeter, 2000). Imagine for example a WLAN user trying to determine the best signal quality in a certain room by stepping around

without knowing the exact location of the access point. This local-searching blind technique is not as efficient as the previously discussed method (Zhao & Guibas, 2004).

Autonomic Context Maintenance

A node i, in S state, acts as follows (see the satisfied state in Figure 1): it either continues communicating with leaders (*dependent* behavior) or re-starts moving at random (*independent* behavior) with $\mathbf{v}_i \sim U(\mathbf{v}_{min}, \mathbf{v}_{max})$. In the former behavior, it is likely that node i constantly follows leaders, also known as tracking optima policy (Eberhart & Shi, 2001). The advantage of such behavior is that: in case node i's context turns obsolete, node i will easier find some leader provided that the latter might be yet reachable (or not far away). By adopting the independent behavior node i has no information in which direction to move towards once context turns obsolete.

Once a neighbor node k, of a node i, in S state obtains better context $\mathbf{y}$ (i.e., $\theta_y > g_j(\mathbf{y}, t) > g_k(\mathbf{y}, t)$) then node i may choose to abandon the existing leader and follow the new leader node k. Specifically, by adopting the dependent behavior, the node i communicates with neighbors with the intention of finding a node k that carries more fresh context than the objectively fresh obtained context. Hence, the node i switches constantly between among leaders. In addition, the node i never transits to state O since its leader is a source (global optimum). However, the main objective in context discovery is to enable nodes to minimize the communication load and explore for as many sources and leaders as possible escaping from local optima. If all nodes adopted the dependent behavior then they would attach to sources resulting in large communication effort for the sources (sources would have to communicate with a large number of nodes) but carrying objectively fresh context. It is of high importance to take into account the inherent efficiency for both behaviors.

The Autonomic Algorithm

The context discovery algorithm implements the idea around the state-based policies for nodes in exploring context. A node i in state O either transits only to state S once a leader with objectively fresh context is found or transits to the immediate state P once a leader with better context is found. As long as a leader carries objectively fresh context then node i transits from state P to S. In state S node i adopts either the independent or the dependent behavior.

The context discovery autonomic algorithm is presented in Algorithm 2, in which node i, in state O, transits to states P and/or S, and, in state S, it adopts the dependent behavior. Initially, all N nodes in the swarm are in state O and are randomly distributed in a given terrain with random velocities in $[\mathbf{v}_{min}, \mathbf{v}_{max}]$. The inertia w is used to controlling the exploration and exploitation abilities of the swarm and eliminating the need for velocity clamping (i.e., if $|\mathbf{v}_i| > |\mathbf{v}_{max}|$ then $|\mathbf{v}_i| = |\mathbf{v}_{max}|$). The inertia is very important to ensure convergent behavior; large values for w facilitate exploration with increased diversity while small values promote local exploitation.

One can adopt a dynamically changing inertia values, i.e., an initially value decreases nonlinearly to a small value allowing for a shorter exploration time (due to context validity rate) with more time spent on refining optima (Peram et al., 2003). That is,

$$w(t+1) = \frac{(w(t) - 0.4)(t_0 - t)}{t_0 + 0.4}$$

$w(0) = 0.9$, t_0 is the maximum number of iterations. In case a node transits to state O then it re-sets w to its initial value. The randomly moving M sources generate context with sensing rate q (in samples/second, Hz) and the thresholds $\theta_l = a$ for the properties Y_l are set. The c_1 and c_2 constants denote how much the *lbest* and *pbest* solutions

influence the movement of the node; usually $c_1 = c_2 = 2$ (Engelbrecht, 2007). The $\mathbf{r}_1$, $\mathbf{r}_2$ are two random vectors with each component be a uniform random number in [0, 1]. In each iteration, a node i in O, or P, adjusts its movement (lines 18, 19) w.r.t. *pbest* and *lbest* (lines 20-28) once interactive communication takes place. If the node i in S adopts:

- Dependent behavior then it adjusts its movement w.r.t lines 21-28,
- Independent behavior then it randomly moves with v_i in $[v_{min}, v_{max}]$ (omit lines 17-28).

The end-criterion of the algorithm can be the number of iterations, the time needed to find fresh context a given portion of nodes, or energy consumption constraints. In our case the end-criterion is time dependent since the validity of context depends on the sensing rate q. Nodes adopting the independent behavior stop searching as long as they obtain fresh context and re-start foraging once context turns obsolete. The end-criterion for the dependent behavior is the minimum mean value $g_+(t)$ for the fitness function g. We require that $g_+(t)$ be as low as possible w.r.t. the a threshold that is,

maximize $\{d(t) = (g_+(t) - a)^2\}$

The $d(t)$ value denotes how much fresh is context. In other words, it reflects the portion of time needed for context to turn obsolete as long as $g_+(t)$ is greater than a. For instance, let two nodes, i and j, carry context $\mathbf{y}$ with $g_i(\mathbf{y}) = a/2$ and $g_j(\mathbf{y}) = a/4$. Objectively, both nodes carry fresh context w.r.t. a. Therefore, node j carries fresher context than node i since node j will carry fresh context for longer time than node i. The convergence $g_+(t_0)$ value denotes a state in which some nodes obtain fresh context for $t \geq t_0$ and depends highly on a: a high value of a denotes a little time for context to turn obsolete. In that case, the nodes may stay for a long in S state. On the contrary, a low value of a (i.e., nodes are interested only for up-to-date context) results in values of $g_+(t)$ close to a; context turns obsolete with a high rate. It is of high interest to examine the efficiency of each behavior.

SIMULATION OF THE PSO-BASED AUTONOMIC CONTEXT DISCOVERY

In this section we assess the behavior for context discovery. The objective in autonomous context discovery is to enable nodes to discover and maintain fresh context. However, the fact of locating sources and leaders in an attempt to carry fresh context is at the expense of the inherent network load due to communication of nodes.

We define as efficiency in discovering context $e(t)$ of a certain behavior the portion of nodes $n(t)$ being in state S out of the communication load $l(t)$ among neighboring nodes exchanging information about context quality, i.e.,

$$e(t) = n(t) / l(t).$$

We require that $e(t)$ assumes high values minimizing the load $l(t)$ and maximizing $n(t)$ w.r.t. the adopted behavior.

The parameters of the reported simulations are:

- A swarm of $N = 100$ nodes,
- $M = 2$ sources,
- $a = 100$ time units,
- A terrain of $L = 100$ spatial units,
- Transmission range $R = 0.01L$,
- The *random waypoint* model for mobility behavior in $[\mathbf{v}_{min}, \mathbf{v}_{max}] = [0.1, 2]$ (Bettstetter et al., 2004), and 1000 runs of the algorithm.

Context turns obsolete every a time units and is sensed by the sources with q ranging from $(2/a)$

Algorithm 2. The context discovery algorithm

```
1.  Set c_1, c_2, N, M, q
2.  Set random x_i(t), threshold θy = θy, t ← 0
3.  For i = 1: N
4.  v_i(t) ~ U(v_min, v_max), k_i ← O
5.  g_i*(y) ← (g_1(y, t) + ··· + g_|Ni|(y, t)) / |N_i|
6.  x_i* ← x_i(t)
7.  g_i#(y) ← max_i{g_l(y, t)}), l ∈ {N_i} ∪ {i}
8.  x_i# ← x_e: e = argmax_i{g_l(y, t)}), l∈{N_i}∪{i}, leader_i←e
9.  Next i
10. While (the end criterion is not met) Do
11. t ← t + 1;
12. For i = 1: N
13. Calculate g_i(y, t)
14. Validate g_i*(y), g_i#(y) //increase validity indicators
15. Next i
16. For i = 1: N
17. Set random unary vectors r_1, r_2
18. x_i(t) ← x_i(t − 1) + v_i(t)
19. v_i(t) ← v_i(t − 1) + c_1 r_1 (x_i* - x_i(t-1)) + c_2 r_2 (x_i# - x_i(t-1))
20. g_Ni(y, t) ← (g_1(y, t) + ··· + g_|Ni|(y, t)) / |N_i|
21. If g_i*(y) < g_Ni(y, t) Then
22. x_i* ← x_i(t)
23. g_i*(y) ← g_Ni(y, t)
24. End
25. If g_i#(y) < max_i{g_l(y, t)}), l ∈ {N_i} Then
26. x_i# ← x_e: e = argmax_i{g_l(y, t)}), l ∈ {N_i}, leader_i←e
27. g_i#(y) ← max_i{g_l(y, t)}), l ∈ {N_i}
28. End
29. If g_i#(y) < g_i(y) < θyThen k_i ← O
30. If g_i(y) < g_i#(y) < θyThen k_i ← P
31. If θy < g_i#(y) Then k_i ← S
32. Next i
33. End While
```

Hz to 1Hz. We require that $g_+(t)$ be lower than a as time passes or, at least, lower than a between consequent intervals of a time units.

Experimenting with Quality of Context for Dependent and Independent Behavior

Figure 2 depicts the $g_+(t)$ value (in time units –t.u.) when all nodes in the swarm adopt the dependent behavior for different values of q. It is observed that all nodes rapidly locate leaders and then carry fresh context denoting the algorithm convergence. The $g_+(t)$ value converges to $g_+(t_0)$ ranging from 14.633t.u. to 40.882t.u. for q ranging from 1Hz to 0.02Hz, respectively. It is worth noting that, for q

Figure 2. The g$_+$(t) value of the dependent behavior for sensing rate q = 0.02Hz, q = 0.05Hz and q = 1Hz

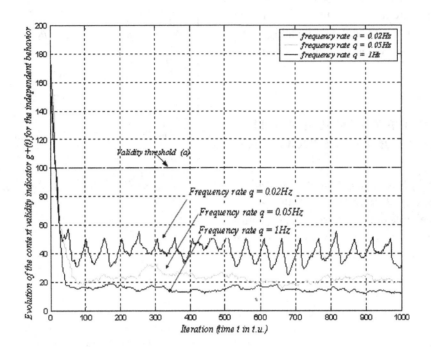

= 1Hz, the $g_+(t_o)$ is 14.633t.u. i.e., 14.633% of the validity threshold a indicating that most nodes can process context for 85.367% of the sensing time before it turns obsolete. Moreover, as q assumes low values (e.g., 0.02Hz), which means that the sources sense context every 50t.u., the value of $g_+(t)$ swings around the 40.882t.u. This indicates that, nodes locate sources whose context turns obsolete after 50t.u. For that reason, the $g_+(t)$ value for such nodes exhibits that behavior. On the other hand, once q assumes high values (e.g., 1Hz), the sources constantly carry up-to-date context. Consequently, nodes that locate sources carry fresh context ($g_+(t)$ converges). The achieved maximum value for $d(t_o)$ is $0.6952.10^4$ for $q=1$Hz, as depicted in Figure 3, compared to $0.3854.10^4$ w.r.t. independent behavior, as discussed later. Evidently, by adopting the dependent behavior, a large portion of the swarm follows leaders and/ or sources carrying objectively fresh context. However, such behavior requires that nodes communicate continuously in order to locate sources

and leaders with more fresh context even if nodes are in state S for maximizing $d(t)$. That leads to additional communication load thus keeping the efficiency to 50% as depicted in Figure 4. Specifically, Figure 4 depicts the value of $e_d(t)$ for the dependent behavior for $q = 1$Hz. Obviously, the inherent communication load of such behavior is high since a large portion of nodes attempts to carry fresh context.

Figure 5 depicts the $g_+(t)$ value of nodes adopting the independent behavior. We illustrate $g_+(t)$ for sensing rates $q = 1$Hz, $q = 0.05$Hz and $q = 0.02$Hz. Evidently, nodes seek for fresh context only when the existing context turns obsolete. This is indicated by the sharp bend of $g_+(t)$ between intervals of a time units for $q = 1$Hz. The periodic behavior of $g_+(t)$ reflects the idea of the independent behavior denoting that a node is about to seek for context only when needed. Hence, between intervals of a time units nodes that are in S state save energy as long as they do not exchange information with others. When context

Figure 3. The d(t) value of the dependent and independent behavior with sensing rate q = 1Hz

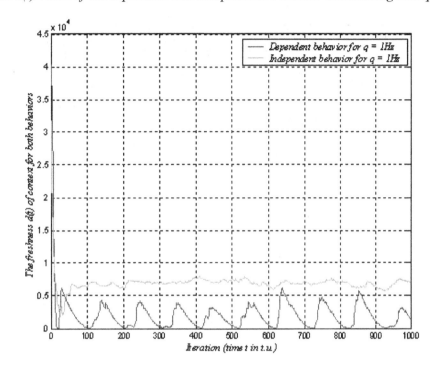

turns obsolete, nodes re-start foraging but having the *pbest* solution as a candidate starting point. This means that, each time context turns obsolete nodes adjust its movement based on the last known *pbest* solution. Hence, they start moving "blindly" as long as their first direction might be the *pbest* position indicating "prolific" neighborhood. For that reason, the maximum value of $g_+(t)$ is close to a in each "period" as depicted in Figure 5. Moreover, the $g_+(t)$ value ranges from 40 t.u. to 100 t.u. compared to the convergence value of $g_+(t_o) = 14.633$t.u. in case of the dependent behavior for $q = 1$Hz. It is worth noting that the value of $g_i^*(y)$ for *pbest* must denote valid context, otherwise node i has to move entirely at random. Moreover, consider the $g_+(t)$ value having $q = 2/a = 0.02$Hz. Specifically, $g_+(t)$ assumes the minimum value every $(a/2) = 50$ t.u., which is greater than the minimum value of $g_+(t)$ achieved for $q = 1$Hz every at.u. In the former case nodes re-start foraging sooner than in the latter case (practically two

times more), thus, the adoption of the *pbest* solution seems more prolific. For that reason, $g_+(t)$ assumes higher minimum values in the former case even though the sensing rate is lower. In such cases, the adoption of the *pbest* solution is of high importance.

Figure 3 depicts also the $d(t)$ value for the independent behavior. The $d(t)$ assumes the maximum value (therefore lower than in the case of the dependent behavior) only when a large portion of nodes carry fresh context. In addition, $d(t)$ assumes zero value regularly every a time units denoting the time that all nodes carry obsolete context. The mean value of $d(t)$ is $0.3854.10^4$, that is 44.56% lower than the convergence value of $d(t_o)$ in the case of the dependent behavior (for the same sensing rate $q = 1$Hz). Hence, the adoption of the independent behavior for context discovery results in 44.56% lower quality of context than that achieved by dependent behavior.

Figure 4. The values of $e_d(t)$ and $e_i(t)$ efficiency in logarithmic scale for q = 1Hz

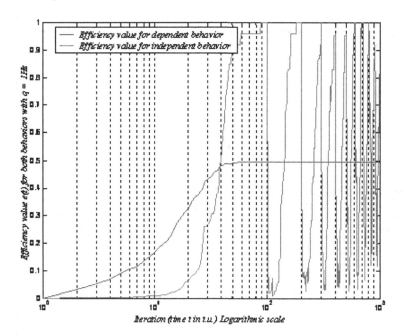

Figure 5. The $g_+(t)$ value of the independent behavior for sensing rates q = 1Hz, q = 0.05Hz and q = 0.02Hz

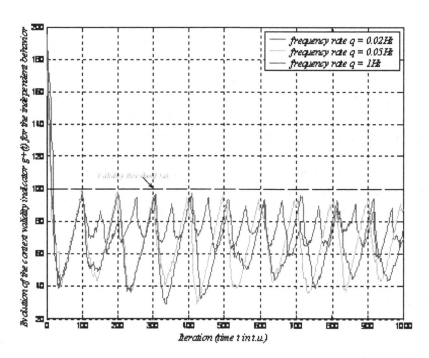

Experimenting with the Efficiency of Context Discovery

By adopting the independent behavior we can achieve high values of efficiency $e_i(t)$ during intervals in which nodes carry fresh context. This is due to the fact that in such intervals nodes stop communicating with each other thus reducing the load $l(t)$. However, when context turns obsolete then $e_i(t)$ assumes a very low value (mean value lower than 0.1) as long as a large portion of nodes do not carry fresh context thus reducing $n(t)$. In Figure 4 the behavior of $e_i(t)$ for sensing rate $q = 1Hz$ is also illustrated. We can observe that $e_i(t)$ ranges from 0.069 (mean value) to 0.93 (mean value) compared to the convergence value of $e_d(t) = 0.5$.

Each behavior can be applied on a context-aware application considering the specific requirements of the application. Once the application needs critically up-to-date context then the adoption of the dependent behavior is preferable. On the other hand, once we are interested in saving energy then nodes can adopt the independent behavior. However, a hybrid scheme combining both behaviors can be adopted. For instance, a portion of nodes can adopt the independent behavior for reducing energy consumption and the rest nodes adopt the dependent behavior maintaining up-to-date information. Another combination refers to the adoption of the dependent behavior for rapidly locating sources and leaders followed by the adoption of the independent behavior till context turns obsolete.

Experimenting with the Random Context Discovery

We also investigate the performance of the algorithm w.r.t. random process. That is, we show the difference of adopting the state-based PSO in context discovery with adopting a random selection of sources in order to explore for context (random behavior). Figure 6 depicts the per cent portion of the $g_+(t)$ value out of the initial value of $g_+(t)$ for experimenting with the independent behavior and the totally random behavior. As shown, the random behavior is not applicable in context discovery once the nodes are not navigated by leaders in areas of fresh context. Specifically,

Figure 6. The portion of g₊(t) value of the independent and random behaviors for sensing rate q = 1Hz

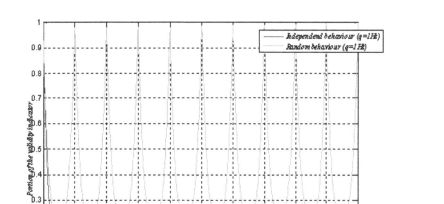

each time context turns obsolete (after 100 t.u.) nodes have to re-initiate the random foraging process for context (the quality indicator has the maximum value) in areas where there is no information about possible sources.

The expected value of the quality indicator does not indicate the convergence nature of the algorithm. Hence, we have to also experiment with the *diversity* metric $\mu(t)$ in context discovery. The PSO attempts to balance between exploration and exploitation; exploration is related to the algorithm's tendency to explore new areas of the context space, while exploitation is the tendency to search a smaller area more thoroughly.

The diversity comes from two sources: one is the difference between the particle's current position and its best neighbour, and the other is the difference between the particle's current position and its best historical value. Although variation provides exploration, it can only be sustained for a limited number of iterations because convergence of the swarm to the best (or the set of best) is necessary to refine the solution (exploitation). The diversity $\mu(t)$ is (Monson, 2006)

$$\mu(t) = \frac{1}{N|Q|} \sum_{i=1}^{N} \sqrt{\sum_{j=1}^{2} \left(x_{ij}(t) - \overline{x}_j(t) \right)^2}$$

which is essentially a measure of the average Euclidean distance of each particle from the centre of mass (the *j*th value of the average point **x**). Diversity is scaled by the length of the longest diagonal $|Q|$ in search space. The $\mu(t)$ value denotes the premature convergence of the algorithm. It indicates how fast the information interaction among nodes PSO leads to the nodes clustering quickly. A low value of $\mu(t)$ along with a satisfactory value of quality of context $g_+(t)$ denotes a mature convergence of swarm. On the other hand, a high value of $\mu(t)$ denotes low interaction among nodes, thus, a little likelihood for nodes to forage fresh context. Figure 7 depicts the $\mu(t)$ value for the independent and random behavior. As shown, in the random behavior the diversity of swarm is nearly constant and assumes higher value w.r.t. the diversity in the independent behavior. That is because, nodes randomly move into the search area without being attracted by some leaders. This has

Figure 7. The diversity value μ(t) of the independent and random behaviors for sensing rate q = 1Hz

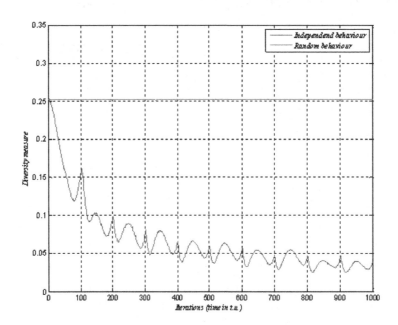

as a consequence an (extremely) high diversity of the swarm, thus, nodes are not able to exploit their interactions in order to located fresh context.

By combining the quality indicator in Figure 6 and the diversity in Figure 7, we can observe that the PSO-based autonomous context discovery algorithm can guarantee mature convergence and explored context of satisfactory quality. Similar conclusion is found by experimenting with the dependent behaviour, but it is not reported due to space limitations.

CONCLUSION

PSO is a simple algorithm with a wide application range on different optimization problems. We deal with context discovery by adopting the decentralized control and self-organization of SI. We provide the mapping between PSO and context discovery, and study how SI-inspired computing can facilitate context exploration. We introduce the time-variant context quality indicator g that refers to the fitness function f in PSO. Hence, each particle-node attempts to carry and maintain fresh context w.r.t. the g indicator. We report the independent and dependent foraging behaviors (strategies) for mobile nodes. The use of such behaviors in conjunction to the local fitness of the neighborhood enables node to discover sources and/or leaders that provide up-to-date contextual information. The discussed state-based algorithm supports such behaviors provided that context turns obsolete over time in a dynamic environment. We evaluated the efficiency and the effectiveness of each behavior. The adoption of each behavior relies on the context-aware application itself: for critically up-to-date context constrained applications the dependent behavior is preferable while, once energy savings are of high importance then the independent behavior exhibits satisfactory results. Our simulation results indicate the applicability of SI in context discovery and the foraging behaviors provide useful tools in auto-

nomics computing. In addition, the adoption of SI for transmission range / power adjustment, so that autonomic context-aware nodes control their energy consumption, is a future work that can be considered in autonomic computing.

REFERENCES

Anagnostopoulos, A., Sekkas, O., & Hadjief-thymiades, S. (2007b). Context fusion: Dealing with sensor reliability. *IEEE Int. Workshop on Information Fusion and Dissemination in Wireless Sensor Networks - IEEE Int. Conference on Mobile Ad-hoc and Sensor Systems*, (pp. 1-7).

Anagnostopoulos, C., Tsounis, A., & Hadjief-thymiades, S. (2007). Context awareness in mobile computing environments. Special Issue on Advances in Wireless Communications Enabling Technologies for 4G, *Wireless Personal Communication Journal, 2*(3), 454-464. Springer.

Anjum, F., & Mouchtaris, P. (2007). *Security for wireless ad hoc networks*. Wiley-Interscience. doi:10.1002/0470118474

Bettstetter, C., Hartenstein, H., & Pérez-Costa, X. (2004). Stochastic properties of the random waypoint mobility model. *ACM/Kluwer Wireless Networks: Special Issue on Modeling and Analysis of Mobile Networks, 10*(5).

Deneubourg, J., Goss, S., Sandini, G., Ferrari, F., & Dario, P. (1990). Self-organizing collection and transport of objects in unpredictable environments. *Symposium on Flexible Automation*, (pp. 1093-1098).

Eberhart, R. C., & Shi, Y. (2001). Tracking and optimizing dynamic systems with particle swarms. *IEEE Congress on Evolutionary Computation*, (vol. 1, pp. 94-100).

Engelbrecht, A. P. (2007). *Computational intelligence: An introduction* (2nd ed.). Wiley.

Hu, X., & Eberhart, R. C. (2001). Tracking dynamic systems with PSO: Where's the cheese? *Proc. Workshop on Particle Swarm Optimization*, (pp. 80-83).

Kennedy, J., & Eberhart, R. (2001). *Swarm intelligence*. San Francisco, CA: Morgan Kaufmann Publishers, Inc.

Matthias, O., & Hanspeter, A. (2000). Biomimetic robot navigation. *Robotics and Autonomous Systems*, *30*(1-2), 133–153. doi:10.1016/S0921-8890(99)00069-X

Monson, C. K., & Seppi, K. D. (2006). Adaptive diversity in PSO. In *Proceedings of the 8th Annual Conference on Genetic and Evolutionary Computation*, GECCO '06. ACM.

Peram, T., Veeramachaneni, K., & Mohan, C. K. (2003). Fitness-distance-ration based particle swarm optimization. *IEEE Symp. Swarm Intelligence,* (pp. 174-181).

Savvides, A., Han, C., & Srivastava, M. (2001). Dynamic fine-grained localization in ad-hoc networks of sensors. *ACM Mobicom*, July 2001, (pp. 166-179).

Zhao, F., & Guibas, L. (2004). *Wireless sensor networks - An information processing approach.* Elsevier Science.

ADDITIONAL READING

Carlishe, A., & Dozier, G. *Adapting Particle Swarm Optimization to Dynamic Environments,* Intl. Conf. Artificial Intelligence, pp.429-434, 2000.

Dorigo, M., & Gambardella, L. M. (1997). Ant Colony Systems: A Cooperative Learning Approach to the Traveling Salesman Problem. *IEEE Transactions on Evolutionary Computation*, *1*(1), 53–66. doi:10.1109/4235.585892

Drogoul, A., & Ferber, J. *From Tom Thumb to the Dockers: Some Experiments With Foraging Robots*, 2nd Int. Conference on Simulation of Adaptive Behavior, pp. 451-459, 1992.

Hu, X., & Eberhart, R. *Adaptive Particle Swarm Optimization: Detection and Response to Dynamic Systems*, IEEE Congress on Evolutionary Computation, USA. pp. 1666-1670, 2002.

LaVille, S. M., Lin, D., Guibas, L. J., Latombe, J. C., & Motwani, R. *Finding an Unpredictable Target in a Workspace with Objects,* IEEE Int. Conf. on Robotics and Automation, pp. 737-742, 1997.

Parker, L. E. (1998). ALLIANCE: An Architecture for Fault-Tolerant Multi-Robot Cooperation. *IEEE Transactions on Robotics and Automation*, *14*(2), 220–240. doi:10.1109/70.681242

Pasino, K., Polycarpou, M., Jacques, D., Pachter, M., Liu, Y., & Yang, Y. (2002). *Cooperative Control for Autonomous Air Vehicles, Cooperative Control and Optimization* (Murphy, R., & Pardalos, P., Eds.). Boston: Kluwer Academics Publishers.

Polycarpou, M., Yang, Y., & Pasino, K. *A Cooperative Search Framework for Distributed Agents,* IEEE Int. Symposium on Intelligent Control, pp.1-6, 2001.

Stone, L. D. (1975). *Theory of Optimal Search.* New York: Academic Press.

Vincent, P., & Rubin, I. A Framework and Analysis for Cooperative Search Using UAV Swarms, ACM Symposium on Applied Computing, 2004.

KEY TERMS AND DEFINITIONS

Context Discovery: The process of locating and exploiting context of better quality w.r.t. a context quality indicator.

Context Quality Indicator: An objective or subjective indicator that quantifies the exploitation of the considering piece of context. A context quality indicator can be the temporal validity of context or the spatial scope of context, the source credibility, and the reliability of the measurement.

Context: Information that refers to the current values of specific parameters that represent the activity / situation of an entity and environmental state, e.g., location, time, humidity, temperature, attending a meeting, driving a car, etc.

Context-Awareness: The ability of a mobile autonomous application to sense, interpret and infer contextual information in order to adapt to its environment.

Contextual Information: see Context definition.

Efficiency in Context Discovery: Efficiency in context discovery is a measure denoting the portion of nodes that have located context of certain quality out of the communication load required to exploring context of such quality.

Particle Swarm Optimization: An optimization algorithm of the swarm intelligence discipline that finds a solution to an optimization problem in a search space.

Swarm Intelligence: The discipline that deals with artificial multi-agent systems composed of agents (entities) that coordinate using decentralized control and self-organization and adopt collective and collaborative behaviors for performing tasks.

ENDNOTE

[1]   This dynamic environment refers to Type III environment (Engelbrecht, 2007).

APPENDIX A: EXERCISES ON THE PSO-BASED AUTONOMIC CONTEXT DISCOVERY

7.1. In this exercise the reader has to implement the Algorithm 2 such that the local fitness of the neighborhood of node i is the maximum fitness of all neighboring nodes leaving the other parameter as is. The maximum local fitness of the neighboring nodes is defined as:

$$g_{N_i}(\mathbf{y}, t) = \max\{g_k(\mathbf{y}, t), k \in N_i - \{i\}\}$$

Compare the $g_+(t)$ value of the dependent only behavior for sensing rate q = 0.02Hz based on such local fitness. Answer to the following:

- Does the algorithn assumes a pre-mature behavior once the node allways follow the neighboring node with the maximum quality of context ?
- Do the nodes enter to the S state sooner when adopting the maximum local fitness of the neighborhood than adopting the mean local fitness of the neighborhood?
- Repeat the simulation by using the minimum local fitness and compare only the $g_+(t)$ value of the independent behavior.

7.2. In this exercise the reader has to implement the Algorithm 2 and experiment with the velocity of the nodes. Specifically, the mobility behavior is the random waypoint model with $\mathbf{v}_i \sim U(\mathbf{v}_{min}, \mathbf{v}_{max})$ and, in our simulations, $[\mathbf{v}_{min}, \mathbf{v}_{max}] = [0.1, 2]$.

- Plot the the $g_+(t)$ value of the dependent and independent behavior for values $\mathbf{v}_{max}$ ranging from 2 to 10 having $\mathbf{v}_{min}$ constant to 0.1.

- If we assume that the increase in velocity results to an additional load (e.g., imagine that mobile nodes are robots), then we can incorporate into the e(t) = n(t) / l*(t) the load l*(t) as the communication load l(t) along with the inherent load of the mobility behavior m(t), that is

$l^*(t) = \gamma l(t) + (1-\gamma)m(t), 1 > \gamma > 0.$

7.3. The γ factor indicates a weighting on l(t) over m(t). For simplicity reasons assume that $\gamma = 0.5$. The inherent load m(t) can be defined as m(t) = v(t)/$\mathbf{v}_{max}$, where v(t) is the selected random velocity of a node at time t. Evidently, for v(t) = $\mathbf{v}_{max}$ the m(t) assumes the maximum value of unity.

- Plot the e(t) = n(t) / l*(t) for both behaviors for context discovery. Especially, focus on the independent behavior since the node in state S is moving randomly.

- At first, compare the diversity μ(t) value for the dependent and random behaviors.

- Secondly, adopt the chaotic sequence of the logistic map

$w(t+1) = 4.w(t).(1-w(t)), w(t) \in (0,1)$

- Plot and compare the $g_+(t)$ value for the above inertia parameter with the one adopted in the chapter for both behaviors.
  - Which behavior assumes lower values in $g_+(t)$ when adopting the chaotic sequence for the interia parameter ?

7.4. In this exercise the reader implements the PSO-based context discovery by introducing a behavior: the semi-collaborative behavior. Such behavior extends both behaviors (independent and dependent) to the point that the node in each state, O, P and S, communicated only to a random subset of the neighboring nodes in order to autonomously decide its future movement. Specifically, let $\zeta \in (0, 1]$ be the probability of querying a neighboring node at time t. That is, if $\zeta = 1$, then we obtain the discussed algorithm in the chapter. For any ζ lower than unity, the node queries only a subset of its neighboring nodes.

- Experiment with both behaviors adopting values for ζ in {0.1, 0.25, 0.5}. Plot the context quality indicator for each behavior.
- Compare the efficiency of context discovery metric for all behaviors, dependent, independent, semi-collaborative dependent and semi-collaborative independent. Note that when $\zeta < 1$, the communication load is obviously lower once not only nodes communicate for exchanging context quality indicators. However, the portion of satisfied nodes might change dramatically.

Chapter 5
Autonomic Computing:
A Fuzzy Control Approach towards Application Development

Harish S. Venkatarama
Manipal Institute of Technology, India

Kandasamy Chandra Sekaran
National Institute of Technology Karnataka, India

ABSTRACT

Autonomic computing (Salehie & Tahvildari, 2005) is a new paradigm to design, develop, deploy, and manage systems by taking inspiration from strategies used by biological systems. An autonomic system has four major characteristics: self-configure, self-heal, self-optimize, and self-protect. The autonomic computing architecture provides a blueprint for developing feedback control loops for self-managing systems. This observation suggests that control theory might provide guidance as to the structure of and requirements for autonomic managers. E-commerce is an area where an Autonomic Computing system could be very effectively deployed. E-commerce has created demand for high quality information technology services, and businesses seek ways to improve the quality of service in a cost-effective way. Properly adjusting tuning parameters for best values is time-consuming and skills-intensive. This chapter describes simulation environments to implement approaches to automate the tuning of MaxClients parameter of Apache web server using fuzzy controllers. These are illustrations of the self-optimizing characteristic of an autonomic computing system.

INTRODUCTION

Autonomic computing is a new paradigm to design, develop, deploy and manage systems by taking inspiration from strategies used by biological systems. The advantage of autonomic computing is that all of the complexity gets hidden from the user. Consider the autonomic nervous system: It tells your heart how many times to beat, checks your blood's sugar and oxygen levels. It adjusts your blood flow and skin functions to maintain the body temperature at the required level. Most important factor is that it does all this without any conscious recognition or effort on our part.

DOI: 10.4018/978-1-60960-845-3.ch005

An autonomic system has four major characteristics: self-configure, self-heal, self-optimize and self-protect (Salehie & Tahvildari, 2005).

Self-configuring is the capability of adapting automatically and dynamically to environmental changes. This characteristic has two aspects

1. Installing, (re-)configuring and integrating large, complex network intensive systems
2. Adaptability in architecture or component level to re-configure the system for achieving the desired quality factors.

Self-healing is the capability of discovery, diagnosing and reacting to disruptions. Such a system must be able to recover by detecting a failed component, taking it off-line to be fixed, and replacing the fixed component into the system without any apparent disruption.

Self-optimizing is the capability to efficiently maximize resource allocation and utilization for satisfying requirements of different users. While, in a short term, self-optimizing can address the complexity of managing system performance, in a long run its components will automatically and proactively seek ways to tune their operations and make themselves more cost efficient.

Self-protecting is the capability of reliably establishing trust, and anticipating, detecting and recovering from the effects of attacks with two aspects

1. Defending the system against correlated problems arising from malicious attacks or cascading failures that remain uncorrected by self-healing measures
2. Anticipating problems based on early reports from sensors and taking steps to avoid or mitigate them.

Briefly, an autonomic system needs to "know itself", must always look for ways to improve itself, must configure and reconfigure itself under varying and unpredictable conditions, must be its own doctor, must be an expert in self-protection, must know its environment and the context surrounding its activity and act accordingly, must adhere to open standards and finally, must anticipate the optimized resources needed to meet a user's information needs while keeping its complexity hidden from the user.

Figure 1 depicts the components and key interactions for a single autonomic manager and a single resource (Diao et al., 2005). The resource, sometimes called a managed element, is what is being made more self-managing. This could be a single system (or even an application within a system), or it may be a collection of many logically related systems. Sensors provide a way to obtain measurement data from resources, and effectors provide a means to change the behavior of the resource. Autonomic managers read sensor data and manipulate effectors to make resources more self-managing. The autonomic manager contains components for monitoring, analysis, planning, and execution. Common to all of these is knowledge of the computing environment, service level agreements, and other related considerations. The monitoring component filters and correlates sensor data. The analysis component processes these refined data to do forecasting and problem determination, among other activities. Planning constructs workflows that specify a partial order of actions to accomplish a goal specified by the analysis component. The execute component controls the execution of such workflows and provides coordination if there are multiple concurrent workflows. In essence, the autonomic computing architecture provides a blue print for developing feedback control loops for self-managing systems. This observation suggests that control theory might provide guidance as to the structure of and requirements for autonomic managers.

E-commerce is an area where an Autonomic Computing system needs to be deployed. E-commerce has created demand for high quality information technology services and businesses seek ways to improve the quality of service in a

Figure 1. Autonomic computing architecture

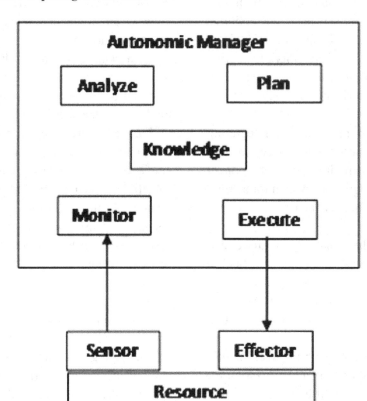

cost-effective way. In a typical e-commerce set up, normally, hundreds or even thousands of customers are always online. The number of customers can fall or rise drastically, sometimes within seconds. It is in the interest of the Service Provider to provide efficient and quick service to the maximum number of customers. Properly adjusting tuning parameters for best values is time-consuming and skills-intensive. Moreover having a fixed value or values for the tuning parameters over different workload intensities is not a good option. It is obviously in the interest of all parties concerned to have maximum utilization of resources irrespective of the usage patterns.

In conventional controllers modeling the system is an essential first step. The modeling process is cumbersome and depends on simplifying assumptions. The effectiveness of the controller depends on the validity of the model obtained. Further, in case of changes to the system, the existing model may no longer be valid and the modeling process may have to be repeated. Fuzzy controllers are exceptionally practical and robust due to its unique ability to accomplish tasks without knowing the mathematical model of the system.

Keeping the above scenarios in mind, this chapter describes simulation environments to implement approaches to automate the tuning of MaxClients parameter of Apache web server using fuzzy controllers for an e-commerce system. This chapter also describes the design and implementation of fuzzy controllers and the results obtained therein. These are illustrations of the self-optimizing characteristic of an autonomic computing system.

BACKGROUND

This section explains, in brief, the basic elements of a feedback control system and the objectives for which a control system is designed. In addition, this section contains a brief overview of fuzzy control.

Control Theoretic Framework

The architecture developed by control theory is about manipulating a target system to achieve a desired objective (Diao et al., 2005). The component that manipulates the target system is the controller. In terms of Figure 1, the target system is a resource, the controller is an autonomic manager, and the objective is part of the policy knowledge.

The essential elements of feedback control system are depicted in Figure 2. These elements are the following.

- Target system, which is the computing system to be controlled.
- Control input, which is a parameter that affects the behavior of the target system and can be adjusted dynamically
- Measured output, which is a measurable characteristic of the target system
- Reference input, which the desired value of the measured output is.

- Error, which is the difference between the reference input and the measured output.
- Controller, which determines the setting of the control input needed to achieve the reference input.

Objectives of Control Systems

Controllers are designed for some intended purpose. We refer to this purpose as the control objective. The most common objectives are the following.

- Regulation: Ensure that the measured output is equal to (or near) the reference input.
- Disturbance rejection: Ensure that disturbances acting on the system do not significantly affect the measured output.
- Optimization: Obtain the "best" value of the measured output.

Concepts of Fuzzy Control

Intelligent control emerged as a viable alternative to conventional model-based control schemes because issues such as uncertainty or unknown variations in plant parameters and structure can be dealt with more effectively. This improves the robustness of the control system. One of the ways of developing an intelligent control system

Figure 2. Control theory architecture

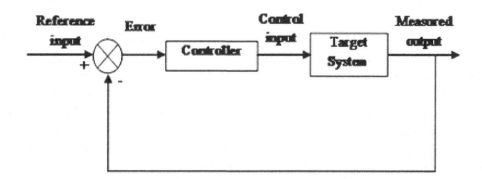

is through Fuzzy control. Fuzzy logic offers the important concept of fuzzy set theory, fuzzy if-then rules and approximate reasoning which deals with imprecision and information granularity.

Any fuzzy control system (Yen & Langari, 2005) involves three main steps –

- Fuzzification
- Inference mechanism
- Defuzzification

The heart of the fuzzy controller involves a set of IF-THEN rules stored in a rule base. The rules are expressed using linguistic variables and linguistic values. For example, "IF *temperature* IS *high* THEN *speed* IS *high*". This means, increase the speed of the fan if temperature is high. The terms *temperature* and *speed* are linguistic variables, while *high* is a linguistic value. Linguistic variables exist in one-to-one correspondence with numeric variables. Linguistic variables take on linguistic values that correspond to the values of the corresponding numeric variables. For example, *temperature* can take on values high, medium or low corresponding to the numeric variable for temperature. Converting the input numeric variables into linguistic values of linguistic variables is known as fuzzification. Membership functions are used for the conversion. Next the inference mechanism invokes each appropriate rule, generates a result for each, then combines the results of all the rules. Defuzzification involves converting the combined result back into a specific numeric output value.

APPLICATION OF FUZZY CONTROL TO ECOMMERCE: AN OVERVIEW

E-commerce is one area where an Autonomic Computing system could be very effectively deployed. E-commerce has created demand for high quality information technology (IT) services.

For example, a "buy" transaction that takes more than a few seconds may cause the customer to abandon the purchase. As a result, businesses are seeking quality of service (QoS) guarantees from their service providers (SPs) (Diao, Hellerstein & Parekh, 2002A). These guarantees are expressed as part of service level agreements (SLAs). SLA is a part of a service contract where the level of service is formally defined. It is a contract that exists between customers and their SP, client or between SPs. Many SLAs include specifications (Diao, Hellerstein & Parekh, 2001) of:

- Revenue that is accrued to the SP for services delivered and
- Costs that are incurred by the SP in the form of rebates to customers if previously agreed constraints are violated or the service is unavailable.

An SLA is characterized by a profit model. Consider a profit model described by 3 parameters

1. r, the revenue received for each completed transaction
2. W, the response time constraint
3. c, the cost incurred if a transaction's response time exceeds W. Such a transaction is called an offending transaction.

Thus, Profit = Revenue – Cost, where

Revenue = r * (number of completed transactions)

Cost = c * (number of offending transactions)

Since demand for services is often unpredictable, providers must sometimes make tradeoffs between losing revenue and incurring penalties. Making such choices is skill intensive and time consuming, and the decisions must be made in real time.

An e-commerce system is basically a client server system. The server being the most important part, it is very advantageous if autonomic computing concepts are incorporated into the server. The system studied here is the Apache web server. In Apache version 2.2 (configured to use Multi-Processing Module prefork), there are a number of worker processes monitored and controlled by a master process (Apache, 2009). The worker processes are responsible for handling the communications with the web clients, including the work required to generate the responses. A worker process handles at most one connection at a time, and it continues to handle only that connection until the connection is terminated. Thus, the worker is idle between consecutive requests from its connected client.

A parameter termed MaxClients limits the size of this worker pool, thereby providing a kind of admission control in which pending requests are kept in the queue. MaxClients should be large enough so that more clients can be served simultaneously, but not so large that resource contention occurs. The optimal value depends on server capacity and the nature of the workload. If MaxClients is too small, there is a long delay due to waits in the queue. If it is too large resources become over utilized which degrades performance as well. The combined effect is that the response time is a concave upward function of MaxClients (Diao, Hellerstein & Parekh, 2002B).

The setting of MaxClients can also be carried out by looking at the profits (Diao, Hellerstein & Parekh, 2002A). Consider an e-commerce system, in which revenues accrue if the admitted requests are processed within the specified deadline and costs are incurred otherwise. If MaxClients is too small, the number of requests that can be processed in a given interval is small. Though the number of violations and hence, costs will be small (mostly zero), profits will be less because of decreased revenue. As MaxClients increases, revenue increases proportionately till the point where the server gets saturated. Thereafter there will be no further increase in revenue but there will be an increase in costs because of increased violations. The combined effect is that profits are concave downwards in the parameter, MaxClients.

In both the above cases, our objective is "Optimization", i.e. obtain the "best value" for MaxClients. This best value depends on the workload, among other things, and as such, its value is unknown beforehand. Moreover, there is no single best value as the workload keeps changing. Thus, we do not have the advantage of comparing the present value of MaxClients with a "reference value". Other techniques have been used in the following sections. The concave upward property is used for obtaining an optimum value of MaxClients for minimizing response time, while the concave downward property is used for setting MaxClients for maximizing profits. This is explained in more detail in the following sections.

MINIMIZING RESPONSE TIME

The time taken by a server to process a request from a client is known as the response time for that request. It includes waiting time in the server queue, if any. The worker processes running in a server are simulated here by processes running under Linux. The time taken by one process to run to completion is called process time. Process time in this simulation is equivalent to response time in a server. In this section, we look into the design and implementation of a fuzzy controller for minimizing process time. This controller can be used with a server to minimize response time.

Design of Fuzzy Controller

We begin by taking a high level view of the system followed by the membership functions for fuzzification and defuzzification. This is followed by a discussion on the fuzzy rules used for the inference mechanism.

The block diagram of the fuzzy control system (Harish & Sekaran, 2009A)(Harish & Sekaran, 2010) is shown in Figure 3. The system being controlled is a linux machine. A number of processes will be running on the machine, the exact number depends on a parameter number-of-processes. Simulation readings are recorded after every interval, called measurement interval (sometimes simply called interval). The time taken by the processes are measured and input to a differentiator whose output is the change-in-process-time (**dt**) between current and previous intervals. The fuzzy controller has two inputs: change-in-process-time (**dt**) and change-in-number-of-processes (**dp**) between intervals. The controller's output is next-change-in-number-of-processes (**dnp**), whose value is taken as change-in-number-of-processes for the next interval. An integrator converts this value into number-of-processes.

Figure 4 shows the triangular membership functions used for the fuzzification of the inputs and defuzzification of the output. In each case, the parameter is divided into 5 intervals called neglarge, negsmall, zero, possmall and poslarge. Neglarge is an abbreviation for "negative large in size". Similarly negsmall, possmall and poslarge are abbreviations. Zero is the name of the interval denoting small changes. The measured numeric values will be multiplied by factors known as the normalized gains, denoted by **gdp** and **gdt**. That is why the x-axis shows -1 and 1 for all the membership functions. The output value obtained will be denormalized by dividing by the normalized gain, gnp, to obtain the actual output value. We have seen that process time is a concave upward function of the number of processes. Hence, a gradient descent procedure is used to minimize process times. This is described using fuzzy rules shown in Table 1.

Since the value of number of processes that minimizes the process time is not known, these rules are described in terms of changes to number of processes and process times values. As an example, consider rule 5. It means that the number of processes has been increased by a large amount (in the beginning of the current measurement interval) and it is observed that the process time has decreased by a large amount by the end of the interval. This means in the process time curve, the operating point is to the left of the minimum, and proceeding in the correct direction. Hence, it is continued to be moved in the same direction. That is, for the next interval, the number of processes is increased further.

It can be seen that for some of the rules, the output of the controller is "zero", which means no action is taken by the controller. Consider rule 3. There is no change in the number of processes,

Figure 3. Block diagram of the fuzzy control system

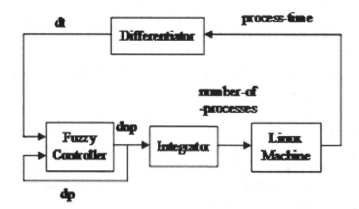

Figure 4. Membership functions for fuzzification (top) and defuzzification (bottom)

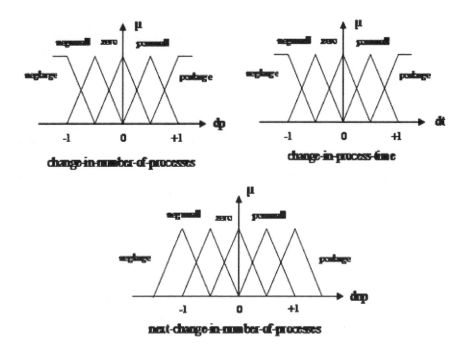

while the process time falls by a large value. This means either the number of requests has fallen or their service demand has fallen. In the former case, there should be no action by the controller, while in the latter case, the controller can respond by increasing the number of processes. In this set up, there is no way the controller can find out the reason. In the interest of stability, it assumes the former and takes no action. The opposite of this occurs in rule 23 where the process time increases by a large amount. Here also the controller does not take any action. In rule 11, the number of processes falls by a large amount, while there is no change in process time. In 15, the number of processes increases by a large amount and once again there is no change in process time. In both these cases, it means the system is under loaded. So the controller does not take any action. For rules 8, 12, 13, 14 and 18 either one or both inputs are small or zero. Hence controller does not take any action.

Thus, rules 1 through 10 take care of the correct situations where as rules 16 through 25 handle the incorrect situations. In rules 16 through 25 the previous action caused the process time to increase, so the direction has to be "reversed". Later the consequents from all the activated rules are weighted using the centre of gravity method to obtain the (normalized) output value.

Implementation

Ubuntu running on a 1.8 GHz Pentium IV desktop is used as the platform for running the simulations. The simulation environment consists of

* A load program to create processes
* A differentiator routine, which finds the difference between process times
* A fuzzy controller program, which finds the optimum value of the number of processes

Table 1. Fuzzy rule base

Rule	IF			THEN
	change-in-number-of-processes	AND	change-in-process-time	next-change-in-number-of-processes
1	neglarge	AND	neglarge	neglarge
2	negsmall	AND	neglarge	negsmall
3	zero	AND	neglarge	zero
4	possmall	AND	neglarge	possmall
5	poslarge	AND	neglarge	poslarge
6	neglarge	AND	negsmall	neglarge
7	negsmall	AND	negsmall	negsmall
8	zero	AND	negsmall	zero
9	possmall	AND	negsmall	possmall
10	poslarge	AND	negsmall	poslarge
11	neglarge	AND	zero	zero
12	negsmall	AND	zero	zero
13	zero	AND	zero	zero
14	possmall	AND	zero	zero
15	poslarge	AND	zero	zero
16	neglarge	AND	possmall	poslarge
17	negsmall	AND	possmall	possmall
18	zero	AND	possmall	zero
19	possmall	AND	possmall	negsmall
20	poslarge	AND	possmall	neglarge
21	neglarge	AND	poslarge	poslarge
22	negsmall	AND	poslarge	possmall
23	zero	AND	poslarge	zero
24	possmall	AND	poslarge	negsmall
25	poslarge	AND	poslarge	neglarge

- An integrator routine, which obtains the value of required number of processes from change in number of processes.

The output of the integrator is the input to the load program. The load program reads its input at the beginning of every measurement interval. The parent process in the load program creates and maintains that many child processes. Creation of each child process corresponds to the arrival of a client in Apache server. Hence, before creating a child process, a parent waits for a small duration. The time taken by the Apache server to service a client is simulated by means of a delay routine. This delay routine is invoked within each child process and the quantum of delay depends on number-of-processes. If there are two child processes running, it takes about 30 seconds for each of them to complete. If there are four pro-

cesses, each of them takes 15 seconds and so on. The optimum value of the number-of-processes is 10 and the process time corresponding to this situation is 6 seconds. Each child process, just before terminating sends the time taken to the differentiator.

In the child process, it first calls a delay, the duration of which depends upon number-of-processes and a parameter called loadfactor. Loadfactor takes a value 1, 2 or 3 to simulate low load, medium load and high load. For a fixed number-of-processes, delay is proportional to the loadfactor. It then sends the time taken to execute the delay, to the differentiator. Just before terminating, a signal is sent to the parent process, which will decrement process-count.

The fuzzy controller program takes 2 inputs, change-in-number-of-processes and change-in-process-time. The value of next-change-in-number-of-processes obtained in the previous measurement interval is taken as the value of change-in-number-of-processes for the current measurement interval. The value of change-in-process-time is obtained from the differentiator. The controller calculates the adjustment required for the number of processes for the next measurement interval.

The measurement interval should be large enough to reduce the effect of transients and also small enough so that the controller is able to quickly respond to changes. A measurement interval of 3 minutes was used. After waiting 2 minutes for the transients to reduce, readings of process time of processes that exited in the last minute are taken. The median of these values was used to further reduce the effect of the transients. For the normalizing gains, large values increase the speed of the controller, but too large values will cause the system to oscillate. After experimenting with a few values, the values selected were **gdp** = **gdnp** = 1/2 and **gdt** = 1/5. This means a change of 2 in the number of processes or a change of 5 seconds in process time is considered to be large.

Results

The simulation was repeated for low load (loadfactor = 1), medium load (loadfactor = 2) and high load (loadfactor = 3). For ease of comparison, the simulation is always started with 2 processes for the first measurement interval and 4 processes for the second interval. Since the controller works only with change-in-number-of-processes and change-in-process-time, it is invoked from the third interval. It is seen that irrespective of the load, controller always adjusts the number of processes for minimum process time, with the minimum value depending on the load.

Table 2 shows the values of the input and output variables, number of processes and process time for loadfactor equal to 1. The minimum value of process time obtained is 4 seconds. The controller, very quickly, converges to this value.

Table 3 shows the results for loadfactor equal to 2. The minimum value of process time obtained is 7 seconds. This value is larger because of the higher loadfactor. Also the controller takes more time to converge.

Table 4 shows the results for loadfactor equal to 3. The minimum value of process time obtained is 10 seconds. Also there is some oscillation, before the controller converges to a stable value.

MAXIMIZING THE PROFIT

It is our goal here to maximize the number of completed transactions, while keeping the number of offending transactions at a minimum, so as to maximize profits. There is no need to minimize the response time, but it should not exceed the

Table 2. For loadfactor = 1

Normalized			next change in no. of processes	no. of processes	process time
change in no. of processes	change in process time	next change in no. of processes			
-	-	-	-	2	15
-	-	-	-	4	9
1.0	-1.2	1.0	2.0	6	6
1.0	-0.6	1.0	2.0	8	4
1.0	-0.4	0.7	1.4	9	4
0.7	0.0	0.0	0.0	9	4

Table 3. For loadfactor = 2

Normalized			next change in no. of processes	no. of processes	process time
change in no. of processes	change in process time	next change in no. of processes			
-	-	-	-	2	30
-	-	-	-	4	16
1.0	-2.8	1.0	2.0	6	11
1.0	-1.0	1.0	2.0	8	7
1.0	-0.8	1.0	2.0	10	6
1.0	-0.2	0.4	0.9	11	7
0.4	0.2	-0.2	-0.4	11	7
-0.2	0.0	0.0	0.0	11	7

given constraint. In fact, we attempt to increase the number of requests processed, subject to the constraint. Processing of a request is simulated here by writing a certain number of bytes to the disk. In this section, we look into the design and implementation of a fuzzy controller for maximizing profits.

Design of Fuzzy Controller

As before, we begin by taking a high level view of the system followed by the membership functions for fuzzification and defuzzification. This is followed by a discussion on the fuzzy rules used for the inference mechanism.

The block diagram of the fuzzy control system (Harish & Sekaran, 2009B) is shown in Figure 5. The system being controlled is a linux machine. A number of processes will be running on the machine, the exact number depends on a parameter number-of-processes. Simulation readings are recorded after every interval, called measurement interval (sometimes simply called interval). The number of completed transactions and the number of violating transactions are used by the profit module for calculating profit. The value of profit is input to a differentiator whose output is the change-in-profit (**dft**) between current and previous intervals. The fuzzy controller has two inputs: change-in-profit (**dft**) and change-in-number-of-processes (**dp**) between intervals. The controller's output is next-change-in-number-of-processes (**dnp**), whose value is taken as the change-in-number-of-processes for the next

Table 4. For loadfactor = 3

Normalized			next change in no. of processes	no. of processes	process time
change in no. of processes	change in process time	next change in no. of processes			
-	-	-	-	2	44
-	-	-	-	4	23
1.0	-4.2	1.0	2.0	6	16
1.0	-1.4	1.0	2.0	8	12
1.0	-0.8	1.0	2.0	10	10
1.0	-0.4	0.7	1.4	11	11
0.7	0.2	-0.4	-0.8	10	10
-0.4	-0.2	-0.2	-0.4	10	10

interval. An integrator converts this value into number-of-processes.

Figure 6 shows the triangular membership functions used for the fuzzification of the inputs and defuzzification of the output. In each case, the parameter is divided into 5 intervals called neglarge, negsmall, zero, possmall and poslarge. Neglarge is an abbreviation for "negative large in size". Similarly negsmall, possmall and poslarge are abbreviations. Zero is the name of the interval denoting small changes. The measured numeric values will be multiplied by factors known as the normalized gains, denoted by **gdp** and **gdft**. That is why the x-axis shows -1 and 1 for all the membership functions. The output value obtained will be denormalized by dividing by the normalized gain, gdnp, to obtain the actual output value. We have seen that profit is a concave downward function of the number of processes. Hence, a hill climbing procedure is used to maximize profits. This is described using fuzzy rules shown in Table 5.

Since the value of number of processes that maximizes the profit is not known, these rules are described in terms of changes to number of processes and profit values. As an example, consider rule 25. It means that the number of processes has been increased by a large amount (in

the beginning of the current measurement interval) and it is observed that the profit has increased by a large amount by the end of the interval. This means in the profit process curve, the operating point is to the left of the maximum, and proceeding in the correct direction. Hence, it is continued to be moved in the same direction. That is, for the next interval, the number of processes is further increased by a large amount.

It can be seen that for some of the rules, the output of the controller is "zero", which means no action is taken by the controller. Consider rule 3. There is no change in the number of processes, while the profit falls by a large value. This means either the number of requests has fallen or the number of violating requests has increased. In the former case, there should be no action by the controller, while in the latter case, the controller can respond by decreasing the number of processes. In this set up, there is no way the controller can find out the reason. In the interest of stability, it assumes the former and takes no action. The opposite of this occurs in rule 23 where the profit increases by a large amount. Here also the controller does not take any action. In rule 11, the number of processes falls by a large amount, while there is no change in profit. In 15, the number of processes increases by a large amount and once again there

Figure 5. Block diagram of the fuzzy control system

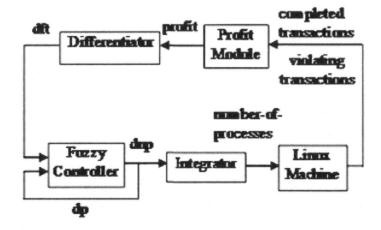

Figure 6. Membership functions for fuzzification (top) and defuzzification (bottom)

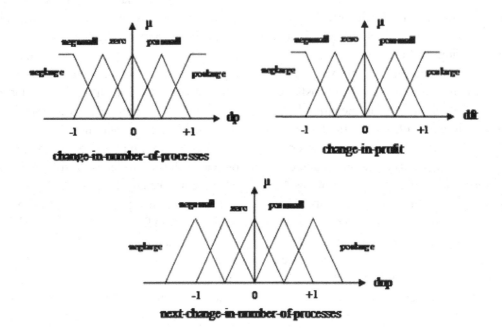

is no change in profit. In both these cases, it means the system is under loaded. So the controller does not take any action. For rules 8, 12, 13, 14 and 18 either one or both inputs are small or zero. Hence controller does not take any action.

Thus, rules 16 through 25 take care of the correct situations where as rules 1 through 10 handle the incorrect situations. In rules 1 through 10 the previous action caused the profit to decrease, so the direction has to be "reversed". Later the consequents from all the activated rules are weighted using the centre of gravity method to obtain the (normalized) output value.

Implementation

Ubuntu running on an 1.8 GHz Pentium IV desktop is used as the platform for running the simulations. The simulation environment consists of

- A load program to create processes
- A profit module for calculating profit values

- A differentiator routine, which finds the difference between profit values
- A fuzzy controller program, which finds the optimum value of the number of processes
- An integrator routine, which obtains the value of required number of processes from change in number of processes.

The working of the simulation environment is almost the same as for the previous controller with one major difference. Here, the time taken by the Apache server to service a client is simulated by means of a routine which writes transaction size number of bytes to the disk. This routine is invoked within each child process. However, at any given time only one process is allowed to write to disk and all the other processes wait for the disk to become free. The number of processes which are able to write to disk within the interval are called completed transactions and the number unable to write are called violating transactions. These two values are sent to the profit module for calculating profit. The profit module contains

Table 5. Fuzzy rule base

Rule	IF			THEN
	change-in-number-of-processes	AND	change-in-profit	next-change-in-number-of-processes
1	neglarge	AND	neglarge	poslarge
2	negsmall	AND	neglarge	possmall
3	zero	AND	neglarge	zero
4	possmall	AND	neglarge	negsmall
5	poslarge	AND	neglarge	neglarge
6	neglarge	AND	negsmall	poslarge
7	negsmall	AND	negsmall	possmall
8	zero	AND	negsmall	zero
9	possmall	AND	negsmall	negsmall
10	poslarge	AND	negsmall	neglarge
11	neglarge	AND	zero	zero
12	negsmall	AND	zero	zero
13	zero	AND	zero	zero
14	possmall	AND	zero	zero
15	poslarge	AND	zero	zero
16	neglarge	AND	possmall	neglarge
17	negsmall	AND	possmall	negsmall
18	zero	AND	possmall	zero
19	possmall	AND	possmall	possmall
20	poslarge	AND	possmall	poslarge
21	neglarge	AND	poslarge	neglarge
22	negsmall	AND	poslarge	negsmall
23	zero	AND	poslarge	zero
24	possmall	AND	poslarge	possmall
25	poslarge	AND	poslarge	poslarge

the profit model which is characterized by r, the revenue per completed transaction and c, the cost per violating transaction. Three profit models are defined. **P1: r = c**, that is, equal weight is assigned to completed and violating transactions; **P2: r = 5 * c**, assigns more weight to completed transactions; **P3: r = c/5**, assigns more weight to offending transactions.

The child waits for the disk to become free and then writes transaction size number of bytes to disk. Just before terminating, it sends a signal to the parent process, which will decrement process-count and increment processed-requests-count.

The fuzzy controller program takes two inputs, change-in-number-of-processes and change-in-profit. The value of next-change-in-number-of-processes is obtained as before. The value of change-in-profit is obtained from the differentiator. The controller calculates the adjustment required for the number of processes for the next measurement interval.

A measurement interval of 60 seconds was used. Too large normalizing gains result in the controller oscillating, while too small ones result in a slow performance. For better performance, different values of normalizing gains were selected for different profit models. For **P1, gdp = gdnp = gdft** = 1/5. For **P2, gdp = gdnp** = 1/5 and **gdft** = 1/25. For **P3, gdp = gdnp** = 1/5 and **gdft** = 1/10.

Results

The simulation was repeated many times with different profit models and transaction sizes. The number of processes for the first and second measurement interval is kept at 155 and 160 respectively. However, for the third simulation the values used are 75 and 80 because of the

Table 6. For profit model P2 and transaction size 10MB

Normalized			next change in no. of processes	no. of processes	profit obtained
change in no. of processes	change in profit	next change in no. of processes			
-	-	-	-	155	775
-	-	-	-	160	800
1	1	1	5	165	825
1	1	1	5	170	850
1	1	1	5	175	875
1	1	1	5	180	870
1	-0.2	-0.4	-2	178	854
-0.4	-0.6	0.4	2	180	852
0.4	-0.1	-0.1	-0.5	180	834

larger transaction size. As before, the controller is invoked from the third interval. Irrespective of different profit models and transaction sizes, the controller always maximizes the profit.

Table 6 shows the input and output variables, number of processes and profit values for profit model **P2** and transaction size 10MB. As mentioned before, the revenue per completed transaction is 5 times the cost per violating transaction. This is the reason for the large profit values. As seen, the number of processes stabilizes at 180.

Table 7 shows the results obtained for the same transaction size and profit model **P1**. In this case, the revenue per completed transaction is equal to the cost per violating transaction. This is the reason for the smaller profit values.

Table 8 shows the results obtained for the same profit model **P1** and transaction size 20MB. The larger transaction size leads to smaller number of processes and profit values.

Table 7. For profit model P1 and transaction size 10MB

Normalized			next change in no. of processes	no. of processes	profit obtained
change in no. of processes	change in profit	next change in no. of processes			
-	-	-	-	155	155
-	-	-	-	160	160
1	1	1	5	165	165
1	1	1	5	170	170
1	1	1	5	175	175
1	1	1	5	180	174
1	-0.2	-0.4	-2	178	178
-0.4	0.8	-0.4	-2	176	176
-0.4	-0.4	0.4	2	178	178
0.4	0.4	0.4	2	180	178
0.4	0.0	0.0	0	180	174

Table 8. For profit model P1 and transaction size 20MB

Normalized			next change in no. of processes	no. of processes	profit obtained
change in no. of processes	change in profit	next change in no. of processes			
-	-	-	-	75	75
-	-	-	-	80	80
1	1	1	5	85	85
1	1	1	5	90	90
1	1	1	5	95	87
1	-0.6	-1	-5	90	90
-1	0.6	-1	-5	85	85
-1	-1	1	5	90	88
1	0.6	1	5	95	79
1	-1.8	-1	-5	90	86

FUTURE RESEARCH DIRECTIONS

In the present work, the simulation of the server was carried out by either calling delays of some duration or writing some number of bytes to the disk. The simulation environment can be improved by using queuing theory concepts for modeling the client and the server. Clients can be modeled by incorporating a workload generator which generates requests such that the time between generations of consecutive requests (inter-arrival time) is exponentially distributed. For each request received by the server, the parent process creates a child process which sleeps for a time (service time) which is exponentially distributed. Thus, the client server architecture can be simulated here as an M/M/1 queue. The advantage here is that high workload can be very easily simulated by reducing the inter-arrival time and/or increasing the service time. Moreover, an exponentially distributed service time represents a worst case scenario. That is, service times in an actual server will normally have less variability than the exponentially distributed service time in an M/M/1 system. Thus, the controller can be subjected to a rigorous testing.

EXERCISES

1. Consider human biological system. Identify the subsystems, which are autonomic in nature and express using block diagrams.
2. In this chapter, simulation is carried out using processes. Repeat the simulation using any other approach. (Hint: simulate client server using M/M/1 queue).
3. In this chapter, fuzzy control is used to minimize process time. Modify this controller to regulate process time, that is, ensure that the process time is at or near to a specified value.

CONCLUSION

In this chapter, simulation environments to illustrate the self-optimizing characteristic of an autonomic computing system are described. Two fuzzy controllers were designed and implemented, one for optimizing quality of service (minimizing response time) and the other for maximizing profit. Experimental results show that a fuzzy algorithm based controller can automatically adjust tuning parameters. It is possible to obtain similar benefits in a server running in real time by incorporating one of these controllers.

REFERENCES

Apache Software Foundation. (2009). *Website.* Retrieved from http://www.apache.org

Diao, Y., Hellerstein, J. L., & Parekh, S. (2001). A business-oriented approach to the design of feedback loops for performance management. *Proceedings of the 12th IEEE International Workshop on Distributed Systems: Operations and Management*, October 2001.

Diao, Y., Hellerstein, J. L., & Parekh, S. (2002A). Using fuzzy control to maximize profits in service level management. *IBM Systems Journal, 41*(3). doi:10.1147/sj.413.0403

Diao, Y., Hellerstein, J. L., & Parekh, S. (2002B). Optimizing quality of service using fuzzy control. *Proceedings of Distributed Systems Operations and Management*. Springer.

Diao, Y., Hellerstein, J. L., Parekh, S., Griffith, R., Kaiser, G. E., & Phung, D. (2005). A control theory foundation for self-managing computing systems. *IEEE Journal on Selected Areas in Communications, 23*(12).

Harish, S. V., & Chandra Sekaran, K. (2009A). Simulation environment for a fuzzy controller based autonomic computing system. *Proceedings of the 2009 IEEE Intl. Conf. on Advanced Computer Control (ICACC 2009)*, Singapore, January 2009.

Harish, S. V., & Chandra Sekaran, K. (2009B). Simulation environment for maximizing profits in an autonomic computing system using fuzzy control. *Proceedings of the 4th Indian Intl. Conf. on Artificial Intelligence (IICAI-09)*, December 16-18, Tumkur, India.

Harish, S. V., & Chandra Sekaran, K. (2010). *Simulation environment for minimizing response time in an autonomic computing system using fuzzy control*. 2010 IEEE Intl. Conf. on Recent Trends in Information, Telecommunication and Computing (ITC 2010), March 2010, Kochi, India.

Salehie, M., & Tahvildari, L. (2005). Autonomic computing: Emerging trends and open problems. *Proceedings of the Workshop on the Design and Evolution of Autonomic Application Software*, 2005.

Yen, J., & Langari, R. (2005). *Fuzzy logic: Intelligence, control and information*. India: Pearson Education.

Chapter 6
Genetic Programming for System Identification

Lavinia Ferariu
Gheorghe Asachi Technical University of Iasi, Romania

Alina Patelli
Gheorghe Asachi Technical University of Iasi, Romania

ABSTRACT

This chapter discusses the features of genetic programming based identification approaches, starting with the connected theoretical background. The presentation reveals both advantages and limitations of the methodology and offers several recommendations useful for making GP techniques a valuable alternative for mathematical models' construction. For a sound illustration of the discussed design scheme, two GP-based multiobjective algorithms are suggested. They permit a flexible selection of nonlinear models, linear in parameters, by advantageously exploiting their particular structure, thus improving the exploration capabilities of GP and the interpretability of the resulted mathematical description. Both model accuracy and parsimony are addressed, by means of non-elitist and elitist Pareto techniques, aimed at adapting the priority of each involved objective. The algorithms' performances are illustrated on two applications of different complexity levels, namely the identification of a simulated system, and the identification of an industrial plant.

INTRODUCTION

The design of mathematical models able to capture the dynamic behavior of industrial plants represents a very difficult task. As the assumptions imposed by working directly with the physical/chemical laws that govern the inner processes of the targeted systems are commonly not satisfied in the industrial environment, this approach cannot be employed for building analytical models, or at least the model structure, at an adequate level of approximation (Fleming & Purshouse, 2002). Therefore, the models are usually determined by means of system identification - a data driven

DOI: 10.4018/978-1-60960-845-3.ch006

methodology which constructs the mathematical description of the plant by using a *finite* number of plant variables' measurements acquired during a *finite* period of time. The aim of system identification is to find a valid model able to capture the most relevant properties of the system, without comprising extraneous blocks which are not plant specific. Even if a limited number of observations are used during the design stage, the resulted model must have good generalization capabilities, meaning it has to describe the behavior of the system in a range of operating conditions as large as possible. Additionally, to decrease the risk of inappropriate further model utilization, a reduced sensitiveness of the model output relative to small variations of the model parameters is recommended, together with increased interpretability. This becomes a very challenging problem, especially if the system features complex nonlinearities, whilst scarce information about its dynamics is *a priori* accessible, and/or large sets of highly dimensional, noisy data are available (Poli et al., 2008).

Note that if the model includes alien parts, it will most likely offer an unsatisfactory approximation on data sets different than those used for model configuration. In this context, in compliance with Occam's razor principle, the identification procedure has to encourage the selection of the simplest model which can ensure the level of accuracy required by the application. Obviously, no model could be a perfect copy of the real system. The mathematical description involves simplifications which are assumed as acceptable only if the requested model accuracy is satisfied. It is also worth mentioning that the model accuracy cannot exceed the accuracy of data acquisition.

Assuming that a representative data set of plant variables measurements has been experimentally collected during plant operation - in such a way as to reflect as much of the system dynamics as possible, the configuration of the model comprises the selection of relevant inputs, the selection of the model structure and the estimation of the

model parameters. These stages can be carried out separately or solved concomitantly, however note that the last alternative provides higher flexibility at the cost of increasing problem complexity. Lastly, the designed model has to be validated on different data sets.

Classical identification approaches deal with only one potential model at a time, restarting the search if the candidate's features are not satisfactory. By doing so, the identification process tends to become time consuming, and more importantly, there is no guarantee that a certain structure selection will turn out to be better, in terms of end model quality, than the previous ones. Moreover, to ensure faster variables reduction and structure selection, most identification approaches investigate only a reduced number of combinations, by using predefined schemes which do not guarantee the achievement of a convenient solution for any particular application. Additionally, the models parameters are commonly computed via a deterministic optimization procedure that strives to minimize the squared error function. Whilst industrial systems feature complex nonlinearities and work in noisy environments, the estimation of parameters usually implies dealing with nonlinear, discontinuous objective functions, as well as large and non-convex search spaces, therefore the risk of failing into a local optimum point or of generating inconvenient solutions results very high (Fleming & Purshouse, 2002).

Genetic programming (GP) offers solutions to many of the drawbacks inherent to classic identification approaches. Basically, it consists in an evolutionary algorithm designed to evolve graph-based individuals. Therefore, the GP-based identification involves the evolution of a population of potential mathematical descriptions of the dynamic system (called individuals), carried out for numerous iterations (generations) (Nedjah et al., 2006; Poli et al., 2008).

As GP works on multiple models at every generation, it provides increased exploration capabilities within vast search spaces of high dimension. Valuable models configured at previous iterations are exploited for producing offspring with potentially better performances. Additionally, transitions from one generation to the next are stochastic in nature and implement the Darwinian principle of the survival of the fittest (Koza, 1992; Bäck et al., 2000; Poli et al., 2008). If an adequate diversity of the population is maintained during the evolutionary loop, the risk of stagnation in local optima points is reduced, making GP able to perform a robust self-adaptation of the population of models.

The new solutions are produced by means of genetic operators which work both at the structural and parametric levels of the encoded models, rendering the three main phases of model configuration (input variable reduction, structure selection and parameter estimation) practically simultaneous. This brings increased flexibility in mixing various model components and permits a more realistic quality assessment of each investigated combination, at the risk of algorithm incapacity of providing an adequate solution in a reasonable time interval. Improved performances in terms of exploration capabilities and convergence speed could be obtained by incorporating additional problem specific knowledge in the standard GP loop. Also, GP may be hybridized with a local optimization procedure, usually targeted at determining the model parameters (Coello Coello et al., 2007), provided that the symbiosis between the structure selection process and the parameter computation is carefully configured.

Note also that GP employs a direct search, therefore it can handle discontinuous and noisy data, with important benefits yielded by the compatibility with realistic formulation of objectives and hypothesis in engineering applications. The algorithm parameters are either self tuned during the evolutionary process, or quite easily determined via "trial and error" procedures (Affenzeler et al., 2009).

Although there is no sound theoretical support regarding the method's convergence, the experimental trials conducted within the context of complex optimization problems show its benefits relative to classical analytical procedures (Fleming & Purshouse, 2002; Poli et al., 2008).

Starting with related theoretical foundations, this chapter glances through the main advantages and challenges of GP-based identification approaches. Insight to the nature of the methodology is provided by means of two multiobjective optimization approaches devoted to the design of nonlinear models, linear in parameters. The performances of the suggested algorithms are highlighted both on simulated and real-life industrial plants and, finally, some remarks are formulated.

BACKGROUND

Fundamentals of System Identification

For a sound understanding of the particularities of GP-based identification methods, firstly, the problem of system identification is revisited. System identification is meant to create a model (M), which best mimics the behavior of a dynamic system, based on a finite set of plant observations. The discussion focuses on the determination of input-output mathematical models defined in discrete-time domain, as only this type of models will be later configured by means of GP. Let us consider a multivariable system with m inputs ($\mathbf{u} \in \Re^m$) and n outputs ($\mathbf{y} \in \Re^n$), therefore the model has to approximate the $\mathbf{u} \rightarrow \mathbf{y}$ mapping which characterizes the plant dynamics. According to the series-parallel identification scheme, the model is defined as

$$\hat{\mathbf{y}}(k) = \mathbf{f}(\mathbf{u}(k), \mathbf{u}(k-1), ..., \mathbf{u}(k-n_u), \mathbf{y}(k-1), ..., \mathbf{y}(k-n_y))$$

Here, $\hat{\mathbf{y}} \in \Re^n$ denotes the output of the model and

$$[\mathbf{u}(k), \mathbf{u}(k-1), ..., \mathbf{u}(k-n_u), \mathbf{y}(k-1), ..., \mathbf{y}(k-n_y)]$$

are the inputs of the model at the sampling instant k, with n_u and n_y specifying the maximum permitted input and output lags. Usually, the case of models with external dynamics is addressed, which means that **f** implements a static mapping and the dynamic behavior of the model results solely from use of the lagged values of plant inputs and outputs. The models with internal dynamics assume that **f** is itself time-variant and set $n_u = 0$, $n_y = 1$. They can lead to more compact representations and sometimes to better performances of accuracy, at the cost of a higher complexity of the design procedure (Iserman, 1997; Ferariu & Voicu, 2005). If $n > 1$, the identification can be carried out independently, for building n different multi-input single-output models, by allowing inter-connections between system outputs:

$$\hat{y}_p(k) = f(\mathbf{u}(k), \mathbf{u}(k-1), ..., \mathbf{u}(k-n_u), \mathbf{y}(k-1), ..., \mathbf{y}(k-n_y))$$
(1)

where $\hat{y}_p \in \Re$ approximates the pth output of the plant, $y_p \in \Re$.

Basically, the identification comprises the following steps:

A. **Selection of relevant observations for model generation and validation.** This is not included in the scope of this chapter. In accordance to input-output formalism, one assumes that both training and validation data sets are available, including representative pairs of system input and output measurements acquired with the same sampling period:
$$\mathbf{D} = \{(\mathbf{u}_k, \mathbf{y}_k) \mid \mathbf{u}_k \in \Re^m, \mathbf{y}_k \in \Re^n, \forall\, k = \overline{1, N}\}$$
and
$$\mathbf{D\_v} = \{(\mathbf{u}_j, \mathbf{y}_j) \mid \mathbf{u}_j \in \Re^m, \mathbf{y}_j \in \Re^n, j = \overline{1, N_v}\}$$
respectively, with $|\mathbf{D}| = N < \infty$, $|\mathbf{D\_v}| = N_v < \infty$ and $\mathbf{D\_v} \cap \mathbf{D} = \varphi$). The training data set **D** comprising few, less noisy representative samples is used for the construction of the model *M* during steps b, c and d. The validation data set **D_v** is em-

ployed at the final stage e, for verifying the generalization ability of *M*, therefore, it has to be as different as possible than **D**, in order to provide challenging testing situations. In the case of linear systems, the shape of persistent inputs and the required sampling period are theoretically configured, if white noise is assumed. Though, for nonlinear systems a complete theoretical background is not yet available. Moreover, note that in many industrial applications, some operating conditions are risky or costly to achieve, so **D** and **D_v** can only be obtained subject to these constraints. Usually, the training samples are spread over the whole accepted range and illustrate static plant exploitation intervals, as well as dynamic operating regions with high variations of system inputs and outputs.

B. **Selection of independent input variables,** also known as variable reduction. It consists in determining the relevant plant variables to be considered as model inputs (independent of the lag) in the subsequent steps of identification. In compliance with (1), this involves establishing the components of **u** and **y** which have significant influence on y_p, $\tilde{\mathbf{u}} = [u_v]_{v \in \{1, ..., m\}} \in \Re^{\tilde{m}}$ and $\tilde{\mathbf{y}} = [y_z]_{z \in \{1, ..., n\}} \in \Re^{\tilde{n}}$, with $m \geq \tilde{m}$, $n \geq \tilde{n}$. If highly dimensional data is acquired, yet the expertise concerning the inner behavior of the system is reduced, the selection is carried out in a supervised manner, using filters, wrappers or embedded methods (Globerson. & Tishby, 2003; Guyon et al., 2006). Note that, for noisy and redundant data, the independent analysis of each variable is not illustrative, as useless variables can become beneficial in specific combinations (Guyon et al., 2006). However, if the approach works directly on subsets of model inputs, the problem becomes NP-hard, so the exhaustive investigation of all possible combinations cannot be performed. The filters use statistic tests (like T-test, F-test, Chi-squared) to analyze the relevance of variables, usually working separately on each potential model input. In contrast, the wrappers operate on subsets of model inputs and eliminate/add specific variables based on cross-validation, whilst the embedded methods merge the steps b, c and d to provide a better control of the end model quality (including its generalisation capabilities), with the cost of high computational effort.

C. **Selection of proper model structure.** The structure of the model is indicated by the mathematical expression implemented by *f*, written with generic parameters. If no *a priori* information is accessible, one can customize a template derived from Kolmogorov's decomposition theorem, able to offer universal approximation capabilities, in other words able to guarantee the *existence* of a model of any desired degree of accuracy, for any continuous, bounded nonlinearity. Unfortunately, even in this case, the model structure must be selected from a large search space of possible architectures, whilst confronted with the difficulty of working on structural elements with no physical significance. Usually, only some potential architectures are investigated, by applying preset constructive or destructive procedures, which add or delete certain structural components (Fleming & Purshouse, 2002). Note that the destructive algorithms have to start with the most complex architecture and this might introduce difficulties related to numerical implementations. Both constructive and destructive methods involve the symbiosis with step d, as the quality of a model can be assessed only if appropriate model parameters are associated. It is worth mentioning that, in compliance with the law of parsimony, the structure has to be as simple as possible in terms of desired accuracy.

D. **Estimation of parameters** is usually formulated as the minimization of the mean squared error computed over the training data set **D**, $\theta^* = \arg\min_{\theta \in S} SSE_{|_D}(M(\theta))$, with

$$SSE_{|_D}(M(\theta)) = \frac{1}{2N}\sum_{i=1}^{N}(\mathbf{y}(k) - \hat{\mathbf{y}}^\theta(k))^T \cdot (\mathbf{y}(k) - \hat{\mathbf{y}}^\theta(k))_{|_D},$$

where $(\cdot)^T$ denotes the transpose operator, $\hat{\mathbf{y}}^\cdot(k))$ represents the output of the model at instant k, using the parameters' set, and the model input vector $[\mathbf{u}_k, \mathbf{u}_{k-1}, ..., \mathbf{u}_{k-n_u}, \mathbf{y}_{k-1}, ..., \mathbf{y}_{k-n_y}]$ built with samples from **D** (eventually, $[\tilde{\mathbf{u}}_k, \tilde{\mathbf{u}}_{k-1}, ..., \tilde{\mathbf{u}}_{k-n_u}, \tilde{\mathbf{y}}_{k-1}, ..., \tilde{\mathbf{y}}_{k-n_y}]$, if several variables have been categorized as irrelevant). Note that for any $i \leq 0$, $\mathbf{u}_i = 0$, $\mathbf{y}_i = 0$, $\tilde{\mathbf{u}}_i = 0$, $\tilde{\mathbf{y}}_i = 0$. If the search space S results highly dimensional, large or nonconvex, the optimization problem becomes very difficult, especially when no rough initial localization of the solution is available and noisy data is used. First order optimization methods can theoretically operate with discontinuous objective functions, yet they lack in accuracy (Fletcher, 1980). Assuming the existence of the derivatives of the objective function, the optima points can be located faster and much more precisely by means of higher order optimization procedures, yet, with a high risk of the search process to stagnate in local optima or to become instable (Fletcher, 1980). A possible alternative would be to use a conjoint optimization scheme, by applying a first order optimization method to locate a rough vicinity of the end solution, followed by a superior order procedure to perform the refined search. However, when complex nonlinearities are involved, employing a sequence of two procedures to compute the model parameters translates by unwanted supplementary computational costs, with no guarantee that the global optimum solution will be found.

E. **Model validation** includes investigations concerning the approximation provided by M on different validation data sets (**D_v**) and other statistical tests.

GP addresses system identification in a global approach, by concomitantly solving the steps b, c and d. The simplest methodology is to formulate the problem as a mono-objective optimization, e. g. to consider the minimization of the empirical risk computed in terms of **D**:

$$M^* = \arg\min_{M \in I_M} SSE_{|_D}(M),$$

$$SSE_{|_D}(M) = \frac{1}{N}\sum_{i=1}^{N}(\hat{\mathbf{y}}(k) - \mathbf{y}(k))^T \cdot (\hat{\mathbf{y}}(k) - \mathbf{y}(k))_{|_D}$$

(2)

Note that the objective function *SSE* indicates the overall model accuracy relative to the training data set, however, if some plant operating areas are preponderantly illustrated in **D**, then the approximation performances of the model obtained in these working conditions have higher impact on *SSE*.

Basics of Genetic Programming

GP represents a class of evolutionary algorithms (Bäck et al. 2000), therefore it can be completely defined by $(I, F, \Omega, \psi, s_r, s_i, \tau, \mu, \lambda)$ items, as briefly explained in the following (Figure 1). I denotes the space of individuals, namely the projection of the problem search space (I_M) provided by the employed encoding. $F : I \to \Re$ represents the fitness function which assesses the adaptation capabilities of the individuals in terms of the imposed objectives. At every generation, t, the algorithm works on a population of μ individuals ($P(t) \in I^\mu$) and produces λ new solutions, called offspring, which are meant to be better adapted than the current ones. To suit this purpose,

stochastic selection (s_r) is employed to fill the recombination pool, preferably with the fittest individuals of $P(t)$, then probabilistic genetic operators (Ω) act on the selected genetic material to generate new individuals. Afterwards, the algorithm inserts the offspring into the population of the next generation, by making use of s_i selection, which implements a deterministic or stochastic competition between the offspring and the old solutions, in the sense that the fittest individuals get greater chances to survive. The stop criterion τ usually refers to the maximum permitted number of generations. ψ is the transition function which specifies all transformations that a population goes through, at a certain generation, as result of successive deployment of genetic and selection operators, $P(t+1) = \psi(P(t))$, with $\psi = s_i \circ \Omega \circ s_r$.

GP was introduced by Koza in 1992. Unlike other evolutionary algorithms, it evolves a population of programs tailored to solve the optimization problem. A program represents an entity which receives several inputs, performs some transformations and produces several outputs. These transformations can refer to arithmetical and logical operations done on various types of variables, with the possibility of iterative and/or recursive execution (Koza, 1992). Therefore, the general template of evolutionary algorithms was customized to work with tree-based individuals, which encode hierarchical programs of different shapes and sizes (considering that a subtree corresponds to a subroutine). Various other encryption schemes have been later investigated (Poli et. al, 2008; Brameier & Banzhaf, 2006; Abraham&Nedjah & Mourelle, 2005) leading to variants of GP (linear GP, graph GP, Cartesian GP, developmental GP, etc.), however the original version suggested by Koza has remained the most common one. For the sake of simplicity, the case of multiple inputs, single – output individuals is addressed in classic GP. In accordance to LISP syntax, the individuals are built as recursive

Figure 1. Standard evolutionary algorithm

$t = 0$, initialize $P(t)$, $|P(t)| = \mu$.

while (τ is not true), do:

      build the recombination pool: $P'(t) = s_r(P(t))$;

      produce new solutions (offspring): $P''(t) = \Omega(P'(t))$, $|P''(t)| = \lambda$;

      insert the new solutions into the population:

           $P(t+1) = s_i(P(t), P''(t))$, such that $|P(t+1)| = \mu$;

      $t = t + 1$;

list the best individual of $P(t)$.

combinations of certain primitives selected from a set of functions and operators, $\mathbf{O} = \{o_1, o_2, \ldots\ldots, o_{NO_{max}}\}$, $NO_{max} < \infty$ and a set of terminals, $\mathbf{x} = \{t_1, t_2, \ldots\ldots, t_{NT_{max}}\}$, $NT_{max} < \infty$ The functions of $\mathbf{O}$ can perform any mathematical mappings, from simple arithmetical or logical operations, to complex domain-specific ones. Usually, loop-based items are not included in $\mathbf{O}$. The terminals are used only as leaves of the trees. Typically, they are variable or constant atoms (Koza, 1992). In the context of symbolic regression, the tree-based structures can be evaluated depth – first, starting from the left, to obtain the reverse Polish form (Affenzeller et al., 2009).

To guarantee that any combination of primitives leads to a valid model, $\mathbf{O}$ and $\mathbf{x}$ have to satisfy the closure property, meaning that any element of $\mathbf{O}$ accepts as input any value and data type returned by any function/operator, as well as any value and data type of the terminals (Koza, 1992). Firstly, type consistency can be solved by means of appropriate type conversions or by restricting the combinations of primitives (allowed at initialization or for offspring generation). Secondly, data consistency is achieved only if any potential tree permits a safe evaluation (Poli et al., 2008). Note that, despite the type inconsistency, data

inconsistency cannot be detected at the stage of tree generation without tree evaluation (excepting the particular case when the problem occurs on a node having a single constant terminal child). To ensure a consistent evaluation, usually, a default protection value is employed or the fitness of any improper individual is penalized, in order to discourage its recombination and survival. However, the generation of invalid individuals results in a significant waste of computational effort, so, if possible, such functions/operators should be avoided.

The optimal solution can be obtained only if all required terminals and functions have been included in $\mathbf{x}$ and $\mathbf{O}$ sets. As GP is mostly applied when scarce information about the optimal solution/program is available, in practical situations, the sufficiency of functions and terminals sets is usually satisfied at the cost of using more primitives than necessary. The extraneous elements make the exploration more difficult, by leading to a larger search space (Koza, 1992). However, working on minimally sufficient sets is not always the best alternative. If some combinations of primitives are known as frequent and valuable structural blocks, then they may be included as independent atomic primitives, for allowing the achievement of more compact representations and for speeding up the generation of well adapted individuals. The difficulty here is to decide the appropriate level of granularity, as these blocks cannot be internally reconfigured by means of GP techniques, as well as to determine which modules are really useful. The library of primitives can be adapted during the evolutionary loop. In this case, the new elements are chosen based on the performances achieved by the individuals which contain the corresponding structural blocks, their inclusion in the primitive set being inherently dependent on all other components of GP which influence the algorithm behavior.

One may consider the fitness function F defined as the relative objective function which compares the performances of each individual with the performances of the rest of the population (Fonseca & Fleming, 1998). The fitness values must be higher for individuals with better performances, as they will play the part of selection probabilities in the process of filling the recombination pool. The most common fitness assignment scheme is the proportional one. However, ranking fitness computation provides higher capabilities in preserving the diversity of the population, as well as a suitable approach for multiobjective optimizations. It establishes the fitness values based on the rank held by each individual in a list sorted according to objective values, thus giving greater chances to currently less adapted individuals (Bäck, 1996), which could become valuable solutions after several genetic transformations. Unfortunately, this fitness assignment is incompliant with available proofs of evolutionary algorithm convergence. Selection for recombination (s_r) usually employs a roulette-based technique. Each individual is assigned to a roulette slice proportional to its fitness. To provide an accurate, consistent and efficient selection, the universal stochastic sampling uses a special rigid block of $|P'(t)|$ needles (with $|P'(t)| \leq |P(t)|$) and builds the whole recombination pool after a single rotation of the roulette. On the contrary, selection for insertion (s_i) is frequently done in

a deterministic manner. Some approaches insert all resulted offspring or only the best $\lambda_s < \lambda$ offspring, and assign the available places to the best individuals of $P(t)$. If $\lambda = \mu$, the algorithm is not elitist, meaning that it does not guarantee the survival of the best solution. Other algorithms choose the best solutions of $P(t) \bigcup P'(t)$. They are elitist in nature, but can excessively encourage the survival of too similar (fittest) solutions, thus disturbing the diversity of the population. Extensive explanations concerning various selection techniques can be found in (Bäck, 1996).

As no *a priori* information about the optimal solution/program is available, the initial population, $P(0)$, is randomly generated and spread over the entire search space. Obviously, any initialization technique will introduce a bias, leading to the impossibility of guaranteeing a uniform distribution in particular implementations (Poli et al., 2008). Usually, the maximum accepted depth of the trees, d, is predefined. The full method introduces only full trees in the initial population, having the same maximum accepted depth d relative to all leaves (Koza, 1992). The individuals could result in various, yet limited, shapes and sizes. Moreover, if d is set much higher than the depth of the optimal tree, a convenient solution is difficult to find. The grow method builds the initial individuals in a more flexible way, as it accepts branches of any depth lower than d (Koza, 1992). Note that if **x** is much more numerous than **O**, the grow method's tendency is to preponderantly generate shorter and asymmetric trees. Langdon suggested to balance the initial population with equal numbers of trees of every depth $1,.., d$ (Poli et al., 2008). The initialization procedure can also call both grow and full methods, each to generate one half of the population or can seed the initial batch of individuals with certain solutions apriorically known as well adapted. Though, the survival of these "good" individuals is not guaranteed, and, if they are much better than the rest of the population, the proportional selection is dramatically disturbed.

GP employs both types of probabilistic genetic operators. Unlike other evolutionary techniques, crossover and mutation can be applied exclusively, not necessarily in sequel. The crossover acts on two selected parents to produce two new offspring. Subtree crossover randomly selects a cutting node inside each parent and interchanges the corresponding subtrees (the cutting point becomes the root node for the swapped subtree), whilst homologous crossover chooses the cutting points only from the parts of the parents having the same shape. Koza (1992) recommends using different probabilities for selecting cutting points of function and terminal type (0.9 and 0.1, respectively). Mutation acts more rarely than crossover, on a single individual: subtree mutation selects a single parent and applies subtree crossover after generating a random second parent; node replacement mutation changes the type of randomly selected nodes with other compatible primitives; hoist mutation replaces the individual with one of its subtrees. Various other types of crossovers and mutations are presented in (Poli et. al, 2008).

Even if crossover does not affect the mean size from parents to offspring, in combination with selection, after only few generations, its action produces significant modifications of the population, in terms of distribution of tree sizes (Poli et al., 2008). One possible explanation is that the crossover favors the production of pairs of offspring of unequal sizes. As shorter trees are usually less adapted, the mean size of the population is increased during the evolutionary loop, unfortunately without important improvement of the objective values. This phenomenon is called bloat and special strategies are suggested to reduce its influence, as basis for an efficient exploration of the search space. Some bloat-control strategies consist in eliminating the offspring which exceed the imposed maximum size or depth, by replacing them with one of the parents, though this means the complex trees gain greater chances to survive, with negative impact on population diversity. Bloat can also be managed by means of special genetic operators - for instance size fair crossover, which randomly selects the cutting point of a parent and then chooses the cutting point of the second parent such that the size/depth of the offspring could remain in the desired range. A more flexible approach is to use anti-bloat selection, by reformulating the problem as a multiobjective optimization, one objective demanding the minimization of tree complexity order (Poli et al., 2008). Details are given in next section.

The theoretical basis of GP is still incipient, though the field is progressing by intensive empirical research. Some results regarding the convergence of the algorithm are available in (Poli et al., 2008; Abraham&Nedjah & Mourelle, 2005). They exploit the Markov chain theory or customize the general Schema Theorem for the case of GP with proportional fitness and particular types of crossover (one-point, homologous, context preserving or size-fair crossover). In practical numerical implementation, when working on finite populations of individuals for a finite number of generations, GP offers no guarantee that the optimal solution will be obtained, even if such particular configurations are used. These models are probabilistic in nature and only indicate how genetic operators and selection work, regardless of the landscape of the fitness function (Poli et al., 2008). Though, the empirical research targets to obtain convenient results in a reasonable time interval, even through several independent runs of the algorithm.

EVOLVEMENT OF DYNAMIC NONLINEAR MODELS

Applicability of GP-Based Identification

As a universal optimization method, GP can be employed for the design of dynamic models, according to (2), if enough lagged plant inputs and outputs are included in the terminal set:

$$\mathbf{x}(k) = [u_1(k), \ldots, u_1(k - n_u), \ldots, u_m(k), \ldots, u_m(k - n_u),$$
$$y_1(k-1), \ldots, y_1(k - n_y), \ldots, y_n(k-1), \ldots, y_n(k - n_y)].$$
$$(3)$$

In this case, each tree-based individual encodes a potential mathematical description of the dynamic plant (1), formulated in compliance with the Polish form.

The approach can benefit of increased flexibility, due to the simultaneous configuration of model inputs, structure and parameters and the implicit self-adaptation capabilities of the evolutionary approach. The main downside is a higher computational effort, which can lead to increased risk of producing inappropriate solutions in a limited period of time. Therefore, the approach is mainly recommended for off-line identification, if classic analytical approaches or other less costly procedures fail. GP based identification is usually employed when scarce information about the model structure is available, inter-dependencies between plant variables are poorly comprehended and/or high model accuracy is required. In all these situations, the automatic fashion in which GP searches for an optimal model usually conducts to a lower total design time, in comparison with the approaches that work on a single potential model at a time. This makes GP a much more valuable alternative, especially if the application requests the design of numerous models (e.g. diagnosis systems based on observer schemes, identification of many component subsystems). However, the main advantage of GP resides in its capacity of providing the self-organization of the model, while using only a finite data training set.

GP is often criticized for its incapacity of guaranteeing the achievement of the optimal solution. Though, recalling the applications mentioned above as suitable for GP appliance, this criticism needs at least a reformulation, whilst no better alternative is known. Moreover, note that GP does not impose severe working restrictions and accepts

a realistic formulation of the engineering problem (multiple and discontinuous objective functions, different types of decision variables, non-convex, large and disjoint search spaces). So, the user has to decide if a convenient (but not optimal) solution of the real problem is preferred over the optimal solution of an idealistic reformulated problem, which in fact is often expected to behave worse in the real environment.

Practitioners could face difficulties in implementing various GP based algorithms, as the efficiency of the exploration results from the symbiosis of initialization, selection, genetic operators and fitness landscape, yet the interconnections between these mechanisms are still incompletely understood. Moreover, given the complete or partial lack of information relative to the shape and size of optimal tree, some difficulties could appear in determining the quality of the result, especially because the convergence towards the optima point is not guaranteed and the algorithm is stochastic.

The use of GP for symbolic regression and identification is continuously encouraged by the successful results reported in the related literature, which highlight the efficiency of this evolutionary technique in dealing with complex optimizations. Some recent examples could be found in (Beligiannis et al. 2005; Cai et al., 2006; Chang et al. 2005; Feng et al., 2006; Han et al., 2006; Lew et al. 2006; Dolinsky et al., 2007; Kishor, et al., 2007; Poli et al. 2008; Winkler et al., 2008).

Recommended GP Customizations

For a suitable creation of mathematical models, two types of GP customizations could be addressed. The first ones are mandatory, as in fact they establish the connection with the optimization problem to be solved (the configuration of the sets of terminals and functions/operators and the implementation of model evaluation routines). The other ones make GP compatible with the particularities of system identification, mainly by incorporating available problem specific knowledge, in order to improve the exploration capabilities and/or the algorithm's speed in finding an appropriate solution, as well as to increase the usefulness of the resulted model.

A key issue of each GP approach is the use of appropriate primitives. The set of terminals (3) results sufficient if it contains all required plant variables and if sufficiently large n_u and n_y maximum lags are chosen. Even if GP does not compulsorily request a minimally sufficient **x** set, the algorithm is capable to provide a more efficient exploration, if unnecessary terminals are rejected. If the selection of model inputs is solved, n_u and n_y can be determined at a slight supplementary cost, as a result of trial and error experiments.

An appropriate initialization of **O,** in terms of sufficiency and closure properties, implies tailoring the set in accordance to the allowed model structure. Additionally, the structure of **O** should be chosen to reduce the risk of producing numerous combinations of primitives which guarantee type and data consistency, yet are incompliant with the application. Generally, the blind initialization of **O** cannot lead to appropriate GP results. If scarce *a priori* information about the model structure is available, a suitable approach is to employ a structural template which has been proven to provide universal approximation capabilities in terms of continuous, bounded nonlinearities. A straightforward mathematical pattern is, for instance, the NLP (**N**onlinear **L**inear in **P**arameter) formalism. NLP models are NARMA (**N**onlinear **A**uto **R**egressive **M**oving **A**verage) based and consist of linear combinations of nonlinear factors called regressors (Wey, et. al 2004),

shown in Box 1, where x_{ij} denotes a terminal and c_{ij} are real coefficients. In this case, $\mathbf{O} = \{+, *\}$ is minimally sufficient and other supplementary problem dependent functions are obviously unnecessary, as the structural components of the model have to be built solely by adequately grouping the lagged plant variables in conveniently shaped products. Another example could be the evolvement of neural models, based on MLP, RBF (Haykin, 1998) or a hybrid MLP – RBF formalism. **O** can be set as minimally sufficient, by using simple operators/functions $\mathbf{O} = \{+, /, *, \exp\}$, yet this is not the most convenient strategy, as almost all combination of its elements do not implement valid aggregations of neurons. To reduce the risk of producing useless individuals, **O** can be more advantageously filled with problem specific functions of variable arity, able to directly perform the input-output mapping characteristic to the allowed neurons:

$$\mathbf{O} = \{\tanh(\sum_{i=1}^{q} w_i z_i + b)\} \text{ for MLP}, \qquad (5)$$

$$\mathbf{O} = \{\exp\left(-\sum_{i=1}^{q}(c_i - z_i)^2 / (2\sigma^2)\right), \sum_{i=1}^{q}(w_i z_i + b)\}$$
for RBF, $\qquad (6)$

$$\mathbf{O} = \{\tanh(\sum_{i=1}^{q} w_i z_i + b), \exp\left(-\sum_{i=1}^{q}(c_i - z_i)^2 / (2\sigma^2)\right), \sum_{i=1}^{q}(w_i z_i + b)\}$$
for hybrid MLP-RBF, $\qquad (7)$

where z_i denotes a input of the function-type node, w_i, b, c_i, σ are the neural parameters (weights, bias, centers and spread, respectively),

Box 1.

$$\hat{y}(k) = c_0 + \sum_{i=1}^{n} c_i x_i + \sum_{i_1=1}^{n}\sum_{i_2=i_1}^{n} c_{i_1} c_{i_2} x_{i_1} x_{i_2} + \cdots + \sum_{i_1=1}^{n} \cdots \sum_{i_l=i_{l-1}}^{n} c_{i_1} \cdots c_{i_l} x_{i_1} \cdots x_{i_l} \qquad (4)$$

and q denotes the arity of the function. The downside is that all model parameters become parameters of functions and GP has no "legal" access to update their value, therefore the estimation of parameters must be solved by hybridization with other local optimization procedures or by modifying the known GP genetic operators. However, in this case, the initialization procedure and the genetic operators can better exploit the content of **O,** for only producing allowed neural structures, especially if a more natural encoding is adopted, such as directed acyclic graphs.

GP is resourceful in providing various structural configurations of the models (including variable reduction), though its capacity of accurately locating the parameters values is reduced. Therefore, hybridization with local optimization procedures is intensively used (Feng et. al, 2006; Kishor et al., 2007) and obviously, the mathematical models which provide linearity in terms of model parameters are preferred from the numerical implementation standpoint.

Note also that the initialization procedure and the genetic operators should guarantee that only permitted model architectures are generated, by incorporating specific restrictions or corrective actions, as all approaches based on penalizing the fitness of undesired trees lead to significant computational effort waste and reduced exploration capacity.

Evaluation of the model can be done in terms of empirical risk, though the accuracy objective (2) cannot guarantee the achievement of a useful model, on its own. System identification also demands compliance with other multiple quality criteria, such as parsimony, noise reduction ratio, interpretability, etc. Both from application and GP standpoint, special attention has to be paid to parsimony. Due to the bloat phenomenon, GP has the "natural" tendency of producing more and more complex trees, which, in fact, encode overfitted models. Therefore, a more realistic approach is the **m**ultiobjective **o**ptimization (MOO). Usually, one objective addresses to model accuracy (*SSE*

minimization) and another one to parsimony (*CF* minimization):

$$M^* = \arg\min_{M \in I_M}\{SSE_{|_D}(M), CF(M)\},$$

$$SSE_{|_D}(M) = \frac{1}{2N}\sum_{i=1}^{N}(\hat{\mathbf{y}}(k) - \mathbf{y}(k))^T \cdot (\hat{\mathbf{y}}(k) - \mathbf{y}(k))_{|_D},$$
$$CF(M) = |M|. \tag{8}$$

The complexity order of a model, $CF(M)$, could be simply defined as the size or the depth of the corresponding tree, yet refined problem specific formulations exploiting the shape of potential trees and the complexity of the nodes can bring more valuable information.

The two objectives indicated in (8) are conflicting, as they conduct to different optima, when separately approached. The problem leads to a standard multiobjective optimization according to the classification suggested in (Knowles & Corne & Deb, 2008). Therefore, it admits an infinite set of Pareto-optimal solutions, each representing a possible tradeoff between accuracy and parsimony (Deb, 2001). The most straightforward approach is to combine all considered objectives into a single one, by using a vector of weights, one for each evaluation function. The immediate advantage is that a SOO (**S**ingle **O**bjective **O**ptimization) is easier to solve than a MOO one, yet the weight vector, necessary to assign specific priorities to each objective function, is seldom available apriorically. The risk of selecting solutions which are useless from application standpoint results very high, so a more efficient alternative is based on Pareto optimality. The Pareto-optimal front is the non-dominated set of solutions defined over the search space (Deb, 2001):

$$PO = \{M_* \in I_M \,|\, \nexists\, M \in I_M\,,\ M \preceq M_*\}, \tag{9}$$

where, in compliance with (8), M_* dominates M (notation $M \preceq M_*$) in the following cases:

$$SSE(M_*) \leq SSE(M), CF(M_*) < CF(M)$$
$$\text{or } SSE(M_*) < SSE(M), CF(M_*) \leq CF(M)$$
$$(10)$$

Note that the dominance is asymmetric, transitive, non-reflexive and illustrates a partial sorting of individuals, meaning that, for two arbitrary solutions M_1 and M_2, one of the following cases can occur: a) $M_1 \preceq M_2$; b) $M_1 \succeq M_2$; c) no solution dominates the other one.

The MOO algorithms are usually configured based on *a posteriori* articulation between search and decision, which means that the optimization algorithm is aimed at producing a diverse set of solutions, situated close to *PO*, from which the user can afterwards choose an appropriate model, in accordance with the particular requirements of the application. As GP works on a population of models at every generation, the diversity of resulted solutions can be better controlled, even during a single run.

Various evolutionary MOO algorithms are presented in (Arkov et al., 2000; Deb, 2001; Rodriguez-Vasquez et. al, 2004; Gustafson and Vanneschi, 2008; Woldesenbet & Yen, 2009). The Pareto techniques are recommended as the most efficient in managing population diversity (Fleming & Purshouse, 2002; Rodriguez-Vasquez et al, 2004; Coello Coello et al., 2007). Basically, they employ the dominance analysis to asses the quality of competing solutions. Non-elitist approaches work solely on the current population to assign the ranks of the individuals, whilst the elitist methods build an external set of elites, by using the non-dominated solutions produced during the evolutionary loop, which stands as a reference for fitness assignment (Deb, 2001).

When addressing multiobjective formulation of system identification, some particularities need to be understood, as basis for efficient tuning of the MOO algorithm. Firstly, the optimization procedure can benefit from the reduced number of objectives. Secondly, obtaining a simple yet less accurate model is of no use, therefore some Pareto optimal solutions of (8) have no practical utilization (Ferariu & Voicu, 2005; Ferariu & Patelli, 2009a). Thus, the natural formulation of the multiobjective optimization problem should consider different priorities for the two involved objectives (Fonseca & Fleming, 1998; Deb, 2001; Rodriguez-Vasquez et al, 2004). As these priorities are difficult to determine apriorically (Rachmawati, 2009), it is recommended to implement certain mechanisms to dynamically balance the selection pressure imposed by the employed objectives during the evolutionary process. These mechanisms should be aimed at implementing the progressive articulation between identification specific decision and evolutionary search.

Models' Self-Management in GP-Based Identification

Considering the particularities of tree-based individuals' evolvement, GP-based identification could be considered as an autonomic computing technique (Tianfield & Unland, 2004). It starts with a self-configured initial population and, progressively, it enriches the batch of solutions with new offspring generated by means of genetic operators. In fact, GP implements an inductive sub-symbolic learning strategy based on observations, being able to produce, on itself, all examples (individuals) needed for learning. The success of the optimization depends on assuring a balance between exploitation and exploration, namely between self-protection of valuable genetic material and variations allowed in the available batch of solutions. These variations, corroborated with selection, ensure the self-configuration of the models and, within dynamic contexts, the self-healing. Summing up, GP provides the self-management of the population (Tianfield & Unland, 2004), being able to handle large scale optimization problems, which involve numerous decision variables, vast search spaces, etc.

When integrated in larger systems, GP inherently brings the essential mechanisms specific to autonomic computing, namely adaptation and complexity transparent from user's standpoint (Tianfield & Unland, 2004). Usually, GP-based algorithms are employed for system parametric adaptation. In autonomic networking, most applications address to off-line synthesis of protocols, dynamic software self-configuration, adaptive routing and scheduling, etc. (Tianfield & Unland, 2004; Miorandi & Yamamoto & De Pellegrini, 2010).

As the approaches presented in this paper can extract complex dependencies from available data sets, many applications can be imagined, dealing with self-configuration of the models characterizing various compound subsystems or external systems which need to interact with the application. The algorithms are compliant with on-line optimizations only if the adaptation process involves slow and reduced variations of already existing solutions.

Design of Nonlinear Models, Linear in Parameters

NLP was intensively used in GP-based identification. The main benefits result from model parameter wise linearity and the simplicity of the resulted sufficient operators set. NLP provides universal approximation capabilities, yet, in the case of complex nonlinearities, high performances relative to accuracy could lead to a very large number of regressors (Wey et al., 2004; Rodriguez-Vasquez et al. 2004; Kishor, et al., 2007). GP is able to produce diverse combination of regressors of various shapes. Though, many of the initial trees or offspring may feature insignificant terms, with little if any influence on the overall accuracy, which have to be eliminated during the evolutionary process, in order to achieve satisfactory model quality. Another disturbing phenomenon that is likely to occur in GP approaches is compensation, which means that the same end accuracy could be

achieved by replacing an entire combination of regressors within the model structure with a single different regressor that influences the estimated output more significantly.

One possible way of identifying and eliminating unnecessary model terms is to hybridize the evolutionary algorithm with a local OLS (Orthogonally Least Squares) procedure, responsible with computing error ratios for each regressor in the current model, and eliminating the least significant ones (Madar *et al*, 2005; Kishor et al., 2007). The approach is greedy in nature as one nonlinear atom, irrelevant with respect to the containing individual at the current generation, may be just one mutation away from becoming useful, in which case its exclusion from the model would be premature. Furthermore, genetic operators may spoil the effects of OLS by introducing random regressors into the model, therefore the symbiosis between the two algorithm stages must be carefully configured.

MOO approaches can provide a more efficient control on the parsimony of the trees, and, therefore on the rejection of insignificant regressors. (Rodriguez-Vasquez et. al, 2004) suggests MOO algorithms which exploits dominance analysis, considering objectives assigned with same or different priorities. The particular requirements of the identification problem are formalized by setting a goal for each objective direction, therefore the quality of individuals is assessed in terms of the distance to the targeted performances. The ranks are determined by counting the dominating solutions for each tree-encrypted model of the population, and, subsequently, the adjustment of the fitness is carried out by means of niching techniques, which encourage the solitary individuals, as a strategy for diversity preservation. The similarity is measured inside the search space. If the objectives are assigned with different priorities, the procedure is applied in sequel, starting with the highest priority. Fitness computation is solved in Deb (2001), by extracting several fronts of different orders from the population. The kth

front, FP_k, includes the nondominated solutions of $P(t) \setminus \bigcup_{i=1}^{k-1} FP_i$, with $k = 1, 2, \ldots$ Naturally, all individuals of FP_i get higher fitness than those placed in fronts FP_j, with $j > i$. To provide better control in spreading the population over the Pareto front, the niching techniques are separately applied inside each front, by computing the distance between the individuals in the objective space.

It is worth mentioning that Pareto methods could be successful only if high diversity of the genetic material is maintained during the evolutionary process. To suit this purpose, some approaches target the production of well adapted, yet diverse offspring, by means of customized genetic operators, such as gene transposition (Chan et al., 2008) or enhanced crossover based on parents' similarity analysis (Gustafson & Vanneschi, 2008). Another alternative consists in adjusting the selection pressure in favor of certain solutions: the knees of the first order front (Rachmawati & Srinivasan, 2009), the offspring which are significantly different than their parents (Chen & Low & Yang, 2009), the solitary individuals of each depicted Pareto front (Deb, 2001).

For getting more insight about GP-based identification, this chapter presents two MOO approaches devoted to NLP models configuration. The algorithms comprise two main types of enhancements, aimed at providing an improved exploration capability and convergence speed, whilst featuring flexibility in generating the potential solutions, in terms of the MOO approach. Some customizations exploit the particular structure of NLP models in order to supply GP with enhanced initialization procedure, genetic operators and parameters computation. Other improvements refer to advanced non-elitist and elitist MOO techniques meant to perform a more flexible adaptation of objectives priorities, in accordance with system identification particularities. Finally, the performances of the approaches are comparatively illustrated on two applications.

NLP Compliant Customizations

The specific form of NLP models (4) permits several advantageous configurations of standard GP. Basically, the parameter wise linearity allows the hybridization with QR decomposition, as basis for providing a faster computation of models parameters. Also, the content of the operators set and the particular shape of regressors enable some customizations of genetic operators, implemented to increase the chance of producing compact and well adapted offspring.

For each tree-encrypted model, QR is employed to solve an algebraic system of linear equations:

$$\begin{bmatrix} \hat{y}_p(1) \\ \hat{y}_p(2) \\ \vdots \\ \hat{y}_N(k) \end{bmatrix} = \mathbf{F}_p \cdot \mathbf{c}_p, \text{ with}$$

$$\mathbf{F}_p = \begin{bmatrix} F_{1p}(\mathbf{x}(1)) & .. & \cdots & F_{rp}(\mathbf{x}(1)) \\ F_{1p}(\mathbf{x}(2)) & .. & \cdots & F_{rp}(\mathbf{x}(2)) \\ \vdots & \vdots & & \vdots \\ F_{1p}(\mathbf{x}(N)) & .. & \cdots & F_{rp}(\mathbf{x}(N)) \end{bmatrix} \text{ and}$$

$$\mathbf{c}_p = \begin{bmatrix} c_{1p} \\ c_{2p} \\ \vdots \\ c_{rp} \end{bmatrix}. \tag{11}$$

Here, F_{ij} are the model regressors, consisting in nonlinear combinations of the terminals, $\mathbf{F}_p$ is the regressor matrix associated to the pth estimated system output, $\mathbf{c}_p$ stands for the parameter vector and N is the length of the training data set, $\mathbf{D}$. As $\mathbf{c}_p$ is provided by QR decomposition, GP's responsibility is to configure $\mathbf{F}_p$, which comprises model structure selection and variable reduction.

In order to assure good search space coverage, as well as to provide the evolutionary algorithm with a rich initial batch of genetic material, the authors build the trees in the initial population based on the set of rules listed in the following (Patelli and Ferariu, 2009a):

1. All elements of the terminal set (3) are included in each tree, while making sure that every terminal node is unique within the containing individual. This way, each tree in the initial population encrypts a different possible combination of all available terminals, further variable reduction and lags configuration being solely decided by evolutionary techniques.

2. Each operator node is forced to accept two children and the terminal selection probability is slightly higher than the operator selection one. This permits to control the chromosome dimension by avoiding the generation of degenerated (hierarchical lists) or unbalanced trees.

3. After all terminal nodes have been inserted in available leaves, the free slots are filled with constants.

The trees that result by means of recursive combinations of primitives (Figure 2) are not necessarily compliant with (4) and (11), meaning that QR decomposition cannot be directly applied for all potential individuals. The transformation of trees from a raw form to a regressive based form (3) makes use of the distributive property of addition over multiplication (Patelli & Ferariu, 2009). In fact, the transformation procedure consists in "lifting" all "+" nodes which are successors of "*" nodes, so that the resulting individual is NLP compliant, and in the same time, mathematically equivalent with the original chromosome. The approach is illustrated in Figure 2, for a single input, single output system model.

An alternate way to deal with raw to regressive adaptation of the trees in the initial population is to replace all badly positioned "+" nodes with "*" nodes (Madar et al., 2005). In spite of its simplicity, this approach may generate large regressors, making it difficult to control individual complexity. More importantly, the method does not guarantee mathematical equivalence between the original tree and the one in the regressive form, which may affect the exploration capability of the algorithm.

The production of offspring is the key stage of any evolutionary technique. A necessary condition for algorithm convergence is to achieve children trees superior to their parents in terms of the considered objectives (Hasegawa & Iba, 2008). The classic version of the genetic operators cannot guarantee this requirement. Therefore, it is advisable to guide the cut point search process, as the computational cost of supplementary preprocessing is lower than the computational cost of generating poorly adapted offspring.

Figure 2. Transformation from raw to regressive form

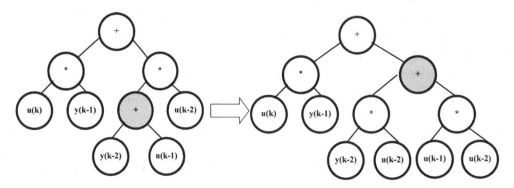

Especially towards the end of the evolutionary loop more individuals get closer to the end solutions, so they start featuring similar regressors, which have survived over the generations in several trees. Ergo, in most likelihood, these nonlinear atoms are useful, with a positive influence relative to the overall performances of the containing chromosomes, and have to be protected from division by crossover (Walker et al., 2008). To do so, the genetic operator is changed to spot similar regressors and exclude all their component nodes from the potential cut point list (Patelli & Ferariu, 2009). In consequence, all the inner nodes of the similar regressor will be eliminated from the accepted cut point set, for both trees, along with the nodes from the regressor root to the tree root. Besides protecting similar useful regressors, the tree preprocessing mechanism described above is aimed at preventing the children from featuring the same regressor more than one time. This situation would lead to singular regression matrices, causing difficulties in computing the optimum set of parameters. The proposed enhanced crossover is exemplified in Figure 3 and Figure 4. Here, the parents (Figure 3) contain one similar regressor (which includes the nodes 5, 6 and 7 in the left tree, and the nodes 4, 5 and 6 in the right tree). Therefore, the eligible cut points remain the following ones: 2 and 4 for the tree on the left, and 3,

7, 8 and 9 for the tree on the right. Assuming that the parents were cut in nodes 4 and 3, respectively, the children resulted after sub-trees' swapping are illustrated in Figure 4.

The other genetic operator, node replacement mutation, is customized to target not only terminal names, but also their exponents (Patelli & Ferariu, 2009). The reason behind that is the avoidance of the compensation phenomenon, which occurs whenever the same model accuracy could be achieved on a less complex structure. Another benefit brought on by enhanced mutation has to do with controlling tree size by encouraging the generation of more compact individuals, in which an entire subtree may be replaced by a single terminal node to a higher exponent.

Techniques for Handling Multiobjective Optimization of Dynamic Models

The multiobjective optimization problem (8) is revisited, by using a mathematical formulation of *CF* tailored to comply with the NLP model (Patelli & Ferariu, 2010):

$$CF(M) = r + \frac{t}{n_u + n_y + 1} - \sum_{q=1}^{r} \lg |\mathbf{c}_p|, \quad (12)$$

Figure 3. Parents with similar regressors

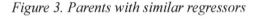
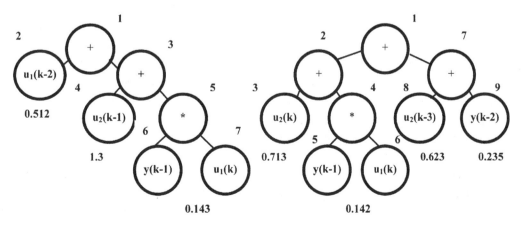

Figure 4. Children generated by enhanced crossover applied on parents presented in Figure 3

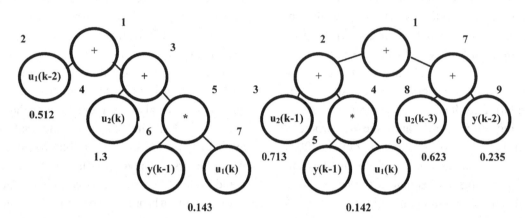

where r stands for the number of regressors within M, t represents the total number of terminals to be found in the tree's structure, n_u and n_y are the input and output lags respectively, and $\mathbf{c}_p$ denote the parameters of M. The second term in (12) represents the ratio between the number of terminals within the model and the total number of terminals in set $\mathbf{x}$, and is meant to penalize the individuals that feature large regressors. Lastly, the third term is aimed at favoring the chromosomes containing relevant regressors, a quality that is evaluated by investigating the values of their associated parameters. To avoid negative values of CF, the training data has been scaled to fit the interval [-1 1].

To dynamically tune the selection pressure imposed by accuracy and complexity criteria, a non-elitist MOO algorithm is proposed. **P**opulation **C**lustering and **A**daptive **M**igration (PCAM) divides the initial population in two "islands" (Ferariu & Patelli, 2009a) which evolve quasi independently. The trees on the first island are solely evaluated relative to *SSE*, as basis for enforcing models' accuracy improvement. The individuals of the second island undergo a conjoint MOO assessment procedure. A preliminary clustering mechanism is employed to split this subpopulation in two groups (Figure 5), as basis for a progressive increasing of the selection pressure imposed by

SSE objective. Therefore, the first group includes the best adapted individuals relative to (8). These models are characterized by moderately low complexity, so their fitness values are computed merely according to *SSE*, whilst the individuals in the second group receive a selection probability via dominance analysis (Ferariu & Patelli, 2009a). The fitness values are linearly scaled so that the trees in the first group will stand a better chance to reproduce than the ones in the second group.

Thresholds g_1 and g_2, that represent the boundaries in between the two groups, are dynamically computed relative to the average performances and the diversity achieved inside the MOO based subpopulation. If the individuals have quite similar performances, meaning the variance of Euclidian distances computed in the objective space between all the trees of MOO subpopulation results low, then g_1 and g_2 correspond to the average of *SSE* and *CF* values, respectively. In the opposite case, when the trees are scattered throughout the objectives space, g_1 is assigned with the mean *SSE* value relative to the two individuals furthest apart, while g_2 is computed in a similar way, considering the *CF* objective. This permits the handling of batches of individuals spread over the entire search space, expected at the beginning of the evolutionary loop, as well as those subpopulations containing some outlier individuals,

Figure 5. Second island population clustering in the objectives space

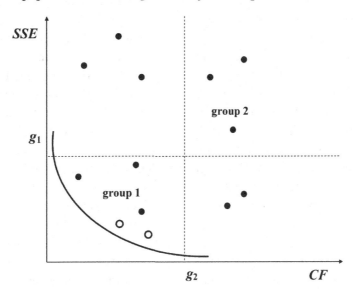

corresponding to undesired solutions (accidentally generated) and/or to non-dominated solutions (with significantly better performances than the other models of the island).

Once every *noMigr* generations, the two islands exchange genetic material according to a migration process with adaptive thresholds. Therefore, simple models are injected in the first subpopulation, targeting their accuracy improvement. Additionally, more and more accurate models are received by MOO-based subpopulation. This translates to g_1 reduction, leading higher priority of *SSE*. Three preset migration rates are considered, as follows: rate1 = 10%, rate2 = 20% and rate3 = 25%. If the average complexity of the SOO population is below that of the MOO population, then many of the simple and accurate trees evolved solely via *SSE* have a good chance of being included in the first group (Figure 5) of the MOO island and the second subpopulation cannot significantly help the first subpopulation with models of low complexity. Therefore, the maximum allowed percentage (25%) of SOO trees will migrate to the MOO population, whilst only 10% will be sent the opposite direction. The second possibility is that of an average SOO complexity comparable to the MOO one, leading to a 20% migration rate in both directions. Finally, if the SOO trees are substantially more complex than the MOO ones, then their chances of being included in group 1 (Figure 5) and of populating the interest region of the first order front are slim. Only 10% of the SOO trees will migrate towards the MOO population, while 25% simpler, yet less accurate trees will be sent the opposite direction (Ferariu & Patelli, 2009b).

Although PCAM algorithm favors the individuals of the first order Pareto front by awarding them with higher fitness values, their participation in the recombination process is not guaranteed, due to the stochastic nature of the selection process. A possible way of counteracting this effect, and of consequently increasing the algorithm's speed, is to store all nondominated individuals throughout the entire algorithm, in a separate archive called elite set, which gets updated at each generation.

As far as elite fitness assignment is considered, an enhanced dominance analysis-based procedure is employed. In order to award solitary trees with higher fitness values than the ones in clusters, pre-determined, fixed cluster radius could be used (Deb, 2001). Instead, the Dynamic Niching and

Elite Clustering (DNEC) algorithm (Patelli & Ferariu, 2010) suggests the dynamic computation of this parameter before each new elite insertion. By considering the radius of a niche equal to the average Euclidian distance in between all elites in the set, after the current insertion, the resulting fitness values will reflect the "remoteness" of a tree much more accurately than in the case of static crowding. The goal of dynamically increasing the weight of the accuracy criterion is also pursued in the case of elitist approaches. To fit that end, the elite set is divided in two separate groups, the boundaries being dictated by the average performances of the individuals in the set. In the objectives space (Figure 5), the intersection of the markers, corresponding to the average *SSE* and *CF* values respectively, defines a point that can be associated to a "dummy individual". Should the two objectives axes be translated so that the origin of the new coordinates system would be the dummy individual, four quadrants could be visualized. All elites situated in the lower left one are closer to the interest zone of the Pareto front and their fitness values will be raised by an amount equal to the mean Euclidian distance between all of them and the dummy individual. The authors have suggested this fitness augmentation technique in order to progressively increase the selection pressure in favor of the individuals characterized by high accuracy, which feature a reduced complexity order. The rest of the elites (1 and 4 in Figure 6) are either too complex or too inaccurate to be of any practical use, therefore their fitness values will remain unaltered.

Experimental Results

The above described algorithms (PCAM and DNEC) were implemented by the authors in C/C++, as this programming language offers an increased flexibility in managing the tree-encrypted models. The experiments started with an academic test case involving a five input, one output, linear dead time system, which was devoted to illustrate algorithms' capacity of automatically configuring model traits unavailable pre-design (like time delay), as well as their efficiency in dealing with a multi input system. The second test consists in the identification of a real industrial nonlinear system and was meant to illustrate the generalization capabilities of the generated models, and the gain in efficiency (speed and memory consumption) brought by the implemented enhancements.

A linear multivariable system with time delay was chosen to test the two suggested evolutionary algorithms on. Its discrete mathematical model is indicated (13 in Box 2), in terms of the sampling period $T_s = 0.05$.

Knowing the desired solution, the generated models are easy to be compared. Additionally, the test case can reveal certain aspects difficult to isolate and analyze when dealing with industrial, complex plants. Note that system (13) admits three poles placed near the boundary of BIBO stability unit circle, two of them being complex. Moreover, a non-minimum phase transfer is provided from inputs u_1, u_2, u_3 and u_5. As the dead time is not apriorically known, the minimally sufficient set of terminals contains 118 elements,

Box 2.

$$y(k) = 0.080u_1(k-21) - 0.185u_1(k-22) + 0.103u_1(k-23) + 0.138u_2(k-21) - 0.278u_2(k-22) + 0.138u_2(k-23)$$
$$- 0.046u_3(k-21) + 0.092u_3(k-22) - 0.046u_3(k-23) + 0.116u_4(k-21) - 0.184u_4(k-22) + 0.070u_4(k-23)$$
$$+ 0.132u_5(k-21) - 0.277u_5(k-22) + 0.144u_5(k-23) + 2.837y(k-1) - 2.699y(k-2) + 0.860y(k-3)$$

$$(13)$$

Figure 6. Elite clustering in objectives space

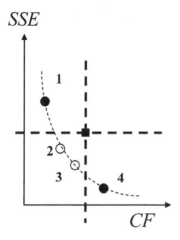

PCAM and DNEC results could be compared against. The resulted model, shown in Box 3, features a Mean Relative Error (MRE) of 1% over the validation data set, yet it contains several "alien" terms, corresponding to the dead time interval, as CMOO was not successful in filtering them out, thus making it necessary to simplify the model post design. Note that *MRE* was computed according to

$$MRE(M) = \frac{1}{N} \sum_{i=1}^{N} \left| \frac{\hat{y}(k) - y(k)}{y(k)} \right|,$$

with $y(k), \hat{y}(k) \in \Re$.

leading to numerous input combinations which must be rejected by GP. The training data set **D** was built considering pulses of different magnitudes and widths, applied on all system inputs, subject to T_s. For validation, the step response (Figure 7) was considered. A Classic **M**ulti **O**bjective **O**ptimization (CMOO) algorithm (which does not employ any of the above mentioned enhancements) was firstly used to obtain a model that

As PCAM and DNEC feature an enhanced complexity objective formulation (12), as well as upgraded genetic operators that, among other effects, help control model parsimony, the models they generated do not feature any extraneous regressors, while achieving a *MRE* of 0.5% over the validation data set. Due to the simplicity of the targeted system, the two models are very similar, therefore only the PCAM generated one is listed, as in Box 4.

Box 3.

$$
\begin{aligned}
y(k) = &\, 0.079u_1(k-21) - 0.178u_1(k-22) + 0.123u_1(k-23) + 0.238u_2(k-21) - 0.275u_2(k-22) + 0.135u_2(k-23) \\
&- 0.050u_3(k-21) + 0.102u_3(k-22) - 0.038u_3(k-23) + 0.110u_4(k-21) - 0.186u_4(k-22) + 0.056u_4(k-23) \\
&+ 0.132u_5(k-21) - 0.279u_5(k-22) + 0.147u_5(k-23) + 2.835y(k-1) - 2.701y(k-2) + 0.857y(k-3) \\
&+ 0.000u_1(k-17) + 0.000u_2(k-5) - 0.003u_5(k-19)
\end{aligned}
$$

(14)

Box 4.

$$
\begin{aligned}
y(k) = &\, 0.085u_1(k-21) - 0.179u_1(k-22) + 0.099u_1(k-23) + 0.138u_2(k-21) - 0.270u_2(k-22) + 0.141u_2(k-23) \\
&- 0.045u_3(k-21) + 0.088u_3(k-22) - 0.043u_3(k-23) + 0.121u_4(k-21) - 0.181u_4(k-22) + 0.065u_4(k-23) \\
&+ 0.130u_5(k-21) - 0.278u_5(k-22) + 0.140u_5(k-23) + 2.830y(k-1) - 2.685y(k-2) + 0.859y(k-3)
\end{aligned}
$$

(15)

Figure 7. Validation data set used for the identification of system (13)

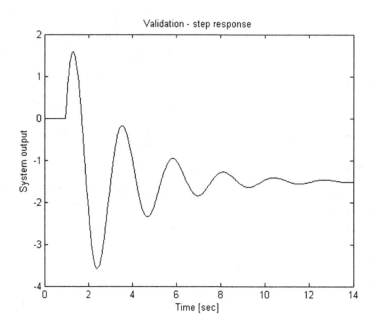

The two proposed approaches are therefore successful in configuring model traits unavailable apriorically, such as dead time and optimum model complexity, while also showing their capacity of generating high quality models even when dealing with multi input systems.

A more refined comparison between the PCAM and DNEC was conducted in the framework of a real industrial plant, namely the **ST**eam **S**ubsystem (STS) of the evaporation station within the sugar factory of Lublin, Poland. Note that the evaporation station has to reduce the content of water of the sucrose juice which passes in sequel through its sections. STS is a one input (steam temperature), one output (steam pressure) nonlinear system (Marcu et al., 2000). No analytical model of STS is available for an adequate level of accuracy. The training data set includes 290 measurements collected during a production shift. It illustrates the maximum possible excitation of the process achievable in normal plant exploitation. **D** was filtered with a low - pass 4th order Butterworth system, and all missing and uncertain values have been replaced by means of polynomial interpola-

tion. To provide a suitable verification of the model generalization capability, the validation data set **D_v** contains measurements acquired in a different month of plant operation (Marcu et al., 2000).

The performances of the suggested approaches were investigated for different sets of algorithm parameters, as listed in Table 1. For each configuration, the most accurate model obtained in the final batch of solutions generated by means of CMOO, PCAM and DNEC are analyzed in Table 2. Here, the accuracy performances of the models are illustrated by *MRE* computed over the training data set.

The first trials (R1→R6) correspond to a minimally sufficient set of terminals or a set of terminals with few supplementary elements. All algorithms lead to quite similar numbers of regressors, though the selected regressors are much simpler in the case of PCAM and DNEC, which make use of enhanced genetic operators and specific MOO techniques for tuning the selection pressure imposed by *CF* during the evolutionary loop. As the maximum allowed lags increase (R7→R9), the individuals become more complex,

Table 1. Testing configurations for CMOO, PCAM, DNEC

Run	Lags	Population size [nr. of individuals]
R1	$n_y = 2\ n_u = 2$	75
R2	$n_y = 2\ n_u = 2$	150
R3	$n_y = 2\ n_u = 2$	500
R4	$n_y = 4\ n_u = 5$	75
R5	$n_y = 4\ n_u = 5$	150
R6	$n_y = 4\ n_u = 5$	500
R7	$n_y = 10\ n_u = 11$	75
R8	$n_y = 10\ n_u = 11$	150
R9	$n_y = 10\ n_u = 11$	500

due to the tree generation process that includes all available terminals in each initial individual. Note that in these cases the set of terminal contains many alien terms, therefore the use of numerous populations and large number of generations is advisable, for enforcing the exploration within the resulted large search space. However, the algorithm features nonlinear behavior, so there is no guarantee of improving the performances of the selected model, by solely raising the number of individuals/generations. The increased tree size

is difficult to control by the CMOO algorithm, therefore the accuracy drops and the number of involved regressors becomes unacceptably high. The enhanced genetic operators allow the PCAM approach to generate trees with a satisfactory *SSE* value, regardless of the amount of redundant genetic material introduced by the extraneous lags. Upgraded crossover maintains an acceptable exploration capacity, while enhanced mutation avoids compensation and encourages the production of models with a low number of fairly simple

Table 2. The steam subsystem - Comparative analysis of CMOO, PCAM and DNEC performances. Here gen indicates the generation when the model was firstly found, r denotes the number of regressors, t the number of terminals in the selected model and MRE is computed according to **D**. *PCAM was run with noMigr = 10.*

Run	CMOO				PCAM				DNEC			
	MRE	*r*	*t*	*gen*	*MRE*	*R*	*t*	*Gen*	*MRE*	*r*	*t*	*gen*
R1	1.41%	5	26	76	1.31%	5	10	50	1.29%	6	9	25
R2	1.39%	7	35	75	1.29%	6	9	45	1.32%	7	11	20
R3	1.65%	6	30	80	1.32%	4	11	55	1.43%	5	12	25
R4	1.73%	9	45	95	1.35%	7	8	60	1.41%	5	10	27
R5	2.05%	12	50	100	1.43%	4	12	56	1.39%	8	13	30
R6	1.35%	13	49	97	1.39%	6	10	46	1.29%	7	12	29
R7	3.45%	17	121	100	1.34%	5	8	57	1.45%	8	9	39
R8	3.86%	21	85	100	1.41%	7	9	62	1.43%	9	10	30
R9	2.56%	19	56	100	1.45%	5	9	49	1.39%	7	10	27

Table 3. Migration interval calibration

noMigr	10	10	10	3	25
g_1	M	M	M	M	m
g_2	M	1.5m	2m	2m	2m
SSE	75.33%	2.55%	1.33%	1.32%	2.85%
R	1	3	7	13	6
Gen	5	40	50	53	61

regressors (each containing a reasonable number of terminals). The DNEC alternative generates models of similar performances relative to the ones produced by PCAM, yet, due to its elitist nature, it can find appropriate models at earlier generations.

The boundaries used to delimit the two groups in the context of population clustering, namely g_1 and g_2 (Figure 5), have a great influence on the PCAM performances. If complexity boundary g_2 is computed as the mean CF values of the individuals, the population will quickly be taken over by trees with only one regressor, leading to the production of unacceptable models (Table 3). Additionally, if migration takes place too often, the algorithm will produce a model much like the one generated by a single objective procedure, as the accuracy criterion is emphasized excessively. On the contrary, if migration is too rare, the final front of non-dominated solutions is similar to the one generated by CMOO, as the selection pressure in favor of the individuals situated on or close to the interest zone is not sufficiently increased.

The DNEC algorithm has an increased ability in selecting simpler individuals, with a better expected generalization capability, due to the fact it stores, in a separate archive, valuable and diverse elites obtained during the entire evolutionary process. This behavior is revealed in Figure 8. The elites chosen by DNEC are generally characterized by smaller CF values than the models belonging to the first group of PCAM's final population. DNEC was also able to preserve a higher variety between its best solutions, with

important benefits on algorithm exploration capacity. However, the best individuals produced by PCAM are not dominated by these elites, all featuring very good accuracy. Additionally, note that the diversity of PCAM's population also results from the individuals belonging to its second group. The nondominated individuals contained by the final CMOO population feature worse SSE and CF values, therefore, for preserving increased visibility, they were not drawn in Figure 8.

As basis for extensive comparison (Table 4, Figure 9 and 10), other nonlinear models were designed using the same training data set and $n_u = n_y = 2$, as indicated in the following. Two of them correspond to homogeneous feed-forward full connected neural networks. The neural architectures were tuned by means of trial and error, assuming a single hidden layer with maximum 20 neurons. The selected **MultiLayer Perceptron** (MLP) has 5 hidden neurons characterized by hyperbolic tangent activation functions. It was trained for 6000 epochs by means of Levenberg-Marquardt procedure. The neural network with **Radial Basis Functions** (RBF) includes 18 Gaussian neurons, iteratively added by the constructive design algorithm. Lastly, the maximal NLP considers all possible regressors generated with $t = 1$ and $t = 2$, for $n_u = n_y = 2$. Being an overfitted model, it provides an excellent approximation on the training data set, but inappropriate behavior on **D_v**. Figures 9 and 10 show that PCAM and DNEC models (generated with a population of 50 individuals, using $n_u = n_y = 2$) are character-

Figure 8. Comparison between the best individuals provided at the end of the evolutionary loop by DNEC and PCAM

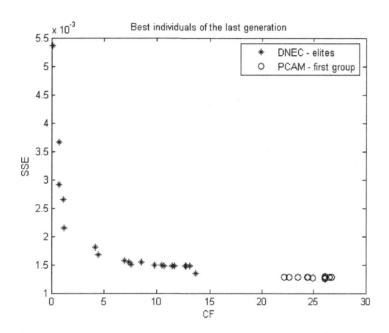

ized by good generalization capabilities, being able to provide accurate approximation on the validation data set. For visibility reasons, the output of the maximal NLP is not included in the comparative plot and the performances of PCAM and DNEC are separately drawn.

In the case of PCAM model, supplementary validation tests were carried out in terms of whiteness and independence residual based analysis. Figure 10 illustrates the autocorrelation of the residue, as well as the cross-correlation computed between the residue and system input, relative to **D_v**. All lagged samples are placed within the region of 99% confidence (marked with dotted line), so one can expect that the model has captured the relevant characteristics of the input-output mapping.

Table 4. Approximation provided by the selected models on the training and the validation data sets. Here, SSE_r corresponds to non-scaled data sets.

Method/model	Training	Validation
	SSE_r	SSE_r
CMOO	1.26	5.1
PCAM	1.19	4.05
DNEC	1.19	3.73
MLP	1.33	5.70
RBF	0.29	4.20
Maximal NLP	≈ 0	$9.73 * 10^{13}$

Figure 9. Approximation provided on validation data set – DNEC compared with MLP and RBF

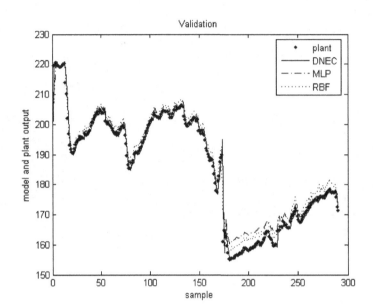

FUTURE RESEARCH DIRECTIONS

GP represents a viable alternative in system identification, however the field is still open to intensive further research. Firstly, the GP standard loop needs improved techniques to make it more efficient in exploring new areas of the search space and in exploiting all valuable structural components which are already encoded in the current batch of individuals. On the one side, this means improvements of inner GP techniques (such as, encoding, genetic operators, selection, initialization), as well as extensive analysis of their symbiosis, by highlighting the effects produced on population diversity, algorithm convergence, magnitude of bloat. Other interesting research topics are related to co-operative evolution, meant to heighten GP adaptability and robustness, and distributed computing, which can increase GP applicability in real-time applications. On the other side, one needs higher adaptability in solving various types of identification problems, by means of the same GP framework. This involves increased flexibility in coping with multiple structural templates, whilst exploiting the characteristics of each particular one.

Self organization of the models seems to be more efficient if approached from a multiobjective optimization perspective, though advanced algorithms tailored to fit the requirements of industrial applications are still needed. Also, in order to allow a refined formulation of the engineering applications, the possibility of operating with numerous objectives demands more rigorous investigations.

GP based algorithms need to gain in scalability, in terms of the capacity of working on large amount of data describing the behavior of complex nonlinear industrial systems with a high number of inputs and outputs.

The chances of GP breaking through the barrier of limited academic research may consist in extended empirical investigations, as well in a heightened theoretical background.

Figure 10. Approximation provided on validation data set – PCAM compared with MLP and RBF

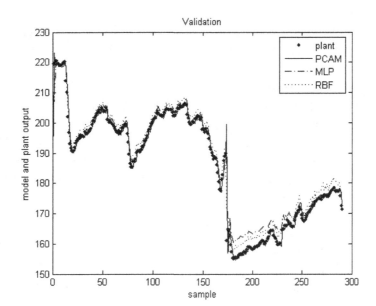

CONCLUSION

In the context of complex identification problems, genetic programming brings some important benefits which basically refer to its inherent capacity of self-organizing the models, without restrictive working hypothesis. This involves compliance with discontinuous, nonlinear objective func-

tions, as well as with large, high dimensional, non-convex search spaces, which are targeted by industrial applications when no rich a priori knowledge about the inner workings of the system is available and the measurements are acquired in a noisy environment. Additionally, GP aims to simultaneously solve variable inputs reduction, model selection and parameters estimation, by

Figure 11. Residual analysis for PCAM model

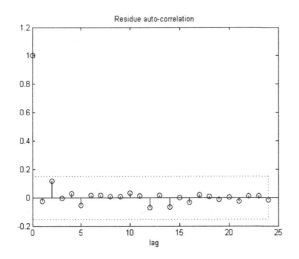
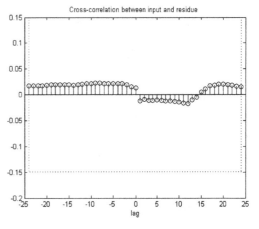

evolving a collection of potential models encrypted as tree-based individuals. This leads to flexibility in generating the competing solutions, as well as to increased exploration capabilities and robustness.

Even if GP-based approaches are intuitive and seem to be simple, they consist in complex interdependencies between encoding, offspring production and selection. Therefore a careful design is required to provide satisfactory results, especially because the theoretical background is not exhaustive. The chapter outlines several recommendations which can be helpful for the design of GP-based identification algorithms. Attention is paid to configurations required by the standard GP loop for approaching the optimization of model accuracy, as well as to enhancements of GP which better exploit the particularities of system identification. In that context, the discussion focuses on the multiobjective optimization of the models, carried out in terms of accuracy and parsimony, for dealing with overfitting and bloat. Pareto techniques based on efficient exploitation of dominance analysis results are presented. They provide increased capacity in describing the shape of the Pareto-optimal front, by preserving the diversity of non-dominated solutions included into the population.

The design methodology is revealed on two multiobjective algorithms – the non-elitist PCAM and the elitist DNEC, which were suggested by the authors in order to provide a valuable gradual combination between the evolutionary search and problem specific decision, by means of adapting the priorities of the involved objectives. Both approaches are applied in the framework of non-linear linear in parameters formalism. They benefit from several GP customizations compliant with NLP models, which consist in enhanced genetic operators and hybridization with QR decomposition. As shown by the experimental trials, PCAM and DNEC are able to select simple and accurate models, without requiring rich preliminary information about the system.

Many applications indicate successful employment of GP based approaches in various engineering applications, though this field still needs further empirical and theoretical investigations.

REFERENCES

Affenzeller, M., Winker, S., Wagner, S., & Beham, A. (2009). *Genetic algorithms and genetic programming – Modern concepts and practical application* (pp. 157–207). Boca Raton, FL: CRC Press. doi:10.1201/9781420011326.ch9

Arkov, V., Evans, C., Fleming, P. J., Hill, V., Norton, J. P., & Pratt, I. (2000). System identification strategies applied to aircraft gas turbine engines. *Annual Reviews in Control, 24*(1), 68–81. doi:10.1016/S1367-5788(00)00004-3

Bäck, T. (1996). *Evolutionary algorithms in theory and practice* (pp. 163–193). New York, NY: Oxford University Press.

Bäck, T., Fogel, D., & Michalewicz, Z. (2000). *Evolutionary computation – Advanced algorithms and operators* (2nd ed., pp. 59–102). Bristol, UK: Institute of Physics Publishing. doi:10.1887/0750306653

Beligiannis, G. N., Skarlas, L. V., Likothanassis, S. D., & Perdikouri, K. G. (2005). Nonlinear model structure identification of complex biomedical data using a genetic-programming-based technique. *IEEE Transactions on Instrumentation and Measurement, 54*(6), 2184–2190. doi:10.1109/TIM.2005.858573

Brameier, M., & Banzhaf, W. (2007). *Linear genetic programming* (pp. 1–191). New York, NY: Springer.

Cai, W., Pacheco-Vega, A., Sen, M., & Yang, K. T. (2006). Heat transfer correlations by symbolic regression. *International Journal of Heat and Mass Transfer, 49*(23-24), 4352–4359. doi:10.1016/j.ijheatmasstransfer.2006.04.029

Chan, T. M., Man, K. F., Kwong, S., & Tang, K. S. (2008). Jumping gene paradigm for evolutionary multiobjective optimisation. *IEEE Transactions on Evolutionary Computation, 12*(2), 143–159. doi:10.1109/TEVC.2007.895269

Chang, Y. S., Park, K. S., & Kim, B. Y. (2005). Nonlinear model for ECG R-R interval variation using genetic programming approach. *Future Generation Computer Systems, 21*(7), 1117–1123. doi:10.1016/j.future.2004.03.011

Chen, G., Low, C. P., & Yang, Z. (2009). Preserving and exploiting genetic diversity in evolutionary programming algorithms. *IEEE Transactions on Evolutionary Computation, 13*(3), 61–673. doi:10.1109/TEVC.2008.2011742

Coello Coello, C. A., Lamont, G. B., & Van Veldhuizen, D. A. (2007). *Evolutionary algorithms for solving multi-objective problems* (2nd ed., pp. 50–150). New York, NY: Springer.

Deb, K. (2001). *Multi - objective optimization using evolutionary algorithms* (pp. 1–150). Chichester, UK: John Wiley & Sons.

Dolinsky, J. U., Jenkinson, I. D., & Colquhoun, G. J. (2007). Application of genetic programming to the calibration of industrial robots. *Computers in Industry, 58*(3), 255–264. doi:10.1016/j.compind.2006.06.003

Feng, X.-T., Chen, B.-R., Yang, C., Zhou, H., & Ding, X. (2006). Identification of visco-elastic models for rocks using genetic programming coupled with the modified particle swarm optimization algorithm. *International Journal of Rock Mechanics and Mining Sciences, 43*(5), 789–801. doi:10.1016/j.ijrmms.2005.12.010

Ferariu, L., & Patelli, A. (2009a). Multiobjective genetic programming for nonlinear systems identification. In Kolehmainen, M., Toivanen, P., & Beliczynski, B. (Eds.), *Adaptive natural computing algorithms: Lecture Notes in Computer Science 5495* (pp. 233–242). Springer. doi:10.1007/978-3-642-04921-7_24

Ferariu, L., & Patelli, A. (2009b). Migration-based multiobjective genetic programming for nonlinear system identification. *Proc. of 5th International Symposium on Applied Computational Intelligence and Informatics SACI 2009,* Timisoara, Romania.

Ferariu, L., & Voicu, M. (2005). Nonlinear system identification based on evolutionary dynamic neural networks with hybrid structure. *Proc. of IFAC Congress,* Praga, Czech Republic.

Fleming, P. J., & Purshouse, R. C. (2002). Evolutionary algorithms in control systems engineering: A survey. *Control Engineering Practice, 10,* 1223–1241. doi:10.1016/S0967-0661(02)00081-3

Fletcher, R. (1980). *Practical methods of optimization* (pp. 1–70). Chichester, UK: John Wiley & Sons.

Fonseca, C. M., & Fleming P. J. (1998). Multiobjective optimization and multiple constraint handling with evolutionary algorithms – Part I: A unified formulation. *IEEE Transactions on Systems, MAN, and Cybernetics – Part A, 28*(1), 26–37.

Globerson, A., & Tishby, N. (2003). Sufficient dimensionality reduction. *Journal of Machine Learning Research, 3,* 1307–1331.

Gustafson, S., & Vanneschi, L. (2008). Crossover-based tree distance in genetic programming. *IEEE Transactions on Evolutionary Computation, 12*(4), 506–524. doi:10.1109/TEVC.2008.915993

Guyon, I., Gunn, S., Nikravesh, M., & Zadeh, L. A. (Eds.). (2006). *Feature extraction- Foundation and applications* (pp. 1–162). Netherlands: Springer.

Han, P., Zhou, S., & Wang, D. (2006). A multiobjective genetic programming/ NARMAX approach to chaotic systems identification. *Proc. The Sixth World Congress on Intelligent Control and Automation, WCICA 2006: Vol. 1,* (pp. 1735-17390).

Hasegawa, Y., & Iba, H. (2008). A Bayesian network approach to program generation. *IEEE Transactions on Evolutionary Computation, 12*(6), 750–764. doi:10.1109/TEVC.2008.915999

Haykin, S. (1998). *Neural networks - A comprehensive foundation* (pp. 1–250). Upper Saddle River, NJ: Prentice Hall.

Iserman, R., Ernst, S., & Nelles, O. (1997). Identification with dynamic neural networks architectures, comparisons, applications. *Proc. of IFAC Symposium on System Identification*, vol. 3, Japan, (pp. 997–1022).

Kishor, N., Singh, M., & Raghuvanshi, A. S. (2007). Genetic programming approach for model structure determination of hydro turbine in closed loop operation. *Proc of. IEEE Congress on Evolutionary Computation 2007* (pp. 2751-2757).

Knowles, J., Corne, D., & Deb, K. (Eds.). (2008). *Multiobjective problem solver from nature – From concepts to applications* (pp. 131–154). Pondicherry, India: Springer. doi:10.1007/978-3-540-72964-8

Koza, J. R. (1992). *Genetic programming – On the programming of computers by means of natural selection* (pp. 73–190). Cambridge, MA: MIT Press.

Lew, T. L., Spencer, A. B., Scarpa, F., Worden, K., Rutherford, A., & Hemez, F. (2006). Identification of response surface models using genetic programming. *Mechanical Systems and Signal Processing, 20*(8), 1819–183. doi:10.1016/j.ymssp.2005.12.003

Madar, J., Abonyi, J., & Szeifert, F. (2005). *Genetic programming for system identification*. Retrieved from http://www.fmt.vein.Hu/softcomp/isda04_gpolsnew.pdf

Marcu, T., Mirea, L., Ferariu, L., & Frank, P. M. (2000). Miscellaneous neural networks applied to fault detection and isolation of an evaporation station. *Proc. of 4th IFAC Symposium on Fault Detection, Supervision and Safety for Technical Processes, SAFEPROCESS*, Budapest, Hungary.

Miorandi, D., Yamamoto, L., & De Pellegrini, F. (2010). A survey of evolutionary and embryogenic approaches to autonomic networking. *Computer Networks, 54*, 944–959. doi:10.1016/j.comnet.2009.08.021

Nedjah, N., Abraham, A., & de Macedo Mourelle, L. (Eds.). (2006). Genetic systems programming –Theories and experiences. *Studies in Computational Intelligence, 13*, 1-129. Netherlands: Springer.

Patelli, A., & Ferariu, L. (2009). nonlinear systems identification by means of genetic programming. *Proc. of European Control Conference ECC 2009*, Budapest, Hungary.

Patelli, A., & Ferariu, L. (2010). Elite based multiobjective genetic programming in nonlinear systems identification. *Advances in Electrical and Computer Engineering, 10*(1), 94–99. doi:10.4316/aece.2010.01017

Poli, R., Langdon, W. B., McPhee, N. F., & Koza, J. R. (2008). *A field guide to genetic programming*, (pp. 1-114). Retrieved from http://www.gp-field-guide.org.uk

Rachmawati, L., & Srinivasan, D. (2009). Multiobjective evolutionary algorithm with controllable focus on the knees of the Pareto front. *IEEE Transactions on Evolutionary Computation, 13*(4), 810–824. doi:10.1109/TEVC.2009.2017515

Rodriguez-Vasquez, K., Fonseca, C. M., & Fleming, P. J. (2004). Identifying the structure of nonlinear dynamic systems using multiobjective genetic programming. *IEEE Transactions on Systems, Man, and Cybernetics. Part A, Systems and Humans, 34*, 531–534. doi:10.1109/TSMCA.2004.826299

Tianfield, H., & Unland, R. (2004). Towards autonomic computing systems. *Engineering Applications of Artificial Intelligence*, *17*, 689–699. doi:10.1016/S0952-1976(04)00113-7

Walker, J. A., & Miller, J. F. (2008). The automatic acquisition, evolution and reuse of modules in Cartesian genetic programming. *IEEE Transactions on Evolutionary Computation*, *12*(4), 397–417. doi:10.1109/TEVC.2007.903549

Wey, H., Billings, S. A., & Lui, J. (2004). Term and variable selection for nonlinear models. *International Journal of Control*, *77*, 86–110.

Winkler, S. M., Affenzeller, M., & Wagner, S. (2008). Fine-grained population diversity estimation for genetic programming based structure identification. *Proc. of the 10th Annual Conference on Genetic and Evolutionary Computation GECCO '08* (pp. 1435-1436).

Woldesenbet, Y. G., & Yen, G. C. (2009). Dynamic evolutionary algorithm with variable relocation. *IEEE Transactions on Evolutionary Computation*, *13*(3), 500–513. doi:10.1109/TEVC.2008.2009031

ADDITIONAL READING

Adra, S. F., Dodd, T., Griffin, I. A., & Fleming, P. (2009). Convergence Acceleration Operator for Multiobjective Optimisation. *IEEE Transactions on Evolutionary Computation*, *13*(4), 825–846. doi:10.1109/TEVC.2008.2011743

Alves da Silva, A. P., & Abrao, P. J. (2002). Applications of Evolutionary Computation in Electric Power Systems. In Proceedings of the 2002 Congress on Evolutionary Computation CEC2002 (pp. 1057-1062).

Ashlock, D. (2006). *Evolutionary Computation for Modeling and Optimization*. New York, NY: Springer.

Buchsbaum, T., & Vossner, S. (2006). Information-Dependent Switching of Identification Criteria in a Genetic Programming System for System Identification. *Proc. of the 9th European Conference on Genetic Programming*, Budapest, Hungary (pp. 300-309).

De Jong, K. A. (2006). *Evolutionary Computation - A Unified Approach*. Cambridge, MA: MIT Press.

Evans, C., Fleming, P. J., Hill, D. C., Norton, J. P., Pratt, I., Rees, D., & Rodriguez-Vazquez, K. (2001). Application of system identification techniques to aircraft gas turbine engines. *Control Engineering Practice*, *9*(2), 135–148. doi:10.1016/S0967-0661(00)00091-5

Fogel, D. (2006). *Evolutionary computation – Toward a New Philosophy of Machine Intelligence* (3rd ed.). Piscataway, NJ: IEEE Press.

Gustafson, S., Burke, E. K., & Krasnogor, N. (2005). On Improving Genetic Programming for Symbolic Regression. *Proceedings of the 2005 IEEE Congress on Evolutionary Computation: Vol. 1* (pp. 912 - 919).

Guyon, I., & Elisseeff, A. (2003). An Introduction to Variable and Feature Selection. *Journal of Machine Learning Research*, *3*, 1157–1182.

Kotanchek, M. E., Vladislavleva, E. Y., & Smits, G. F. (2009). Symbolic Regression via GP as a Discovery Engine: Insights on Outliers and Prototypes. In Riolo, R. L., O'Reilly, U.-M., & McConaghy, T. (Eds.), *Genetic Programming Theory and Practice VII, Genetic and Evolutionary Computation* (pp. 55–72). Springer.

Madar, J., Abonyi, J., & Szeifert, F. (2005). Genetic Programming for the Identification of Nonlinear Input-Output Models. *Industrial & Engineering Chemistry Research*, *44*(9), 3178–3186. doi:10.1021/ie049626e

Purshouse, R., & Fleming, P. (2006). On the Evolutionary Optimization of Many Conflicting Objectives. *IEEE Transactions on Evolutionary Computation*, *11*(6), 770–784. doi:10.1109/TEVC.2007.910138

Zhang, V., Wu, Z.-M., & Yang, G.-K. (2004). Genetic programming-based chaotic time series modeling. *Journal of Zhejiang University. Science*, *5*(11), 1432–1439. doi:10.1631/jzus.2004.1432

KEY TERMS AND DEFINITIONS

Evolutionary Algorithm: An iterative optimization algorithm which works on a population of potential solutions, produces new solutions by means of genetic operators and encourages the survival of the fittest ones to the next iteration.

Genetic Programming: An evolutionary algorithm that evolves a population of hierarchical encrypted individuals.

System Identification: Construction of a model that mimics the dynamic behavior of the plant, using a finite data set of plant variables measurements.

Model Parsimony: Simplicity of the model in terms of its structure.

Multiobjective Optimization: A problem demanding the simultaneous optimization of different objective functions.

Pareto Optimal Solution: A solution which, within the framework of multiobjective optimizations, cannot be improved in terms of an objective direction, without deteriorating the performances in terms of at least another remaining objective direction.

Non-Dominant Solution: A solution of a set which is not worst in terms of all objectives than any other solution of the set.

APPENDIX: EXERCISES

1. GP is employed for configuring MISO Hammerstein models (Figure 12), whilst considering a set of possible nonlinear static functions, denoted Nf_1, Nf_2, ... Is this structural template advantageous from a GP standpoint? Motivate the response in terms of involved primitive sets. Discuss the case when Nf_1, Nf_2, .. are inserted in the operators' set, as well as the case when Nf_1, Nf_2, .. are used to generate some specific terminals. The comparison can involve issues related to closure property, phenotypic validity of the offspring, configuration of genetic operators.

Figure 12. Hammerstein model

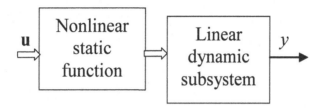

2. Considering a certain sampling period, GP is used to determine the discrete model of a linear dynamic system with apriorically known dead time. Indicate sufficient sets of primitives, considering that the dynamic behavior is implemented:

A.   with external delay blocks only;
B.   with external and internal delay blocks.

Discuss the approaches relative to both phenotypic and genotypic validity aspects.

3. Let us consider the NLP - based design algorithm applied for the identification of a SISO dynamic system. The best model is indicated below, in terms of three distinct sampling periods:

$$y(k) = 0.03343 \cdot u(k-1) + 0.08642 \cdot u(k-2) - 0.5476 \cdot y(k-1) - 0.1353 \cdot y(k-2), \text{ for } T_s = 2.$$

$$y(k) = 0.03963 \cdot u(k-1) + 0.03582 \cdot u(k-2) + 1.439 \cdot y(k-1) - 0.7408 \cdot y(k-2), \text{ for } T_s = 0.3.$$

$$y(k) = 0.001228 \cdot u(k-1) + 0.001208 \cdot u(k-2) + 1.941 \cdot y(k-1) - 0.9512 \cdot y(k-2),$$
for $T_s = 0.05$.

These models are used to generate different training data sets (denoted $\mathbf{D}_1$, $\mathbf{D}_2$ and $\mathbf{D}_3$ respectively), by simulating the step response over the time interval $[0, T_f]$, $T_f = 12$. Note that $\mathbf{D}_1$ is not representative and $\mathbf{D}_3$ contains more samples than necessary.

A. Indicate an arbitrary tree - based individual which can be produced by the initialization procedure, transform the initial individual to regressive one - if necessary - and compute the parameters by means of QR decomposition, considering $\mathbf{D}_1$, $\mathbf{D}_2$ and $\mathbf{D}_3$. Compare the resulted *SSE* values and discuss the influence of the training data set over QR procedure's performances.

B. Comment the expected downsides, assuming the following settings: $n_u = 2$, $n_y = 2$, $T_f = 20$; $n_u = 3$, $n_y = 4$, $T_f = 12$; $n_u = 1$, $n_y = 1$, $T_f = 12$; $n_u = 3$, $n_y = 4$, $T_f = 12$.

4. Let us consider the PCAM algorithm. At a certain generation, one assumes the following performances of the individuals included in the MOO and SOO subpopulations, respectively:

$$MOO : \{(SEF, CF)| (0.1; 3.2), (0.4; 2), (1; 2.7), (0.5; 4.3), (1.25; 1.5), (0.7; 2.2), (0.4; 3.7),$$
$$(0.2; 2.3), (0.5; 1.6), (0.3; 2.1)\},$$

$$\mathbf{SOO} : \{(SEF, CF)| (0.1; 3.2), (0.4; 2), (1; 2.7), (0.5; 4.3), (1.25; 1.5), (0.7; 2.2), (0.4; 3.7),$$
$$(0.2; 2.3), (0.5; 1.6), (0.3; 2.1)\}.$$

Apply the clustering algorithm on the MOO subpopulation and depict the Pareto-fronts. Compute the fitness values for all the individuals and select the emigrants, considering that the migration procedure is activated.

5. DNEC algorithm is applied to solve a multiobjective optimization problem, in terms of *SEF* and *CF* objective functions. Let us consider a set **SE** of individuals having the following performances:

$$\mathbf{SE} : \{(SEF, CF)| (0.4; 3.2), (0.4; 2), (0.4; 2.1), (0.3; 2.7), (0.35; 2.5)\} .$$

Can **SE** be considered an elite set? Eliminate the extraneous individuals, if necessary, and determine the dummy individual in the resulted elite set. Compute the fitness for all the elites.

6. Let us consider the identification of a nonlinear MISO plant, with $\mathbf{u} \in \Re^2$ and $y \in \Re$. One of the prerequisites of the identification problem is that no regressor of the optimal model can simultaneously contain all the inputs of the system. Indicate how the suggested design procedure can be tuned to incorporate this aprioric information.

Section 2
Formal and Practical Aspects of Autonomic Networking

Chapter 7
Formal Specification and Verification of Self-Configuring P2P Networking:
A Case Study in Mobile Environments

Phan Cong-Vinh
NTT University, Vietnam

ABSTRACT

In mobile environments (MEs) such as vehicular ad hoc networks (VANETs), mobile ad hoc networks (MANETs), wireless sensor networks (WSNs), and so on, formal specification of self-configuring P2P networking (SPN) emerges as a need for programming, and verifying such mobile networks. Moreover, well-specified SPN in MEs becomes a requirement of developing middleware for the mobile networks. The chapter is a reference material for readers who already have a basic understanding of the MEs for their applications and are now ready to know how to specify and verify formally aspect-oriented self-configuring P2P networking (ASPN) in MEs using categorical language, assured that their computing needs are handled correctly and efficiently. ASPN in MEs is presented in a straightforward fashion by discussing in detail the necessary components and briefly touching on the more advanced components. Several explanatory notes and examples are represented throughout the chapter as a moderation of the formal descriptions. Significant properties of ASPN in MEs, which emerge from the specification, create the firm criteria for verification.

INTRODUCTION

In mobile environments (MEs) such as vehicular ad hoc networks (VANETs), mobile ad hoc networks (MANETs), wireless sensor networks (WSNs) and

so on, *self-configuring P2P networking* (SPN), which is seen as a fundamental paradigm of mobile computing, is currently on the spot as one of the priority research areas and research activities are booming nowadays (Denko, Yang, & Zhang, 2009; Xhafa, 2009).

DOI: 10.4018/978-1-60960-845-3.ch007

Although this networking paradigm is potentially very powerful using nature-inspired computational intelligence (Vinh, 2009a, 2009c, 2009d, 2011b), there are still many aspects of designing such mobile networks that are not yet well understood. Thus investigating SPN in MEs emerges as a need, on the one hand, for managing the mobile networks, but on the other hand, for modeling, specifying, programming, and verifying such mobile networks. Moreover, well-established SPN in MEs becomes a requirement of developing middleware for the mobile networks. Hence this chapter is intended to present a rigorous approach to SPN in MEs on how SPN in MEs can be specified and verified formally. In other words, our aim is to formalize SPN in MEs using categorical language for developing and verifying SPN in MEs. Especially, taking advantage of aspect-oriented approach, SPN in MEs is primarily investigated based on this aspect-orientation such that we firstly construct aspects of SPN in MEs. Secondly, categorical specification for *aspect-oriented self-configuring P2P networking* (ASPN) in MEs is developed. Thirdly, by the categorical specification, significant properties of ASPN in MEs are built as strong criteria for verification. Finally, a mechanism of verification for ASPN in MEs is illustrated.

Furthermore, this chapter breaks new ground in dealing with ASPN in MEs taking advantage of categorical approach – a firm formal method applicable to a wide variety of ASPN in MEs. While the dealing with this subject is normally very formal (Vinh, 2009c), the chapter goes across some categorical structures straightforwardly, leading the readers to an understanding of what it means to give a rigorous approach to ASPN in MEs.

The chapter is a reference material for readers who already have a basic understanding of the MEs for their applications and are now ready to know how to specify and verify formally ASPN in MEs using categorical language, assured that their computing needs are handled correctly and efficiently.

ASPN in MEs is presented in a straightforward fashion by discussing in detail the necessary components and briefly touching on the more advanced components. Several explanatory notes and examples are represented throughout the chapter as a moderation of the formal descriptions. Significant properties of ASPN in MEs, which emerge from the specification, create the firm criteria for verification.

We attempt to make the presentation as self-contained as possible, although familiarity with the notion of MEs is assumed. Acquaintance with categorical language and the associated notion of aspect-orientation is useful for recognizing the results, but is almost everywhere not strictly necessary.

The rest of this chapter is organized as follows: In section of Basic Concepts, we recall preliminaries from the category theory used in the chapter. Section of Formal Specification of ME Peers presents formal specification of ME peers including the formal structures of P2P, self-configuration, aspect-orientation and ASPN in MEs using categorical language. In section of Formal Verification of ME Peers, we present formal verification of ME peers including a mechanism of verification based on specification and an illustration in detail. In section of Notes and Remarks, we briefly discuss a direction of further developments in the future. A short summary and further investigations are given in section of Summary. Finally, exercises and further reading are recommended at the end of chapter.

BASIC CONCEPTS

In this section, we recall some concepts from the category theory (Asperti & Longo, 1991; Bergman, 1998; Adamek, Herrlich, & Strecker, 2009; Levine, 1998; Lawvere & Schanuel, 1997) used in this chapter.

Category Definition

Category as a Graph

A category **C** can be viewed as a graph (*Obj(C)*, *Arc(C)),.s,t*) where

- *Obj(C)* is the set of nodes we call *objects*,
- *Arc(C)* is the set of edges we call *morphisms* and
- *s,t* : *Arc(C)*→ *Obj(C)* are two maps called *source* (or *domain*) and *target* (or *codomain*), respectively.

We write $f:_X \longrightarrow_Y$ when f is in *Arc(C)*, $s(f) =$ X and $t(f) =_Y$.

Explanation on Terminology

An object in the category is an algebraic structure such as a set. We are probably familiar with some notations for finite sets: {*Student A, Student B, Student C*} is a name for the set whose three elements are *Student A, Student B,* and *Student C*. Note that the order in which the elements are listed is irrelevant.

A morphism ^{f} in the category consists of three things: a set X, called the source of the morphism; a set ^{y}, called the target of the morphism and a rule assigning to each element X in the source an element ^{y} in the target. This ^{y} is denoted by f(X), read "^{f} of X ". Note that the morphism is also called the *map, function, transformation, operator* or *arrow*. For example, let X = {*Student A, Student B, Student C*}, Y ={*Math, Physics, Chemistry, History*} and let ^{f} assign each student his or her favorite subject. The following internal diagram is an illustration.

{*Student A*   *Student B*   *Student C*}

f=favorite subject

{*Math*   *Chemistry*   *History*   *Physics*}

(1)

This states that the favorite subject of the *Student C* is *History*, written by f (*Student C)=History*, while *StudentA* and *Student B* prefer *Chemistry*. There are some important properties of any morphism

- From each element in the source {*Student A, Student B, Student C*} there is exactly one arrow leaving.
- To an element in the target {*Math, Physics, Chemistry, History*} there may be zero, one or more arrows arriving.

It is possible that the source and target of the morphism could be the same set. The following internal diagram is an example.

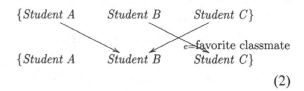

{*Student A*   *Student B*   *Student C*}

{*Student A*   *Student B*   *Student C*}

e=favorite classmate

(2)

and, in the case, the morphism is called an *endomorphism* whose representation is available as in:

{*Student A* ⟶ *Student B* ⟵ *Student C*}

(3)

Identity Morphism and Composition of Morphisms

Associated with each object *x* in *Obj(C)*, there is a morphism I_x = X → X, called the *identity* morphism on X, and to each pair of morphisms f: X→ Y and g: Y → Z, there is an associated morphism $f; g$: Y →Z Z, , called the *composition* of f with g. The representations in (4) include the external diagrams of identity morphism and composition of morphisms.

$$
\overset{1_x}{\underset{x}{\bigcirc}}
\qquad
\underbrace{x \xrightarrow{f} y \xrightarrow{g} z}_{f;g}
\tag{4}
$$

Explanation on Terminology

Here are the corresponding internal diagrams of the identity morphism.

$$
\begin{array}{ccc}
\{Student\ A & Student\ B & Student\ C\} \\
\downarrow & \downarrow{}^{1_x} & \downarrow \\
\{Student\ A & Student\ B & Student\ C\}
\end{array}
\tag{5}
$$

or

$$
\{Student\ A \qquad Student\ B \qquad Student\ C\}
\tag{6}
$$

and here, the composition of morphisms is described in the internal diagram,

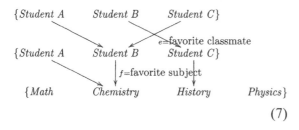

$$
\tag{7}
$$

or, in the external diagram $x \xrightarrow{e} x \xrightarrow{f} y$.

From diagram (7), we can obtain answers for the question "What should each student support to his or her favorite classmate for subject?". In fact, the answers are such as "*Student A* likes *Student B, Student B* likes *Chemistry*, so *Student A* should support *Chemistry*", "*Student B* likes *Student C, Student C* likes *History*, so *Student B* should support *History*" and "*Student C* likes *Student B, Student B* likes *Chemistry*, so *Student C* should support *Chemistry*".

The composition of two morphisms e and f means that e and f are combined to obtain a third morphism $x \xrightarrow{e;f} y$. This is represented in the following internal diagram.

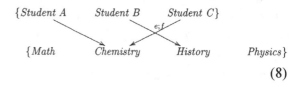

$$
\tag{8}
$$

where, for example, $e;f(Student\ B)=History$ is read as "the favorite subject of the favorite classmate of *Student B* is *History*".

Identity and Associativity for Composition of Morphisms

The following equation must hold for all objects X, Y in $Obj(\mathbf{C})$ and morphism f: X→Y in $Arc(\mathbf{C})$:

$$
Identity: \qquad 1_x; f = f = f; 1_y
$$

$$
1_x\bigcirc x \xrightarrow{f} y \;=\; x \xrightarrow{f} y \;=\; x \xrightarrow{f} y \bigcirc 1_y
\tag{9}
$$

The following equation must hold for all objects X, Y and z in $Obj(\mathbf{C})$ and morphisms f: X→Y, g: Y→Z and h:Z → T in $Arc(\mathbf{C})$:

$$
Associativity: \qquad (f;g); h = f; (g; h)
$$

$$
\underbrace{x \xrightarrow{f} y \xrightarrow{g} z}_{f;g} \xrightarrow{h} T \;=\; x \xrightarrow{f} y \underbrace{\xrightarrow{g} z \xrightarrow{h} T}_{g;h}
\tag{10}
$$

Functor

Functor is a special type of mapping between categories. Functor from a category to itself is called an *endofunctor*. Note that, in this chapter, when the notion of endofunctor dominates throughout in use, then we can name them as the functor, for short, without any confusion. The functors are also viewed as morphisms in a category, whose objects are smaller categories.

A *multifunctor* is a generalization of the functor concept to *n* arguments. Specially, a *bifunctor* is a multifunctor with $n = 2$.

There are two kinds of functors distinguished by the way they treat morphisms to be *covariant* and *contravariant*. A functors $\top$ covariant if for each source morphism $x \xrightarrow{f} y$ the target morphism has the form $\top x \xrightarrow{\top f} \top y$. A functor $\top$ is contravariant if for each source morphism $x \xrightarrow{f} y$ the target morphism has the form $\top x \xleftarrow{\top f} \top y$.

Homomorphism

Let $\top$ be a functor with algebraic objects such as algebras $a\colon \top X \to X$ and $b\colon \top Y \to Y$. A *homomorphism of algebras* (also called a *map of algebras*) from (X, a) to (Ψ, b) is a function $f\colon X \to Y$ between the carrier sets x and y such that the equation $a; f = \top f; b$ holds. That is, the following diagram commutes:

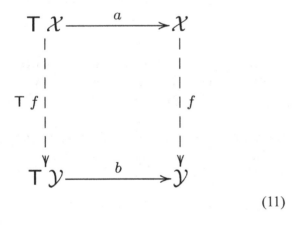

(11)

Isomorphism

A morphism $f\colon X \to Y$ in the category $\mathbf{C}$ is an *isomorphism* if there exists a morphism $g\colon Y \to X$ in that category such that $f;g = 1x$ and $g; f = 1y$.

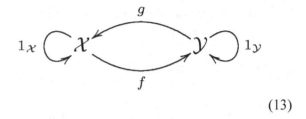

(12)

That is, if the following diagram commutes.

(13)

Natural Isomorphism

Let $\mathbf{C}$ and $\mathbf{C}'$ be two categories. Consider a parallel pair:

$$\mathbf{C} \underset{\top'}{\overset{\top}{\rightrightarrows}} \mathbf{C}'$$

(14)

of functors of the same variance. Two functors of $\top$ and $\top$ are *naturally equivalent* (also called *naturally isomorphic*) if there is an inverse pair of natural isomorphisms between them. In other words, the inverse pair of natural isomorphisms between $\top$ and $\top'$ is a pair:

$$\top \underset{\zeta_-}{\overset{\eta_-}{\rightleftarrows}} \top'$$

(15)

such that for each object X in $\mathbf{C}$ the morphisms

$$T\,\mathcal{X} \xrightarrow[\zeta x]{\eta x} T'\,\mathcal{X}$$

$$(16)$$

are an inverse pair of isomorphisms in **C'**.

FORMAL SPECIFICATION OF ME PEERS: A CASE STUDY

For ME peers, their formal structures of *P2P*, *self-configuration* and *aspect-orientation* are achieved when ASPN is specified. In this way, for forming ASPN, we start with considering *self-configuring P2P networking* (SPN) for ME peers and then refactor SPN to discover common factors (called *aspects*) of SPN using categorical language.

P2P Networking for ME Peers

We present this subsection concentrating on parallel composition of ME peers and on P2P networking for ME peers together with the notion of commutative diagram chasing.

Parallel Composition of ME Peers and its Algebraic Axioms

Parallel processing, which is one of the significant features of MEs, requires dividing a service into ME peers that can run simultaneously, but such services in ME peers often must deal with challenges as decentralization, networking links of varying latencies, unpredictable failures and dynamicity in distributed heterogeneous environments.

Definition 1

A parallel composition *of ME peers is a binary operation (denoted as -||-) between two ME peers which groups them together as being parallel in MEs. Hence, let a and b be arbitrary ME peers, then a||b denotes that a is parallel to b.*

It follows that the parallel composition of a sequence of ME peers $a_1, a_2, ..., a_n$ (denoted as $a_1 || a_2 || (... || a_n)...)))$ is simply written as $a_1 || a_2 || ... || a_n$ or $||1 \leqslant i \leqslant n\, a_i$. Sometimes, the notation of $||_0$ is used to denote a special ME peer *skip* that has no effect on any state of MEs, and drops immediately.

The algebraic axioms governing the behavior of $a||b$ are very simple and regular (Roscoe, 1997; Hoare, 2004 ; Xu & He, 1994). The following are three axioms related to our development in this section.

Axiom on symmetry: This axiom expresses the logical *symmetry* between two ME peers:

$$a||b = b||a \qquad (17)$$

Axiom on associativity: This axiom shows that when three ME peers are assembled, it does not matter in which order they are put together:

$$(a||b)||c = a||(b||c) \qquad (18)$$

Axiom on identity: Composition with *skip* makes no difference

$$a||skip = a \qquad (19)$$

P2P Networking for ME Peers

For every ME peer a and b, if a is parallel to b then we define a labeled arrow from a to b as $a \xrightarrow{a||b} b$ in which its label is $a||b$. Category of ME peers is founded upon the abstraction of the labeled arrow called *morphism*. Here, the labeled arrow "$\xrightarrow{a||b}$" is the morphism between a and b. We usually use two following diagrams to specify this morphism.

$$a \xrightarrow{a||b} b \qquad \text{or} \qquad a \parallel b : a \longrightarrow b \qquad (20)$$

where source and target of the morphism $a||b$ are the ME peers a and b, respectively. Such directional structures occur widely in representation of this chapter.

By describing structures in terms of the existence and characteristics of morphisms -||-, categorical structures of ME peers achieve their wide applicability. The usual method of mathematical description is by reference to the internal structure of ME peers. The applicability of this description is then limited to ME peers supporting such structure. Categorical descriptions make no assumption about the internal structure of ME peers, but they purely ensure that whatever structure of ME peers is preserved by the morphisms -||-. In this sense, categorical representations are data independent descriptions. Thus the same description may apply to whatever can be seen as ME peers in a category.

A category of ME peers, which is a fundamental and abstract way to describe peers in MEs and their relationships, is composed of

- A set of ME peers (also called *objects*) together with
- A set of morphisms (sometimes called *arrows*) -||- between ME peers.

Morphisms -||- are to be composable, that is, if $a||b:a \longrightarrow b$ and $b||c:b \rightarrow c$, then there is a parallel composition $a||b||c$ such that the axioms on associativity in (18) and on identity in (19) are satisfied.

Category of ME peers is thus a directed graph with the parallel composition and identity structure. This leads to the following formal definition of the category, named **MEPr**, of ME peers. We name this category **MEPr** to refer to "ME peers".

Category **MEPr** is a graph (ParPeerSet, ParRel, *s*, *t*) consisting of

- ParPeerSet is the set of ME peers (considered as nodes),
- ParRel is the set of parallel compositions (considered as edges) and

- *s, t*: ParRel $\longrightarrow$ ParPeerSet are two maps called *source* (or *domain*) and *target* (or *codomain*), respectively.

such that the following axioms (also called *coherence statements*) hold:

(Associativity) If $a||b$ and $b||c$ then $(a||b)||c = a||(b||c)$. For notational convenience, this can be written as:

$$\frac{a \parallel b \text{ and } b \parallel c}{(a \parallel b) \parallel c = a \parallel (b \parallel c)} \qquad (21)$$

(Identity) For every ME peer *a*, there exists a morphism $a||skip$ called the identity morphism for *a*, such that for every morphism $a||b$, we have

$$a||skip||b = a||b = a||b||skip \qquad (22)$$

We write $a||b: a \longrightarrow b$ when $a||b$ is in ParRel and $s(a||b)=a$ and $t(a||b)=b$.

Property 1. *The category* **MEPr** *is exactly a P2P network of ME peers*

It follows that, from a mathematical viewpoint, the category **MEPr** is seen as

Property 2. *The category* **MEPr** *is a complete graph*

Commutative Diagram Chasing

Categorical characteristics are often expressed in terms of commutative diagrams and justifications take the form of *diagram chasing*. Informally, a diagram is a picture of some ME peers and morphisms in the category **MEPr**. Formally, a diagram is a graph whose nodes are labeled with ME peers of **MEPr** and whose edges are labeled with morphisms of **MEPr** in such a way that source and target ME peers of an edge are labeled with source and target ME peers of the labeling morphism.

Example: Axioms on symmetry in (17), on associativity in (18) and on identity in (19) are respectively represented by the following commutative diagrams:

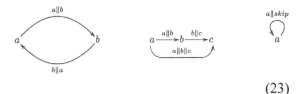

$$(23)$$

Example: The representations in (24) as below include the commutative diagrams of the Equation (22).

$$a\|skip \;\circlearrowleft\; a \xrightarrow{a\|b} b \;\;=\;\; a \xrightarrow{a\|b} b \;\;=\;\; a \xrightarrow{a\|b} b \circlearrowright b\|skip$$

$$(24)$$

and the equation $(a\|b\|c)\|d = a\|(b\|c\|d)$ is diagrammatically represented as in (25)

$$a \xrightarrow{a\|b} b \xrightarrow{b\|c} c \xrightarrow{c\|d} d \;\;=\;\; a \xrightarrow{a\|b} b \xrightarrow{b\|c} c \xrightarrow{c\|d} d$$
$$\underbrace{a\|b\|c} \qquad\qquad \underbrace{b\|c\|d}$$

$$(25)$$

A path in a diagram is a non-empty sequence of edges and their labeling morphisms such that the target peer of each edge is the source peer of the next edge in the sequence.

Example: The central diagram in (23) contains the path $a \xrightarrow{a\|b} b \xrightarrow{b\|c} c$, the right diagram in (25) contains the paths $a \xrightarrow{a\|b} b \xrightarrow{b\|c} c \xrightarrow{c\|d} d$ and $a \xrightarrow{a\|b} b \xrightarrow{b\|c\|d} d$.

Each path determines a morphism by composing the morphisms along it. A diagram is said to *commute* if, for every pair of peers x, y every path from x to y determines the same morphism through composition.

Example: The following diagram commutes then this amounts to the equation in (22) to hold.

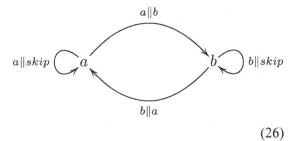

$$(26)$$

In a similar way, the following diagram,

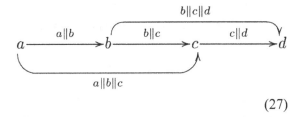

$$(27)$$

commutes then, in other words, the equation $(a\|b\|c)\|d = a\|(b\|c\|d)$ must hold.

Self-Configuring P2P Networking (SPN) for ME Peers

The category **MEPr**, which consists of the set **ParPeerSet** of ME peers together with morphisms -‖- in the set **ParRel**, generates P2P structure of ME peers. This P2P structure of ME peers is dynamic in nature because ME peers can be dynamically added to or dropped from the P2P structure. For such every change, *self-configuration* (Vinh, 2009a, 2009b, 2007) for the P2P structure of ME peers occurs. In this context, self-configuring P2P networking (SPN) for ME peers is formed by the P2P structure of ME peers and its self-configuration.

Let *OP= {add, drop}* be the set of operations making a P2P structure of ME peers change, in which *add* and *drop* are defined as follows:

Adding an ME Peer

Adding an ME peer into a P2P structure of ME peers is performed by the operation *add*, which is defined as a function of type *add:* $\mathsf{ParPeerSet} \times \mathsf{ParRel} \rightarrow \mathsf{ParRel}$ (28)

or, in the alternative form, as a curried function of type

add: $\mathsf{ParPeerSet} \rightarrow \mathsf{ParRel} \rightarrow \mathsf{ParRel}$ (29)

That is, *add* takes an ME peer of type $\mathsf{ParPeerSet}$ and returns a function of type $\mathsf{ParRel} \rightarrow \mathsf{ParRel}$. In other words, a partial application of *add* to an ME peer in $\mathsf{ParPeerSet}$ returns a function of type $\mathsf{ParRel} \rightarrow \mathsf{ParRel}$.

We know that *currying* is the technique of transforming a function that takes multiple arguments (or more accurately an n-tuple as argument) in such a way that it can be called as a chain of functions each with a single argument. Currying makes the function *add* easy to be defined and hence the curried form in (29) is a preferred specification.

The function *add* obeys the following axioms: For all $i \in \mathsf{IN}_0$,

$$\begin{cases} add(b)(\|_{1 \leqslant i \leqslant n}\, a_i) = (\|_{1 \leqslant i \leqslant n}\, a_i) \parallel b & \text{for } i \geqslant 1 \\ add(b)(\|_0) = (\|_0) \parallel b = skip \parallel b = b & \text{when } i = 0 \end{cases}$$

Example:

$add(b)(a) = a \parallel b$

$add(b)(add(a)(\|_0)) = a \parallel b$

$add(c)(a \parallel b) = a \parallel b \parallel c$

Dropping an ME Peer

Dropping an ME peer out of a P2P structure of ME peers is performed by the operation *drop*, which is defined as a function of type

drop: $\mathsf{ParPeerSet} \times \mathsf{ParRel} \rightarrow \mathsf{ParRel}$ (30)

or, in the alternative form, as a curried function of type

drop: $\mathsf{ParPeerSet} \rightarrow \mathsf{ParRel} \rightarrow \mathsf{ParRel}$

(31)

That is, *drop* takes an ME peer of type $\mathsf{ParPeerSet}$ and returns a function of type $\mathsf{ParRel} \rightarrow \mathsf{ParRel}$. In other words, a partial application of *drop* to an ME peer in $\mathsf{ParPeerSet}$ returns a function of type $\mathsf{ParRel} \rightarrow \mathsf{ParRel}$

The function *drop* obeys the following axioms: For all $i \in \mathsf{IN}_0$,

$$\begin{cases} drop(b)(\|_{1 \leqslant i \leqslant n}\, a_i) = \|_{1 \leqslant i \leqslant (n-1)}\, a_i & \text{when there exists } a_i = b \\ drop(b)(\|_{1 \leqslant i \leqslant n}\, a_i) = \|_{1 \leqslant i \leqslant n}\, a_i & \text{for all } a_i \neq b \end{cases}$$

It follows that $drop(b, \|_0) = \|_0 = skip$.
Example:

$drop(a,a) = \|_0$

$drop(b,\, a \parallel b \parallel c) = a \parallel c$

$drop(d, a \parallel b \parallel c) = a \parallel b \parallel c$

A Sequence of Self-Configurations

A sequence of self-configurations is completely defined when operations *add* and *drop* are executed on SPN as illustrated in the following diagram:

(32)

In the context of **MEPr**, self-configurations are known as *homomorphisms* from an **MEPr** to another **MEPr** to preserve the P2P structure of ME peers. In other words, self-configuration is a map from a ParRel to another ParRel of the same type that preserves all the parallel structures of ME peers.

Aspects of SPN for ME Peers

A SPN composed of $n+1$ ME peers a_i, $\forall 0 \leqslant i \leqslant n$, is denoted by $\|_{0 \leqslant i \leqslant n} a_i$, whose subscript relates to ME peer number.

Aspect-Oriented Development of SPN for ME Peers

Aspect-oriented development of the SPN $\|_{0 \leqslant i \leqslant n} a_i$ is really a refactoring process (or decomposing process) to discover so-called common factors of $\|_{0 \leqslant i \leqslant n} a_i$. Such a refactoring process can be more referred to (Vinh & Bowen, 2007 ; Vinh, 2007). Those common factors are called *aspects* (Kiczales et al., 1997). In fact, an aspect A is viewed as a self-configuration on $\|_{0 \leqslant i \leqslant n} a_i$ including $n+1$ peers a_i, $\forall 0 \leqslant i \leqslant n$.

We define an *application* of A to $\|_{0 \leqslant i \leqslant n} a_i$ (denoted by $A(\|_{0 \leqslant i \leqslant n} a_i)$) to determine the resulting SPN $\|_{0 \leqslant i \leqslant n} a_i = A(\|_{0 \leqslant i \leqslant n} a_i)$, where $x = n-1$ or $x = n+1$. That is,

$$A(\|_{0 \leqslant i \leqslant n} a_i) = \|_{0 \leqslant i \leqslant x} a_i = \begin{cases} \|_{0 \leqslant i \leqslant n-1} a_i & \text{when } x = n-1 \text{ and} \\ \|_{0 \leqslant i \leqslant n+1} a_i & \text{when } x = n+1 \end{cases}$$

Aspects of SPN and its application. From the self-configurations in the set $OP = \{add, drop\}$ and the sequence of self-configurations (32) considered in a previous subsection, common factors are decomposed to be $add(\_)$ and $drop(\_)$. Thus, $add(\_)$ and $drop(\_)$ are defined as aspects on $\|_{0 \leqslant i \leqslant n} a_i$.

In this case, the application of $add(\_)$ to $\|_{0 \leqslant i \leqslant n} a_i$ is written $add(\_) (\|_{0 \leqslant i \leqslant n} a_i)$ and, in the same way, $drop(\_)(\|_{0 \leqslant i \leqslant n} a_i)$ specifies an application of $drop(\_)$ to $\|_{0 \leqslant i \leqslant n} a_i$.

We use the notation $\cdot$A to denote a transition when applying the aspect A on SPN of ME peers. In this way, when we write $\|_0 \cdot_{add(a)} a$, for example, which means that a change from $\|_0$ to a occurs after applying the aspect $add(a)$ on $\|_0$. Moreover, when we write:

$$\|_0 \vdash_{add(a)} a \vdash_{add(b)} a \| b \vdash_{add(c)} a \| b \| c \vdash_{drop(b)} a \| c \vdash_{add(d)} a \| c \| d$$

that is understood as an application process of the aspects A=$add(\_)$or A=$drop(\_)$ by which the change happens.

Category of P2P Networks and Specification Properties

A category whose objects are categories **MEPr** and whose morphisms are self-configurations is called the category **Cat(MEPr)** of P2P networks. The category **Cat(MEPr)** is constructed as follows:

Objects as categories **MEPr**: Let *ObjCat* be the set of categories **MEPr**. That is,

$ObjCat = \{$**MEPr**|**MEPr** is a category of ME peers$\}$ (33)

- *Morphisms as self-configurations*: Associated with each pair of categories **MEPr** and **MEPr'** in *ObjCat*, self-configuration $h:$**MEPr** $\rightarrow$ **MEPr'** to map every P2P structure to another is a self-configuration from **MEPr** to **MEPr'** such that for all parallel compositions $a\|b$ in **ParRel** it holds that $h(a\|b)=h(a)\|h(b)$.

For each pair of self-configurations $h:$**MEPr** $\rightarrow$ **MEPr'** and $k:$**MEPr** $\rightarrow$ **MEPr'**, there is an associated self-configuration $h \cdot k:$**MEPr** $\rightarrow$ **MEPr'**, the composition of $h$with k (and read as "h before k"), such that for all parallel compositions $a\|b$ in **ParRel** it holds that $k)h(a\|v))$- $k(h(a)\|b)) = k(h(a)\|h(b)) = k(h(a))\|k(h(b))$.

Associated with each **MEPr** in *ObjCat*, self-configuration $id_{\text{MEPr}}:$ **MEPr**$\rightarrow$**MEPr'** to map every P2P structure to itself is defined as an identity self-configuration from **MEPr** to **MEPr** such that for all parallel compositions $a\|b$ in **ParRel** it holds that

$$id_{\text{MEPr}}(a\|b)=id_{\text{MEPr}}(a)\|id_{\text{MEPr}}(b)=a\|b.$$

As a result, for every P2P structure and the self-configurations $h:$ **MEPr** $\rightarrow$ **MEPr'**, $k:$ **MEPr** $\rightarrow$ **MEPr''** and $g:$ **MEPr''**$\rightarrow$**MEPr'''**, the following equations must hold

Associativity: $(h \cdot k) \cdot g = h \cdot (k \cdot g)$

Identity: $id_{\text{MEPr}} \cdot h = h = h \cdot id_{\text{MEPr}}'$

These two equations amount to two following commutative diagrams, respectively.

$$(34)$$

and

$$(35)$$

These are all the basic ingredients we need for the category **Cat(MEPr)** of P2P networks defined.

Property 3. *Every self-configuration h: **MEPr** $\rightarrow$ **MEPr**′ and g: **MEPr**″$\rightarrow$**MEPr**‴ in the category **Cat(MEPr)**, there exist unique self-configurations x: **MEPr**″$\rightarrow$**MEPr** and y:**MEPr**′$\rightarrow$**MEPr**‴ in **Cat(MEPr)** such that the following equation holds:*

$$x \cdot h \cdot y : \text{MEPr}'' \longrightarrow \text{MEPr}''' = g : \text{MEPr}'' \longrightarrow \text{MEPr}'''$$

$$(36)$$

It follows that the self-configurations id_{MEPr}: **MEPr**$\rightarrow$**MEPr** and id_{MEPr}: **MEPr**′$\rightarrow$**MEPr**′ are identity self-configurations, then the equation holds (see Box 1).

Property 4. *For all self-configurations x and y in **Cat(MEPr)**, if $x \cdot h \cdot y = x \cdot h' \cdot y$, then $h = h'$.*

The properties 3 and 4 of self-configurations in **Cat(MEPr)** (also called *specification properties*) direct toward a mechanism of verification as presented in the next section .

Extensional monoidal structure of category **Cat(MEPr)** and specification properties

Further to the category **Cat(MEPr)** of P2P networks, we investigate the extensional monoidal structure of the category **Cat(MEPr)** of P2P networks. The operation "·" defines an extensional monoidal structure on the category **Cat(MEPr)**. In fact, **Cat(MEPr)** equipped with the following multifunctor defines an extensional monoidal category. (Note that we name a monoidal category "extensional monoidal category" when it is equipped with a *multifunctor*, in general, for a distinction from a normal monoidal category just with a *bifunctor*)

Cat(MEPr)×**Cat(MEPr)**×**Cat(MEPr)**→ **Cat(MEPr)** $\qquad (38)$

which, called composition operation, is associative up to a natural isomorphism, and an identity self-configuration *id* which is both a left and right identity for the multifunctor "·", again, up to natural isomorphism. The associated natural isomorphisms are subject to some coherence conditions which ensure that all the relevant diagrams commute. We consider the facts in detail as below.

Property 5. *The composition operation "·" is associative up to three natural isomorphism* α, β, γ, *called associative ones, with components:*

$\alpha(h,k,g,d,e)$	:	$(h \cdot k \cdot g) \cdot d \cdot e$	$\longrightarrow$	$h \cdot (k \cdot g \cdot d) \cdot e$
$\beta(h,k,g,d,e)$	:	$h \cdot (k \cdot g \cdot d) \cdot e$	$\longrightarrow$	$h \cdot k \cdot (g \cdot d \cdot e)$
$\gamma(h,k,g,d,e)$	:	$(h \cdot k \cdot g) \cdot d \cdot e$	$\longrightarrow$	$h \cdot k \cdot (g \cdot d \cdot e)$

Box 1.

$$id_{\text{MEPr}} \cdot h \cdot id_{\text{MEPr}'} : \text{MEPr} \longrightarrow \text{MEPr}' = h : \text{MEPr} \longrightarrow \text{MEPr}' \qquad (37)$$

Sometimes, the natural isomorphisms α, β, γ *are also represented as:*

$\alpha(h,k,g,d,e)$	:	$(h \cdot k \cdot g) \cdot d \cdot e$	$\cong$	$h \cdot (k \cdot g \cdot d) \cdot e$
$\beta(h,k,g,d,e)$	:	$h \cdot (k \cdot g \cdot d) \cdot e$	$\cong$	$h \cdot k \cdot (g \cdot d \cdot e)$
$\gamma(h,k,g,d,e)$	:	$(h \cdot k \cdot g) \cdot d \cdot e$	$\cong$	$h \cdot k \cdot (g \cdot d \cdot e)$

The coherence conditions for three natural isomorphisms α, β, and γ are thought of as the diagram (39) commuting for all self-configurations h, k, g, d, e, f and p in **Cat(MEPr)**.

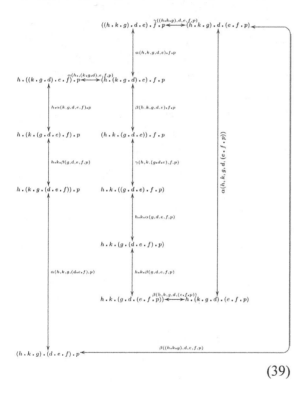

(39)

Property 6. *Every self-configuration h:* **MEPr** → **MEPr'** *has* id_{MEPr} *and* id_{MEPr}' *as left and right identity self-configurations, respectively. There is a natural isomorphism* λ, *called identity one, with components as in Box 2.*

The coherence condition for the identity natural isomorphism λ is considered as the diagram (41) commuting for all self-configurations h, k and g in **Cat(MEPr)**.

The coherence condition states that two or more natural isomorphisms between two given multifunctors are equal based on the existence of which is given or follows from general characteristics. Such situations are ubiquitous in parallelism of ME peers in SPN. Coherence conditions, which are formulated and studied in categorical structures of parallelism of ME peers, are also called *specification properties*.

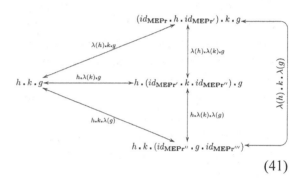

(41)

FORMAL VERIFICATION OF ME PEERS: A CASE STUDY

In this section, a mechanism of verification based on the specification of ME peers is constructed in order to check whether a model of ME peers through its transformations even still meets such specification. Then, an illustration is presented and explained in detail.

Box 2.

$$\lambda(h) : id_{\text{MEPr}} \cdot h \cdot id_{\text{MEPr}'} \longleftrightarrow h \quad \text{or} \quad \lambda(h) : id_{\text{MEPr}} \cdot h \cdot id_{\text{MEPr}'} \cong h \tag{40}$$

Representation of Verification Mechanism

In the context of MEs, formal verification is the act of proving or disproving the correctness of intended ME peers underlying an ASPN with respect to specification properties 3 - 6 in the previous section. In other words, the mechanism of verification refers to the following problem: Given a model of ME peers underlying an ASPN, test automatically whether this model meets specification properties 3, 4, 5 and 6.

In order to solve such a problem algorithmically, the model of ME peers must be formulated in the categorical language. To this end, it is formulated as a categorical structure to check whether this categorical structure satisfies specification properties 3, 4, 5 and 6.

It follows that the following corollary supports verification of ME peers.

Corollary 1. *Let H be specification of ASPN in MEs and G a given structure of ME peers then*

$$\frac{H, G \models Homomorphism\ from\ H\ to\ G}{G \models specification\ properties\ 3, 4, 5\ and\ 6}$$
$$(42)$$

Note that the notation of $\models$ is read as "satisfy". Hence the meaning of (42) is understood as if H and G satisfy a relation of homomorphism from H to G then G satisfies the specification properties stemming from the formal specification H of ME peers. This mechanism of verification is general and can be applied to all kinds of ME peers. Hence a verifying problem is to check whether a homomorphism from the specification of ASPN in MEs to a given structure of ME peers is satisfied.

For exemplifying the mechanism of ME peers verification expressed in this subsection, we consider the following typical illustration and explanations.

Illustration

We illustrate this subsection concentrating on verifying structure of choice among ME peers and necessary explanations.

Choice Among ME Peers

We present a *choice* operation of ME peers (denoted as $a \square b$), for which the environment can control which of a and b will be selected, provided that this control is exercised on the very first action. If this action is not a possible first action of a, then b will be selected; but if b cannot engage initially in the action, a will be selected. If, however, the first action is possible for both a and b, then the choice between them is nondeterministic. Of course, if the event is impossible for both a and b, then it just cannot happen.

It follows that, for a sequence of ME peers $b_1, b_2, ..., b_n$, a choice of these ME peers $b_1 \square b_2$ ($... \square b_n$)...) is simply written as $b_1 \square b_2 ... \square b_n$ or $\square_{1 \leqslant i \leqslant n} b_i$. Sometimes, the notation of $\square_0$ is used to denote a special peer *stop* that never actually engages in any of the events.

The algebraic axioms directing the behavior of $a \square b$ are exceptionally simple and ordinary (Roscoe, 1997 ; Hoare, 2004). The following are three axioms related to our illustration in this section.

Axiom on symmetry: This axiom expresses the logical *symmetry* between two peers

$$a \square b = b \square a \qquad (43)$$

Axiom on associativity: This axiom shows that when three peers are assembled, it does not matter in which order they are put together

$$(a \square b) \square c = a \square (b \square c) \qquad (44)$$

Axiom on identity: Choice with *stop* makes no difference

$$a \square stop = a \qquad (45)$$

$\square_{1 \leqslant i \leqslant n} b_i$ **as a P2P structure.** Obviously, $\square_{1 \leqslant i \leqslant n} b_i$ is exactly a category of ME peers $b_i \in$ N composed of

- A set $\{b_i | i \in N\}$ of ME peers $b_i \in$ N (also called *objects*) together with
- A set of morphisms (sometimes called *arrows*) $\_\square\_$ between ME peers $b_i \in$ N.

Morphisms $\_\square\_$ are to be composable, that is, if $a \square b$: $a \rightarrow b$ and $b \square c$: $b \rightarrow c$, then there is a choice composition $a \square b \square c$ such that the axioms on associativity in (44) and on identity in (45) are satisfied. Hence $\square_{1 \leqslant i \leqslant n} b_i$ is a complete graph with the choice composition and identity structure. This leads to the following corollary

Corollary 2. $\square_{1 \leqslant i \leqslant n} b_i$ *is exactly a P2P structure of ME peers* $b_i \in$ N.

Some operations on $\square_{1 \leqslant i \leqslant n} b_i$. Let $OPR = \{+, -\}$ be the set of operations making $\square_{1 \leqslant i \leqslant n} b_i$ change, in which $+$ and $-$ are defined as follows:

Operation +

Adding a peer into $\square_{1 \leqslant i \leqslant n} b_i$ is performed by the operation $+$, which is defined as a curried function of type

$$+: \mathsf{ChoicePeerSet} \rightarrow \mathsf{ChoiceRel} \rightarrow \mathsf{ChoiceRel} \qquad (46)$$

That is, $+$ takes a peer of type $\mathsf{ChoicePeerSet}$ and returns a function of type $\mathsf{ChoiceRel} \rightarrow \mathsf{ChoiceRel}$. In other words, a partial application of $+$ to a peer in $\mathsf{ChoicePeerSet}$ returns a function of type $\mathsf{ChoiceRel} \rightarrow \mathsf{ChoiceRel}$.

The function $+$ obeys the following axioms: For all $i \in N_0$,

$$\begin{cases} +(a)(\square_{1 \leqslant i \leqslant n} b_i) = (\square_{1 \leqslant i \leqslant n} b_i) \square a & \text{for } i \geqslant 1 \\ +(a)(\square_0) = (\square_0) \square a = stop \square a = a & \text{when } i = 0 \end{cases}$$

Operation −

Dropping a peer out of $\square_{1 \leqslant i \leqslant n} b_i$ is performed by the operation $-$, which is defined as a curried function of type

$$-: \mathsf{ChoicePeerSet} \rightarrow \mathsf{ChoiceRel} \rightarrow \mathsf{ChoiceRel} \qquad (47)$$

That is, $-$ takes a peer of type $\mathsf{ChoicePeerSet}$ and returns a function of type $\mathsf{ChoiceRel} \rightarrow \mathsf{ChoiceRel}$. In other words, a partial application of $-$ to a peer in $\mathsf{ChoicePeerSet}$ returns a function of type $\mathsf{ChoiceRel} \rightarrow \mathsf{ChoiceRel}$.

The function $-$ obeys the following axioms: For all $i \in N_0$,

$$\begin{cases} -(a)(\square_{1 \leqslant i \leqslant n} b_i) = \square_{1 \leqslant i \leqslant (n-1)} b_i & \text{when there exists } b_i = a \\ -(a)(\square_{1 \leqslant i \leqslant n} b_i) = \square_{1 \leqslant i \leqslant n} b_i & \text{for all } b_i \neq a \end{cases}$$

It follows that $-(a)(\square_0) = \square_0 = stop$.

Self-Organizing $\square_{1 \leqslant i \leqslant n} b_i$

A sequence of self-configurations on $\square_{1 \leqslant i \leqslant n} b_i$ is completely defined when operations $+$ and $-$ are executed on $\square_{1 \leqslant i \leqslant n} b_i$ as illustrated in the following diagram:

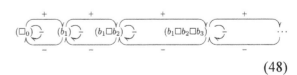

$$(48)$$

In the context of $\square_{1\leqslant i\leqslant n} b_i$, self-configurations $+$ and $-$ are seen as homomorphic relations among $\square_{1\leqslant i\leqslant n} b_i$ to preserve the choice structures of ME peers. In other words, self-configurations $+$ and $-$, which map a choice structure of ME peers in **ChoiceRel** to another choice structure also in **ChoiceRel**, respect all the choice structures of ME peers.

Homomorphism from a Sequence of Self-organizations on $\square_{1\leqslant i\leqslant n} a_i$ *to* $\square_{1\leqslant i\leqslant n} b_i$

Let $\left\langle \|_{1\leqslant i\leqslant n} a_i, (add, drop) \right\rangle$ and $\left\langle \square_{1\leqslant i\leqslant n} b_i, (+, -) \right\rangle$ be two sequences of self-organizations on $\|_{1\leqslant i\leqslant n} a_i$ and $\square_{1\leqslant i\leqslant n} b_i$, respectively, then homomorphism is a function f from $\left\langle \|_{1\leqslant i\leqslant n} a_i, (add, drop) \right\rangle$ to $\left\langle \square_{1\leqslant i\leqslant n} b_i, (+, -) \right\rangle$ that respects their algebraic structures. In other words, f is defined as

$$f\colon \left\langle \|_{1\leqslant i\leqslant n} a_i, (add, drop) \right\rangle \longrightarrow \left\langle \square_{1\leqslant i\leqslant n} b_i, (+, -) \right\rangle$$

such that:

$$f(add : a_{i+1} \longrightarrow \|_{0\leqslant i\leqslant n} a_i \longrightarrow \|_{0\leqslant i\leqslant n} a_{i+1})$$
$$\overset{def}{=}$$
$$f(add) : f(a_{i+1}) \longrightarrow f(\|_{0\leqslant i\leqslant n} a_i) \longrightarrow f(\|_{0\leqslant i\leqslant n} a_{i+1})$$
$$(49)$$

where

- $f(add) \overset{def}{=} +$
- $f(a_{i+1}) \overset{def}{=} b \in$ **ChoicePeerSet**
- $f(\|_{0\leqslant i\leqslant n} a_i) \overset{def}{=} \square_{0\leqslant i\leqslant n} b_i$
- $f(\|_{0\leqslant i\leqslant n} a_i + 1) \overset{def}{=} (\square_{0\leqslant i\leqslant n} b_i)\square b$

and

$$f(drop : a_i \longrightarrow \|_{0\leqslant i\leqslant n} a_i \longrightarrow \|_{0\leqslant i\leqslant n} a_{i-1})$$
$$\overset{def}{=}$$
$$f(drop) : f(a_i) \longrightarrow f(\|_{0\leqslant i\leqslant n} a_i) \longrightarrow f(\|_{0\leqslant i\leqslant n} a_{i-1})$$
$$(50)$$

where

- $f(drop) \overset{def}{=} -$
- $f(a_i) \overset{def}{=} b_i \in$ **ChoicePeerSet**
- $f(\|_{0\leqslant i\leqslant n} a_i) \overset{def}{=} \square_{0\leqslant i\leqslant n} b_i$
- $f(\|_{0\leqslant i\leqslant n} a_i - 1) \overset{def}{=} \square_{0\leqslant i\leqslant n} b_i - 1$

That is, the defined function f makes the following diagram commute. It follows that f is a homomorphism.

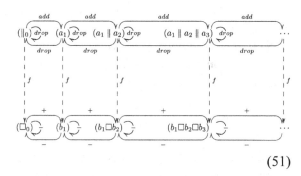

$$(51)$$

As a result of corollary 1, $\left\langle \square_{1\leqslant i\leqslant n} b_i, (+, -) \right\rangle$ satisfies the specification properties 3, 4, 5 and 6.

NOTES AND REMARKS

Formalizing ASPN in MEs is a purposeful abstraction of mobile software engineering. It allows us to understand a mobile software system precisely. Beyond its use as documentation, ASPN in MEs can also be used to generate artifacts. Moreover, a formal foundation of ASPN in MEs allows to generate parts of mobile software systems. Thus, the usage of ASPN in MEs, transformations of

ASPN in MEs, and code generation are becoming more and more important for applications. Among the most significant representatives for ASPN in MEs, categorical approach is a formal development methodology based on transformations of ASPN in MEs. Currently this approach is not yet well understood, but categorically related techniques show that they are quickly changing and that corresponding discusses arise frequently. Most important, there is crucial need for validation and verification (V&V) techniques in the context of ASPN in MEs. This demand is to identify the mutual impact of ASPN in MEs and V&V such that how can ASPN in MEs support development of V&V techniques and how to integrate V&V techniques with ASPN in MEs.

Hence the main discusses about ASPN in MEs and V&V should be focused on potential overlaps and mutual benefits for both subjects such that do a transformation of ASPN in MEs express what the initial requirements want to describe? Are the artifacts generated by abstraction of ASPN in MEs correct with respect to constraints such as security, time, performance, and so on? Is the result of linking several transformations of ASPN in MEs even still correct? How can categorical language support well V&V in testing ASPN? Through transformations of ASPN in MEs can V&V support the whole mobile software engineering process from initial requirements to source code?

SUMMARY

In this chapter, based on categorical structures, we have rigorously specified aspect-oriented self-configuring P2P networking (ASPN) in mobile environments (MEs) from which its useful properties supporting verification emerge.

For forming ASPN in MEs, we have considered the formal structures of P2P, self-configuration, aspect-orientation and self-configuring P2P networking (SPN) for ME peers and then refac-

tored SPN to discover common factors (called *aspects*) of SPN using categorical language. Most important, from such categorical structures, four specification properties of ASPN in MEs have appeared as strong criteria for verification.

Based on the four specification properties, a mechanism of verification has been constructed in order to answer whether a networking system in MEs through its transformations even still meets such specification properties. This mechanism expresses that if there exists a homomorphic relation from the specification of ASPN in MEs to a given networking system, then the networking system satisfies the four specification properties of ASPN in MEs.

Our further investigations have also been suggested to develop validation and verification (V&V) techniques in the context of ASPN in MEs, to identify the mutual impact of ASPN in MEs and V&V, and to integrate ASPN in MEs with V&V.

EXERCISES

1. For each of the properties/corollaries stated in the chapter, show that their statements are rational.

2. A sequence of self-configurations is completely defined when operations *add* and *drop* are executed on SPN as illustrated in the following diagram H:

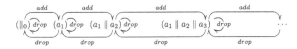

Let K be a structure of peers $\{0,1\}$ as follows

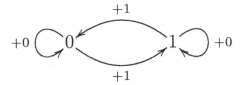

Then show that

A. *H* and *K* satisfy a relation of homomorphism from *H* to *K*
B. *K* satisfies specification properties 3,4,5 and 6

FURTHER READING AND CONCLUSION

In software engineering, formal methods refer to mathematically rigorous techniques for the specification, development (also called synthesis) and verification of software systems (Bowen & Hinchey, 2004). While this chapter is built on a very large achievement of existing work, it mainly stems from the following four sources.

In formal specification techniques, firstly, we are interested in Hoare's CSP (Hoare, 2004), Milner's work (Milner, 1989) on calculus of concurrent programming, and Baeten and Weijland's work (Baeten & Weijland, 1990) on Algebra of Communicating Processes (ACP) among others.

Among results of formal verification techniques, secondly, we take account of Sifakis and Queille's work (Queille & Sifakis, 1982) on *model checking* which in turn was influenced by Ben-Ari, Manna and Pnueli (Ben-Ari, Manna, & Pnueli, 1981) in verification of concurrent programs using the temporal logics.

Furthermore, thirdly, we are especially interested in *verified software synthesis* (Woodcock, 2006) that is really a verification technique aimed toward and integrated into synthesis steps. Beside the current post-synthesis verification techniques, we can also perform a verifying software synthesis to guarantee correct synthesis (Vinh & Bowen, 2008). The difference with post-synthesis verification is that the knowledge about *which* synthesis step has been performed is used to its advantage during verification. However, the knowledge about *how* the synthesis was performed is unknown.

Finally, choosing which underlying specification and verification techniques requires a close look at concrete challenges in MEs. Hence, our interest centers on Michel's categorical approach to distributed systems (Michel, 1989) and our work (Vinh, 2009c, 2011a) on parallel programming in large scale distributed networks taking advantage of category theory. In fact, categories were first described by Samuel Eilenberg and Saunders Mac Lane in 1945 (Lawvere & Schanuel, 1997), but have since grown substantially to become a branch of modern mathematics. Category theory spreads its influence over the development of both mathematics and theoretical computer science. The categorical structures themselves are still the subject of active research, including work to increase their range of practical applicability.

ACKNOWLEDGMENT

Thank you to the anonymous reviewers for their helpful comments and valuable suggestions which have contributed to the final preparation of the chapter.

REFERENCES

Adamek, J., Herrlich, H., & Strecker, G. (2009). *Abstract and concrete categories*. Dover Publications.

Asperti, A., & Longo, G. (1991). *Categories, types and structures*. MIT Press.

Baeten, J. C. M., & Weijland, W. P. (1990). *Process algebra* (1st ed.). Cambridge University Press.

Ben-Ari, M., Manna, Z., & Pnueli, A. (1981). The temporal logic of branching time. In *Proceedings of the 8th ACM Sigplan-Sigact Symposium on Principles of Programming Languages (POPL '81)* (pp. 164–176). New York, NY: ACM.

Bergman, G. M. (1998). *An invitation to general algebra and universal constructions*. Berkeley, CA: Henry Helson.

Bowen, J., & Hinchey, M. (2004). Formal methods. In A. T. Jr. (Ed.), *Computer science handbook* (2nd ed., pp. 106-1–106-25). USA: Chapman & Hall/CRC, ACM.

Denko, M. K., Yang, L. T., & Zhang, Y. (Eds.). (2009). *Autonomic computing and networking* (1st ed.). Springer, USA.

Hoare, C. (2004). *Communicating sequential processes*. Prentice Hall.

Kiczales, G., Lamping, J., Menhdhekar, A., Maeda, C., Lopes, C., Loingtier, J., et al. (1997, 10 June). Aspect-oriented programming. In M. Aksit & S. Matsuoka (Eds.), *Proceedings of 11th European Conference on Object-Oriented Programming (ECOOP)* (vol. 1241, pp. 220–242). Jyvaskyla, Finland: Springer-Verlag.

Lawvere, F., & Schanuel, S. (1997). *Conceptual mathematics: A first introduction to categories* (1st ed.). Cambridge University Press.

Levine, M. (1998). Categorical algebra . In Benkart, G., Ratiu, T., Masur, H., & Renardy, M. (Eds.), *Mixed motives* (*Vol. 57*, pp. 373–499). USA: American Mathematical Society.

Michel, R. (1989). A categorical approach to distributed systems expressibility and knowledge. In *Proceedings of the Eighth Annual ACM Symposium on Principles of Distributed Computing (PODC '89)* (pp. 129–143). New York, NY: ACM.

Milner, R. (1989). *Communication and concurrency* (1st ed.). Prentice Hall.

Queille, J. P., & Sifakis, J. (1982, April). Specification and verification of concurrent systems in CESAR. In M. Dezani-Ciancaglini & U. Montanari (Eds.), *Proceedings of the 5th International Symposium on Programming* (vol. 137, pp. 337–351). Springer-Verlag.

Roscoe, A. W. (1997). *Theory and practice of concurrency* (1st ed.). Prentice Hall.

Vinh, P. (2007). Homomorphism between AOMRC and Hoare model of deterministic reconfiguration processes in reconfigurable computing systems. *Scientific Annals of Computer Science*, *17*, 113–145.

Vinh, P. (2009a, May). Formal aspects of Self-* in autonomic networked computing systems . In Denko, M. K., Yang, L. T., & Zhang, Y. (Eds.), *Autonomic computing and networking* (1st ed., pp. 381–410). Springer, USA. doi:10.1007/978-0-387-89828-5_16

Vinh, P. (2009b). *Dynamic reconfigurability in reconfigurable computing systems: Formal aspects of computing* (1st ed.). Saarbrucken, Germany: VDM Verlag Dr. Muller.

Vinh, P. (2009c, May). Formalizing parallel programming in large scale distributed networks: From tasks parallel and data parallel to applied categorical structures. In F. Xhafa (Ed.), *Parallel Programming, Models and Applications in Grid and P2P Systems* (1st ed., vol. 17, pp. 24–53). IOS Press.

Vinh, P. (2009d, January). Categorical approaches to models and behaviors of autonomic agent systems. [IJCiNi]. *International Journal of Cognitive Informatics and Natural Intelligence*, *3*(1), 17–33. doi:10.4018/jcini.2009010102

Vinh, P. (2011a). Aspect-oriented self-configuring P2P networking in mobile environments: A formal specification and verification. In P. Alencar & D. Cowan (Eds.), *Handbook of research on mobile software engineering: Design, implementation and emergent applications* (1st ed.). Hershey, PA: IGI Global.

Vinh, P. (2011b). Autonomic agent systems: Categorical models and behaviors . In Wang, Y. (Ed.), *Transdisciplinary advancements in cognitive mechanisms and human information processing* (1st ed.). Hershey, PA: IGI Global. doi:10.4018/978-1-60960-553-7.ch002

Vinh, P., & Bowen, J. (2007, 6–8 June). A formal approach to aspect-oriented modular reconfigurable computing. In *Proceedings of 1st IEEE & IFIP International Symposium on Theoretical Aspects of Software Engineering (TASE)* (pp. 369–378). Shanghai, China: IEEE Computer Society Press.

Vinh, P., & Bowen, J. (2008, June). Formalization of data flow computing and a coinductive approach to verifying flowware synthesis. *LNCS Transactions on Computational Science, 4750*(1), 1–36. doi:10.1007/978-3-540-79299-4_1

Woodcock, J. (2006, October). First steps in the verified software grand challenge. *IEEE Computer, 39*(10), 57–64.

Xhafa, F. (Ed.). (2009). *Parallel programming, models and applications in Grid and P2P systems* (1st ed., vol. 17). IOS Press.

Xu, Q., & He, J. (1994, 5–7 January). Laws of parallel programming with shared variables. In D. Till (Ed.), Proceedings of the 6th Refinement Workshop. Springer-Verlag.

KEY TERMS AND DEFINITIONS

Aspect-Orientation: A software development focuses on the identification, specification and representation of crosscutting concerns and their modularization into separate functional units as well as their automated composition into a working system.

Formal Methods: A particular kind of mathematically-based techniques for the specification, development and verification of software and hardware systems.

Formal Specification: A mathematical description of software or hardware that may be used to develop an implementation. It describes what the system should do, not (necessarily) how the system should do it.

Formal Verification: An act of proving or disproving, using mathematically-based techniques, the correctness of intended algorithms underlying a system with respect to a certain formal specification or property.

Middleware: Computer software that connects software components or applications.

Mobile Computing: A comprehensive term describing ability of systems to use information processing technology while moving, as opposed to portable computers, which are only practical for use while deployed in a stationary configuration.

P2P Networking: Any distributed networking structure composed of participants (so-called peers) that make a portion of their resources (such as processing power, disk storage or network bandwidth) directly available to other network participants, without the need for central coordination instances (such as servers or stable hosts).

Self-Configuration: A process by which computer systems or networks automatically adapt their own configuration of components without human direct intervention. Self-configuration technologies are expected to permeate among the next generation of computer systems or networks.

Chapter 8
Logical Methods for Self-Configuration of Network Devices

Sylvain Hallé
Université du Québec à Chicoutimi, Canada

Roger Villemaire
Université du Québec à Montréal, Canada

Omar Cherkaoui
Université du Québec à Montréal, Canada

ABSTRACT

The goal of self-configuration consists of providing appropriate values for parameters that modulate the behaviour of a device. In this chapter, self-configuration is studied from a mathematical logic point of view. In contrast with imperative means of generating configurations, characterized by scripts and templates, the use of declarative languages such as propositional or first-order logic is argued. In that setting, device configurations become models of particular logical formulæ, which can be generated using constraint solvers without any rigid scripting or user intervention.

INTRODUCTION

Despite the tremendous development of network services and functionalities over the years, the configuration and deployment of network elements such as routers and switches remains a mostly manual task. An intricate knowledge of each devices' and services' inner workings and dependencies between configuration parameters

DOI: 10.4018/978-1-60960-845-3.ch008

is required from the network engineer in order to successfully run even basic use cases. The addition of a new device or the deployment of a new service to an existing infrastructure requires repetitive but careful manipulation of multiple configuration parameters on many elements, and even such a cautious work can spawn unpredicted side effects that are discovered by trial and error.

The wish for systems behaving automatically can be traced back to the foundations of control theory (Maxwell, 1867). The application of such principles to software systems started being studied in the late 20th century (Williams & Nayak, 1996). The advent of increasingly powerful devices showing complex behaviours and myriad configuration states led researchers to raise a "Call to action" for the development of systems following radically different design principles. The study of self-configuration and self-healing as a field in itself got its kick-start with IBM's Autonomic Computing initiative0F[1] in the early 2000s. Rather than relying on manual configuration, inter-operation, and repair of computer systems, Autonomic Computing pushes forward the concept of mimicking properties of the autonomic nervous system. Among the so-called "self-*" capabilities that should be exhibited by such systems, we mention self-configuration, self-healing, self-deployment, self-management, and so on.

The application of the Autonomic Computing and Networking (ACN) paradigm (Parashar & Hariri, 2004) to computer networks offers a promising means to release the burden of knowledge and tedious manipulations currently needed from engineers. It has long been argued that Internet Service Provider environments are becoming too complex to manage on an individual system-to-system basis (Melcher & Mitchell, 2004). By definition, self-governed devices can automatically modulate their behaviour in reaction to inconsistencies in the state of the network, or to changes in its topology or management policies.

ACN Through Self-Configuration

In this chapter, we focus on the implementation of *self-configuration* through formal methods. (Narain, 2004) describes a typical self-configuration architecture, called a *service grammar*, shown in Figure 1. Under such an architecture, specific system requirements, expressed in plain English, are first translated into some machine-readable notation, called a *requirements language* (1). This language serves as a reference, or *goal*,

that must be reached by the autonomic system. This language is first fed to a synthesis engine (3), whose task is to generate a first instance of a system configuration satisfying the requirements (4). This configuration is then applied to the actual devices (5), possibly with the help of some vendor-specific adaptor that transforms the formal system configuration into actual commands and parameters.

Conversely, the devices' configurations are periodically retrieved to update the formal system configuration. Changes to the configuration are detected by the diagnosis engine (6), which relays them back to the synthesis engine (7). Should some of the changes invalidate the requirements, the synthesis engine regenerates a new, valid system configuration and sends any modifications back to the appropriate devices.

It shall be noted that this architecture consists only of a few minor additions to the core cycle 4–6–7, which is nothing but a *feedback loop* in the traditional, control-theoretic sense (Hellerstein et al., 2004). Hence, as such, self-configuration can be seen as an application of control theory to information systems, and in particular network devices.

In turn, other autonomic, self-* properties are partly subsumed by the previous architecture. For example, **self-deployment** is achieved by iterating through the system a first time, starting from an empty configuration. Similarly, *self-healing* is a particular case of self-configuration, where harmful modifications to the devices' configurations are detected by the diagnosis engine, and corrected through the generation of a new configuration that re-establishes the network's conformance to its requirements.

ACN Through Self-Configuration

This framework supposes that system requirements be expressed in a way that makes possible reasoning and computation about them. Although the service grammar architecture provides an

Figure 1. A self-configuration architecture for network devices, inspired from Narain (2004)

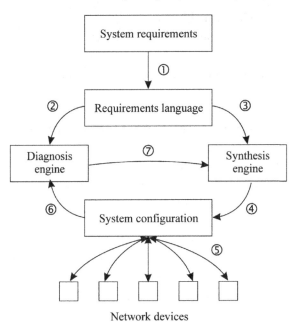

Network devices

appealing model for analyzing and designing multiple facets of ACN systems, there exists tremendous variability in the requirements languages used by different proposed solutions. Boutaba et al. (2009) point to the lack of formal foundations for what they call *knowledge management*.

Indeed, formal aspects of ACN have seldom been studied. Wang (2007) describes formal aspects of ACN from a behavioural perspective, while Cong-Vinh (2009) characterizes self-* facets using category theory. This chapter rather takes a *logical* point of view, and attempts to describe how self-configuration and related self-* properties can be studied and realized through the use of appropriate logical formalisms.

We shall see that such a viewpoint provides several advantages. First, it provides a unified framework for expressing both the *state* of a network, and *constraints* that such a network must fulfil to be in working order. Second, the use of logical notations allows us to tap onto readily available constraint solvers to automatically generate configurations satisfying a set of properties,

thereby achieving self-configuration. Finally, theoretical results about logical formalisms can be used to infer important properties of autonomic systems. These claims will be illustrated by the means of a running example.

BACKGROUND

In this section, we develop a configuration example based on Virtual Local Area Networks and the Virtual Trunking Protocol. We express configuration "self-rules" for a configuration of this type to be functional. This example will later be used to show how we can find the appropriate configuration of a device in a self-configuring and self-healing context.

Virtual Local Area Networks and the Virtual Trunking Protocol

Switches allow a network to be partitioned into logical segments through the use of Virtual Local Area Networks (VLAN). This segmentation is independent of the physical location of the users in the network. The ports of a switch can be assigned to a particular VLAN. Ports that are assigned to the same VLAN are able to communicate at Layer 2 of the OSI model, while ports not assigned to the same VLAN require Layer 3 communication. There can be numerous VLANs on a single switch and all the stations of a VLAN can be distributed on many switches.

Switches that need to share Layer 2 intra-VLAN communication need to be connected by a *trunk*, using popular protocols such as IEEE 802.1Q (2003) and VTP. A trunk is an interface that has the capability to carry the traffic of many VLANs. Only a trunk will allow two stations assigned to the same VLAN but connected to different switches to communicate at layer 2. The trunk will have two interfaces, one on each switch, these interfaces should be encapsulated in the same mode.

In principle, for a VLAN to exist on a switch, it has to be manually created by the network engineer on the said switch. This means that if a VLAN is to exist on several switches, it has to be created on every one of these switches. Otherwise, a port assigned to a non-existing VLAN is deactivated. The Virtual Trunking Protocol (VTP) has been developed on Cisco devices to centralize the creation and deletion of VLANs in a network into a VTP *server*. This server takes care of creating, deleting, and updating the status of existing VLANs to the other switches sharing the same VTP *domain*. The clients that are in the same VTP domain of the server will update their VLAN list according to the update. The switches that are in transparent mode will simply ignore the transmission but will nevertheless broadcast it so that other switches might get it.

Our configuration example involves a simple VTP setup, shown in Figure 2. We assume a minimal set of information about this network:

1. There are three devices, named switch-1, switch-2, and switch-3
2. A trunk links interface eth1-0 on switch-1 and interface eth2-0 on switch-2
3. A trunk links interface eth1-1 on switch-1 and interface eth3-0 on switch-3

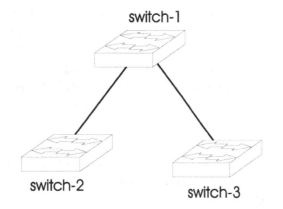

Figure 2. A simple cluster of switches in the same VLAN. The links are VLAN trunks

switch-1

switch-2   switch-3

4. Possible VTP domain names are "domain-1", "domain-2" and "domain-3"
5. The available encapsulation protocols are 802.1Q and ISL for all the trunks

We call these assertions the description of the initial *environment*.

Constraints on VLAN Configurations

Obviously, this initial setup is not sufficient for VTP to work on the network. The next natural step would consist of manually entering commands to enable VTP, or to write scripts that replay these commands to allow some form of batch processing. However, this script will do nothing but concretize a number of constraints, or VTP "self-rules", that must be true across this network.

First, in order to have a working VTP configuration, the network needs a unique VTP server; all other switches must be VTP clients. This will allow us to centralize VLAN creation and deletion on our server, and calls for a first set of two self-rules:

VTP Self-Rule 1 *The VTP must be activated on all switches.*
VTP Self-Rule 2 *There is a unique VTP server.*

We impose that all switches be in the same VTP domain, and that if two switches are connected by a trunk, then this trunk must be encapsulated in the same mode on both interfaces. This gives us two more constraints that should be true in all times:

VTP Self-Rule 3 *All switches must be in the same VTP domain.*
VTP Self-Rule 4 *The interfaces at both ends of a trunk should be defined as such and encapsulated in the same mode.*

Intuitively, a valid VLAN configuration for the network of Figure 2 will consist of any assignment of parameter values that defines:

- A VTP mode and VTP domain for each switch…
- A switchport mode and encapsulation protocol for each interface…

…that complement the environment declarations and are consistent with the VTP self-rules. Any procedure that can generate such an assignment automatically will hence fill the role of the synthesis engine in the framework of Figure 1, and exhibit the self-configuration property we are seeking.

Existing Approaches

The SELFCON project (Boutaba et al., 2001) developed a self-configuring environment based on the Directory-enabled Networking (DEN) (Strassner, 1999) principles, where devices register at a centralized directory server that notifies them of changes in configuration policies or network state. Similarly, the AUTONOMIA (Hariri et al., 2003) environment provides an autonomic architecture for automated control and management of networked applications

In Pujolle & Gaïti (2004), a suite of protocols compatible with TCP/IP is described that could be implemented into autonomic, agent-based "smart routers" that take decisions about which protocol in the suite should be used to optimize some user-defined goals. All these projects describe an infrastructure in terms of high level concepts and do not concentrate on the representation, validation and actual generation of configurations and rules, but rather provide an environment in which these operations can take place. The agent approach is extended in Gaïti et al. (2005) from a quality of service perspective.

In Golab & Boutaba (2004), the parameters of an optical network are automatically reconfigured based on link traffic using regression techniques. However, the range of legal values of these parameters is fixed and known in advance and the reconfiguration only aims at finding an optimal adjustment of existing values: the network itself is supposed to be properly working at any moment. Our work rather attempts to structurally modify a configuration by adding and removing parameters. Moreover, in our situation, the legal range of values changes from time to time and our method attempts to discover that range from the configuration rules.

The GulfStream software system (Fakhouri et al., 2001) provides a dynamic topology discovery and failure detection for clusters of switches in multiple VLANs; the approach is not based on the examination of the configuration of other switches, but rather on the broadcasting of Beacon and heartbeat messages between VLAN peers and is somewhat restricted to this particular situation.

Logic-Based ACN

The representation of VLAN operation as a set of rules paves the way for formulating self-configuration broadly as a *constraint satisfaction problem*. The leitmotiv for this chapter is simple. Given:

- some language L to describe constraints
- a set of configuration parameters $\bar{x}$ whose values need to be found
- φ, a description of the constraints on $\bar{x}$ expressed in the language L
- P, a procedure that finds values for $\bar{x}$ that satisfy φ

then the computation of $P(\varphi, \bar{x})$ allows an element to autonomously find appropriate values for its configuration. Such a general formulation presents an advantage: as we mentioned, the computation of P is nothing but a constraint satisfaction problem. Therefore, representing the configuration guidelines in a language L for which an algorithm P exists allows us to leverage any available CSP tool to perform self-configuration. This has been argued independently argued in various works under different names: Foley et al. (2006) describes a "constraint-based framework", and Lehtihet et al. (2005) proposes a "goal language".

The use of a constraint solver for configuration specification has been extensively argued by Narain (2005), who describes six possible purposes for this approach:

1. Configuration Synthesis: to produce a configuration from a set of constraints φ, compute $P(\varphi, \bar{x})$ and take the result $\bar{x}$.
2. Requirement Strengthening: to reconfigure a network with a set of additional constraints ψ, compute $P(\varphi \wedge \psi, \bar{x})$ (that is, the constraints of *φ and ψ* together) and take the result $\bar{x}$.
3. Component Addition: modify an existing set of constraints φ, to reflect, for example, the addition of a new component in the network. Submit the resulting new constraints, φ', to the solver, compute $P(\varphi', \bar{x})$ and take the result $\bar{x}$.
4. Requirement Verification: to make sure that a network fulfilling the constraints φ cannot cause a particular, undesirable situation described as ξ, compute $P(\varphi \wedge \xi, \bar{x})$ and observe the absence of a solution for $\bar{x}$.
5. Configuration Error Detection: model the current configuration of a network by a set of assignments, γ, and make sure that $P(\varphi \wedge \gamma, \bar{x})$ returns a solution —that is, take the current state of the system as a constraint in its own right. If not, then the current state of the network violates the constraints in φ.
6. Configuration Error Fixing: if a configuration does not fulfil φ, compute $P(\varphi, \bar{x})$ and take the solution $\bar{x}$ closest to the current configuration.

In particular, our study will show that logical formalisms are particularly appropriate for that task. The *declarative* nature of logical formalisms, which concentrates on "what", makes them well suited to describe constraints and relationships. Furthermore, logic, by avoiding early rigid procedural ("how") decisions, keeps flexibility in the choice of values for as long as possible. This chapter will therefore concentrate on logical formalisms that offer procedures to automatically solve constraints.

In this respect, logic-based configuration should be seen as a subset of *model-based* self-configuration, which uses a formal, mathematical model of a system as a basis for deriving its configuration (Williams & Nayak, 1996). Based on examples, the chapter will then proceed to show successively how various languages L can be used to describe configurations of autonomic devices, and present existing, off-the-shelf CSP solvers for these languages. In the present case, we restrict ourselves to mathematical logic as a means of modelling the system, and resort to logical algorithmic methods for synthesizing configurations. The satisfaction of logical constraints is called *model building* and is a theory that has been extensively studied (Caferra et al., 2004).

Why Use Logic-Based ACN?

Logical formalisms have been thoroughly studied. For example, theoretical results about first-order logic tell us that, the problem of finding a finite model for an arbitrary set of constraints is undecidable –that is, unless a tool uses a restricted form of first-order logic, its algorithm is bound to be imperfect (Mendelson, 1997; Grädel et al., 2007). On the other hand, checking that a finite structure satisfies a given set of constraints can be done in time typically polynomial in the size of this structure. Therefore checking an existing structure or validating a heuristically found candidate can be done rapidly. These kinds of global results are seldom available for *ad hoc* methods used in most configuration management products. In this sense, many drawbacks and shortcomings of logical formulations of self-configuration are already well documented, which is not usually the case with most commercial-grade configuration management products. With logical approaches, one can hence concentrate on issues specific to applying logic to self-configuration and not on the analysis of the global methodology.

What Logic-Based ACN is Not

We seize the opportunity to mention other approaches which achieve autonomic networking through means that can be perceived as related to logic-based ACN.

Scriptable Configuration Management

Many automated methods of configuring systems use a predefined bank of "scripts", "templates" or "recipes" (Steenkiste & Huang, 2006), that can be instantiated with different parameters. One example is the well-established configuration system Cfengine (Burgess & Couch, 2006). Our approach also differs from it in that only the desired properties of the configuration are expressed in a declarative way, but no action or script must be specified by the user. The method we present automatically determines the proper actions to take on the configuration in order to fulfil the desired rules.

In this respect, a more recent configuration management tool called Puppet1F[2] provides a declarative language that specifies a configuration with a sequence of constant values. Periodically, each device retrieves its configuration's declaration, and the Puppet engine finds all the differences between this declaration and the device's current state. It then applies whatever modification is necessary to make the system conformant to its declaration: for example, if a file is specified to exist and does not, the engine creates it.

Other approaches use rules in the if-then form. For example, Virgilio et al. (2007) describes a web information system that uses rules to automatically transform the contents of a page according to the display characteristics of a particular mobile device. The rules are of the form condition-action. The IETF also prescribes these kinds of rules as

the basis for *policy-based* management of network resources (Moore et al., 2001).

As argued by Narain (2005), condition-action, or if-then rules, can be seen as a middle ground between hard scripts and fully declarative specifications. Yet, they are not appropriate for the autonomic functionalities we seek, since are a procedural encoding of the logic, and ultimately have to embed all the work of a requirement solver. Scripting languages traditionally used for configuration management are not deemed appropriate for the same reason.

Topological or Numerical Configuration

A lot of work has been published about self-configuration applied to wireless sensor networks. In this context, the word "configuration" generally refers to the topological arrangement of the different elements forming the sensor mesh, and not the logical parameters that regulate the behaviour of a device in itself. It is therefore only faintly related to the present work.

In the same way, other self-configuration works are focused on the fine-tuning of numerical parameters with the goal of optimizing particular metrics of a network. This is the case of Steenkiste & Huang (2006), who describe a framework for automatically optimizing the latency of a network. The work we present in this chapter is not directly usable for optimizing parameters, but rather strives to find a *working* combination of parameters, which can then be fine-tuned using other methods.

Automated Theorem Proving

Automated Theorem Proving (ATP) (Newborn, 2000) is the dual of model finding. Instead of finding an appropriate assignment for parameters given some constraints, theorem provers attempt to demonstrate that a set of constraints will *always* be fulfilled, no matter what values are used. Popular theorem provers include Otter (Kalman, 2001),

Vampire (Riazanov & Voronkov, 1999), Equinox (Baader et al., 2005).

For example, Feamster & Balakrishnan (2003) use a logical formulation of BGP configurations, while Bush & Griffin (2003) formalize Virtual Private Networks (VPN) using first-order logic. However, both use this logical formulation to *prove* properties about the respective networks. For example, Bush shows that if the SYMMETRIC, SSAA and SCOPE properties (formally defined in their paper) hold, then the STRONG-ISOLATION property holds. They use these results to provide invariants about VPN configurations that can then be checked on actual configurations.

In our framework, these results would be obtained by automatically demonstrating *theorems* about a set of logic formulæ, and be accomplished through ATP. This technique, though, cannot be used directly to infer working configurations of VPNs. It shall be noted that, while theorem provers frequently require interaction with a user to develop a proof of some theorem, the tools and methods we present in this chapter are in comparison completely automated, a fundamental requirement in the use of logical methods for autonomic purposes.

MODELLING OF SELF-RULES WITH PROPOSITIONAL LOGIC

Although the term "logic" technically refers to a large number of languages, the most common form of such logic that comes to the mind is *propositional logic*. Propositional logic is the logic of Boolean variables (propositions) that are either true (•) or false (⊥). These variables can be combined with traditional connectives: ∧ ("and"), ∨ ("or") and ¬ ("not"). The meaning of these connectives is defined by truth tables. This way, simple variables can be combined to form compound statements, whose truth value can be computed from the values of their underlying variables.

As simple as this logic may seem, it can be used to directly encode self-configuration constraints.

VTP Constraints in Propositional Logic

Let us consider our VLAN configuration problem. In this context, the switch's configuration must be represented as values of some propositional variables. Let us first suppose there exist S different switches, labelled 1, 2, ..., S, D VTP domains, labelled 1, 2, ..., D, and a total of I interfaces on all switches, labelled 1, 2, ..., I. For any switch i, we can define a boolean variable a_i which is true when that switch is in VTP mode "server", and a boolean variable b_i which is true when switch i is in VTP mode "client". VTP is activated on this switch when VTP mode is either server or client, and this must be true of all switches 1, 2, ..., S. With those variables, constraint VTP Self-Rule 1 can be expressed as follows:

Propositional VTP Self-Rule 1

$$\bigwedge_{i=1}^{S}(a_i \wedge b_i)$$

where $\bigwedge_{i=1}^{S}$ represents the iterated conjunction

$$(a_1 \vee b_1) \wedge (a_2 \vee b_2) \wedge \ldots \wedge (a_S \vee b_S).$$

For VTP Self-Rule 2, we have in fact two conditions. One of the switches must first be a server, which is expressed by $a_1 \vee \ldots \vee a_S$. Furthermore this server must be unique. Therefore, for any two switches i, j, at most one should be a server, which can be expressed as $\neg(a_i \wedge a_j)$. Taking the logical conjunction of these expressions, yields a propositional formula expressing VTP Self-Rule 2:

Propositional VTP Self-Rule 2

$$(a_1 \vee \ldots \vee a_S) \wedge \bigwedge_{i=1}^{S-1} \bigwedge_{j=i+1}^{S} \neg(a_i \wedge a_j)$$

Since propositional logic offers a unique data type, booleans, more complex data, such as VTP domain name or trunk encapsulation mode, must be encoded using a sequence of boolean variables. For instance, one can introduce for every encapsulation mode *m* and every switch *i*, a new boolean variable $e_{i,m}$, which is true when switch *i* is using encapsulation mode *m*. With such variables, VTP Self-Rule 4 could be encoded as a propositional formula. The complete formalization of the VTP example is shown in Figure 3.

Configuration Through Model Finding

Once the environment and configuration properties have been represented as a set of Boolean formulæ, the process of finding an appropriate configuration amounts to computing an *assignment* for each of the variables that *satisfies* all the formulæ. In the case of propositional logic, an assignment gives a value (• or ⊥) to each of the a_i, b_i, and so on; this assignment satisfies the constraints if the formulæ in Figures 3 and 4 evaluate to • when each variable is replaced with its given value.

As an example, take propositional VTP self-rule 1. A possible assignment for the variables could be $a_1 = a_2 = a_3 = •$, and all the *b*'s set to ⊥. One can see that, when replacing the values into the formula, it indeed evaluates to •. Such an as-

Figure 3. VTP constraints, encoded as propositional logic formulæ

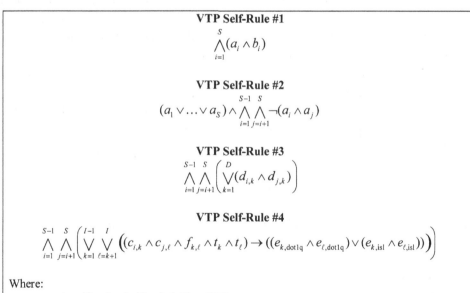

VTP Self-Rule #1

$$\bigwedge_{i=1}^{S}(a_i \wedge b_i)$$

VTP Self-Rule #2

$$(a_1 \vee \ldots \vee a_S) \wedge \bigwedge_{i=1}^{S-1} \bigwedge_{j=i+1}^{S} \neg(a_i \wedge a_j)$$

VTP Self-Rule #3

$$\bigwedge_{i=1}^{S-1} \bigwedge_{j=i+1}^{S} \left(\bigvee_{k=1}^{D} (d_{i,k} \wedge d_{j,k}) \right)$$

VTP Self-Rule #4

$$\bigwedge_{i=1}^{S-1} \bigwedge_{j=i+1}^{S} \left(\bigvee_{k=1}^{I-1} \bigvee_{\ell=k+1}^{I} \left((c_{i,k} \wedge c_{j,\ell} \wedge f_{k,\ell} \wedge t_k \wedge t_\ell) \rightarrow ((e_{k,\text{dot1q}} \wedge e_{\ell,\text{dot1q}}) \vee (e_{k,\text{isl}} \wedge e_{\ell,\text{isl}})) \right) \right)$$

Where:
- a_i: true if and only if switch *i* is a VTP server
- b_i: true if and only if switch *i* is a VTP client
- $c_{i,j}$: true if and only if interface *j* belongs to switch *i*
- $d_{i,j}$: true if and only if switch *i* belongs to VTP domain *j*
- $e_{i,\text{dot1q}}$ and $e_{i,\text{isl}}$: are true if and only if the encapsulation protocol for interface *i* is 802.1Q and ISL, respectively
- $f_{i,j}$: true if and only if interface *i* is connected to interface *j*
- t_i: true if and only if interface *i* is configured as a VTP trunk

Figure 4. Environment declarations, encoded as propositional logic formulæ

$$c_{1,1} \wedge c_{1,2} \wedge c_{2,3} \wedge c_{3,4}$$

$$f_{1,3} \wedge f_{2,4}$$

signment therefore satisfies VTP self-rule 1. Intuitively, one can see why: this assignment sets switch-1 as a VTP server ($a_1 = \bullet$), and all other switches as well ($a_2 = a_3 = \bullet$). Since VTP self-rule 1 asks for each switch to be either a VTP client or a VTP server, such an assignment is appropriate.

It is not appropriate, however, for VTP self-rule 2. The same assignment of values to the a's will naturally make VTP Self-rule 2 evaluate to $\bot$, since the formula can only be true if exactly one (and not all) of the a_i is set to $\bullet$. This again matches intuition, since VTP self-rule 2 requires only one VTP server, and our previous assignment sets all switches as servers.

Eventually, one can see that an assignment of values to all variables, such that all formulæ evaluate to $\bullet$, will indeed correspond to a situation where the configuration of each switch follows the requirements for VTP. Hence, finding a *model* –that is, a satisfying assignment– of the set of Boolean expressions is equivalent to configuring VTP.

The manual calculation of such an assignment quickly becomes tedious. For n variables, one possibly needs to evaluate 2^n assignments until the correct one is found, if any. To this end, *Boolean satisfiability solvers* (commonly named "SAT solvers") have been developed, which exhaustively search for possible assignments.

Contrary to what one might believe, SAT solving enjoys a great popularity due to the availability of efficient and widely available tools. The introduction of highly efficient optimization techniques, such as conflict-directed backjump-

ing and learning (Silva & Sakallah, 1999) and watched literals (Moskewicz et al., 2001) led them to being used to solve very large industrial problems. SAT-solver improvement can even be followed at an annual competition of available tools.2F[3] Popular solvers that have been used in various applications include Chaff (Moskewicz et al., 2001), Limmat (Biere), Berkmin (Goldberg & Novikov, 2002) and MiniSAT (Eén & Sörensson, 2003). The reader is referred to (Biere et al., 2009) for further background on the method.

However, the constraints in Figure 3 are true of any working VTP network. Hence, a SAT solver given these constraints will find a working configuration for *some* network. We rather want to find a configuration for the network in Figure 2, whose initial setup was described earlier. We must therefore add statements representing this initial setup as additional constraints.

For example, interface 1 belongs to switch-1. It is connected to switch-2's interface 2. This can be represented by $c_{1,2} \wedge f_{1,2} \wedge f_{2,2}$. The rest of these assertions is shown in Figure 4. Therefore, the set of formulæ is divided into two groups:

- Expressions that state universal conditions on a network are called *constraints*. This is what Boutaba et al. (2009) called *meta-knowledge*.

- Expressions that describe the state of a particular network are called *environment definitions*; this is what Boutaba et al. (2009) call *instance-knowledge*.

As an illustration, we performed experiments with the MiniSAT solver on sample VTP problems similar to the one described in this chapter. We generated network topologies for a varying number of switches, labelled 1 to S, with initial conditions that switch-i is connected with interfaces to switches $i+1$ and $i+2$. We then produced the corresponding Boolean formulæ, and sent them to MiniSAT to search for a valid VTP configuration. For each switch, MiniSAT had to find proper values for VTP modes, trunks, VTP domains and encapsulation protocols. The running times are shown in Table 1.

One can see that these running times are negligible. Indeed, SAT solvers are used on problems with millions of clauses and variables, and are accustomed to run for minutes, if not hours at a time on a single problem instance. In comparison, the modelling of the VTP configuration problem, even for a network of fifteen switches, is very small: it takes less than 1/6th of a second to configure a switch in that context.

Formal Consequences of Propositional Modelling

The first consequence of using propositional logic to model configurations is straightforward:

Theorem 1. *Self-configuration using propositional logic is an NP-complete problem.*

Table 1. Configuration time per switch for networks of varying number of switches, using the Boolean modelling of constraints and the MiniSAT satisfiability solver

Number of devices	Time per switch (ms)
3	5
5	6
10	40
15	156

Proof

Formally demonstrating NP-completeness involves a two-step reasoning. First, one must show that an already-known NP-complete problem can be reduced to self-configuration. To this end, we take Boolean satisfiability (SAT; *cf.* Garey & Johnson, 1979); it suffices to observe that any propositional formula can be converted into an equivalent description of some network in a straightforward manner. Second, self-configuration must be shown to belong to the NP complexity class; it suffices to remark that any solution (that is, any assignment of values to configuration parameters) can be verified against the original constraints in polynomial time, by simply re-translating them into their logical equivalents.

As straightforward as this conclusion may seem, we shall stress that formal computational complexity results seldom exist for existing, *ad hoc* self-configuration approaches. For example, proving any complexity results for custom-built languages, such as Cfengine's or Puppet's, remains an open and non-trivial problem. A consequence of logical modelling of configurations and constraints is therefore an easy and precise characterization of its computational load.

Moreover, once the configuration properties and initial state are represented in a Boolean notation, the actual process of finding a satisfying assignment is completely tackled by the SAT solver. This removes the need for purpose-built, *ad hoc* algorithms and implementations, to rather tap into industrial-grade, thoroughly optimized (and generally free) tools.

In some cases, existing features of SAT solvers can even be used to solve issues that are still open in the autonomic realm. For example, (Bahati & Bauer, 2008) tackle the problem of policy changes at runtime, where the introduction of slight modifications to the set of requirements force the modification of existing configuration elements. They describe an algorithm that tries to take advantage of the fact that the previous state of the system fulfilled the former requirements to incrementally find a solution to the new ones. It so happens that on the logical side, a similar problem has already been studied and implemented in the form of *incremental* SAT solvers (Whittemore et al., 2001), which can take advantage of pre-computed solutions to similar problems when searching for an assignment to a new set of formulæ. By representing the configuration problem into a Boolean satisfiability problem as above, and by sending this problem to an incremental SAT solver, the issue of policy changes at runtime can be managed out-of-the-box, without the need for developing a specific algorithm to this end.

MODELLING OF SELF-RULES WITH FIRST-ORDER LOGIC

One can easily see that even if propositional logic can encode any finite data types, writing out the formulæ can become cumbersome as the data types get more complex. One therefore usually prefers a more expressive logic, allowing to directly express constraints in a more convenient way. We now turn our attention to a more expressive logic, namely first-order logic.

In addition to the propositional logical connectives, first-order logic provides:

1. Arbitrary elements over a domain $\mathcal{D}$. In the following, we assume this domain is finite, although there exist theories that consider statements over infinite domains.

2. A finite list of predicate symbols $p_1, p_2, \ldots$ Each predicate is a function $\mathcal{D}k \to \{\bullet, \perp\}$; the value k is called the *arity* of that particular predicate. Intuitively, a predicate associates each k-uplet of input parameters to a truth value.

3. First-order predicates. The expression $\exists x$: $\varphi(x)$ states that there exists some element $d \in \mathcal{D}$ such that φ is true when all occurrences of x are replaced by d. Similarly, $\exists x$: $\varphi(x)$

asserts the same property, but for all elements $d \in \mathcal{D}$.

VTP Constraints in First-order Logic

Equipped with these additional tools, it is possible to formulate the VTP constraints in a much more compact notation. In the present case, the domain $\mathcal{D}$ will contain a finite number of device names, possible values for configuration parameters, IP addresses, and so on. VTP Self-Rule #1 becomes the following:

First-Order VTP Self-Rule 1

$$\forall s_1 : device(s_1) \rightarrow (IsVTPServer(s_1) \vee IsVTPClient(s_1))$$

This rule simply expresses that for every element s1, if s1 is a device name, then either this device name fulfils predicate IsVTPServer, or this device fulfils predicate IsVTPClient. Note that we still haven't defined predicates device, IsVTPServer and IsVTPClient; however, assuming they follow their intuitive meaning, the previous first-order expression faithfully expresses VTP Self-Rule #1. Indeed, it states that every device should be either a VTP server or a VTP client.

Similarly, VTP Self-Rule #2 can be expressed in first-order logic as follows:

First-Order VTP Self-Rule 2

$$\exists s_1 : device(s_1) \wedge IsVTPServer(s_1) \wedge$$
$$(\forall s_2 : device(s_2) \wedge s_1 \neq s_2) \rightarrow IsVTPClient(s_2))$$

Using the same predicates as above, this second expression states that there exists a device which is a VTP server, and such that all other devices are VTP clients. This ensures the presence of exactly one VTP server among all possible devices.

We postpone the presentation of Self-Rules 3 and 4 for the moment, and switch our focus on the predicates IsVTPServer and IsVTPClient.

Figure 5. VTP constraints, encoded as first-order logic formulæ

VTP Self-Rule #1

$$\forall s_1 : \text{device}(s_1) \rightarrow (IsVTPServer(s_1) \vee IsVTPClient(s_1))$$

VTP Self-Rule #2

$$\forall s_1 : \text{device}(s_1) \wedge IsVTPServer(s_1) \wedge (\forall s_2 : (\text{device}(s_2) \wedge s_1 \neq s_2) \rightarrow IsVTPClient(s_2))$$

VTP Self-Rule #3

$$\forall s_1 \forall s_2 : (\text{device}(s_1) \wedge \text{device}(s_2)) \rightarrow SwitchesInSameVTPDomain(s_1, s_2)$$

VTP Self-Rule #4

$$\forall s_1 \forall s_2 : (\text{device}(s_1) \wedge \text{device}(s_2)) \rightarrow$$
$$(\exists i_1 \exists i_2 : (\text{interface}(s_1, i_1) \wedge \text{interface}(s_2, i_2) \wedge InterfacesConnected(i_1, i_2)$$
$$IsTrunk(i_1) \wedge IsTrunk(i_2)) \rightarrow SameEncapsulation(i_1, i_2))$$

Predicate definitions

$$IsVTPClient(S) \equiv \exists x : (\text{vtp\_mode}(S, x) \wedge x = \text{"client"})$$
$$IsVTPServer(S) \equiv \exists x : (\text{vtp\_mode}(S, x) \wedge x = \text{"server"})$$
$$IsTrunk(I) \equiv \exists x : \text{switchport\_mode}(I, x) \wedge x = \text{"trunk"}$$
$$SameEncapsulation(I_1, I_2) \equiv$$
$$\forall x : \text{switchport\_encapsulation}(I_1, x) \leftrightarrow$$
$$\text{switchport\_encapsulation}(I_2, x)$$

These predicates can also be defined using other first-order expressions. For example, here is the IsVTPClient predicate:

$$IsVTPClient(S) \equiv \exists x : (\text{vtp\_mode}(S, x) \wedge x = \text{"client"})$$

This formula states that for all S, the predicate IsVTPClient(S) is true exactly when the predicate vtp_mode(S, "client") is true. One can see that the predicate IsVTPClient is defined by a first-order formula that refers to another predicate, vtp_mode. The IsVTPServer predicate is defined in a similar way:

$$IsVTPServer(S) \equiv \exists x : (\text{vtp\_mode}(S, x) \wedge x = \text{"server"})$$

One can use similar definitions for VTP Self-rules 3 and 4, as well as remaining predicates. The complete system of constraints is shown in Figure 6. One should contrast the legibility of these expressions with their respective propositional formulation in Figure 3. In addition to expressiveness, first-order modelling also brings increased clarity.

As for propositional logic, we also need to express the environment as additional first-order formulæ. We first define the unary predicate device(x) to identify switch names. Hence, we want device(x) to be true exactly when x is either "switch-1", "switch-2" or "switch-3", and false for any other input symbol. This can be done easily by means of two first-order formulæ:

Figure 6. Environment declarations, encoded as first-order logic formulæ

$$device(\text{“switch-1”}) \wedge device(\text{“switch-2”}) \wedge device(\text{“switch-3”})$$

$$\forall x : device(x) \rightarrow (x = \text{“switch-1”} \vee x = \text{“switch-2”} \vee x = \text{“switch-3”})$$

$$\forall i \, \forall x : switchport\_encapsulation(i,x) \rightarrow (x = \text{“dot1q”} \vee x = \text{“isl”})$$

$$InterfacesConnected(\text{“eth1-0”}, \text{“eth2-0”})$$

$$InterfacesConnected(\text{“eth1-1”}, \text{“eth3-0”})$$

$$\forall x \, \forall y : InterfacesConnected(x,y) \rightarrow$$

$$((x = \text{“eth1-0”} \wedge y = \text{“eth2-0”}) \vee (x = \text{“eth1-1”} \wedge y = \text{“eth3-0”}))$$

$device(\text{“switch-1”}) \wedge device(\text{“switch-2”}) \wedge device(\text{“switch-3”})$

$\forall x: device(x) \rightarrow (x = \text{“switch-1”} \vee x = \text{“switch-2”} \vee x = \text{“switch-3”})$

Configuration Through Model Finding

The conjunction of constraints and environment definitions constitutes a set of assertions about a given network. A *model* is a set of values and predicates that satisfy these assertions. As for propositional logic, there exist tools which, given a set of assertions, try to find a model that suits these assertions. In this case, a model of first-order formulæ will consist of a set of constants, a set of predicates, and the complete definition of the predicates for all values in the domain. For example, given the assertions:

$device(\text{“switch-1”}) \wedge device(\text{“switch-2”}) \wedge device(\text{“switch-3”})$

a satisfying assignment for VTP Self-Rule 1 would need to define the behaviour of IsVTPServer for both switch-1, switch-2, and switch-3. A possible definition is given in Box 1.

In turn, the fact that IsVTPServer("switch-1") is true entails that vtp_mode("switch-1", "server") holds, and so on. Following the same rationale as for propositional logic, one can realize that a complete assignment satisfying all VTP self-rules and all environment definitions will indeed qualify as an appropriate VTP configuration.

Analog to SAT solvers for propositional logic, there exist "model finders" for first-order logic. Some of the most well-known first-order model finders are Mace (McCune, 1994), Paradox (Claessen & Sörensson, 2003), and SEM(Zhang & Zhang, 1996). Figure 7 shows the graphical user interface for Mace4, along with a plain-text representation of the first-order formulæ shown in Figure 6. If a set of formulæ given to Mace is contradictory, no model can be found, and Mace eventually warns the user of this fact. On the contrary, if one or more models exist, Mace usually finds one and displays it to the user, in a notation similar to its input.

Box 1.

x	IsVTPServer(x)
switch-1	•
switch-2	•
switch-3	•

It shall be noted that some predicates have not yet been associated with any constraints. This is the case for predicate vtp_mode, which, apart from its appearance in the definition of IsVTPServer and IsVTPClient, is not constrained in any other way. By finding a model, Mace will "fill the blanks", and provide a complete definition for all the predicates that are under-constrained.

Figure 8 shows a partial output for a model satisfying the VTP constraints. In particular, it shows the definition of the vtp_mode predicate. Internally, Mace uses positive integers in place of any symbolic constant or string. The table shows for which of these tuples of values the relation vtp_mode holds. In this particular example, numbers 3 and 4 represent the values "client" and "server", respectively, while numbers 0, 1 and 2 represent the values "switch-1", "switch-2" and "switch-3". Therefore, Mace correctly assigned VTP mode "server" to exactly one switch (in this case, switch 1), and gave VTP mode "client" to the remaining two switches. Since our set of constraints did not specify which switch was to be the server, Mace's choice is arbitrary.

Therefore, if configuration constraints and environment definitions are both expressed as first-order constraints, Mace fulfils exactly the role of the synthesis engine shown in Figure 1.

An important side note is that a first-order solver will provide a definition of any under-constrained predicate. Therefore, one need not require values for VTP modes and domains, given a topology; the reverse operation can also be done. For example, one can provide a set of switches with their encapsulation protocols and VTP domains already defined in the environment, and not give any constraint on the InterfacesConnected predicate. In such a case, Mace will rather fill the blanks for this predicate, and hence find a suitable subset of switches that can be connected to form a valid VLAN.

As long as the data being managed is finite, an automatic translation into propositional logic will allow the use of efficient SAT solvers. Propositional logic is also often used as the target language in which other more expressive formalisms can be automatically translated. This translation approach is, for instance, used with the tools Mace

Figure 7. The Prover9-Mace4 graphical interface

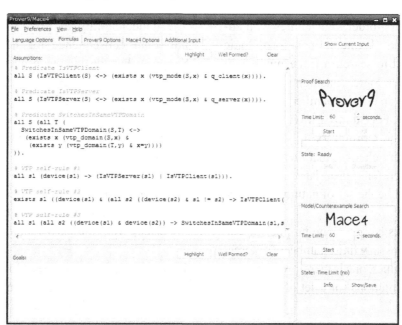

Figure 8. A model provided by Prover9- Mace4

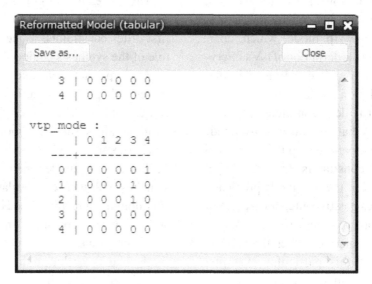

(McCune, 1994) and Alloy (Jackson, 2006), which allow more involved and natural input languages, in which complex constraints can be easily expressed. The running times for our VTP example with Mace are therefore similar to SAT solving shown in the previous section.

Formal Consequences of First-Order Modelling

The richness of first-order logic comes with additional drawbacks. While propositional logic solvers only need to search a finite number of models, first-order logic constraints may only have models with an infinite number of elements in their domain $\mathcal{D}$. For example, no finite domain can ever satisfy the formula $\forall x \exists y: y > x$, since it requires for every element that there exists an even greater element (an appropriate model for this expression would be the set of natural numbers, which is infinite).

Since networks have a finite number of elements and only a possibly finite number of different parameters and values, one is therefore interested in finding *finite* solutions for a set of first-order

formulæ. This wish is thwarted by an observation demonstrated by Trakhtenbrot in the 1950s:

Theorem 2 (From (Trakhtenbrot, 1950))

For any first-order language including a relation symbol that is not unary (other than the equality relation), satisfiability over finite structures is undecidable.

The undecidability of first-order logic has an important consequence for self-configuration. Suppose that the language used for describing self-rules includes any *binary* predicate $p(x,y)$, defined for tuples of values x and y. Such predicates can be used for multiple purposes: checking that two IP addresses have the same mask, verifying that the distance (in terms of "hops") between two devices is above a certain threshold value, and so on. Then any self-configuration procedure P dealing with such a language is *bound* to be imperfect. More precisely, either:

1. It cannot be guaranteed to provide the correct configuration every time, i.e. there exist situations where a satisfying assignment

exists but *P* cannot find it (and vice versa); or

2.   It cannot be guaranteed to terminate every time —that is, for some configurations, *P* might fall into an infinite loop.

Note that this consequence stems not from the inability for a programmer to write a correct self-configuration procedure, but rather from a formal property of the underlying specification language. Only in exceptional cases (such as the VTP example, when the only binary predicate used is $p(x,y) \equiv x = y$) can the decidability of the problem be restored.

This result, in turn, translates into interesting consequences from a control-theoretic point of view. For example, a number of works have studied the property of *self-stabilization* of autonomic systems (Brukman et al., 2007; Boutaba et al., 2009; Anthony, 2009), as defined by Dijkstra (1974). Self-stabilization is the capability for a system to arrive at a legitimate state in a finite number of steps. The same idea was recently presented under the name of *convergence* (Couch & Sun, 2003). From the above remark, one can easily notice the connection between a self-stabilizing system and the decidability of its specification language. If the representation logic is undecidable, then a model-finding procedure for it either might not reach a legitimate state every time, or might simply not find a state to settle on, thus violating self-stabilization. By this simple argument, one can again see the power of logic-based modelling for drawing fundamental conclusions about autonomic systems.

Alternate First-Order Languages

Alternate works using variants of first-order logic have also been proposed. For the reader knowing the Prolog language (Bratko, 2000), many expressions in Figure 6 look a lot like Prolog statements. Indeed, Narain et al. (2003) and Couch & Gilfix (1999) use Prolog to model configuration con-

straints of network elements, and use Prolog's resolution engine to find appropriate values for missing parameters. Take for example, the following Prolog *database*:

```
mortal(X):- man(X).
man(socrates).
man(aristotle).
```

Sending Prolog the query mortal(X) will find all values of X that must satisfy the predicate, drawing any required inferences from the assertions defined in its database. In this particular case, Prolog enumerates X=socrates, then X=aristotle, which are the two values that must satisfy the mortal predicate. Taking this reasoning further, one can imagine how configuration values can be found using an appropriate representation of the problem.

This, however, is only partially true. Narain (2005) remarks that Prolog is less expressive than first-order logic, and in particular cannot express existential quantification over values. Our configuration example shows that existential quantification is indeed required, as is exemplified by VTP Self-Rule 3. Therefore, no Prolog rule can ever be written with exactly the same meaning as VTP Self-Rule 3.

In a similar vein, Loo et al. (2005) suggest the use of *Datalog*, a declarative database querying language with similar semantics, for so-called *declarative routing*. We shall also point that *ontologies* can be used to represent configuration constraints. For example, the Web Ontology Language (OWL) (W3C, 2004), the Structure of Management Information (SMI) (McCloghrie et al., 1999) and Guidelines for Definition of Management Objects (GDMO, 1992) are all possible languages for describing network elements, their configurations and relations between various configuration parameters. However, SMI and GDMO lack a formal semantic, and are therefore inappropriate for automated reasoning and generation of configurations. On its side, OWL uses first-order logic to represent its constraints; barring a few adaptations, our presentation therefore applies to this language as well.

An interesting family of logics, used among others by OWL, is called *Description Logics* (DL). DLs emerged from the problem of knowledge representation in Artificial Intelligence. A well-known instance of DL is the logic $\mathcal{ALC}$ (Baader et al., 2007), which allows the definition of relationships and conditions between objects using a syntax reminiscent of set theory. Co*ncepts,* the equivalent of first-order predicates, can be combined with operators such as intersection ($\sqcap$), union ($\sqcup$), and inclusion ($\sqsubseteq$). Individual instances of ob*jects c*an be linked by binary relations called ro*les.* For example, to express the fact that each device is either a VTP server or a VTP client, on writes the following $\mathcal{ALC}$ sentence:

$\mathcal{ALC}$ **VTP Self-Rule 1** ∀**Dev**ice.(IsVTPServer ⊔ IsVTPClient)

When translated into classical first-order logic, this expression becomes exactly First-order VTP Self-rule #1. Similarly, one can succinctly express that there is only one VTP server:

$\mathcal{ALC}$ **VTP Self-Rule 2 1D**evice.IsVTPServer

This expression has no "simple" translation into first-order logic. To express that only one x is such that both device(x) a*n*d IsVTPServer(x) a*re* true, one must resort to a slightly more involved expression stating that any y su*ch* that y $\neq$ x cannot have both these predicates true. This is indeed what First-order VTP Self-rule #2 expressed.

A first advantage of $\mathcal{ALC}$'s syntax is that quantification is implicit; most of the quantifiers required in FOL can be dispensed with, which results in simpler formulæ. Another appealing characteristic of $\mathcal{ALC}$ is the separation of its knowledge base into termino*logical axioms (TBox)* and and asserti*onal axioms (ABox).* Intuitively, the TBox contains declarations of general

relationships that apply to classes of objects, while the ABox declares facts about individual instances of objects. This distinction corresponds, almost word for word, to the constraints and environment definitions used in self-configuration. For instance, the previous two self-rules belong to the TBox, while the following two environment definitions belong to the ABox:

```
switch1: Device
⟨eth1-0,eth2-0⟩: interfaces_connected
```

A second advantage of this logic is its complexity. There exist many direct mappings between $\mathcal{ALC}$ and equivalent first-order formulæ, yet in actuality $\mathcal{ALC}$ is a strict subset of first-order logic. While the demonstration of this fact is beyond the scope of this chapter, it yields an interesting consequence: satisfiability of $\mathcal{ALC}$ is no longer undecidable, and shifts down to the PSPACE-complete complexity class (Schmidt-Schauß & Smolka, 1991). However, this restricted expressiveness does not impact on the constraints described in our running example, which can all be expressed with appropriate DL formulæ.

Finally, many open source frameworks, such as Protégé (Knublauch et al., 2004), provide functionalities for editing OWL knowledge bases. The latest version of this framework comes built in with HermIT (Motik et al., 2007), a reasoner for $\mathcal{ALC}$ that allows users to execute queries on a DL knowledge base. Other free reasoners exist, such as Pellet (Sirin et al., 2007), FaCT++ (Tsarkov & Horrocks, 2006), RACER (Haarslev & Möller, 2001).

OTHER APPROACHES

While propositional and first-order logic represent classical and appealing formalisms for self-configuration, a number of alternate logics can be successfully used for that purpose. In this section, we briefly overview three alternate formalisms that have been used to achieve self-configuration.

Self-Configuration with Alloy

By definition, a first-order expression like $\forall x$ must apply for all the values in the domain $\mathcal{D}$. This creates a problem if this domain contains elements of different types, such as interface names, switch names, and parameter values. One can see from the expression of first-order logic constraints that a number of predicates are required simply to take care of the type of a *value*. For example, VTP Self-Rule #1 must be "guarded" by the device() predicate, to make sure that the only values s1 to which the formula applies are switch names. It would not make sense to check this rule by giving to s1 an interface name. As we have seen, quantification in the description logic $\mathcal{ALC}$ is always done over roles; for *example*, the expression $\forall$Device.C will make sure that condition C is true, *but* only for objects that are Devices (or fill the Device "role").

Another elegant extension of first-order logic is implemented in an object-oriented constraint solver called Alloy (Jackson, 2003), which precisely takes care of such typing. In Alloy, one first defines signatures *through n*ested data types declarations, similar to type definitions in an object-oriented programming language. For example, the switch and interface data types can be declared as follows:

```
sig switch {
 name: string,
 vtpMode: mode
}
sig interface {
 name: string,
 belongsTo: switch,
 connectedTo: interface,
 encapsulationMode: encapsulation
 mode: trunkmode
}
```

Following these declarations, an interface has a name, points to exactly one switch, is connected to exactly one other instance of interface, and so on. Similar declarations can be made for switches and encapsulation modes.

Once this data structure is defined, Alloy uses first-order logic to express constraints on these structures. For example, VTP Self-Rule #2 becomes the following Alloy expression:

```
pred VTPActivated()
 {no disj s1,s2:switch | s1.vtpMode =
server && s2.vtpMode = server}
```

This formula states that no pair of different switches s1, s2 are such that both have their vtp-Mode field set to "server". Remark how quantification, in Alloy, operates over values of a specific type (in this case, the switch type), and not to the whole domain of possible elements. Moreover, one can easily refer to subfields of a particular object using familiar "dot" notation: the VTP mode of a particular switch s1 is obtained with s1.vtpMode. This should be contrasted with classical first-order modelling, where the VTP mode of a particular switch is obtained through the binary predicate vtp_mode(s, x), *where* s is *a* switch name passed as an argument to the predicate.

The modelling of other VTP constraints, using this syntax, is straightforward. Alloy can then be run on configurations of varying number of elements, through a command like run VTPActivated for 3 switch, 2 domain, 5 interface, which will then try to find a model consisting of the said number of each element satisfying constraint VTPActivated. This approach has been used by Narain (2005) to generate valid configurations of routers implementing a Virtual Private Network (VPN), using 16 configuration constraints and computing a configuration for up to 50 routers and 50 interfaces; the reported running times amount to roughly 3.6 seconds per router.

Self-Configuration with XML Schemas

Alloy represents an increase in legibility of properties by allowing some form of structuring over the otherwise "flat" structure of unary or binary relations over a set of values. As explained in Hallé et al. (2004), the configuration of network devices such as routers and switches can be pushed further and be represented as a *tree*, where each node is a pair composed of a name and a value. This tree represents the hierarchy of parameters inherent to the configuration of such devices. As

an example, Figure 9 shows a tree representation of the configuration of switch-1 in the network of Figure 2.

A particular example of a tree structure is an XML document. XML has become an ubiquitous, general-purpose representation language for so-called *semi-structured data*, and is the foundation for network management protocols such as Net-conf (Enns, 2006), that uses this format to fetch and modify the configuration of a device. It is therefore natural to seek logical methods for self-configuration over such tree structures.

Figure 9. A portion of the configuration of the switch-1 in the network of Figure 2. The configuration of switch-2 and switch-3 differs in the VTP mode and trunk information.

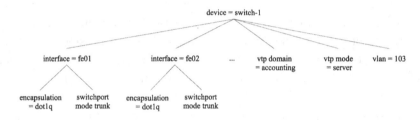

Figure 10. A graphical representation of a schema (left), and an instance of XML document satisfying that schema (right)

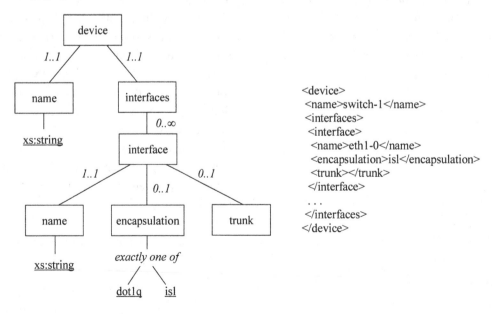

As an example, the left part of Figure 10 shows a simple XML Schema. It specifies that a device element must contain exactly one name element, whose content is a string representing the device's name. It must also contain exactly one interfaces element, which in turn may have an arbitrary number of interfaces descriptions. Each of these interfaces has a name and possibly an encapsulation mode and trunk element, indicating that this interface is configured as a trunk. One can imagine additional elements, such as a connected tag listing the interface names to which this particular interface is connected, and so on.

In turn, the right side of Figure 10 shows a particular instance of XML document that satisfies this schema. A tool called TAXI (Testing by Automatically generated XML Instances) has been developed to automatically produce valid instances of XML Schemas (Bertolino et al., 2006). It has been used in the field of web services, to automatically generate XML documents with given structure to be sent as an input to a web service to test. However, one can see that generating satisfying instances of an appropriate XML Schema can also be used to perform self-configuration for the VTP example, following the recurring principle demonstrated in this chapter.

Self-Configuration with Tree Logics

There is, however, a small drawback to the use of XML Schemas. While in Figure 10, the encapsulation and trunk elements are represented as optional, they are actually dependent on each other. It does not make sense to include a trunk element without encapsulation, and vice versa. Moreover, structural and cardinality constraints cannot capture more complex dependencies, such as the fact that two *connected* switches must have identical protocols in the encapsulation elements for the two interfaces that link them. Therefore, XML Schema alone fails to represent all the required constraints for realistic self-configuration situations.

A number of solutions have been proposed to complement XML Schema with the ability of specifying such constraints. Schematron (sch, 2004), TQL (Cardelli & Ghelli, 2001) and most notably the XML Path Language (XPath (Clark & DeRose, 1999)) and XML Query Language (XQuery (Boag et al., 2005)) have been developed as standard notations for retrieving parts of XML documents. They can also be used to compute Boolean queries over documents, which can in turn be used to verify constraints about them. For example, here is a simple XQuery expression:

```
for $x in /device/interfaces/inter-
face
 if (empty($x/trunk))
  then return (empty($x/encapsula-
tion))
  else return (not(empty($x/encapsu-
lation)));
```

This expression tells that for every interface element, the trunk element is present if and only if the encapsulation element is present. The expression returns true exactly when this condition is met.

XQuery is a powerful language, sufficient for representing all the VTP constraints as Boolean expressions similar to this one. For the purpose of this chapter, it is therefore natural to look for a "model finder" that can automatically generate XML documents satisfying Boolean XQuery expressions.

It turns out that the richness of XQuery also makes it a harsh environment for model generators. Since XQuery provides first-order quantifiers, the existence of a finite model is undecidable —in fact, it has been shown that XQuery is "as complex as possible" by proving its Turing-completeness (Gottlob et al., 2003).

We have already exposed the consequences of undecidability for self-configuration. However, since the full power of XQuery is seldom required, extensive research has been done on restricted *fragments* of the language that could restore decidability. Each of them differs from the others in the set of features they support: first-order quantification on node values ($\exists$), "next-sibling" relation ($\rightarrow$), number and type of Boolean connectives ($\vee$, $\neg$, $\wedge$), "child" relation ($\downarrow$), recursion or transitive closure ($*$), equality between node values ($=$). For example, the XQuery expression above requires quantification, disjunction and negation, and would therefore be representable by any fragment that includes $\exists$, $\vee$ and $\neg$. Decidability results for various fragments are summarized in Table 2.

Two notable proponents deserve mention. The first one is the ΔX language (Benedikt et al., 2002), based on XPath and XML Schema, that allows the expression of complex relationships between elements in an XML document. ΔX can be used to write *integrity constraints* about a document, that are then checked automatically whenever the document is modified. Using such a principle, one can ensure, for example, that a working VTP configuration remains valid after some changes are applied to the network. It does not, however, tell *what* modifications must be made to restore validity in case integrity becomes violated. As such, this solution can hence be used for *requirement verification* or *configuration error detection*.

The second related language is called Configuration Logic, and was developed specifically to represent network constraints over configurations represented as tree structures. Its syntax resembles that of firstorder logic: CL formulæ use the traditional Boolean connectives of predicate logic: $\wedge$ ("and"), $\vee$ ("or"), $\neg$ ("not"), $\rightarrow$ ("implies"), to which two special quantifiers are added. The universal quantifier, identified by [ ], indicates a path in the tree and imposes that a formula be true for all nodes at the end of that path. Likewise, the existential quantifier, identified by $\langle \rangle$, indicates a path in the tree and imposes that a formula be true for some node at the end of that path. For example, the following CL formula defines the predicate SameEncapsulation, which verifies that the encapsulation on a VLAN trunk is either IEEE 802.11Q or ISL, and that both ends use matching protocols.

```
SameEncapsulation(I1, I2) ≡
  [I₁ ; switchport encapsulation = x₁]
  ⟨I₂ ; switchport encapsulation = x₂⟩
    (x₁ = dot1q ∧ x₂ = dot1q) _ (x₁ =
  isl ∧ x₂ = isl)
```

Algorithms have been developed to automatically find a configuration satisfying a CL formula

Table 2. Satisfiability results for various related logics. The † symbol indicates that the result concerns finite structures or finite domains.

Fragment	Satisfiability	References
$\{\neg, \vee, \downarrow\}$	Decidable	Calcagno et al., 2003
$\{\neg, \vee, \downarrow, \rightarrow, =\}$	Decidable	Marx, 2005
$\{\wedge, \downarrow, \rightarrow\}$	NP-complete	Hidders, 2003
$\{\vee, \downarrow, \rightarrow\}$	NP-complete	Lakshmanan et al., 2004
$\{\neg, \wedge, \downarrow, \rightarrow\}$	NP-hard	Hidders, 2003
$\{\neg, \vee, \downarrow, \rightarrow, =, *\}$	EXPTIME-complete †	Marx, 2004
$\{\neg, \vee, \downarrow, \rightarrow, *\}$	EXPTIME-complete †	Afanasiev et al., 2005
$\{\neg, \vee, \downarrow, \rightarrow, \exists\}$	NEXPTIME-complete †	Hallé & Villemaire, 2008
mCTL*	2EXPTIME-complete †	Kupferman & Vardi, 2006
$\{\neg, \vee, \downarrow, \exists\}$	Undecidable	Conforti & Ghelli, 2004; Charatonik & Talbot, 2001

(Hallé & Villemaire, 2008), and this use has been suggested in an autonomic context. The VTP example in this chapter has been formalized as a set of CL formulæ in Hallé et al. (2006).

OPEN ISSUES

Although the concept of using logic to enable self-configuration of network devices is appealing, it is also subjected to a number of issues. Too often, relevant information about the proper configuration of various devices and services is scattered across hundreds of pages of documentation and is expressed in natural language. Some important details might even remain undocumented and be only known through informal communication channels such as mailing lists or even word of mouth. On the contrary, logic-based approaches to self-configuration rely on the fact that all configuration constraints are known in advance and fed to the synthesis engine.

In the case where this information is not readily available in an appropriate format, the task of eliciting and formalizing constraints from various sources might be time-consuming. Moreover, as we have seen, the use of logic is a departure from traditional, imperative and script-like languages that are well-known to network engineers and technicians. As a result, the formalization of configuration constraints can be seen as too steep a learning curve for organizations to invest resources in it, despite the promise of later benefits such as self-configuration.

This, in turn, lifts the veil over a second issue: the lack of a standard, agreed-upon notation for expressing such constraints. This chapter enumerated half a dozen possible formalisms based on various mathematical logics, each with its pros and cons: the same logic might not be appropriate to all tasks. Promising candidates include the DMTF's Common Information Model3F[4] (CIM); however, while the model leaves room for expressing so-called "policies", it only provides basic template classes for expressing them in a free-form notation. The choice of the actual formal policy language is left to the implementation.

While the prospect of an industry-wide formal standard for configuration *constraints* looks improbable for the near future, the issue could be mitigated by methods similar to those used in the Semantic Web community, such as *ontology mapping*. In such a situation, translators between various ontology languages allow information collated from various sources to be mapped into constructs of a single language.

We end this chapter by mentioning a few topics which, while not properly being issues, warrant additional work. The first is management of *dynamic* configuration constraints, where the desirable state of the network (and hence the properties that it must satisfy) changes over time. Similarly, the logic-based approach described in this chapter only specifies the goal state to achieve, without dealing with *sequential* aspects of the configuration. Yet, it is well-known that some changes to a configuration need to be performed in a specific order, and that some devices might even require to be set up before others. A more complete self-configuration solution should eventually formalize, and take care of, such ordering constraints. Finally, "fuzzy" goal descriptions, involving the optimization of various evaluation functions over real-valued intervals, could further refine the set of allowable configurations.

CONCLUSION

As the reader is now able to realize, there exists a myriad of formalisms, based on mathematical logic, that can be used to represent the configuration of network elements, as well as *constraints* on these elements. Based on the VTP example described as an introductory remark, one can see that even the simplest of such formalisms, namely propositional logic, can already be used for the efficient generation of configuration parameters, thereby achieving self-configuration. Increasing the expressiveness of the requirements language to first-order, and then tree logics, has the additional benefit of allowing the specification of multiple levels of abstraction, thereby improving the readability and compactness of the problem.

The most important side effect of such a logical approach is the potential for direct reuse of multiple techniques and theoretical results in the autonomic computing domain. Decision procedures and model finding tools that are readily available can be used off-the-shelf for self-configuration purposes. Moreover, various logics, including propositional and first-order logic, have extensively been studied over the past centuries. Interesting results about these logics apply directly to self-configuration problems when one of them is used as the specification language —for example, we have shown how the decidability of the decision procedure for a logic is closely related to the concept of self-stabilization in autonomic systems.

REFERENCES

W3C. (2004). *OWL Web ontology language overview*. Retrieved from http://www.w3.org/TR/owl-features/

Afanasiev, L., Blackburn, P., Dimitriou, I., Gaiffe, B., Goris, E., Marx, M., & de Rijke, M. (2005). PDL for ordered trees. *Journal of Applied Non-Classical Logics*, *15*(2), 115–135. doi:10.3166/jancl.15.115-135

Anthony, R. J. (2009). Policy-based autonomic computing with integral support for self-stabilisation. *Int. J. of Autonomic Computing*, *1*(1), 1–33. doi:10.1504/IJAC.2009.024497

Baader, F., Baumgartner, P., Nieuwenhuis, R., & Voronkov, A. (2005). 05431 Abstracts collection - Deduction and applications. In F. Baader, P. Baumgartner, R. Nieuwenhuis, & A. Voronkov (Eds.), *Deduction and applications*, vol. 05431 of *Dagstuhl Seminar Proceedings*. Internationales Begegnungs- und Forschungszentrum für Informatik (IBFI), Schloss Dagstuhl, Germany.

Baader, F., Horrocks, I., & Sattler, U. (2007). Description logics. In Van Harmelen, F., Lifschitz, V., & Porter, B. (Eds.), *Handbook of knowledge representation*. Elsevier.

Bahati, R. M., & Bauer, M. A. (2008). Adapting to run-time changes in policies driving autonomic management. In *ICAS*, (pp. 88–93). IEEE Computer Society.

Benedikt, M., Bruns, G., Gibson, J., Kuss, R., & Ng, A. (2002). *Automated update management for XML integrity constraints*.

Bertolino, A., Gao, J., Marchetti, E., & Polini, A. (2006). Systematic generation of XML instances to test complex software applications. In Guelfi, N., & Buchs, D. (Eds.), *RISE, LNCS 4401* (pp. 114–129). Springer.

Biere, A. (n.d.). *The Limmat SAT solver*. Retrieved from http://fmv.jku.at/limmat/

Biere, A., Heule, M., van Maaren, H., & Walsh, T. (Eds.). (2009). *Handbook of satisfiability. Frontiers in Artificial Intelligence and Applications* (*Vol. 185*). IOS Press.

Boag, S., Chamberlin, D., Fernández, M. F., Florescu, D., Robie, J., & Siméon, J. (2005). *XQuery 1.0: An XML query language*. W3C working draft. Retrieved from http://www.w3.org/TR/xquery/

Boutaba, R., Omari, S., & Virk, A. P. S. (2001). SELFCON: An architecture for self-configuration of networks. *Journal of Communications and Networks*, *3*(4), 317–323. Retrieved from http://bcr2.uwaterloo.ca/~rboutaba /publications.htm.

Boutaba, R., Xiao, J., & Zhang, Q. (2009). *Toward autonomic networks: Knowledge management and self-stabilization*, (pp. 239–260).

Bratko, I. (2000). *Prolog programming for artificial intelligence* (3rd ed.). Addison-Wesley.

Brukman, O., Dolev, S., Haviv, Y. A., & Yagel, R. (2007). Self-stabilization as a foundation for autonomic computing. In *ARES*, (pp. 991–998). IEEE Computer Society.

Burgess, M., & Couch, A. (2006). Modeling next generation configuration management tools. In *LISA*, (pp. 131–147). USENIX.

Bush, R., & Griffin, T. (2003). *Integrity for virtual private routed networks*. In INFOCOM.

Caferra, R., Leitsch, A., & Peltier, N. (2004). *Automated model building. Applied Logic Series*. Springer.

Calcagno, C., Cardelli, L., & Gordon, A. D. (2003). *Deciding validity in a spatial logic for trees* (pp. 62–73). TLDI.

Cardelli, L., & Ghelli, G. (2001). A query language based on the ambient logic. In Sands, D. (Ed.), *ESOP, LNCS 2028* (pp. 1–22). Springer.

Charatonik, W., & Talbot, J.-M. (2001). The decidability of model checking mobile ambients. In Fribourg, L. (Ed.), *CSL, LNCS 2142* (pp. 339–354). Springer.

Cisco. (n.d). *Configuring VTP*. Retrieved from http://www.cisco.com/en/US/products/hw / switches/ps708/products_configuration_ guide_ chapter09186a008019f048.html

Claessen, K., & Sörensson, N. (2003). New techniques that improve MACE-style model finding. In *Proc. of Workshop on Model Computation (MODEL)*.

Clark, J., & DeRose, S. (1999). *XML path language (XPath) version 1.0*. W3C recommendation. Retrieved from http://www.w3.org/TR/xpath

Conforti, G., & Ghelli, G. (2004). Decidability of freshness, undecidability of revelation. In Walukiewicz, I. (Ed.), *FoSSaCS, LNCS 2987* (pp. 105–120). Springer.

Cong-Vinh, P. (2009). *Formal aspects of Self-* in autonomic networked computing systems*, (pp. 381–410).

Couch, A. L., & Gilfix, M. (1999). It's elementary, dear Watson: Applying logic programming to convergent system management processes. In *LISA*, (pp. 123–138). USENIX. Retrieved from http://www.usenix.org/publications/library /proceedings/lisa99/couch.html

Couch, A. L., & Sun, Y. (2003). On the algebraic structure of convergence. In Brunner, M., & Keller, A. (Eds.), *DSOM, LNCS 2867* (pp. 28–40). Springer.

DAC. (2001). *Proceedings of the 38th Design Automation Conference, DAC 2001,* Las Vegas, NV, USA, June 18-22, 2001. ACM.

Denko, M. K., Yang, L. T., & Zhang, Y. (Eds.). (2009). *Autonomic computing and networking*. Springer.

Dijkstra, E. W. (1974). Self-stabilizing systems in spite of distributed control. *Communications of the ACM, 17*(11), 643–644. doi:10.1145/361179.361202

Eén, N., & Sörensson, N. (2003). An extensible sat-solver. In Giunchiglia, E., & Tacchella, A. (Eds.), *SAT, LNCS 2919* (pp. 502–518). Springer.

Enns, R. (2006). *Netconf configuration protocol*. IETF internet draft. Retrieved from http://www.ietf.org/internet-drafts/draft-ietf-netconf-prot-12.txt

Fakhouri, S. A., Goldszmidt, G. S., Kalantar, M. H., Pershing, J. A., & Gupta, I. (2001). Gulfstream - A system for dynamic topology management in multi-domain server farms. In *CLUSTER*, (pp. 55–62). IEEE Computer Society.

Feamster, N., & Balakrishnan, H. (2003). Towards a logic for wide-area internet routing. *Computer Communication Review, 33*(4), 289–300. doi:10.1145/972426.944767

Foley, S. N., Fitzgerald, W. M., Bistarelli, S., O'Sullivan, B., & Foghlú, M. Ó. (2006). Principles of secure network configuration: Towards a formal basis for self-configuration. In Parr, G., Malone, D., & Foghlú, M. Ó. (Eds.), *IPOM, LNCS 4268* (pp. 168–180). Springer.

Gaïti, D., Pujolle, G., Salaün, M., & Zimmermann, H. (2005). Autonomous network equipments. In Stavrakakis, I., & Smirnov, M. (Eds.), *WAC, LNCS 3854* (pp. 177–185). Springer.

Garey, M. R., & Johnson, D. S. (1979). *Computers and intractability: A guide to the theory of NP-completeness.* W.H. Freeman.

Golab, W., & Boutaba, R. (2004). *Optical network reconfiguration using automated regression-based parameter value selection.* In ICN.

Goldberg, E. I., & Novikov, Y. (2002). Berkmin: A fast and robust sat-solver. In *DATE*, (pp. 142–149). IEEE Computer Society.

Gottlob, G., Koch, C., & Pichler, R. (2003). The complexity of XPath query evaluation. In *PODS*, (pp. 179–190). ACM.

Grädel, E., Kolaitis, P. G., Libkin, L., Marx, M., Spencer, J., & Vardi, M. Y. … Weinstein, S. (2007). *Finite model theory and its applications.* Texts in Theoretical Computer Science. An EATCS Series. Springer.

Haarslev, V., & Möller, R. (2001). RACER system description. In Goré, R., Leitsch, A., & Nipkow, T. (Eds.), *IJCAR, LNCS 2083* (pp. 701–706). Springer.

Hallé, S., Deca, R., Cherkaoui, O., & Villemaire, R. (2004). Automated validation of service configuration on network devices. In Vicente, J. B., & Hutchison, D. (Eds.), *MMNS, LNCS 3271* (pp. 176–188). Springer.

Hallé, S., & Villemaire, R. (2008). Satisfying a fragment of XQuery by branching-time reduction. In *TIME*, (pp. 72–76). IEEE Computer Society.

Hallé, S., Wenaas, É., Villemaire, R., & Cherkaoui, O. (2006). Self-configuration of network devices with configuration logic. In D. Gaïti, G. Pujolle, E. S. Al-Shaer, K. L. Calvert, S. A. Dobson, G. Leduc, & O. Martikainen (Eds.), *Autonomic networking, LNCS 4195* (pp. 36–49). Springer.

Hariri, S., Xue, L., Chen, H., Zhang, M., Pavuluri, S., & Rao, S. (2003). An autonomic computing environment. In *IPCCC*. AUTONOMIA.

Hellerstein, J. L., Diao, Y., Parekh, S., & Tilbury, D. M. (2004). *Feedback control of computing systems.* Wiley. doi:10.1002/047166880X

Hidders, J. (2003). Satisfiability of XPath expressions. In Lausen, G., & Suciu, D. (Eds.), *DBPL, LNCS 2921* (pp. 21–36). Springer.

IEEE. (2003). *802.11Q: Virtual bridged local area networks standard.* Retrieved from http://standards.ieee.org/getieee802/download/802.1Q-2003.pdf

International Organization for Standardization. (1992). *Guidelines for definition of management objects.* (Tech. rep. ISO/IEC 10165-2:1992).

Jackson, D. (2003). Alloy: A logical modelling language. In Bert, D., Bowen, J. P., King, S., & Waldén, M. A. (Eds.), *ZB, LNCS 2651* (p. 1). Springer.

Jackson, D. (2006). *Software abstractions: Logic, language, and analysis.* MIT Press.

Kalman, J. A. (2001). *Automated reasoning with Otter.* Rinton Press.

Knublauch, H., Fergerson, R. W., Noy, N. F., & Musen, M. A. (2004). The Protégé OWL plugin: An open development environment for Semantic Web applications. In McIlraith, S., Plexousakis, D., & Van Harmelen, F. (Eds.), *ISWC, LNCS 3298* (pp. 229–243). Springer.

Kupferman, O., & Vardi, M. Y. (2006). *Memoryful branching-time logic* (pp. 265–274). LICS.

Lakshmanan, L. V. S., Ramesh, G., Wang, H., & Zhao, Z. (2004). On testing satisfiability of tree pattern queries. In C. Koch, J. Gehrke, M. N. Garofalakis, D. Srivastava, K. Aberer, A. Deshpande, D. Florescu, C. Y. Chan, V. Ganti, C.-C. Kanne, W. Klas, & E. J. Neuhold (Eds.), *VLDB*, (pp. 120–131). ACM.

Lehtihet, E., Derbel, H., Agoulmine, N., Ghamri-Doudane, Y., & van der Meer, S. (2005). Initial approach toward self-configuration and self-optimization in ip networks. In Royo, J. D., & Hasegawa, G. (Eds.), *MMNS, LNCS 3754* (pp. 371–382). Springer.

Loo, B. T., Hellerstein, J. M., Stoica, I., & Ramakrishnan, R. (2005). Declarative routing: Extensible routing with declarative queries. In Guérin, R., Govindan, R., & Minshall, G. (Eds.), *SIGCOMM* (pp. 289–300). ACM.

Marx, M. (2004). XPath with conditional axis relations. In Bertino, E., Christodoulakis, S., Plexousakis, D., Christophides, V., Koubarakis, M., Böhm, K., & Ferrari, E. (Eds.), *EDBT, LNCS 2992* (pp. 477–494). Springer.

Marx, M. (2005). Conditional XPath. *ACM Transactions on Database Systems*, *30*(4), 929–959. doi:10.1145/1114244.1114247

Maxwell, J. C. (1867). On governors. *Proceedings of the Royal Society of London*, *16*, 270–283. doi:10.1098/rspl.1867.0055

McCloghrie, K., Perkins, D., & Schoenwaelder, J. (1999). *Structure of management information, version 2* (SMIv2). (IETF Tech. rep 2578). Retrieved from http://tools.ietf.org/html/rfc2578

McCune, W. (1994). *A Davis-Putnam program and its application to finite first-order model search: Quasigroup existence problems*. Tech. rep., Argonne National Laboratory. Retrieved from http://www-unix.mcs.anl.gov/AR/mace/

Melcher, B., & Mitchell, B. (2004). Towards an autonomic framework: Self-configuring network services and developing autonomic applications. *Intel Technology Journal*, *4*, 279–290.

Mendelson, E. (1997). *Introduction to mathematical logic* (4th ed.). Springer.

Moore, B., Ellesson, E., Strassner, J., & Westerinen, A. (2001). *Policy core information model – Version 1 specification*. (IETF Tech. rep RFC 3060). Retrieved from http://tools.ietf.org/html/rfc3060

Moskewicz, M. W., Madigan, C. F., Zhao, Y., Zhang, L., & Malik, S. (2001). Engineering an efficient SAT solver. In *DBL (2001)* (pp. 530–535). Chaff.

Motik, B., Shearer, R., & Horrocks, I. (2007). A Hypertableau Calculus for $\mathcal{SHIQ}$. In *Proc. of the 20th International Workshop on Description Logics, DL 2007*, (pp. 419–426). Bozen/Bolzano University Press.

Narain, S. (2004). *Towards a foundation for building distributed systems via configuration*. Retrieved February 11th, 2010, from http://www.argreenhouse.com/papers /narain/Service-Grammar-Web-Version.pdf

Narain, S. (2005). Network configuration management via model finding. In *LISA*, (pp. 155–168). USENIX.

Narain, S., Cheng, T., Coan, B. A., Kaul, V., Parmeswaran, K., & Stephens, W. (2003). Building autonomic systems via configuration. In *Active Middleware Services* (pp. 77–85). IEEE Computer Society.

Newborn, M. (2000). *Automated theorem proving: Theory and practice*. Springer.

Parashar, M., & Hariri, S. (2004). Autonomic computing: An overview. In J.-P. Banâtre, P. Fradet, J.-L. Giavitto, & O. Michel (Eds.), *UPP, LNCS 3566* (pp. 257–269). Springer.

Pujolle, G., & Gaïti, D. (2004). Intelligent routers and smart protocols. In Aagesen, F. A., Anutariya, C., & Wuwongse, V. (Eds.), *INTELLCOMM, LNCS 3283* (pp. 16–27). Springer.

Riazanov, A., & Voronkov, A. (1999). Vampire. In Ganzinger, H. (Ed.), *CADE, LNCS 1632* (pp. 292–296). Springer.

Schematron. (2004). *ISO/IEC specification FDIS 19757-3*. Retrieved from http://www.schematron.com/spec.html

Schmidt-Schauß, M., & Smolka, G. (1991). Attributive concept descriptions with complements. *AI, 48*(1), 1–26.

Silva, J. P. M., & Sakallah, K. A. (1999). Graps: A search algorithm for propositional satisfiability. *IEEE Transactions on Computers, 48*(5), 506–521. doi:10.1109/12.769433

Sirin, E., Parsia, B., Grau, B. C., Kalyanpur, A., & Katz, Y. (2007). Pellet: A practical OWL-DL reasoner. [Elsevier.]. *Software Engineering and the Semantic Web, 5*(2), 51–53. doi:10.1016/j.websem.2007.03.004

Steenkiste, P., & Huang, A.-C. (2006). *Recipe-based service configuration and adaptation* (pp. 189–210). CRC Press.

Strassner, J. (1999). *Directory enabled networks*. New Riders Publishing.

Tasrkov, D., & Horrocks, I. (2006). FaCT++ description logic reasoned: System description. In Furbach, U., & Shankar, N. (Eds.), *IJCAR, LNCS 4130* (pp. 292–297). Springer.

Trakhtenbrot, B. A. (1950). Impossibility of an algorithm for the decision problem in finite classes. *Doklady Akademii Nauk SSSR, 70*, 569–572.

Virgilio, R. D., Torlone, R., & Houben, G.-J. (2007). Rule-based adaptation of web information systems. *World Wide Web (Bussum), 10*(4), 443–470. doi:10.1007/s11280-007-0020-2

Wang, Y. (2007). Toward theoretical foundations of autonomic computing. *International Journal of Cognitive Informatics and Natural Intelligence, 1*(3), 1–16. doi:10.4018/jcini.2007070101

Whittemore, J., Kim, J., & Sakallah, K. A. (2001). A new incremental satisfiability engine. In *DBL (2001)* (pp. 542–545). SATIRE.

Williams, B. C., & Nayak, P. P. (1996). *A model-based approach to reactive self-configuring systems* (*Vol. 2*, pp. 971–978). AAAI/IAAI.

Zhang, J., & Zhang, H. (1996). System description: Generating models by SEM. In McRobbie, M. A., & Slaney, J. K. (Eds.), *CADE, LNCS 1104* (pp. 308–312). Springer.

ENDNOTES

[1] http://www.research.ibm.com/autonomic
[2] http://reductivelabs.com/products/puppet
[3] http://www.satcompetition.org
[4] http://www.dmtf.org/standards/cim

Chapter 9
Bio–Inspired Techniques for Topology Control of Mobile Nodes

Cem Safak Sahin
City University of New York, USA

Elkin Urrea
City University of New York, USA

M. Umit Uyar
City University of New York, USA

ABSTRACT

In this chapter, we introduce a topology control mechanism based on genetic algorithms (GAs) within a mobile ad hoc network (MANET). We provide formal and practical aspects of convergence properties of our force-based genetic algorithm, called FGA. Within this framework, FGA is used as a decentralized topology control mechanism among active running software agents to achieve a uniform spread of autonomous mobile nodes over an unknown geographical terrain. FGA can be treated as a dynamical system in order to provide formalism to study its convergence trajectory in the space of possible populations. Discrete time dynamical system model is used for calculating the cumulative effects of our FGA operators such as selection, mutation, and crossover as a population of possible solutions evolves through generations. To demonstrate applicability of FGA to real-life problems and evaluate its effectiveness, we implemented a simulation software system and several different testbed platforms. The simulation and testbed experiment results indicate that, for important performance metrics such as normalized area coverage (NAC) and convergence rate, FGA can be an effective mechanism to deploy nodes under restrained communication conditions in MANETs operating in unknown areas. Since FGA adapts to the local environment rapidly and does not require global network knowledge, it can be used as a real-time topology controller for realistic military and civilian applications.

DOI: 10.4018/978-1-60960-845-3.ch009

INTRODUCTION

Autonomous systems represent a blend of software and machinery to create intelligent platforms for complex real world problems without human control and guidance. These systems must be self-sufficient and capable of adapting their behavior to rapidly changing and most likely unfamiliar environments.

A *mobile ad hoc network* (*MANET*) consists of an autonomous system of mobile nodes which dynamically form a network without any pre-existing structure. These mobile entities are geographically dispersed and equipped with wireless transmitters and receivers to communicate with each other within the MANET. The communications among the mobile nodes are generally established through multi-hop routing due to the limited range of transmission capabilities of each individual node. Since the mobile nodes move arbitrarily in a MANET, the network topology may change dynamically and unpredictably. One way of maintaining a uniform distribution of mobile nodes over any terrain is to provide the nodes with the ability to adapt their speeds and movement directions based on their local neighbor nodes and surroundings (e.g., number of neighbors, neighbors' locations, obstacles within node sensing range, etc.).

It is easy to envision many applications for GA-based topology control approach ranging from military to commercial applications, such as search and rescue missions (e.g., locating humans trapped in rubble after an earthquake), controlling unmanned vehicles and transportation systems, clearing mine-fields, and spreading military assets (e.g., robots, mini-submarines, etc.) under harsh and bandwidth-limited conditions. In these applications a large number of mobile nodes can gather information from multiple viewpoints simultaneously, allowing them to share information and adapt to the environment quickly and comprehensively. A common objective among these applications is the uniform distribution of autonomous mobile nodes operating on geo-graphical areas without prior geographical terrain knowledge. The topology control of autonomous mobile nodes faces extra challenges in MANETs since: (*a*) due to mobility, local terrain may change dramatically in a short time-span during an operation, (*b*) the number of mobile nodes may increase or decrease unpredictably due to malfunctions, (*c*) mobile nodes may not have access to neither navigation maps or GPS devices, but can only have limited information collected from local neighbors, and (*d*) nodes may be deployed into a terrain from a single entry point (rather than random or other types of initial distributions often seen in existing research).

Genetic algorithms (*GA*s) are adaptive heuristic search algorithms which have been demonstrated to be useful tools in a variety of search and optimization problems. GAs premise on the evolutionary ideas of natural selection and search for the *best individuals* within a *population* as the GA evolves toward the *fittest* solution or optimum result in an entire problem space (Holland, 1995; Mitchell, 1996). We introduce a *force-based GA* called *FGA* as a topology control mechanism in MANETs (see, for example, Sahin et al., 2008; Urrea et al., 2009; Sahin et al., 2010; Sahin, 2010). In this framework, each mobile node runs FGA to decide its next speed and movement direction based on its current local information to obtain a uniform distribution. The *objective function* used in FGA is inspired by the equilibrium of the molecules in physics where each molecule tries to be in the balanced position and to spend minimum energy to protect its own position. FGA uses the objective function (also called *fitness* function) to quantify the optimality of a solution (*chromosome*) and rank it against all the other chromosomes.

We implemented simulation software to evaluate FGA's effectiveness and applicability to real-life problems. In addition, in the Bio-inspired Computing Laboratory at the City College of New York, we built several testbeds to study the convergence properties of various GA-based topology control mechanisms, including FGA, in

MANETs. Our testbeds use different technologies and components namely FPGA Virtex-II™ with laptops and desktops and small robots (iRobots™) controlled by gumstix™ processors (Dogan et al., 2008; Dogan et al., 2009).

This chapter is organized as follows. In Background, we review prior research on the use of GAs on mobile node deployment, target localization in MANETs, and swarm robotics. In the next section, Our Force-Based GA, we briefly explain working principals of a simple GA and outline our FGA approach. The section of Dynamical System Model introduces formal models for convergence properties of FGA. Simulation experiment results are in Simulation Experiments for FGA. Overviews of our different testbeds are presented in Testbed Implementations.

BACKGROUND

Recently, distribution of mobile nodes has attracted attention of researchers due to the proliferation of MANET applications. In Winfield (2000), mobile nodes are required to disperse into a physically bounded area, take sensor readings, and then communicate the sense data back to a single collection point. A potential-field-based approach is used to deploy the mobile agents where the fields are constructed such that each node is repelled by both obstacles and other nodes in Howard and Sukhatme (2002). Blough et al. (2004) test the performance of different network parameters (e.g., average route length, network capacity, and connectivity) for Brownian-like, intentional movement, and random way movement algorithms. In Hasircioglu et al. (2008), evolutionary algorithms are used to calculate off-line path planning for unmanned aerial vehicles in a 3-D terrain. GAs are used for selection of MANET parameters in Montana and Redi (2005). Chen and Zalzala (1995) present a GA to optimize mobile robot motion. Khanna et al. (2006) propose a reduced complexity GA for optimizing sensor networks

to create a maximum number of sensor clusters with cluster-heads using a GA.

GAs have also been widely used in different distributed and swarm robotic applications. In Shinchi et al. (2000), a GA guides autonomous mobile robots to move in a highway without any collision. Similarly, Garro et al. (2006) use bio-inspired algorithms for robotic path planning application. An adaptive GA for mobile robots is proposed in Gesu et al. (2004) to identify targets while avoiding obstacles using the information from their cameras and light sensors. In Pugh and Martinoli (2005), performance evaluation of a noise-resistant particle swarm optimization for the unsupervised robotic learning is presented. Tuci et al. (2006) illustrate a complex transporting problem requiring collaboration for small autonomous mobile robots using neural networks.

Schema theory (Holland, 1995), Markov chains, and dynamic system model are widely used to provide a formal structure for analyzing GAs. For example, in Aytug et al. (1997), GA convergence time behaviour is modeled with a Markov chain to show the effectiveness of binary and higher cardinality representation of a search space. Nix and Vose (1992) provide one of the first modes for a simple GA and show how to incorporate selection, mutation, and crossover with transition matrix. Vose (1998) uses the dynamical system model to create the state of the current population from past populations. Nakama (2008) investigates the convergence properties of GAs applied to fitness functions perturbed by multiple sources of additive noise. Baras and Tan (2004) use Gibb's sampler simulated annealing process to control of autonomous swarms.

Different mobility models (e.g., random waypoint, random way group mobility, manhattan mobility, and freeway mobility) have been studied for mobile node movements (Bai and Helmy, 2006). Lin et al. (2004) propose a technique, based on renewal theory, for analyzing mobility models in ad hoc networks and apply their method to random waypoint mobility. Camp et al. (2002) provide relation between various mobility models and their effects on performance of ad hoc network. The mobility model used in our analysis is adapted from Hokelek et al. (2008).

There are fundamental differences between our approach and the existing research cited above. Our FGA controls the topology in a MANET without a central controller or the global knowledge of the entire network; FGA only utilizes information from neighboring nodes and local terrain to make movement and speed decisions to converge toward a uniform node distribution. Since FGA adapts to its immediate environment rapidly and does not require global network knowledge, it can be used as a real-time topology controller for realistic military and civilian applications. Furthermore, fully distributed characteristic of FGA makes it resilient to mobile node losses. Another significant difference is that no prior knowledge of the terrain is needed for FGA.

OUR FORCE-BASED GENETIC ALGORITHM

GAs are a class of stochastic search algorithms forming a subset of *bio-inspired computation* algorithms. GAs mimic the way biological trait information is transferred and improved under *selection* pressure in nature. The desired phenotype traits (that is, those of *individuals*) are selected by the evaluation of a specified *fitness* (i.e., *objective*) function. Individuals with a higher objective function score are more likely to be selected for *breeding* process by the GA. According to the theory of evolution, only those individuals in a population who are better suited to the environment are likely to survive and generate offspring, thereby transmitting their superior genetic information to new generations (Holland, 1995; Mitchell, 1996). The GAs, utilizing this principal of survival of the fittest, are typically applied to problems where deterministic methods are not present or cannot provide satisfactory results. GAs are essentially

composed of a set of individual chromosomes (called a *population*) and biologically inspired operators that create a new (and potentially better) population from an old one in a *generation*.

A GA evolves toward a (sub)optimum solution using an iterative procedure. Instead of working with a single candidate solution in each *iteration* (i.e., *generation*), it works with a number of candidate solutions (i.e., a population). Another important property of GAs is that they can work effectively with a randomly generated initial population for enumerable or large problem spaces (problem space may even have a couple of disconnected pieces like an *island model*). These properties make GAs perfect candidates for the problems (e.g., mobile node deployment in MANETs) where the environment continuously changes, only limited information is available and there is no global source for the dynamically changing problem space.

The following example describes the steps in a simple GA to provide the working principals of GA-based applications. Before running a GA, a fitness function is set up to evaluate the quality of each chromosome. First a population of N individuals is randomly generated and evaluated using a fitness score. The population is then sorted by their fitness values. In tournament and crossover, individuals are selected for breeding using probabilities proportional to their fitness scores (i.e., *roulette wheel selection*). The offspring are added to a pool consisting of candidate solutions for a new population. The offspring in the pool are then evaluated based on their fitness scores. Only the better performing individuals are accepted into the newly created population. With a small probability, mutation occurs on randomly selected individuals such that the chromosome is randomly altered. The elite individual has the best fitness value in the previous population and is typically chosen for the newly created population without applying any genetic operator. Thus, the fitness score in the new population is better than, or at least the same as, the previous one. The population undergoes the same process without the initialization step for many generations until a termination criterion is satisfied (e.g., convergence tolerance of the best individuals reaching a certain preset limit or reaching a limit on the number of generations).

In Sahin et al. (2008) and (2010), we introduced our force-based GA (FGA), which is inspired by the force-based molecule distribution in physics in which each molecule attempts to remain in a balance position and to spend minimum energy to protect its own position (Heo and Varshney, 2003). The fitness function of FGA is similar to molecular forces: each node is exposed to a force applied by its neighboring nodes (i.e., the mobile nodes located within its communication range of R_{com}) proportional to the distance between them. At the equilibrium, the aggregate force applied to a given node by its neighbors should be zero. If the summed force value is not zero, this non-zero virtual force value is used in fitness calculations by our FGA to find the node's next speed and movement direction. The force from a closer neighbor node is expectedly greater than the force from a further node. The force exerted on a node N_i by a node N_j is calculated as:

$$F_{ij} = \begin{cases} F_{\max}, & if \ d_{ij} = 0 \\ \varphi(d_{th} - d_{ij}), & if \ 0 < d_{ij} < d_{th} \\ 0, & if \ d_{th} \le d_{ij} \le R_{com} \end{cases} \qquad (1)$$

where d_{ij} is the Euclidean distance between N_i and N_j, d_{th} is the threshold to define the local neighborhood, and ϕ is the mean node degree for N_i (Sahin et al., 2008). The fitness function f_i is given as the sum of all the partial virtual forces that node N_i exerts on its k neighboring nodes.

$$f_i = \sum_{j=1}^{k} F_{ij} \qquad (2)$$

As seen from Equations 1 and 2, the goal of FGA is to find a set of parameter values (i.e., a chromosome) for node speed and direction that minimize the fitness f_i. These equations also show that the force on a node depends on the distance between the node, the location, and number of neighboring nodes within its communication range. Another important observation from Equations 1 and 2 is that there is no need for global knowledge to calculate fitness value of a node.

Each node in a MANET runs FGA as a software agent and follows simple rules to distribute uniformly while providing fully connected network, although there is no centralized control structure dictating how an individual node should behave. Autonomous decisions by each node for its speed and direction are determined by our FGA based on local neighborhood information.

Mobility Model

In our approach, adopted from the mobility model introduced by Hokelek et. al (2008), each autonomous mobile node runs FGA as an independent software agent such that FGA assigns the speed and movement direction of a mobile node based on its local neighborhood information (see section Estimating Behaviour of FGA). In our mobility model, we have a hexagonal terrain as a two-dimensional geographical area of $(d_{\max} \times d_{\max})$ composed of logical hexagonal cells, where a unique Cartesian coordinate pair <x,y> is assigned to each one of the cells. For example, in Figure 1, there are 64 hexagonal cells and seven mobile nodes, each of which can move into six different directions (i.e., D_0 through D_5). A wireless communication link between two mobile nodes is represented by a vector whose dimensions are in terms of layers. One layer is equal to the center-to-center distance between two neighboring cells. In general, for a mobile node in location <0,0> and another mobile node in location <x,y>, the link state between these nodes is <x-0,y-0> = <x,y>. For example, in Figure 1, for a mobile node N_3 in location <3,4> and another node N_1 in location <1,6>, the vector

Figure 1. Six nodes distributed within an 8x8 area partitioned into hexagonal cells (R_{com} =3)

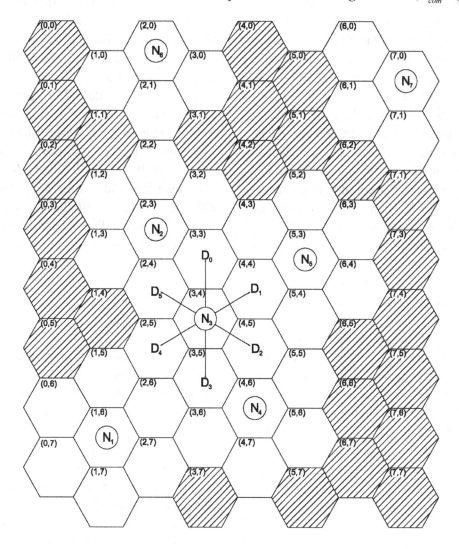

representing wireless link between these nodes is <2-$1,4$-$6> = <2,$-$2>$.

A wireless link with the state of $<x,y>$ ($0 < x,y < d_{max}$) between two mobile nodes is called *available* if two nodes are communicating with each other; otherwise the link is said to be *unavailable*. For a wireless link $<x,y>$ connecting two mobile nodes, after one time unit, each mobile node moves one of its six neighbor cells with a probability of 1/6 for each direction (i.e., D_0 through D_5). There are 36 possible next link states, and, as some of the will result in the same vector, only 19 possible combinations as shown in Table 1 (Urrea et al.,

2009). If R_{com} is a positive integer representing the communication range of a node, and R is the center-to-center distance between two neighboring cells, a wireless link can be available only if $R \leq R_{com}$ (The wireless link is unavailable if there is an obstacle between two mobile nodes).

The number of available links of a node is called its *degree*. In Figure 1, N_3 communicates with N_1, N_2, N_4, and N_5 if R_{com}=3; hence, the degree of N_3 is 4 for R_{com}=3 (the cells that are not within the transmission range of any MANET node are colored in shaded-gray). After one time unit each mobile node moves into one of its six

Table 1. The probability distribution for a wireless link to switch from state $<x,y>$ to state $<x',y'>$

x',y'	x,y	$x-1,y$	$x-1,y-1$	$x,y-2$	$x+1,y-2$	$x+1,y-1$	$x+1,y$	$x,y-1$	$x+2,y-2$	$x+2,y-1$
Probability	6/36	2/36	2/36	1/36	2/36	2/36	2/36	2/36	1/36	2/36

x',y'	$x+1,y+1$	$x,y+1$	$x+1,y$	$x,y+2$	$x-1,y+2$	$x-1,y+1$	$x-1,y+2$	$x-2,y+1$	$x-2,y$
Probability	2/36	2/36	1/36	1/36	2/36	2/36	1/36	2/36	1/36

directions with a certain speed. Speed and direction information are assigned by FGA based on local neighborhood information. The mobile node stays as immobile if FGA assigns the speed of a mobile node as zero. In our mobility model a mobile node is not allowed to move beyond the area boundaries. For example, N_6 can only move directions D_2, D_3, and D_4 in Figure 1.

Without loss of generality, all mobile nodes are assumed to be identical and broadcast periodic light-weight messages to one-hop neighbors within their communication ranges, where each message includes the node's location, direction, and speed (The results presented here can easily be extended for MANETs with heterogeneous nodes).

Chromosome Encoding

A chromosome (*genome*) is encoded as a string which defines a proposed solution to the problem that the GA is trying to solve. The chromosome is divided into genes which are short blocks of adjacent bits that encode a particular parameter of a mobile node in an application. In FGA, the chromosome encodes feasible settings for a mobile node's speed and direction. The chromosome length is set to 5-bit, which requires a solution space with size of $2^5=32$. Without using this simplification, the solution space of our model would be $2^{18}=262,144$, which is impractical to show in this paper.

In our hexagonal mobility model (see section Mobility Model), a node can move into one of six directions as seen in Figure 1. These directions in binary are encoded as 0 = (000) representing north, 1 = (001) as northeast, 2 = (010) as southeast, 3 = (011) as south, 4 = (100) as southwest, and 5 =

(101) as northwest. Binary string 6 = (110) and 7 = (111) are considered invalid. Four different node speeds are defined: 0 = (00) as immobile, 1 = (01) as slow speed, 2 = (10) as normal speed and 3 = (11) as fast. For example the chromosome string of 14 = (10010) means that the node will move to two hexagonal cells southwest of its current location.

Each mobile node runs FGA separately to generate new chromosomes representing candidate solutions for the next generation. These candidates are then sorted based on their fitness values. Lower values of fitness indicate better solutions which are composed of speed and direction. After FGA runs several generations, the speed and direction from the best chromosome in the last generation are given to a mobile node as the new parameters of its next movement.

DISCRETE-TIME DYNAMICAL SYSTEM MODEL

For a given fitness function of a GA, discrete-time dynamical system model uses the information from past populations to create the state of the current population (Vose, 1998). To estimate the expected next populations, we can calculate the probability distribution over the set of possible populations defined by the genetic information from past populations. As the number of generations of a population grows, the probability that the next state of a population will be the targeted one approaches to one since the chance that copies of the best chromosome will be included in the population increases.

Estimating Behaviour of FGA

We construct a discrete-time dynamical system model for our decentralized topology control mechanism using Vose's model to calculate the cumulative effects of FGA as a population progresses through multiple generations (Vose, 1998). This model provides expected next population distribution and a relatively safe indication of the actual FGA behavior.

Let Ω denote the search space, and n the cardinality of Ω. Then, using a fixed-length binary string representation, $\Omega = \{0, 1\}^{\ell}$, where ℓ is the string length. We will identify the elements of Ω with the integers in the range of $[0, n)$. A population P can be represented as an incidence vector: $P = <P_0, P_1, P_2, ...,P_{n-1}>$ where P_k is the number of copies of individual $k \in \Omega$ in the population. Hence, $\sum_{k=0}^{n-1} P_k = N$ where N is the population size. To obtain a more general representation, we can also describe the population as a vector $p = <p_0, p_1, p_2, ...,p_{n-1}>$ where p_k is the proportion that an individual $k \in \Omega$ appears in the population P. For example, for $\ell=2$, suppose a population consists of $<10,00,01,10,11,00,10,10,11,10>$. In this case, we have $N=10$ and p=$<2/10,1/10,5/10,2/10>$.

Population vectors have the following properties: (*i*) p is an element of the vector space R^n; (*ii*) each entry p_k must lie in the range $[0,1]$; and (*iii*) the sum of all of entries should be equal to one. The set of all vectors in R^n that satisfy these properties is called a *simplex* and denoted by Λ that can be seen as either the set of population-size-independent representations of populations, or the set of probability distributions over Ω. In general, $\Lambda= \{p \in R^n: p_t \geq 0$ and $\sum_{i=0}^{n-1} p_i =1\}$.

We can now view the actions of our FGA on a population as a trajectory of vectors $p \in R^n$. When $n = 2$, the simplex is a straight line segment in the plane R^2, running from $<1,0>$ to $<0,1>$to. All real populations correspond to points within the simplex. However, since components in the corresponding population vectors must be rational

numbers not all points in the simplex correspond to finite populations.

FGA can be represented as a heuristic function $G(p)$: $\Lambda \longrightarrow \Lambda$ where $G(p)$ contains all the details of selection, crossover, and mutation operators represented by F, C, and U heuristic functions, respectively. In other words, $G(p) = U(C(F(p)))$ represents the discrete-time dynamical system. $G(p)$can be interpreted as the *expected* next generation population where $G(p)_k$ is the *probability* that $k \in \Omega$ is selected to be part of it. Now we proceed to describe act of the three heuristic functions in more detail.

Selection Operator

Selection is the first operator in our FGA. In nature, the stronger organisms have a higher probability of reproducing than the weak ones and, hence, propagate their genetic material more effectively to the next generation. In other words, the selection procedure gives preference to fitter individuals (i.e., in FGA, the chromosomes with a lower value of fitness function, Equation 2). Let $p = <p_0, p_1, p_2, ...,p_{n-1}>$ be the current population vector and the probability $P_r(k)$ that any individual k will be selected for the next population is given by:

$$P_r(k) = \frac{f_k p_k}{\sum_{i=0}^{n-1} f_i p_i} \qquad (3)$$

where f_i represents the fitness value of individual $i \in \Omega$. Then, using matrices, the selection heuristic function $F(p)$: $\Lambda \longrightarrow \Lambda$ can be expressed as:

$$F_r(p) = \frac{diag(f)p}{f^T p} \qquad (4)$$

where f is the fitness function expressed as a vector, $diag(f)$ is the diagonal matrix with entries from vector f along its diagonal, and $f^T p$ is the average fitness of the population p. For example, let $\ell =$

2, $N=10$, $P=<2,1,5,2>$, and fitness function $f(x) = x^2$. Therefore the population vector is given as $p=<1/5, 1/10,1/2,1/5>$. Using Equation 4, we calculate $F(p)$ as follows:

$$F(p) = \cfrac{\begin{bmatrix} 0 & 0 & 0 & 0 \\ 0 & 2 & 0 & 0 \\ 0 & 0 & 4 & 0 \\ 0 & 0 & 0 & 9 \end{bmatrix}\begin{bmatrix} 0.2 \\ 0.1 \\ 0.5 \\ 0.2 \end{bmatrix}}{\begin{bmatrix} 0 & 1 & 4 & 9 \end{bmatrix}\begin{bmatrix} 0.2 \\ 0.1 \\ 0.5 \\ 0.2 \end{bmatrix}} = \cfrac{\begin{bmatrix} 0 \\ 0.1 \\ 2.0 \\ 1.8 \end{bmatrix}}{3.9} = \begin{bmatrix} 0 \\ 0.0256 \\ 0.5128 \\ 0.4615 \end{bmatrix}$$

Crossover Operator

Crossover operator is defined between two chromosomes from a given generation. It is used to generate two new offspring as possible candidates to be included in the next generation. Crossover operator does not change the number of 0s or 1s in a given chromosome pair, but only mixes them up. In *one-point crossover*, a crossover point is chosen at random from the range of $[0, \ell-1]$. Using this crossover point, a new chromosome is created by merging the parts of the original parent chromosomes. For example, if we perform crossover operation on parent chromosomes of $<a_0, a_1, a_2, a_3>$ and $<b_0, b_1, b_2, b_3>$ with a crossover point of two, the offspring chromosomes would be $<a_0, a_1, a_2, a_3>$ and $<b_0, b_1, b_2, b_3>$. Although, there are other crossover techniques (e.g., two-point crossover) (Holland, 1995; Mitchell, 1996), one-point crossover is the most popular one. FGA uses one-point crossover.

Crossover can be seen as a binary string or *mask* where any linear crossover operator is represented by a vector $m \in \Omega$ so that the offspring of parents a and b are $a \otimes m \oplus b \otimes \overline{m}$ and $a \otimes \overline{m} \oplus b \otimes m$, where $\otimes$ and $\oplus$ are bit-wise

multiplication and addition operators, respectively. The effects of applying the one-point crossover can be represented with the crossover heuristic function $C(p)$: $\Lambda \longrightarrow \Lambda$ such that the kth element of $C(p)$ is the probability that individual $k \in \Omega$ results from applying crossover to population p. Consequently, $C(p)$ can be is found by summing over all the possible ways that this mixing can happen. Hence,

$$C(p)_k = \sum_{i,j} p_i p_j r(i,j,k) \qquad (5)$$

where, $i,j \in \Omega$ are two (parent) individuals, and $r(i,j,k)$ is the probability of forming (offspring) chromosome k from (parent) chromosomes i and j. One-point crossover is not symmetric such that $r(i,j,k) \neq r(j,i,k)$. However, for (offspring) chromosome k and (parent) chromosomes i and j, we can define a symmetric mixing matrix M_k as: $M_k = 0.5 \cdot (r(i,j,k)+ r(j,i,k))$. Therefore,

$$C(p)_k = p^T M_k p \qquad (6)$$

Continuing with the example from the previous section, we identify two valid masks of $m \in \Omega$ for $\ell=2$ that characterize one-point crossover. They are $m = 2 = (10)$ and $m = 3 = (11)$ with probabilities μ_c and $(1-\mu_c)$, respectively. We now calculate $r(i,j,0)$, the probability that individuals i and j perform crossover to form individual $0 = (00)$:

$$r(i,j,0) = \begin{bmatrix} 1 & \mu_c & 0 & 0 \\ 1-\mu_c & 0 & 0 & 0 \\ 1 & \mu_c & 0 & 0 \\ 1-\mu_c & 0 & 0 & 0 \end{bmatrix}$$

We now proceed to calculate $r(i,j,0)$, the probability that individuals j and i perform one-point crossover to form individual (offspring) $0 = (00)$:

$$r(j,i,0) = \begin{bmatrix} 1 & 1-\mu_c & 1 & 1-\mu_c \\ \mu_c & 0 & \mu_c & 0 \\ 0 & 0 & 0 & 0 \\ 0 & 0 & 0 & 0 \end{bmatrix}$$

We now combine matrices $r(i,j,0)$ and $r(j,i,0)$ to find the symmetric matrix of M_0:

$$M_0 \frac{1}{2} r(i,j,0) + r(j,i,0) =$$

$$\begin{bmatrix} 1 & 0.5 & 0.5 & (1-\mu_c)/2 \\ 0.5 & 0 & \mu_c/2 & 0 \\ 0.5 & \mu_c/2 & 0 & 0 \\ (1-\mu_c)/2 & 0 & 0 & 0 \end{bmatrix}$$

M_k for each individual $k \in \Omega$ is obtained in the same manner as M_0. Hence,

$$C(p) = <p^T M_0 p, p^T M_1 p, p^T M_2 p, \ldots, p^T M_{n-1} p,>.$$

Please note that the probabilities in each matrix M_0 represent all possible ways of generating an offspring 0 from parents i and j using the crossover rate of μ_c. Therefore, the entry values in all other matrices M_k for $k=1,2,\ldots,n-1$ are the same as those in M_0, but shuffled differently according to the permutation matrix of α_k. Consequently, we only have to calculate mixing matrix M_0 to capture the entire effect of one-point crossover for each $k \in \Omega$ as $M_k = \alpha_k M_0 \alpha_k^T$.

To determine permutation matrix α_k, we first consider each individual within Ω as a group under bitwise addition. In the example from the previous section, the group table for bitwise addition is presented in Table 2.

The element $0 = (00)$ is the identity in this group. The corresponding permutation matrices for the other individual of $\ell=2$ are:

Table 2. Bitwise addition

	00	01	10	11
00	00	01	10	11
01	01	00	11	10
10	10	11	00	01
11	11	10	01	00

$$\alpha_0 = \begin{bmatrix} 1 & 0 & 0 & 0 \\ 0 & 1 & 0 & 0 \\ 0 & 0 & 1 & 0 \\ 0 & 0 & 0 & 1 \end{bmatrix} \quad \alpha_1 = \begin{bmatrix} 0 & 1 & 0 & 0 \\ 1 & 0 & 0 & 0 \\ 0 & 0 & 0 & 1 \\ 0 & 0 & 1 & 0 \end{bmatrix}$$

$$\alpha_2 = \begin{bmatrix} 0 & 0 & 1 & 0 \\ 0 & 0 & 0 & 1 \\ 1 & 0 & 0 & 0 \\ 0 & 1 & 0 & 0 \end{bmatrix} \quad \alpha_3 = \begin{bmatrix} 0 & 0 & 0 & 1 \\ 0 & 0 & 1 & 0 \\ 0 & 1 & 0 & 0 \\ 1 & 0 & 0 & 0 \end{bmatrix}$$

We can observe that for any given α_k, a value of one is set for an element (x,y) of α_k such that any bitwise operation between parents i and j results in k; otherwise a zero is assigned in α_k. For example, suppose in our continuing example, in α_2 element $(1,3)$ is set to one because parents 01 and 11 result in $01 \oplus 11 = 10(2)$.

Now, let us continue with our example from the previous section. Suppose the one-point crossover rate is defined as $\mu_c = 0.4$. The complete set of mixing matrices for the crossover operator is:

$$M_0 = \begin{bmatrix} 1 & 0.5 & 0.5 & 0.3 \\ 0.5 & 0 & 0.2 & 0 \\ 0.5 & 0.2 & 0 & 0 \\ 0.3 & 0 & 0 & 0 \end{bmatrix} \quad M_1 = \begin{bmatrix} 0 & 0.5 & 0 & 0.2 \\ 0.5 & 1 & 0.3 & 0.5 \\ 0 & 0.3 & 0 & 0 \\ 0.2 & 0.5 & 1 & 0 \end{bmatrix}$$

$$M_2 = \begin{bmatrix} 0 & 0 & 0.5 & 0.2 \\ 0.5 & 0 & 0.3 & 0 \\ 0.5 & 0.3 & 1 & 0.5 \\ 0.2 & 0 & 0.5 & 0 \end{bmatrix} \quad M_3 = \begin{bmatrix} 0 & 0 & 0 & 0.3 \\ 0 & 1 & 0.2 & 0.5 \\ 0 & 0.2 & 0 & 0.5 \\ 0.3 & 0.5 & 0.5 & 1 \end{bmatrix}$$

Now, we calculate $C(p)$ using Equation 3 as:

$$C(p) = \langle F(p)^T M_0 F(p), F(p)^T M_1 F(p), F(p)^T M_2 F(p), F(p)^T M_3 F(p), \rangle$$

$$C(p) = \begin{bmatrix} 0.0053 \\ 0.0204 \\ 0.5076 \\ 0.4668 \end{bmatrix}$$

Mutation Operator

Typically, mutation operator is defined as randomly modifying a bit, with a small probability, to preserve diversity in a population and to protect against getting stuck in local optima with many individuals with similar chromosomes (Holland, 1995; Mitchell, 1996). Mutation can also be defined by means of mutation masks. For an individual $j (j \in \Omega)$, the result of mutation operator using a mutation mask $m \in \Omega$ is represented as $j \oplus m$ where $\oplus$ is the bit-wise addition operator. The mutation heuristic function is defined by giving a probability distribution $\mu \in \Lambda$ over mutation masks. In other words, μm is the probability that $m \in \Omega$ is applied to a given individual j. Given a population $p \in \Lambda$, the mutation heuristic $U(p)$: $\Lambda \longrightarrow \Lambda$ is defined as:

$$U(p)_k = \sum_{j \in \Omega} \mu_{j \oplus k} p_j \tag{7}$$

Where $\mu_{j \oplus k}$ is the probability that an individual j mutates to an individual k using a mutation mask $m \in \Omega$. The contribution of mutation can also be described in terms of a $(n \times n)$ matrix U (called *mutation matrix*) that directly gives the effect of mutation on a population vector. Hence, the mutation heuristic can simply be shown as $U(p)k = Up$.

In our numerical example, for $\mu_m = 0.1$, the mutation matrix U is

$$U = \begin{bmatrix} (1-\mu_m)^2 & \mu_m(1-\mu_m) & \mu_m(1-\mu_m) & \mu_m^2 \\ \mu_m(1-\mu_m) & (1-\mu_m)^2 & \mu_m^2 & \mu_m(1-\mu_m) \\ \mu_m(1-\mu_m) & \mu_m^2 & (1-\mu_m)^2 & \mu_m(1-\mu_m) \\ \mu_m^2 & \mu_m(1-\mu_m) & \mu_m(1-\mu_m) & (1-\mu_m)^2 \end{bmatrix}$$

$$U = \begin{bmatrix} 0.81 & 0.09 & 0.09 & 0.01 \\ 0.09 & 0.81 & 0.01 & 0.09 \\ 0.09 & 0.01 & 0.81 & 0.09 \\ 0.01 & 0.09 & 0.09 & 0.81 \end{bmatrix}$$

Now, we calculate $U(p)$ as:

$$U(p) = UC(p) =$$
$$\begin{bmatrix} 0.81 & 0.09 & 0.09 & 0.01 \\ 0.09 & 0.81 & 0.01 & 0.09 \\ 0.09 & 0.01 & 0.81 & 0.09 \\ 0.01 & 0.09 & 0.09 & 0.81 \end{bmatrix} \begin{bmatrix} 0.0053 \\ 0.0204 \\ 0.5076 \\ 0.4668 \end{bmatrix} = \begin{bmatrix} 0.0564 \\ 0.0641 \\ 0.4538 \\ 0.4257 \end{bmatrix},$$

The matrix above shows the expected next generation population for all four chromosomes of length $\ell = 2$ in our numerical example. Chromosomes 2=(10) and 3=(11) have a high probability of surviving and therefore be part of the next generation population with probabilities of 0.4538 and 0.4257, respectively.

Dynamical System Model for our FGA

For the analysis of our GA-based approach using dynamical system model (Urrea, 2010), let us start from the initial mobile node distribution shown in Figure 2, where all mobile nodes remain in their positions at all times except node N_3 (i.e., it is the only node running FGA to improve its fitness value with respect to its neighboring nodes). To predict the behaviour of our FGA using dynamical system model (see section Estimating Behaviour of FGA), let us use chromosome of shorter length,

ℓ=5 bits, rather than the 18-bit chromosomes adopted in our implementations. As explained in The Chromosome section, the chromosomes represent the different combinations of speed and movement directions of mobile nodes. When the length of chromosome is set to ℓ=5, which requires a solution space Ω with size of 2^{ℓ}=32.

The normalized fitness values for FGA using Equations 1 and 2 for all chromosomes of length ℓ=5 is shown in Table 3. For instance, chromosome 6=<00110> for the mobile node N_3 represents

a movement to northeast with speed of two. As a result, N_3 will move from hexagonal cell <3,3> to <5,2> as seen in Figure 2. The fitness value is f_6=0.8000 as shown in Table 3. Since FGA handles this topology control problem as a minimization problem (i.e., a chromosome with a smaller fitness value has more chance to survive than the one with a higher fitness value), f_6 has a little expectation to transfer its genetic material to next generation. For example, chromosome 10 (f_{10}=0.1815) has higher change to produce off-

Figure 2. Six nodes distributed within an 8x8 hexagonal area and all nodes are immobile except N_3 (R_{com} =3)

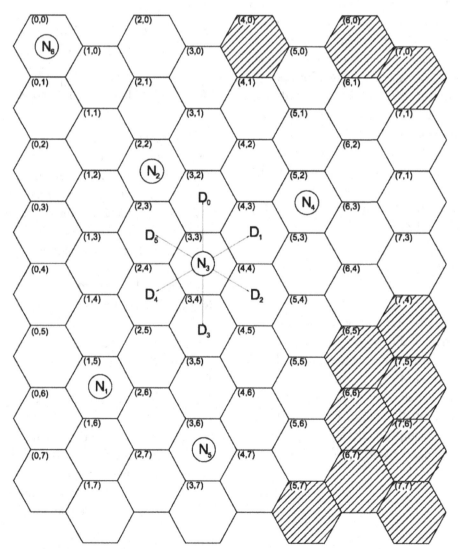

Table 3. FGA's normalized fitness value for all 32 chromosomes of length, $\ell=5$

$f_0=0.7262$	$f_8=0.7262$	$f_{16}=0.7262$	$f_{24}=1.0000$
$f_1=0.5446$	$f_9=0.3631$	$f_{17}=0.7262$	$f_{25}=1.0000$
$f_2=0.5446$	$f_{10}=0.1815$	$f_{18}=0.5446$	$f_{26}=1.0000$
$f_3=0.1815$	$f_{11}=0.0000$	$f_{19}=0.3631$	$f_{27}=1.0000$
$f_4=0.7262$	$f_{12}=0.7262$	$f_{20}=0.7262$	$f_{28}=1.0000$
$f_5=0.5446$	$f_{13}=0.7262$	$f_{21}=0.5446$	$f_{29}=1.0000$
$f_6=0.8000$	$f_{14}=0.5446$	$f_{22}=0.3631$	$f_{30}=1.0000$
$f_7=0.1865$	$f_{15}=0.9631$	$f_{23}=0.0908$	$f_{31}=1.0000$

spring (so that copy its genetic material) than chromosome 6 ($f_6=0.8000$).

Let us start with a random initial population P (size of 10) which is composed of chromosomes <0,3,7,3,26,10,26,23,26,30>. We can calculate $F(p)$ for our GA-based algorithms with Equation 2. After applying the selection operator to this population P, chromosome 3 (with two copies in the initial population) has the highest probability (0.3673) of being selected for crossover by roulette wheel selection process. On the other hand, chromosome 26 (with three copies in the initial population) has no change to be selected so that transfer its genetic material to the next generations because of its high fitness value of $f_{26}=1.0000$. Using Equation 4 with a crossover probability of $\mu_c=0.5$, we calculate $C(p)$ as shown in Figure 3 (b). We also observe from Figure 3 (b) that chromosome 3 still remains as the individual with the highest probability of survival after crossover operation. Also notice that the most of 32 chromosomes have non-zero probabilities compared to the values $F(p)$ in Figure 3 (a). It means that our FGA developed a non-zero possibility of survival for many individuals after crossover operation applied into the population P. For a mutation probability $\mu_m=0.001$, U_p is (calculated by using Equation 5) shown in Figure 3 (c). Chromosome 3 has the highest probability of surviving and, therefore to be a part of the next generation population, with probability of 0.3511 after the first generation if formed.

Figures 4 (a)-(c) show the expected population distribution after 40 generations. Chromosome 11=<01011> has the highest probability to survive in the entire solution space with a probability of 0.8491 after 40 generations. We observe the similar result from where the expected generation of population for all 32 chromosomes of length $\ell=5$ during 40 generations are displayed (The probabilities of crossover (μ_c) and mutation (μ_m) are set to 0.5 and 0.001, respectively). In Figures 4 and 5 chromosome 11 represents N_3 bearing south east with a speed of three so that we expect N_3 to be located in cell <6,5> (in Figure 2) at ($t+1$) after running FGA.

Figures 6 and 7 examine the effect of crossover and crossover in our GA-based approach. They show the expected population distributions of chromosome 11=<01011>, the test chromosome in our example, for different crossover and mutation rates. Figure 6 shows that changes in the value of crossover rate do not have a major impact on the expected population distributions of chromosome 11. On the other hand, small changes in the mutation rate cause a significant impact in the FGA's trajectory as seen in Figure 7. As mutation increases, chromosome 11 gets weaker, and it is more likely that it (and any offspring) will die out.

In this section, we analyzed the convergence and cumulative effects of GA operators as a population evolves through several generations for our FGA. Using Vose's discrete-time dy-

Figure 3. Expected population distribution after (a) F(p)$_0$, (b) C(p)$_0$, and (c) U(p)$_0$ operators for population vector p at the 1st generation

$$
\mathcal{F}(p)_0 = \begin{bmatrix} 0.0614 \\ 0 \\ 0 \\ 0.3673 \\ 0 \\ 0 \\ 0 \\ 0.1836 \\ 0 \\ 0 \\ 0.1836 \\ 0 \\ 0 \\ 0 \\ 0 \\ 0 \\ 0 \\ 0 \\ 0 \\ 0 \\ 0 \\ 0.204 \\ 0 \\ 0 \\ 0 \\ 0 \\ 0 \\ 0 \\ 0 \end{bmatrix}
\quad
\mathcal{C}(p)_0 = \begin{bmatrix} 0.0449 \\ 0.0091 \\ 0.0383 \\ 0.3105 \\ 0.0019 \\ 0.002 \\ 0.0118 \\ 0.19 \\ 0.0043 \\ 0.0005 \\ 0.1189 \\ 0.0454 \\ 0.0001 \\ 0.0001 \\ 0.0014 \\ 0.0108 \\ 0.0035 \\ 0.0003 \\ 0.0052 \\ 0.0225 \\ 0.0017 \\ 0.0016 \\ 0.0121 \\ 0.1546 \\ 0.0001 \\ 0 \\ 0.0057 \\ 0.0007 \\ 0 \\ 0 \\ 0.0002 \\ 0.0017 \end{bmatrix}
\quad
\mathcal{U}(p)_0 = \begin{bmatrix} 0.0585 \\ 0.0041 \\ 0.0059 \\ 0.3511 \\ 0.0006 \\ 0.0018 \\ 0.0018 \\ 0.1801 \\ 0.0024 \\ 0.0001 \\ 0.1747 \\ 0.0053 \\ 0 \\ 0 \\ 0.0018 \\ 0.0018 \\ 0.0006 \\ 0.0001 \\ 0.0001 \\ 0.0055 \\ 0 \\ 0.002 \\ 0.002 \\ 0.1958 \\ 0 \\ 0 \\ 0.0018 \\ 0.0001 \\ 0 \\ 0 \\ 0 \\ 0.002 \end{bmatrix}
$$

(a) $\qquad\qquad$ (b) $\qquad\qquad$ (c)

Figure 4. Expected population distribution after (a) F(p)$_{40}$, (b) C(p)$_{40}$, and (c) U(p)$_{40}$ operators for population vector p at 40 generations

$$
\mathcal{F}(p)_{40} = \begin{bmatrix} 0 \\ 0.0007 \\ 0.0011 \\ 0.0476 \\ 0 \\ 0 \\ 0 \\ 0.0024 \\ 0.0003 \\ 0.0156 \\ 0.0383 \\ 0.8919 \\ 0 \\ 0.0001 \\ 0.0003 \\ 0.0004 \\ 0 \\ 0 \\ 0 \\ 0.001 \\ 0 \\ 0 \\ 0 \\ 0.0002 \\ 0 \\ 0 \\ 0 \\ 0 \\ 0 \\ 0 \\ 0 \\ 0 \end{bmatrix}
\quad
\mathcal{C}(p)_{40} = \begin{bmatrix} 0 \\ 0.0014 \\ 0.0023 \\ 0.0539 \\ 0 \\ 0.0001 \\ 0.0001 \\ 0.0026 \\ 0.0009 \\ 0.0234 \\ 0.0447 \\ 0.8491 \\ 0 \\ 0.0003 \\ 0.0007 \\ 0.0093 \\ 0 \\ 0 \\ 0.0001 \\ 0.0014 \\ 0 \\ 0 \\ 0 \\ 0.0002 \\ 0 \\ 0.0002 \\ 0.0005 \\ 0.0087 \\ 0 \\ 0 \\ 0 \\ 0.0001 \end{bmatrix}
\quad
\mathcal{U}(p)_{40} = \begin{bmatrix} 0 \\ 0.0013 \\ 0.002 \\ 0.0539 \\ 0 \\ 0.0001 \\ 0.0001 \\ 0.0029 \\ 0.0008 \\ 0.0235 \\ 0.045 \\ 0.8492 \\ 0 \\ 0.0003 \\ 0.0008 \\ 0.009 \\ 0 \\ 0 \\ 0.0001 \\ 0.0015 \\ 0 \\ 0 \\ 0 \\ 0.0002 \\ 0 \\ 0.0002 \\ 0.0005 \\ 0.0086 \\ 0 \\ 0 \\ 0 \\ 0.0001 \end{bmatrix}
$$

(a) $\qquad\qquad$ (b) $\qquad\qquad$ (c)

Figure 5. Expected population distribution for chromosomes of length ℓ=5 (with μ_c=0.5 and μ_m=0.001) after 40 generations

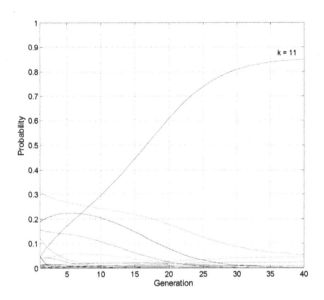

Figure 6. Expected population distribution of chromosome 11 = <01011> for different crossover rates (shown as c) after 40 generations

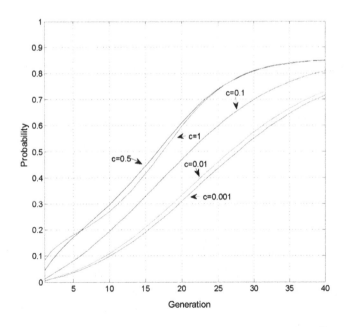

Figure 7. Expected population distribution of chromosome 11 = <01011> for different mutation rates after 40 generations

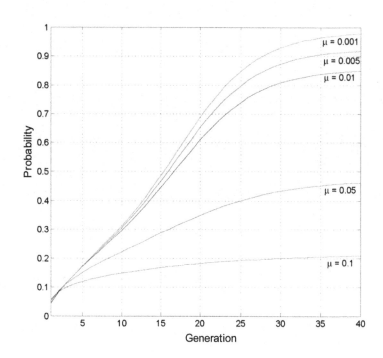

namical model (Vose, 1998), we studied the expected behavior of our FGA framework over multiple generations. A simple scenario for FGA was evolved up to 40 generations to show the better chromosomes life cycles in the generations.

SIMULATION EXPERIMENTS FOR FGA

In this section we present simulation software and testbed experiments to analyze effectiveness and convergence of our FGA approach. For simplicity, we assume that all mobile nodes have the same capability including communication range (R_{com}) and movement capabilities (i.e., speed and directions) for simulation experiments.

GA Simulation Software

We implemented simulation software in Java to study the effectiveness of our distributed GA-based framework for a uniform distribution of knowledge sharing mobile nodes. Eclipse SD-K™ version 3.2.0 was used as the development environment, and Mason, a fast discrete-event multi-agent simulation library core developed by George Mason University ECJLab, was chosen as the visualization tool (i.e., GUI) and multi-agent library.

The current simulation software implementation has more than 4,000 lines of algorithmic Java code. Our software design philosophy was to build a GA-based application to which a programmer can easily add new features (e.g., different types of crossover operators, or different rules for mutation operators, etc.) and new evolutionary approaches. Our simulation software runs as a multi-agent application which imitates a real-time topology control mechanism. Therefore, the results from our simulation software match closely to those from our real testbed experiments as shown by Dogan et al. (2009).

Figure 8. Graphical user interface for our GA software package (a) a screen shot of user input, and (b) a screen shot from an initial mobile node distribution for FGA

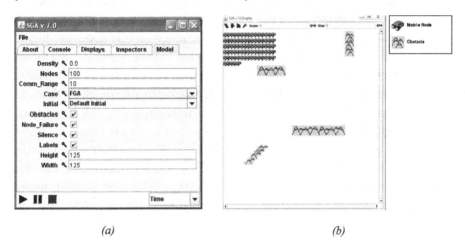

(a)   *(b)*

Sample screen shots of the graphical user interface of our simulation software are shown in Figures 8 (a)-(b). User-defined input parameters for our software include (Figure 8 (a)):

a.   **N:** total number of mobile nodes,
b. R_{com}: communication range,
c. T_{max}: maximum number of iterations,
d.   **Initial deployment type:** currently there are three different initial deployment strategies for the mobile nodes: (*i*) start from the northwest corner, (*ii*) place the nodes randomly in a given area, and (*iii*) start from a given coordinate (e.g., the center of the area) in the terrain,
e. d_{max}: size of the geographical terrain,
f.   Obstacle inclusion (on user defined locations),
g.   Random node failures,
h.   Silent mode (i.e., no communication among mobile nodes for given time periods).

Figure 8 (b) displays a sample initial deployment of mobile nodes starting from the northwest sector of a given terrain. Note that the northwest initial deployment option represents a more realistic approach of the topology control problem for the knowledge sharing nodes than other deployment possibilities over an unknown terrain. For example, in an earthquake rescue, a mine clearing mission, a military mission in hostile area, or a surveillance operation, all nodes may be forced to enter the operation area from the same vicinity rather than random or central node deployment.

Our simulation software also has the ability to run experiments using a previously used initial mobile node distribution and initial conditions from previous runs (i.e., the initial data for each mobile node includes a starting coordinate, speed, and direction). This ability is important since each experiment is repeated many times to eliminate the noise in the collected data and provide an accurate stochastic behaviour of GA-based algorithms. The mobile agents can move with one of four different speeds (i.e., immobile, slow, normal, and fast) to any of the six possible directions in the hexagonal lattice.

Simulation Experiment Results

We designed FGA such that each mobile node's movement is only affected by its current neighbors' positions and the obstacles in the communication range. Due to this flexibility, we expect that mobile nodes will be adaptive to the changes in their environment including node density, node failures, terrain shape, and obstacles. Figure 8 (b) shows an example simulation experiment for 80 mobile nodes, each with communication range of $R_{com} = 10$, the initial mobile node deployment and the positions of the obstacles. For more realistic results, simulation software does not allow the nodes to communicate through the obstacles even if they are close to each other. Each of our simulation experiments was run for $T_{max} = 1000$ time units, and was repeated for 50 times so as to avoid transient results from the natural non-deterministic behaviour of GA-based applications.

To analyze the performance and effectiveness of our FGA approach, we set up a scenario in which a team of mobile nodes enters an unknown geographical area (e.g., building rubble due to an earthquake). The goal of the mobile nodes is to uniformly spread over the terrain (in spite of obstacles/debris) to provide visual information using their cameras in a search and rescue mission. During this operation some randomly chosen mobile nodes may malfunction. In Figure 9, malfunctioned mobile nodes are highlighted as blue circles. In the experiment, the mobile nodes at the southeast corner will be collapsed under building debris due to aftershocks at times T = 400 and T = 600 time units. These destroyed nodes are shown as yellow circles in Figure 9. Following the aftershocks, the remaining mobile nodes reconfigure their positions to compensate for the missing area coverage. The final node distribution is shown in Figure 9, after T = 1000 time units (i.e., after node positions are readjusted). Although a total of 14 nodes have become disabled, the network is still fully connected and the remaining 66 nodes are still reachable by other mobile nodes through either a one-hop or multi-hop communication.

Normalized area coverage (NAC) is an important performance metric to define the effectiveness of our FGA approach. NAC is defined as the ratio

Figure 9. Final distribution of mobile nodes after T = 1000 time units

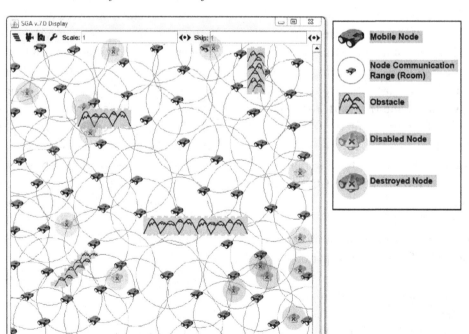

of union of covered areas (the area within at least one mobile node's communication range) and the total geographical terrain:

$$NAC = \frac{\sum_{i=1}^{n} A_i}{A} \qquad (8)$$

where A_i is the area covered by a mobile node N_i, and A is the total geographical terrain. NAC is a real number between zero and one, where one means that the geographical area is fully covered by mobile nodes.

If a node is located well inside the geographical area, the full area of a circle around the node with a radius of R_{com} is counted as the covered region (i.e., πR_{com}^2) (assuming that there are no other nodes overlapping with this node's coverage). If, however, a node is located near the boundaries of the geographical area, then only the partial area of the terrain covered by that node is included in NAC computation. For example, Figures 10 (a)-(b) show two nodes with a separation distance of $d_x > R_{com}$ and $d_y = R_{com}$, respectively. Let $A_T(2)$ denote the total area covered by these two nodes shown in Figure 10 where the gray region is counted only once. As the separation distance between nodes N_1 and N_2 increases, $A_T(2)$ gets larger and the overlapping region becomes smaller. The largest value for $A_T(2)$ is reached when $d = 2R_{com}$ as seen in Equation 9.

However, this separation distance is infeasible because the two nodes are now too far apart and cannot communicate with each other. Therefore, the allowable separation distances among mobile nodes are bounded by R_{com} so that the mobile nodes can communicate each other, collect the necessary local information to run FGA and find a feasible speed and direction for their next movements. As explained in Our Force-based Genetic Algorithms section, the goal of fitness function in FGA is to minimize the aggregated force on the corresponding node. Another constraint is that each node needs to communicate with its neighbors to exchange local information. To satisfy these two constraints, the distance between mobile nodes, at the perfect case, must be R_{com} to provide maximum area coverage.

$$A_T(2) = \bigcup_{i=1}^{n} A_i = A_1 + A_2 - (A_1 \cap A_2) \qquad (9)$$

where A_1 and A_2 are the areas of the first node (N_i) and second node (N_j), respectively.

For the general case, the area covered by n nodes is

$$A_T(n) = \bigcup_{i=1}^{n} A_i = \sum_{j=1}^{n} (-1)^{j-1} S_j$$
$$= S_1 - S_2 + \dots + (-1)^{j-2} S_{j-1} + (-1)^{j-1} S_j \qquad (10)$$

Figure 10. Intersection of two mobile nodes (a) $d_x > R_{com}$ and (b) $d_y = R_{com}$)

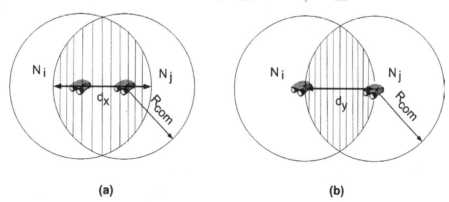

(a)   (b)

where

$$S_1 = A_1 + A_2 + \ldots A_n$$

$$S_{12} = \sum_{i=1}^{n-1} \sum_{j=i+1}^{n} A_i \cap A_j$$

…

$$S_n = A_1 \cap A_2 \cap \ldots \cap A_n$$

Figure 11 shows the improvement in NAC through time for the earthquake experiment above as the mobile nodes perform FGA. The blue line in Figure 11 represents that the mobile nodes successfully deploy themselves around the obstacles. At time T = 1000, the NAC value reaches ~99%. The NAC values when the mobile nodes malfunction are shown by the red line in Figure 11. We observe that the mobile nodes reach 97% area coverage at time T = 400. Once first aftershock damaged the mobile nodes at the southeast corner of the geographical terrain, NAC value drops because of the lost mobile nodes, which recovers after 200 time units to the NAC value of 95%. Similarly, after the second aftershock at time T = 600, the drop of NAC value is compensated by the remaining mobile nodes at approximately 300 time units.

TESTBED IMPLEMENTATIONS FOR FGA

Most of the research in wireless ad-hoc networks is based on software tools simulating network environments under strictly controlled conditions rather than implementing realistic testbeds due to their extreme cost of design, operation and difficulty of adapting real-time topology changes. To study the effectiveness of our GA-based algorithms and to prove the results of our simulation software, we implemented two different testbeds using FPGA Virtex-II™ and small robotic units (iRobots™) controlled by gumstix™ processors with wireless capabilities.

Testbed with iRobot™ and gumstix™

In this testbed implementation shown in Figures 12 (a)-(d), we used iRobots™ Create robots as the hardware platform. Each robot is equipped with an onboard gumstix™ computer acting as the brain of the iRobot™; all of our GA-based mobility commands including speed and direction, and wireless communication codes run on the gumstix™ computer. Figure 12 (a) shows the gumstix™ computer with an iRobot™. The

Figure 11. Normalized area coverage after T=1000 time units (N=80 and R_{com}=10)

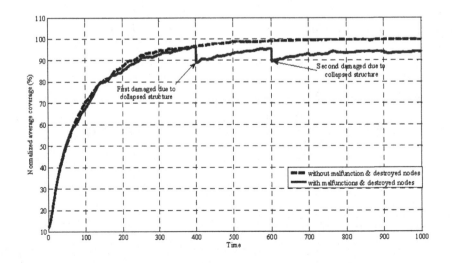

connection among the gumstix™ computers is established on the fly and immediately starts functioning. Once the wireless connection is established, all nodes communicate to each other using UDP broadcast at software level. To study the performance of our FGA with different network densities, we developed this testbed using multiple machines (i.e., iRobot™ controlled by the gumstix™) that emulate wireless mobile nodes (Dogan et. al, 2008). Feasibility of this testbed architecture along with our FGA algorithm for self-spreading of nodes have been studied with an experiment of nine real integrated single-board gumstix™ computers and automated iRobots™ as shown in Figures 12 (b)-(d). The initial positions of iRobots™ are displayed in Figure 12 (b). Figures 12 (c) and (d) show two snapshots of movements of iRobots™ by using our GA.

Testbed Using FPGA Devices

We implemented this testbed platform using Xilinx ML310™ development boards with Virtex-II Pro™ FPGA devices, laptops and desktops (Dogan et. al., 2009). It uses off-the-shelf wireless PCI cards that complies with the PCI Local Bus Specification version 2.3 on the Xilinx ML310™ with Power PC Virtex-II™ Pro based Processor running VxWorks™. We choose wireless hardware support (Atheros AR521x chipset™) under network devices 802.11a/b/g components and wireless mode support to include component support for ad-hoc IBSS to build the driver module into VxWorks™ real-time kernel.

This testbed allows us to implement and study different scenarios of our FGA for uniform node distribution. It is programmed in C++ and runs in both Windows and Linux operating systems. The experiments using this testbed represent realistic MANET conditions where each node has autonomous mobility and wireless communication capabilities. Software in all mobile nodes is configured with identical characteristics. Each mobile node broadcasts a periodic heartbeat message to the maximum radial distance allowed by the configured communication ranges. The collected local

Figure 12. Mobile node spreading experiments using iRobots™ controlled by gumstix™ processors (a total of 30 time units elapsed)

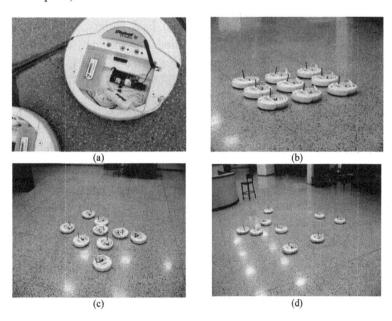

neighborhood information is then used by each mobile node as an input for our FGA to decide the next speed and direction. Detection and avoidance of node collision, prevention of excessive coverage overlaps, and out-of-boundary area coverage are considered as an add-on for effective GA-based solution evaluation. In order to emulate mobility, the TCP packets exchanged among nodes are dropped intentionally when the virtual distance between a source and a destination is greater than the configured communication range. Each mobile node moves independently from all others based on the results of its own FGA.

FUTURE RESEARCH DIRECTIONS

Future extensions of this work will include more precise analytic models of FGA behavior to provide a better understanding of convergence properties. Also applications to aerial vehicles and submarine systems are within the scope of this research.

SUMMARY

In this chapter, we outlined a GA-based topology control approach for efficient, reliable, and effective self-deployment of mobile nodes in MANETs. Our FGA controls the mobile node's speed and direction using local neighborhood information without a global controller. We presented a dynamical system model to formally analyze the convergence of FGA. Experiments results from our simulation software and two different testbed implementations showed that FGA delivers promising results for uniform node distribution of knowledge sharing mobile nodes over unknown geographical areas in MANETs.

ACKNOWLEDGMENT

This work has been supported by U.S. Army Communications-Electronics RD&E Center. The contents of this document represent the views of the authors and are not necessarily the official views of, or are endorsed by, the U.S. Government, Department of Defense, Department of the Army, or the U.S. Army Communications-Electronics RD&E Center.

This work has been partially supported by the National Science Foundation grants ECS-0421159 and CNS-0619577.

The authors would like to acknowledge the contributions of the City College of New York students Cevher Dogan, Jumie Yuventi, and Yahao Chen who worked on various stages of our testbed design and implementations.

REFERENCES

Aytug, H., Bhattacharrya, S., & Koehler, G. J. (1997). A Markov chain analysis of genetic algorithms with power of 2 cardinality alphabets. *European Journal of Operational Research, 96*(1), 195–201. doi:10.1016/S0377-2217(96)00121-X

Bai, F., & Helmy, A. (2006). A survey of mobility modeling and analysis in wireless ad hoc networks. In Safwat, A. (Ed.), *Wireless ad hoc and sensor networks* (pp. 1–30). Berlin, Germany: Springer.

Baras, J. S., & Tan, X. (2004). Control of autonomous swarms using Gibbs sampling. *In Proceeding of 43rd IEEE Conference on Decision and Control* (pp. 4752-4757).

Blough, D. M., Resta, G., & Santi, P. (2004). A statistical analysis of the long-run node spatial distribution in mobile ad hoc networks. *Wireless Networks, 10*(5), 543–554. doi:10.1023/B:WINE.0000036457.00804.e9

Camp, T., Boleng, J., & Davies, V. (2002). A survey of mobility models for ad hoc network research. *Wireless Communications & Mobile Computing (WCMC): Special issue on Mobile Ad Hoc Networking: Research. Trends and Applications*, 2(5), 483–502.

Chen, M., & Zalzala, A. (1995). Safety considerations in the optimization of the paths for mobile robots using genetic algorithms. *In Proceeding of 1ˢᵗ International Conference on Genetic Algorithms in Engineering Systems: Innovations and Applications* (pp. 299-306). London, UK: Institution of Electrical Engineers.

Dogan, C., Sahin, C. S., Uyar, M. U., & Urrea, E. (2009). Testbed for node communication in MANETs to uniformly cover unknown geographical terrain using genetic algorithms. In M. Suess et al. (Eds.), *Proceedings of the NASA/ESA Conference on Adaptive Hardware and Systems* (pp.273–280). Los Alamos, NM: IEEE Computer Society.

Dogan, C., Uyar, M. U., Urrea, E., Sahin, C. S., & Hokelek, I. (2008). Testbed implementation of genetic algorithms for self spreading nodes in MANETs. In H. R. Arabnia & Y.Mun (Ed.), *Proceedings of the 2008 International Conference on Genetic and Evolutionary Methods* (pp. 10–16). CSREA Press.

Garro, B. A., Sossa, H., & Vazquez, R. A. (2006). Path planning optimization using bio-inspired algorithms. In *Proceeding of IEEE 5ᵗʰ Mexican International Conference on Artificial Intelligence* (pp. 319–330). Washington, DC: IEEE Computer Society.

Gesu, V., Lenzitti, B., Bosco, G., & Tegolo, D. (2004). A distributed architecture for autonomous navigation of robots. *In Proceeding of 5th IEEE International Workshop on Computer Architectures for Machine Perception* (pp. 190-194). Washington, DC: IEEE Computer Society.

Hasircioglu, I., Topcuoglu, H. R., & Ermis, M. (2008). 3-D path planning for the navigation of unmanned aerial vehicles by using evolutionary algorithms. In M. Keijzer (Ed.), *Proceeding of the 10ᵗʰ Annual Conference on Genetic and Evolutionary Computations* (pp.1499–1506). New York, NY: ACM.

Heo, N., & Varshney, P. (2003). *A distributed self spreading algorithm for mobile wireless sensor networks* (pp. 1597–1602). IEEE Wireless Communications and Networking.

Hokelek, I., Uyar, M. U., & Fecko, M. A. (2008). On stability analysis of virtual backbone in mobile ad hoc networks. *Springer Wireless Networks*, 14(1), 87–102. doi:10.1007/s11276-006-7831-4

Holland, J. H. (1995). *Hidden order: How adaptation builds complexity*. New York, NY: Addison-Wesley.

Howard, M. A., & Sukhatme, G. (2002). Mobile sensors network deployment using potential fields: A distributed, scale solution to the area coverage problem. In E. Pagello et al. (Eds.), *Proceedings of the 6th International Symposium on Distributed Autonomous Robotic Systems* (pp. 299-308). The Netherlands: IOS Press.

Khanna, R., Liu, H., & Chen, H. (2006). Self-organization of sensor networks using genetic algorithms. *International Journal of Sensor Networks*, 1(3-4), 241–252. doi:10.1504/IJSNET.2006.012040

Lin, G., Noubir, G., & Rajaraman, R. (2004). Mobility models for ad hoc network simulation. *In Proceedings of Twenty-third Annual Joint Conference of the IEEE Computer and Communications Societies, INFOCOM'04* (pp. 454-463).

Mitchell, M. (1996). *An introduction to genetic algorithms*. Boston, MA: MIT Press.

Montana, D., & Redi, J. (2005). Optimizing parameters of a mobile ad hoc network protocol with a genetic algorithm. In H. Beyer (Ed.), *Proceeding of the 7th Annual Conference on Genetic and Evolutionary Computations* (pp. 1993–1998). New York, NY: ACM.

Nakama, T. (2008). Markov chain analysis of genetic algorithms applied to fitness functions perturbed by multiple sources of additive noise. *Studies in Computational Intelligence, 149,* 123-136. Berlin, Germany: Springer.

Nix, A. E., & Vose, M. D. (1992). Modeling genetic algorithms with Markov chains. *Annals of Mathematics and Artificial Intelligence, 5*(1), 79–88. doi:10.1007/BF01530781

Pugh, J., & Martinoli, M. (2007). Parallel learning in heterogeneous multi-robot swarms. In D. Thierens et al. (Eds.), *Proceeding of IEEE 2007 Congress on Evolutionary Computation* (pp. 3839–3846). New York, NY: ACM.

Sahin, C. S. (2010). *Design and performance analysis of genetic algorithms for topology control problems.* The Graduate Center of the City University of New York, Ph.D. Thesis, in progress.

Sahin, C. S., Urrea, E., Uyar, M.U., Conner, M., Bertoli, G., & Pizzo, C. (2010). Design of genetic algorithms for topology control of unmanned vehicles. *Special Issue of the International Journal of Applied Decision Sciences (IJADS) on Decision Support Systems for Unmanned Vehicles, 3*(3).

Sahin, C. S., Urrea, E., Uyar, M. U., Conner, M., Hokelek, I., Bertoli, G., & Pizzo, C. (2008). Genetic algorithms for self-spreading nodes in MANETs. In M. Keijzer (Ed.), *Proceedings of the 10th Annual Conference on Genetic and Evolutionary Computation* (pp. 1141-1142). New York, NY: ACM.

Shinchi, T., Tabuse, M., Kitazoe, T., & Todaka, A. (2000). Khepera robots applied to highway autonomous mobiles. *Artificial Life and Robotics, 7*(3), 118–123. doi:10.1007/BF02481159

Tuci, E., Gross, R., Trianni, V., Mondada, F., Bonani, M., & Dorigo, M. (2006). Cooperation through self-assembly in multi-robot systems. *ACM Transactions on Autonomous and Adaptive Systems, 1*(2), 115–150. doi:10.1145/1186778.1186779

Urrea, E. (2010). *Knowledge sharing agents using genetic algorithms in mobile ad hoc networks.* The Graduate Center of the City University of New York, Ph.D. Thesis, in progress.

Urrea, E., Sahin, C. S., Uyar, M. U., Conner, M., Hokelek, I., Bertoli, G., & Pizzo, C. (2009). Bio-inspired topology control for knowledge sharing mobile agents. *Ad Hoc Networks, 7*(4), 677–689. doi:10.1016/j.adhoc.2008.03.005

Vose, M. D. (1998). *The simple genetic algorithm: Foundations and theory.* Cambridge, MA: MIT Press.

Winfield, A. F. (2000). *Distributed sensing and data collection via broken ad hoc wireless networks of mobile robots* (pp. 273–282). Proceedings of Distributed Autonomous Robotic Systems.

Chapter 10
Niche:
A Platform for Self-Managing Distributed Applications

Vladimir Vlassov
KTH Royal Institute of Technology, Sweden

Ahmad Al-Shishtawy
KTH Royal Institute of Technology, Sweden

Per Brand
Swedish Institute of Computer Science, Sweden

Nikos Parlavantzas
Université Européenne de Bretagne, France

ABSTRACT

We present Niche, a general-purpose, distributed component management system used to develop, deploy, and execute self-managing distributed applications. Niche consists of both a component-based programming model as well as a distributed runtime environment. It is especially designed for complex distributed applications that run and manage themselves in dynamic and volatile environments. Self-management in dynamic environments is challenging due to the high rate of system or environmental changes and the corresponding need to frequently reconfigure, heal, and tune the application. The challenges are met partly by making use of an underlying overlay in the platform to provide an efficient, location-independent, and robust sensing and actuation infrastructure, and partly by allowing for maximum decentralization of management. We describe the overlay services, the execution environment, showing how the challenges in dynamic environments are met. We also describe the programming model and a high-level design methodology for developing decentralized management, illustrated by two application case studies.

DOI: 10.4018/978-1-60960-845-3.ch010

INTRODUCTION

Autonomic computing (Horn, 2001) is an attractive paradigm to tackle the problem of growing software complexity by making software systems and applications self-managing. Self-management, namely self-configuration, self-optimization, self-healing, and self-protection, can be achieved by using autonomic managers (IBM, 2006). An autonomic manager continuously monitors software and its execution environment and acts to meet its management objectives. Managing applications in dynamic environments with dynamic resources and/or load (like community Grids, peer-to-peer systems, and Clouds) is especially challenging due to large scale, complexity, high resource churn (e.g., in P2P systems) and lack of clear management responsibility.

This chapter presents the Niche platform (Niche, 2010) for self-managing distributed applications; we share our practical experience, challenges and issues, and lessons learned when building the Niche platform and developing self-managing demonstrator applications using Niche. We also present a high-level design methodology (including design space and steps) for developing self-managing applications.

Niche is a general-purpose, distributed component management system used to develop, deploy, and execute self-managing distributed applications or services in different kinds of environments, including very dynamic ones with volatile resources. Niche is both a component-based programming model that includes management aspects as well as a distributed runtime environment.

Niche provides a programming environment that is especially designed to enable application developers to design and develop complex distributed applications that will run and manage themselves in dynamic and volatile environments. The volatility may be due to the resources (e.g., low-end edge resources), the varying load, or the action of other applications running on the same infrastructure. The vision is that once the infrastructure-wide Niche runtime environment has been installed, applications that have been developed using Niche, can be installed, and run with virtually no effort. Policies cover such issues as which applications to scale down or stop upon resource contention. After deployment the application manages itself, completely without human intervention, excepting, of course, policy changes. During the application lifetime the application is transparently recovering from failure, and tuning and reconfiguring itself on environmental changes such as resource availability or load. This cannot be done today in volatile environments, i.e., it is beyond the state-of-the-art, except for single machine applications and the most trivial of distributed applications, e.g., client/server.

The rest of this chapter is organized as follows. The next section lays out the necessary background for this work. Then, we discuss challenges for enabling and achieving self-management in a dynamic environment characterized by volatile resources and high resource churn (leaves, failures and joins of computers). Next, we present Niche. We provide some insight into the Niche design ideas and its architecture, programming model and execution environment, followed by a presentation of programming concepts and some insight into the programming of self-managing distributed applications using Niche illustrated with a simple example of a self-healing distributed group service. Next, we present our design methodology (including design space and design steps) for developing a management part of a self-managing distributed application in a decentralized manner, i.e., with multiple interactive autonomic managers. We illustrate our methodology with two demonstrator applications, which are self-managing distributed services developed using Niche. Next, we discuss combining a policy-based management (using a policy language and a policy engine) with hard-coded management logic. Finally, we present some conclusions and our future work.

BACKGROUND

The benefits of self-managing applications apply in all kinds of environments, and not only in dynamic ones. The alternative to self-management is management by humans, which is costly, error-prone, and slow. In the well-known IBM Autonomic Computing Initiative (Horn, 2001) the axes of self-management were self-configuration, self-healing, self-tuning and self-protection. Today, there is a considerable body of work in the area, most of it geared to clusters.

However, the more dynamic and volatile the environment, the more often appropriate management actions to heal/tune/reconfigure the application will be needed. In very dynamic environments self-management is not a question of cost but feasibility, as management by humans (even if one could assemble enough of them) will be too slow, and the system will degrade faster than humans can repair it. Any non-trivial distributed application running in such an environment must be self-managing. There are a few distributed applications that are self-managing and can run in dynamic environments, like peer-to-peer file-sharing systems, but they are handcrafted and special-purpose, offering no guidance to designing self-managing distributed applications in general.

Application management in a distributed setting consists of two parts. First, there is the initial deployment and configuration, where individual components are shipped, deployed, and initialized at suitable nodes (or virtual machine instances), then the components are bound to each other as dictated by the application architecture, and the application can start working. Second, there is dynamic reconfiguration when a running application needs to be reconfigured. This is usually due to environmental changes, such as change of load, the state of other applications sharing the same infrastructure, node failure, node leave (either owner rescinding the sharing of his resource, or controlled shutdown), but might also be due to software errors or policy changes. All the tasks

in the initial configuration may also be present in dynamic reconfiguration. For instance, increasing the number of nodes in a given tier will involve discovering suitable resources, deploying and initializing components on those resources and binding them appropriately. However, dynamic reconfiguration generally involves more, because firstly, the application is running and disruption must be kept to a minimum, and secondly, management must be able to manipulate running components and existing bindings. In general, in dynamic reconfiguration, there are more constraints on the order in which configuration change actions are taken, compared to initial configuration when the configuration can be built first and components are only activated after this has been completed.

A configuration may be seen as a graph, where the nodes are components and the links are bindings. Components need suitable resources to host them, and we can complete the picture by adding the mapping of components onto physical resources. This is illustrated in Figure 1. On the left we show the graph only, the abstract configuration, while on the right the concrete configuration is shown. The bindings that cross resource boundaries will upon use involve remote invocations, while those that do not can be invoked locally. Reconfiguration may involve a change in the concrete configuration only or in both the abstract and concrete configurations. Note, that we show the more interesting and challenging aspects of reconfiguration; there are also reconfigurations that leave the graph unchanged but only change the way in which components work by changing component attributes.

We now proceed with some examples of dynamic reconfiguration. In these dynamic environments, a resource may announce that it is leaving and a new resource will need to be located and the components currently residing on the resource moved to the new resource. In this case only the concrete configuration is changed. Alternatively, when there is an increase in the number of service components in a service tier this will change the

Figure 1. Abstract (left) and concrete (right) view of a configuration. Boxes represent nodes or virtual machines, circles represent components.

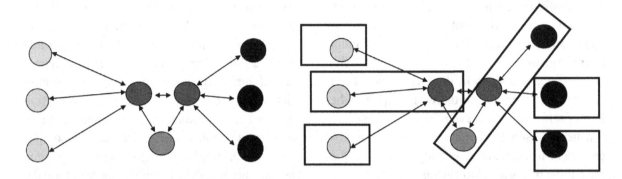

abstract (and concrete) configuration by adding a new node and the appropriate bindings. Another example is when a resource fails. If we disregard the transient broken configuration, where the failed component is no longer present in the configuration and the bindings that existed to it are broken, an identical abstract configuration will eventually be created, differing only in the resource mapping. In general, an application architecture consists of a set of suitable abstract configurations with associated information as to the resource requirements of components. The actual environment will determine which one is best to deploy or to reconfigure towards.

Note that in Figure 1 only the top-level components are shown. At a finer level of detail there are many more components, but for our management we can ignore components that are always co-located and bound exclusively to co-located components. Note, that we ignore only those that are always co-located (in all configurations). There are components that might be co-located in some concrete configurations (when a sufficient capable resource is available) but not in others. In Figure 1, on the right, a configuration is shown with one machine hosting 3 components; in another concrete configuration they might be mapped to different machines.

We use an architectural approach to self-management, with particular focus on achieving self-management for dynamic environments, enabling the usage of multiple distributed cooperative autonomic managers for scalability and avoiding a single-point-of failure or contention.

RELATED WORK

The increasing complexity of software systems and networked environments motivates autonomic system research in both, academia and industry, e.g., (J. O. Kephart & Chess, 2003; Roy et al., 2007; Horn, 2001; Parashar & Hariri, 2005). Major computer and software vendors have launched R&D initiatives in the field of autonomic computing.

The main goal of autonomic system research is to automate most system management functions, including configuration management, fault management, performance management, power management, security management, cost management, SLA management, and SLO management.

There is vast research on building autonomic computing systems using different approaches (Parashar & Hariri, 2005), including control theoretic approach; architectural approach; multi-agent systems; policy-based management; management using utility-functions. For example, authors of (Hellerstein, Diao, Parekh, & Tilbury, 2004) apply the control theoretic approach to design computing systems with feedback loops. The architectural approach to autonomic computing (White, Hanson, Whalley, Chess, & Kephart, 2004) suggests specifying interfaces, behavioral requirements, and interaction patterns for architectural elements, e.g., components. The approach has been shown to be useful for autonomous repair management (Bouchenak et al., 2005). A reference architecture for autonomic computing is presented in (Sweitzer & Draper, 2006). The authors present patterns for applying their proposed architecture to solve specific problems common to self-managing applications. The analyzing and planning stages of a control loop can be implemented using utility functions to make management decisions, e.g., to achieve efficient resource allocation (J. O. Kephart & Das, 2007). Authors of (J. Kephart et al., 2007) and (Das et al., 2008) use multi-objective utility functions for power-aware performance management. Authors of (Abdelwahed & Kandasamy, 2006; Bhat, Parashar, Khandekar, Kandasamy, & Klasky, 2006) use a model-predictive control technique, namely a limited look-ahead control (LLC), combined with a rule-based managers, to optimize the system performance based on its forecast behavior over a look-ahead horizon. Policy-based self-management (Chan & Arnold, 2003; Feng, Wasson, & Humphrey, 2007; Agrawal, Calo, Lee, Lobo, & Res., 2007; Kumar et al., 2007) allows high-level specification of management objectives in the form of policies that drive autonomic management and can be changed at run time.

Some research is focused on interaction and coordination between multiple autonomic managers. An attempt to analyze and understand how multiple interacting loops can manage a single system has been done in (Roy et al., 2007) by studying and analyzing existing systems such as biological and software systems. By this study the authors try to understand the rules of a good control loop design. A study of how to compose multiple loops and ensure that they are consistent and complementary is presented in (Cheng, Huang, Garlan, Schmerl, & Steenkiste, 2004). The

authors presented an architecture that supports such compositions.

There are many research projects focused on or using self-management for software systems and networked environments, including projects performed at the NSF Center for Autonomic Computing (The Center for Autonomic Computing, 2010) and a number of European projects funded by European Commission such as RESERVOIR, SELFMAN, Grid4All and others.

There are several industrial solutions (tools, techniques and software suites) for enabling and achieving self-management of enterprise IT systems, e.g., IBM® Tivoli®[1] and HP's OpenView, which include different autonomic tools and managers to simplify management, monitoring and automation of complex enterprise-scale IT systems. These solutions are based on functional decomposition of management performed by multiple cooperative managers with different management objectives (e.g., performance manager, power manager, storage manager, etc.). These tools are specially developed and optimized to be used in IT infrastructure of enterprises and datacenters.

The area of autonomic computing is still evolving. Still there are many open research issues such as development environments to facilitate development of self-managing applications, efficient monitoring, scalable actuation, and robust management.

In our work we focus on enabling and achieving self-management for large-scale distributed systems in dynamic environments (dynamic resources and load) using an architectural approach to self-management with multiple distributed cooperative autonomic managers.

OUR APPROACH

We, like many others, use the feedback control loop approach to achieve self-management. Referring back to Figure 1 we can identify the constituent parts of what is needed at runtime.

Container: Each available machine has a container (the boxes in the figure). The container hosts running components and directs actuation (control) commands addressed to a particular component. The container can be told by management to install a new component. Ideally the container can completely isolate and protect components from one another (particularly important when components belonging to different applications are hosted in the same container). This can be achieved by using Virtual Machine technology (currently the containers in Niche do not guarantee this).

Sensing: Management needs to sense or be informed about changes in the application state. Some events are independent of the application type. For example, the failure of a machine (or container) necessarily entails failure of the hosted components, as does the leave of a machine. Other events are application-specific, with a component programmed to report certain events to management (via the management interface of the component). There is a choice with application-independent events (failure and leaves) if the reporting to management is on the level of the container/machine (in which case the management must make the appropriate mapping to components), or on the level of the individual components.

Resource Discovery: Management needs to sense or be informed about changes in available resources, or alternatively management needs to be able, upon need, to discover free (or underutilized) resources. This could be seen as part of sensing, but note that in general more than a single application is running on the same infrastructure and resource discovery/allocation is an infrastructure-wide service, in contrast to sensing as described above which is directly linked to components in a given application.

Actuation: Management needs to be able to control applications and the components that they are composed of.

Management Hosting: Management needs to be hosted as well. In general the management of a single application is divided into one or more management elements. These management elements are programs that are triggered by some event, perform some planning, and thereafter send the appropriate actuation commands to perform the required reconfiguration.

In a static and constrained environment, these elements of the runtime support may be straightforward or even trivial. For instance, if management is centralized, then the management should know exactly where each application component is hosted, and it is straightforward to send the appropriate command message to a component at its known host. If management is decentralized, it is possible that a component has been moved as a result of the action of another management element without the first management element having been made aware of this. If management never moves, then it is straightforward to find it, and deliver sensing messages to it. If all resources are known statically, then management will always know what resources are potentially available. However, as explained in the next section, to handle dynamic environments we cannot make such simplifying assumptions and the five described elements of the runtime are non-trivial.

The runtime support for management is, of course, only part of the story. Developing the management for a distributed application is a programming task, and a programming model is needed. This will be covered later in the section about the Niche platform.

CHALLENGES

Achieving self-management in a dynamic environment characterized by volatile resources and high churn (leaves, failures and joins of machines) is challenging. State-of-the-art techniques for self-management in clusters are not suitable. The challenges are:

1. *Resource discovery*: Discovering and utilizing free resources;
2. *Robust and efficient sensing and actuation*: Churn-tolerant, efficient and robust sensing and actuation infrastructure;
3. *Management bottleneck:* Avoiding management bottleneck and single-point-of-failure;
4. *Scale.*

In our driving scenarios resources are extremely volatile. This volatility is partly related to churn. There are many scenarios where high churn is expected. In community Grids and other collaborations across the Internet machines may be at any time removed when the owner needs the machine for other purposes. At the edge both the machines and the networks are less reliable.

There are other aspects of volatility. Demanding applications may require more resources than are available in the current infrastructure and additional resources then need to be obtained quickly from an external provider (e.g., Cloud). These new resources need to be integrated with existing resources to allow applications to run over the aggregated resources. Furthermore we do not assume over provisioning within the infrastructure - it may be working close to available capacity so that even smaller changes of load in one application may trigger a reconfiguration as other applications need to be ramped up or down depending on the relative priorities of the applications (according to policy). We see the need for a system-wide infrastructure where volatile resources can efficiently be discovered and utilized. This infrastructure (i.e., the resource discovery service) itself also needs to be self-managing.

The sensing and actuation infrastructure needs to be efficient. The demand for efficiency rules out, at least as the main mechanism, a probing monitoring approach. Instead, the publish/subscribe paradigm needs to be used. The sensing and actuation infrastructure must be robust and churn-tolerant. Sensing events must be delivered (at least once) to subscribing management elements, irrespective of failure events, and irrespective of whether or not the management element has moved. In a dynamic environment it is quite normal for a management element to move from machine to machine during the lifetime of the application as resources leave and join.

It is important that management does not become the bottleneck. For the moment, let us disregard the question of failure of management nodes. The overall management load for a single application depends on both the size of the system (i.e., number of nodes in the configuration graph) and the volatility of the environment. It may well be that a dynamic environment of a few hundred nodes could generate as many events per time unit as a large data centre. The standard mechanism of a single management node will introduce a bottleneck (both in terms of management processing, but also in terms of bandwidth). Decentralization of management is, we believe, the key to solving this problem. Of course, decentralization of management introduces design and synchronization issues. There are issues on how to design management that requires minimal synchronization between the manager nodes and how to achieve that necessary synchronization. These issues will be discussed later in the section about design methodology.

The issue of failure of management nodes in centralized and decentralized solutions is, on the other hand, not that different. (Of course, with a decentralized approach, only parts of the management fail). If management elements are stateless, fault-recovery is relatively easy. If they are stateful, some form of replication can be used for fault-tolerance, e.g., hot standby in a cluster or state machine replication (Al-Shishtawy, Fayyaz, Popov, & Vlassov, 2010).

Finally, there are many aspects of scale to consider. We have touched upon some of them in the preceding paragraphs, pointing out that we have to take into account the sheer number of environmental sensing events. Clearly the system-wide resource discovery infrastructure needs to scale.

But there are other issues to consider regarding scale and efficiency. We have used two approaches in dealing with these issues. The first, keeping in mind our decentralized model of management, is to couple as loosely as possible. In contrast to cluster management systems, not only do we avoid maintaining a centralized system map reflecting the "current state" of the application configuration, we strive for the loosest coupling possible. In particular, management elements only receive event notifications for exactly those events that have been subscribed to. Secondly, we have tried to identify common management patterns, to see if they can be optimized (in terms of number of messages/events or hops) by supporting them directly in the platform as primitives, rather than as programmed abstractions when and if this makes for a difference in messaging or other overhead.

NICHE: A PLATFORM FOR SELF-MANAGING DISTRIBUTED APPLICATIONS

In this section, we present Niche, which is a platform for development, deployment, and execution of component-based self-managing applications. Niche includes a distributed component programming model, APIs, and a runtime system (including a deployment service) that operates on an internal structured overlay network. Niche supports sensing changes in the state of components and an execution environment, and it allows individual components to be found and appropriately manipulated. It deploys both functional and management components and sets up the appropriate sensor and actuation support infrastructure.

Niche has been developed assuming that its runtime environment and applications might execute in a highly dynamic environment with volatile resources, where resources (computers, virtual machines) can unpredictably fail or leave. In order to deal with such dynamicity, Niche leverages self-organizing properties of the underlying structured overlay network, including name-based routing and the DHT functionality. Niche provides transparent replication of management elements for robustness. For efficiency, Niche directly supports a component group abstraction with group bindings (one-to-all and one-to-any).

There are aspects of Niche that are fairly common in autonomic computing. Firstly, Niche supports the feedback control loop paradigm where management logic in a continuous feedback loop senses changes in the environment and component status, reasons about those changes, and then, when needed, actuates, i.e., manipulates components and their bindings. A self-managing application can be divided into a functional part and a management part tied together by sensing and actuation. Secondly, the Niche programming model is based on a component model, called Fractal component model (Bruneton, Coupaye, & Stefani, 2004), in which components can be monitored and managed. In Fractal, components are bound and interact functionally with each other using two kinds of interfaces: (1) server interfaces offered by the components; (2) and client interfaces used by the components. Components are interconnected by bindings: a client interface of one component is bound to a server interface of another component. Fractal allows nesting of components in composite components and sharing of components. Components have control (management) membranes, with introspection and intercession capabilities. It is through this control membrane that components are started, stopped, configured. It is through this membrane that the components are passivated (as a prelude to component migration), and through which the component can report application-specific events to management (e.g., load). Fractal can be seen as defining a set of capabilities for functional components. It does not force application components to comply, but clearly the capabilities of the programmed components must match the needs of management. For instance, if the component is both stateful and not capable of passivation (or checkpointing) then management will not be able to transparently move the component.

The major novel feature of Niche is that, in order to enable and achieve self-management for large-scale dynamic distributed systems, it combines a suitable component model (Fractal) with a Chord-like structured overlay network to provide a number of robust overlay services. Niche leverages the self-organizing properties of the structured overlay network, e.g., automatic correction of routing tables on node leaves, joins and failures. The Fractal model supports components that can be monitored and managed through component introspection and control interfaces (called controllers in Fractal), e.g., lifecycle, attribute, binding and content controllers. The Niche execution environment provides a number of overlay services, notably, name-based communication, the key-value store (DHT) for lookup services, a controlled broadcast for resource discovery, a publish/subscribe mechanism for event dissemination, and node failure detection. These services are used by Niche to provide higher level abstractions such as name-based bindings to support component mobility; dynamic component groups; one-to-any and one-to-all group bindings, and event based interaction. Note that the application programmer does not need to know about the underlying overlay services, this is under the hood, and his/her interaction is through the Niche API.

An important feature of Niche is that all architectural elements such as component interfaces, singleton components, components groups, and management elements, have system-wide unique identifiers. This enables location transparency, transparent migration and reconfiguration (rebinding) of components and management elements at run time. In Niche, components can be found, monitored and controlled – deployed, created, stopped, rebound, started, etc. Niche uses the DHT functionality of the underlying structured overlay network for its lookup service. This is especially important in dynamic environments where components need to be migrated frequently as machines leave and join frequently. Furthermore, each container maintains a cache of name-to-location mappings. Once a name of an element is resolve to its location, the element (its hosting container) is accessed directly rather than by routing messages though the overlay network. If the element moves to a new location, the element name is transparently resolved to the new location.

We now proceed to describe both the Niche runtime and, to a lesser extent, the Niche programming model. The Niche programming model will be presented in more detail in the following section interleaved with examples.

Building Management with Niche

Niche implements (in the Java™ programming language[2]) the autonomic computing reference architecture proposed by IBM in (IBM, 2006), i.e., it allows building MAPE-K (Monitor, Analyze, Plan and Execute; with Knowledge) control loops. An Autonomic Manager in Niche can be organized as a network of *Management Elements (MEs)* that interact through events, monitor via sensors and act via actuators (e.g., using the actuation API). The ability to distribute MEs among Niche containers enables the construction of decentralized feedback control loops for robustness and performance.

A self-managing application in Niche consists of functional and management parts. Functional components communicate via component bindings, which bind client interfaces to server interfaces; whereas management elements communicate mostly via a publish/subscribe event notification mechanism. The functional part is developed using Fractal components and component groups, which are controllable (e.g., can be looked up, moved, rebound, started, stopped, etc.) and can be monitored by the management part of the application. The management part of an application can be constructed as a set of interactive or independent control loops each of which monitors some part of the application and reacts on predefined events such as node failures, leaves or joins, component failures, and group membership events; and application-specific events such as component load change events, and low storage capacity events.

In Figure 2, we show what an abstract configuration might look like when all management elements are passive in the sense that they are all waiting for some triggering events to take place. The double-headed arrows in the functional part are bindings between components (as the concrete configuration is not shown the bindings may or may not be between different machines). The management elements have references to functional components by name (e.g., component id) or are connected to actuators. The management and functional parts are also "connected" by sensors (this is also actually by name, because management, as well as functional components can migrate) In the picture there are sensors from the A group of functional components (A1, A2 and A3) to two management elements (sensors connected to the other management elements are not shown). The management architecture in Figure 2 is flat, and later we show how management can be structured hierarchically (see section *Development of Self-*

Managing Applications Using Niche), which is important for larger more complex applications.

The form of a management element is show in Exhibit 1, together with a high level description of the features available in the Niche actuation API.

Actuation is a sequence of invocations (actions) that are listed in Exhibit 2 (in no specific order). Note that all of the following actions are provided in the Niche actuation API. The list is extensible with user-defined actions.

For implementing the touchpoints (sensors and actuations), Niche leverages the introspection and dynamic reconfiguration features of the Fractal component model in order to provide sensing and actuation API abstractions. Sensors and actuators are special components that can be attached to the application's functional components. There are also built-in sensors in Niche that sense changes in the environment such as resource and component failures, joins, and leaves, as well as modifications in application architecture such as creation of a group.

The application programmer also needs to install/deploy management elements (components). To a large degree this is done in an analogous

Figure 2. Abstract configuration of a self-managing application

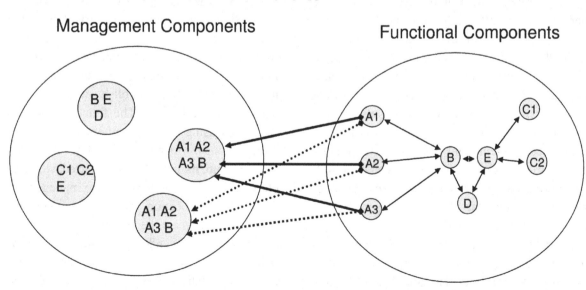

Exhibit 1. Niche actuation API

```
loop
    wait SensorEvent
        change internal state    // e.g., for monitoring and aggregation
            analyze/plan
        actuate
```

Exhibit 2. Actuation

```
reconfigure existing components    // functional components / changing con-
crete configuration only
passivate/move existing components
discover resources                            // functional components / chang-
ing configuration.
allocate and deploy new components on a given resource
kill/remove existing components
remove/create bindings
add subscriptions/sensors        // may cause sensors to be installed
remove subscriptions
discover resources                        // management components
allocate resources and deploy new management elements
trigger events                            // for management coordination
```

manner to dealing with functional components. There are two important differences, however. One concerns allocating resources to host management components, and the other concerns connections between management elements. In Niche the application programmer usually lets the Niche runtime find a suitable resource and deploy a management component in one step. Niche reserves a slice of each machine for management activity so that management elements can be placed anywhere (ideally, optimally so as to minimize latency between the management element and its sensors and references). Note that this assumes that the *analyze/plan* step in management logic are computationally inexpensive. Secondly there are other ways to explicitly share information between management elements, and they are rarely bound to one another (unless they are always co-located).

In Figure 2, there are no connections between management elements whatsoever, therefore the only coordination that is possible between managers is via stigmergy. Knowledge (as in MAPE-K) in Niche can be shared between MEs using two mechanisms: first, the publish/subscribe mechanism provided by Niche; second, the Niche DHT to store/retrieve information such as references to component group members, name-to-location mappings. In section *A Design Methodology for Self-Management in Distributed Environments*, we discuss management coordination in more detail in conjunction with design issues involved in the decentralization of management.

Although programming in Niche is on the level of Java, it is both possible and desirable to program management at a higher level (e.g., declaratively). Currently in Niche such high-level language support includes a declarative ADL (Architecture Description Language) that is used for describing initial configurations at a high-level which is interpreted by Niche at runtime for initial deployment. Policies (supported with a policy language and a corresponding policy engine) can also be used to raise the level of abstraction on management (see section *Policy-Based Management*).

Execution Environment

The Niche execution environment (see Figure 3) is a set of distributed *containers* (hosting components, groups and management elements) connected via the structured overlay network, and a number of *overlay services* including name-based communication, resource discovery, deployment, a lookup service, component group support, the publish/subscribe service for event dissemination including predefined event notification (e.g., component failures). The services allow an application (its management part) to discover and to allocate resources, to deploy the application and reconfigure it at runtime, to monitor and react on changes

in the application and in its execution environment, and to locate elements of the application (e.g., components, groups, managers). In this section, we will describe the execution environment. We begin with the aspects of the execution environment that the application programmer needs to be aware of. Thereafter we will describe the mechanisms used to realize the execution environment, and particularly the overlay services. Although the application programmer does not need to understand the underlying mechanisms they are reflected in the performance/fault model. Finally in this section, we describe the performance/fault model and discuss how Niche meets the four challenges discussed in section *Challenges*.

Programmer View

Containers

The Niche runtime environment is a set of distributed containers, called Jade[3] nodes, connected via the Niche structured P2P overlay network. Containers host functional components and management elements of distributed applications executed

Figure 3. Niche architecture

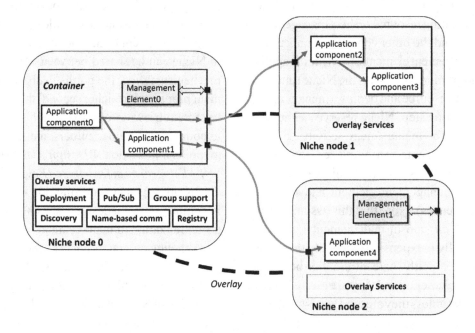

in Niche. There are two container configurations in the current Niche prototype: (1) the JadeBoot container that bootstraps the system and interprets given ADL (*.fractal) files describing initial configuration of an application on deployment; (2) the JadeNode container, which does not include the ADL interpreter but supports a deployment API to deploy components programmatically.

We use a Webcache PHP application (deployed on an Apache server) to maintain a list of nodes used as access points to join the overlay network. The URL of the Webcache is a part of the configuration information to be provided when installing and configuring the Niche platform. When started, a new Jade node sends an HTTP request to the Webcache to get an address of any of the Jade nodes that can be contacted to join the overlay.

Niche allows a programmer to control the distribution of functional components and management elements among Niche containers, i.e., for every component or/and ME, the programmer can specify the container (by a resource id) where that element should reside (e.g., to co-locate components for efficiency). If a location is not specified, the deployment service of the Niche runtime environment will deploy (or move on failure) an ME on any container selected randomly or in a round-robin manner. Collocation of an ME with a controlled component in the same container allows improving performance of management by monitoring and/or controlling the component locally rather than remotely over the network.

Group Support

Niche provides support for component groups and group bindings. Components can be bound to groups via one-to-any (where a member of the group is chosen at random) or one-to-all bindings. The use of component groups is a fairly common programming pattern. For instance, a tier in a multi-tier application might be modeled as a component group. The application programmer needs to be aware of the fact that component groups are supported directly in the runtime for efficiency reasons (the alternative would be to program a group abstraction).

Resource Discovery and Deployment Service

Niche is an infrastructure that loosely connects available physical resources/containers (computers), and provides for resource discovery. The Niche execution environment is a set of containers (hosting components and managers), which upon joining and leaving the overlay, inform the Niche runtime environment and its applications in a manner completely analogous to peer-to-peer systems (e.g., Chord).

For initial deployment and runtime reconfiguration Niche provides a deployment service (including resource discovery) that can be performed either by the ADL interpreter given an ADL (possibly incomplete) description of architecture of an application to be deployed; or programmatically using a deployment Niche API. ADL-driven deployment of an application does not necessary deploy the entire application but rather some primary components that in their turn can complete deployment programmatically by executing deployment process logic. A deployment process includes resource discovery, placement and creation of components and component groups, binding component and groups, placement and creation of management elements, subscription to predefined or application-specific events. The deployment service (API) uses the Niche resource discovery service to find resources (Niche containers) with specified properties to deploy components.

All planned removal of resources, like controlled shutdown, should be done by performing a leave action a short time before the resource is removed. It is generally easier for management to perform the necessary reconfiguration on leaves than on failures. Hopefully, management has had the necessary time to successfully move (or kill) the components hosted by the resource by the time the resource is actually removed from the infrastructure (e.g., shut down).

Management Support

In addition to resource discovery and deployment services described above, runtime system support for self-management includes a publish/subscribe service used for monitoring and event-driven management; and a number of server interfaces to manipulate components, groups, and management elements, and to access overlay services (discovery, deployment, and pub/sub).

The publish/subscribe service is used by management elements for publishing and delivering of monitoring and actuation events. The service is accessed though NicheActuatorInterface and TriggerInterface runtime system interfaces described below. The service provides built-in sensors to monitor component and node failures/leaves and group membership changes. The sensors issue corresponding predefined events (e.g., ComponentFailEvent, CreateGroupEvent, MemberAddedEvent, ResourceJoinEvent, ResourceLeaveEvent, ResourceStateChangeEvent), to which MEs can subscribe. A corresponding pub/sub API allows the programmer also to define application-specific sensors and events. The Niche runtime system guarantees event delivery.

The runtime system provides a number of interfaces (available in each container) used by MEs to control the functional part of an application and to access the overlay services (discovery, deployment, pub/sub). The interfaces are automatically bound by the runtime system to corresponding client interfaces of an ME when the management element is deployed and initialized. The set of runtime interfaces includes the following interfaces (Niche, 2010):

- NicheActuatorInterface (named "actuator") provides methods to access overlay services, to (un)bind functional components, to manipulate groups, to get access to components in order to monitor and control them (i.e., to register components and MEs with names and to lookup by names). Methods of this interface include, but are not limited to, discover, allocate, deallocate, deploy, redeploy, subscribe, unsubscribe, register, lookup, bind, unbind, create group, remove group, add to group;
- TriggerInterface (named "trigger") used to trigger events;
- NicheIdRegistry (named "nicheIdRegistry") is an auxiliary low-level interface used to lookup components by system-wide names;
- OverlayAccess (named "overlayAccess") is an auxiliary low-level interface used to obtain access to the runtime system and the NicheActuatorInterface interface.

When developing a management part of an application, the developer should mostly use the first two interfaces. Note that in addition to the above interfaces, the programmer also uses a component and group APIs (Fractal API) to manipulate component and groups for the sake of self-management. Architectural elements (components, groups, MEs) can be located in different Niche containers; therefore invocations of methods of the NicheActuatorInterface interface as well as group and component interfaces can be remote, i.e., cross container boundaries. All architectural elements (components, groups, management elements) of an application are uniquely identified by system-wide IDs assigned on deployment. An element can be registered at the Niche runtime system with a given name to be looked up (and bound with) by its name.

Execution Environment: Internals

Resource Discovery

Niche applications can discover and allocate resources using an overlay-based resource discovery mechanism provided by Niche. Currently the Niche prototype uses a full broadcast (i.e., sends an inquiry to all nodes in the overlay) which scales poorly. However, there are approaches to make broadcast-based discovery more efficient and scalable, such as an incremental controlled broadcast e.g., (El-Ansary, Alima, Brand, & Haridi, 2003).

Mobility and Location Transparency

The DHT-based lookup (registry) service built into Niche is used to keep information (metadata) on all identifiable architectural elements of an application executed in the Niche environment, such as components, component groups, bindings, management elements, subscriptions. Each architectural element is assigned a system-wide unique identifier (ID) that is used to identify the element in the actuation API. The ID is assigned to the element when the element is created. The ID is used as a key to lookup information about the element in the DHT of the Niche overlay. For most of the element types, the DHT-based lookup service contains location information, e.g., an end-point of a container hosting a given component, or end-points of containers hosting members of a given component group. Being resolved, the location information is cached in the element's handle. If the cached location information is invalid (the element has moved to another container), it will be automatically and transparently updated by the component binding stub via lookup in the DHT. This enables location transparency, transparent migration of component, members of component groups, and management elements at runtime. In order to prevent losing of data on failures of DHT nodes, we use a standard DHT replication mechanism.

For example, Figure 4 depicts steps in executing a (remote) method invocation on a component located in a remote container. Assume a client interface of component *A* in node 0 is bound to a server interface of component *B* in node 1; whereas the information about the binding of *A* to *B* (i.e., the end-point of *B*) is stored at node 2. When *A* makes its first call to *B* (Step 1), the method call is invoked on the binding stub of *B* at node 0 (Step 2). The stub performs lookup, using the binding ID as a key, for current location of

component *B* (Step 3). The lookup result, i.e., the end-point reference of *B*, is cached at node 0 for further calls. When the reference to *B* is resolved, the stub makes a remote call to the component *B* using the reference. All further calls to *B* from node 0 will use the cached end-point reference. If, for any reason, *B* migrates to another container (not shown in Figure 4), the location of *B* will be updated in the DHT, and the stub of *B* in node 0 can lookup the new location in the next call to component *B*. If a node hosting component *B* fails, a component failure event will be sent to all subscribers, including a manager (if any) responsible for restoring component *B* in another container. In this case, component *A*, which is bound to *B*, does not need to be informed; rebinding of *A* to the new instance of *B* is done transparently to *A*.

Location information is stored in the Niche DHT in the form of a data structure called *Set of Network References*, SNR, which represents a set of references to identifiable Niche elements (e.g., components, component groups). A component SNR contains one reference, whereas an SNR of a component group contains references to members of the corresponding group. SNRs are stored under their names (used as keys) in the Niche DHT-based key-value store. SNRs are used to find Niche elements by names and can contain either direct or indirect references. A direct reference contains the location of an element; whereas an indirect reference refers to another SNR identified by its name. The indirect reference must be resolved before use. An SNR can be cached by a client in order to improve access time to the referenced element(s). Niche transparently detects out-of-date (invalid) references and refreshes cache contents when needed. Niche supports transparent sensing of elements referenced in an SNR. When a management element is created to control (sense and actuate) functional components referenced by the SNR, the Niche runtime system transparently deploys sensors and actuators for each component. Whenever the references in the

Figure 4. Steps of method invocation in Niche

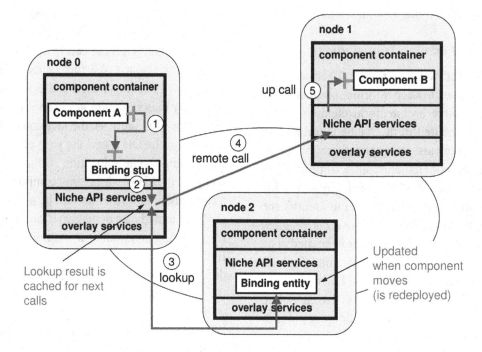

SNR are changed, the runtime system transparently (un)deploys sensors and actuators for the corresponding components. For robustness, SNRs are replicated using a DHT replication mechanism. The SRN replication provides eventual consistency of SNR replicas, but transient inconsistencies are allowed. Similarly to handling of SNR caching, the framework recognizes out-of-date SNR references and retries SNR access whenever necessary.

Groups are implemented using SNRs containing multiple references. Since a group SNR represents a group, a component bound to the group is actually bound to the group SNR. An invocation through "one-to-any" or "one-to-all" group binding is performed as follows. First, the target group name (the name of the group binding) is resolved to its SNR that contains references to all members of the group. Next, in the case of the one-to-any binding, one of the references is (randomly) selected and the invocation request is sent to the corresponding member of the group. In the case of the one-to-all binding, the invocation

request is sent to all members of the group, i.e., to all references in the group SNR. Use of SNRs allows changing the group membership (i.e., growing or shrinking the group) transparently to components bound to the group. Niche supports monitoring of group membership and subscribing to group events issued by group sensors when new members are added or removed from the monitored groups.

Meeting the Challenges

In this section, we discuss how Niche meets the four challenges (see Section *Challenges*) for self-management in dynamic and volatile environments. The challenges are chiefly concerned with the non-functional properties of the execution environment, so we shall also present the performance/fault model associated with the basic operations of Niche. For most operations the performance model is in terms of network hops, ignoring local computation which is insignificant. Sometimes the number of messages is also taken into account. Clearly, the best that can be obtained for any remote operation is one or two hops, for asynchronous and synchronous operations, respectively.

Resource Discovery

Niche is an infrastructure that loosely connects available physical resources (computers), and provides for resource discovery by using the structured overlay. Using total broadcast to discover resources means that at most it take $O(\log N)$ hops to find the required resource(s) (where N is the number of physical nodes). However, the total number of messages sent is large, $O(N)$. In large systems controlled incremental interval broadcast can be used to decrease the number of messages sent, at the price of greater delay if and when the discovery search needs to be expanded (i.e., when searching for a rare type of available resource). Finally, we note that, often there is actually little net increase in the number of messages, as the resource discovery messages are sent along the same links that continuously need to be probed anyway for overlay self-management.

The use of a structured overlay allows Niche to deal with the first challenge (*Resource discovery*).

Mobility and Location Transparency

In Niche all the architectural elements are potentially mobile. In much of the Niche actuation API, element identifiers are passed to Niche. An example would be to install a sensor on a given component. Associated with the element identifier is a cached location. If the cached entry is correct, then the action is typically one or two hops, i.e., the minimum. However, due to the action of other management elements the cached location may be invalid in which case a lookup needs to be performed. In the worst case a lookup takes $\log N$ hops (where N is the number of physical nodes). What is to be expected depends on the rate of dynamicity of the system. Additionally if the rate of churn is low the overlay can be instrumented

so as to decrease the average lookup hops (by increasing the size of routing table at the price of increasing the self-management overhead of the overlay itself).

In our view, the network or location transparency of element identifiers is an important requisite for efficient decentralization of management and directly relates to the second (*Robust and efficient sensing and actuation*) and third (*Management bottleneck*) challenges of the previous section. Management elements do not need to be informed when the components that they reference are moved, and neither do sensors need to be informed when the management elements that they reference are moved. For example, in a dynamic environment both a given component and a related management element might be moved (from container to container) many times before the component triggers a high-load event. In this case a DHT-lookup will occur, and the event will reach the management element later than it would be if the location of architectural elements was kept up-to-date, but fewer messages are sent.

Sensing and Actuation

The sensing and actuation services are robust and churn-tolerant, as Niche itself is self-managing. Niche thus meets the second challenge (*Robust and efficient sensing and actuation*). Niche achieves this by leveraging the self-management properties of an underlying structured overlay. The necessary information to relay events to subscribers (at least once) is stored with redundancy in the overlay. Upon subscription Niche creates the necessary sensors that serve as the initial detection points. In some cases, sensors can be safely co-located with the entity whose behavior is being monitored (e.g., a component leave event). In other cases, the sensors cannot be co-located. For instance, a crash of a machine will cause all the components (belonging to the same or different applications) being hosted on it to fail. Here the failure sensors need to be located on other nodes. Niche does all this transparently for the developer; the only thing the application developer must do is to use the Niche API to ensure that management elements subscribe to the events that it is programmed to handle, and that components are properly programmed to trigger application-specific events (e.g., load change).

Self-management requires monitoring of the execution environment, components, and component groups. In Niche monitoring is performed by the push rather than pull method for the sake of performance and scalability (the fourth challenge: *Scale*) using a publish/subscribe event dissemination mechanism. Sensors and management elements can publish predefined (e.g., node failure) and application-specific (e.g., load change) events to be delivered to subscribers (event listeners). Niche provides the publish/subscribe service that allows management elements to publish events and to subscribe to predefined or application-specific events fired by sensors and other MEs. A set of predefined events that can be published by the Niche runtime environment includes resource (node) and component failure/leave events, group change events, component move events, and other events used to notify subscribers (if any) about certain changes in the execution environment and in the architecture of the application. The Niche publish/subscribe API allows the programmer to define application specific events and sensors to issue the events whenever needed. A list of subscribers is maintained in an overlay proxy in the form of an SNR (a Set of Network References described above). The sensor triggers the proxy which then sends the events to subscribers.

Decentralized and Robust Management

Niche allows for maximum decentralization of management. Management can be divided (i.e., parallelized) by aspects (e.g., self-healing, self-tuning), spatially, and hierarchically. Later, we present the design methodology and report on use-case studies of decentralized management. In our view, a single application has many loosely synchronized managers. Niche supports the mobility of management elements. Niche also provides the execution platform for these managers; they typically get assigned to different machines in the Niche overlay. There is some support for optimizing this placement of managers, and some support for replication of managers for fault-tolerance. Thus Niche meets, at least partly, the challenge to avoid the management bottleneck (the third challenge: *Management bottleneck*). The main reason for the "at least partly" in the last sentence, is that more support for optimal placement of managers, taking into account network locality, will probably be needed (currently Niche recognizes only some special cases, like co-location). A vanilla management replication mechanism is available in the current Niche prototype, and, at the time of writing this chapter, work is ongoing on a robust replicated manager scheme based on the Paxos algorithm, adapted to the Niche overlay (Al-Shishtawy, Fayyaz, Popov, & Vlassov, 2010).

Groups

The fact that Niche provides support for component groups and group bindings contributes to dealing with the fourth challenge (*Scale*). Supporting component groups directly in the runtime system, rather than as a programming abstraction, allows us to adapt the sensing and actuation infrastructure to minimize messaging overhead and to increase robustness.

DEVELOPMENT OF SELF-MANAGING APPLICATIONS USING NICHE

The Niche programming environment enables the development of self-managing applications built of functional components and management elements. Note that the Niche platform (Niche,

2010) uses Java for programming components and management elements.

In this section, we describe in more detail the Niche programming model and exemplify with a Hello World application (singleton and group). The Niche programming model is based on *Fractal*, a modular and extensible component model intended for designing, implementing, deploying, and reconfiguring complex software systems. Niche borrows the core Fractal concepts, which are components, interfaces, and bindings, and adds new concepts related to group communication, deployment, and management. The following section discusses the main concepts of the Niche programming model and how they are used. Then we describe typical steps of developing a self-managing application illustrated with an example of programming of a self-healing group service.

Niche Programming Concepts

A self-managing application in Niche is built of functional components and management elements. The former constitute the functional part of the application; whereas the latter constitute the management part.

Components are runtime entities that communicate exclusively through named well-defined access points, called *interfaces,* including control interfaces used for management. Component interfaces are divided into two kinds: *client interfaces* that emit operation invocations and *server interfaces* that receive them. Interfaces are connected through communication paths, called *bindings*. Components and interfaces are named in order to lookup component interfaces by names and bind them.

Components can be *primitive* or *composite*, formed by hierarchically assembling other components (called *sub-components*). This hierarchical composition is a key Fractal feature that helps managing the complexity of understanding and developing component systems.

Another important Fractal feature is its support for extensible reflective facilities, allowing inspection and adaptation of the component structure and behavior. Specifically, each component is made of two parts: the *membrane*, which embodies reflective behavior, and the *content*, which consists of a finite set of sub-components. The membrane exposes an extensible set of *control interfaces* (called controllers) for reconfiguring internal features of the component and to control its life cycle. The control interfaces are server interfaces that must be implemented by component classes in order to be manageable. In Niche, the control interfaces are used by application-specific management elements (namely, sensors and actuators), and by the Niche runtime environment to monitor and control the components, e.g., to (re)bind, change attributes, and start. Fractal defines the following four basic control interfaces: *attribute, biding, content,* and *life-cycle controllers*. The *attribute controller* (AttributeController[4]) supports configuring named component properties. The *binding controller* (BindingController) is used to bind and unbind client interfaces to server interfaces, to lookup an interface with a given name, and to list all client interfaces of the component. The *content controller* (ContentController) supports listing, adding, and removing sub-components. Finally, the *life-cycle controller* (LifeCycleController) supports starting and stopping the execution of a component and getting the component state.

The core concepts of the Fractal component model are illustrated in Figure 5 that depicts a client-server application HelloWorld, which is a composite Fractal component containing two sub-components, Client and Server. The client interface of the Client component is bound to the server interface of the Server component. Membranes of components contain control interfaces. Note that on deployment, the composite, the Client, and the Server components can be placed in different containers.

Building a component-based application involves programming primitive components and

Figure 5. A composite fractal component HelloWorld with two sub-components client and server

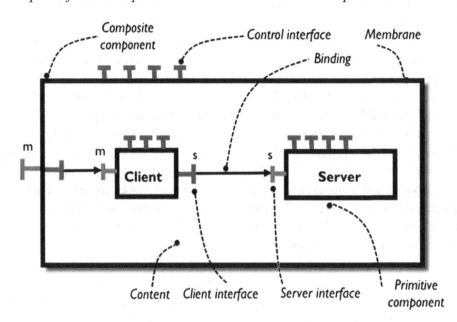

assembling them into an initial configuration either programmatically, using methods of the NicheActuatorInterface interface of the Niche runtime environment; or declaratively, using an Architecture Description Language (ADL) (Fractal ADL, 2009). In the former case, at least one (startup) component must be described in ADL to be initially deployed and started by the ADL interpreter. The startup component can deploy the remaining part of the application by executing a deployment and configuration workflow programmed using the Niche runtime actuation API, which allows the developer to program complex and flexible deployment and configuration workflows. The ADL used by Niche is based on Fractal ADL, an extensible language made of modules, each module defining an abstract syntax for a given architectural concern (e.g., hierarchical containment, deployment). Primitive components are programmed in Java.

Niche extends the Fractal component model with abstractions for group communication (*component group, group bindings*) as well as abstractions for deployment and resource man-

agement (*package, node*). All these abstractions are described later in this section.

A management part of a Niche application is programmed using the *Management Element (ME)* abstractions that include *Sensors, Watchers, Aggregators, Managers, Executors* and *Actuators*. Note that the distinction between Watchers, Aggregators, Managers and Executors is an architectural one. From the point of view of the execution environment they are all management elements, and management can be programmed in a flat manner (managers, sensors and actuators only). Figure 6 depicts a typical hierarchy of management elements in a Niche application. We distinguish different types of MEs depending on the roles they play in self-management code. *Sensors* monitor components through interfaces and trigger events to notify appropriate management elements about different application-specific changes in monitored components. There are sensors provided by the Niche runtime environment to monitor component failures/leaves (which in turn may be triggered by container/machine failures and leaves), component groups (changes in membership, group creations), and container failures. *Watchers* receive notification events from a number of sensors, filter and propagate them to *Aggregators*, which aggregate the information, detect and report symptoms to Managers. A symptom is an indication of the presence of some abnormality in the functioning of monitored components, groups or environment. *Managers* analyze the symptoms, make decisions and request Executors to act accordingly. *Executors* receive commands from managers and issue commands to *Actuators*, which act on components through control interfaces. Sensors and actuators interact with functional components via control interfaces (e.g., life-cycle and biding controllers), whereas management elements typically communicate by events using the pub/sub service provided by the Niche runtime environment. To manage and to access Niche runtime services, MEs use the NicheActuatorInterface interface bound to the Niche runtime environment which provides useful service and control methods such as dis-

cover, allocate, de-allocate, deploy, lookup, bind, unbind, subscribe, and unsubscribe. To publish events, MEs use the TriggerInterface interface of the runtime environment. Both client interfaces, NicheActuatorInterface and TriggerInterface, used by an ME are automatically bound to corresponding server interfaces of the Niche runtime environment when the ME is deployed (created). In order to receive events, an ME must implement the EventHandlerInterface server interface and subscribe to the events of interest.

Development Steps

When developing a self-managing distributed component-based application using Niche, the developer makes the following steps.

Development of architecture of the functional and management parts of the application. This step includes the following work: definition and design of functional components (includ-

Figure 6. Hierarchy of management elements in a Niche application

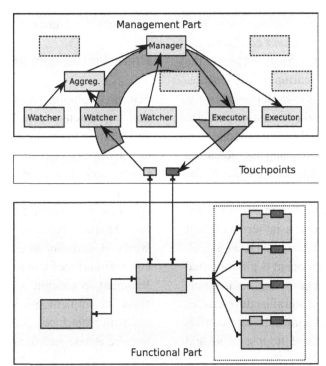

ing server and client interfaces) and component groups, assigning names to components and interfaces, definition of component and group bindings, definition and design of management elements including algorithms of event handlers for application-specific management objectives, definition of application-specific monitoring and actuation events, selection of predefined events issued by the Niche runtime environment, definition of event sources and subscriptions.

Description of (initial) architecture of functional and management parts in ADL, including components, their interfaces and bindings. Note that it is not necessary to describe the entire configuration in ADL, as components, groups and management elements can be deployed and configured also programmatically using the Niche actuation API rather than the ADL interpreter.

Programming of functional and management components. At this stage, the developer defines classes and interfaces of functional and management components, implements server interfaces (functional), event handlers (management), Fractal and Niche control interfaces, e.g., life-cycle and binding controllers.

Programming a (startup) component that completes initial deployment and configuration done by the ADL interpreter. An initial part of the application (including the startup component) described in ADL in Step 2 is to be deployed by the ADL interpreter; whereas the remaining part is to be deployed and configured by the programmer-defined startup component using the actuation interface NicheActuatorInterface of the Niche runtime system. Completion of the deployment might be either trivial if ADL is maximally used in Step 2, or complicated if a rather small part of the application is described in ADL in Step 2. Typically, the startup component is programmed to perform the following actions: bind components deployed by ADL, discover and allocate resources (containers) to deploy components; create, configure and bind components and groups; create and

configure management elements and subscribe them to events; and start components.

Programming of Functional Components and Component Groups

This section demonstrates how the above concepts are practically applied in programming the simple client-server HelloWorld application (Figure 4) which is a composite component containing two sub-components, Client and Server. The application provides a singleton service that prints a message (the greeting *"Hello World!"*) specified in the client call. In this example, the server component provides a server interface of type Service containing the *print* method. The client component has a client interface of type Service and a server interface of type Main containing the *main* method. The client interface of the client component is bound to the server interface of the service component. The composite Hello-World component provides a server interface that exports the corresponding interface of the client component; its main method is invoked when the application is launched.

Primitive Components

Primitive components are realized as Java classes that implement server interfaces (e.g., Service and Main in the HelloWorld example) as well as any necessary control interfaces (e.g., Binding-Controller). The client component class called ClientImpl, implements the Main interface. Since the client component has a client interface to be bound to the server, the class implements also the BindingController interface, which is the basic control interface for managing bindings. The code fragment in Exhibit 3 presents the ClientImpl class that implements the Main and the binding controller interfaces. Note that the client interface Service is assigned the name "s".

Exhibit 3. ClientImpl

```
public class ClientImpl implements Main, BindingController {
        private Service service; // Client interface to be bound to server in-
terface of Server component
        private String citfName = "s"; // Name of the client interface
        // Implementation of the Main interface
        public void main (final String[] args) {
                service.print ("Hello world!"); // call the service to print
the greeting
        }
        // All methods below belong to the Binding Controller interface with
the default implementation
        // Returns names of all client interfaces of the component
        public String[] listFc () {
                return new String[] { citfName };
        }
        // Returns the interface to which the given client interface is bound
        public Object lookupFc(final String citfName) throws NoSuchInterface-
Exception {
                if (!this.citfName.equals(citfName)) throw new NoSuchInterface
Exception(itfName);
                return service;
        }
        // Binds the client interface with the given name to the given server
interface
        public void bindFc(final String citfName, final Object sItf) throws
NoSuchInterfaceException {
                if (!this.citfName.equals(citfName)) throw new NoSuchInterface
Exception(itfName);
                service = (Service)sItf;
        }
        // Unbinds the client interface with the given name
        public void unbindFc (final String citfName) throws NoSuchInterfaceEx-
ception {
                if (!this.citfName.equals(citfName)) throw new NoSuchInterface
Exception(itfName);
                service = null;
        }
}
```

Exhibit 4. ServerImpl

```
public class ServerImpl implements Service {
public void print (final String msg) {
    for (int i = 0; i < count; ++i)
      System.err.println("Server prints:" + msg);
  }
}
```

The server component class, called ServerImpl, implements only the Service interface as shown in Exhibit 4.

Assembling Components

The simplest method to assemble components is through the ADL, which specifies a set of components, their bindings, and their containment relationships, and can be used to automatically deploy a Fractal system. The main concepts of the ADL are component definitions, components, interfaces, and bindings. The ADL description of the HelloWorld application with the singleton service presented in Exhibit 5.

Component Groups and Group Bindings

Niche bindings support communication among components hosted in different machines. Apart from the previously seen, one-to-one bindings, Niche also supports *groups* and *group bindings*, which are particularly useful for building decentralized, fault-tolerant applications. Group bindings allow treating a collection of components, the group, as a single entity, and can deliver invocations either to all group members (*one-to-all* semantics) or to any, randomly-chosen group member (*one-to-any* semantics). Groups are dynamic in that their membership can change over time (e.g., increase the group size to handle increased load in a tier).

Exhibit 5. ADL description of the HelloWorld application

```
<definition name="HelloWorld">
        <interface name="m" role="server" signature="Main"/>
        <component name="client">
          <interface name="m" role="server" signature="Main"/>
            <interface name="s" role="client" signature="Service"/>
            <content class="ClientImpl"/>
  </component>
        <component name="server">
            <interface name="s" role="server" signature="Service"/>
            <content class="ServerImpl"/>
        </component>
        <binding client="this.m" server="client.m" />
        <binding client="client.s" server="server.s" />
</definition>
```

Figure 7. HelloGroup application

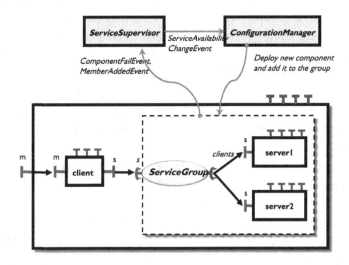

Exhibit 6. HelloGroup application

```
<definition name="HelloGroup">
        <interface name="m" role="server" signature="Main"/>
        <component name="client">
                <interface name="m" role="server" signature="Main"/>
                <interface name="s" role="client" signature="Service"/>
                <content class="ClientImpl"/>
        </component>
        <component name="ServiceGroup">
                <interface name="s" role="server" signature="Service"/>
                <interface name="clients" role="client" signature="Service"
cardinality="collection"/>
                <content class="GROUP"/>
  </component>
        <component name="server1">
    <interface name="s" role="server" signature="Service"/>
    <content class="ServerImpl"/>
  </component>
  <component name="server2">
    <interface name="s" role="server" signature="Service"/>
    <content class="ServerImpl"/>
  </component>
  <binding client="this.r" server="client.r" />
  <binding client="client.s" server="group.s" bindingType="groupAny"/>
  <binding client="group1.clients1" server="server1.s"/>
  <binding client="group1.clients2" server="server2.s"/>
</definition>
```

Groups are manipulated through the Niche API, which supports creating groups, binding groups and components, and adding/removing group members. Moreover, the Fractal ADL has been extended to enable describing groups as part of the system architecture.

Figure 7 depicts the HelloGroup application, in which the client component is connected to a group of two stateless service components (server1 and server2) using one-to-any invocation semantics. The group of service components provides a service that prints the "Hello World!" greeting by any of the group members on a client request.

The initial configuration of this example application (without management elements) can be described in ADL as seen in Exhibit 6.

As seen in this description, the service group is represented by a special component with content "GROUP". Group membership is then represented as binding the server interfaces of members to the client interfaces of the group. The bindingType attribute represents the invocation semantics (one-to-any in this case). Groups can also be created and bound programmatically using the Niche actuation API (namely the NicheActuatorInterface client interface bound to the Niche runtime system). As an example, the Java code fragment presented in Exhibit 7 illustrates group creation performed by a management element.

Programming of Management Elements

The management part of a Niche application is programmed using the Management Element (ME) abstractions that include Sensors, Watchers, Aggregators, Managers, Executors and Actuators. MEs are typically reactive event-driven components; therefore developing of MEs is mostly programming event handlers, i.e., methods of the EventHandlerInterface server interface that each ME must implement in order to receive

Exhibit 7. Java code fragment

```
// Code fragment from the StartManager class
// References to the Niche runtime interfaces bound on init or via binding
controller
private NicheIdRegistry nicheIdRegistry;
private NicheActuatorInterface myActuatorInterface;
...
// Lookup the client component and all server components by names
ComponentId client = (ComponentId) nicheIdRegistry.lookup("HelloGroup _0/client");
ArrayList<ComponentId> servers = new ArrayList();
servers.add((ComponentId) nicheIdRegistry.lookup("HelloGroup _0/server1");
servers.add((ComponentId) nicheIdRegistry.lookup("HelloGroup_0/server2");
// Create a group containing all server components.
GroupId groupTemplate = myActuatorInterface.getGroupTemplate();
groupTemplate.addServerBinding("s", JadeBindInterface.ONE_TO_ANY);
GroupId serviceGroup = myActuatorInterface.createGroup(groupTemplate, servers);
// Bind the client to the group with one-to-any binding
myActuatorInterface.bind(client, "s", serviceGroup, "s", JadeBindInterface.ONE_TO_ANY);
```

sensor events (including user-defined events and predefined events issued by the runtime system) and events from other MEs. The event handler is eventually invoked when a corresponding event is published (generated). The event handlers can be programmed to receive and handle events of different types. A typical management algorithm of an event handler includes, but not necessarily and not limited to, a sequence of conditional if-then(-else or -else-if) control statements (management logic rules) that examine rule conditions (IF clause) based on information retrieved from the received events or/and its internal state (which in turn reflects previous received events as part of monitoring activity); make a management decision and perform management actions and issue events (THEN clause) (see section *Policy-Based Management*).

When programming an ME class, the programmer must implement the following three *server* interfaces: the InitInterface interface to initialize an ME instance, the EventHandlerInterface interface to receive and handle events; and the MovableInterface interface to get a checkpoint, when the ME is moved and redeployed for replication or migration (the checkpoint is passed to a new instance through its InitInterface). To perform control actions, to subscribe and publish events, an ME class must include the following two *client* interfaces: the NicheActuatorInterface interface, named "actuator"; and the TriggerInterface interface, named "trigger". Both client interfaces are bound to the Niche runtime system when the ME is deployed either through its InitInterface or via the BidingController interface.

When developing the management code of an ME (event handlers) to control the functional part of an application and to subscribe to events, the programmer uses methods of the NicheActuatorInterface client interface that includes a number of actuation methods such as discover, allocate, de-allocate, deploy, create a component group, add a member to a group, bind, unbind, subscribe, unsubscribe. Note that the program-

mer can subscribe/unsubscribe to predefined built-in events (e.g., component failure, group membership change) issued by built-in sensors of the Niche runtime system. To publish events, the programmer uses the TriggerInterface client interface of the ME.

For example, Figure 7 depicts the HelloGroup application that provides a group service with self-healing capabilities. Feedback control in the application maintains the group size (a specified minimum number of service components) despite node failures, i.e., if any of the components in the group fails, a new service component is created and added to the group so that the group always contain the given number of servers. The self-healing control loop includes the Service Supervisor aggregator that monitors the number of components in the group, and the Configuration manager that is responsible to create and add a new service component on a request from the Service Supervisor. Figure 8 depicts a sequence of events and control actions of the management components. Specifically, if one of the service components of the service group fails, the group sensor issues a component failure event received by the Service Supervisor (1), which checks whether the number of components has dropped below a specified threshold (2). If so, the Server Supervisor fires the Service-Availability-Change event received by the Configuration Manager (3), which heals the component, i.e., creates a new instance of the server component and adds it to the group (4). When a new member is added to the group, the Service Supervisor, which keeps track of the number of server components, is notified by the predefined Member-Added-Event issued by the group sensor (5, 6).

The shortened Java code fragment presented in Exhibit 8 shows the management logic of the Configuration Manager responsible for healing of a failed server component upon receiving a Service-Availability-Change event issued by the Service Supervisor (steps 3 and 4 in Figure 8)

Figure 8. Events and actions in the self-healing loop of the HelloGroup application

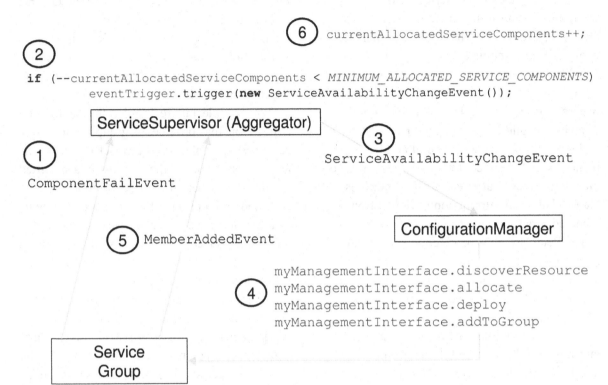

While MEs interact with each other mostly by events, sensors and actuators are programmed to interact with functional components via interface bindings. Interfaces between sensors and components are defined by the programmer, who may choose to use either the push or pull methods of interaction between a sensor and a component. In the case of the push method, the component pushes the sensor to issue an event. In this case, the component's client interface is bound to the corresponding sensor's server interface. In the case of the pull method, a sensor pulls the state from a component. In this case, the sensor's client interface is bound to a corresponding component's server interface. A sensor and a component are auto-bound when the sensor is deployed by a watcher. Actuation (control actions) can be done by MEs either through actuators bound to functional components or directly on components via their control interfaces using the Niche actuation API. Actuators are programmed in a similar way as sensors and are deployed by executors. By analogy to sensors, an actuator can be programmed to interact with a controlled component in the push and/or pull manner. In the former case (push), the actuator pushes a component through component's control interfaces, which can be either application-specific interfaces defined by the programmer or the Fractal control interfaces, e.g., LifeCycleController and AttributeController. In the case of the pull-based actuation, the controlled component checks its actuator for actions to be executed.

Deployment and Resource Management

Niche supports component deployment and resource management through the concepts of *component package* and *node*. A component package

Exhibit 8. Healing of a failed server component

```
// Code fragment from the ConfigurationManager class
public class ConfigurationManager implements EventHandlerInterface, MovableIn-
terface,
    InitInterface, BindingController, LifeCycleController {
private static final String DISCOVER_PREFIX = "dynamic:";
// Reference to the Actuation interface of the Niche runtime (automatically
bound on deployment).
private NicheActuatorInterface myManagementInterface;
...
public void init(NicheActuatorInterface managementInterface) { // invoked by
the runtime system
                myManagementInterface = managementInterface;
        }
public void init(Serializable[] parameters) { // invoked by the runtime system
on deployment
        initAttributes = parameters;
        componentGroup = (GroupId) initAttributes[0];
        serviceCompProps = initAttributes[1];
        nodeRequirements = DISCOVER_PREFIX + initAttributes[2];
}
...
public void eventHandler(Serializable e, int flag) { // event handler, invoked
on an event
                // For any case, check event type, ignore if it is not the
event of interest (should not happen)
                if (! (e instanceof ServiceAvailabilityChangeEvent)) return;
                // Find a node that meets the requirements for a server compo-
nent.
                try {
                        newNode = myManagementInterface.oneShotDiscoverResour
ce(nodeRequirements);
                } catch (OperationTimedOutException err) {
                        ... // Retry later (the code is removed)
                }
                // Allocate resources for a server component at the found
node.
                try {
                        List allocatedResources = myManagementInterface.
allocate(newNode, null);
                } catch (OperationTimedOutException err) {
```

continued on following page

269

Exhibit 8. Continued

```
                        ... // Retry later (the code is removed)
            }
            ...
        String deploymentParams = Serialization.serialize(serviceCompProps);
                // Deploy a new server component instance at the allocated
node.
            try {
                    deployedComponents = myManagementInterface.
deploy(allocatedResource,
                                                    deploymentParams);
                } catch (OperationTimedOutException err) {
                ... // Retry later (the code is removed)
                }
                ComponentId cid = (ComponentId) ((Object[]) deployedCompo-
nents.get(0))[1];
                // Add the new server component to the service group and start
the server.
                myManagementInterface.update(componentGroup, cid,
                                NicheComponentSupportInterface.ADD_
TO_GROUP_AND_START);
            }
```

is a bundle that contains the executables necessary for creating components, the data needed for their correct functioning as well as metadata describing their properties. A node is the physical or virtual machine on which components are deployed and executed. A node provides processing, storage, and communication resources, which are shared among the deployed components.

Niche exposes basic primitives for discovering nodes, allocating resources on those nodes, and deploying components; these primitives are designed to form the basis for external services for deploying components and managing their underlying resources. In the current prototype, component packages are OSGi™[5] bundles (OSGi Service Platform Release 4, 2010) and managed resources include CPU time, physical memory, storage space, and network bandwidth. The Fractal ADL has been extended to allow specifying packages and resource constraints on nodes. These extensions are illustrated in the ADL extract presented in Exhibit 9, which refines the client and composite descriptions in the HelloGroup example (added elements are show in Bold).

The packages element provides information about the OSGi bundles necessary for creating a component; packages are identified with their unique name in the OSGi bundle repository (e.g., "ClientPackage v1.3"). The virtual-node element describes resource and location requirements of components. At deployment time, each virtual node is mapped to a node (container) that conforms to the given resource requirements specified in the resourceReqs attribute. The necessary bundles are then installed on this node and the associated component is created. In the example, the client and the composite components are co-located at a node with memory larger than 1GB and CPU speed larger than 1Ghz.

```
<definition name="HelloGroup">
        <interface name="m" role="server" signature="Main"/>
        <component name="client">
    <interface name="m" role="server" signature="Main"/>
    <interface name="s" role="client" signature="Service"/>
    <content class="ClientImpl"/>
    <packages>
                    <package name="ClientPackage v1.3" >
                            <property name="local.dir" value="/tmp/j2ee"/>
                </package>
    </packages>
    <virtual-node name="node1" resourceReqs="(&(memory>=1)(CPUSpeed>=1))"/>
        </component>
 <!-- description of other components and bindings  (is not shown) -->
  ...
        <virtual-node name="node1">
</definition>
```

Initialization of Management Code

The ADL includes support for initializing the management part of an application in the form of *start manager* components. Start managers have a predefined definition "StartManagementType" that contains a set of client interfaces corresponding to the Niche API. These interfaces are implicitly bound by the system after start managers are instantiated. The declaration of a start manager is demonstrated in the ADL extract presented in Exhibit 10, which refines the HelloGroup example.

Typically, the start manager contains the code for creating, configuring, and activating the set of management elements that constitute the man-

agement part of an application. In the HelloGroup example, the management part realizes self-healing behavior and relies on an aggregator and a manager, which monitors the server group and maintains its size despite node failures. The start manager implementation (the StartManager class) then contains the code for deploying and configuring the elements of the self-healing loop shown in Figure 7 (i.e., ServiceSupervisor and ConfigurationManager). The code is actually located in the implementation of the LifeCycleController interface (startFc operation) of the startup manager, as seen in Exhibit 11.

Exhibit 10. Declaration of a start manager

```
<component name="StartManager" definition="org.ow2.jade.StartManage-
mentType">
        <content class=" helloworld.managers.StartManager"/>
        </component>
```

Exhibit 11. LifeCycleController interface

```
// Code fragment from the StartManager class of the HelloGroup application
public class StartManager implements BindingController, LifeCycleController {
// References to the Niche runtime interfaces bound on init or via binding control-
ler
private NicheIdRegistry nicheIdRegistry;
private NicheActuatorInterface myActuatorInterface;
…
public void startFc() throws IllegalLifeCycleException { // Invoked by the Niche
runtime system

        …
        // Lookup client and servers, create service group and bind client to the
group (code is not shown)
        GroupId serviceGroup = myActuatorInterface.createGroup(...);
...
        // Configure and deploy the Service Supervisor aggregator
  GroupId gid = serviceGroup;
  ManagementDeployParameters params = new ManagementDeployParameters();
        params.describeAggregator(ServiceSupervisor.class.getName(), "SA", null,
                                        new Serializable[] { gid.getId() });
        NicheId serviceSupervisor = myActuatorInterface.
deployManagementElement(params, gid);
        // Subscribe the aggregator to events from group
        myActuatorInterface.subscribe(gid, serviceSupervisor, ComponentFailEvent.
class.getName());
        myActuatorInterface.subscribe(gid, serviceSupervisor, MemberAddedEvent.
class.getName());
        // Configure and deploy the Configuration manager
  String minimumNodeCapacity = "200";
  params = new ManagementDeployParameters();
        params.describeManager(ConfigurationManager.class.getName(), "CM", null,
                                        new Serializable[] { gid, fp, minimumNo-
deCapacity });
        NicheId configurationManager = myActuatorInterface.
deployManagementElement(params, gid);
        // Subscribe the manager to events from the aggregator
        myActuatorInterface.subscribe(serviceSupervisor, configurationManager,
                                                ServiceAvailabilityChan-
geEvent.class.getName());
  …
}
```

Support for Legacy Systems

The Niche self-management framework can be applied to legacy systems by means of a *wrapping* approach. In this approach, legacy software elements are wrapped as Fractal components that hide proprietary configuration capabilities behind Fractal control interfaces. The approach has been successfully demonstrated with the Jade management system, which relied also on Fractal and served as a basis for developing Niche (Sicard, Boyer, & De Palma, 2008). Another example of the use of a "legacy" application (namely the VLC[6] program) in a self-managing application developed using Niche, is the gMovie demo application that performs transcoding of a given movie from one format to another. The description and the code of the gMovie application can be found in (Hannesson, 2009) and (Niche, 2010).

To briefly illustrate the wrapping approach, consider an enterprise system composed of an application server and a database server. The two servers are wrapped as Fractal components, whose controllers are implemented using legacy configuration mechanisms. For example, the lifecycle controllers are implemented by executing shell scripts for starting or stopping the servers. The attribute controllers are implemented by modifying text entries of configuration files. The connection between the two servers is represented as a binding between the corresponding components. The binding controller of the application server wrapper is then implemented by setting the database host address and port in the application server configuration file.

The wrapping approach produces a layer of Fractal components that enable observing and controlling the legacy software through standard interfaces. This layer can be then complemented with a Niche-based management system (e.g., sensors, actuators, managers), developed according to the described methodology. Of course, the degree of control exposed by the Fractal layer to the management system depends heavily on the legacy system (e.g., it may be impossible to dynamically move software elements). Moreover, the wrapping approach cannot take full advantage of Niche features such as name-based communication and group bindings. The reason is that bindings are only used to represent and manage connections between legacy software elements, not to implement them.

A DESIGN METHODOLOGY FOR SELF-MANAGEMENT IN DISTRIBUTED ENVIRONMENTS

A self-managing application can be decomposed into three parts: the functional part, the touchpoints, and the management part. The design process starts by specifying the functional and management requirements for the functional and management parts, respectively. In the case of Niche, the functional part of the application is designed by defining interfaces, components, component groups, and bindings. The management part is designed based on management requirements, by defining autonomic managers (management elements) and the required touchpoints (sensors and actuators). Touchpoints enable management of the functional part, i.e., make it manageable.

An Autonomic Manager is a control loop that continuously monitors and affects the functional part of the application when needed. For many applications and environments it is desirable to decompose the autonomic manager into a number of cooperating autonomic managers each performing a specific management function or/and controlling a specific part of the application. Decomposition of management can be motivated by different reasons such as follows. It avoids a single point of failure. It may be required to distribute the management overhead among participating resources. Self-managing a complex system may require more than one autonomic manager to simplify design by separation of concerns. Decomposition can also be used to enhance the management performance by running different management tasks concurrently and by placing the autonomic managers closer to the resources they manage.

We define the following iterative steps to be performed when designing and developing the management part of a self-managing distributed application in a decentralized manner given the management requirements and touchpoints.

Decomposition: The first step is to divide the management logic into a number of management tasks. Decomposition can be either functional (e.g., tasks are defined based which self-* properties they implement) or spatial (e.g., tasks are defined based on the structure of the managed application). The major design issue to be considered at this step is granularity of tasks assuming that a task or a group of related tasks can be performed by a single manager.

Assignment: The tasks are then assigned to autonomic managers each of which becomes responsible for one or more management tasks. Assignment can be done based on self-* properties that a task belongs to (according to the functional decomposition) or based on which part of the application that task is related to (according to the spatial decomposition).

Orchestration: Although autonomic managers can be designed independently, multiple autonomic managers, in the general case, are not independent since they manage the same system and there exist dependencies between management tasks. Therefore they need to interact and coordinate their actions in order to avoid conflicts and interference and to manage the system properly. Orchestration of autonomic managers is discussed in the following section.

Mapping: The set of autonomic managers are then mapped to the resources, i.e., to nodes of the distributed environment. A major issue to be considered at this step is optimized placement of managers and possibly functional components on nodes in order to improve management performance.

In this section, our major focus is on the orchestration of autonomic managers as the most challenging and less studied problem. The actions and objectives of the other stages are more related to classical issues in distributed systems such as partitioning and separation of concerns, and optimal placement of modules in a distributed environment.

Orchestrating Autonomic Managers

Autonomic managers can interact and coordinate their operation in the following four ways as discussed below and illustrated in Figure 9: indirect interactions via the managed system (stigmergy); hierarchical interaction (through touch points); direct interaction (via direct bindings); sharing of management elements.

Stigmergy

Stigmergy is a way of indirect communication and coordination between agents (Bonabeau, 1999). Agents make changes in their environment, and these changes are sensed by other agents and cause them to do more actions. Stigmergy was first observed in social insects like ants. In our case, agents are autonomic managers and the environment is the managed application.

The stigmergy effect is, in general, unavoidable when you have more than one autonomic manager and can cause undesired behavior at runtime. Hidden stigmergy makes it challenging to design a self-managing system with multiple autonomic managers. However, stigmergy can be part of the design and used as a way of orchestrating autonomic managers.

Hierarchical Management

By hierarchical management we mean that some autonomic managers can monitor and control other autonomic managers. The lower level autonomic managers are considered to be a managed

Figure 9. Interaction patterns

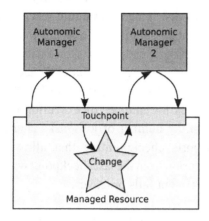

a. The stigmergy effect.

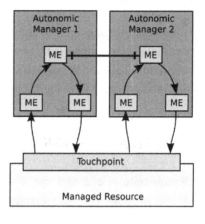

b. Direct interaction.

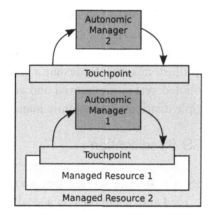

c. Hierarchical management.

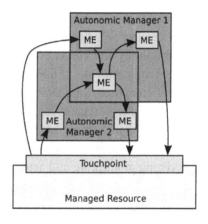

d. Shared Management Elements.

resource for the higher level autonomic manager. Communications between levels take place using touchpoints. Higher level managers can sense and affect lower level managers.

Autonomic managers at different levels often operate at different time scales. Lower level autonomic managers are used to manage changes in the system that need immediate actions. Higher level autonomic managers are often slower and used to regulate and orchestrate the system by monitoring global properties and tuning lower level autonomic managers accordingly.

Direct Interaction

Autonomic managers may interact directly with one another. Technically this is achieved by direct communication (via bindings or events) between appropriate management elements in the autonomic managers. Cross autonomic manager bindings can be used to coordinate autonomic managers and avoid undesired behaviors such as race conditions or oscillations.

Shared Management Elements

Another way for autonomic managers to communicate and coordinate their actions is by sharing management elements. This can be used to share state (knowledge) and to synchronize their actions.

DEMONSTRATOR APPLICATIONS

In order to demonstrate Niche and our design methodology, we present two self-managing services developed using Niche: (1) a robust storage service called YASS – Yet Another Storage Service; and (2) a robust computing service called YACS – Yet Another Computing Service. Each of the services has self-healing and self-configuration capabilities and can execute in a dynamic distributed environment, i.e., the services can operate even if computers join, leave or fail at any time. Each of the services implements relatively simple self-management algorithms, which can be extended to be more sophisticated, while reusing existing monitoring and actuation code of the services. The code and documentation of YASS and YACS services can be found at (Niche, 2010).

YASS (Yet Another Storage Service) is a robust storage service that allows a client to store, read and delete files on a set of computers. The service transparently replicates files in order to achieve high availability of files and to improve access time. The current version of YASS maintains the specified number of file replicas despite nodes leaving or failing, and it can scale (i.e., increase available storage space) when the total free storage is below a specified threshold. Management tasks include maintenance of file replication degree; maintenance of total storage space and total free space; increasing availability of popular files; releasing extra allocate storage; and balancing the stored files among available resources.

YACS (Yet Another Computing Service) is a robust distributed computing service that allows a client to submit and execute jobs, which are bags of independent tasks, on a network of nodes (computers). YACS guarantees execution of jobs despite nodes leaving or failing. YACS scales, i.e., changes the number of execution components, when the number of jobs/tasks changes. YACS supports checkpointing that allows restarting execution from the last checkpoint when a worker component fails or leaves.

Demonstrator I: Yet Another Storage Service (YASS)

In order to illustrate our design methodology, we have developed a storage service called YASS (Yet Another Storage Service), using Niche. The case study illustrates how to design a self-managing distributed system monitored and controlled by multiple distributed autonomic managers.

YASS Specification

YASS is a storage service that allows users to store, read and delete files on a set of distributed resources. The service transparently replicates the stored files for robustness and scalability.

Assuming that YASS is to be deployed and provided in a dynamic distributed environment, the following management functions are required in order to make the storage service self-managing in the presence of dynamicity in resources and load: the service should tolerate the resource churn (joins/leaves/failures), optimize usage of resources, and resolve hot-spots. We define the following tasks based on the functional decomposition of management according to self-* properties (namely self-healing, self-configuration, and self-optimization) to be achieved:

- Maintain the file replication degree by restoring the files which were stored on a failed/leaving resource. This function provides the self-healing property of the service so that the service is available despite of the resource churn;

• Maintain the total storage space and total free space to meet QoS requirements by allocating additional resources when needed. This function provides self-configuration of the service;

• Increasing the availability of popular files. This and the next two functions are related to the self-optimization of the service.

• Release excess allocated storage when it is no longer needed.

• Balance the stored files among the allocated resources.

YASS Functional Design

A YASS instance consists of front-end components and storage components as shown in Figure 10. The front-end component provides a user interface that is used to interact with the storage service. Storage components represent the storage capacity available at the resource on which they are deployed.

The storage components are grouped together in a storage group. A user issues commands (store,

read, and delete) using the front-end. A store request is sent to an arbitrary storage component (using one-to-any binding between the front-end and the storage group) which in turn will find some r different storage components, where r is the file's replication degree, with enough free space to store a file replica. These replicas together will form a file group containing the r storage components that will host the file. The front-end will then use a one-to-all binding to the file group to transfer the file in parallel to the r replicas in the group. A read request is sent to any of the r storage components in the group using the one-to-any binding between the front-end and the file group. A delete request is sent to the file group in parallel using a one-to-all binding between the front-end and the file group.

Enabling Management of YASS

Given that the functional part of YASS has been developed, to manage it we need to provide touchpoints. Niche provides basic touchpoints for manipulating the system's architecture and resources, such as sensors for resource failures and component group creation; and actuators for deploying and binding components. Beside the

Figure 10. YASS functional design

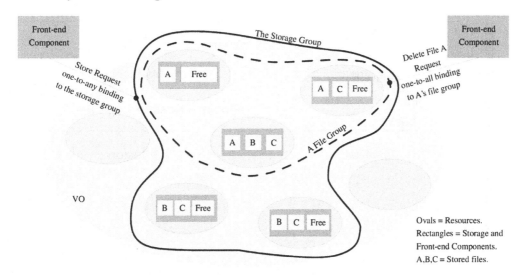

basic touchpoints the following additional, YASS specific, sensors and actuators are required:

- A load sensor to measure the current free space on a storage component;
- An access frequency sensor to detect popular files;
- A replicate-file actuator to add one extra replica of a specified file;
- A move-file actuator to move files for load balancing.

Self-Managing YASS

The following autonomic managers are needed to manage YASS in a dynamic environment. All four orchestration techniques described in the previous section on design methodology, are demonstrated below.

Replica Autonomic Manager

The replica autonomic manager is responsible for maintaining the desired replication degree for each stored file in spite of resources failing and leaving. This autonomic manager adds the self-healing property to YASS. The replica autonomic manager consists of two management

elements, the File-Replica-Aggregator and the File-Replica-Manager as shown in Figure 11. The File-Replica-Aggregator monitors a file group, containing the subset of storage components that host the file replicas, by subscribing to resource fail or leave events caused by any of the group members. These events are received when a resource, on which a component member in the group is deployed, is about to leave or has failed. The File-Replica-Aggregator responds to these events by triggering a replica change event to the File-Replica-Manager that will issue a find and restore replica command.

Storage Autonomic Manager

The storage autonomic manager is responsible for maintaining the total storage capacity and the total free space in the storage group, in the presence of dynamism, to meet QoS requirements. The dynamism is due either to resources failing/leaving (affecting both the total and free storage space) or file creation/addition/deletion (affecting the free storage space only). The storage autonomic manager reconfigures YASS to restore the total free space and/or the total storage capacity to meet the requirements. The reconfiguration is done by allocating free resources and deploying additional

Figure 11. Self-healing control loop for restoring file replicas

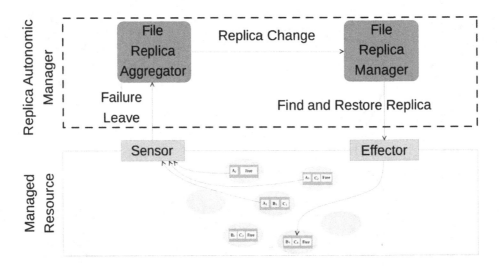

storage components on them. This autonomic manager adds the self-configuration property to YASS. The storage autonomic manager consists of Component-Load-Watcher, Storage-Aggregator, and Storage-Manager as shown in Figure 12. The Component-Load-Watcher monitors the storage group, containing all storage components, for changes in the total free space available by subscribing to the load sensors events. The Component-Load-Watcher will trigger a load change event when the load is changed by a predefined delta. The Storage-Aggregator is subscribed to the Component-Load-Watcher load change event and the resource fail, leave, and join events (note that the File-Replica-Aggregator also subscribes to the resource failure and leave events). The Storage-Aggregator, by analyzing these events, will be able to estimate the total storage capacity and the total free space. The Storage-Aggregator will trigger a storage availability change event when the total and/or free storage space drops below a predefined threshold. The Storage-Manager responds to this event by trying to allocate more resources and deploying storage components on them.

Direct Interactions to Coordinate Autonomic Managers

The two autonomic managers, replica autonomic manager and storage autonomic manager, described above seem to be independent. The first manager restores files and the other manager restores storage. But it is possible to have a race condition between the two autonomic managers that will cause the replica autonomic manager to fail. For example, when a resource fails the storage autonomic manager may detect that more storage is needed and start allocating resources and deploying storage components. Meanwhile the replica autonomic manager will be restoring the files that were on the failed resource. The replica autonomic manager might fail to restore the files due to space shortage if the storage autonomic manager is slower and does not have time to finish. This may also prevent the users, temporarily, from storing files.

If the replica autonomic manager would have waited for the storage autonomic manager to finish, it would not fail to recreate replicas. We used direct interaction to coordinate the two autonomic managers by binding the File-Replica-Manager to the Storage-Manager.

Figure 12. Self-configuration control loop for adding storage

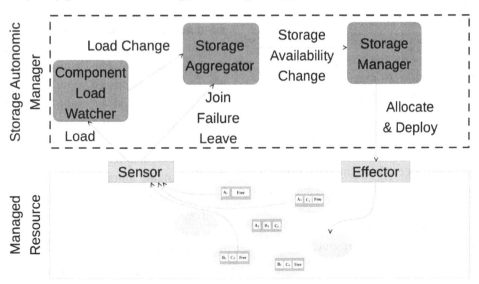

Before restoring files the File-Replica-Manager informs the Storage-Manager about the amount of storage it needs to restore files. The Storage-Manager checks available storage and informs the File-Replica-Manager that it can proceed if enough space is available or ask it to wait.

The direct coordination used here does not mean that one manager controls the other. For example, if there is only one replica left of a file, the File-Replica-Manager may ignore the request to wait from the Storage-Manager and proceed with restoring the file anyway.

Optimizing Allocated Storage

Systems should maintain high resource utilization. The storage autonomic manager allocates additional resources if needed to guarantee the ability to store files. However, users might delete files later causing the utilization of the storage space to drop. It is desirable that YASS be able to self-optimize itself by releasing excess resources to improve utilization.

It is possible to design an autonomic manager that will: detect low resource utilization, move file replicas stored on a chosen lowly utilized resource, and finally release it. Since the functionality required by this autonomic manager is partially provided by the storage and replica autonomic managers we will try to augment them instead of adding a new autonomic manager, and use stigmergy to coordinate them.

It is easy to modify the storage autonomic manager to detect low storage utilization. The replica manager knows how to restore files. When the utilization of the storage components drops, the storage autonomic manager will detect it and will deallocate some resource. The deallocation of resources will trigger, through stigmergy, another action at the replica autonomic manager. The replica autonomic manager will receive the corresponding resource leave events and will move the files from the leaving resource to other resources.

We believe that this is better than adding another autonomic manager for the following two reasons: first, it allows avoiding duplication of functionality; and second, it allows avoiding oscillation between allocating and releasing resources by keeping the decision about the proper amount of storage at one place.

Improving File Availability

Popular files should have more replicas in order to increase their availability. A higher level availability autonomic manager can be used to achieve this through regulating the replica autonomic manager. The autonomic manager consists of two management elements. The File-Access-Watcher and File-Availability-Manager are shown in Figure 13. The File-Access-Watcher monitors the file access frequency. If the popularity of a file changes dramatically it issues a frequency change event. The File-Availability-Manager may decide to change the replication degree of that file. This is achieved by changing the value of the replication degree parameter in the File-Replica-Manager.

Balancing File Storage

A load balancing autonomic manager can be used for self-optimization by trying to lazily balance the stored files among storage components. Since knowledge of current load is available at the Storage-Aggregator, we design the load balancing autonomic manager by sharing the Storage-Aggregator as shown in Figure 14. All autonomic managers we discussed so far are reactive. They receive events and act upon them. Sometimes proactive managers might be also required, such as in this case. Proactive managers are implemented in Niche using a timer abstraction. The load balancing autonomic manager is triggered, by a timer, every x time units. The timer event will be received by the shared Storage-Aggregator that will trigger an event containing the most and least loaded storage components. This event will be received by the Load-Balancing-Manager that

Figure 13. Hierarchical management used to implement the self-optimization control loop for file availability

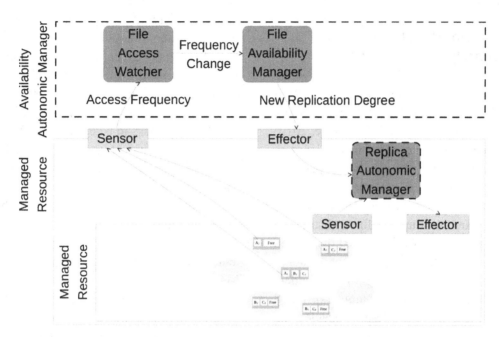

Figure 14. Sharing of management elements used to implement the self-optimization control loop for load balancing

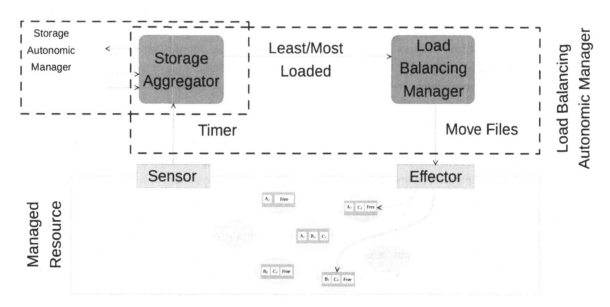

will move some files from the most to the least loaded storage component.

Demonstrator II: Yet Another Computing Service (YACS)

This section presents a rough overview of YACS (Yet Another Computing Service) developed using Niche (see (Hannesson, 2009; Niche, 2010) for more detail). The major goal in development of YACS was to evaluate the Niche platform and to study design and implementation issues in providing self-management (in particular, self-healing and self-tuning) for a distributed computing service. YACS is a robust distributed computing service that allows a client to submit and execute jobs, which are bags of independent tasks, on a network of nodes (computers). YACS guarantees execution of jobs despite nodes leaving or failing. YACS supports checkpointing that allows restarting execution from the last checkpoint when a worker component fails or leaves. The YACS includes a checkpoint service that allows the task programmer to perform task checkpointing whenever needed. Furthermore, YACS scales, i.e., changes the number of execution components, whenever the number of jobs/tasks changes. In order to achieve high availability, YACS always maintains a number of free masters and workers so that new jobs can be accepted without delay.

YACS executes jobs, which are collections of tasks, where a task represents instance of work of a particular type that needs to be done. For example, in order to transcode a movie, the movie file can be split into several parts (tasks) to be transcoded independently and in parallel. Tasks are programmed by the user and can be programmed to do just about anything. Tasks can be programmed in any programming language using any programming environment, and placed in a YACS job (bag of independent tasks) using the YACS API.

Figure 15 depicts YACS architecture. The functional part of YACS includes distributed Masters (only one Master is shown in Figure 15) and Workers used to execute jobs. A user submits jobs via the YACS Frontend component, which assigns jobs to Masters (one job per Master). A Master finds Workers to execute tasks in the job. When all tasks complete, the user is notified, and results of execution are returned to the user through the YACS frontend. YACS is implemented in Java, and therefore tasks to be executed by YACS can be either programmed in Java by extending the abstract Task class, or wrapped in a Task subclass. The execute method of the Task class has to be implemented to include the task code or the code that invoke the wrapped task. The execute method is invoked by a Worker that performs the task. When the method returns, the Worker sends to its Master an object that holds results and final status of execution. When developing a Task subclass, the programmer can override checkpointing methods to be invoked by the checkpoint service to make a checkpoint or by the Worker to restart the task from its last checkpoint. Checkpoints are stored in files identified by URLs.

There are two management objectives of the YACS management part: (1) self-healing, i.e., to guarantee execution of jobs despite of failures of Masters and Workers, and failures and leaves of Niche containers; (2) self-tuning, i.e., to scale execution (e.g., deploy new Masters and Workers if needed whenever a new Niche container joins the system).

The management elements responsible for self-healing include Master Watchers and Worker Watchers that monitor and control Masters and Workers correspondingly (see Figure 15). A Master Watcher deploys a sensor for the Master group it is watching, and subscribes to the component failure events and the state change events that might come from that group. A State Change Event contains a checkpoint (a URL of the checkpoint file) for the job executed by the Master. Master failures are reported by the Component Fail Event that causes the Watcher to find a free Master in the Master group and reassign the failed group to it,

Figure 15. Architecture of YACS (yet another computing service)

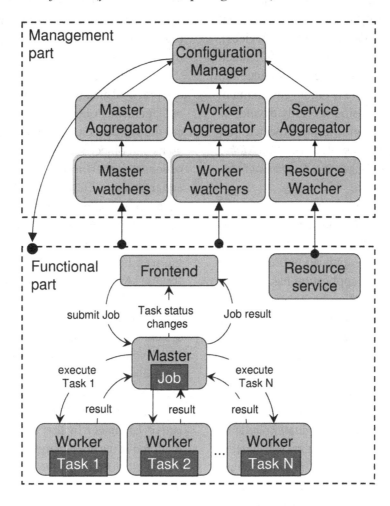

or to deploy a new Master instance if there are no free Masters in the group. The job checkpoint is used to restart the job on another Master. A Worker Watcher monitors and controls a group of Workers and responsible for healing Workers and restarting tasks in the case of failures. A Worker Watcher performs in a in a similar way as a Master Watcher described above.

The management elements responsible for self-tuning include Master-, Worker- and Service- Aggregators and the Configuration Manager, which is on top of the management hierarchy. The self-tuning control loop monitors availability of resources (number of Masters and Workers) and adds more resources, i.e., deploys Masters and Workers on available Niche containers upon

requests from the Aggregators. The Aggregators collect information about the status of job execution, Master and Workers groups and resources (Niche containers) from Master, Worker and Service Resource Watchers. The Aggregators request the Configuration Manager to deploy and add to the service more Masters and/or Workers when the number of Masters and/or Workers drops (because of failures) below predefined thresholds or when there are not enough Masters and Workers to execute jobs and tasks in parallel.

Evaluation

In order to validate and evaluate the effectiveness of Niche, in terms of efficacy and overheads, the

Niche execution environment and both demo applications, YASS (Yet Another Storage Service) and YACS (Yeat Another Computing Services), were tested and evaluated on the Grid5000 testbed (https://www.grid5000.fr/). The performance and overhead of the Niche execution environment was evaluated mostly using specially developed test programs: These confirm the expected performance/fault model presented in section *Niche: a Platform for Self-Managing Distributed Applications*.

The effectiveness of Niche for developing and executing self-managing applications was validated by YASS, YACS, and, in particular, with the gMovie demo application built on top of YACS. The gMovie application has been developed to validate the functionality and self-* (self-healing and self-configuration) properties of YACS, as well as to validate and evaluate effectiveness and stability of the Niche execution environment. The gMovie application performs transcoding of a given movie from one format to another in parallel on a number of YACS workers. Results of our validation and evaluation indicate that the desired self-* properties, e.g., self-healing in the presence of failures and resource churn can be obtained, and that the programming is not particularly burdensome. Programmers with varying experience were able to learn and understand Niche to the point that they could be productive in a matter of days or weeks. For results of performance evaluation of YACS, the reader is referred to (Hannesson, 2009).

POLICY BASED MANAGEMENT

So far in our discussion we have shown how to program management logic directly in the management elements using Java (in addition to ADL for initial deployment). However, a part of the analysis and planning phases of the management logic can also be programmed separately using policy languages. Note that currently the developer has to implement the rest of management logic (e.g., actuation workflow) in a programming language (e.g., Java) used to program the management part of a self-managing application.

Policy-based management has been proposed as a practical means to improve and facilitate self-management. Policies are sets of rules which govern the system behaviors and reflect the business goals and objectives. Rules dictate management actions to be performed under certain conditions and constraints. The key idea of policy-based management is to allow IT administrators to define a set of policy rules to govern behaviors of their IT systems, rather than relying on manually managing or ad-hoc mechanics (e.g., writing customized scripts) (Agrawal, Giles, Lee, & Lobo, 2005). In this way, the complexity of system management can be reduced, and also, the reliability of the system's behavior is improved.

The implementation and maintenance (e.g., replacement) of policies in a policy-based management are rather difficult, if policies are embedded in the management logic and programmed in its native language. In this case, policy rules and scattered in the management logic and that makes it difficult to modify the policies, especially at runtime. The major advantages of using a special policy language (and a corresponding policy engine) to program policies are the following:

- All related policy rules can be grouped and defined in policy files. This makes it easier to program and to reason about policy-based management.
- Policy languages are at a higher level than the programming languages used to program management logic. This makes it easier for system administrators to understand and modify policies without the need to interact with system developers.
- When updating policies, the new policies can be applied to the system at run time without the need to stop, rebuild or redeploy the application (or parts of it).

In order to facilitate implementation and maintenance of policies, language support, including a policy language and a policy evaluation engine, is needed. Niche provides ability to program policy-based management using a policy language, a corresponding API and a policy engine (Bao, Al-Shishtawy, & Vlassov, 2010). The current implementation of Niche includes a generic policy-based framework for policy-based management using SPL (Simplified Policy Language) (SPL Language Reference, 2009) or XACML (OASIS[7] eXtensible Access Control Markup Language (XACML) TC, 2009). Both languages allow defining policy rules (rules with obligations in XACML, or decision statements in SPL) that dictate the management actions that are to be enforced on managed resources and applications in certain situations (e.g., on failures). SPL is intended for management of distributed systems; whereas XACML was specially designed for access control rather than for management. Nevertheless, XACML allows for obligations (actions to be performed) conveyed with access decisions (permit/denied/not-applicable); and we have adopted obligations for management.

The policy framework includes abstractions (and corresponding API) of policies, policy-managers and policy-manager groups. A policy is a set of if-then rules that dictate what should be done (e.g., publishing an actuation request) when something has happened (e.g., a symptom that require management actions has been detected). A Policy Manager is a management element that is responsible for loading policies, making decisions based on policies and delegating obligations (actuation requests) to Executors. Niche introduces a policy-manager group abstraction that represents a group of policy-based managers sharing the same set of policies. A policy-manager group can be created for performance or robustness. A Policy Watcher monitors the policy repositories for policy changes and request reloading policies. The Policy Engine evaluates policies and returns decisions (obligations).

Policy-based management enables self-management under guidelines defined by humans in the form of management policies that can be easily changed at run-time. With policy-based management it is easier to administrate and maintain management policies. It facilitates development by separating of policy definition and maintenance from application logic. However, our performance evaluation shows that hard-coded management performs better than the policy-based management due to relatively long policy evaluation latencies of the latter. Based on our evaluation results, we recommend using policy-based management for high-level policies that require the flexibility to be able to be rapidly changed and manipulated by administrators at deployment and runtime. Policies can be easily understood by humans, can be changed on the fly, and separated from development code for easier management.

Policy based management can be introduced to the management part of an application by adding a policy manager in the control loop. Figure 16 depicts an example on how to introduce a policy manager in the Storage Autonomic Manager used in the YASS demonstrator (see Figure 12). The policy manager receives monitoring events such as total load in the system. The policy manager then evaluates the policies using the policy engine. An example of a policy used by the Storage Autonomic Manager for releasing extra storage is shown below. Exhibit 12 shows one policy from the policy file written in SPL. When a policy fires (the condition is true) the state of the manager may change and actuation events may be triggered.

CONCLUSION

The presented management framework enables the development of distributed component based applications with self-* behaviors which are independent from application's functional code, yet can interact with it when necessary. The framework provides a small set of abstractions

Figure 16. YASS self-configuration using policies

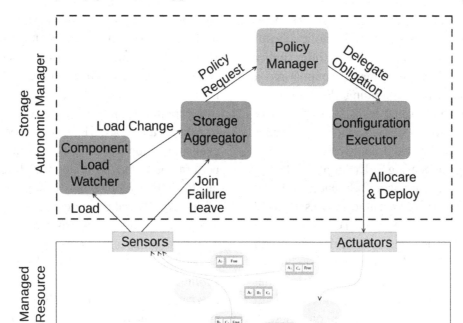

that facilitate robust and efficient application management even in dynamic environments. The framework leverages the self-* properties of the structured overlay network which it is built upon. Our prototype implementation and demonstrators show the feasibility of the framework.

In dynamic environments, such as community Grids or Clouds, self-management presents four challenges. Niche mostly meets these challenges, and presents a programming model and runtime execution service to enable application developers to develop self-managing applications.

Exhibit 12. Releasing extra storage

```
Policy {
        Declaration {
                lowloadthreshold = 500;
        }
        Condition {
                storageInfo.totalLoad <= lowloadthreshold
        }
        Decision {
                manager.setTriggeredHighLoad(false) &&
                manager.delegateObligation("release storage")
        }
}:1;
...
```

The first challenge is that of the efficient and robust resource discovery. This was the most straightforward of the challenges to meet. All resources (containers) are members of the Niche overlay, and resources can be discovered using the overlay.

The second challenge is that of developing a robust and efficient sensing and actuation infrastructure. For efficiency we use a push (i.e., publish/subscribe) rather than a pull mechanism. In Niche all architectural elements (i.e., both functional components and management elements) are potentially mobile. This is necessary in dynamic environments but it means that delivering sensing events and actuation commands is non-trivial. The underlying overlay provides efficient sensing and actuation storing locations in a DHT-like structure, and through replication (as in a peer-to-peer system) sensing and actuation is robust. In terms of messaging all sensing and actuation events are delivered at least once.

The third challenge is to avoid a management bottleneck or single-point-of-failure. We advocate a decentralized approach to management. Management functions (of a single application) should be distributed among several cooperative autonomic managers that coordinate (as loosely-coupled as possible) their activities to achieve the overall management objectives. While multiple managers are needed for scalability, robustness, and performance, we found that they are also useful for reflecting separation of concerns. We have worked toward a design methodology, and stipulate the design steps to take in developing the management part of a self-managing application including spatial and functional partitioning of management, assignment of management tasks to autonomic managers, and co-ordination of multiple autonomic managers.

The fourth challenge is that of scale, by which we meant that in dynamic systems the rate of change (join, leaves, failure of resources, change of component load etc.) is high and that it was

important to reduce the need for action/communication in the system. This may be open-ended task, but Niche contained many features that directly impact communication. The sensing/actuation infrastructure only delivers events to management elements that directly have subscribed to the event (i.e., avoiding the overhead of keeping management elements up-to-date as to component location). Decentralizing management makes for better scalability. We support component groups and bindings to such groups, to be able to map this useful abstraction to the best (known) efficient communication infrastructure.

FUTURE WORK

Our future work includes issues in the areas of platform improvement, management design, management replication, high-level programming support, coupled control loops, and the relevance of the approach in other domains.

Currently, there are many aspects of the Niche platform that could be improved. This includes better placement of managers, more efficient resource discovery, and improved containers, the limitations of which were mentioned in section on the Niche platform (e.g., enforcing isolation of components).

We believe that in dynamic or large-scale systems that decentralized management is a must. We have taken a few steps in this direction but additional case studies with the focus on the orchestration of multiple autonomic managers for a single application need to be made.

Robustifying management is another concern. Work is ongoing on a Paxos-based replication scheme for management elements. Other complementary approaches will be investigated, as consistent replication schemes are heavyweight.

Currently, the high-level (declarative) language support in Niche is limited. ADLs may be used for initial configuration only. For dynamic reconfiguration the developer needs to use the Niche API directly, which has the disadvantage of being somewhat verbose and error-prone. Workflows could be used to lift the level of abstraction.

There is also the issue of coupled control loops, which we did not study. In our scenario multiple managers are directly or indirectly (via stigmergy) interacting with each other and it is not always clear how to avoid undesirable behavior such as rapid or large oscillations which not only can cause the system to behave non-optimally but also increase management overhead. We found that it is desirable to decentralize management as much as possible, but this probably aggravates the problems with coupled control loops. Although we did not observe this in our two demonstrators, one might expect problems with coupled control loops in larger and more complex applications. Application programmers should not need to handle coordination of multiple managers (where each manager may be responsible for a specific aspect). Future work might need to address the design of coordination protocols that could be directly used or specialized.

There is another domain, one that we did not target, where scale is also a challenge and decentralization probably necessary. This is the domain of very large (Cloud-scale) applications, involving tens of thousands of machines. Even if the environment is fairly stable the sheer number of involved machines will generate many events, and management might become a bottleneck. It would be of interest to investigate if our approach can, in part of wholly, be useful in that domain.

FURTHER READING

For more information on topics covered in this chapter and on previous Niche-related work, see (Al-Shishtawy, 2010; Al-Shishtawy et al., 2010; Bao et al., 2010; Al-Shishtawy et al., 2008; Brand et al., 2007). For more information on Niche, in-

cluding documentation, code (available as open source) and demo applications, demo videos, see (Niche, 2010).

EXERCISES

1. Define management objectives that could be assigned to autonomic managers in the following applications: a web server, a storage service using a storage Cloud, a compute service using a compute Cloud, a content distribution network (e.g. a video-on-demand, live media streaming).

2. Define touch-points (sensors and actuators) and management elements in the systems of Exercise 1. In particular, define what should be monitored and what should be controlled in the systems in order to meet management objectives? Design control algorithms for autonomic managers. *Optional:* Implement one of the systems using Niche.

3. Consider the design of the YASS (Yet Another Storage Service) application described in Section *Demonstrator I: Yet Another Storage Service (YASS)*. Add a new management objective, e.g., to achieve good load balancing by balancing access requests among YASS storage components, or to improve access time by limiting the maximum number of concurrent downloads. For the new objective, define required touch-points (sensors and actuators) and design an autonomic manager. Does it conflict with other managers? Discuss possible way to orchestrate the managers in order to avoid conflicts if any. *Optional:* Implement the extension of YASS using Niche.

4. Design a distributed application with self-management capabilities (e.g., a distributed key-value store, or a peer-to-peer photo sharing application). First, develop architecture of the functional part of the application, and,

next, design its management part by performing the design steps described in Section *A Design Methodology for Self-Management in Distributed Environments*. In particular, define management objectives, corresponding management tasks, required touch-points (sensors and actuators), and management algorithms.

5. Design and compare the following two possible architectures of the management part of the application in Exercise 4: (i) a single autonomic manager that performs all management tasks; (ii) a set of autonomic managers assigned different management tasks. For the second approach, discuss how the managers must interact in order to achieve their management objectives without conflicts. *Optional:* Implement one of the architectures using Niche.

6. Describe in SPL the management policy for the manager of the helloGroup example described in Section *Development of Self-Managing Applications Using Niche*. Modify the policy so that if there are no available resources to deploy additional services the policy manager will send a notification email to the service administrator.

ACKNOWLEDGMENT

We thank Konstantin Popov and Joel Höglund (SICS), Noel De Palma (INRIA), Atli Thor Hannesson, Leif Lindbäck, and Lin Bao, for their contribution to development of Niche and self-management demo applications using Niche. This research has been supported in part by the FP6 projects Grid4All (contract IST-2006-034567) and SELFMAN (contract IST-2006-034084) funded by the European Commission. We also thank the anonymous reviewers for their constructive comments.

REFERENCES

Abdelwahed, S., & Kandasamy, N. (2006). A control-based approach to autonomic performance management in computing systems. In Parashar, M., & Hariri, S. (Eds.), *Autonomic computing: Concepts, infrastructure, and applications* (pp. 149–168). CRC Press. doi:10.1201/9781420009354.ch8

Agrawal, D., Calo, S., Lee, K.-W., Lobo, J., & Res, T. W. (2007, June). Issues in designing a policy language for distributed management of it infrastructures. In *Integrated network management, 2007. IM'07. 10th IFIP/IEEE International Symposium* (pp. 30-39).

Agrawal, D., Giles, J., Lee, K., & Lobo, J. (2005, June). Policy ratification. In T. Priol & M. Vanneschi (Eds.), *Policies for distributed systems and networks, 2005. Sixth IEEE Int. Workshop* (pp. 223- 232).

Al-Shishtawy, A. (2010). Enabling and achieving self-management for large scale distributed systems. Licentiate thesis, Royal Institute of Technology (KTH), Stockholm, Sweden.

Al-Shishtawy, A., Fayyaz, M. A., Popov, K., & Vlassov, V. (2010, October). Achieving robust self-management for large-scale distributed applications. In *Self-Adaptive and Self-Organizing Systems (SASO), 2010 4th IEEE International Conference* (pp. 31-40).

Al-Shishtawy, A., Höglund, J., Popov, K., Parlavantzas, N., Vlassov, V., & Brand, P. (2008, July). Enabling self-management of component based distributed applications. In Priol, T., & Vanneschi, M. (Eds.), *From Grids to service and pervasive computing* (pp. 163–174). Springer, US. doi:10.1007/978-0-387-09455-7_12

Al-Shishtawy, A., Vlassov, V., Brand, P., & Haridi, S. (2009, August). A design methodology for self-management in distributed environments. In *IEEE International Conference on Computational Science and Engineering, 2009* (vol. 1, pp. 430-436). Vancouver, BC: IEEE Computer Society.

Bao, L., Al-Shishtawy, A., & Vlassov, V. (2010, September). Policy based self-management in distributed environments. *Self-Adaptive and Self-Organizing Systems Workshop (SASOW), 2010 Fourth IEEE International Conference* (pp. 256-260).

Bhat, V., Parashar, M., Khandekar, M., Kandasamy, N., & Klasky, S. (2006, Sept.). A self-managing wide-area data streaming service using model-based online control. In *7th IEEE/ACM International Conference on Grid computing* (pp. 176-183).

Bonabeau, E. (1999). Editor's introduction: Stigmergy. *Artificial Life*, 5(2), 95–96. doi:10.1162/106454699568692

Bouchenak, S., Boyer, F., Krakowiak, S., Hagimont, D., Mos, A., Stefani, J.-B., et al. (2005, October). Architecture-based autonomous repair management: An application to J2EE clusters. In *SRDS'05: Proceedings of the 24th IEEE Symposium on Reliable Distributed Systems* (pp. 13-24). Orlando, Florida.

Brand, P., Höglund, J., Popov, K., de Palma, N., Boyer, F., & Parlavantzas, N. (2007). The role of overlay services in a self-managing framework for dynamic virtual organizations. In Danelutto, M., Fragopoulou, P., & Getov, V. (Eds.), *Making Grids work* (pp. 153–164). Springer, US.

Bruneton, E., Coupaye, T., & Stefani, J.-B. (2004, February 5). *The fractal component model* (Technical Report). France Telecom R&D and INRIA.

Chan, H., & Arnold, B. (2003). A policy based system to incorporate self-managing behaviors in applications. In *OOPSLA'03: Companion of the 18th Annual ACM SIGPLAN Conference on Object-Oriented Programming, Systems, Languages, and Applications* (pp. 94-95). New York, NY, USA.

Cheng, S.-W., Huang, A.-C., Garlan, D., Schmerl, B., & Steenkiste, P. (2004). An architecture for coordinating multiple self-management systems. In *WICSA'04* (p. 243). Washington, DC, USA.

Das, R., Kephart, J. O., Lefurgy, C., Tesauro, G., Levine, D. W., & Chan, H. (2008). Autonomic multi-agent management of power and performance in data centers. In *AAMAS'08: Proceedings of the 7th international joint conference on autonomous agents and multiagent systems* (pp. 107-114). Richland, SC: International Foundation for Autonomous Agents and Multiagent Systems.

El-Ansary, S., Alima, L. O., Brand, P., & Haridi, S. (2003, October). Efficient broadcast in structured P2P networks. In *Peer-to-Peer Systems II* (p. 304-314). Berlin, Germany: Springer.

Feng, J., Wasson, G., & Humphrey, M. (2007, Sept.). Resource usage policy expression and enforcement in grid computing. In *8th IEEE/ACM International Conference on Grid Computing, 2007* (pp. 66-73).

Hannesson, A. T. (2009). *YACS: Yet another computing service using Niche*. Master of Science Thesis, Royal Institute of Technology (KTH), Stockholm, Sweden. Retrieved from http://niche.sics.se/trac/raw-attachment/wiki/WikiStart/YACS_thesis__athan.pdf

Hellerstein, J. L., Diao, Y., Parekh, S., & Tilbury, D. M. (2004). *Feedback control of computing systems*. John Wiley & Sons. doi:10.1002/047166880X

Horn, P. (2001, October 15). *Autonomic computing: IBM's perspective on the state of information technology.*

IBM. (2006, June). *An architectural blueprint for autonomic computing*, 4th edition. Retrieved from http://www-01.ibm.com/software/tivoli/autonomic/pdfs/AC Blueprint White Paper 4th.pdf

Kephart, J., Chan, H., Das, R., Levine, D., Tesauro, G., Rawson, F., et al. (2007, June). Coordinating multiple autonomic managers to achieve specified power-performance tradeoffs. In *Fourth International Conference on Autonomic Computing, 2007* (p. 24).

Kephart, J. O., & Chess, D. M. (2003, January). The vision of autonomic computing. *Computer, 36*(1), 41–50. doi:10.1109/MC.2003.1160055

Kephart, J. O., & Das, R. (2007). Achieving self-management via utility functions. *IEEE Internet Computing, 11*(1), 40–48. doi:10.1109/MIC.2007.2

Kumar, V., Cooper, B. F., Eisenhauer, G., & Schwan, K. (2007). iManage: Policy-driven self-management for enterprise-scale systems. In *Middleware '07: Proceedings of the ACM/IFIP/USENIX 2007 International Conference on Middleware* (pp. 287-307). New York, NY: Springer-Verlag.

Niche. (2010). *Website*. Retrieved from http://niche.sics.se/

OW2 Consortium. (2009). *Fractal ADL*. Retrieved October 2009, from http://fractal.ow2.org/fractaladl/

Oasis. (2009). *eXtensible Access Control Markup Language TC* (XACML). Retrieved October 2009, from http://www.oasis-open.org/committees/xacml/

OSGi. (2010). *Service platform release 4*. Retrieved June 2010, from http://www.osgi.org/Specifications/HomePage

Parashar, M., & Hariri, S. (2005). Autonomic computing: An overview. In *Unconventional Programming Paradigms* [Springer Verlag.]. *Lecture Notes in Computer Science, 3566*, 257–269. doi:10.1007/11527800_20

Roy, P. V., Haridi, S., Reinefeld, A., Stefani, J.-B., Yap, R., & Coupaye, T. (2007, Oct). *Self management for large-scale distributed systems: An overview of the SELFMAN project*. In FMCO'07: Software Technologies Concertation on Formal Methods for Components and Objects. Amsterdam, The Netherlands.

Sicard, S., Boyer, F., & De Palma, N. (2008). Using components for architecture-based management: The self-repair case. In *ICSE '08: Proceedings of the 30th International Conference on Software Engineering* (pp. 101-110). New York, NY: ACM.

SPL. (2009). *Language reference*. Retrieved October 2009, from http://incubator.apache.org/imperius/docs/spl_reference.html

Sweitzer, J. W., & Draper, C. (2006). Architecture overview for autonomic computing. In Parashar, M., & Hariri, S. (Eds.), *Autonomic computing: Concepts, infrastructure, and applications* (pp. 71–98). CRC Press.

The Center for Autonomic Computing. (2010). *Website*. Retrieved from http://www.nsfcac.org/

White, S. R., Hanson, J. E., Whalley, I., Chess, D. M., & Kephart, J. O. (2004). An architectural approach to autonomic computing. In *Proc. International Conference on Autonomic Computing* (pp. 2-9).

KEY TERMS AND DEFINITIONS

ADL: Architecture Description Language, a language to define a configuration or subconfiguration consisting of software components, the bindings between them, their resource requirements and various configuration constraints.

Churn: In overlay networks (e.g. DHTs) churn is the continuous turnover in the nodes that participate in the overlay as nodes join, leave or fail.

Component: In software engineering a component is a software package or a module that encapsulates a set of related functions or data. Applications are composed of multiple components, where the division into components should reflect a separation of concerns. With regard to system-wide co-ordination, components communicate with each other via interfaces.

Component Model: There are many variations in languages and tools for component-based programming. These are reflected in the component model which specifies, among other things, the semantics and syntax of the interfaces through which components interact. Examples of component models are Fractal, Microsoft® COM (Component Object Model), and CORBA. Components models vary as to capabilities of the management interface to components and runtime access mechanisms.

Container: In Niche, a container is the process that hosts running components (both functional and management components), providing the services through which components interact (bindings or events).

Distributed Hash Table (DHT): A distributed hash table (DHT) is a scalable distributed system that provides hash table functionality to store key/value pairs on a set of cooperating computers (nodes) and to retrieve the value associated with a given key. Requests to store/retrieve values can be issued at any node in the DHT. Maintenance of the mapping from keys to values is distributed among the nodes participating in the DHT so that each participating node is responsible for portion of the items, which it stores locally. DHTs can scale to a large number of nodes and tolerate nodes joins, leaves and failures.

Management Element: In Niche, a management element (ME) is a component in the management part of an application. An autonomic manager is built of a network of management elements that, typically, communicate using events and are connected to the functional part of the application through touchpoints (sensors, actuators). Management elements can be divided into watchers, aggregators, managers and executors, depending on their roles.

Overlay Network: An overlay network is a computer network built on top of another network (underlay). Overlay nodes are connected to each other with virtual links, where each virtual link may span any number of links in the underlay.

Resource Discovery: The process of finding suitable resources in a dynamic system. In a dynamic system the set of available resources is continuously changing and are not known a priori.

Structured Overlay: Structured overlays are a class of overlay networks in which virtual links between overlay nodes follow a given structure. This structure ensures that any overlay node can efficiently route a message to a destination (another overlay node). The structured pattern of virtual links is continuously maintained by a distributed algorithm making the overlay self-organizing, preserving the structure by correction of routing tables on node leaves, joins and failures.

Touchpoints: In Autonomic Computing the points of contact between the management and functional parts of an application (or between management and the system being managed). Touchpoints may be divided into sensors and actuators, depending on the direction of information/control flow where sensors provide information to management and actuators operate on the system as directed by management.

ENDNOTES

[1] Tivoli® is a registered U.S. trademark of IBM®.

[2] Oracle® and Java™ are registered trademarks of Oracle and/or its affiliates..

[3] Called Jade for historical reasons. Jade is a cluster-based environment for autonomic management developed at INRIA, France, parts of which were adapted and integrated into Niche.

[4] The Niche API documentation can be found at http://niche.sics.se/.

[5] OSGi is a trademark or a registered trademark of the OSGi Alliance in the United States, other countries, or both.

[6] VLC media player is a trademark owned by the VideoLAN non-profit organization.

[7] OASIS is a trademark of OASIS, the open standards consortium.

Chapter 11

A Guideline for Realizing the Vision of Autonomic Networking:
Implementing Self–Adaptive Routing on Top of OSPF

Gábor Rétvári
Budapest University of Technology and Economics, Hungary

Felicián Németh
Budapest University of Technology and Economics, Hungary

Ibrahim Hokelek
Telcordia Technologies, Inc., USA

Mariusz Fecko
Telcordia Technologies, Inc., USA

Arun Prakash
Fraunhofer Institute for Open Communication Systems, Germany

Ranganai Chaparadza
Fraunhofer Institute for Open Communication Systems, Germany

Michał Wódczak
Telcordia Technologies, Inc., USA

Bruno Vidalenc
Alcatel-Lucent Bell Labs, France

ABSTRACT

Autonomicity, realized through control loop structures operating within network devices and the network as a whole, is an enabler for advanced and enriched self-manageability of communication systems. Unfortunately, very little practical knowledge is currently available that would guide a network engineer through realizing this ambitious vision. In this survey, we intend to fill this gap by providing a practical guideline for building truly autonomic systems. Our main motivation is the recognition that it is not necessary to rebuild the whole network infrastructure out of piecemeal-designed, autonomic-aware protocol components. Instead, the framework of Autonomic Networking is broad enough to accommodate many of, if not all, existing off-the-shelf network technologies. This is because sophisticated network protocol

DOI: 10.4018/978-1-60960-845-3.ch011

machinery is usually quite capable self-managing entity in itself, complete with all the basic components of an autonomic networking element, like embedded control loops, decision-making modules, distributed knowledge repositories, et cetera. What remained to be done to achieve the desired autonomic behavior is to open up of some of these intrinsic control loops and incorporate them into external decision making logics. We demonstrate this idea on the example of building advanced self-adaptive routing mechanisms on top of OSPF. First, we present a generic framework for autonomic networks, designed to integrate well-tested, legacy network technology and modern, inherently autonomic-aware functionality into a single feature-rich self-managing infrastructure. Then, we cast an illustrious legacy network technology, the Open Shortest Path First (OSPF) routing protocol, in this framework, we identify the control loops intrinsic to it, and we describe the way these can be incorporated into higher level control loops. Finally, we demonstrate this design process through two illustrative case studies, namely, adding risk-awareness and autonomic routing resilience to the OSPF routing protocol.

INTRODUCTION

To our days, networked systems, like business intranets, Web systems, cloud computing facilities, or the Internet itself, have reached a point where they are no longer just playing grounds for hackers, early adopters, network researchers, and other enthusiasts, but fundamental and omnipresent information infrastructures, indispensable for carrying on our everyday life. However, recently this ever-growing information infrastructure has become quite a challenge to operate efficiently and cost-effectively, while also ensuring that the services delivered meet the quality requirements of the users.

Some believe that it is the growing complexity, stemming from increasing host heterogeneity, mobility and diversity, that causes the recent boost in network management expenditures experimented by operators. Others believe that it is the sheer size of contemporary networks, the need for frequent system deployments, and hardware and software instabilities, that seem today to overwhelm network management staffs and skyrocket operational spending. And still others believe that the real root of the increasing burden is the changing landscape of killer applications and shifting user demands, from email and Web to peer-to-peer and real-time multimedia, all presenting unpredictable, wildly varying workload and unique quality of service requirements to the network. Whoever turns out

to be right, one thing is certainly true: together, these issues make it really difficult for human operators, however skilled, to install, deploy, maintain and troubleshoot, that is, to overlook, the essential network infrastructure.

Instead of wasting expensive human resources to deal with everyday network management jobs, many of which can easily be automated, networks themselves should be better put in charge of managing themselves. A Self-managing Network, or Autonomic Network, should be engineered in such a way that traditional network management functions, and the basic network functions they act upon, like routing, forwarding, monitoring, supervision, fault-detection and fault-removal, etc, are made to autonomously respond to system failures, security threats, sudden traffic fluctuations, etc., affecting the reliable and effective operation of the network. These reactive feedback processes then would enable the network to co-operatively achieve and maintain some well-defined network goals, set by the operator. As such, even the traditional network management functions become incorporated into the overall network architecture and diffused into the very fabric of the network. This is in sharp contrast to the conventional network management school of thought, where a distinct management plane is engineered separately from the other functional planes of the network.

The term "autonomic" is taken from biology. After all, nature has already evolved mechanisms to cope with the complexity, scale, heterogeneity, dynamism and unpredictability, of large, interconnected systems. Autonomic networking is, consequently, roughly modeled after the human autonomous nervous system, which overlooks basic bodily functions, like the human respiratory system, blood pressure, body temperature, etc., without any conscious effort whatsoever. The key goal of autonomic networking is to achieve that same level of autonomicity, responsiveness and stability, using highly decentralized and heterogeneous network architectures that self-configure, self-optimize, self-heal and self-protect without any particular human intervention.

There are basically two approaches to reach this goal, a revolutionary and an evolutionary.

The revolutionary approach is based on the assumption that a fundamental redesign is inevitable to achieve the required level of self-management at all the different levels of node and network functionality. New concepts, functional planes and entities, and their associated architectural design principles and abstractions are thus required and, so the argument follows, a clean slate design process must be initiated (Greenberg et al, 2005, Chaparadza, 2008). The evolutionary approach, on the other hand, attempts to take into account the colossal inertia behind legacy network technologies, manifested in the enormous installed base, the vast amount of operational experience and monetary and mental investment. Thus, instead of substituting all these legacy equipment and technology with piecemeal-designed, autonomic-aware components in one turn, the evolutionary approach seeks ways to draw an incremental path towards future's evolved autonomic networks. This promises with smoother upgrades with no flagship day at all, less operational and capital expenditures, and overall a much more pleasant route towards future, self-managing systems.

Exactly how such a promotion of a legacy network protocol, devised long ago with absolutely no regard to autonomicity, to a self-managing technology should happen, and the vastness and complexity of difficulties this raises, can be spectacularly demonstrated on the case of the Open Shortest Path First (OSPF) routing protocol (Moy, 1998).

OSPF is perhaps the most successful routing protocol for the IP suite. It is a link-state routing protocol, with two-level routing hierarchy, support for basically any type of medium IP supports, an integrated neighbor discovery and keep alive protocol, reliable link state flooding, fast shortest path routing algorithm, support for multipath routing, etc. Accordingly, the OSPF protocol rapidly gained ground after its inception, and it has been enjoying unparalleled popularity in the networking community to our days. Only in special environments, like extremely large ISP backbones or heterogeneous, multiprotocol networks, other routing protocols are preferred, like the Intermediate-System-to-Intermediate-System (IS-IS) routing protocol (Oran, 1990).

A key enabler in the success of the OSPF routing protocol is the inherent capability for self-management built into it from the bottom up. Self-management, in the case of OSPF, means that the routers, participating in the distributed process of IP routing, perform various management tasks autonomously, independently of any higher level control function or manual intervention. A quintessential self-management operation built into OSPF is self-adaptation to the network topology at hand: routers running OSPF autonomously discover network topology, disseminate topology information and compute shortest paths to produce consistent routing tables, and this self-adaptation mechanism is completely independent of external control or human supervision of any kind. There are several other self-management functionality hard-wired into OSPF, like autonomous detection of neighbors (auto-discovery), autonomous advertisement of capabilities (self-advertisement), adaptation to failures and outages (self-healing), etc. This is so much so that we could as well view

OSPF as a truly autonomous, distributed network protocol entity itself: never again was a protocol able to take off and perform the complex task of routing table maintenance with so little manual supervision. In reality, once network interfaces are properly brought up and supplied with unique IP addresses, and OSPF is made aware of the interfaces it should use, the protocol is up and running, with full support for basic network routing. Only for complex operations, like link weight adjustment, multiple administrative areas, or interfacing with inter-domain routing protocols, does OSPF need special configuration and manual intervention on the part of the network operator.

One could argue, however, that in fact the autonomous capabilities built into OSPF are a bit over the point, as sometimes these self-management functions may work against, instead of cooperating with, the network operator. This is because for a network operator to achieve her network-level performance objectives, she needs to be in full control of the network. However, once OSPF with its intrinsic self-management functionality comes into the picture, the management actions taken on the part of the network operator and the self-management actions carried out by OSPF might easily end up interfering with each other. For instance, the policy of OSPF to provision the forwarding paths exclusively over shortest paths might differ from the policy seen by the operator as optimal. Thus, network operators have for a long time been working around OSPF's shortest path routing by tweaking the link weights for obtaining the desired routing pattern (Fortz and Thorup, 2000).

Clearly, fulfilling network-level objectives is much easier with direct control over the configuration of the data plane. Therefore, the decision logic should not be hard-wired into protocols like OSPF, but rather it should be re-factored into an external, pluggable control logic, which should be fed by monitoring information from the network and whose output should then be communicated back to the routers. This modularization of net-work fabric and control intelligence is exactly the most important promise of autonomic networking. However, in order to be able to incorporate a legacy network function, like OSPF, into an autonomic network framework, one must be very well aware of the inherent self-management functionality built into it. Without first discovering how OSPF performs autonomous adaptation to external and internal stimuli by itself, anyone willing to deploy autonomic networking functionality on top of OSPF might easily find himself needlessly re-implementing autonomic functionality already present in OSPF, or blindly interfering with OSPF's intrinsic control loops.

This suggests that the evolutionary approach to autonomic networking hides quite some traps. The most important goal of the present survey is, therefore, to give a comprehensive guide into the hand of practitioners and theorists on how to build autonomic networks out of legacy network technology. We identify the most compelling motivations for doing so and the benefits one could achieve, we reveal the most important design principles and best practices, and we describe the pitfalls that might be encountered during this process.

Our main tool is an all-encompassing framework for autonomic networking, able to incorporate legacy, well-tested network technologies as well as new, inherently autonomic-aware network functionality, and integrate them into a single self-managing entity. For this purpose, we adopt the Generic Autonomic Network Architecture (GANA), proposed recently by the EFIPSANS project, as it delivers the required level of genericity and abstraction (Chaparadza, 2007). GANA is, thusly, the main topic of interest in the first part of this survey.

We chose OSPF in our guideline as the basis onto which we construct autonomic functions, due to its large installed base and relatively rich internal self-management capability. The second part of this survey is, therefore, devoted to take a look at OSPF from a novel point of view: we reinterpret

OSPF in an autonomic networking context. We identify the control loops implemented by the OSPF protocol engine, and we discuss the most important control loop, the self-adaptation control loop, in huge detail. We also discover the state of the art in various extensions and improvements to OSPF's intrinsic self-adaptation mechanism and we discuss how OSPF could be exploited for implementing self-adaptive routing, what decision logics and control mechanisms would be necessary, and we delve into some implementation details.

No guidelines are complete without thorough and illustrative case studies, and we immediately give two of them. Our first case study addresses a fundamental deficiency of contemporary OSPF-based networks and network management systems, namely that unreliable and frequently failing components, like flapping physical interfaces or router processor ventilation fans, can harm the operation of an entire site and easily deteriorate the end user experience, affecting the profitability of a network in a very serious way. We present a risk-aware routing technique that has the ability to take into account and address the dynamicity of the risks endangering networks, and to practice real-time risk-assessment inside a node and in a network as a whole. This lets the network to proactively employ strategies to avoid failures, damages, outages and service unavailability when the probability of failure changes. Our second case study is concerned with improving the convergence time of OSPF, should a failure occur despite of the efforts of the risk-mitigation module. Currently, OSPF applies a self-adaptation method that is based on reactive, global response to failures. The IP Fast ReRoute technique, we introduce lastly in this survey, promises with reducing the re-convergence time to mere milliseconds, thanks to the enriched self-adaptation control loop and the advanced fast, local, proactive resilience algorithm. For both case studies we detail the required autonomic behaviors, we present a completely worked-out GANA-compliant autonomic infrastructure real-

izing those behaviors and we summarize some implementation experiences. Finally, we sketch some possible directions of future research and we draw the conclusions.

BACKGROUND

The last years have seen strong operator interests moving fast towards all-IP converged Next Generation Networks (NGN). This trend is on the rise. With the advent of Voice-Over-IP, IMS (IP Multimedia Subsystem), programmable networking, Universal Mobile Telecommunications System (UMTS) and its vision for IP-based UMTS access and core networks, and many other developments, IP has ever been receiving more and more serious attention. On the other hand, IP-based networks and services are becoming more and more complex to manage (Strassner et al, 2006, Chaparadza, 2007).

Autonomic networking is targeting at complexity issues related to network management. In short, autonomic systems engineering is about designing systems that exhibit so-called self-managing properties in order to make the systems themselves tackle those management complexities that are otherwise difficult or daunting to be handled by the network operations personnel. Other areas where autonomic networks excel at are self-adaptability, and context or situation driven behavior in systems, services and applications.

Self-managing systems are usually designed around the concept of a control loop, which consists of an autonomic manager or decision-making entity governing the behavior of the underlying physical resource according to pre-defined policies. Information flows upwards from the managed resource towards the decision-making entity, which, after analyzing the monitoring data, plans and feeds back appropriate response to the managed entity, in a way as to realize some self-management function. The concept of control loops is so fundamental in autonomics that almost any sorts of autonomic behavior, presenting itself anywhere in a self-managing system, implies the presence of a control loop somewhere in the system, either in an explicit, well-observable form or in a distributed, diffused fashion.

The concept of autonomics originates from the architectural blueprint for autonomic computing of IBM (IBM, 2003). This initiative was aimed at the efficient, resilient and responsive operation of enterprise information technology infrastructures. Later, this concept evolved to cover distributed information services, and finally the entire diverse area of computer networks (Raymer et al, 2008).

The research area of autonomic networking is becoming widely investigated across the industry and academia sectors. This trend is spectacularly demonstrated by the recent proliferation of related research projects. The EC FP6 ANA Project (ANA, 2006) is concerned with an all-encompassing autonomic network architecture, facilitating for dynamically adapting the network according to the actual economical and social needs (Bouabene et al, 2010). The EC FP6 Haggle Project (Haggle, 2006) also defines new autonomic network architecture, but specifically concentrates on opportunistic communications (Scott et al, 2006). The EC FP7 Autonomic Internet Project (AutoI, 2008) applies the principles of autonomicity to define a new, service-aware, self-managing Internet (Bassi et al, 2007). As part of its activity, the EC FP7 4WARD Project (4WARD, 2008) also aims at autonomicity: the project deals with embedding inherent management capabilities into network devices, achieving self-management and self-organization through the autonomous interaction of connected devices (Pentikousis et al, 2009). There are numerous other activities concerned with autonomic networking is some forms (Raymer et al, 2008), and consequently up to our days many different autonomic network architectures and reference models have come to existence, (see, e.g., Tianfield, 2003, Suzuki et al, 2005, Strassner et al, 2006, Balasubramaniam et al, 2006, Davy et al, 2006, Cheng et al, 2006, Siekkinen et al, 2007, Tizghadam et al, 2008, Derbela et al, 2009).

The ideas these autonomic network architectures are built on vary on a wide spectrum, from the traditional autonomic-manager-based, through agent-based and biologically inspired, all the way to control theoretical approaches. One theme, however, is recurring across the majority of these frameworks: they are looking at the problem of designing and implementing autonomic behaviors as separate add-on functions, built from inherently autonomic-ready components. In other words, most of the architectures available in the literature represent clean-slate, revolutionary approaches to autonomic networking.

A fundamentally different way to tackle the problem was chosen by the EC FP7 EFIPSANS Project (EFIPSANS, 2007). Instead of a clean slate approach, the project aims at extending existing, off-the-shelf network protocols, above all, IPv6, for the purposes of designing and building autonomic networks and services. As part of this activity, a new reference model for autonomic networks, the so called Generic Autonomic Network Architecture (GANA), has been defined (Chaparadza, 2007). GANA is, principally, evolvable, meaning that it is much better suited to serve as a basis for an incremental upgrade of legacy network technologies than its alternatives (Chaparadza et al, 2009).

There have been some sporadic attempts in the literature at realizing autonomic routing functions on top of OSPF (Rétvári et al, 2009). Most of these efforts concentrate on the self-optimization aspect of autonomic networking, in particular, on efficient and robust OSPF traffic engineering (Antic et al, 2010, Tizghadam et al, 2010). Apart from these, very little knowledge is available on how to build autonomic systems around legacy technology. One notable exception is (Mortier and Kiciman, 2006), which gives valuable pragmatic considerations for the designer of self-managing systems, learnt from operational experiences with legacy networking technology, like OSPF and

TCP. It is the belief of the authors that the practical guidelines given in this survey will complete those considerations with important, real-world insight on how to design truly autonomic systems.

For a broader look on self-managing networks, comprehensive surveys on autonomic networking and other, related aspects, the reader is referred to the Additional Reading section at the end of this survey.

The Generic Autonomic Network Architecture

The success of telecommunications, computer networking, and the Internet, has been based on the fact that reference models, such as the Open System Interconnection Reference (OSI) and TCP/IP models, were established, which guarantee a common understating of the underlying concepts, the basic modules constituting the network stack, and the interactions between them. This allowed the implementation of interoperable systems, and hence the flourishing of cheap, multi-vendor network infrastructures. Unfortunately, neither of the well-established architectural models was designed with self-management in mind, since autonomic computing and networking are relatively fresh paradigm shifts in systems and network management. Therefore, new architectural reference models are required. Recently, such an architectural reference model for autonomic networking and self-management, dubbed the Generic Autonomic Network Architecture (GANA), has emerged from the EC-funded EFIPSANS project (EFIPSANS, 2007, Chaparadza, 2007).

GANA, like most existing autonomic network architectures, is centered around the concept of control loop structures operating within network devices and the network as a whole, in order to realize advanced and enriched self-manageability. Two crucial concepts in GANA are the autonomic decision element (DE), and its assigned managed entities (MEs). A decision element is the central component in the control loop, which implements the decision logic driving the control loop over the management interfaces of the MEs. Therefore, in GANA self-management functionalities are always implemented by, and associated with, DEs. Consequently, the act of designing an autonomic behavior in GANA boils down to assigning managed entities to decision elements, implementing the management interfaces, and engineering suitable control intelligence in the DE.

Figure 1 shows the generic model of an autonomic networked system and its associated control loop. This model was derived from the IBM Monitoring-Analysis-Planning-Execution (MAPE) model (Bell, 2004), specifically for addressing the autonomic networking domain. The model adopts the concept of a decision element as the autonomic element, similar to the role of an Autonomic Manager in the IBM MAPE model. It also adopts the concept of a managed entity to mean a managed resource, or an automated task in general, instead of a Managed Element, which is only associated with a Network Element (NE). In contrast, in GANA MEs are not only associated with a physical network resource, but they also include protocol modules or even a complete autonomic functionality the DE acts upon.

Figure 1 illustrates the organization of a control loop in GANA. In the control loop, state information flows upwards, from the managed resource or the managed automated task, towards the decision element that manifests the control intelligence in the loop. The decision element musters data from its information suppliers, namely, from managed entities, monitoring components and other knowledge repositories, analyzes it and assembles it into an abstract view and, based on the network management goals and policies it received from its upper layer, triggers and executes some appropriate behavior on its associated managed entity.

The figure suggests an important property of GANA, which is in sharp contrast to the IBM MAPE model, namely the possible distributed nature of the information suppliers that feed a DE

Figure 1. A generic model of abstract autonomic networked system

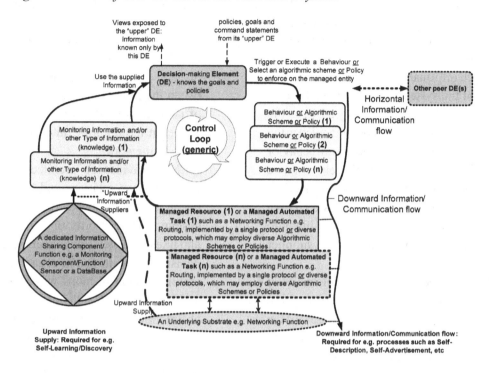

with information that can be used to autonomically manage the associated MEs. This makes it possible to more liberally associate the decision-making-logics with managed resources and organize control loops, and thusly distribute knowledge and functionality to a larger extent. On the other hand, the flexibility in the way decision elements and managed entities can be interconnected requires standardized, interoperable information sharing interfaces between them, in order to ensure the undisrupted flow of information. Hence, one of the key aims of the EFIPSANS project is to provide specifications for the autonomic components in the architecture and to standardize the communication interfaces between them.

The figure also illustrates the fact that the actions taken by the DE do not all necessarily involve triggering some behavior or enforcing a policy on the MEs, that is, changing the behavior thereof. Instead, some of the actions executed by the DE may involve communication between the DE and other entities in the node or network architecture,

e.g., other DEs in the system. This is indicated by the extended span of the arrow "Downward Information or Communication flow" and the "Horizontal Information/Communication flow" to other DEs, as well as the fact that a DE also exposes information to its upper DE and receives information, in the form of policies, goals and other command statements, from its upper DE. For example, the DE may need to self-describe and self-advertise to other DEs in order to be discovered or to discover other DEs. This suggests (as shall be later discussed in more detail) that control loops in GANA can be organized into hierarchical, compound control loop structures, in which higher-level DEs execute management actions on lower-level DEs. This also means that a managed entity may be of a physical nature, or may have the nature of an automated task in an abstract sense, represented by an ME or a DE.

In GANA, an autonomic behavior is defined as an action of the DE in an attempt to regulate the behavior of the MEs associated with it. The autonomic behavior is either spontaneously started by the DE, or it can be triggered by the receipt of information from the information suppliers of the DE, i.e., its associated MEs or sibling, peer, or upper DEs. Such information can be events relevant to the state of the system, security threats, etc. A behavior triggered spontaneously by a DE, on the other hand, is simply a spontaneous transition in the finite state machine describing the overall behavior of the DE. Examples of autonomic behaviors are self-description, self-advertisement, self-healing, and self-configuration, all triggered by a DE. An autonomic behavior, therefore, always binds to a DE and possibly to other information supplier components of the control loop.

Besides the specification of the elements of the autonomic architecture and the management interfaces between them, the other key goal of the EFIPSANS project is the produce standardizable specifications for autonomic behaviors, governing the way various components interact in order to move the system towards the desired management goal. The detailed model of the GANA decision element and managed entity, the management interfaces, and their fundamental operations, are given in (Chaparadza et al, 2008).

GANA is a holistic reference model for autonomic networking and self-management, lending itself readily to both clean-slate design approaches as well as incremental, evolutionary architectural designs and refinements. Exactly this friendliness towards the evolutionary upgrade path is why we chose GANA as the basic reference model in this survey. Besides, the genericity of GANA also facilitates for the evolution of the framework based on the experiences gained from concrete implementations. In this context, "generic" means that in GANA the model and specification of the building blocks and interfaces leave out the implementation-oriented details.

As a summary, GANA is designed to fulfill the following key requirements:

- GANA serves as reference model, which describes the basic concepts of autonomic networks, the types and structure of functional entities (DEs and MEs) it consists of, and the management interfaces between them. This is achieved as the result of consolidating different understandings, and even terminology, into one single generic framework.

- GANA provides an architectural model, describing the relations and hierarchy between the components of an autonomic system. In other words, the model captures and fixes the levels of abstractions at which decision elements can be organized into hierarchical control-loops within a network architecture. GANA defines four levels of abstractions, described later in this survey (Chaparadza et al, 2009).

- GANA substantiates the specification, and even the standardization, of autonomic behaviors (self-* features) the system needs to exhibit in order to attain the required level of self-management.

- GANA serves as a commonly shared reference model, from which further architectural refinements for either clean-slate-based or evolutionary ways of realizing autonomics can be pursued. The aspect of being "commonly shared" also addresses the fact that the concepts of the reference model are agnostic to any specific technology or implementation detail.

- GANA incorporates design-for-evolvability principles, which allow the DEs to be refined as new requirements for autonomicity emerge and new implementation experiences are gathered. For instance, it may be necessary to improve the cognitive and learning properties of the DEs, or to distinguish and fix those interfaces of DEs that must remain constant during time (i.e. fundamentally mandatory interfaces).

In (Chaparadza et al, 2009), the authors present further rationales behind the development of GANA as a standardizable architectural reference model for autonomic network engineering. Furthermore, in (Chaparadza, 2008, Chaparadza et al, 2008, Chaparadza et al, 2009) GANA is contrasted against today's best known approaches to autonomic networking, such as those presented in (ANA, 2006, Bell, 2004, Bullot et al, 2008, Clark et al, 2003, Strassner et al, 2006).

However useful GANA is as a reference model, several questions still remain difficult to address within the scope of it, and are left open to be decided by the human designer. It is of question, for instance, how to ensure that the decision-making processes for autonomic behaviors are conflict-free and stable. In addition, it is a challenge to design appropriate human-machine interfaces and define the perspectives and views offered to end-users and operators of self-managing networks. Such an interface would be used, for instance, to allow humans to define network-level objectives, governing the overall behavior of the network. And perhaps the most important question is also left open: to determine the design principles that enable intrinsic-management within the devices, and within the network as a whole. GANA can not give any particular help here, apart from providing a modularized reference model and fixing down the mental model for the designer. From there, the detailed definition of the particular autonomic behaviors, and the algorithms realizing them, will for a long time remain a work of art rather than a systematic, automatable engineering process. The case studies provided later in this survey are aimed at easing this untrivial and complex design challenge.

The Building Blocks of GANA and Their Relations

The Generic Autonomic Network Architecture introduces autonomic manager components, known as decision elements, for different abstraction levels of functionality. These autonomic manager components are designed following the principles of hierarchical, peering, and sibling relationships among each other within a node or network. Moreover, these components are capable of performing autonomic control of their associated managed entities, as well as co-operating with each other in driving the self-managing features of the network. By defining appropriate abstractions for self-management functionality, the inherent complexity of the design of autonomic networks can be broken down into designing piecemeal self-contained modules and specifying the interactions between them. This is greatly eased by the hierarchical levels of abstraction in GANA, as described below.

In GANA, the four hierarchical levels are assigned, at which DEs, MEs, control loops and their associated dynamic adaptive behaviors can be placed. The levels of abstractions are as follows:

- **Protocol-level:** the lowest level of self-management, usually associated with the network protocol itself (whether monolithic or modular). There is growing opinion, however, that future protocols need to be simpler, with no decision logic embedded that may interact in an undesired way with decision logic of other protocols. This means that there is a need to rather implement decision logic at a level higher, outside the individual protocols' level.

- **Abstracted function-level:** the level directly above the protocol-level, which abstracts some protocols and mechanisms associated with a particular compound network function, like routing, forwarding, mobility management, etc.

- **Node-level:** the level of the device's overall functionality and behavior, i.e., a node or system as a whole.

- **Network-level:** the level of the network's overall functionality and behavior (the highest level).

Figure 2 illustrates that, at the node-level of self-management properties, the lower level decision elements, operating at the level of abstracted networking functions, become the managed entities of the main DE of the node. This implies that the node's main DE has access to the information exposed by the lower level DEs, and uses its overall knowledge to influence the lower level DEs to take certain desired decisions, which may in turn further influence desired behaviors on their associated MEs, down to the lowest level of individual protocol behavior. Apart from these hierarchical master-slave relationships, a "sibling" relationship between DEs is also permitted. A sibling relation simply means that the entities are created or managed by the same upper level DE. This also means that the entities having a sibling relation can still form other types of peer relationships within the autonomic node or with other entities hosted by other nodes in the network, according to the protocol defined for their needs to communicate with other DEs.

To understand the concept of the abstract control loop hierarchies in GANA, consider the case of routing. At the lowest level, the protocol level, we find the routing protocols themselves.

These may be autonomic-compliant, modern routing protocols, or legacy routing technology like OSPF, IS-IS or the Border Gateway Protocol (BGP). All the self-management functionality these protocols embody, manifested by the control intelligence, control loops, and the associated managed resources existing in the protocol machinery, are represented in the model as protocol-level DEs, protocol-intrinsic control loops, and protocol-level MEs (managed functions of the protocol), respectively. Note that these abstract components do not necessarily exist in the actual protocol engine in a clear, well-defined set of modules and interactions. Instead, they can be just virtual representations of the self-management functionality built into the protocol's overall functionality, which still needs to expose a management interface to its associated upper DE. This abstraction makes it possible to easily incorporate existing network protocols into the GANA model, opening the way to build complete autonomic management and control structures onto them. This abstraction will be the tool we shall use in the next section to analyze the self-management capability of OSPF in large detail.

Figure 2. Hierarchical, peering, sibling relationships and interfaces of DEs in GANA

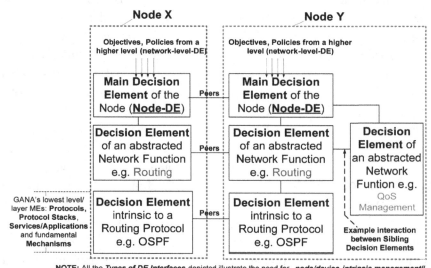

NOTE: All the *Types of DE Interfaces* depicted illustrate the need for „*node/device-intrinsic management*" and „*network-intrinsic management or in-network management*" in Self-Managing Future Networks

Staying at the example of routing, the second level, the abstracted function level, contains all the autonomic elements needed to realize the complex task of routing within a network device. For instance, the device might run several routing protocols side by side, e.g., an intra-domain protocol like OSPF in parallel with an inter-domain protocol like BGP, and the function-level decision element's task is to manage the individual protocols and orchestrate the interaction thereof (e.g., arbitrate route import and export between the protocols) abstracting away the specifics of the individual protocols. Above the function level there is the node-level DE, whose task is to coordinate the broad and diverse operations needed to operate a complex network device, such as a router.

The network level represents the highest level of autonomicity. There are various ways to engineer the control intelligence at this level. There may exist a logically centralized network-level decision element, hosted on special hardware whose resources are dedicated exclusively to network state data analysis and management operations. This DE would be meant to manage the whole network and should work in harmony with autonomous self-management at lower levels of the control loop hierarchy (i.e., the node level, abstracted function level and protocol level). An alternative way for organizing network-level decision making logics, accommodated by GANA, would be to adopt the distributed model proposed in the 4D network architecture (Greenberg et al, 2005). In this architecture, network management lives outside of network devices in an isolated "decision cloud", which is supposed to know the objectives, goals and policies to be enforced to the network. The lower-level DEs, the node-level DEs in this case, would export information to the decision cloud, which, in turn, would enforce control on the DEs at the node level, which may again have an effect of inductive decision changes on the lower-level DEs all the way down to protocol-level decisions. There are basically two ways to

realize this model. In the simplest case, decision making intelligence is distributed between several DEs in the decision cloud. Or, possibly, the network-level DEs might be completely absent, in which case the main decision elements of nodes would work cooperatively to self-organize into a virtual network level DE and manage the network as a result of their emergent behavior. This latter implementation strategy, however, might be severely restricted in capability, due to resource limitations of the nodes and the problem of longer convergence time with some distributed decision-making algorithms.

A key design principle incorporated into the GANA architectural hierarchy of DEs is that of coordinated access-control to the lowest level of managed entities. This is realized through synchronization among DEs and arbitration mechanisms at the intermediate levels in the hierarchy down to the decision elements at the function level. The DEs at the function level then directly access the lowest level managed entities, consisting of the network protocols and mechanisms themselves.

There are some important guidelines one must keep in mind when designing multi-level control loop hierarchies in order to avoid adverse interference, oscillation, and other unwanted interaction between the control loops at different levels (Mortier and Kiciman, 2006). These guidelines are not specific to autonomic networking, but general guidelines for designing stable control systems stemming from the field of control theory:

- Establish well-defined valid operating regions of particular control loops;
- Decouple control systems by ensuring that they control different independent outputs based on independent inputs;
- If decoupling is not possible, then tune the coupled control systems so that they impose control at very different timescales.

This latter option might help decouple systems that are otherwise inherently entangled. This design principle, when applied to the GANA architecture, implies that going up in the GANA hierarchy the control loops get slower, while we find the fastest control loops at the lowest level of the hierarchy. Lower-level DEs expose aggregated information, based on which upper-level DEs produce management actions of global, node- and network-wide scope. These are then propagated down in the DE hierarchy, decomposed into local-scope actions at every level down to the function-level DEs, which then arbitrate and enforce the actions to the lowest-level managed entities.

Another useful design aid in building multi-level control loop hierarchies is Formal Description Techniques (FDTs). A model-driven approach can help addressing potential stability problems of control-loops at design time. Additionally, modeling and validation of autonomic behaviors of DEs using FTDs, such as the ITU-T SDL language, enables the design, model-checking and verification

of DEs, and the validation, simulation and partial code-generation of autonomic behaviors of DEs.

Control loop hierarchies provide one possible way to look at the relations and organization of the components in an autonomic architecture. Another useful perspective is supplied by the division of the functionalities in the framework into distinct functional planes. Inspired by the 4D architecture (Greenberg et al, 2005), GANA defines four functional planes: the Decision Plane; the Discovery Plane; the Dissemination Plane and the Data Plane (Chaparadza, 2008, Chaparadza et al, 2008). Of particular interest in this survey is the GANA Decision Plane, defined as follows. The Decision Plane makes all decisions driving a node's local, or the system's network-wide, behavior, including reachability, load balancing, access control, security, and interface configuration. Replacing the traditional management plane, the decision plane operates in real time on a

Figure 3. The structure of a GANA node and instantiation case of a function level routing management DE for autonomic routing functionality

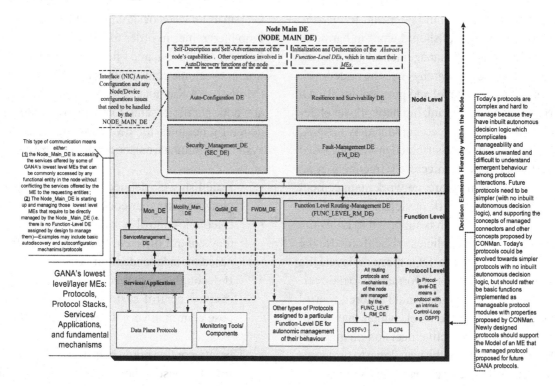

network-wide view of the topology, the traffic, events, context and context changes, network objectives, goals and policies, and the capabilities and resource limitations of the devices of a network in some administrative scope (Greenberg et al, 2005). Consequently, the Decision Plane in GANA consists of the autonomic elements, i.e., the decision elements.

Figure 3 illustrates the structure of a GANA node, its DEs and the service layer view in GANA. The Node-Main-DE consists of sub-DEs, whose management operations affect all the lower-level entities in some way. On the function level, the following DEs are required: Service Management DE, Monitoring DE, Mobility Management DE, QoS Management DE, Forwarding Management DE and the Routing Management DE (see a taxonomy and terminology for GANA DEs in Table 1). The interfaces between the DEs are omitted for the purposes of presenting a simplified picture.

Instantiation of Routing Management Decision Elements for Autonomic Routing

GANA is a generic framework, designed to abstract diverse aspects of self-management. For concrete, autonomic network functions, however, such as routing management, forwarding management or QoS management, a thorough specialization of the general framework is necessary, in the course of which we apply the basic abstractions of the reference model to the network function under consideration, we designate the DEs and MEs necessary to implement that function and we delineate their relations, possibly organized into a hierarchical control loop structure. Below, we show the instantiation of GANA routing management DEs to the case of autonomic, self-adaptive routing (see Figure 4).

Easily, at the lowest level, the protocol level, we find the routing protocols and mechanisms themselves with their intrinsic control loops. These can be legacy routing protocols, like OSPF, IS-IS

Table 1. A taxomomy and terminology for decision elements in the GANA reference model

Short name	Long name	Description
FUNC_LEVEL_RM_DE	Function-level Routing Management Decision Element	The autonomic manager in the fast, node-local control loop coordinating all the routing functions of the node
NET_LEVEL_RM_DE	Network-level Routing Management Decision Element	The controller in the slower, network-wide control loop, managing the routing functionality on a broader scope than its node-local counterpart
NODE_MAIN_DE	Node-level Main Decision Element	The main decision element in a device, overlooking al the self-management behavior implemented within the device.
NODE_LEVEL_FM_DE	Node-level Fault-Management Decision-Element	Manages the node's self-healing function through the automation of fault-management (fault-detection, fault-isolation, and fault-removal), as part of the NODE_MAIN_DE
NET_LEVEL_FM_DE	Network-level Fault-Management Decision Element	Implements the network's global self-healing function using network-wide state information.
NODE_LEVEL_RS_DE	Node-level Resilience & Survivability Decision Element	Manages a device's resilience mechanisms in order to *(i)* proactively prevent failures through prediction of the possible failure cases, and *(ii)* reactively adapt to faults should prediction be unsuccessful
NET_LEVEL_RS_DE	Network-level Resilience & Survivability Decision-Element	Oversees the network's resilience mechanisms using global network fitness information and risk assessment information from network devices. Works in close collaboration with the NET_LEVEL_FM_DE.

Figure 4. Autonomicity as a feature in routing functionality in an IPv6 based network

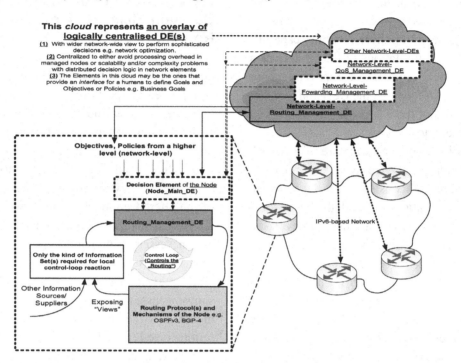

or BGP, integrated into the self-managing network. Or, in a clean slate approach, the protocol level control loops might be completely absent, in which case higher level control loops resolve all the routing tasks of the device. At these higher levels, in general, two types of control loops are required for managing and controlling the routing behavior. The first type is a node-local control loop that consists of a Function-level Routing Management Decision Element (FUNC_LEVEL_RM_DE) embedded inside an autonomic router. This DE is meant to process only that kind of information that is required to enable the node to react autonomically, by adjusting the behavior of the individual routing mechanisms required to be running on the node. The FUNC_LEVEL_RM_DE reacts to information exposed by its managed entities, i.e., the underlying routing protocols. In a nutshell, the function-level routing management DE implements self-configuration and dynamic adaptation features specific to the routing functionality of the autonomic node.

Due to scalability, overhead and complexity issues that arise when attempting to make the routing management DE of a node to process huge amounts of information for the control loop, a second type of DEs, in particular, a logically centralized decision element outside the routing nodes may be required in order to relieve the burden. This logically centralized DE is called the Network-level Routing Management DE, or NET_LEVEL_RM_DE for short. In such a case, a network-wide slower control loop is deployed in addition to the faster node-local control loop, with both types of loops working together in managing the routing behavior via the interaction of their associated routing management DEs.

The node-local FUNC_LEVEL_RM_DE focuses on addressing those limited routing management issues for which the node needs to react fast. At the same time, it listens to control from the NET_LEVEL_RM_DE of the outer, slower control loop, which has wider network-views and dedicated computational power, and thus is able to compute routing specific policies and new parameter values to be used by individual routing protocols of the node. The NET_LEVEL_RM_DE disseminates the computed values and parameters to multiple node-scoped FUNC_LEVEL_RM_DEs of the network-domain, which then directly influence the behavior of the targeted MEs, that is, the routing protocols within a routing device. The interaction between the two types of routing management DEs is achieved through the NODE_MAIN_DE of a node, which verifies those interactions against the overall security policies of the device. In turn, the node-scoped routing management DE relays information describing the actual state of the device, or the events and incidents affecting its behavior, to the network-level routing management DE for further reasoning.

Observe that the interaction of the network-level and the function-level routing management DEs in fact realizes a hierarchical control loop structure. This example therefore demonstrates the modeling power of GANA in its full glory. Besides, it exemplifies an important design principle: the higher we go up the control loop hierarchy, the broader the global knowledge a DE is required to have to be able to take proper decisions in managing its associated MEs. These MEs, however, can really be DEs at a lower level of the control loop hierarchy, which may in turn inductively trigger specialized actions, resulting from decomposing the upper level decision action of broader sense to locally valid management actions, on lower level MEs, down to the level of protocols.

There are a number of ways to realize the interaction between GANA DEs and protocol MEs such as OSPF. The standard NETCONF protocol can be used in the GANA framework in such a way that the NODE-MAIN-DE of a node can use the NETCONF Agent to interact with NETWORK-LEVEL-DEs, which would need to use the NETCONF Manager to communicate configuration data to individual nodes. The NETWORK-LEVEL-DEs can convey a configuration or policy specification file to the NETCONF

Manager for dissemination to nodes. On the target node, the NODE-MAIN-DE needs to receive the configuration file via the NETCONF Agent and apply the configuration operations required. In the NETCONF batch mode a list of required operation calls can be stored in a text file that can be read by NETCONF manager and executed automatically. Any GANA DE that requires exchanging some XML structured data can use this feature. After performing self-configuration procedures required for protocols, DEs would need the possibility to autonomically adapt the behavior of the managed protocols, like OSPF. This should be done via the manipulation of parameters defined for the management of the protocol (either via an SNMP MIB or CLI), and this self-adaptation behavior carried out by the DEs should be performed using SNMP operations, provided that the set of parameters being manipulated at a time is not so big to warrant the use of NETCONF instead.

OSPF as Building Block in Self-Adaptive Autonomic Networks

So far, we have presented the GANA framework and we have showed how GANA can be specialized to specific network functions, like routing management. We have also seen that at the lowest level of the GANA control loop hierarchy, the protocol level, we find the control loops intrinsically embedded into the network protocols themselves. In this section, we show particular cases of such protocol-intrinsic control loops, namely, the control loops driving the self-* behavior embedded into the OSPF protocol. This enumeration of the autonomic behavior inside OSPF will be crucial in the later developments in this survey, because it substantiates our view of OSPF as an entity, capable to self-management to some extent. Furthermore, it allows us to open up some of the intrinsic control loops of OSPF and incorporating them into broader control loops with decision making logics at higher levels of the GANA hierarchy, without the danger of re-implementing, or interfering with, OSPF's intrinsic self-management functions.

In what follows, we shall concentrate on Internet-Protocol-based networks, due to OSPF being mostly IP-centric. We shall use the IP reference model and terminology: for instance, network nodes will be called routers, an end-system's name will be network host, packet forwarding will sometimes be referred to as routing, etc. Naturally, most of the arguments made in the sequel are valid for other network technology as well, like Ethernet, Multi-Protocol Label Switching, etc. A basic familiarity with OSPF on the part of the reader is necessary to get a good understanding of this section. For the precise specification of the protocol, see (Moy, 1998).

Intrinsic Self-Management Functions in OSPF

Routing is the process of ensuring global reachability between routers and hosts. In the beginning, routing tables were provisioned manually. This practice led to daunting management complexity as networks grew, and it was quite prone to human errors. The very purpose of introducing routing protocols was to mitigate this management burden by automating the process of setting up routing tables. In some sense, autonomic networking can be seen as an extension of this idea to the extreme: make the systems themselves tackle all the management complexities, not just routing, that are otherwise difficult to handle manually. For this, the network needs to be able to self-provision and self-manage to some extent. Such self-* functionality involve, for instance, self-adaptation to changes in the operational conditions, self-healing to repair or circumvent failures, self-optimization for improving performance related aspects of networking, etc. Below, we show that many of these autonomic behaviors can readily be identified in the Open Shortest Path First (OSPF) routing protocol (Moy, 1998). The enumeration is given in roughly the same order as the corresponding

self-* function appears in the course of the real operation of the protocol

Auto-Discovery: routers running OSPF discover their immediate neighborhood by using the Hello protocol. Neighboring routers periodically exchange Hello packets, so that each router is aware of all the routers connected to any one of the links or LANs attached to its interfaces. This auto-discovery mechanism is pretty extensive, covering every aspect of routing except for one very important issue. Namely, the auto-discovery capabilities built into OSPF lack support for box-level discovery. This means that routers do not autonomously self-detect their interfaces, and manual configuration is needed to make a router aware of the interfaces it should involve in OSPF message passing (see more on this issue later).

Self-description: in OSPF, routers self-describe their capabilities in the Hello packets they generate. In particular, the Hello packet contains information regarding the highest version of OSPF the router's implementation supports, plus a bitfield to describe OSPF extensions the router understands. This makes it possible to eliminate the chance of misconfiguration arising from letting routers using divergent OSPF versions speak to each other. Additionally, self-description makes it possible to seamlessly deploy protocol extensions.

Self-advertisement: routers generate so called Link State Advertisements (LSAs) to advertise their forwarding services into the network. These LSAs convey information on the individual routers making up the topology, with their identity, attached interfaces, IP addresses, etc.; the links and LANs connecting the routers with their type (broadcast, Non-Broadcast-Multiple-Access, point-to-point); administrative link cost, etc. OSPF variants, like OSPF-TE, the Traffic Engineering extensions to OSPF (Katz et al, 2003) and OSPF-TE-GMPLS, the OSPF extensions in support of Generalized Multi-Protocol Label Switching (Kompella and Rekhter, 2005) add their respective type of link state information to LSAs, involving the link's transmission capacity, free capacity, protection type, the forwarding services offered by the router, the multiplexing/demultiplexing capability of interfaces, etc. It is by passing these LSAs around between routers using a reliable, acknowledged flooding protocol that OSPF synchronizes routing information across the domain. This mechanism basically maintains a distributed, versioned, massively parallel Link State Database (LSDB), shared and synchronized amongst routers, which ensures that, in steady state, each router holds exactly the same copy of the graph topology of the network and thusly consistent forwarding paths are selected.

Self-configuration and self-organization: self-configuration involves setting up and maintaining some configuration parameter by the protocol itself, that otherwise would be handled by the network operator. Self-organization is a method by which entities autonomously organize themselves into groups or hierarchies. A good example of self-configuration and self-organization in OSPF is the election of Designated Routers. In order to reduce the amount of protocol traffic on LANs that connect multiple routers, OSPF mandates that each router synchronizes with only a single neighbor, the Designated Router, instead of having to exchange signaling information with all the other neighbors. This Designated Router is also responsible for generating an LSA on behalf of the LAN. The actual Designated Router (and the Backup Designated Router, which is just what its name says, the backup of the Designated Router) is elected autonomously, by means of the Hello protocol, without the need to be configured manually by the network operator.

Self-healing: an operational network is constantly subjected to disturbances from the environment, most important amongst these is the intermittent and unavoidable failures of network devices and transmission media. To come over failures, OSPF implements a simple but efficient self-healing mechanism: once a router detects that a node or link went down (through not getting

Hello packets for a certain amount of time from a specific direction), it immediately advertises the changed topology information into the domain, leading to a global recalculation of routing tables with the failed node or link removed from the topology. Although this self-healing mechanism might be somewhat slow due to the need to deliver the LSA to the furthest part of the network to achieve correct global response, it is highly effective and is able to keep up reachability as long as the network remains connected, irrespective of the number and type of failures occurring.

Self-adaptation: the most important self-management functionality implemented by OPSF is undoubtedly self-adaptation to the topology at hand. This means that routes are not provisioned statically with regard to the underlying network topology, but instead OSPF is able to dynamically maintain correct, consistent and loop-free forwarding tables over an arbitrary topology. Self-adaptation is, therefore, the most important property of OSPF and the very purpose the protocol was designed in the first place. In the sequel, we shall discuss this self-adaptation control loop in more detail.

One could as well keep on listing the various autonomic behaviors built into OSPF further (e.g., self-protection, etc.), but we believe that the above examples were sufficient enough to demonstrate the richness of OSPF in terms of self-management. In fact, OSPF implements, either in its entirety or only partially, pretty much every possible autonomic behavior, with the notable exception of box-level auto-discovery and self-optimization. The lack of self-optimization means, for instance, that OSPF is not able to readjust forwarding paths in order to mitigate or eliminate congestions or load-balance traffic, that is, to optimize the performance of the network. In order to equip OSPF with self-optimization functionality, we shall need to incorporate it into an external control loop, as shall be discussed later on.

Self-Adaptation in OSPF

Self-adaptation to the underlying topology, to topology changes and to other stimuli effecting routing, is the main purpose of a routing protocol. Below, we interpret the main self-adaptation control loop implemented by OSPF in the context and terminology of autonomic networking.

The basic operation of the self-adaptation control loop of OSPF is as follows. When OSPF takes off, or when the underlying topology changes, that is, a link or node goes down or comes up again, the auto-discovery mechanism of OSPF (i.e., the Hello protocol), through observing the neighborhood of the router, initiates the self-advertisement functionality to flood the (changed) network state information throughout the network. Routers, upon the receipt of new LSAs, calculate new routing tables based on refreshed routing information,

which makes it possible to always self-adapt to the actual network topology.

In the context of autonomic networking, and GANA in particular, this self-adaptation mechanism is a typical example of an embedded, protocol-intrinsic control loop, with the OSPF protocol acting as a virtual distributed decision element that is scattered all over domain. In fact, just about every constituent of the Monitoring-Analysis-Planning-Execution model of autonomic control loops can be readily identified in the self-adaptation control loop of OSPF, as depicted in Figure 5:

- The Managed Entity is represented by the collective set of all routing tables in the network, which are then used to update the Forwarding Information Bases (FIBs). The routing tables are the entity on which the control loop's effector operates.

Figure 5. The self-adaptation control loop of OSPF in terms of the MAPE model

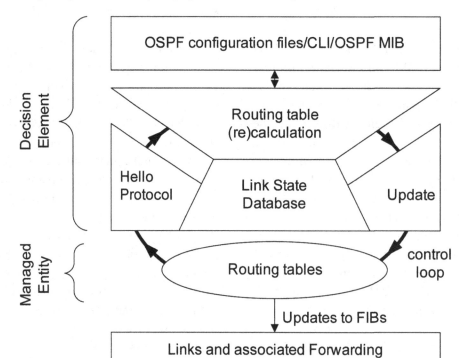

- Monitoring of the links and interfaces and their forwarding capability is implemented by the Hello protocol.
- The Analyze and Planning function is broadly mapped to the process of routing table (re)calculation.
- Execution corresponds to the process of updating the forwarding tables across the routers with the next-hops obtained during the last routing table (re)calculation.
- Knowledge is manifested in this self-adaptation control loop by the collective set of the LSDBs of the routers. Note that, however, OSPF pays special attention to always keep the LSDBs at each router consistent, synchronized and up-to-date, therefore the Knowledge component is in fact replicated throughout the network instead of being unified at a central knowledge base.
- Sensors and Effectors for higher level decision elements to monitor and control the self-adaptation of OSPF are represented by the management interfaces of OSPF, including, usually, a set of OSPF configuration files, a command line interface (CLI) plus versatile, standardized Management Information Bases (MIB).

Extensions to the Intrinsic Self-Adaptation Control Loop of OSPF

The self-adaptation mechanism built into OSPF is somewhat basic, although quite straight-to-the-point: it only involves tracking topology changes. However, it does not contain mechanisms, knowledge, services, algorithms or other protocol machinery to self-adapt other aspects of routing to the actual environment, or to adapt the self-adaptation control loop itself when changing conditions make it necessary. Below, we give a brief overview of the state-of-the-art as to how the research community proposes to extend the basic self-adaptation control loop of OSPF beyond its present capabilities. Note that the survey below

lists only those proposals that build the extensions right into OSPF itself, and do not involve those ones that organize OSPF into an external control loop with separate decision element somewhere in the GANA hierarchy (we discuss the latter option in the next section).

Self-adaptation to changing resource availability: it has for a long time been pointed out as one of the major shortcomings of OSPF-type link-state routing protocols that the self-adaptation mechanism they implement is somewhat static. This means that OSPF self-adapts only to the (changing) topology, but not to the changing operational conditions, the amount and type of actual ingress or egress traffic, QoS criteria, Service Level Agreements, or the actual amount of free resources available in the network. This makes OSPF routing invariant to the variations and fluctuations of daily user traffic, or its changing/evolving embedment into a vibrant sociocultural and economic environment. This often leads to suboptimal routing: traffic tends to concentrate along shortest paths while, at the same time, complete portions of the network remain greatly under-utilized. Various attempts have been made to address the problem of dynamic routing in the context of OSPF. The basic idea is to add further information to the link state, most importantly, the amount of provisionable resources at network elements, and select routes that avoid overloaded components. A good example is QoSPF, the Quality of Service extensions to OSPF (Apostolopoulos et al, 1999), or recent standardization efforts, like OSPF-TE (Katz et al, 2003) and OSPF-TE-GMPLS (Kompella and Rekhter, 2005). Another aspect of self-adaptation in OSPF is considering the reliability and risks of failure of network components along the forwarding path. Obviously, a path that consists of frequently failing routers or unreliable wireless links, however short in terms of administrative cost, is of no use to the end-user. Instead, the anticipated availability of the path should be taken into consideration when selecting forwarding paths, and this will be precisely the main motivation behind the design of the risk-aware routing technique we shall present as the first case study in this survey.

Self-adaptation and multipath routing: the basic mode of operation in OSPF is to always select the minimum cost path towards a destination, where path cost is understood in terms of some administrative cost, preset for each network link. Where ambiguity arises, that is, when there exist more than one shortest paths to a destination, one path is selected somewhat randomly. In the Equal-Cost-MultiPath (ECMP) mode, however, a router is allowed to use all the potential shortest paths to the destination, by splitting traffic roughly equally amongst the available next-hops. Unfortunately, however, OSPF-ECMP still does not qualify as a self-adaptive multipath routing protocol, because traffic is not balanced with respect to available resources along the paths, but instead it is split evenly. Additionally, the path-diversity of ECMP is somewhat insufficient, because in many topologies it is only a rare accident that multiple shortest paths become available to a destination. OSPF-OMP, the OSPF Optimized-MultiPath extensions (Villamizar, 1999) is aimed at overcoming these difficulties: it improves path diversity by not confining itself to shortest paths but instead utilizing all loop-free paths, and it makes self-adaptation sensitive to varying operational conditions by dynamically readjusting traffic shares at individual forwarding paths with respect to actual resource availability along that path.

Fast self-adaptation and self-healing: as mentioned earlier, the self-adaptation control loop in OSPF involves a tedious global resynchronization of Link State Databases plus additional recalculations of the routing tables. This scheme of "global, reactive response" makes the convergence of the control loop slow, which yields that the reaction to failures is a lengthy process in OSPF. Furthermore, the auto-discovery process, responsible for detecting the error in the first place, adds its own fair share of slugishness to the process (the smallest granularity of the Hello protocol timers is 1 sec,

basically pushing the convergence time into the order of seconds). To speed up the convergence process, a localized, proactive approach should be taken instead of a global, reactive one, and this is exactly the way the IP Fast ReRoute (IPFRR, Shand and Bryant, 2010) suite of standards are set to remedy the situation. In IPFRR, OSPF pre-computes detours with respect to each potentially failing component and stores the next-hops in an alternative forwarding table. By using an explicit, fast detection mechanism like Bidirectional Forwarding Detection (BFD, Katz and Ward, 2010), discovering a failure is possible within milliseconds of its occurrence. If an error is detected, OSPF switches to this alternative table and suppresses global response by withholding the fresh LSA in the hope that the failure is transient. Should the failure go away soon after, OSPF switches back to the original forwarding table and everything goes on as normal as if no failure happened. Only when a failure persists for a longer period of time, global re-convergence is initiated. IPFRR proved highly efficient in practice, bringing down failure recovery to the order of milliseconds (Enyedi et al, 2009). However, neither IPFRR comes without its own set of limitations and problems, the gravest of which seems to be the substantial additional management burden it presents to the network operator, the increased signaling traffic caused by failure detection mechanisms and the adverse transient phenomena that arises during global re-convergence due to LSDB-synchronization delays. The second case study presented later in this survey, therefore, will concentrate incorporating OSPF and IPFRR into a GANA-based autonomic, self-managing network architecture, to provide autonomic routing resilience with fast convergence time and minimal transients.

Self-adaptation with partial or outdated link-state information: a basic assumption lying in the heart of the design of OSPF is that the information in the Link State Database is always consistent and up-to-date. Otherwise, self-adaptation might suffer as certain destinations might become unreachable and transient or even persistent routing loops might emerge. The assumption of consistency and freshness, however, might not always hold. For instance, in order to limit the amount of signaling traffic exchanged between nodes in order to save valuable battery power in a fixed or slowly changing wireless network, it would be plausible to tweak the self-advertisement mechanism so that routers hold precise information only in a limited vicinity, and the further they look the more inaccurate the link state information. As a packet travels hop by hop in the network, it will always "see" locally accurate link state, leading to, hopefully, close to optimal shortest path forwarding. For pointers on how to change the intrinsic self-adaptation of OSPF, see FishEye State Routing (Pei et al, 2000) or XL Link State (Levchenko et al, 2008).

OSPF for Implementing Truly Self-Adaptive Routing

So far, we have seen that OSPF implements a solid number of self-* functions intrinsically, by means of control loops embedded deep into the protocol machinery. The most important of these, the self-adaptation control loop, is an efficient and robust control loop and, considering the numerous extensions to this control loop on their way to standardization and large-scale deployment, OSPF is expected to need only very little governance from higher layers to achieve its full potential. This is not to say that OSPF, on its own, qualifies as an autonomic, self-managing protocol entity, only that certain functionality it embeds can be interpreted, to some extent, within the context of autonomic networking frameworks, like GANA. To truly realize the vision of autonomic, self-managing routing, the intrinsic self-management functionality of OSPF is, unfortunately, insufficient. Therefore, further decision elements are needed, decoupled from OSPF and implemented at higher layers of the GANA control loop hierarchy, either because, due to implementation considerations, decision making would be very difficult to

engineer into OSPF proper, or the decision making process would make use of external information that is simply not available at the lowest level of the DE hierarchy OSPF resides at in the GANA architecture. Or, one might deliberately choose not to embed certain control loops into OSPF in order to better modularize the architecture, to separate managed and managing functionality from each other, to ease swapping or changing the decision making process, etc.

Below, we discuss some additional control loops that could further improve the efficiency and robustness of OSPF. The difference from the previous discussions will be that the control loops discussed in this section will rely on a separate decision element at higher layers of the DE hierarchy in GANA, instead of having decision making hard-wired into OSPF itself.

Auto-discovery and self-configuration: as mentioned earlier, auto-discovery in OSPF lacks box-level discovery. This means that there is no way for a router to learn autonomously the set of functional interfaces it has, and configure the OSPF protocol properly on those interfaces. Unless OSPF is explicitly told so, by means of manual configuration, intervention at the CLI or through central network management, an OSPF-speaking router will not use an interface, even if, by all measures, it legitimately could. The reasons for this are multi-faceted. First, whether to run or not run OSPF on a specific interface is a crucial configuration issue, dependent on high-level network engineering policies and it has important security implications as well. There are various configuration parameters (e.g., timers, link cost, authentication, link type, etc.) that quite commonly need manual tweaking too. Additionally, every interface must uniquely be associated with a specific OSPF area, retaining the consistency of the network via the Backbone Area, and this also must be handled through explicit configuration. Therefore, OSPF must be involved in an auto-discovery and self-configuration control loop: a router would send its identity, authentication tokens, and some router-specific data upstream, and would get back a routing profile with a complete set of configuration parameters to set, including the list of interfaces to initiate the OSPF protocol at, timer settings, authentication keys, link costs, etc.

Self-configuration: as discussed previously, the network operator can tweak the operation of OSPF with considerable detail and granularity, through configuration parameters. Monitoring, setting, and readjusting from time to time these configuration parameters might benefit the operation and the performance of the network. The main enabler for this is OSPF's timer mechanism, which allows the network operator to manipulate the way certain events are scheduled.

For instance, in networks with limited resources the signaling traffic generated by OSPF might put too much burden on the network infrastructure, leading to premature drainage of battery power, congestion along low-capacity links, etc. Thus, relying on monitoring data the Network-level Routing Management DE might instruct OSPF to slow down LSA propagation. The OSPF parameters to adjust to achieve this are *MinLSInterval*, *MinLSArrival* and *RxmtInterval*, see Appendix A and C in (Moy, 1998). (Note that the latter two parameters are protocol constants, or architectural constants, which means that they are not marked as user configurable in the OSPF standard, though, they could be easily made to be so in implementations.) The Hello protocol could be tweaked to generate smaller keep-alive traffic in slowly changing environments or between high-reliability interfaces where failures only rarely show up (OSPF parameter: *HelloInterval*, *RouterDeadInterval*). To save precious battery power at wireless nodes, OSPF routing table recalculations could also be throttled leading to smaller computational burden on the CPU (note that the OSPF standard does not provide an OSPF parameter to throttle SPF calculations, but implementations usually do).

Self-optimization: in OSPF, link costs completely determine, through the shortest path al-gorithm, the emergent forwarding paths and thus have crucial impact on the way user traffic flows through the network. Even though link costs are set to a constant, default value almost universally in today's OSPF deployments, it not necessarily needs to be so. Constant cost setting (either to a default constant or a static value reciprocal to the link capacity as recommended by router vendors) leads to a routing pattern that is completely and adversely independent of the operating conditions (i.e., the load at network links, the amount of incoming user traffic, etc.). This often leads to inefficient data forwarding. In order to improve the performance of the network, link costs could (and should) be regularly updated to better reflect the actual operational circumstances, and this could be done by organizing OSPF into a self-optimization control loop (Antic et al, 2010, Tizghadam et al, 2010). In this control loop, either the node-level routing management DE in the router itself, or the network-level routing management DE implemented in the decision cloud, could readjust the link costs when the need arises (OSPF parameter: *Interface output cost*). The difference between the two approaches is the amount of monitoring data available to the DE based on which link cost recalculation can be done. If the link costs are readjusted at the node level (the first option), only knowledge available to that node can be used in the readjustment. For instance, cost of overloaded or heavily used local interfaces could be increased, while the cost of underutilized local interfaces could be decreased, but no information on the load at links in remote parts of the network could be used in this process. Unfortunately, careless local intervention into the shortest path structure, apart from over-provisioning the network with excess signaling traffic, usually leads to global oscillations and instability (Khanna and Zinky, 1989). Hence, it is better to readjust link costs at the network level, as fostered by the discipline of OSPF traffic engineering (Fortz and Thorup, 2000, Rétvári et al, 2007). It is important to note that, as theoretical results confirm, it is hopeless to drive the network right to optimal performance, due to the inherent limitations and inflexibility of shortest path routing. Yet, one can go pretty close to the optimum (Fortz and Thorup, 2000), and this is more than enough in most of the cases.

Self-organization: routers in an OSPF domain can be separated into distinct administrative scopes, called OSPF areas, with complete topology information available inside the area but only limited, summarized information flooding between them. This makes it possible to reduce the signaling overhead of OSPF; better modularize the network; eliminate excess signaling in stub areas (parts of the network with a single ingress/egress router); etc. In a bandwidth-constrained network, the area structure could be readjusted every time it is believed that the signaling overhead of OSPF could be reduced that way. Note that, however, changing area boundaries on the fly may lead to routing loops and transient spillage of reachability, making this self-organization function less appealing from the practical standpoint. Curiously, even the *raison d'etre* of areas has been questioned quite vigorously in the near past (Thorup, 2003).

Inter-domain self-adaptation: interaction between intra-domain and inter-domain routing has for a long time been a hardly understood and thus heavily researched question. The reason for this is that the two are not completely independent from each other: a simple change of an intra-domain forwarding path might have far-reaching consequences, causing routing updates in a significant portion of the entire Internet (Teixeira et al, 2004). Additionally, many of the changes of external routes are advertised into the routing domain, often causing the fluctuation of ingress traffic or outgoing traffic. It would be plausible, thusly, to try to readjust the interaction between intra- and inter-domain routing based on detailed knowledge of topology, monitoring data, network mining data, predicted profiles, AS paths, BGP policies, etc. The ideal entity to carry out such inter-domain optimization would be the Network-level Routing Management DE. However, currently there exists very little understanding as to how changing some aspects of this interaction effects the rest of the network (i.e., how changing route filters, route maps, the flooding scope of external-LSAs, etc., impacts the network holistically), which makes designing, implementing and optimizing such an inter-domain self-adaptation control loop quite a task.

CASE STUDIES

In the previous section, we showed that one of the most widely known network routing protocols, the OSPF routing protocol, includes a fair number of traits that qualify as some forms of self-management function. Apart from the main control loop, the self-adaptation control-loop, we have shown examples of auto-discovery, self-healing, self-configuration, etc., both within the OSPF protocol machinery itself, as well as existing as a separate control loop in the GANA architecture, of which OSPF is simply a managed entity.

In this section, we focus our attention exclusively to issues regarding routing management. In particular, we present two completely worked out case studies aiming at enriching OSPF's intrinsic self-adaptation capability by organizing it into a GANA control loop. For each case study, we give a motivation leading to the development of the autonomic behavior under consideration, we enumerate the elements needed to realize the corresponding control loops, and, taking concrete, real-life scenarios, we give the process model of how the various components in the control loop interact in order to realize the desired management goals. Finally, we share some initial implementation experience and basic measurement and simulation results, in order to testify the usefulness of the self-managing architecture at hand.

The intention of these case studies is not to give an exhaustive and accurate specification of the autonomic behaviors under consideration, which would then be amenable to interoperable implementations. Instead, the aim is to increase the reader's familiarity with the basic components of the GANA framework, to demonstrate the mental process of designing and building autonomic systems, and to shed light on the intricate and sometimes subtle steps involved in this process in an easy to follow manner.

Risk-Aware Self-Adaptive Routing Over OSPF

Today's network technologies, network management systems and associated network management practices constrain network operators in exercising fault-management in a static manner, without having the ability to take into account the dynamicity of the risks endangering their networks. The reason for this is that the routing function does not take into account the risk of failure of a network device, link, or other component, which is a problem when failure eventually occurs. For instance, in the case of OSPF failures are reactively handled by the self-adaptation mechanism, thanks to the Hello protocol that periodically sends Hello messages to detect failures. However, due to the delay between the occurrence of the failure and OSPF's eventual global convergence, user traffic may experience loss of packets, temporary routing loops, asymmetrical routing, or routing black holes, and other routing transients.

Deploying risk-assessment functions inside a node, and the network as a whole, is therefore a requisite. Such risk-assessment functions provide real-time risk-level information to the nodes and the network, in order to proactively employ strategies to avoid failures, damages, outages and eventual service unavailability, when the probability of failure changes. Additionally, in response to the risk assessment information gathered from the network, risk-aware self-adaptation behaviors must be triggered to adjust the operation of the network to the incurred risk. An example of such an adaptation strategy is adaptive traffic engineering mechanisms at the routing level that dynamically tune OSPF link costs in order to adapt to the risk-levels in the physical devices.

The risk-aware self-adaptation feature, demonstrated in the case study below, aims to avoid failures by using timely and accurate risk-level information to proactively adapt OSPF link costs, prompting the traffic to avoid devices with certain risk-level. This mechanism bypasses the fault management slowness and avoids the visible impact of failure on the traffic flows. Failure anticipation also benefits recovery speed, since the preventive failure bypass enables to isolate failure before it causes damages.

Design of a Risk-Aware, Self-Adaptive Routing Functionality in GANA

There are basically two ways to handle outages in a fault-tolerant network infrastructure. A proactive approach is to prepare for the occurrence of failures, and apply predictive actions in an attempt to prevent the failure from happening. A reactive approach, on the other hand, involves acting only after the failure has shown up. The action usually means simply circumventing the failed component. The self-adaptive failure-mitigation architecture we sketch below is capable of applying both the proactive and the reactive approach.

The architecture consists of two basic functional blocks, the Risk Assessment Module (RAM) and Fault Masking Functions (FMF), which, in close cooperation, orchestrate the self-healing function of the network. The Risk Assessment Module, implemented in every network device, is responsible for continuously monitoring the device in an attempt to quantify its actual fitness, to evaluate the evolution of the state of the device in time, to estimate the probability of its failure based on recent fitness data, to quantify the severity of a possible failure, and to spread real-time risk level assessment information within the network. The Fault Masking Functions, in response to the risk levels collected from the network, perform proactive and reactive measures in an attempt to prevent failures from occurring, to minimize their severity, and to adapt to failures once they happened by relocating functionality from the failed device to backup resources.

Every device in the network is associated with a risk model, based on which its risk is assessed and risk-mitigation is performed. The risk model is expected to be implemented within the device by the manufacturer, ready to supply monitoring data and other system parameters usable for failure-prediction. A good example of such functionality is the Self-Monitoring, Analysis, and Reporting Technology (S.M.A.R.T.), a standardized monitoring, fault-detection and reporting system for computer hard disks. Based on the data obtained from the risk model, a special report, the so called risk description, is originated by the device to describe its fitness, which is then collected by the fault-management logic. This logic then analyzes the collected data by means of Bayesian networks, time series analysis, statistical methods, etc., to extract meaningful information regarding the possibility of the failure of the device in the near future. The risk description sent by the device comprises the identity of the affected device, the origin of the report (e.g., S.M.A.R.T.), the nature of the possible failure (human misconfiguration, hardware error or a natural disaster), the severity, a list of impacted services and functions, and possibly other parameters. The severity is measured in discrete levels of criticality, the so called risk levels. Quantizing risk levels simplifies the exploitation of the risk information and lifts the burden on the self-adaptation mechanism by avoiding frequent OSPF transients. A possible choice for discrete risk levels would be "normal", "moderate/alarm", "high" and "maximum" risk of failure, each one associated with failure probability thresholds.

There are various parameters forewarning a failure, like abnormal sensor readings, extraordinary log entries, etc., that are observed by the RAM to quantify the health of a device, and to predict a failure. Perhaps most important of these is the temperature of different components in the device, like the temperature of the CPU, the chassis, the power supply, network controllers, hard drives, etc. Indeed, a high temperature reading can be the result of an air conditioner failure, cooling system malfunction, or may even come from dirty filter, all of which will eventually lead to an overheating, causing a failure. Apart from this, component temperature is a value easily available in today's operating systems, via the Advanced Configuration and Power Interface (ACPI) or similar interfaces. Being such a telltale parameter forewarning a failure, we shall use the CPU temperature below as the only risk level parameter included in the risk descriptions. For each risk level we assign an operating region, with the understanding that if the observed parameter, the CPU temperature for now, is in the operating region then the corresponding risk level is in effect. Thusly, we have a normal, moderate, and high-risk operating region, and we have failure threshold above which the device is deemed dysfunctional.

The other functional block involved in the risk-aware self-adaptation control loop is the Fault Masking Function (FMF). This module is responsible for analyzing risk assessment information coming from the network, and performing appropriate proactive or reactive steps. The adaptation itself is carried out by tuning OSPF link costs in order to dynamically adapt to risk levels in the network elements and the network. The cost of reliable links is set small, while the cost of risky components is set high, always reflecting the actual risk levels arriving from the network, thereby causing traffic to flow through reliable, low cost paths. Exactly how to enforce the risk level in OSPF link costs, nevertheless, is an intriguing question. An option would be to use the risk level directly as the link cost. Unfortunately, this solution would compel the operator to use the risk exposure metric as the only optimization parameter, forbidding other traffic engineering strategies to be reflected in the link cost. It is, therefore, more advisable to combine the usual, operator-defined metrics, such as link capacity, delay, etc., with the new risk level metric. The composite approach allows the operator to apply the traffic engineering strategies he desires most of the time, while benefiting from failure mitigation in case of a failure. Herein, we do not delve into the ramifications of the link cost computation algorithm itself, good pointers are (Francois et al, 2007) and (Rétvári et al, 2007).

The control logic is realized through a close collaboration between several decision elements implemented in the devices (node level) as well as at the network level. The Resilience and Survivability Decision Elements, the home of the Risk Assessment Module, compute and monitor the risk level of the network components, and send risk descriptions around in the network. These DEs remain in close cooperation with Fault Management Decision Elements, realizing the Fault Masking Function based on the risk descriptions collected from the network, and the Routing Management Decision Elements, responsible for adjusting OSPF link costs in concert with perceived risk levels. For a summary on the names of the DEs used throughout this survey, we refer the reader back to Table 1.

The risk model, which is used by the NODE_LEVEL_RS_DE and NET_LEVEL_RS_DE for the computation and correlation of local and global risks, is assumed to be built into the DEs at design time. Based on this risk model, the NODE_LEVEL_RS_DE calculates the risks for the device, with respect to the information collected from the underlying MEs and DEs and provided by the monitoring components. Once the risk assessment information is computed, it is disseminated to the NODE_LEVEL_FM_DE to see whether local risk mitigation actions need to be performed. Since some failures might be impossible to handle locally at the node level, the NODE_MAIN_DE can decide to disseminate the risk description to upper layers in the control loop hierarchy. This is decided by checking whether the risk level associated with the device, or some of

its components, has crossed a certain threshold of severity. If it has, then the NODE_MAIN_DE will send the risk description to an overlay information repository, which is assumed to be present in the GANA architecture providing subscription based information retrieval services to any interested DEs. The NET_LEVEL_RS_DE is subscribed to receive risk reports from this repository, based on which it refreshes the network's global risk description, which is then put back into the repository. Other network-level DEs are assumed to also be subscribed to receive either a part or the complete aggregated and correlated global risk information from the overlay repository. Based on this information, global risk mitigation actions can be performed by the NET_LEVEL_FM_DE and the NET_LEVEL_RM_DE.

A Demonstration Scenario

Next, we demonstrate how the decision elements collaborate in realizing the self-healing function on a scenario quite common in today's network operations practice: the overheating of a CPU in a router. We discuss the steps of how the network adapts the routing to the increasing risk level of the overheating router, starting from the steady state of the network, through reducing the load on the affected router to alleviate the burden and mitigate the effects of a possible failure, all the way to the eventual shut down of the router. We divide this process into three essential steps:

- **Local risk evaluation and alarms:** executed when the risks are moderate and only require alarms to be sent to the network-level DEs without requiring any specific risk mitigation actions.
- **Local risk assessment and local risk mitigation actions:** risk assessment and mitigation actions confined to a network device, without network-wide self-adaptation;
- **Global risk assessment and global risk mitigation actions:** executed when local

risk mitigation is impossible, requiring global risk assessment and mitigation by the network-level decision elements.

Consider the simple network depicted in Figure 6. Let us assume that, initially, all the devices in the network have successfully performed the self-configuration and auto-discovery processes. The network is now fully functional with the routers performing their routine tasks. During the auto-configuration process, when the network gets partitioned into OSPF areas, both CR1 and BR1 are available as viable area border router candidates based on their capabilities. For some reason (as decided by NET_LEVEL_RM_DE), BR1 is chosen to play the role of a border router, while CR1 is assigned the role of a core router. Consequently, CR1 does not have an OSPF adjacency with CR4, i.e. there is no exchanging of OSPF messages, though, the link is configured to forward data. Bob, a user, is connected to CR4 in

Area 1, while other users, Alice, Charlie and Dave, are connected to BR4 in another area.

Scene 1: Local Risk Evaluation and Alarms – Temperature of BR1 Reaches Threshold Limit, Moderate Risk of Router Failure – Risk Level: Moderate/Alarm

After some time, all the routers with the exception of BR1 are functioning properly. The hardware temperature in BR1, however, has just reached its threshold limit. This is indicated by the thermometers shown next to the routers in Figure 7. As it can be seen, all the routers' thermometers with the exception of BR1 show normal operating temperature readings.

Based on the information supplied by monitoring components and from the underlying DEs and MEs, the NODE_LEVEL_RS_DE of each router computes the risk description for the router. Based on the severity of the risk description, the NODE_MAIN_DE may decide to escalate and disseminate

Figure 6. Initial state of the network - auto-configuration and auto-discovery of the network has been completed. Risk-level: NORMAL/LOW.

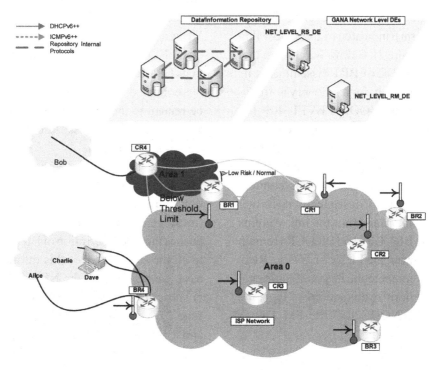

Figure 7. Temperature of BR1 reaches threshold limit – Moderate risk of router failure. Risk-level: Moderate/Alarm.

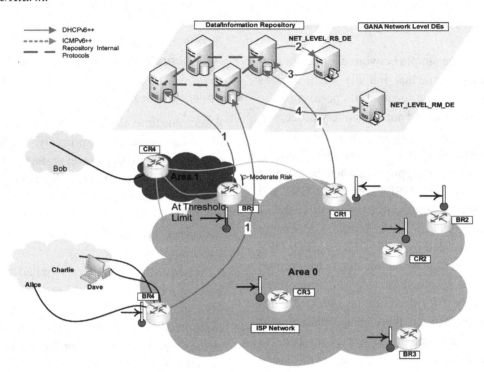

the risk description to the overlay information repository for further risk analysis by NET_LEVEL_RS_DE. The current risk level of BR1 is "Moderate" (Alarm) (indicated by the yellow flag next to BR1 in Figure 7). Below, we assume that the NODE_MAIN_DE of BR1 disseminates its risk description, but only for cautionary notification purposes, as the NODE_LEVEL_RS_DE considers this risk to be transient, and expects the CPU temperature of BR1 to return to its normal operating range. Similar decision is made by the NET_LEVEL_RS_DE, based on the assessment of BR1's risk description. Consequently, no further control action is taken, and thus the link-weights between the links BR1-CR1 and BR1-CR4 remain unchanged. However, the FUNC_LEVEL_RM_DE of BR1 may compute the need for additional monitoring and prioritize this action or trigger the operations of the NODE_LEVEL_FM_DE or both.

In addition to the risk description from BR1, two more routers, CR1 and BR4, also disseminate their risk description to the information repository. We assume that the risk description disseminated by the NODE_MAIN_DE of BR1 is due to the rise in its CPU temperature, while the risk description disseminated by CR1 and BR4 may or may not be related to the risks of BR1. Router CR4 may also disseminate its risk description (though not shown in the figure).

The sequence of message exchanges is as follows. First, all the routers upload their risk description to the central information retrieval repository (message 1). In response, the overlay repository pushes the risk description of BR1, CR1 and BR4, to all the subscribers of this information. In this case, we assume that the NET_LEVEL_RS_DE is subscribed to receive risk descriptions (message 2). The NET_LEVEL_RS_DE aggregates and correlates the risk descriptions, based on which it computes the global risk description for the network, and publishes it back to the overlay repository (message 3). The NET_LEVEL_RS_DE notes the risk level of BR1 as "Moderate" (Alarm) in its aggregated risk description for the network. The overlay repository pushes a part or the complete global risk description to the NET_LEVEL_RM_DE (message 4). In this scene, NET_LEVEL_RM_DE does not provide any solution to BR1, as the risk level is "Moderate" (Alarm). The NET_LEVEL_RM_DE registers the occurrence of such a risk (to be used in future computations) in the network.

Scene 2: Local Risk Evaluation, and Local Risk Mitigation Actions – Temperature of BR1 Crosses Threshold Limit, High Risk of Router Failure

To continue the scenario, we now assume that the hardware temperature increases further. This could be due to the presence of external problems, such as router fan or cooling failure rather than router operation per se.

The message sequence is as follows. As the hardware temperature of BR1 goes beyond the threshold limit, the NODE_LEVEL_RS_DE computes a new risk description for the node and disseminates it simultaneously to both the overlay information repository, the underlying DEs and the NODE_LEVEL_FM_DE (message 1 in Figure 8). The risk level of BR1 is now "High Risk" (indicated by the orange flag next to BR1 in Figure 8). Based on the risk description obtained from NODE_MAIN_DE, the FUNC_LEVEL_RM_DE of BR1 computes the cost of the links BR1-CR1 and BR1-CR4 (message 2a). The new link costs are computed by the "Risk Aware Link Cost Computation" block of the FUNC_LEVEL_RM_DE. In the meantime, the overlay repository pushes the risk description to the NET_LEVEL_RS_DE (message 2b). The DE performs the same actions as described previously, and updates the global risk description data in the overlay repository (message 3). The NET_LEVEL_RS_DE notes the risk

level of BR1 as "High Risk" in its aggregated risk description for the network. The repository now pushes parts or the complete form of this updated risks description to the other network level DEs (message 4). In this scene, NET_LEVEL_RM_DE does not provide any solution to BR1 as it is aware of the severity of the risks of BR1 and its implications. Nevertheless, NET_LEVEL_RM_DE registers the occurrence of such a risk (to be used in future computations) in the network.

Once a new link cost is computed for the risk mitigation action, the FUNC_LEVEL_RM_DEs change the link cost between BR1-CR1 and BR1-CR4. This is indicated by the orange color of the links. Link State Advertisements indicating the new link costs are sent throughout the network and routing tables are updated based on this. This new link cost aggressively discourages the forwarding of a large volume of traffic along the links of BR1, and forces the other routers to forward the majority of traffic along other paths, minimizing the traffic flowing through BR1. A possible way to achieve this is the OSPF Stub Router Advertisement option (Retana et al, 2001). The link costs of the other links in the network remain unchanged. This behavior is kept until the current risk is mitigated, and till the link costs have been restored to their previous value. By minimizing the traffic through BR1, the risk of packets being lost due to router failure is minimized. The node thus self-adapts its routing behavior and consequently it's forwarding behavior, and influences the routing and forwarding behavior of its neighbors, with respect to the local risks evaluation. All services to Bob remain unaffected throughout this scene.

Scene 3: Global Risk Evaluation and Global Risk Mitigation Actions – Temperature of BR1 Reaches High Value, Maximum Risk of Router Failure

To continue our scenario, we assume that the temperature of BR1 further increases as indicated

Figure 8. Temperature of BR1 crosses threshold limit – High risk of router failure. Risk-level: High.

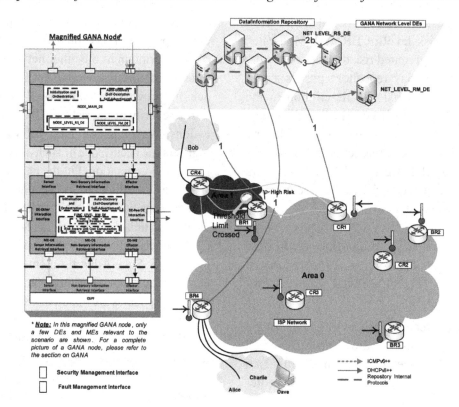

by the thermometer of BR1 in Figure 9. If BR1 remains in operation, then the network faces the risk of losing a critical area border router between Area 0 and Area 1, which may affect the reachability between areas negatively. Therefore, it is best to turn off BR1 completely to prevent permanent hardware failure and promote another router to ABR in the place of BR1.

The message sequence from message 1 to message 4 is the same as described previously. The current risk level of BR1 is set as "Maximum Risk" (indicated by the red flag next to BR1 in Figure 9). As the risk level is "Maximum Risk", the node disseminates the risk description without performing other node based risk mitigation actions that could further compromise the operability of the node. Based on the previous and current global risk descriptions, the NET_LEVEL_RM_DE now predicts that BR1 has a high probability of failure. Based on this, it instructs a role change

for the routers in the network. The NET_LEVEL_RM_DE issues different messages, one to BR1 (message 5a), the other to CR1 (message 5b), the third to CR4 (message 5c) and the fourth to the other routers (BR4, CR3, BR2, BR3, CR2) in Area 0. Through message 5a, BR1 is instructed to shut down to prevent further damage to the router. With message 5b, CR1 is instructed to reconfigure to the role of a border router (the role previously played by BR1) and also configure its link CR1-CR4. With message 5c, CR4 is instructed to re-configure its link interface (CR4-CR1) with respect to the new role of CR1 (the new BR1). The other core-routers are instructed to change their link costs to reflect the requirements of the new network topology and to achieve their network goals. This is indicated by "dot & dashed-green" link connecting the core-routers, a "thick light green" link connecting CR4 to CR1 (the new BR1), and a "broken red" link with an

Figure 9. Temperature of BR1 reaches a very high value – Maximum risk of router failure. Risk-level: Maximum.

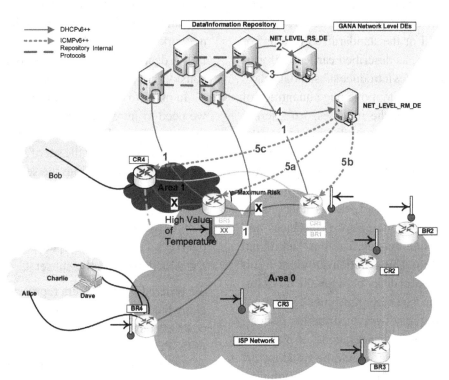

X between BR1 (now XX) to CR4 and CR1 (the new BR1).

The new topology and the link costs are kept until the current risk has mitigated, and BR1 has rebooted. By shutting down BR1 and reconfiguring the CR1 to play its role of ABR, the risk of packets being lost due to router failure is minimized. The network thus self-adapts its routing behavior and consequently, it's forwarding behavior. All services to Bob remain unaffected throughout this scene.

Implementation of the Risk-Aware Routing Functionality in GANA

Next, we discuss some important questions regarding the implementation of risk-aware routing within the GANA framework, and then we highlight the importance of such a solution by taking a concrete, real-life example.

One of the most important goals of the case studies presented in this survey is to demonstrate that adding new functionality to legacy network technology does not necessarily require modifications to the legacy technology under consideration. Instead, by incorporating it into autonomic control loops, the legacy protocol can be used the unaltered, yet new functionality can be realized by driving the legacy equipment via its management interfaces by higher level intelligence. This is exactly the case with the risk-aware self-adaptation method presented above: it does not require any modification to OSPF at all, but instead uses OSPF's standard behavior to act on the routes traffic takes in order to minimize its exposure to risks.

To accomplish this, three additional functional blocks are needed: the risk assessment module, the fault masking functions, and the link weight assignment functionality living in the routing management decision elements. There are various strategies to arrange the communication between these modules. For instance, OSPF could be driven through the CLI or the standardized Netconf or SNMP interfaces, as described earlier. Unfortunately, such interfaces introduce substantial delays and make it difficult to move huge quantities of information between the modules. An alternative would be to build the modules right into the routing protocol platform. This does not mean the modification of the OSPF code in any regards; this just means that the routing software platform, which hosts OSPF, BGP and perhaps other routing protocols as standalone protocol instances and lets them run side-by-side, can host additional functionality too. This solution provides minimal communication delay between the modules, crucial to attain fast response times to changes in risk level, but raises grave portability issues.

Based on these considerations, a plausible implementation strategy would be to adopt the second option and build link weight assignment functionality into the routing platform, due to its need for fast response time to minimize additional delays and its need for operating directly on the OSPF Link State Database. Risk assessment and fault masking, on the other hand, may live in separate processes, and inter-process communication could be used between the modules.

Next, we turn to evaluate the effects of risk-aware routing in our demonstration scenario introduced above. Consider the network depicted in Figure 6, and suppose that there are 3 traffic flows provisioned in the network, each of 10Gbit/s bandwidth. One traffic instance flows from CR4 toward CR2, another one from BR2 to BR4, and the last one from CR1 to BR3, respectively. Additionally, suppose that the link costs are set in the network so that the flows take the following paths: *Flow*1={CR4, BR1, CR1, CR2}, *Flow*2={BR2, CR2, CR3, BR4}, *Flow*3={CR1, CR3, BR3}. What we shall do next is to compute a so called link exposure index, which expresses the vulnerability of traffic to possible failures in the network,

and use that index to demonstrate the usefulness of the autonomic risk-adaptive routing technique. We shall consider the router as the only atomic network element in this demonstration that can fail. A deeper evaluation would require, at least, considering links and line cards as well.

In order to calculate the traffic risk exposure, we need to introduce some notation. We define the network topology as a weighted simple graph $G = (N,E)$, where N is the set of routers and E the set of links. Let F denote the set of traffic flows carried by the network G, where a unique traffic flow $f_i \in F$ is defined by its ingress node $In(f_i) \in N$, its destination node $Out(f_i) \in N$, and its throughput $W(f_i)$. The forwarding path followed by a flow $f_i \in F$ is defined as the subset $C_{f_i} \subseteq N$, that is, the ordered list of routers representing each hop along the shortest path in terms of the OSPF link costs as computed by the shortest path algorithm of OSPF.

To be able to evaluate the traffic risk exposure, we need to define the probability of the failure of a node, and consequently, of a flow. The probability of failure of a node during the time window T is defined as $Pnode(n_i)$. Failure prediction performance is usually in the range 60-80% (Li et al, 2007), thus, there exists a non-null probability of failure for a node that is considered safe by failure prediction. For this reason, we will use $Pnode(n_i)$ = 1% for a non-risky node. In the same way, a failure prediction does not always lead to a real failure. Given that the current failure prediction mechanisms generate less than 35% of false positives (Li et al, 2007), we choose $Pnode(n_i)$ = 65% for risky routers, i.e., that are likely to fail during the time window T.

The failure of a traffic flow f_i is characterized by the inability for the network to carry the data flow towards its destination and results from the failure of at least one router on the shortest path C_{f_i} of the flow f_i. For the computation of the failure probability $Pflow(f_i)$ of a flow f_i, we make the assumption that node failures are independent events, that is, $Pnode(n_i \cap n_j) = Pnode(n_i) * Pnode(n_j)$. The probability of failure of a flow f_i during the time window T is calculated by using the complementary of the probability that any of the routers constituting its shortest path fail:

$$Pflow(f_i) = 1 - \left(\prod_{\forall ni \in C_{f_i}} (1 - Pnode(n_i)) \right).$$

The traffic risk exposure index is expressed as the weighted average of the flow failure probabilities weighted by the bit rate of each flow. The resulting indicator takes into account the importance of the flow in the entire amount of traffic carried by the network, in order to provide a "per-bit" average risk exposure. The resulting formula is:

$$E(G, F) = \frac{\left(\sum_{\forall f_i \in (F)} Pflow(f_i) * w(f_i) \right)}{\sum_{\forall f_i \in (F)} w(f_i)}.$$

To illustrate the advantages of the risk-adaptation scheme, we first compute the impact of a single failure prediction on the failure probability of each flow with and without risk-aware routing, and we quantify the impact of risk-aware routing on the reduction of the risk exposure. The failure probability for all flows in normal conditions (if no future failure is detected on the flow paths), is lower than 4%: $Pflow(flow1) = 3.9\%$, $Pflow(flow2) = 3.9\%$, $Pflow(flow1) = 3.0\%$, (see corresponding values in Table 2).

Table 3 summarizes the global traffic risk exposure by measuring the impact of a single failure prediction for each node and for all flows, with and without the risk-aware routing. The average risk exposure value of a single failure prediction is also provided as a general indicator.

The differences in the risk exposures (highlighted in italic in the tables) stem from the fact that the network topology provides an alternative, safer path in case of failure of the nodes BR1 and CR3. On the other hand, other failure predictions do not influence the risk exposure since there is no existing alternative path. The ability of risk-aware routing to decrease the traffic risk exposure, therefore, is naturally bounded by the number of disjoint paths between a pair of nodes. The average node degree is thus an important parameter in the capacity to provide alternative paths to avoid risky nodes, and ultimately, to increase the network robustness and reliability.

Next, we quantify how much risk-aware self-adaptation benefits the performance of the network. The basic quantity we use to characterize this effect will be the amount of traffic loss obviated by the preventive action of risk-aware routing in contrast to the standard OSPF case. Easily, the benefit here is the additional availability that is experienced as better service level by the end user.

As mentioned previously, the intrinsic self-adaptation control loop of OSPF consists of four basic steps: failure detection through the Hello protocol, LSA flooding, shortest path first computation, and updating of the RIB and FIB. If no risk-aware self-adaptation is used, then the network must resort to this standard self-adaptation

Table 2. Impact of a single failure prediction on the failure probability of each flow

	Flow1			Flow2				Flow3		
Router	BR1	CR1	CR2	BR2	CR2	CR3	BR4	CR1	CR3	BR3
Standard	*0,66*	*0,66*	0,66	0,66	0,66	*0,66*	0,66	0,66	*0,66*	0,66
Risk-aware	*0,04*	*0,03*	0,66	0,66	0,66	*0,04*	0,66	0,66	*0,03*	0,66

Table 3. Traffic risk exposure E(G,F)

	No failure	BR1	BR2	BR3	BR4	CR1	CR2	CR3	Average
Standard routing	0,04	*0,24*	0,24	0,25	0,24	*0,45*	0,45	*0,45*	*0,33*
Risk-aware routing	0,04	*0,04*	0,24	0,25	0,24	*0,25*	0,45	*0,04*	*0,21*

mechanism of OSPF, and consequently packets will be lost during it takes each of the above four steps to complete. We have also seen that the major cause of the slowness of OSPF self-adaptation is the failure detection mechanism, that is, the Hello protocol. Recall that *HelloInterval* is the OSPF parameter determining the emission rate of Hello messages, and the *RouterDeadInterval* parameter is the multiple of Hello timers, after which a link is declared as "down". The slowness of OSPF's self-adaptation comes from the fact that these parameters can only be configured with the granularity of seconds. The *HelloInterval* is usually set to 10 seconds, and the *RouterDeadInterval* is usually set to four times the *HelloInterval* (but see Francois et al, 2005 for an in-depth discussion of the setting of these timers). Such configurations lead to tens of seconds of unavailability only due to the failure detection process, completely dominating the convergence time of OSPF. Consequently, we will only consider packet losses during the failure detection time, since other phases' duration are negligible compared to it. Moreover, packet losses during the other three steps are hard to quantify,

because these losses mostly arise due to transient routing loops, which do not appear systematically.

Based on these considerations, we estimate the amount of packet loss during the failure detection time, with *HelloInterval* timers following a 10, 5 and 0,33 seconds setting. The following formula details the minimum time to detect a failure, when all packets sent to the failed node are lost.

$$Min(Td) = (\frac{RouterDeadInterval}{HelloInterval} - 1) * HelloInterval$$

Min(Td) takes respectively the values 30, 15 and 1 seconds. The evaluation of packet losses resulting of a single router failure $Lp(n_i)$ is computed with the following formula:

$$Lp(n_i) = Min(Td) * \left(\sum_{\forall f_i \in F \cap n_i \in C_{f_i}} w(f_i) \right)$$

Table 4 summarizes the amount of packet loss suffered by the 3 previously defined traffic flows of 10 Gbit/s each, after a single failure. Current IP

Table 4. Amount of packet loss in Gbit

	Router failure	BR1	BR2	BR3	BR4	CR1	CR2	CR3
OSPF restoration without risk-aware routing	10s timer	300	Flow2*	Flow3	Flow2	*Flow3+300*	Flow2&3	*600*
	5s timer	150	Flow2	Flow3	Flow2	*Flow3+150*	Flow2&3	*300*
	Subsecond timer	10	Flow2	Flow3	Flow2	*Flow3+10*	Flow2&3	*20*
OSPF restoration with risk-aware routing	10s timer	0	Flow2	Flow3	Flow2	*Flow3*	Flow2&3	*0*
	5s timer	0	Flow2	Flow3	Flow2	*Flow3*	Flow2&3	*0*
	Subsecond timer	0	Flow2	Flow3	Flow2	*Flow3*	Flow2&3	*0*

* The traffic flow is indefinitely stopped with an amount of packet loss corresponding to (Flow Throughput * Time of reparation).

restoration is compared with the expected benefit of the risk-aware routing scheme using failure prediction, with the three different values of *HelloInterval* timer and the *RouterDeadInterval* set to 4 times the *HelloInterval*.

These comparisons highlight, in a practical way, the expected gain of risk-aware routing. The solution proves useful especially in the case of true failure prediction, by steering traffic away from risky hot-spots and by reducing the amount of packet loss where rerouting is possible. The study also helped in identifying the intrinsic limits of the solution in the case where no alternative path is available. It is important to note that, in this situation, neither risk-aware routing nor the classical OSPF restoration mechanism will be able to reestablish the traffic flow connectivity.

To conclude, risk-aware routing allows rerouting traffic to reduce the traffic risk exposure, in order to help the basic IP restoration mechanism to mitigate the consequences of a failure on the traffic. Like IP restoration, risk aware routing too is limited by the network topology, and may introduce side effects like congestion along the alternative routes and the deterioration of the QoS-level of certain flows. Addressing the issues of congestion and QoS management in conjunction with the risk-aware routing is an interesting topic for future research.

Autonomic Routing Resilience through the IP Fast Re-Route Mechanism

Despite all the efforts of the self-adaptive failure mitigation function in a network, there may still occur unpredictable, and hence unexpected, outages in an operational network. Such outages then cause service disruptions, temporal unavailability, routing blackholes, QoS degradation and similar adverse phenomena, all affecting the end-user experience in a negative way. In a modern self-managing network, therefore, it is essential to deploy a fast, reliable and secure self-healing

functionality. The case study we present in the section addresses just this concern. In particular, by incorporating OSPF and the IP Fast ReRoute mechanism into a GANA-style control loop, we construct an autonomic resilience architecture.

In case of a failure, the self-adaptation control-loop in OSPF is likely to cause momentary route instability and service interruption during the time it takes for routing tables at all routers to converge to new routes. Since OSPF's global and reactive response makes the convergence of the control loop slow, IP Fast ReRoute (IPFRR) extensions have been proposed within the IETF to minimize the harmful effects of link or node failures (Shand and Bryant, 2010). IPFRR works by redirecting traffic to pre-computed repair paths in a timely fashion. This avoids the delay caused by the global convergence of OSPF, and hence transient failures, flapping interfaces and similar temporal outages making up the majority of the failure cases in an operational network. Meanwhile, OSPF's global re-convergence mechanism is suppressed, and only after a failure turns out to be permanent OSPF's global re-convergence is initiated.

In the IPFRR framework, Loop-Free Alternates (LFAs) have been widely accepted as a viable solution (Atlas and Zinin, 2008). Loop-Free Alternates is based on the idea that if a router redirects packets from the default path, affected by a failure, to a neighboring router that is closer to the destination in terms of OSPF costs than itself (an LFA), then the neighboring router will not send the packet back, which might otherwise yield a routing loop. Instead, the packet will, hopefully, arrive to the destination sidestepping the failed network component.

Unfortunately, LFAs do not provide a complete solution to the suite of problems IP Fast ReRoute addresses.

First, LFAs can only partially cover the failure scenarios, in that they are limited to a single failure or failures within a single shared risk link group. What is more, it is not guaranteed that an LFA always exists, leaving some failures impossible to repair. For pointers on alternative IPFRR schemes, see (Bryant and Shand, 2005, Bryant and Shand, 2006, Wang and Nelakuditi, 2007, Enyedi et al, 2009), and the surveys in (Raj and Ibe, 2007) and (Gjoka et al, 2007).

Second, during the re-convergence of OSPF from LFAs to the new OSPF routes, micro-loops, routing blackholes and other detrimental transients can show up if the update of the Forwarding Information Bases at the routers is not done in the right order. To avoid this, the Ordered FIB Update method (oFIB, Francois and Bonaventure, 2008) was proposed, which provides loop-free convergence by correctly sequencing the FIB updates on the routers. See (Bryant and Shand, 2006) for other methods to provide loop-free switching from LFAs to new OSPF routes.

Third, by LFA being a pure OSPF-based fast reroute mechanism, it relies on the auto-discovery function in OSPF to detect topology changes. Although the timers of this process can be tuned to achieve sub-second detection time (Cisco, 2002), statically configured smaller timers are not a preferable option in many networks as they can cause routing instability under interface flapping conditions, create false positives, and increase signaling overhead by sending frequent Hello packets and network-wide flooding of more Link State Advertisements (LSAs). By using an explicit fast probe mechanism, such as IETF's Bidirectional Forwarding Detection (BFD, Katz and Ward, 2010), a failure event can be detected within milliseconds of its occurrence. Still, false positives and intense signaling traffic remain.

Fourth, IPFRR through LFAs is specifically aimed at fixed, wired OSPF networks. For fixed or slowly changing mobile, multi-hop wireless networks, however, it is a bad fit. Compared to wired networks, wireless mobile multi-hop networks are much smaller in size, but experience far more frequent routing table updates due to blockage, mobility, interference, etc. A relatively long convergence time significantly drops the throughput performance of wireless mobile networks, since

limited bandwidth resources will not be efficiently used until a new route is converged. One could attempt to reduce the convergence time into the sub-second range by setting configurable routing protocol timers appropriately, however, smaller timers will not only significantly increase the signaling overhead in bandwidth limited wireless networks but also decrease the stability of routing protocols during frequent topology changes. Hence, IPFRR protocols must be specifically designed considering the unique requirements of wireless mobile multi-hop networks.

The case study discussed below is aimed precisely at addressing the above needs, by providing IPFRR in wireless multi-hop networks that happen to use OSPF. Note that, however, the architecture applies equally well to wired IP networks. An ideal, but unrealistic, IPFRR mechanism would have zero reroute delay, create no extra overhead, either be micro-loop free or handle all micro-loops, be backward compatible, require minimum amount of processing power and memory, and cover all failure scenarios. We attempt to get as close to these requirements as possible. Building on the concept of LFAs, we introduce the concept of remote LFAs to extend the IPFRR mechanism with complete alternate path coverage. To alleviate the signaling burden caused by the fast failure detection mechanisms, a prediction-based mechanism is used. This enables proactive handover to a pre-computed LFA in the face of a deteriorating OSPF primary path without the need for fast Hellos or BFD.

The IPFRR method will be realized within the GANA architecture as a fast self-healing autonomic behavior, by adding suitable extensions to the self-adaptation and auto-discovery control loops of OSPF. The fast-self healing mechanism works as follows. OSPF will not necessarily change routes when a wireless link becomes unstable, because its link failure criteria, designed for wired networks, may not have been met. In such cases, the IPFRR mechanism temporarily and locally switches to a more reliable route via the pre-computed LFAs until the link quality improves. If the conditions of the unstable link further deteriorate, OSPF will commit to a route change by initiating its global re-convergence process. The formation of micro-loops and other routing transients is avoided by *(i)* sending fast failure notification to the affected routers before re-routing any data over LFAs, and *(ii)* calculating next hops for LFAs identical to new routing table entries that would be calculated by OSPF for a particular failure.

Below, we sketch an IPFRR-based fast self-healing function for self-managing networks. As shall be shown, the use of IPFRR within GANA facilitates the instantiation of autonomic behaviors that can make the network act like a living organism, able to handle different situations without the need for any external intervention. This way, a dynamic wireless mobile multi-hop network is expected to exercise resilience by assuring that data flows can be routed virtually seamlessly, independent of temporary problems that might have occurred.

Design of a Fast Self-Healing Functionality in GANA

The success of end-to-end packet delivery, from the routing perspective, depends mainly on the existence of loop-free forwarding tables and availability of links with sufficient resources along the path. Any violation of these two criteria results in end-to-end application disruption until either a link with sufficient resources becomes available, or the underlying routing protocols calculate new loop-free forwarding tables.

The following cases of wireless link condition changes can cause application disruption: *(i)* link emerging and failure events due to node mobility and resource deployments and failures; *(ii)* temporary link disruptions due to peculiarities of wireless medium; and *(iii)* variations in link congestion levels due to varying link capacities and user demands. Traditional routing protocols,

like OSPF, have built-in, yet slow, self-adaptation mechanism with respect to the first type of wireless link condition change, and IPFRR methods promise to speed up this mechanism significantly. Link status changes under the second and third categories, however, are mostly ignored by the majority of existing routing protocols. Unfortunately, these failure cases, if not addressed adequately, might degrade the link forwarding capability significantly. The fast reroute mechanism described next can be immediately used to deal with the link status changes under the first and second categories and can be extended to cope with the case of link congestion variations as well.

In order to speed up the convergence of the routing tables to loop-free routes after topology changes, OSPF needs to be extended with several autonomic components as illustrated in Figure 10. In this framework, OSPF's conventional self-adaptation mechanism detects and reacts to topology changes in a long time scale, by using stable timers. In the meantime, the self-healing functionality achieves faster convergence by employing two complementary mechanisms: *(i)* prediction, quick detection and controlled dissemination of topology changes, and *(ii)* quick repair of the forwarding tables at routers by replacing the affected routing table entries with their pre-computed loop-free alternatives. The routing table entries need to be updated either when the LSDB (Link State Database) changes due to failure notification messages received from neighboring routers, or when the status of a local interface changes. Here, changes in local interface states (e.g., local link failures) are quickly detected by a pro-active cross-layer detection mechanism, which is developed by integrating probe and prediction modules as described next.

A bi-directional link is considered failed if it does not function properly in either of its transmit or receive direction, or both. The prediction module and the probe module, both of which belong to the link layer of the IPFRR function, are re-

Figure 10. IPFRR control flow within a single node

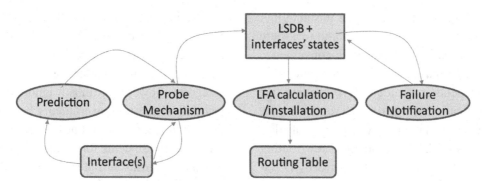

sponsible for the timely detection and prediction of such failures.

The prediction module collects real-time physical and link layer data from wireless channels, such as Received Signal Strength Indicator (RSSI) and Bit Error Rate (BER) via its interface to the radio hardware. Based on this monitoring data, the prediction module implements proactive methods to prognosticate link quality. It also enables proactive fast reroute in the face of a deteriorating primary path with minimal bandwidth overhead. The other component of the IPFRR architecture, the probe mechanism, sends small Hello messages between neighboring nodes to verify the status of local links. The Hello interval of the explicit probe mechanism is adaptively controlled by the output of the prediction module. The idea is to monitor the link quality more aggressively, by exchanging Hello messages more frequently, when the prediction module indicates that the quality of a wireless channel is deteriorating. While prediction provides an early indication of wireless channel quality with minimal bandwidth consumption by using local information such as RSSI and BER, the probe mechanism provides a more accurate status of a wireless channel at the expense of additional bandwidth overhead by transmitting Hello packets over the channel. The final failure decision is made by the probe mechanism based on the probe lost statistics, and it triggers the installation of LFAs and dissemination of failure notification messages in the neighborhood of the router.

Note, however, that special care must be taken when installing LFAs in the routing table as there are two control loops that act on the same routing table entries simultaneously: OSPF's intrinsic routing self-adaptation control loop installing the routes computed from the LSDB, and the fast self-healing control loop installing LFAs. An inconsiderate design, thus, might yield that OSPF blindly overrides LFAs, preventing the fast self-healing actions to take effect, or the other way around. Similar interference shows up in legacy router implementations that run multiple routing protocols side-by-side working on the same routing table. The conventional method to deal with such problems is to assign priority levels (called administrative distances in the routing terminology) to the individual routing protocols, and let the final forwarding table be constructed by merging the Routing Information Bases (RIBs) of the different protocol instances based on their administrative distances. A standard setting for priorities is, for instance, the following: static routes are configured with lower administrative distances then OSPF routes, meaning that static routes override OSPF routes, provided they pertain to the same destination prefix. This same mechanism can be exploited for our purposes here: the IPFRR module enjoys a higher preference, that is, smaller administrative distance, than the legacy routing protocol, and consequently LFAs override OSPF routes when link layer modules send a failure notification. When eventually the

OSPF self-adaptation control loop kicks in, the IPFRR module withdraws its routes, letting the OSPF routes to take effect.

As mentioned previously, LFAs do not cover all possible failure scenarios. This is because it is not guaranteed that a router has a neighbor that is closer to the destination than itself, providing an LFA. If this rule was violated, then there would be a strong chance of forming routing loops, as the neighbor, unaware of the failure, would send the redirected traffic along its default route back to the router. In such cases, the router does not have an option to which to redirect traffic affected by a failure. A possible way to overcome this issue is to extend the concept of LFAs by so called remote LFAs. According to this method, a router can send fast failure notifications to neighbors, and if the neighbor has an LFA with respect to some destination node, then it can grant that LFA to the router. We do not go into further details on how to compute remote LFAs and the failure case coverage attainable using them, the reader is referred to (Cevher et al, 2010) for a exhaustive treatment of these problems. Hereinafter, this granted remote LFA will also be referred to as an LFA.

As a summary, the IPFRR-based fast self-healing mechanism introduces a new, fine grained control loop into the GANA architecture, which, in close collaboration with OSPF's built in slow self-adaptive control loop, manages the routing table entries autonomously in order to respond to failures in a timely fashion. This new self-healing control loop nicely fits into the GANA architecture, as demonstrated below:

- The Managed Entity is represented by all the routing tables in the network.
- Monitoring of the interfaces and their forwarding state is implemented by the probe and prediction mechanisms, which are finer grained compared to OSPF.
- Analyze/Plan is mapped to the LFA calculation process.

- Execution corresponds to the process of installing LFAs.
- Knowledge is represented by the collective set of LSDBs, obtained from local OSPF processes.

It is instructive to contrast this control loop with OSPF's intrinsic self-adaptation control loop depicted in Figure 5.

Finally in this section, we mention that, by incorporating OSPF and the IPFRR mechanism into higher level GANA control loops, one can implement additional useful autonomic behaviors. An illustrative example is exploiting the availability of LFAs to supply additional path diversity to mobile nodes. In wireless networks, diversity techniques achievable through cooperative transmission allow more than one intermediary node to assist in the transmission between two other neighbors (Dohler et al, 2004), potentially enhanced with additional routing information (Wódczak, 2007, Wódczak, 2008, Doppler et al, 2009). This way, extra resilience can be provisioned through the exploitation of the alternative paths, which typically would be only applied in case of failure. In other words, one can imagine situation where, based on the current status of the wireless mobile multi-hop network, the Routing Management Decision Element would normally force route change based on the options available from IPFRR (Liakopoulos et al, 2008). However, thanks to the fact that information coming from IPFRR is preprocessed to put LFAs into cooperative groups, it is still possible to keep the connection via a diversified set of paths despite some problems with maintaining non-cooperative links.

A Demonstration Scenario

In order to give a better understanding of the fast self-healing functionality and its interaction with OSPF, we present a brief demonstration scenario below. Consider the 5-node ring topology depicted in Figure 11, and suppose that the link costs are the

Figure 11. An example 5-node ring topology

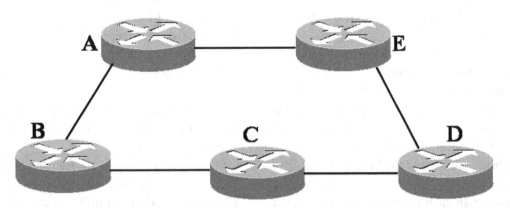

same throughout the network. We assume that each router runs OSPF as its link state routing protocol besides the IPFRR mechanism described in the previous section. We shall describe the sequence of actions taking place after the link between router B and C fails.

Figure 12 shows the OSPF routing tables (RTs) and the LFAs available at router A and B, when all five links are functional. Figure 13 shows the routing table OSPF will finally converge to after link B-C fails. For example, B will route its traffic destined to D via the path B-C-D in normal case. However, when the link between B and C fails, routing entries for the destinations C and D at B (and C at A) will be affected, eventually converging to the grayed entries shown in Figure 13. Until that finally occurs, though, it is the responsibility of the IPFRR-based fast self-healing component to keep up persistent global reach-

ability in the network by installing proper LFAs in the FIB.

This happens by letting all nodes pre-computing LFAs for all anticipated topology changes, and installing them as temporary forwarding table fixes as soon as the corresponding topology change becomes apparent, either through their own detection or through receiving a failure notification from their neighbors. The temporary forwarding table updates last until the routing protocols converge to new routes or until the IPFRR mechanism determines that the topology change was intermittent and routing updates are no longer necessary. Installation of temporary forwarding table changes is achieved in the most affected area first, and then carefully extended in the neighborhood of the failure to minimize unwanted routing loops.

As shown in Figure 12, LFAs for the destinations C and D at router B and for the destination

Figure 12. OSPF routing tables at router A (a) and B (b), and pre-computed LFAs at router A (c) and router B (d), before link B-C fails

	OSPF RT at A	
Dest	**via**	**cost**
B	B	1
C	B	2
D	E	2
E	E	1

(a)

	OSPF RT at B	
Dest	**via**	**cost**
A	A	1
C	C	1
D	C	2
E	A	2

(b)

	LFAPs at A for link failure of B-C	
Dest	**via**	**cost**
C	E	3

(c)

	LFAPs at B for link failure of B-C	
Dest	**via**	**cost**
C	A	4
D	A	3

(d)

Figure 13. OSPF RTs at B and A after link B-C fails

	OSPF RT at A	
Dest	**via**	**cost**
B	B	1
C	E	3
D	E	2
E	E	1

(a)

	OSPF RT at B	
Dest	**via**	**cost**
A	A	1
C	A	4
D	A	3
E	A	2

(b)

D at router A are pre-calculated and stored, readily available for forwarding table updates when the link B-C fails. Note that the entry for the destination C at B is initially not an LFA, because an LFA for the destination C does not exist in this failure scenario. However, by B sending a fast failure notification message to A that has a pre-computed LFA to C, B grants the existence of an LFA to C via itself (a remote LFA). Router B switches to this remote LFA, which is immediately reflected in the FIB through overwriting the forwarding table entry originally installed there by OSPF (recall that IPFRR routes have higher preference than OSPF routes). This forwarding entry will remain in effect until either the failure turns out to be intermittent and goes away, or eventually OSPF's slow self-adaptation control loop converges.

Implementation of the Fast Self-Healing Functionality in GANA

There are two options to implement the IPFRR mechanism within the GANA architecture. First, IPFRR may be implemented as a software module running on a general purpose processor external to the router and hence the OSPF process, and information exchange between the IPFRR and the OSPF processes may be accomplished using standard management interfaces. For instance, the standard router CLI could be used for installing LFAs, and the Simple Network Management Protocol (SNMP) can be invoked for retrieving the LSDB and other relevant information. A second option would be to create a new process within the router platform and arrange the information exchange between the two processes via the standard inter-process communication infrastructure of the router platform. While the first option can support multiple routing platforms and different OSPF implementations, it may cause the IPFRR convergence time to suffer substantial additional delay. This is because standard management interfaces are slow. For example, it can take about 500 ms for a Cisco Internetwork Operating System (IOS) command to become effective. This delay can be avoided if the IPFRR technology is implemented within the router platform proper. However, this option needs larger implementation efforts and it is not portable at all.

Herein, we take the first approach, that is, we will describe an implementation of IPFRR as an external process and we shall use SNMP and the CLI to communicate with OSPF. For an implementation based on the second option, the reader is referred to (Cevher et al, 2010), where the IPFRR module is implemented within the eXtensible Open Router Platform (XORP, XORP, 2004).

Figure 14 shows the same example network we used previously, with an expanded view of router B. The network consists of five emulated wireless mobile nodes. Each node consists of a Cisco router representing the Wide Area Network (WAN) router running IOS Release 12.3, the IP-FRR module implemented on standalone general purpose computer, traffic source and sink, and a radio hardware.

The IPFRR module is implemented as a multi-threaded program written in Java where there are six threads: *(i)* main IPFRR, *(ii)* link verifier sender, *(iii)* link verifier receiver, *(iv)* failure notification sender, *(v)* failure notification receiver, and *(vi)* LFA installer. The main IPFRR thread periodically reads the network topology from the router's LSDB, runs the alternate path calculation algorithm to calculate local and remote LFAs, and store them in temporary routing table objects to be immediately installed to the WAN router when actual link failures are detected. The link verifier sender periodically sends small-sized UDP request (REQ) messages to all of its im-

mediate neighbors and waits for their reply (REP) messages. A neighbor's link verifier receiver immediately sends a REP message when it receives a new REQ. By using REQ and REP messages, several statistics can be determined and dynamically maintained. In particular, the round trip time of the link is used to compute a timeout value, after which a packet is declared lost. The main SHA checks these statistics periodically and declares a failure if the number of lost REP messages exceeds a certain threshold within a timeout period. Upon the detection of a failure, the main SHA creates two new threads: one for installing LFAs and another for sending failure notification messages to remote nodes over TCP. The LFA installer, not surprisingly, installs LFAs to the WAN router by issuing a set of IOS commands.

The convergence time is measured by running a session, quite similar to a ping application, between routers A and B. When the link between routers A and B goes away, the primary path A-B (and hence the session between them) fails. Once the failure is detected, router A (B) first propagates

Figure 14. Expanded view of a single node

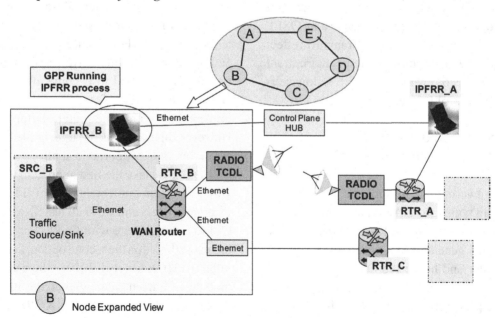

the failure information to router E (C) which has already pre-computed a remote LFA for this particular failure and installs its pre-computed LFAs. As a result, the session is rerouted through the alternate path A-E-D-C-B (B-C-D-E-A). In this experiment, sub-second convergence time could be achieved, not counting the failure detection time, which is a significant improvement compared to OSPF's convergence time, which is usually in the range of seconds.

FUTURE RESEARCH DIRECTIONS

The future for autonomic self-managing networks seems bright. At the moment, there does not appear to be any other way to tackle the increasing management burden imposed by complex modern network infrastructures to the network management personnel and systems. It is therefore expected that more and more self-managing devices will show up in operational networks, and research must support network operators in building truly autonomic systems out of these components.

Further research for achieving advanced autonomic and self-managing behavior for routing functionality in general, based on the GANA approach, is mainly on the design and implementation of an advanced management interface to the routing protocols and mechanisms of a node. That would enable the Function-level Routing Management DE's logic to operate on rich information exposed to it by the underlying routing protocol (e.g., OSPF), and to regulate different behavioral features of the protocol through the same interface based on context and cognition. Another challenge is on designing a logic for a DE that controls multiple routing instances of different protocols simultaneously, for example, an OSPF and BGP instance operating side-by-side in the same network device. To achieve these goals, the GANA framework itself could be further refined and enhanced, for instance, by semantic models and ontologies for representing network-wide knowledge, formal descriptions for the decision elements based on which state machines could be derived and implementations could be automatically generated, and standardized interface specifications for DE-to-DE and DE-to-ME communications. Much of this research has already been undertaken in the course of the EC FP7 EFIPSANS project (EFIPSANS, 2007).

In the future, the case study on risk driven self-adaptation would be extended in the direction of incorporating advanced risk-models. In addition, it would be desirable to tune the self-adaptation features of GANA to handle multiple router failures and various other types of risks that affect routing in the network. A future implementation, furthermore, should be extended to take into account the load and capacity of links, which may prevent the network from rerouting traffic from a risky path to a potentially congested one, causing more harm than if no rerouting would have been done at all. Another way of improvement would be to take into account the QoS constraints in conjunction with risk-aware routing, to favor a flow with guaranteed QoS against best effort traffic when the remaining capacity is limited. The fast self-healing mechanism, on the other hand, could be extended further in the direction of providing a higher level of built-in resilience through additional path diversity, with the use of cooperative transmission exploiting the availabile LFAs before there would be a need to switch to one of them in normal operation.

CONCLUSION

In this survey, we gave a practical guideline for realizing autonomic behaviors in self-managing networks. Our motivation was the observation that it is not necessary to completely re-implement all networking functionality from scratch in order to realize the vision of autonomic networking. Instead, it is more convenient to take an evolutionary road towards future's self-managing networks. A way we can achieve this is to design a suitable, generic framework for autonomicity that is able to capture not just modern, inherently autonomic-ready networking functionality, but traditional, legacy networking technology as well. Then, one can simply design autonomic behaviors around legacy hardware and software using the mental model supplied by the autonomic framework. This evolutionary approach promises with a smooth, incremental deployment plan for self-management in future networks.

We demonstrated this idea using the Generic Autonomic Network Architecture as the holistic framework for autonomicity, and the venerable Open Shortest Path First routing protocol as the legacy network technology. We saw that OSPF already includes a fair number of traits that qualify as some forms of self-management. Apart from the main control loop, the self-adaptation control loop, we showed examples of auto-discovery, self-healing, self-configuration, etc., all within OSPF. However, these control loops were designed piece-meal and are deeply hidden in the very substrate of the network protocol engine. In order to enrich OSPF's built-in functionality with advanced self-management capability, one needs to open up the implicit control loops, buried deeply into OSPF, and re-engineer them into explicit control loops, which communicate over standardized interfaces with heavily optimized and flexible decision-making-logics implemented by autonomic decision elements at higher layers of the GANA hierarchical model.

The process of integrating protocol-intrinsic and external control loops, though, hides quite some covert traps. In particular, special care must be taken to prevent the external control decision making logics to interfere with the internal control loops, to facilitate seamless information exchange between legacy and new networking technology, and to ensure that the multi-level control loop remains stable and conflict-free. Therefore, the specification and implementation of autonomic behaviors, and the algorithms realizing them, do not easily lend themselves to a systematic design process. Instead, building autonomic behaviors is much rather a work of art today, posing an untrivial and complex design challenge for the human engineer. To ease this process, we provided two completely worked-out case studies, demonstrating how to enhance OSPF's self-adaptation capability with useful new functionality. Our first case study addressed the need for risk-aware routing in operational networks, allowing the network to self-adapt to risk levels, fitness data and other monitoring information collected from the network. The second case study was concerned with realizing fast and efficient self-healing functionality in multi-hop wireless networks. Both case studies included a motivation for implementing the autonomic functionality under consideration, a GANA-based reference model for realizing it, and additional discussions on implementation details and operational experiences.

Taking a broader look, it turns out that not just OSPF, but basically any network protocol in existence today is designed around some forms of self-management and self-adaptation control loop. A marked example is the Transmission Control Protocol (TCP) flow control protocol. Many of these protocols therefore, similarly to the case of OSPF, readily lend themselves to be incorporated into higher level control loops to implement beneficial autonomic behaviors in addition to their inherent self-management capability. We believe that the design guidelines given in this survey will help the networking community realize this ambitious vision.

REFERENCES

Alamouti, S. M. (1998). A simple transmit diversity technique for wireless communications. *IEEE Journal on Selected Areas in Communications, 16*(8), 1451–1458. doi:10.1109/49.730453

Antic, M., Maksic, N., Knezevic, P., & Smiljanic, A. (2010). Two phase load balanced routing using OSPF. *IEEE Journal on Selected Areas in Communications, 28*(1), 51–59. doi:10.1109/JSAC.2010.100106

Apostolopoulos, G., Kama, S., Williams, D., Guerin, R., Orda, A., & Przygienda, T. (1999). *QoS routing mechanisms and OSPF extensions.* RFC 2676.

Atlas, A., & Zinin, A. (2008). *Basic specification for IP fast-rerorute: Loop-free alternates.* IETF RFC 5286.

Balasubramaniam, S., Barrett, K., Strassner, J., Donnelly, W., & van der Meer, S. (2006). *Bio-inspired policy based management (bioPBM) for autonomic communication systems.* In 7th IEEE Workshop on Policies for Distributed Systems and Networks.

Ballani, H., & Francis, P. (2007). Conman: A step towards network manageability. *SIG-COMM Comput. Commun. Rev., 37*(4), 205–216. doi:10.1145/1282427.1282404

Bassi, A., Denazis, S., Galis, A., Fahy, C., Serrano, M., & Serrat, J. (2007). *Autonomic Internet: A perspective for future internet services based on autonomic principles.* In 2nd IEEE International Workshop on Modelling Autonomic Communications Environments, MACE'07, San José, California, USA.

Bell, J. (2004). *Understand the autonomic manager concept.* Retrieved from http://www.ibm.com/developerworks/library/ac-amconcept/

Bouabene, G., Jelger, C., Tschudin, C., Schmid, S., Keller, A., & May, M. (2010). The autonomic network architecture (ANA). *IEEE Journal on Selected Areas in Communications, 28*(1), 4–14. doi:10.1109/JSAC.2010.100102

Bryant, S., & Shand, M. (2005). *IP fast reroute using tunnels.* Internet Draft.

Bryant, S., & Shand, M. (2006). *A framework for loop-free convergence.* Internet Draft.

Bryant, S., Shand, M., & Previdi, S. (2006). *IP fast reroute using not-via addresses.* Internet Draft.

Bullot, T., Khatoun, R., Hugues, L., Gati, D., & Merghem-Boulahia, L. (2008). A situatedness-based knowledge plane for autonomic networking. *International Journal of Network Management, 18*(2), 171–193. doi:10.1002/nem.679

Cevher, S., Chen, T., Hokelek, I. (2010). *An integrated soft handoff approach to IP fast reroute in wireless mobile networks.* COMSNETS 2010.

Chaparadza, R. (2007). *Evolution of the current IPv6 towards IPv6++: IPv6 with autonomic flavours. Annual Review of Communications, 60.* International Engineering Consortium.

Chaparadza, R. (2008). Requirements for a generic autonomic network architecture (GANA), suitable for standardizable autonomic behavior specifications for diverse networking environments. *Annual Review of Communications, 61.* International Engineering Consortium (IEC).

Chaparadza, R., Papavassiliou, S., Aristomenopoulos, G., Kastrinogiannis, T., Grammatikou, M., Argyropoulos, C., … Vidalenc, b. (2008). *Second draft of autonomic behaviours specifications (abs) for the diverse networking environments.* EFIPSANS Deliverable.

Chaparadza, R., Papavassiliou, S., Kastrinogiannis, T., Vigoureux, M., Dotaro, E., & Davy, A. … Wilson, M. (2009). Creating a viable evolution path towards self-managing future Internet via a standardizable reference model for autonomic network engineering. In R. Chaparadza (Ed.), *Towards the future Internet - A European research perspective,* (pp. 313–324). IOS Press.

Cheng, Y., Farha, R., Kim, M., Leon-Garcia, A., & Won-Ki-Hong, J. (2006). A generic architecture for autonomic service and network management. *Computer Communications, 29*(18), 3691–3709. doi:10.1016/j.comcom.2006.06.017

Cheng, Y., Leon-Garcia, A., & Foster, I. (2008). Toward an autonomic service management framework: A holistic vision of SOA, AON, and autonomic computing. *Communications Magazine, 46*(5), 138–146. doi:10.1109/MCOM.2008.4511662

Cisco Systems. (2002). *OSPF support for fast hello*. Retrieved from http://www.ciscosystems.com.ro/en/US/docs/ios/12_0s/feature/guide/fasthelo.html

Clark, D. D., Partridge, C., Ramming, J. C., & Wroclawski, J. T. (2003). A knowledge plane for the internet. In *SIGCOMM '03: Proceedings of the 2003 Conference on Applications, Technologies, Architectures, and Protocols for Computer Communications*, (pp. 3–10). New York, NY: ACM.

IBM Corporation. (2003). *An architectural blueprint for autonomic computing*.

Davy, S., Barrett, K., Balasubramaniam, S., van der Meer, S., Jennings, B., & Strassner, J. (2006). Policy-based architecture to enable autonomic communications - A position paper. *Proceedings of IEEE CCNC, special session on Autonomic Communications*, Las Vegas, USA.

Derbela, H., Agoulminea, N., & Salaunb, M. (2009). ANEMA: Autonomic network management architecture to support self-configuration and self-optimization in IP networks. *Computer Networks, 53*(3), 418–430. doi:10.1016/j.comnet.2008.10.022

Dohler, M., Gkelias, A., & Aghvami, H. (2004). A resource allocation strategy for distributed MIMO multi-hop communication systems. *IEEE Communications Letters, 8*(2), 99–101. doi:10.1109/LCOMM.2004.823425

Doppler, K., Osseiran, A., Wódczak, M., & Rost, P. (2007). *On the integration of cooperative relaying into the WINNER system concept*. IST Mobile and Wireless Communications Summit.

Doppler, K., Redana, S., Wódczak, M., Rost, P., & Wichman, R. (2009). Dynamic resource assignment and cooperative relaying in cellular networks: Concept and performance assessment. *EURASIP Journal on Wireless Communications and Networking*.

Enyedi, G., Szilágyi, P., Rétvári, G., Császár, A. (2009). *IP fast reroute: Lightweight not-via without additional addresses*. INFOCOM'09.

FP6. (n.d.). *The FP6 ANA Project*. Retrieved from http://www.ana-project.org

FP6. (n.d.). *The FP6 Haggle Project*. Retrieved from http://www.haggleproject.org

FP7. (n.d.). *The FP7 4WARD Project*. Retrieved from http://www.4ward-project.eu

FP7. (n.d.). *The FP7 Autonomic Internet (AutoI) Project*. Retrieved from http://ist-autoi.eu/atoi

FP7. (n.d.). *The EC FP7 EFIPSANS Project*. Retrieved from http://www.efipsans.org

Fortz, B., & Thorup, M. (2000). *Internet traffic engineering by optimizing OSPF weights* (pp. 519–528). INFOCOM.

Francois, P., & Bonaventure, O. (2008). *Loop-free convergence using ordered FIB updates*. Internet Draft.

Francois, P., Filsfils, C., Evans, J., & Bonaventure, O. (2005). Achieving sub-second IGP convergence in large IP networks. *SIGCOMM Computer Communication Review, 35*(3), 35–44. doi:10.1145/1070873.1070877

Francois, P., Shand, M., & Bonaventure, O. (2007). Disruption free topology reconfiguration in OSPF networks. In *Proc. IEEE INFOCOM*, Anchorage, AK.

Greenberg, A., Hjalmtysson, G., Maltz, D. A., Myers, A., Rexford, J., & Xie, G. (2005). A clean slate 4D approach to network control and management. *SIGCOMM Computer Communication Review*, *35*(5), 41–54. doi:10.1145/1096536.1096541

Heckmann, O., et. al. (2002). *How to use topology generators to create realistic topologies*. Technical Report.

Hökelek, I., Cevher, S., Fecko, M. A., & Gurung, P. (2008). *Testbed implementation of loop-free soft handoff in wireless battlefield networks*. ASC 2008.

Hökelek, I., Fecko, M.A., Gurung, P., Samtani, S., Staikos, A., Bowcock, J. (2007). *Seamless softhandoff in wireless battlefield networks using local and remote LFAPs*. MILCOM 2007.

Jennings, B., van der Meer, S., Balasubramaniam, S., Botvich, D., Foghlu, M. O., Donnelly, W., & Strassner, J. (2007). Towards autonomic management of communications networks. *IEEE Communications Magazine*, *45*, 112–121. doi:10.1109/MCOM.2007.4342833

Katz, D., Kompella, K., & Yeung, D. (2003). *Traffic engineering (TE) extensions to OSPF version 2*. RFC 3630.

Katz, D., & Ward, D. (2010). *Bidirectional forwarding detection*. Internet Draft.

Khanna, A., & Zinky, J. (1989). The revised ARPANET routing metric. *SIGCOMM Comput. Commun. Rev.*, *19*(4), 45–56. doi:10.1145/75247.75252

Kompella, K., & Rekhter, Y. (2005). *OSPF extensions in support of generalized multi-protocol label switching (GMPLS)*. RFC 4203.

Levchenko, K., Voelker, G. M., Paturi, R., & Savage, S. (2008). XL: An efficient network routing algorithm. *SIGCOMM Comput. Commun. Rev.*, *38*(4), 15–26. doi:10.1145/1402946.1402962

Li, Y., Gujrati, P., Lan, Z., & Sun, X. (2007). Fault-driven re-scheduling for improving system-level fault resilience. In the *Proceedings of International Conference on Parallel Processing, ICPP '07*, (p. 39).

Liakopoulos, A., Zafeiropoulos, A., Polyrakis, A., Grammatikou, M., González, J. M., Wódczak, M., & Chaparadza, R. (2008). *Monitoring issues for autonomic networks: The EFIPSANS vision*. European Workshop on Mechanisms for the Future Internet 2008.

Mortier, R., & Kiciman, E. (2006). Autonomic network management: Some pragmatic considerations. In *INM '06: Proceedings of the 2006 SIGCOMM workshop on Internet network management*, (pp. 89–93). New York, NY: ACM.

Moy, J. (1998). *OSPF version 2*. RFC 2328.

Oran, D. (1990). *OSI IS-IS intra-domain routing protocol*. RFC 1142.

Pei, G., Gerla, M., & Chen, T. W. (2000). Fisheye state routing: A routing scheme for ad hoc wireless networks. In *Proceedings of ICC 2000*, New Orleans, LA.

Pentikousis, K., Meirosu, C., Miron, A., & Brunner, M. (2009). Self-management for a network of information. In *Proc. IEEE International Conference on Communication (ICC) Workshops*, Dresden, Germany, (pp. 1-5).

Raymer, D., Meer, S. v., & Strassner, J. (2008). From autonomic computing to autonomic networking: An architectural perspective. In *Proceedings of the Fifth IEEE Workshop on Engineering of Autonomic and Autonomous Systems*.

Retana, A., Nguyen, L., White, R., Zinin, A., & McPherson, D. (2001). *OSPF stub router advertisement*. RFC 3137.

Rétvári, G., Bíró, J. J., & Cinkler, T. (2007). On shortest path representation. *IEEE/ACM Transactions on Networking, 15*(6), 1293–1306. doi:10.1109/TNET.2007.900708

Rétvári, G., Németh, F., Chaparadza, R., & Szabó, R. (2009). OSPF for implementing self-adaptive routing in autonomic networks: A case study. *Modelling Autonomic Communications Environments. Lecture Notes in Computer Science, 5844,* 72–85. doi:10.1007/978-3-642-05006-0_6

Scott, J., Hui, P., Crowcroft, J., & Diot, C. (2006). Haggle: A networking architecture designed around mobile users. In *Proceedings of The Third Annual IFIP Conference on Wireless On-demand Network Systems and Services* (WONS 2006), Les Menuires, France.

Shand, M., & Bryant, S. (2010). *IP fast reroute framework*. RFC 5714.

Siekkinen, M., Goebel, V., Plagemann, T., Skevik, K.-A., Banfield, M., & Brusic, I. (2007). Beyond the future Internet - Requirements of autonomic networking architectures to address long term future networking challenges. In *11th IEEE International Workshop on Future Trends of Distributed Computing Systems* (FTDCS'07), (pp. 89-98).

Sterritt, R. (2005). Autonomic computing. *Innovations in Systems and Software Engineering, 1*(1), 79–88. doi:10.1007/s11334-005-0001-5

Sterritt, R., Parashar, M., Tianfield, H., & Unland, R. (2005). A concise introduction to autonomic computing. *Advanced Engineering Informatics, 19*(3), 181–187. doi:10.1016/j.aei.2005.05.012

Strassner, J. C., Agoulmine, N., & Lehtihet, E. (2006). *FOCALE – A novel autonomic networking architecture*. In Latin American Autonomic Computing Symposium (LAACS), Campo Grande, MS, Brazil.

Suzuki, J., & Suda, T. (2005). A middleware platform for a biologically inspired network architecture supporting autonomous and adaptive applications. *IEEE Journal on Selected Areas in Communications, 23*(2), 249–260. doi:10.1109/JSAC.2004.839388

Teixeira, R., Shaikh, A., Griffin, T., & Rexford, J. (2004). Dynamics of hot-potato routing in IP networks. *SIGMETRICS Perform. Eval. Rev., 32*(1), 307–319. doi:10.1145/1012888.1005723

Thorup, M. (2003). *OSPF areas considered harmful*. Internet Draft.

Tianfield, H. (2003). Multi-agent based autonomic architecture for network management. In *Proceedings of IEEE International Conference on Industrial Informatics,* INDIN 2003, (pp. 462-469).

Tizghadam, A., & Leon-Garcia, A. (2008). AORTA: Autonomic network control and management system. In *IEEE Conference on Computer Communications Workshops*, INFOCOM, (pp. 1-4).

Tizghadam, A., & Leon-Garcia, A. (2010). Autonomic traffic engineering for network robustness. *IEEE Journal on Selected Areas in Communications, 28*(1), 39–50. doi:10.1109/JSAC.2010.100105

Villamizar, C. (1999). *OSPF optimized multipath (OSPF-OMP)*. Internet Draft.

Wang, J., & Nelakuditi, S. (2007). *IP fast reroute with failure inferencing*. INM'07, Kyoto, Japan.

Wódczak, M. (2007). *Extended REACT – Routing information enhanced algorithm for cooperative transmission*. IST Mobile and Wireless Communications Summit 2007.

Wódczak, M. (2008). *Cooperative relaying in an indoor environment*. ICT Mobile Summit 2008.

XORP. (n.d.). *The eXtensible open source router platform (XORP) Project*. Retrieved from http://xorp.org

Zinin, A. (2005). *Analysis and minimization of microloops in link-state routing protocols.* Internet Draft.

ADDITIONAL READING

Babaoglu, O., Canright, G., Deutsch, A., Caro, G. A., Ducatelle, F., & Gambardella, L. M. (2006). Design patterns from biology for distributed computing. *ACM Trans. Auton. Adapt. Syst.*, *1*(1), 26–66. doi:10.1145/1152934.1152937

Boutaba, R., Martin-Flatin, J.P., Hellerstein, J.L., Katz, R.H., Pavlou, G., Chin-Tau Lea. (2010). Recent advances in autonomic communications, special issue of the IEEE Journal on Selected Areas in Communications, vol. 28, no. 1, pp. 1-3.

Dobson, S., Denazis, S., Fernandez, A., Gati, D., Gelenbe, E., & Massacci, F. (2006). A survey of autonomic communications [TAAS]. *ACM Transactions on Autonomous and Adaptive Systems*, *1*(2), 223–259. doi:10.1145/1186778.1186782

Gjoka, M., Ram, V., and Yang, X. (2007). Evaluation of IP Fast Reroute Proposals, in IEEE/Create-Net/ICST COMSWARE 2007.

Raj, A., & Ibe, O. C. (2007). A survey of IP and multiprotocol label switching fast reroute schemes. *Elsevier Computer Networks*, *51*(8), 1882–1907. doi:10.1016/j.comnet.2006.09.010

Tcholtchev, N., Grajzer, M., and Vidalenc, B. (2009). Towards a Unified Architecture for Resilience, Survivability and Autonomic Fault-Management for Self-Managing Networks, Mona workshop 2009.

KEY TERMS AND DEFINITIONS

Autonomic Behavior: An action of the decision element in an attempt to regulate the behavior of the managed entity associated with it, in order to realize some self-* function.

Autonomic Network: A network that autonomously responds to external and internal events affecting the reliable and effective operation of it, in a way as to achieve some defined network goals.

Control Loop: A reactive feedback process, in the course of which a decision-making-logic observes the state and drives the behavior of some physical or abstract network resource according to pre-defined policies.

Decision Element: An autonomic manager component implementing the decision-making-logic that drives a control loop over the management interfaces of its associated managed entities.

Decision Plane: The collection of all decision elements deployed in the network, collectively representing the network-wide decision-making intelligence driving the network's overall behavior.

Managed Entity: A physical network resource or abstract network function, like routing, forwarding, etc., or a lower-level decision element, being managed through a control loop.

Chapter 12
Network–Aided Session Management for Adaptive Context–Aware Multiparty Communications

Josephina Antoniou
University of Cyprus, Cyprus

Christophoros Christophorou
University of Cyprus, Cyprus

Jose Simoes
Fraunhofer FOKUS, Germany

Andreas Pitsillides
University of Cyprus, Cyprus

ABSTRACT

Recent years, from about the early 2000s, have been characterized by global broadband penetration, Fixed-Mobile-Convergence, Triple Play, and content provisioning over All-IP multimedia networks. Increasing demands in group-based multimedia sessions and market forces are fuelling the design of the future Internet, which is expected to fundamentally change the networking landscape in the upcoming years. Context, understood as sensed information that changes over time, has already led, to some extent, to service adaptation in terms of recognizing and using simple context, e.g. location. Context may also include network or personal state, location, or weather. To allow for session adaptation, it is important to use network and user context to enhance the existing service, keeping the user satisfied throughout the session.

DOI: 10.4018/978-1-60960-845-3.ch012

INTRODUCTION

The current chapter addresses enhanced Session Management (SM) for multiparty communications, i.e. how to setup and modify a multi-party session that may respond to context changes and adapt to satisfy the users of a service group. By using the users' situation information, i.e. environment and network context, the chapter plans to illustrate ways to provide more accurate sessions for mobile communities. An evolved SM functional entity, aided by the network, can support the establishment of context-aware multiparty sessions in a heterogeneous environment in an efficient way. Works of the authors that have led to the current chapter include (Antoniou et al., 2009; Antoniou et al., 2009b; Antoniou et al., 2009c; Simoes et al., 2009) performed within and supported by the ICT-funded C-CAST (C-CAST, 2008) project. The chapter ends with the methodology stemming from this work representing a practical framework that can be used to investigate similar research objectives, and lists adaptations that may be achieved from this methodology.

Session Management and Multiparty Communications

In terms of group-based sessions, efficiency of session setup and session modification requires a correct definition of user groups. Nowadays, it is common to cross areas where there exists overlapping of different network access technologies, such as Wi-Fi, 3G and WiMax. The efficiency of the grouping operation (creation of a set of users to receive a given session) may depend on parameters, such as access technology, since for instance, 3G networks have lower bandwidth capabilities than Wi-Fi and WiMax networks. Thus, sub-grouping could be performed and the same service session could be delivered with different throughput (e.g., using different *codings* of

the same content) to adapt to the current network capabilities. In addition to network traffic, other types of context should also be used to improve sub-grouping, such as noise, terminal location and speed, user's priority and network preferences, user's terminal capabilities, quality of received signal etc.

SM manages all the user-to-content and content-to-user relationships. In fact, it provides the necessary signalling to deliver content to its consumers, handling different types of events, specifically: session initiation, modification, termination and mobility. SM thus participates in dynamic changes, e.g. switching between different content for the same group of users because of new quality constraints. Since SM is closely interlinked with media delivery, it is responsible to ensure that content is delivered to its customer and is thus, appropriate to handle the coupling of context-awareness and multiparty communications.

There are two key issues that must be considered for achieving context-aware, adaptive multiparty communications: (a) Context-to-content matching and, (b) Session handling based on context information. We consider issue (a) to be out of scope for the current chapter, which concentrates on (b), the session enhancement. In addition, the chapter plans to address enhanced SM so that its key functionality is to motivate the creation of user subgroups, i.e. subsets of the same content group based on network, user and environment context to the extent that these are necessary for efficiency. A new session may adapt to the context of the user and the environment as well as to the context of the network. For the last adaptation, SM is aided by the network itself, which handles the selection of the best access network (when more than one access networks are available) for a particular user service request, based on dynamically collected network information.

Context Awareness

Sensor networks opened the doors to a world where everything is sensed. There are sensors for movement, temperature, etc. The information made available by the sensors allows building efficient, context-aware systems. There is already a link between context and mobile systems. Many services utilize user context to deliver accurate information to the end-users, e.g. location based services. An important use of context information is that it allows the creation of communities that are looking for the same information, making them appropriate candidates for the use of multicasting. The work carried out in (Aguiar & Gomes, 2008) addresses the impact of context, sensors and wireless networks in the telecommunications field. Several scenarios are proposed highlighting the possible synergies between the defined areas.

Context-aware, personalized sessions can be influenced by varying context, allowing users access sessions based on their location, preferences, profile and capabilities (Sigrid et al., 2000). The authors of (Kwon et al., 2006) propose a Point-to-Multipoint SM scheme using Session Initiation Protocol (SIP) in MPLS-based Next Generation Network service stratum. This scheme is simple and flexible to join, modify, and leave session for NGN multicast service. Article (Dong & Newmarch, 2005) proposes and develops a new mechanism that supports Web services SM by using SIP. This means adding session information in the SOAP header element and using SIP to manage the session state for Web services.

So far, SM has been autonomous and well separated from context, even for sessions carrying context-aware services. Certainly, SM has not been using context information for improving the connections of the multiparty sessions. Thus, an enhanced SM that supports the initiation, modification, termination and mobility of adaptive, context-aware multiparty sessions in a heterogeneous environment is needed. The chapter addresses an enhanced SM, which can select

the appropriate media coding for a set of users according to the particular quality they support, or use environment noise measures to increase or decrease the audio quality.

Furthermore, in next generation networks, where multiple access networks coexist, access network selection using context-based algorithms is necessary to enable the optimization of both terminal and network (Jesus et al., 2008). Although many proposals base the decision process on radio signal properties (e.g. [Pavlahan et al., 2000]), this is only one of the many criteria in such selection schemes. Some proposals suggest context-aware decisions (Jesus et al., 2008). Moreover, the majority of related work focuses entirely on network selection algorithms, not concerning other important mechanisms crucial to support the decisions e.g. QoS management, to enable the complete network re-configuration triggered by context. This lack of high-level perspective is addressed in more recent proposals, (Chen & Yang, 2007). We consider the support of context-aware selection to aid the context-aware, multiparty SM in this chapter, where the group membership is a main issue, but being flexible enough to support any parameter envisioned.

Media Adaptation

The technological advances and market developments in the wireless communications area during the last years led to the 4th Generation (4G) Networks which encompasses network heterogeneity. In a wireless heterogeneous network, a plethora of different Radio Access Technologies (RATs) will have to co-exist, overlap and be inter-connected in an all-IP framework and many Internet appliances such as handheld computers, personal digital assistants (PDAs) and smart phones will emerge as pervasive computing devices. In a pervasive computing environment, people can take their pervasive devices anywhere, using them in various environments to access information and perform different tasks without the constraints of time and location. As users are beginning to rely more heavily on pervasive devices, the way information is used and accessed will soon revolutionized, enabling low-cost and ubiquitous access to Internet content and services. However, before we can take full advantage of these devices, there are many technical problems that need to be resolved.

Most multimedia web content was designed and organized with desktop computers and high-speed network networks in mind. They usually contain rich media data such as images, audio, and video, which are not suitable for those pervasive devices with limited display capability, process power and network bandwidth. As a result, Internet access is still constrained on these devices, and users frequently experience frustration when their devices are unable to handle certain media types or the data takes a long time to download in small-bandwidth networks such as GPRS. Therefore, in order to provide service to users with pervasive devices, the quality of the media presentation and the delivery scheme often needs to be adjusted according to the network bandwidth and the capabilities of those devices.

Furthermore, the growing plenitude of multimedia information also calls for personalization of the multimedia presentation according to the user's individual preference. Context-based media adaptation technology is mainly concerned with selecting different qualities of single media types or selecting different media types, and then delivering information to different context, such as location, device capability, network bandwidth, user preference, etc. With media adaptation technology, multimedia information can be filtered, transformed, converted or reformed to make it universally accessible by different devices, and to provide personalized content to different users. Ideally, pervasive devices could transparently adapt to the environment and their user's preference, providing adapted information and services to their users.

In order to increase accessibility of multimedia information, many media processing techniques can be used to enable media adaptation. Several existing systems apply image-processing techniques to adapt the embedded images of a web page according to client display. Some other techniques, such as text summarization, video-to-image transformation, are applied in some multimedia applications. Based on different standards and perspectives, there are a lot of techniques that can be used for media adaptation (Lei & Georganas, 2001). Some of these techniques are briefly described below.

Media Adaptation Based on the Target Context

Media adaptation to technical infrastructure: Technical infrastructure includes device capabilities and network connections. Current pervasive devices vary widely in their features such as screen size, resolution and colour depth, computing power, storage and software. They also use a variety of network connections range from cable to wireless, with different effective bandwidth and network latency. Media adaptation technology should be able to provide an appropriate presentation to different devices. For example, in order to display images on devices with a small screen and limited display capability, reducing the size or resolution for each image will help to fit the image on the small screens of devices.

Media adaptation to user preferences (based on the target context): For a specific multimedia presentation, individual users may have different requirements on the level of details or some other parameters. For example, given a medical tele-learning system, both a professor and a student are interested in a surgery, but the professor wants to get the in-depth multimedia material for his lecture, while the student only needs an abstraction of the same material to pass the upcoming exam.

Media Adaptation According to When Different Media Alternatives are Created

Static adaptation: At authoring time, multimedia formation is pre-processed and stored in multiple versions that differ in quality and processing requirements. At presentation time, the appropriate version will be selected at run-time depending on the user's context. In order to eliminate extra processing overhead at presentation time, most current web sites create multiple versions of information at authoring time. However, the drawback of this technique is high consumption of disc space that cannot be possible in every case.

Dynamic adaptation: Multimedia information is processed and delivered on the fly. The available alternatives are determined for the specific context at presentation time. For example, when network bandwidth is not enough, we can drop less important data and give a summarization of the multimedia presentation. As we have mentioned before, the diversity of devices and network connections will make it difficult and expensive to create multimedia content separately for each individual type of device at authoring time. Moreover, the nature of network connections is not always known at authoring time. Therefore, technologies that can dynamically adapt multimedia information to diverse client devices and network connections will become critical. More recently, scalable video coding (SVC) is being developed. With this technique, encoding rate can change dynamically according to network condition.

Media Adaptation According to the Media Types Involved in the Adaptation

Single media element adaptation: A lot of current best-effort adaptation techniques are considered with switching between different qualities or formats of single media elements. For example, most images can be significantly compressed without an appreciable decrease in quality. GIF-to-JPEG or color-to-grayscale transformations could be able to simply reduce the physical size of an image.

Cross-media adaptation: Single media element adaptation is limited to an inherent lower bound, i.e., the lowest acceptable technical quality of the respective media type (Boll et al., 1999). Cross-media adaptation is the process of transforming the content from one media type to another so that the content can be processed by a particular device. For instance, most handheld computers are not capable of handling video data due to their hardware and software constraints. Transforming video into sets of images and extracting audio or caption will enable the devices to access the information contained in the video. In this case, users will be able to receive useful information in whatever form their devices can handle.

Media Adaptation According to the Abstract Presentation Level

Semantic Adaptation: In principle, semantic adaptation is a selective process. Based on available and requested information, multiple pieces of information are combined into a complete presentation. Semantic adaptation is affected by the semantic structure of a presentation, which determines the relative data in the final presentation. For example, most current e-commerce web sites usually contain many images of banners, logos, and advertisements. These data often consume a good deal of network bandwidth, and are redundant or not of interest to a user. If we can define the semantic structure of the web page at authoring time, and then generate a new version of web page by removing redundant objects, the efficiency of information delivery will be improved.

Physical adaptation: Physical adaptation of media is defined as the combination of conversion, scaling and distillation processes guided by the characteristic of media format and physical QoS.

ADAPTIVE CONTEXT-AWARE SESSIONS

The convergence of different RATs in 4G networks, created an environment where the Network Operators need to manage the resources of different RATs simultaneously and provide to the end users independence and flexibility with the possibility to connect to the "best" point of attachment anytime, anywhere and anyhow. Moreover, most multimedia web content currently used contains rich media data such as images, audio, and video, which are sometimes not suitable for those pervasive devices with limited display capability, process power and network bandwidth.

As a result, Internet access is still constrained on these devices, and users frequently experience frustration when their devices are unable to handle certain media types or the data takes a long time to download in small-bandwidth networks such as GPRS. Therefore, in order to provide service to users with pervasive devices moving within a heterogeneous network environment, the quality of the media presentation (i.e. the content coding) and the radio access technology (i.e. WiMAX, WiFi, UMTS, etc.) used to provide this content often needs to be adjusted according to the current network conditions (i.e. available network bandwidth, etc.) and the capabilities of those devices matched with the available content coding for a particular service group.

In the sections that follow, we deal with this issue and describe an algorithm that provides both at session setup and also during the session, efficient RAT and content coding selection functionality, for the users receiving a multicast service. The algorithm describes how the network aids the enhanced SM for a multiparty communication, since the sub-dividing of a user service group so that it is best supported by different access networks is translated at the session levels into different multiparty sessions, and hence different content flows to the service subgroups.

Network-Aided Session Setup

At the Session Level

The context-awareness in the SM entity comes from the recognition of context as triggers or the capability to receive any context requested, e.g. for initiating a context-aware session. Therefore, the SM entity has functionalities based on interfaces with other system functional entities, necessary to enable this awareness of context information:

Primarily, the SM needs to interact with the entity responsible for identifying the service groups, i.e. the groups of users that will receive the same content. Through this interface the SM must receive identification for the service group, together with separate identifications for the individual users that comprise the particular group. Consequently, the SM must be able to interact with the entity responsible for Content Processing and Delivery. The SM sends the group identification received in the step described above, to the Content Processing and Delivery entity, and the identification is used by this entity to collect some general content information for the group e.g. whether the content that will be received by the particular group is video or audio, as well as some more specific information, e.g. the coding(s) and bitrate(s) in which the particular content is available. Thus, the SM entity acquires descriptive information on the content that will be transmitted to the group.

Once the content description has been acquired, the SM needs to check which of the available content codings the users are capable (device context) and willing (user context) to support. Device and User context information is collected at a broker system entity, i.e. an entity in the converged architecture that accumulates all context information received from various context producing entities (for instance the user terminals in this case). The Context Broker entity contains the required device and user context, therefore the SM entity requests for each user in the service group its capabilities and preferences, including coding options supported/preferred by the user device (e.g. resolution, coding options supported). Once this particular context information is obtained per user, the SM entity can match the content codings/formats in which the content is available, i.e. received from the Content Processing and Delivery (CtPD) entity, to the content codings/formats that each of the group users is capable or willing to support. This matching will results in a list of particular content codings per each user, which may be viewed as an initial refinement of the original service group to sub-groups of users according to the supported content. This is the first step of the sub-grouping process. The sub-grouping will continue in the network where further refinements will additionally consider network and environment context (e.g. current QoS capabilities based on user location and current network load).

The sub-grouping is initiated in the SM entity but is further refined and concluded in the Network Management (NM) entity, since network and environment context are more appropriately collected at that system level. Consequently, the SM entity must support interface functionality to exchange information with the NM entity. Over this interface the SM entity will send the list of users and their supported content codings (once the matching of content availabilities and content capabilities is performed), and will receive the finalized context-based sub-grouping of the original service group by which only one content coding will be selected for each user in the original service group. This will enable a context-aware session for each multicast sub-group to be setup. Furthermore, in the case that context changes at any level, the session is modified accordingly, since the system allows the context information to be propagated through to the content. Session Modification is further explored in the next section.

Figure 1 illustrates the above/described session setup procedure through appropriate signal flows. In this illustration the SM entity is separated into two functional modules: The SM Enabler (SME)

and the Session Use Management (SUM). In terms of functionality the SME is the SM functional module that accepts context information through requests or triggers and responds by creating/modifying/terminating the sub-group sessions. In other words, it handles the interfaces between the SME and the entity providing the identification of the original service groups, the entity responsible for matching a group context to the appropriate content, the SME and NM, the entity that knows the network, the SME and the Context Broker entity, where all context information subsides, as well as the SME and CtPD, the content processing and delivery entity. Finally, the SME needs to interact with the SUM, which is the sub-module responsible for handling the SIP-specific tasks of the Session Manager, such as inviting the users and the Media Delivery Function to sessions. Once the Core Entity of the SME determines the matching between available content formats and user capabilities in terms of supporting content formats, resulting in candidate files per user in the service group, SUM takes over, which is responsible of first inviting the users to a session and to invite the CtPD to deliver the content to these users.

At the Network Level

The current section focuses on the network role during session setup and especially the algorithm, which is responsible for selecting the access network to assign each of the service group users. Intelligence and context-awareness are integrated in this algorithm to facilitate it to be autonomous, self-adaptable and self-controlled. By considering the instantaneous users' and network's context, the intelligence integrated in the algorithm predicts trends in users' and network's behaviour and dynamically adapts its operations to any situation, aiming to provide the end users with seamless service continuity and best possible QoS while at the same time achieve efficient network capacity and performance. The algorithm will be imple-

Figure 1. Session management related messages in session initiation

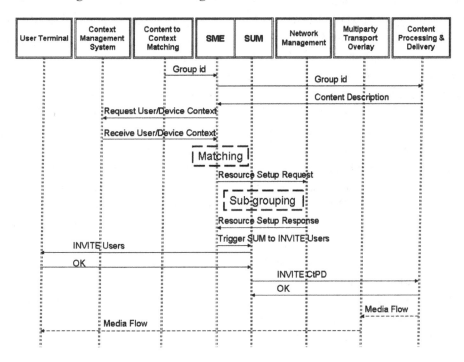

mented in the Network Interface Selection (NIS) component and run in the Core Network of the Network Operator. The algorithm is summarized in Figure 2.

Upon a trigger is received (Start 1), NIS acquires and stores in the SQL Database (2) all the necessary context information related to the users that belong to the service group (i.e. Current con-

Figure 2. RAT and content coding selection process

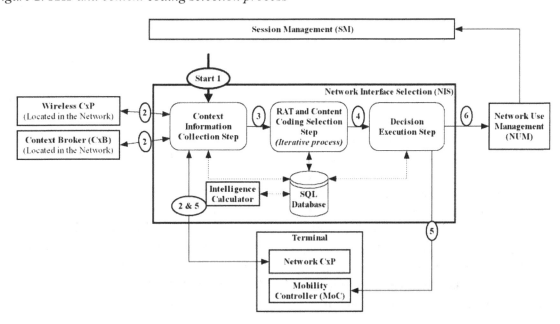

nection, RATs within reach, signal strength received, speed, etc. – this context is retrieved from the Terminal through the Network Context Provider (CxP) and also through the Context Broker located in the Network) and the network (i.e. available capacity and current load in the RATs, QoS that can currently be supported by the RATs, etc – this context is retrieved from the Wireless CxP). Then, based on the instantaneous context received, an iterative process is followed (3), in which different transmission combinations (i.e. different possible ways of which RAT will support which group of users and which content coding they will receive) that can be used for the multicast service provision are formed and the capacity requirements of each is estimated. The transmission combination that best serves all the users with the required QoS, obeys all the rules defined by the Intelligence Calculator and uses the least amount of heterogeneous radio resources, is selected and executed (4). The rules referred above are dynamically generated, by using some intelligence, and aim to facilitate a decision that will eliminate any possibility for undesirable events, that can influence the network performance (like congestion, overloading, etc.) or the quality experienced by the users (i.e. call drop, QoS degradation, etc.), to occur. Once the final decision is made, the users' Terminals are informed (through the Mobility Controller) about the selected interface (5). The Terminals activate the selected interface (i.e. WiFi, UMTS, WiMAX), connects to the selected RAT and receive an IP Address. This IP Address is reported back to NIS through the Network CxP. Once all users' Terminals are activated and connected to the selected interface and an IP address for them is allocated, NIS reports its decision along with the IP Addresses of the users, to the Network Use Management (NUM) module, in order to establish the multicast paths and reserve the required resources. Finally NUM, triggers the SM in order to establish the sessions.

Throughout the description of the algorithm, we use some terms such as "candidate" RAT,

"capable" RAT and Common Radio Resource Units. These terms are explained next.

"Candidate" RAT

Sometimes, even if the RAT is within the Terminal's reach, this does not necessarily mean that it can serve the user at that specific time with the required QoS (cannot be considered at that specific time as "candidate"); the RAT's received channel quality may not be adequate at that specific time (i.e. the signal is not strong enough), in order for the Terminal to decode the signal correctly. The channel quality of a RAT can be estimated by the Terminals by having the RAT's pilot channel as a channel quality estimation reference. Having this as a reference, the RAT will be considered as "candidate" if:

RAT's pilot channel quality received > minimum pilot channel quality required + (C x pilot channel quality alteration rate)

The minimum pilot channel quality required (measured in dB) defines the minimum RAT's pilot channel quality that should be received by the Terminal for guaranteeing a reliable reception of the content with the required QoS. On the other hand, the C x pilot channel quality alteration rate is used as a Safety Margin in order to accommodate the mobility of the Terminals within the network and avoid any QoS degradation and frequent vertical handovers by guaranteeing that the channel quality of this RAT will still be adequate for a period of at least C seconds. The value of time C defines the time required in order to reliably switch a Terminal from one RAT to another (i.e. execute a vertical handover) plus a period of time that the Terminal must stay connected with the RAT before triggering another handover. The value of the aforementioned parameters will be estimated by the Network Operator during the Radio Network Planning and provided to the algorithm upon a request.

On the other hand, the pilot channel quality alteration rate experienced by the Terminal, will be estimated by the Terminal during its mobility, by considering the previous and the instantaneous pilot channel quality measurements, and reported to the algorithm upon a request. This value indicates how quickly (in dB/sec) the channel quality experienced from the RAT degrades or improves during the user's mobility. In order to avoid any inefficiency due to pilot channel measurement errors, it is important to apply filtering on the measurements to average out the effect of fast fading. Appropriate filtering can increase the performance significantly. As long filtering periods can cause a delay in the handover procedure, the length of the filtering period has to be chosen as a trade-off between measurement accuracy and this delay. Also, the speed of the user matters. The slower the user is moving the harder it is to average out the effects of fast fading. Often a filtering period of 200 ms is chosen.

"Capable" RAT

Note that even if the RAT has been identified as "candidate" this does not necessarily mean that it is "capable" to provide the service to the user with the requested QoS. For example the QoS (i.e. bid rate, delay guarantees, etc.) that can currently be supported by the RAT might not be adequate to support the QoS requirements of the service, or the available capacity is not enough to support the user. Also the RAT might be overloaded, or predicted to be congested if a connection with it is established. Also the speed of the user matters; i.e. WiFi cannot support vehicular speeds. Thus, factors like the aforementioned must be considered by the algorithm in order to indicate which of the "candidate" RATs are also "capable" to support the service.

Common Radio Resource Units (Common RRUs)

A Radio Resource Unit (RRU) can be defined by the set of basic physical transmission parameters necessary to support a signal waveform transporting end user information corresponding to a reference service. These physical transmission parameters depend on the multiple access technique being used. For example in FDMA (Frequency Division Multiple Access), a RRU is equivalent to a certain bandwidth within a given carrier frequency while in TDMA (Time Division Multiple Access), a RRU is equivalent to a pair of a carrier frequency and a time slot. Then again, in CDMA (Code Division Multiple Access), a RRU is defined by a carrier frequency, a code sequence and a power level. Consequently, if we transmit the same content in different RATs, different amount of RRUs will be allocated for each RAT. However, the "price" of these RRUs is not necessarily the same. For example, assuming that "K" amount of RRUs are required to transmit the content in WiFi (RRUWiFi) and "L" amount of RRUs are require to transmit the same content in UMTS (RRUUMTS), even if "K" is greater (>) than "L" this does not necessarily mean that it is also considered to be more "expensive"; i.e. the "price" of one (1) RRUWiFi might be considered by the Network Operator equal to 1/5 of the RRU-UMTS "price". Also another factor that can further influence the actual RRU "price" is the current conditions of the RAT. For example, weights can be used during the estimation of RRUs' "price" that will further adjust the their "price" based for example on the current load and available capacity in the RAT, current load and available radio resources in the Cells/Access Points attached to the RAT, etc. (e.g. the RRUs' "price" of overloaded RATs will become more "expensive"). Therefore, a function must be defined that will consider all the aforementioned and express the RRUs of each RAT into a common metric (referred as Common RRUs) in order to have the same metric for comparison. Note that through time the "price" of the RRUs will be dynamically adjusted according to the current network conditions. This function will be defined by the Network Operator itself and provided to the NIS component.

Before the multicast session starts, SM triggers NIS component for session setup, by sending to it a "Group Session Setup request" message. The information that can be included (but not limited to) in the "Group Session Initiation request" message are:

- **RequestID:** The identification of the specific request – i.e. "Group Session Setup request"
- **ContentID:** The ID of the particular content indented for the service group
- **List of Content codings:** List of content codings available for this ContentID. For each content coding the following info is provided:
  ○ *Content Coding ID*
    ▪ Bit Rate of the content
    ▪ Delay Requirements
    ▪ Jitter Delay Requirements
    ▪ Loss requirements
- **List of Users:** List of the users that belong to the service group. For each user included in the list, the following info is provided:
  ○ *UserID:* The identification of the user
  ○ *List of Content Codings* that the user's Terminal can support:
    ▪ Content Coding ID 1
    ▪ Content Coding ID 2
    ▪ …..

Once the request is received, the algorithm is executed in three steps:

1. *Context Information Collection step:* During this step all the necessary users' and network's context information is collected and stored in the SQL Database.

2. *RAT and Content Coding Decision step:* During this step, by using an iterative process, the transmission combination (i.e. the RAT that will serve each user and the content coding that each user will receive) that will used for the multicast service provision is selected. The aim here to select a transmission combination that provides with the least amount of radio resources required the best possible QoS to the users and enhances the overall network performance.

3. *Decision Execution Step:* This step includes all the activities and signalling required for the, transmission combination selected, during the *RAT and Content Coding Decision step*, to be adopted.

Context Information Collection Step

Upon a trigger for Group Session Setup request is received by NIS, a table is created in the SQL Database in which all the information related to the Content and the instantaneous context of the users that belong to the service group, will be stored. We will refer to this table as Users Context Information Table (UCIT) and will be uniquely identified having as a key the ContentID of the particular content. The UCIT along with the information that can be included (and not limited to) is shown in Figure 3. All the information included in the request will be extracted and stored in the UCIT.

For each coding available for this ContentID, one column will be created in the UCIT and mapped with its Content Coding ID (i.e. one subgroup is created for each coding available for this Content ID). Then, for each user that belongs to the service group (i.e. these users are included in the "List of Users" of the session setup request), the NIS creates a record for him in the column mapped to the highest content coding quality their Terminal is capable to support (since one of the aims of our algorithm is to serve the user with the best possible QoS). Note that these subgroups are the "initial" and not the "final" one. The "final"

Figure 3. User context information table (UCIT)

ContentID (Identifying the service group that this table is created for)			
All Content Codings that the content intended to this service group can be made available			
Content Coding ID 1 - Bit Rate of the content (i.e. 128 Kbits/sec) - Delay Requirements - Jitter Delay Requirements - Loss requirements	*Content Coding ID 2* - Bit Rate of the content (i.e. 64 Kbits/sec) - Delay Requirements - Jitter Delay Requirements - Loss requirements	*Content Coding ID 3* - Bit Rate of the content (i.e. 32 Kbits/sec) - Delay Requirements - Jitter Delay Requirements - Loss requirements	...
One column for each Content Coding available for this ContentID (i.e. one Subgroup for each Content Coding ID)			
Content Coding ID 1 *One Record for each user that belongs to this Subgroup*	*Content Coding ID 2* *One Record for each user that belongs to this Subgroup*	*Content Coding ID 3* *One Record for each user that belongs to this Subgroup*	

One Record for each user that belongs to this Subgroup					
UserID 1					UserID 2
Content Codings that can be supported (based on its Terminal capabilities)					
Content Coding ID 1		*Content Coding ID 2*		......	
Speed					
Location					
Direction					
Current Connection					
IP Address	*Type of RAT*	*RAT ID*	*Cell ID/Access Point ID*	*Time of connection establishment/modification*	
RATs within reach					
RAT ID 1 *Type of RAT 1* *Cell ID/Access Point ID* *Pilot Channel quality received* *Pilot channel quality Alteration Rate experienced* *Amount of capacity (radio resources) required** *Additional Load Introduced in RAT and Cell/Access Point** *Common Radio Resource Units Required** *Capable? (YES or NO)**		*RAT ID 2* *Type of RAT 2* *Cell ID/Access Point 1 ID* *Pilot Channel quality received* *Pilot channel quality Alteration Rate experienced* *Amount of capacity (radio resources) required** *Additional Load Introduced in RAT and Cell/Access Point** *Common Radio Resource Units Required** *Capable? (YES or NO)**		....	...
RAT Selected * - Type of RAT - RAT ID - Cell ID/Access Point ID					
* Parameters that will be estimated during the RAT and Content Coding Decision Step					

subgroups will be formed during the RAT and Content Coding Decision step (see *RAT and Content Coding Decision Step* section), based on the instantaneous users' and network's context information and the rules defined by the Intelligence Calculator.

Once the "initial" subgroups are created (i.e. the users have been included to the subgroup mapped to the highest content quality their Terminal can receive), NIS acquires from the Context Broker (CxB) information concerning the Current Connection of the users (IP Addresses, Type of RAT, RAT ID and Cell ID/Access Point ID the users is currently connected to and the time this connection was established or last modified) and notifies them to report to it their instantaneous context.

Once a report is received, the NIS extracts the context information included and stores them in the related user's record in the UCIT. The report that the users will send to NIS can include (but not limited to) the following information:

- **RequestID:** The identification of the specific request – i.e. "Context Reporting"
- **UserID:** The identification of the user
- **ContentID:** The ID of the particular content that the user will receive
- **List of RATs:** List of the RATs within the Terminal's reach. For each RAT the following information will be included:
  - *Type of RAT:* i.e. WiFi, UMTS, WiMAX, etc

○ *RAT ID:* The identification of the RAT

○ *Cell ID/Access Point ID:* The identification of the Cell or Access Point through which the Terminal is connected to the RAT.

○ *Pilot channel quality received (dB)*

○ *Pilot channel quality alteration rate (dB/sec)*

• **Speed:** Speed of the Terminal – estimated using GPS

• **Current Location:** The current location of the Terminal – estimated using GPS

• **Direction:** Direction of the Terminal – estimated using GPS

Note that the Terminal might receive signal from more than one Cells or Access Points that belong to the same RAT. However, in order to simplify analysis and enhance comprehension we assume that the Terminal will report only the one with the stronger signal strength. Nevertheless, this algorithm with minor enhancements can be applied and work efficiently even if more than

one Cells/Access Points belonging to the same RAT are reported by the user.

Once the context information reported by the user are stored in the related user's record, for each RAT reported (i.e. included in the "List of RATs"), NIS creates in the SQL Database (if not already done), a table in which all the instantaneous context information related to the RAT and its attached Cells/Access Points will be stored. We will refer to this table as RAT Context Information Table (RATCIT). The structure of the RATCIT along with the information that can be included (but not limited to) is shown in Figure 4. The context information related to the RATs will be acquired from the Wireless CxP located in the Network. Note that all the RATCITs combined provides to NIS the instantaneous context of the network.

It is worth mentioning that during the session, all RATCITs will be updated continuously by the Wireless CxP, by reporting to NIS once a change occurs. Thus, the RATCITs will always provide to the NIS the instantaneous context of the network. Also, during the session, in order to address any variations on the users' context, the UCITs will

Figure 4. Radio access technology context information table (RATCIT)

RAT ID				
Type of RAT				
Capabilities of the RAT				
Maximum Terminal's speed supported	*Multicast Capable?*	*Maximum number of users that can be supported*	*Maximum throughput that can be supported*	*...*
QoS requirements that can be currently supported by this RAT				
Bit Rates that can be supported	*Delay guarantees*	*Jitter Delay guarantees*	*Packet loss guarantees*	
Current Load in the RAT				
Total Load allowed in the RAT (set by the Network Operator)				
List of rules that must be obeyed within this RAT				
List of all the Cells/Access Points that belong to this RAT				
Cell ID 1/Access Point ID 1		*Cell ID 2/ Access Point ID 2*		
Current Load				
Total Load Allowed in Cell (set by the Network Operator)			*...*	*...*
Available Capacity/Bandwidth				
List of rules that must be obeyed within this Cell/Access Point				

be updated either periodically or due to an event (i.e. if a rule defined by the Intelligence Calculator is violated and immediate actions for transmission combination adaptation is required), after a broadcast notification by the NIS to the users. However, the information previously included in the UCIT will not be deleted but instead will be time-stamped and moved to a History Context Storage Table (HCST), created in the SQL Database. The information included in the HCST will be used by the Intelligence Calculator for locating patterns that will facilitate it to predict trends to undesirable events (i.e. overloading, congestion, QoS degradation, call drops, etc., in certain RATs and Cells/Access Points) that is likely to occur in a short time and generate rules in order for these events to be avoided.

As illustrated in Figure 4, a list of rules is generated for each RAT and for each Cell/Access Point that belongs to the RAT. These rules are generated dynamically and updated continuously by the Intelligence Calculator during the session based on the instantaneous context information of the users and network's current conditions and the patterns located using the context information located in the HCST. These rules will facilitate NIS to select (at session initiation) or modify (during the session – see *Network-Aided Session Modification*) the transmission combination in such a way that any possibility for any undesirable event that can influence the network performance or the quality experienced by the users, to be eliminated. A simple scenario is the one that follows. By considering the instantaneous context of the users (i.e. location, direction, speed, ContentID and QoS of the content they are receiving, etc.) and their daily mobility pattern (extracted from the HCST), the Intelligence Calculator predicts that a great amount of users travelling in a train and belonging to the same service group will disembarked in the same station in a very short time and a connection with the UMTS cell that covers the station's area will be required. By considering the related RATCIT, the Intelligence

Calculator indicates that the capacity currently available in the cell is not enough to support all these users and also the current load in the UMTS network will not allow all of them to be admitted thus resulting in network's overloading and call drops, if measures are not taken immediately. Thus, once these trends are predicted, rules are immediately generated for the affected RAT and Cell (i.e. rules like reduce the load in the UMTS network less than 40%, ensure 20% of the Cell's capacity for the specific service group) and placed in the related RATCIT in the SQL Database. The NIS checks if the current conditions in the specific Cell and UMTS network violates these rules and, if yes, immediate actions are taken in order to settle the RAT's and Cell's current conditions to the rules defined.

Moreover, since more than one service groups can be established in the network, the available radio resources and the load permitted to be introduced in the RATs and Cells/Access Points must be shared among these service groups. Thus the Intelligence Calculator, through time, by considering the instantaneous context information included within all the UCITs and the RATCITs, dynamically shares the available amount of radio resources and permitted load, by generating rules that define the maximum amount of the available radio resources (i.e. capacity) that can be devoted and also the maximum load that can be introduced in each RAT and Cell/Access Point, for each service group.

The NIS, both at session setup and also continuously during the session, monitors the rules defined in the RATCITs and selects (at session setup) or modifies (during the session - by handover some users to another RAT or switch some users from higher content quality to lower content quality subgroups) the transmission combination in such a way that all the rules will be obeyed.

RAT and Content Coding Decision Step

As indicated in the previous section during the Context Information Collection step, "initial" subgroups are created based only on the users' Terminal capabilities (i.e. the users were included in the subgroup mapped to the highest content coding quality their Terminal can receive). The users' and network's context information as well as the rules defined by the Intelligent Calculator were ignored. Using these "initial" subgroups for the multicast service provision will likely lead to congestion, overloading, call drops etc., since the available capacity, the current load, current QoS capabilities of the RATs, the channel quality received by the users, the speed of the user and other parameters that play a vital role on the service provision efficiency, have not been considered. Therefore, within this step an iterative process will be performed in which all these parameters will be considered, aiming to select the transmission combination (i.e. form the final "subgroups and select the RAT that will serve each user) that will achieve the best possible QoS for the users, use as less radio resources as possible and obey all the rules defined by the Intelligence Calculator.

The steps and activities performed for selecting the transmission combination that will be used for the multicast service provision are described below.

Step 1: For each user included in each subgroup indicate its "capable" RATs

For each subgroup, created in the UCIT, in which at least one user is included, do the following:

Step 1.1: For each user included in the subgroup, indicate which of the RATs reported are capable to support the service with the required QoS:

   a.   Check if the RAT is considered as *"candidate"* to support the user, if the *speed of the user* can be supported by the RAT and if the *QoS* (i.e. bit rate, delay guarantees, loss guarantees, etc.) that can currently be supported by this

RAT, is adequate to support the QoS requirements of the content coding indented for the subgroup:

   i.   If not, reject this RAT and set it as "NOT capable"

   ii.   If yes, indicate this RAT as "likely capable" and estimate the *amount of radio resources required* and the *additional load that will be introduced* in the RAT and the Cell/Access Point, in case a connection (unicast) with it is established.

   b.   For each RAT indicated for the user as "likely capable", by considering the rules the Intelligence Calculator have defined in the related RATCIT concerning the *maximum amount of the available radio resources* that can be devoted and also the *maximum load* that can be introduced in each RAT and Cell/Access Point, for each service group, check if the *amount of radio resources required* is available in the RAT's Cell/Access Point and also if the *additional load* that will be introduced in the RAT and the Cell/Access Point keeps the total load of the RAT and the Cell/Access Point below the amount of load permitted for them.

   i.   If not, reject this RAT and set it as "NOT capable"

   ii.   If yes, set this RAT as "capable"

In case all the RATs reported by the user are rejected, then this user will be instantly moved to the subgroup mapped to the content coding with the next lower content coding quality the user's Terminal can support and the same procedure will be repeated until at least one "capable" RAT for this user is found. It is also important to note that some RATs that were considered in the previous iteration as "NOT capable" to support the user, now with lower QoS requirements, might be considered as "capable".

At the end of Step 1, the "capable" RATs of each user are identified and also subgroups are slightly modified. However, the RAT that will serve each user is not yet selected and also the subgroups created are not yet the final. An iterative process will follow, until the final decision of which RAT will support each user is made and also the "final" subgroups are formed.

Step 2: For each Subgroup, form all "possible" <User, RAT> combinations that can be used to provide the content to the users belonging to the subgroup.

For each subgroup created in the UCIT in which at least one user is included, do the following:

Step 2.1: By considering the *capable RATs* indicated for each user, form all "possible" <User, RAT> combinations (i.e. different combinations of which RAT will support which user) that can be used to provide the selected content coding to the users belonging to the subgroup. For each <User, RAT> combination estimate:

- The *total amount of radio resources required* in each Cell/Access Point

- The *additional load* that will be introduced in each RAT and Cell/Access Point

Figure 5 illustrated below, gives a simple example of how the "possible" <User, RAT> combinations are formed for a subgroup. For simplicity, in this example, we assume only 3 users (User 1, 2 and 3) included in Subgroup 1 and located in an area with three RATs overlapped; a WiFi, a UMTS and a WiMAX. The capable RATs assumed for each user are:

- **User 1:** WiFi, UMTS, WiMAX;
- **User 2:** UMTS;
- **User 3:** UMTS, WiMAX.

Based on this example, six possible <User, RAT> combinations are formed (see Figure 5).

Note that some RATs (i.e. UMTS using MBMS (Multimedia Broadcast Multicast Service) system) that are multicast capable can support the users within the cell, if considered more efficient, using common resources (i.e. by establishing a common channel that will be shared by all the users within the Cell/Access Point). Thus, during the estimation of the aforementioned values, in case the RAT is

Figure 5. Forming the "possible" <User, RAT> combinations

	RAT& Cell/Acc. P. / User	WiFi/Acc. P. ID	UMTS/Cell ID	WiMAX/Cell ID		
Possible <User, RAT> Comb. 1	1	X			Add. Load in RAT: WiFi: A%, UMTS:B%, WiMAX:0%	Acceptable? (YES or NO)
	2		X		Add. Load in Cell/Acc. P.: WiFi: C%, UMTS:D%, WiMAX: 0%	Common RRUs Required:
	3		X		Radio Res. Req. in Cell/Acc. P.: WiFi: E, UMTS: F, WiMAX: 0	WiFi: Q, UMTS: R, WiMAX: 0
Possible <User, RAT> Comb. 2	1		X		Add. Load in RAT: WiFi: 0%, UMTS: G%, WiMAX: 0%	Acceptable? (YES or NO)
	2		X		Add. Load in Cell/Acc. P: WiFi: 0%, UMTS: H%, WiMAX: 0%	Common RRU Required:
	3		X		Radio Res. Req. in Cell/Acc. P: WiFi: 0, UMTS: J, WiMAX: 0	WiFi: 0, UMTS: S, WiMAX: 0
Possible <User, RAT> Comb. 3	1			X	Add. Load in RAT: WiFi: 0%, UMTS: B%, WiMAX: T%	Acceptable? (YES or NO)
	2		X		Add. Load in Cell/Acc. P.: WiFi: 0%, UMTS: D%, WiMAX: U%	Common RRUs Required:
	3		X		Radio Res. Req. in Cell/Acc. P.: WiFi: 0, UMTS: F, WiMAX: V	WiFi: 0, UMTS: R, WiMAX: W
Possible <User, RAT> Comb. 4	1	X			...	...
	2		X			
	3			X		
Possible <User, RAT> Comb. 5	1		X		...	...
	2		X			
	3			X		
Possible <User, RAT> Comb. 6	1			X	...	...
	2		X			
	3			X		

multicast capable, the NIS first checks if the use of common resources in the specific Cell/Access Point is justified. Note that the channel selection criteria threshold (i.e. the total downlink transmission power required, in the case of UMTS using MBMS system) is pre-estimated by the Network Operator during Radio Network Planning and already provided to the NIS component. If based on the channel selection criteria threshold defined the use of common resources is justified, the total amount of radio resources required along with the additional load that will be introduced in the RAT and the Cell/Access Point, is acquired from the Network Operator (these values are usually fixed and pre-estimated by the Network Operator).

Step 3: For each Subgroup verify the "acceptable" <User, RAT> combinations that can be used to provide the content to the users belonging to the subgroup:

"Possible" <User, RAT> combinations are all those that can provide the service to the users with the required QoS. However, the "acceptable" <User, RAT> combinations is a subset of the "possible" <User, RAT> combinations that obey all the rules defined by the Intelligence Calculator in the related RATCITs. Note that this step will run in parallel with Step 2.

For each subgroup created in the UCIT, do the following:

Step 3.1: Once a "possible" <User, RAT> combination is formed, check if it obeys all the rules defined in the related RATCITs for this service group, and if yes declare it as "acceptable". For example, for the <User, RAT> combination the following is verified:

- The amount of radio resources required in each Cell/Access Point involved in the <User, RAT> combination, is less than the amount available and devoted by the rules for this service group in this Cell/Access Point.

- The additional load that will be introduced in each RAT and each Cell/Access Point involved in the <User, RAT> combination, keeps the total load of the RAT and the Cell/Access Point below the amount of load allowed and permitted by the rules in this RAT and Cell/Access Point, for this service group.

If the aforementioned are verified, the <User, RAT> combination is indicated as "acceptable" and the amount of Common Radio Resource Units (Common RRUs) required for it are estimated.

Step 3.2: At the end of Step 3, check if at least one *"acceptable"* <User, RAT> combination is verified for the subgroup. If not, do the following until at least one *"acceptable"* <User, RAT> combination is verified:

a. Move a number of users from higher content quality subgroups to lower content quality subgroups that their Terminals can support. The users that will be moved will be chosen from those that were assigned to the RATs or Cell/Access Points that the rules were violated. This is done in order to reduce the radio resource requirements and the load introduced in the affected RATs and Cells/Access Points. Moreover, in order to avoid frequent vertical handovers of users (which is a process that degrades considerably the QoS experienced by the users), the users that will be chosen first for switching to another subgroup are those that have the oldest *"Time of connection establishment/modification"* value (i.e. those that their connection was not altered for the longest period of time). This value is stored in the related user's record in the UCIT (see Figure 3) and denotes the exact point in time the connection of the user was either initially established or last altered (e.g. due to a handover). Moreover, the number of users that will be moved can either be fixed (i.e. five users per iteration) or can be decided dynamically by NIS based on the amount of radio resources that needs to be released or the amount of load that needs to be reduced. Although this dynamic approach will introduce some complexity in the algorithm, it is expected to provide a more efficient and faster subgrouping process. However, this is an issue that require more investigation and will be studied in future work.

b.   For the affected subgroups (i.e. the subgroups that users were removed or added), execute *Step 1 – Step 3* again. Note that during this iteration the radio resource requirements, the load that will be introduced in the RATs and the Cells/Access Points and any other parameters estimated during the previous iteration, will not be estimated again considering all the users in the subgroup, but it will be adjusted accordingly by considering only the users that were removed or added (this is done in order to reduce the processing time).

The algorithm will transit to Step 4 only if at least one "acceptable" <User, RAT> combination is verified for each subgroup. If not, the above iterative procedure will follow, until at least one "acceptable" <User, RAT> combination is verified for each subgroup.

Step 4: By considering all the "acceptable" <User, RAT> combinations verified for all Subgroups, form all "possible groups" of <User,

RAT> combinations, that can be used for the content provision to the service group:

After Step 3 is finished, NIS has a number of "acceptable" <User, RAT> combinations that can be used for each Subgroup. However, the amount of radio resources devoted and the amount of load permitted to be introduced in the RATs and Cells/Access Point for this service group must be further shared among the subgroups created for it. Thus, the NIS, in order to select the "acceptable" <User, RAT> combination that will be used for one subgroup, will have to consider all other "acceptable" <User, RAT> combinations verified for all the other subgroups as well. Therefore, similarly to step 2, the following steps will be performed:

Step 4.1: By considering the "acceptable" <User, RAT> combinations verified for each subgroup, form all *"possible groups"* of <User, RAT> combinations (we will refer to these as *"possible" transmission combinations*) that can be used to provide the indented content to the service group. For each *"possible" transmission combination* formed, estimate:

   ◦   The *total amount of radio resources that will be required* in each Cell/Access Point
   ◦   The *additional load that will be introduced* in each RAT and Cell/Access Point

Step 5: Verify the "acceptable groups" of <User, RAT> combinations that can be used for the content provision to the service group:

Similarly to Step 2 and Step 3, Step 5 will run in parallel with Step 4.

Step 5.1: Once a "possible group" of <User, RAT> combinations is formed, check if it obeys all the rules defined in the related RATCITs for this service group. If yes, declare it as an "acceptable group" (we will refer to this as an *"acceptable" transmission combination*) and estimate the total amount of *Common Radio Resource Units* required for it.

Step 5.2: If none of the *"possible groups"* of <User, RAT> combinations is verified as an *"acceptable group"*, do the following:

a. Similarly to Step 3, from the RATs or the Cells/Access Points that the rules were violated, move a number of users from higher content quality to lower content quality subgroups.

b. Execute Step 1 – Step 5.

The algorithm will transit to Step 6 if at least one *"acceptable" transmission combination* is verified for this service group. If not, the above iterative procedure will follow, until at least one is verified.

Step 6: Select the transmission combination that will be used for the content provision to the service group:

At the end of Step 5, the algorithm has verified a number of *"acceptable" transmission combinations* that can be used for the content provision to the users belonging to the service group and also the total amount of *Common Radio Resource Units* required for each is estimated. At the end of this step, the one with the least amount of Common Radio Resource Units required will be selected.

Note that at the end of this step the RAT and Cell/Access Point that will serve each user that belong to the service group is decided and also the final subgroups are formed. The RAT and Cell/Access Point decided to serve the user will be indicated in the *"RAT Selected"* field of the related user's record in the UCIT. Also the content coding that each user will receive is mapped to the subgroup the user is included.

Once the final decision is made, the Decision Execution step will be initiated in order for this decision to be adopted.

Decision Execution Step

Once the transmission combination (i.e. the RAT that will serve each user is decided and the final subgroups are formed) that will be used for the multicast service provision to the users belonging to the service group is decided, the following activities will be performed:

NIS checks for each user that belongs in the service group if the *"RAT selected"* for him (i.e. RAT Type, RAT ID, Cell/Access Point ID) differs from the one the user is currently connected to (indicated in the *"Current Connection"* field of his related record in the UCIT). In case another RAT is selected for him than the one currently connected, NIS notifies the user's Terminal about the new interface (i.e. the type of RAT, RAT ID and Cell ID/Access Point ID) selected for the user. The user's Terminal activates the interface selected (i.e. the RAT type - WiFi, UMTS, WiMAX, etc.) and connects with the selected RAT (i.e. the RAT ID) and Cell/Access Point (i.e. the Cell ID/Access Point ID) and receive a new IP Address. This new IP Address will be reported back to the NIS and updated in the *"Current Connection"* field of the related user's record in the UCIT along with the new *Type of RAT*, *RAT ID* and *Cell ID/Access Point ID* that will serve him. However, in case the interface selected for the user is the same as the one the user is currently connected, the user do not have to be notified since the selected interface is already activated in the user's Terminal, a connection with the selected RAT and Cell/Access Point is already established and an IP Address is already allocated for this user. Note that for those users that another interface than the one currently used is selected, the value of the *"Time of connection establishment/modification"* field, concerning the *"Current Connection"* of the user, will be updated to the current time (as indicated in *RAT and Content Coding Decision Step*, the value of this field will be considered during *Step 3* and *Step 5* of the *RAT and Content Coding Selection step* for selecting the users that will be switched to another RAT or lower content quality subgroups – aim to avoid frequent handovers of the users).

Once all users' Terminals are activated and connected to the selected interface and an IP address for them is allocated, NIS reports its decision (i.e. the RAT decided to serve each user and the final subgroups formed), along with the IP Addresses of the users, to the Network Use Management (NUM) module in order to identify and select the paths that will be used to distribute the content to the users.

When the paths are selected, the enforcement of resource reservation is triggered (i.e. the Multicast addresses to be used are obtained and resource reservation is performed) and the multiparty transport overlay is enforced by passing the list of overlay nodes (i.e. the nodes that the data path will go through) together with the multicast/unicast IP addresses forming the branches of the overlay tree.

Then the transport port(s) for the multicast branch(es) are allocated and the enforcement is confirmed by enforcing the multicast and QoS in the nodes.

At the end, the IP Addresses are translated to identifications for the users and the subgroups are returned to the SM to establish the sessions.

Network-Aided Session Modification

At the Session Level

The SM is capable of adapting itself and the existing sessions whenever there is a trigger containing a new context that requires the session to be updated to a new state. This trigger can come spontaneously from another component (such as NM) or can derive from previously subscribed context information. In case the NM is involved, all the resource reservation must be reconfigured. Figure 6 shows the interaction between the involved entities.

Specifically, session modification when new context information is available (Figure 6) is achieved in five steps, which are described next.

Step 1: The SME is triggered with the information that a particular user is suffering from network congestion (previously subscribed to this context). According to the existing sub-groups, it decides to downgrade the user to another sub-group containing the same media files but coded in a lower bitrate version. Optionally, it can inform the NM to reconfigure the overlay tree and QoS settings accordingly. We are also assuming that the newly decided sub-group media type was already setup for the current group.

Step 2: When all decisions are taken, the SME sends a SIP INVITE (through the SUM) message towards the involved user, containing the new multicast address to join.

Step 3: Before joining the new multicast address, the user leaves the previously joined address.

Steps 4 and 5: The user joins the new multicast address and informs the SME that the process went without any problems. At this point in time, the user should be receiving the new low bitrate media stream (B instead of A).

At the Network Level

In this section we overview the Network role in session modification, separating between modifications caused by a user joining/leaving a group and ones caused by user mobility.

During the session, optimum multicast service provisioning should be maintained despite the changes occurring in the users' and network's context or the mobility of the users within the network. Therefore, during the session, the transmission combination used should be modified, in order to accommodate the mobility of the users and the changes in the context, and provide the multicast service in an optimum way. During the session the following events are considered:

Figure 6. Session modification when there is a change in relevant context information

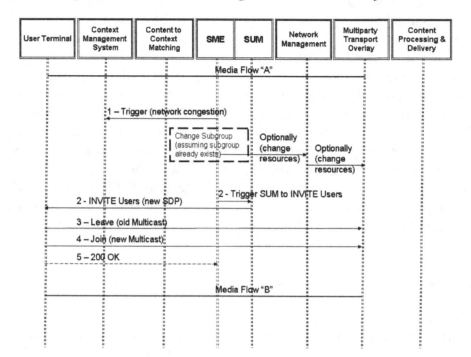

- Users join or leave the multicast service
- Mobility of the users within the network
  - Terminal Triggered Handover
  - Network Triggered Handover

Users Join or Leave the MBMS Service

During the session, users might want to join or leave a multicast service. In case a user or a group of users wants to join a specific multicast service, NIS will receive a "Join Request" message, similar to the one received for session setup (see *At the Network Level*). However, in this message the List of content codings available for the specific ContentID will not be included since they are already known to the NIS from the session setup phase. Upon this message is received, the same steps and activities described in the *At the Network Level* section will be performed, but in this case considering only the users that were included in the join request message, in order to select for them the RAT that will serve them and subgroup that the users will join.

If a user or group of users want to leave a multicast service, NIS will receive a "Leave Request" message including the ContentID related to the specific multicast service, and the List of the users' IDs that want to leave the service. Upon receiving this message, NIS just deletes the users' records created in the UCIT. Note that the resources allocated for these users will be released and the multicast trees will be updated by the Network Use Management (NUM) module.

Mobility of the Users Within the Network

During the session, optimum network capacity and performance, as well as continuity of the multicast services shall be maintained despite the mobility of the group members within the landscape of different Radio Access Technologies (i.e. WiFi, UMTS, WiMAX, etc). Handover is the key concept of providing the aforementioned. There are many reasons in which a user terminal handover from one RAT to another may be triggered. The basic reason is when the air interface of the serving

RAT no longer fulfils the desired criteria to support the service with the requested QoS and thus the terminal in this case, based on some certain criteria (i.e. handover thresholds) initiates actions in order to handover to another RAT. This is done in order to improve the quality of the connection and avoid any QoS degradation (we will refer to this sort of handover as Terminal Triggered Handover). However, most of the criteria behind handover triggering may also rely on the instant networking and environment context of the user and also the overall network conditions. When the aforementioned parameters are considered as the criteria in the handover trigger the aim is not only to fulfil the QoS requested (i.e. avoid any QoS degradation) but also to provide enhanced overall network capacity and performance. This type of handover is triggered by the Network (we refer to this sort of handover as Network Triggered Handover).

Terminal Triggered Handover

There are a lot of reasons that a Terminal can trigger a handover to another RAT, i.e. due to QoS, user's network preferences or other context reasons. The simplest example is when the Terminal, based on certain thresholds, indicates that the signal quality received from the serving RAT will not be adequate in a short time in order to guarantee the reception of the content with the requested QoS and thus must handover to another RAT. Another example is when the Terminal, during its mobility, detects that a RAT appeared within its reach is included in the user's Network Preference list, and a connection with it is preferred. Also, another example is when the interface from which the Terminal is receiving the service started malfunctioning (i.e. the WiFi interface of the Terminal in not working properly) and the connection is likely to be dropped. In these cases the handover request is triggered by the Terminal and it is up to the NIS to accept or reject the handover request based on how critical this handover request is. Therefore, when

the Terminal indicates the need for a handover will compile a "Handover request" message including also the reason that the handover is needed and sent it to NIS for execution. The "Reason for handover" included in the message will assist NIS to indicate how critical the need for handover to another RAT is in order to prioritize the request (i.e. if the handover is for QoS reasons then the handover will be directly accepted and a new RAT will be decided for the Terminal immediately). Also it is worth indicating that in case the handover is triggered due to "QoS reasons" and some of the RATs included in the "List of RATs" belongs to the User's Network Preference list then these RATs will be first in order. The information that can be included (but not limited to) in the "Handover Request" message is:

- **RequestID:** The identification of the specific request – i.e. "Handover Request"
- **UserID:** The identification of the user
- **ContentID:** The ID of the particular content that the user is receiving
- **Reason for Handover:** This will indicate to NIS how critical is the handover request. i.e.:
  ○ *QoS Reason*
  ○ *User's Network Preference Reason*
  ○ *Other Reasons ....*
- **List of RATs:** List of the RATs within the Terminal's reach. For each RAT the following information will be included:
  ○ *Type of RAT:* i.e. WiFi, UMTS, WiMAX, etc
  ○ *RAT ID:* The identification of the RAT
  ○ *Cell ID/Access Point ID:* The identification of the Cell or Access Point through which the Terminal is connected to the RAT.
  ○ *Pilot channel quality received (dB)*
  ○ *Pilot channel quality alteration rate (dB/sec)*

* In case the handover is requested due to "QoS Reason", the Terminal will report all the RATs/Cells/Access Points within its reach (including first in the list the one that the user is currently using). In case the handover is requested due to "Network Preference Reason" the Terminal will report only the RAT/Cell/Access Point that a connection to it is requested.

- **Speed:** Speed of the Terminal – estimated using GPS

Upon the handover request message is received, it is up to NIS to decide if the handover request will be accepted or rejected, based on the criticality of the handover, the instantaneous context of the network (included in the RATCITs) and the rules that should be obeyed in the network. In case more than one handover requests is received at the same time, priority will be given to those that were triggered for "QoS Reason".

Information Collection Step

When the NIS receives a handover request message, will first check the reason the handover was requested and include it either in the "high priority" queue (i.e. if the handover request is for QoS reason) or the "low priority" queue (i.e. user's network preferences). Requests from "low priority" queue will be executed only when the "high priority" queue is empty. If a request sitting in the "low priority" queue is not executed, for example, in the next one second from the time it was received then this request will be removed from the list and respond back to the Terminal that the request was rejected. The Terminal can request the handover again after a small period of time.

NIS will carry out one handover request at a time starting from those included in the "high priority" queue. For each handover request, NIS first locates in the UCIT the record of the user that requested the handover and updates the information included, with those contained in the handover

request message. It is worth mentioning that the RATCITs are always updated by the RATs once a change occurs, thus always providing to NIS the instantaneous context of the network. When the UCIT is updated with the new user's context values, the *RAT and Content Coding Selection step* is initiated in order to select the RAT that will serve the user, and if necessary, a new content coding (with lower quality depending on the load and resources available in the target RAT) for the user to receive.

RAT and Content Coding Decision Step

For each RAT included in the "List of RATs", NIS checks which of them are "candidate" and moreover "capable" to support the user. Also based on the rules defined by the Intelligent Calculator in their related RATCIT check which of them can accept the connection and provide the service to the user the required QoS of the content's coding he is currently receiving. For each RAT that can accept the connection estimate the *Common Radio Resource Units* required for each and select the one with the least amount of *Common Radio Resource Units* required. Note that if none of them can accept the user then this user will be instantly moved to a lower content quality subgroup that his Terminal can support and the same procedure will be repeated until at least one RAT that can accept the connection for this user is found.

Decision Execution Step

At the end of the aforementioned procedure, one of the following might be decided for the user:

1. Another *RAT* and the same *Content Coding*
2. Another *RAT* and another *Content Coding* (with lower quality)
3. The same *RAT* and another *Content Coding* (with the lowest content quality)
   - This case will be decided in case none of the other RATs can admit the user and thus the only solution to gain

some time before the connection is dropped is to keep him connected to the same RAT but with a lowest content quality (using a lower content quality can increase the coverage the user can move within the cell before the connection brakes) until at least one RAT can accept the connection.

In case another RAT is selected for the user than the one currently connected, the user is notified to activate the selected interface and connect to the RAT selected. The new IP Address acquired by the Terminal is reported back to the NIS and updated in the "Current Connection" field of the related user's record in the UCIT along with the new Type of RAT, RAT ID and Cell ID/Access Point ID that will serve him. Also, the value of the "Time of connection establishment/modification" field, concerning the "Current Connection" of the user, will be updated to the current time. Then NIS reports its decision (i.e. the RAT that will serve the user and the content coding that the user will receive), along with the IP Address of the user, to the Network Use Management (NUM) module in order to update, if necessary, the multicast paths and allocate the required resources. At the end, the SM is informed in order to modify the sessions accordingly.

Network Triggered Handover

Through time a lot of changes can occur altering the users' and the network's context and also the rules that should be obeyed within the network, possibly making the current transmission combination used not acceptable anymore (i.e. some of the rules defined in the RATCITs are violated), or even making another transmission combination more efficient than the one currently used. Thus NIS during the session, in order to address these variations, must either periodically (period T) or after an event (i.e. when the rules are violated), acquire the users' and network's new context,

form new transmission combinations that based on the new rules defined are considered as "acceptable" and estimate the capacity requirements of each. The one that is considered at the moment as the most efficient (i.e. the one that provides to the users the best possible QoS and enhances the overall network performance with the least amount of radio resources required) is selected and the appropriate actions are executed (by triggering a handover of a user or a group of users to another RAT or selecting another content coding for them to receive) in order to adapt the transmission combination currently used to the one just selected.

Note that the periodicity of reporting (period T) is a parameter that highly influences efficiency and should be chosen as a tradeoff between the capacity, uplink noise/load introduced and the Terminal's battery consumption (due to context information reporting) efficiency. For example, the more frequent the reporting (i.e. the smaller the value set for the period T), the higher the capacity gain that can be achieved but the more the Terminal's battery consumption and the more the uplink noise and load introduced. Since not only the downlink capacity but also the uplink interference/load and the Terminal's battery life are also considered as critical factors in the service provision efficiency, the period T should be wisely chosen by the Network Operator in order to avoid scarifying the efficiency of the one factor over the other.

Information Collection Step

As indicated above, NIS algorithm can be triggered either periodically (period T) or due to an event. The aim of periodical based triggering is to address, during the session, the variations occurring in the users' and network's context and use through time the most efficient transmission combination for the multicast service provision. On the other hand, the aim of event based triggering, is to take immediate actions in a certain

RATs or Cells/Access Points that the rules set by the Intelligence Calculator are violated, in order to eliminate any possibility for undesirable events, that can influence the network performance (like congestion, overloading, etc.) or the quality experienced by the users (i.e. call drop, QoS degradation, etc.), to occur.

The event based triggering differs from the periodical based triggering since not all users that belong to the service group will be notified for reporting. Only those users that are connected or in range, of let say, 2 RATs away from the affected RATs and Cells/Access Points (i.e. from those RATs and Cells/Access Points that the rules were violated) will be notified for reporting. This is done in order to minimize the uplink load introduced and the processing time required for a decision to be made, since with this kind of triggering immediate actions are required in order to avoid any inefficiency in the network performance or the QoS received by the users.

Once a report is received, the NIS extracts the context information included and stores them in the related user's record in the UCIT. However, the information previously included will not be deleted but instead will be time-stamped and moved to a History Context Storage Table (HCST), created in the SQL Database. As indicated in 2.2.1, this history context information is used by the Intelligence Calculator for locating patterns that will facilitate it to predict trends in the users' and network's behaviour and generate rules that will assist NIS to select a transmission combination that will eliminate any possibility for undesirable events, that can influence the network's performance or the quality experienced by the users, to occur.

RAT and Content Coding Selection Step

Once the Content Information Collection step is finished, NIS will execute the same steps described in the *RAT and Content Coding Decision Step* section in order to form and indicate the "acceptable" transmission combinations that can

be used for the multicast service provision and select the one that is considered at the moment as the most efficient. Note that in case of the event based Network Handover Triggering, only the users that were notified for reporting will be considered. Once the decision is made the Final Decision Execution Step is triggered.

Final Decision Execution Step

At the end of the RAT and Content Coding Selection step, one of the following can be decided for the users:

1. Another *RAT* and another *Content Coding* (with either higher or lower quality)
2. Another *RAT* and the same *Content Coding*
3. The same *RAT* and another *Content Coding* (with either higher or lower quality)
4. The same *RAT* and the same *Content Coding* (i.e. the status of the user will stay the same).

In case another RAT is selected for the user than the one currently connected, the user's Terminal is notified (through the Mobility Controller) to activate the selected interface and handover to the new RAT selected. The new IP Address acquired by the Terminal is reported back to the NIS and updated in the "Current Connection" field of the related user's record in the UCIT along with the new Type of RAT, RAT ID and Cell ID/Access Point ID that will serve him. Once all users are connected to the RAT selected for them, the NUM is informed about the new transmission combination selected in order to update the multicast paths and release or allocate the required resources. Note that for the users that another RAT or another Content Coding was selected the value of the "Time of connection establishment/modification" field, concerning the "Current Connection" of the user, will be updated to the current time. At the end, the SM is informed in order to modify the sessions accordingly.

Multiparty Content Propagation

The previous sections introduced the context-aware management processes and how context is used to adapt multimedia delivery across heterogeneous networks. To complete the cycle of context-aware multiparty delivery, it is important to understand how the content is propagated throughout the different components involved in this task. In this sense, besides overviewing the capabilities of such entities and focus on their interactions, we will describe some of the decisions and limitations found during the engineering design process.

Layered Approach

Due to the amount of components involved in the multiparty delivery system, to simplify the explanation of content propagation, we will address this topic by analyzing the different layers involved, namely session, network and transport.

Session Layer

As explained earlier, all communications start through the Session Manager (SM) and are signaled via SIP. In this sense, the content propagation is no exception. After initially matching the available content formats (in a generic way, it means that this format exists in the content repository or the content processor is capable of performing transcoding) with the users device capabilities and performing the necessary network resource reservations and configurations, the SM will give the instructions for the media to be streamed from the Content Processor and Delivery (CtPD) until the user.

Besides receiving a list of sub-groups indicating which users will receive each type of media and to which IPs and ports they should connect or expect media from (depending if the multimedia will be delivered using multicast or unicast, respectively), depending on the application, the

SM can either send an INVITE in parallel to both the users and the CtPD, send the INVITE first to the users or vice-versa (first to the CtPD). In the case of a live streaming session, the latter makes more sense. (the users are invited first in Figure 1).

The behavior may differ slightly when considering unicast or multicast technologies. The differences occur on both the terminal and the infrastructure side. Based on the information provided in the Session Description Protocol (SDP) part of the SIP INVITE message, the client can extract the IP address that will deliver the media. Therefore, if the address refers to a multicast IP (most terminals identify this automatically), the terminal will send an ICMP JOIN message and from that moment it will automatically be prepared to receive media. However, if the address corresponds to a unicast IP (unicast is only used in case the user device does not support multicast or it is more efficient/convenient for the network), the SM will wait for the 200 OK message that indicates which port the user device will be expect to receive media. In both cases (unicast and multicast) the 200 OK message is sent, but only when it is unicast the information is leveraged to the network layer so that the overlay network can be adapted accordingly (this process will be explained later in detail). When a modification or termination of the multimedia stream occurs, the procedure is very identical, as the changes do not occur at the session level.

On the network side, there is a single SIP IN-VITE corresponding to a single group of contents (session). Although sub-grouping occurs on the session level, it is signaled as different streams from the same session. This approach brings great benefits in comparison to a SIP session per sub-group. The first is related with the amount of information circulating in the network. The second and most obvious is related with synchronization issues. Assuming that the different sub-groups belong to the same session, and that users will receive media from at least two different sub-groups (one for audio and one for video), it is crucial that they are streamed in parallel and not sequentially. Obviously, there are mechanisms to overcome these issues (like increasing the playback buffer on the client side), but the goal is to reduce entropy whenever possible. The last reason relates to a limitation on the CtPD streaming capabilities. If there is a need to modify a session and move a user from a sub-group to another that is not yet created, the CtPD needs to be able to start streaming from the moment (in time) that the content is being played (this problem only occurs on non live streaming). As our solution works with pre-processed files and not real-time transcoding, there is a need to start all possible content formats from the beginning, otherwise adaption can only occur with a limited number of content versions (the ones created initially).

As it is possible to assess from the first 3 streams described, the content type is specified as well as destination IPs and ports. For the CtPD this means that these files need to be streamed to these addresses, which correspond to the overlay source nodes (better described further ahead). The following two streams have a null address description. This means that the CtPD will have to start the stream of these files, however not to any node in the network but to a ghost local address. In other words, the stream will hit a "black hole" and be discarded at localhost. Alternatively, it can be streamed to another local area machine and the packets will be dropped there. The decision of opting between these two options depends on the CPU vs. throuput limitations of the machine where the CtPD is running. Please notice that the architecture supports more than one CtPD and the load balancing between them is done by the Session Manager using a configuration file.

Network Layer

Despite not performing a direct role, there are a series of events occurring at the network layer that will impact the way the content is propagated throughout the network until the end user. With the

role of performing network resource reservation and enforcement, the NM (NM) is responsible for choosing the right network, path and content to each user according to a set of context related variables. In this sense, it controls directly the transport layer, which is where the media packets are forwarded from one node to another.

Transport Layer

Due to the design decision of separating the multi-media streams into different primitive media types (audio, video and subtitles), the transport layer assumes a preponderant role for the performance of media propagation. By applying this concept, both audio and video (for the same multimedia content being played at the client device) travel through different paths, which can bring unexpected behavior when combining both streams at the end device. Therefore, it is preponderant that Quality of Service is assured to avoid transmission and synchronization issues.

Nevertheless, that transport layer implements its own mechanisms to prevent some problems and to increase the overall efficiency on the network side. On current operators implementations, one of the biggest problems on group communications is that not all routers support multicasting, limiting in this way the applicability of such technology on the application side. Consequently, our work proposes a Multiparty Transport Overlay (MTO), which aims at providing a generic, scalable, and efficient transport service for group communications by applying the overlay paradigm at the transport layer. MTO allows hiding the heterogeneity of underlying networks in terms of IP multicast capabilities or IPv4/v6 support, thus allowing any user to participate in a multiparty delivery session irrespective of the network he/she is attached to and in a transparent manner to the application. MTO enables the dynamic creation of an overlay tree, composed of Overlay Nodes (ON), between the source and the group members. The branches of the MTO tree are made of transport connections (unicast or multicast) over which the ON forwards the content to be delivered towards the group members.

There are three types of ONs; all controlled by a fourth entity called the MTO Controller:

- *Source Overlay Node (S-ON):* it represents the functional component of the MTO tree that receives the application data flow directly from the source.
- *Leaf Overlay Node (L-ON):* it represents the functional component of the MTO tree that is the last hop ON from the source to the receiver.
- *On-tree Overlay Node (O-ON):* it represents the functional component of the MTO tree that is on the path between the S-ON and L-ON.
- *MTO Controller (MTO-Ctrl):* it represents the functional component of the MTO tree which is in charge of generating port numbers of multiparty transport connections of the MTO tree and pushing them to the IPT as well as to the different ONs of the MTO tree. The MTO-Ctrl also interacts with the IPT module to manage the MTO tree (creation, update, and deletion).

The branches of the MTO tree are made of transport connections (identified by a unicast source address and port, and a unicast/multicast destination address and port) over which overlay nodes forward the content to be delivered towards the group members. Each ON is forwarding content from one incoming transport connection to one or multiple transport connections based on its own forwarding table. One MTO tree is dynamically established to support one particular multiparty delivery session.

To better understand the overall content propagation flow, Figure 7 shows an example MTO tree made of multiple multicast and unicast transport connections, providing multiparty delivery from a source to a set of receivers in a mobile hetero-

geneous network. Connecting it with the initial assumptions at the session layer, it is now easy to understand that the CtPD will stream all content to different overlay source nodes (controlled by SM and NM modules).

Proposed Methodological Approaches

Despite the differences found between our work and other research initiatives, there are common points that should be emphasized and used as reference for future explorations. Although some have been specified in this article, based on specific components, most of the ideas behind this work can be generalized and abstracted for further extensions. Next we present the methodology stemming from this work representing a practical framework that can be used to investigate similar research objectives, and adaptations that may be achieved from this methodology.

The Methodology

Based on the work done at the different layers involved, application, session, network and transport, we propose a methodology for context-aware multiparty delivery. Figure 8 depicts the relationships between the different steps involved and abstracts these from any of the components previously introduced. This will allow future work to implement the same functionalities according to the specifics of their own projects and needs.

Furthermore, other works described earlier in *Adaptive Context-Aware Sessions* are already using some of these steps. Basically the system context-awareness architecture depicted in Figure 8 and highlighted in a cloud is based on the producer consumer role paradigm. The system is built upon three basic functional entities: Context Consumer (CxC), Context Broker (CxB) and Context Provider (CxP), where a CxP is a source of the context information, a CxB is an arbitral node handling the context data as a reference point

Figure 7. Example of multiparty transport overlay

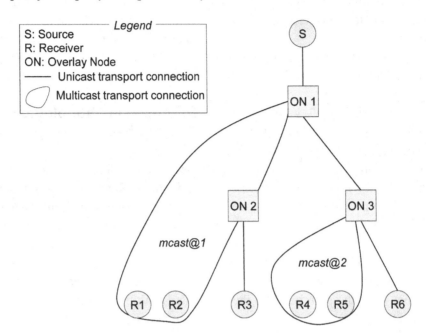

for the overall context in a smart space and CxCs are consumers of context information. The decoupling of provisioning and consumption is important as it impacts on the overall scalability of the system.

Assuming that deployment of the previously mentioned context-awareness is in place, and every time the system is requested to initiate a new session setup (start multimedia delivery to a group of users), it should acquire context information from all the users involved in this session. In parallel, it should request the metadata information regarding the content available to be delivered (formats available, duration, frame rates, etc.). Based on this, a compatibility matching can be done between both intermediaries (the user device and media delivery server) involved in the multimedia session.

Once this is done, the system needs to ascertain what the most appropriate quality for each user is. This can be done by evaluating user network conditions, internal resources, business rules or other information. After this process, the system has the required information to make decisions

regarding user grouping. Therefore, for each user the system should choose the most appropriate media format for each multimedia type available (audio, video, subtitles). These decisions consider all the variables previously evaluated. Once the decisions are taken, the enforcement takes place. Together with the enforcement decisions, the lower layers should inform the upper ones about the final decisions and consequently notify it with the required parameters to establish the session with both the users and the content repositories. Because such systems are not static, the system permanent monitoring and evaluation enables automatic regrouping when the initial conditions change.

When the users are distributed across the different sub-groups, the component responsible for the signaling and session management should invite the users, informing them where and how they should connect or receive the different multimedia types, respectively. Once the users are ready, a similar procedure is done towards the content multimedia delivery servers. If the content being streamed is live, then the session

Figure 8. Proposed methodology for context-aware multimedia delivery

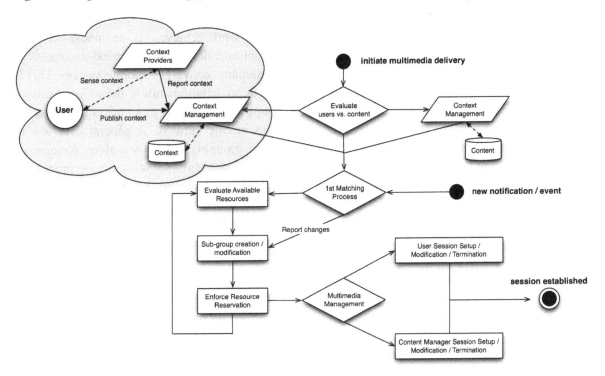

setup process between the user and the server is done in parallel to reduce the delay. After this process, the multimedia sessions are established.

If the system is notified about some context change (e.g., user changes device, network conditions are very low, etc.) it should have the capability to adapt accordingly. For example, if the environment around the user is too noisy, based on the user preferences, the system should automatically modify a multimedia session containing audio and video, to a single video session with embedded subtitles. Using such methodology allows the achievement of a balanced way of increasing multimedia delivery personalization together with efficiency.

Adaptations Achieved

Based on the developed components, proposed architecture and methodologies specified, our work establishes common ground for multimedia network-aided session management for adaptive context-aware multiparty communications and shows how using context information may enable different adaptations for context-aware multiparty delivery, namely:

Adaptation in access network selection, including (a) context-aware RAT selection for mobile terminals aiming at enhanced network capacity and performance, and (b) 802.21 and SIP-based Terminal Mobility between accesses triggered by network or terminal.

Adaptation in routing path selection, consisting in selecting the best multiparty delivery path based on network characteristics (bandwidth, load, delay, jitter, loss rate, multicast capabilities, etc.) and QoS needs from the session.

Adaptation in media coding selection (called subgrouping), consisting in efficient and scalable selection of best media coding per sub-groups of users based on available content formats, device capabilities (e.g. codecs, resolutions supported), user preferences, and network QoS capabilities.

Adaptation in user device selection, with context-aware SIP-based User Session Mobility between terminals triggered by network or terminal.

Adaptation in transport connection type, based on a Multiparty Transport Overlay (MTO) providing an efficient transport service for group communications by hiding heterogeneity of underlying networks in terms of IP multicast capabilities or IPv4/v6 support. MTO tree configuration and update is driven by characteristics of multiparty delivery paths to receivers.

Adaptation in transport reliability, through an adaptive FEC-based reliable transport service well suited for streaming services with stringent latency constraints.

Adaptation in QoS support, through dynamic QoS enforcement along the multiparty delivery tree (with unicast and multicast branches).

CONCLUSION AND FUTURE RESEARCH DIRECTIONS

The use of context allows the definition of mobile communities that are characterized by requiring the same content. The users in similar situations should receive the same data. The mobile system should be enhanced to create multiparty sessions that allow content delivery to such groups of users. Session Management provides the necessary signalling to deliver a specific content to its consumers, handling different types of events regarding session control. Session Management thus participates in dynamic changes such as switching between different content. This chapter has addressed enhanced Session Management for multiparty communications, in particular, how to setup and modify a multi-party session that may respond to context changes and adapt to satisfy the users of a service group, and further how the

content is propagated to the users of a context-aware service group.

The work achieves, in an innovative way, self-optimization through context-awareness in a multiparty converged mobile system. This is done through the dynamic re-definition of service groups (subgrouping) in a converged heterogeneous mobile network. A general overview of the sub-grouping process was given, focusing on particular aspects of the sub-grouping process. In particular, we have shown how the process begins at the session level, is refined at the network level, and is finally propagated at the service level to the content. The use cases of session initiation and session modification are considered. Moreover, as a result of the subgrouping, the content received by each defined sub-group has been adapted to the users' preferences, situations and contexts, as well as the relevant network capabilities and context, reflected in the network selection algorithm presented, achieving improvements both for network resource usage and user experience.

This work is currently being implemented within the C-CAST project (C-CAST, 2008). More specifically, the elements required to perform and enforce sub-grouping both on the session and network level are being implemented: context providers, session and network management, multiparty transport overlay and IP Transport. The interfaces between the elements are also defined and currently under implementation. Future work aims, also within the scope of the project, to finish implementation of the sub-grouping mechanism in order to collect relevant performance measures. Furthermore, specific sub-modules participating in this self-optimization process are planned to be individually enhanced and evaluated.

ADDITIONAL EXERCISES

1. Consider the session initiation message flow chart at the session level provided in

Figure 1. Let there be a new user that must be added in the previously initiated session. Using the proposed methodology, prepare a draft session modification message flow chart, where the session will be modified to include the new user.

- ○ Which adaptations have been used from the adaptations mentioned in *Adaptations Achieved* section? Can you identify any new adaptations that would be necessary for the session modification procedure?
- ○ Describe a scenario where ten users that are registered for the same multiparty service are divided into three different sub-groups, because of their context. Please consider, environment, network and user context in your answer.

2. In the above described scenario, consider some users to have only unicast capabilities while others to be able to receive in multicast mode? How would you deal with such different user capabilities? How could this be detected? How could this be handled?

3. Consider an advertising scenario where a media agency wants to provide a series of personalized advertisements during the Football World Cup 2010 final match. Using the proposed methodology and assuming there are four different content files, each of them is available on three different codecs (ignore subtitles for this exercise), please draw the sequence diagram for the session initiation of the aforementioned scenario. Presuming that the heterogeneity of environmental, network and user context is high, what would be the maximum number of sub-groups that could be created by the system?

4. Consider the procedure of RAT and content coding selection performed at the network level. The Radio Access Technology and the content coding that each user will receive is not straightforward but depends on different parameters related to the network's and user's context. Describe these parameters and also propose additional ones that you believe would be beneficial (and why) during this RAT and content coding selection procedure.

5. The intelligence used in the RAT and content coding selection algorithm dynamically defines rules which aim to facilitate a decision that will eliminate any possibility for undesirable events, that can influence the network performance (like congestion, overloading, etc.) or the quality experienced by the users (i.e. call drop, QoS degradation, etc.), to occur. Describe some scenarios in which this intelligence is essential justifying your answer.

REFERENCES

Aguiar, R., & Gomes, D. (2008). Quasi-omniscient networks: Scenarios on context capturing and new services through wireless sensor networks. *Wireless Personal Communications, 45*, 497–509. doi:10.1007/s11277-008-9474-5

Antoniou, J., Christophorou, C., Jannetau, C., Kelil, M., Sargento, S., & Neto, A. … Simoes J. (2009c, October). *Architecture for context- aware multiparty delivery in mobile heterogeneous networks.* International Conference on Ultra Modern Telecommunications 2009, St. Petersburg, Russia.

Antoniou, J., Christophorou, C., Neto, A., Sargento, S., Pinto, F. C., & Carapeto, N. F. … Pitsillides A. (2009b, October). *Context-aware self-optimization in multiparty converged mobile environments.* 3rd International Conference on Autonomic Computing and Communication Systems, Limassol, Cyprus.

Antoniou, J., Riede, C., Pinto, C. F., & Pitsillides, A. (2009). *Context aware multiparty session support for adaptive multicasting in heterogeneous mobile networks*. Second International Conference Mobilware'09. Berlin, Germany: Springer.

Boll, S., Klas, W., & Wandel, J. (1999, October). A cross-media adaptation strategy for multimedia presentations. *Proc. of ACM Multimedia '99.*

C-CAST. (2008). *ICT-2007-216462 C-CAST (Context Casting) project*. Retrieved from http://www.ict-ccast.eu

Chen, Y., & Yang, Y. (2007). A new 4G architecture providing multimode terminals always best connected services. *Wireless Communications, 14,* 36–41. doi:10.1109/MWC.2007.358962

Dong, W., & Newmarch, J. (2005). Adding session and transaction management to Web services by using Sip. *Proceedings of the IADIS International Conference e-Society 2005,* (pp. 299-306). IADIS Press, Portugal. ISBN/ISSN: 9728939035

Jesus, V., Sargento, S., & Aguiar, R. L. (2008). Any-constraint personalized network selection. In *Personal, Indoor and Mobile Radio Communications Symposium,* (pp. 1-6). Cannes, France: IEEE Press.

Kwon, Y. H., Park, H. J., Choi, S. G., Choi, J. K., & Lee, H. S. (2006, July). P2MP session management scheme using SIP in MPLS-based next generation network. *The Joint International Conference on Optical Internet and Next Generation Network,* COIN-NGNCON 2006, (pp.183-185).

Lei, Z., & Georganas, N. D. (2001, May). Context-based media adaptation in pervasive computing. *Proceedings of Canadian Conference on Electrical and Computer Engineering* (CCECE).

Pahlavan, K., Krishnamurthy, P., Hatami, A., Ylianttila, M., Makela, J. P., Pichna, R., & Vallstron, J. (2000). Handoff in hybrid mobile data networks. *Personal Communications, 7,* 34–47. doi:10.1109/98.839330

Sigrid, B., Poi, M., & Tore, U. (2000). *A simple architecture for delivering context information to mobile users*. In Workshop on Infrastructure for Smart Devices - How to Make Ubiquity an Actuality, Bristol.

Simoes, J., Sargento, S., Antoniou, J., Christophorou, C., Janneteau, C., Carapeto, N., & Neto, A. (2009, September). *Context-aware control for personalized multiparty sessions in mobile multihomed systems*. 5th International Mobile Multimedia Communications Conference (MobiMedia '09), London.

Chapter 13

On Using Multiagent Systems for Spectrum Sharing in Cognitive Radios Networks

Usama Mir
Université de Technologie de Troyes, France

Leila Merghem-Boulahia
Université de Technologie de Troyes, France

Dominique Gaïti
Université de Technologie de Troyes, France

ABSTRACT

In modern day wireless networks, spectrum utilization and allocation are static. Generally, static spectrum allocation is not a feasible solution considering the distributed nature of wireless devices, thus some alternatives must be ensured in order to allocate spectrum dynamically and to mitigate the current spectrum scarcity. An effective solution to this problem is cognitive radio (CR), which seeks the empty spectrum portions and shares them with the neighboring devices. The CR devices can utilize the available spectrum more efficiently if they try to work together. Therefore, in this work, we review a number of dynamic spectrum allocation techniques, especially those using multiagent systems and game-theoretical approaches, and investigate their applicability to CR networks. The distributed nature of these two domains makes them suitable for CR networks. In fact, the idea of dynamic spectrum sharing using these techniques is not entirely new and several interesting approaches already exist in literature. Thus, in our study we try to focus on existing spectrum sharing literature and cooperative multiagent system for CR networks. We are particularly interested in showing how the distributed nature of multiagent system can be combined with cognitive radios in order to alleviate the current static spectrum usage as well as maintaining cooperation amongst the CR nodes. Moreover, our work includes the description of various scenarios in which spectrum sharing is an essential factor and hence must be performed in a dynamic and opportunistic manner. We also explain the working of our proposed spectrum allocation approach using multiagent system cooperation in one of these scenarios and verify its formal behavior using Petri net modeling.

DOI: 10.4018/978-1-60960-845-3.ch013

1.1 INTRODUCTION

Modern day wireless systems are moving from static and centralized control to distributed and autonomous networks, where the devices may work more dynamically and they can opportunistically select the available spectrum/bandwidth by having frequent interactions and information exchanges with their neighboring devices. By autonomous networks (Schmid, Eggert, Brunner & Quit, 2005), we mean that the control and information are fully distributed and the wireless devices have the capabilities of self organization and adaptability to cope with frequent network changes. Most commonly, the devices are meant to be infrastructure independent and are designed to enable inter-device interactions using multi hops heterogeneous elements. The primary and most common objectives of deploying these autonomous infrastructures is to develop systems having autonomous behaviors and to integrate different kinds of devices together in order to permit the technological mobility between the interconnected domains.

The above mentioned opportunistic and autonomous behaviors are now becoming both possible and necessary by the introduction of cognitive radio (CR) technology (Mitola, 2000)(Mitola & Maguire Jr., 1999) in the wireless network domains and through the advances in the field of Distributed Artificial Intelligence (Weiss, 2000) by exploring the concepts of multiagent systems (Wooldridge, 2002). These cognitive radio devices can then be used in a wide variety of network domains (WLAN, WiRAN, MANETs). In addition, an efficiently designed CR with a software agent deployed on it would be capable of interacting with neighboring radios to form a dynamic, loosely-coupled and collaborative network. Then, these radios work together to collectively reach the goals that are difficult to achieve by an individual radio. Further, the deployment of a multiagent system provides an incentive to conceptualize and design new spectrum sharing solutions for wireless networks. This incentive is particularly attractive and equally important to create spectrum sharing solutions that work in dynamic, distributed and open wireless networks domains. To mention one of the many exciting examples, a mobile phone having no license for spectrum usage can still use the unutilized spectrum portion of a licensed (or paid) user via CR capabilities and later can share its spectrum portion with the neighboring users using a multiagent system (MAS) (Jiang, Ivan & Anita, 2007).

In this work, we propose a thorough study of various spectrum sharing techniques available in literature. Our study moves around two parts. In the first part, we try to focus on introducing CR networks along with CR user's basic functionalities and capabilities. This section also includes the introduction of various concepts related to MAS coordination. Our second part focuses on presenting several spectrum sharing studies using game-theoretical and MAS approaches and capturing the different ways of applying these techniques for cognitive radio networks. Note that to a larger extent, the idea of using MAS over CR networks is not entirely new and some of the already proposed solutions have been suggested in the literature (Jiang, Ivan & Anita, 2007)(Kloeck & Jondra, 2006)(Tonmukayakul & Weiss, 2005). Nevertheless, we not only view the multiagent systems usage over CR networks, but take this view a step further and introduce a framework, where the devices having agents can cooperate with each other in order to have an efficient use of the available spectrum.

In our research, we specifically focus on introducing various functions related to CR networks and then try to emphasize on one of the important CR function i.e. spectrum allocation. Different techniques have been successfully proposed to share the unused spectrum in a dynamic way. Since a CR node is capable of sensing and utilizing only a small portion of the nearby available spectrum, we suggest that in order to have better spectrum usage, the nodes have to work together by having series of frequent interactions. This cooperative behavior will result in higher quality spectrum allocations, as the devices will have more knowledge about the neighboring devices spectrum usage.

In addition to proposing a cooperative spectrum sharing framework, another objective of this chapter is to elucidate the working of MAS and to elaborate various cooperation mechanisms, including the contract net protocol, cooperative game-theory, that can be applied in distributed network settings. To this end, we view the static spectrum allocation as a core issue in CR networks and suggest a cooperative architecture to deal with this problem. We also propose several important scenarios in which the techniques like game-theory and multiagent systems can be applied for dynamic spectrum sharing.

The organization of our chapter is as follows. We introduce the concepts of cognitive radio networks in Section 1.2. A rich amount of literature previously exists on utilizing game-theoretical approaches in various domains, thus considering the scope of our chapter, we try to focus on introducing basic concepts of multiagent systems

and its coordination mechanisms in Section 1.3. In Section 1.4, we present a state of the art review of various spectrum sharing approaches using game-theoretical and multiagent system-based studies. Some spectrum sharing scenarios along with our cooperative multiagent system architecture along with its modeling using Petri nets are depicted in Section 1.5. Finally we conclude the chapter in Section 1.6.

1.2 COGNITIVE RADIO

Cognitive radio (CR) was firstly defined by *Mitola* (Mitola, 2000) as *"a radio that employs model-based reasoning to achieve a specified level of competence in radio-related domains."* Generally, a CR is considered to be an intelligent wireless network component that is aware of its surroundings through its sensing part, may adapt to the present environment by examining the radio frequency (RF) signals and can learn by interacting with its neighboring devices. Figure 1 clears the fact that a CR is basically aware of its neighboring radio environments, having the capabilities of adapting

Figure 1. Basic elements of a CR

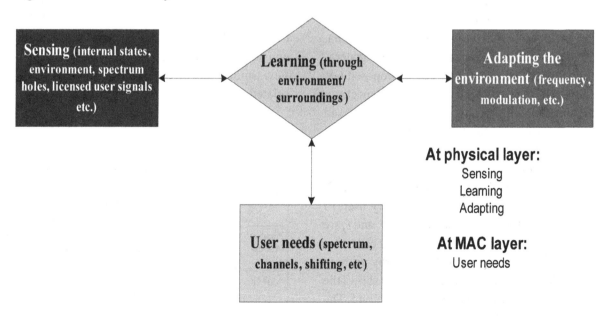

to these surroundings according to the changes. To adapt, a CR continuously senses or monitors its environment. It contains the knowledge of the priorities, procedures and needs of its users by learning over time and finally can generate the possible solutions in order to facilitate the necessary communications with its neighboring devices.

As detailed in (Mitola & Maguire Jr., 1999), CR offers a novel way to solve static spectrum utilization problems. A CR user monitors the radio environment in order to identify those radio spectrum portions that are not in use by the legacy primary users and provides the incentives for making these unused bands available to perform the services required by the user. The unutilized spectrum portions are known as the *spectrum holes* or *white spaces*. In (Haykin, 2006), *Haykin* has given his assessment about a spectrum hole as *"a band of frequencies assigned to a primary user, but at a particular time and specific geographic location, the band is not being utilized by that user."* The definition clearly identifies that the functionality of a CR user circles around these *white spaces*. It is also obvious that the first priority to using these bands must always stay with the legacy primary users and the CR user can only utilize it in an opportunistic manner without causing any interference to the primary users.

In relation to the above assessments, the initial demonstration of CR was given by DARPA (Dana, 1996), as an important element of next generation network program. The newly proposed CR senses the empty spectrum portions (spectrum sensing), communicates and shares the sensed portion (spectrum sharing) and leaves the channel when the legacy licensed user arrives (spectrum mobility). Table 1 and Figure 2 provide a general idea of CR device's basic functions. In Figure 2, two different access-points (or primary users) I and J and mobile-nodes (or CR users) j_1 and j_2 are shown respectively. Both the CR users can sense the transmission signals of their nearby primary users. At first, the double arrowed line shows the spectrum sharing of user k_1 and k_2 at portion 1. The

two lines with circle heads depict the arrival of primary user J who wants to re-utilize its spectrum. Therefore the users k_1 and k_2 have detected the empty spectrum space of nearby primary user I by sensing its transmission signals (as shown by the lines with arrows). Both the users are moving from spectrum portion 1 to 2 to carry on their working. The dotted lines show the spectrum mobility of users k_1 and k_2 from portion 1 to 2. These processes of spectrum sensing, sharing and mobility may continue in the same fashion for more complex scenarios with an increasing number of primary and CR user devices. If CR users arrive in a situation where they cannot find an alternative spectrum portion to carry on their operation (in case of primary user arrival), then they have to vacate the current spectrum portion without causing any collisions or interferences to the legacy users. To give more details, our following subsections provide an introductory state of the art review on CR user's basic functions.

1.2.1. Spectrum Sensing

Spectrum sensing refers to detecting the available empty spectrum portions in order to fill the unutilized *spectrum holes* and continuously sensing the primary users' signals to avoid any unwanted interferences (Sahai & Cabric, 2005) (Yucek & Arslan, 2007). This area has received considerable research attention in the recent past. Few studies have investigated the hypothesis related to detecting empty spectrum portions

Table 1. CR functionalities

CR functions	Description
Sensing	Detection of empty spectrum portions or "spectrum holes" by sensing licensed user signals
Sharing/ Allocation	Sharing the sensed spectrum portions with other CR users or coexisting with them on the same channel
Mobility	Leaving or vacating the spectrum portion when the legacy licensed user arrives

Figure 2. A simple example showing various CR functions

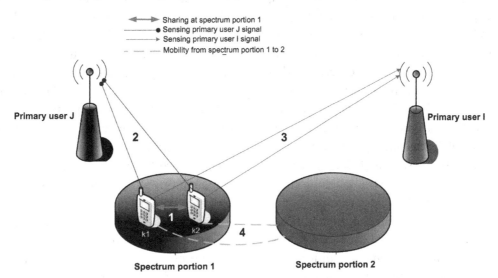

(in a non-cooperative way) as a combination of primary user signal, the additive white Gaussian noise and the signal gain (Ghasemi & Sousa, 2005) (Sahin, Guvenc & Arslan, 2009). The others have drawn their focus towards matched filter detection (Bouzegzi, Ciblat & Jallon, 2008)(Sahai, Hoven & Tandra, 2004), a technique where the primary user signal is known in advance to a CR user and the corresponding match filter generates a high value of gain which maximizes the received signal-to-noise (SNR) ratio. However, matched filter detection technique performs poorly when the information about primary user signal is not accurate. In contrast to matched filter detection, the work presented in (Bixio, Oliveri, Ottonello & Regazzoni, 2009)(Cabric, Mishra & Brodersen, 2004)(Lunden, Koivunen, Huttunen & Poor, 2009) is based on cyclostationary sine waves detection. The detected primary user signals have periodic (or cyclic) shapes, which are considered to be correlated with the pre-estimated sine waves. If both the pre-estimated and detected waves correlate, then there is a possibility of primary user's presence. Other techniques based on detecting primary user's signal as energy (or power) also exist in spectrum sensing literature (Digham, Alouni & Simon, 2007)(Sahai, Hoven, Mishra & Tandra,

2006). In these techniques, the received signal is passed through a bandpass filter. The filter output is then integrated and compared with the threshold value to determine the presence of primary user. However energy detection can only determine the presence of power as primary user's signal, rather it cannot differentiate several signal types.

In distinction to the above studies, cooperative spectrum sensing (Rania, Mokhtar, Khatun, Ali & Ramli, 2009)(Unnikrishnan & Veeravalli, 2008) is based on the fact that there must be some amount of inter-node coherence and coordination, such that the limitations of non-cooperative approaches (e.g. the limited information exchange and the decision making without considering other nodes, etc.) are minimized. Generally, in cooperative approaches a centralized controller (or base-station) cooperates with other devices for getting all the required information about primary user's received signals. Each device gives its information to the controller which is later responsible for sharing the current primary user's arrival information with the other neighboring nodes. Whenever the CR users access any sensed channel, they are awarded with a reward which is equal to the total bandwidth of the accessed channel.

According to (Mishra, Sahai & Brodersen, 2006), cooperative sensing is similar to signal sensing and relaying in traditional wireless networks where a transmitted signal from source to destination is sensed by each device located within the signal's route, which in turn further transmits or "relays" the received signal towards its destination. At the end, the destination node gets the combined signal through multiple relaying nodes over several transmission paths. If during sensing, some cooperation exists between source, destination and relaying devices then several unwanted interferences can be avoided and the traditional hidden and exposed terminal problems can be cured. Table 2 summarizes some of the differences, advantages and disadvantages of cooperative and non-cooperative sensing.

1.2.2. Spectrum Sharing

Sharing the sensed spectrum portion with the neighboring nodes or coexisting with the legacy primary user, is the essence of spectrum allocation (Cao & Zheng, 2008). Generally, after performing spectrum sensing, the spectrum must be properly allocated amongst the CR users. This process mitigates the effects of current static spectrum assignment problems (Akyildiz, Lee, Vuran & Mohanty, 2006). In the recent past, several dynamic spectrum sharing approaches have been proposed using different techniques such as game-theory, multiagent systems, auctions, medium access control protocols, etc. Considering the scope of our work, game-theoretical and multiagent sys-

tems based spectrum sharing will be explained in Section 1.4, thus this subsection briefly focuses on the other commonly used approaches.

In (Adomavicius & Gupts, 2005), a local bargaining strategy (a concept inspired from bargaining in electronic markets (Bui, Gachet, Sebastian, 2006)) is used for utilizing spectrum opportunistically, where the CR users self-organize themselves into small bargaining groups. The group formation process starts by the initiator CR node, sending a bargaining group formation request for a subset of spectrum portions (or channels), to the neighboring nodes. The interested devices acknowledge the request and the bargaining group is formed. The group is later dismissed at the primary user's arrival or after completely utilizing the channels for the agreed time period. Likewise, the works proposed in (Gaurav, Kasbekar & Sarkar, 2009) (Yongle, Wang, Liu & Clancy, 2008) consider market-based auctions (Adomavicius & Gupts, 2005) for dynamic spectrum sharing. The CR users submit their bids (based on SNR) to the centralized auctioneer, which shows their willingness for spectrum sharing. The auctioneer then allocates the spectrum based on the received bids. The ultimate aim of using auctions is to provide an incentive to CR users to maximize their spectrum usage (and hence the utility), while allowing network to achieve *Nash Equilibrium*.

Beside from market-based approaches, the medium access control (MAC) (Kumar, Raghavan & Deng, 2006) solutions, too, have been used into the field of spectrum sharing. In fact, some authors suggest that the spectrum sharing prob-

Table 2. Cooperative vs. non-cooperative sensing

Sensing Types	Description	Advantages	Limitations
Cooperative sensing	Spectrum is detected cooperatively by a bilateral inter-node information exchange	• More accurate detection • Multi-path fading effects are minimized	Information exchange overhead
Non-cooperative sensing	Spectrum is sensed independently through local observations	• Requires less information exchange and processing time • Less complex implementation issues	• Inaccurate signal observations • Interferences due to lack of primary user's signal information

lems are similar to MAC issues (Akyildiz, Lee, Vuran & Mohanty, 2006), where several users try to access the same channel and their access should be coordinated with the neighboring users to avoid interferences. In MAC-based spectrum sharing (Huang, Jing, & Raychaudhuri, 2009) (Ma, Han & Shen, 2005), when a CR node is using a specific channel, both the transmitter and the receiver send a busy tone signal through the associated control channel, such that the signal interferences should be avoided. Moreover, in (Huang, Jing, & Raychaudhuri, 2009), for control channel estimation, fast fourier transform-based radio designs are used which theoretically enable CR receivers to detect the carrier frequency and the bandwidth of a signal without causing interference to the neighboring devices. While, in (Ma, Han & Shen, 2005), the authors use a global plan to exchange the control information between CR devices. However, maintaining global controls by having large sets of frequent information exchange causes overheads for devices and hence complicates their architecture.

In order to increase the throughput capacity of various spectrum bands i.e. several devices can simultaneously transmit on the same bands, multi-channel MAC protocols are proposed in literature. These protocols are divided into single rendezvous (SGV) (Chen, Sheu & Yang, 2003) and multiple rendezvous (So & Walrand, 2005) approaches (MRV). In SGV, all the devices rendezvous at a single control channel for information exchange that can become a bottleneck. Contrary, in MRV, several control channels are used for information exchange reducing the overhead of bottleneck, but causing the problem of transmitter and receiver interferences. The complete comparison of multichannel MAC protocols along with their complexities, advantages and limitations can be found in (Mo, Wilson, So & Walrand, 2005).

1.2.3. Spectrum Mobility

As initiated in (Akyildiz, Lee, Vuran & Mohanty 2008), the spectrum mobility is based on the concept of leaving the licensed band when a legacy primary user arrives. This type of mobility occurs more frequently under ad-hoc conditions, where a CR device may also leave the neighborhood due to its user's mobility (Akyildiz, Lee, & Chowdhury, 2009). Several other intrinsic difficulties arise in using the CR devices under ad-hoc infrastructures, which require reexamining in depth all the aspects such as the topology changes, adaptation of routing protocols, continuity and quality of service issues. Further, the spectrum utilization breakage caused by the CR user's movement is imminent and techniques must be developed in order to find another spectrum band in cases of mobility. As spectrum mobility is a new research area with hardly any research being performed in exploring its aspects in detail, one can suggest the techniques of either monitoring the primary user's activity in advance (i.e. pessimistic or proactive approaches) or to take the decision of finding another band exactly when the mobility occurs (i.e. optimistic or reactive approaches), in order to minimize spectrum mobility (Akyildiz, Lee, & Chowdhury, 2009). Thus, in-depth analysis needs to be done to solve the aforementioned issues and to move further in order to examine this hot research area in details.

Above discussion clears that all the CR functions must be performed robustly and on run-time bases, due to the dynamic nature of modern day networks. For these reasons, we are required to develop efficient and sophisticated approaches to give more autonomy and decision power to each CR user. Further, these users will work with greater dynamism and accuracy, if they cooperate with their neighboring devices to have a more precise knowledge about the relative unutilized spectrum and the corresponding primary user devices' characteristics.

1.3. MULTIAGENT SYSTEMS

The intention of applying distributed artificial intelligence (DAI) techniques to the modern network domains has always been an interesting prospect. Generally, in DAI based applications, many entities work together through coordination and communication to solve particular problems. At first, the problem to be solved is decomposed into several parts and then distributed to participating devices (or agents). Secondly, a subset of agents forming a multiagent system (Figure 3), provides the required cooperation and autonomy to solve the decomposed tasks. Obviously, there exist several definitions of agent and MAS (Ioannis, Athanasiadis, Pericles & Mitkas, 2004)(Weiss, 2000)(Wooldridge, 2002), thus by summarizing these, we offer our own assessment about agent as a loosely coupled system, having the capabilities of performing a task autonomously based on the knowledge received from its environment and/or through other agents' interactions. These autonomous agents work together to form an MAS. As stated in (Nilsson, Russel & Norvig, 1996), an MAS can be similar to a human society, where each human (or agent) has eyes and ears for sensing and hands, feet, legs and other organs for acting. These humans have to interact and talk with each other in order to survive in their society and similar is the case for agents, where they can be partially independent, but may be dependent on other agents' information and support to solve their assigned tasks. For example, in fire alarming applications (Roman-Ballesteros & Pfeiffer, 2007)(Zhang, Deng, Wang, Wittenburg & Xing, 2002), one agent could perform signalization while another can gather sensory data. These two types of agents then work together (forming an MAS) to indicate the presence of "fire" in the building, by turning on the nearby alarm.

An MAS can be partially independent, with the agents having fewer relations to one another. Partially independent systems involve very less cooperation; however agents can cooperate with no intention of doing so. On the other hand, MAS (in many cases) is cooperative where the agents (having less knowledge about their environment) interact with each other. Figure 3 shows an example of two different kinds of multiagent systems. On the left of the figure, all the agents are connected in a distributed and decentralized manner and no single agent has priority over the others. The agents are directly connected with one another via inter-agent cooperation. The right side

Figure 3. A basic diagram showing two different and inter-connected MAS environments

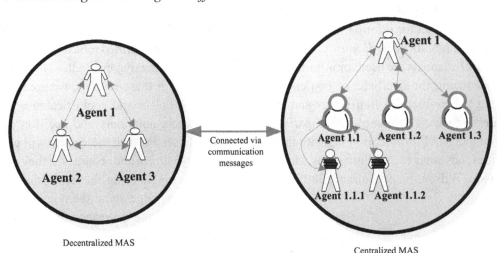

Decentralized MAS

Connected via communication messages

Centralized MAS

of Figure 3 delineates the example of MAS connected in a centralized way. The agents are hierarchically divided into several levels according to their capabilities and priorities. There is no direct communication between the agents rather they only communicate via centralized agent that is able to impose controls and constraints on them. For instance, consider an example of cooperative foraging, where multiple robotic agents are assigned the tasks of rock samples gathering and later bringing them back to the parent robot (or controller agent). If each robot instantaneously knows all rock discoveries, with the knowledge of where the other robots will choose to forage, they could be programmed to operate identically to a basic centralized configuration. As *Jennings et al* (Jennings, Sycara & Wooldridge, 1998) suggested, few real-world problem domains permit such reductions with agents having incomplete information about the environment, lack of centralized control, decentralized and distributed information, and asynchronous computation.

The classification of MAS applications, utilizations and characteristics is shown in Table 3. Looking at Table 3, we observe that the researchers have applied MAS to several domains, which are highly related to our daily life routine. The distinct and adaptable characteristics of MAS make it suitable for solving many modern day network related problems and issues. The focus of our next sections, especially the proposition of our approach (Section 1.5.5) is also inspired by these adherent and efficient MAS features.

1.3.1. Multiagent System Coordination

Coordination is as fundamental in MAS as it is in other parts of nature. For instant, consider a bunch of clusters where multiple machines work together to solve several multi-threaded tasks or to speed up the computation by a considerable amount. In our atmosphere, we can see a group of ducks maintaining "v" shape while flying. All

Table 3. Mutliagent systems examples, applications and characteristics

VARIOUS examples of MAS utilization in several domains
• In mobile and telecommunication networks in which agents are used to provide efficient communication facilities and better QoS features via call forwarding and signaling (Chen, Cheng & Palenc, 2009).
• In wireless sensor and ad-hoc networks, where nodes cooperate in rough terrains and emergency situations, to solve their problems (Mailler & Lesser, 2003).
• Information handling in Internet, where multiple agents are responsible for information filtering and gathering (Zhang, Lesser & Shenoy, 2009).
• In bio-informatics, where several agents work together to monitor the activities of human body and to report these activities to the doctors (Ren, Ding, Shen & Zhang, 2008).
• Analysis of business processes and supply-chain management between enterprises, where agents represent the people or the distinct departments involved in these processes in different stages and at different levels (Wang & Song, 2008).
• For vehicular networks (Weyns, Holvoet & Helleboogh, 2007).

Some dedicated examples of applying MAS to autonomous networks	Basic characteristics of MAS
• For e-medicine and healthcare (Annicchiarico, Cortés & Urdiales, 2008)(Laleci, Dogac, Olduz, Tasyurt, Yuksel & Okcan, 2008)(Tianfield, 2003) • For grid computing (Guo, Gao, Zhu & Zhang, 2006)(Li & Rudder, 2008) • For maintaining Quality of Service control in decentralized environments (Pour, 2006)(Wolf & Holvoet, 2003) • For network security and maintenance (Hamidi & Mohammadi, 2006)(Hentea, 2007)(Ramanujan & Capretez, 2005)	• MAS is autonomous i.e. it self-organizes itself to find the best solution for the assigned problems without any intervention. • MAS is flexible, since it can be modified and reconstructed, without the need for detailed rewriting of the application. • MAS is most of the times failure proof, usually due to the redundancy of agents and the self-managed features. • MAS provides an infrastructure to enable the cooperation and negotiation between the participating agents. The agents can be either cooperative or self-interested. • MAS is open and most of the times distributed i.e. no centralized entry is responsible for controlling the agents' access, rights and behaviors.

these are coordination examples, in which each entity coordinates its activity with the others to maintain its existence. Formulating an MAS based on coordination allows inter-agent activities to be clearly identified. Coordination consists of several categories including cooperation, which is a coordination activity between non-antagonistic (non-competitive) agents and competition (or negotiation) which is based on coordination between self-interested/competitive agents. In addition, according to (Durfee & Lesser, 1989), coordination is a key concept which differentiates multiagent systems from other related disciplines such as distributed computing, object-oriented systems, and expert systems. The authors of (Durfee & Lesser, 1989) have proposed the basic goals for MAS coordination including: (1) the tasks which should be executed in parallel by various agents, augmenting the rate of task completion, and (2) the interference which should be minimized between the decomposed tasks such that the participating agents' conflicts are reduced. Similar explanation of cooperation is been given in (Weiss, 2000), where the authors present the concept of coordination by first decomposing the task into several subtasks and then assigning the related subtasks

to matching agents (i.e. the agents having the desired problem solving capabilities). In Figure 4, we provide a hierarchical overview of various cooperation and competition mechanisms, along with the reference material can be found in (Denning & Martell, 1998)(Weiss, 2000). Following, we explain summarily rest of the approaches, along with their short definitions in Table 4.

Blackboard Approaches

Cooperative blackboard systems (or hierarchical blackboards) can be easily understood by quoting the human expertise example. The main problem which is to be solved is first written on the *blackboard*. Each person puts his/her expertise regarding the problem by getting sufficient information. The process of adding contributions continues until the problem is solved. Basically, blackboard system consists of three parts including a *knowledge source (KS)* that works as a module in order to provide the specific expertise needed by the application, a *blackboard* which contains the information of partial solutions and finally a *control shell* to maintain the coherence between various knowledge sources. All these parts work

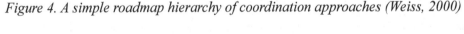

Figure 4. A simple roadmap hierarchy of coordination approaches (Weiss, 2000)

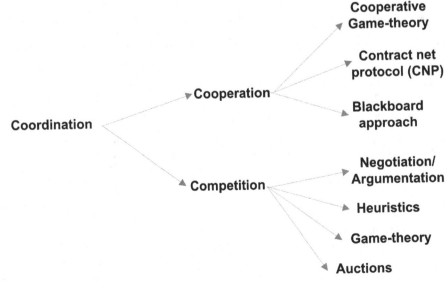

Table 4. Short descriptions of cooperative and competitive approaches

Approaches	Description
Blackboard approaches	The problem to be solved is put on the centralized blackboard (or data structure) and each participating agent contributes with its knowledge until a sufficient solution to the corresponding problem is found.
Game-theory	A mathematical method for decision making and distributed problem solving between the sets of participating agents. In cooperative game-theory the agents make their actions in order to maximize the global utility of the whole game.
Contract net protocol (CNP)	A cooperation protocol for task allocation and sharing using a series of exchange of messages between the manager and contractor agents.
Argumentation	A kind of negotiation that allows agents to *critique* or *argue* on some matter i.e. the agents can exchange more valuable information according to their belief or knowledge regarding some matter.
Heuristics	Are the rules of thumbs which provide empirical outcomes (such as implementations and evaluations) to game-theoretic results.
Auctions	Are the market-based mechanisms for resource assignment and sharing by having several exchanges of bids and awards between the agents.

together to solve the assigned problems. The blackboard systems are proved to be very useful in order to solve the problems with the agents having uncertain or less knowledge about their environment, but sometimes their centralized nature can become a serious bottleneck.

Cooperative and Non-Cooperative Game-Theory

Game-theory is a combination of rules and concepts aimed at analyzing the situations to determine the best course of actions for its participating players. Considering multiagent systems, game-theory is used to analyze the interactive process between the agents (working as players). Generally, in cooperative games the agents make their moves as to maximize the utility of the whole game, while in non-cooperative games, the main goal of the agents is to increase their individual profits. More explanatory details about game-theory can be found in Section 1.4.1.

Argumentation

Argumentation is a kind of negotiation that allows agents to *critique* or *argue* on some matter i.e. the agents can exchange more valuable information according to their belief or knowledge regarding

the problem to be solved. This arguing provides agents the ability to change the view of other agents related to their utility functions. The strong arguing process can change the stance of other agents and they can reach more valuable solutions. However, it is sometimes difficult for programmers to build the agents having the capabilities of argumentation.

Heuristic-Based Approaches

Heuristics are mathematical solutions which provide empirical outcomes (such as implementations and evaluations) to game-theoretic results. In more precise words, to understand the working behavior of a game, each and every outcome of its participating agents has to be modeled and heuristic is an efficient way for this modeling. In contrary, heuristics need huge amount of simulations for obtaining each possible outcome of its players whether it is essential or not. This limitation increases the complexity in building the agents with heuristic behaviors.

Auctions

Inspired from market-based selling and buying of goods, auction is considered to be an efficient way to allocate scarce resources between highly competitive agents. The auctions create an environment for the agents, in which the *buyer agents* send bids to number of *seller agents*, in order to get the required resources. The submitted bids are then compared and the agent with the highest bid wins the award. It then pays the required price for the amount of resources it has acquired. Though, the auctions seem to be quite simple in their working, but at the same time the agents can send false information in order to get higher rewards and it is therefore difficult to maintain an element of trust between them.

1.3.2. Contract Net Protocol

The simplest and distributed way for task allocation via agents' cooperation is contract net protocol (CNP) (Sugawardana, Hirotsu, Kurihara & Fukuda, 2008). The collection of agents in CNP is referred to as *contract net* and the task execution is done as to make a *contract* between these subsets of agents. Each agent can acquire either the role of a *manager* or a *contractor* based on its requirements. The *manager* is responsible for (at first) initiation of the task and then monitoring its execution by exchanging a series of messages.

On the other hand, the *contractor* executes the assigned tasks. Generally, the *manager* wants its goals to be solved, so it sends a *Call for Proposals (CfP)* or a *task announcement* message to its neighboring contractor agents. As specified by *Smith* in (Smith, 1980), a *CfP* message has four slots including: an *eligibility specification slot* (contains a list of eligible contractors), a *task abstraction slot* (is the brief description of the task to be executed), a *bid specification slot* (contains a brief description of essential bids) and *time slot* (refers to the deadline to receiving contractors' responses). This *CfP* message can be generally broadcasted, it can be sent to a subset of agents (limited broadcast) or it may only be sent to one agent (point-to-point). In response to *CfP*, all the eligible contractors send their *proposals* by looking at the *task announcement slot*. The *manager* selects the best *proposal* and the *contract* is then made between the *manager* and the selected *contractor*. The selected *contractor* solves the assigned task either by itself or by further decomposing it into several subtasks and assigning them to other *contractors*. The message passing used to make a contract between a manager and several contractors is shown in Figure 5.

Figure 5. Working of contract net protocol

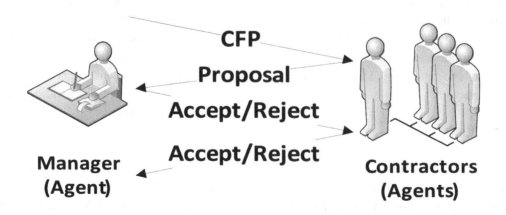

CNP and its extensions (Aknine, Pinson & Shakun, 2004) have also been used in certain autonomous applications. The initial work of *Smith* (Smith & Davis, 1981) on building cooperation based contracts for distributed problem solving in computer networks is one example. Then, the contract net extension method proposed by *Sandholm and Lesser* in (Sandholm & Lesser, 1995) elaborates the working of CNP in autonomous e-commerce applications. Currently, the approach presented in (Qureshi & Terzopoulos, 2008), for camera-based sensor networks, shows how the randomly placed sensor nodes can form several autonomous groups using CNP and can efficiently monitor the nearby environment.

In short, the above detail is an introduction to cognitive radios, multiagent systems, and their applications in relation with autonomous networks. A rather precise state of the art review of various CR functions and multiagent system coordination is also presented. For most of the later sections, we will focus on different dynamic spectrum allocation mechanisms in CR networks using both multiagent systems and game-theoretic approaches. Section 1.5 will explicitly deal with the introduction of different scenarios where the advantages of dynamic and opportunistic spectrum allocations can be exploited.

1.4. SPECTRUM SHARING/ ALLOCATION: THE STATE OF THE ART

Dynamic spectrum allocation and sharing (Bennis, Lara, Wijting & Thilakawardana, 2009) (Cao & Zheng, 2008)(Ma, Han & Shen, 2005) is considered to be the ideal solution to overcome the current spectrum scarcity problem. Future CR network architectures should also be scalable and cooperative enough, in order to provide the best possible spectrum allocation solutions, to fit into modern day applications. The ultimate aim is to increase spectrum utilization through the use of more efficient allocation and sharing schemes, to optimize QoS provision, and to increase the spectrum usage. Once in place, CR users will benefit from these features by being able to access the required services when and where needed, at an affordable cost. Simultaneously, for CR devices, the best possible solution can only be achieved when elements of the radio network are properly configured and suitable spectrum allocation algorithms are applied. In other words, efficient management of the whole reconfiguration decision process is necessary, in order to exploit the advantages provided by dynamic spectrum usage.

Categorically, spectrum allocation and sharing can be viewed as a subset of radio resource management (Dimitrakopoulos, Demestichas, Grandblaise, Mößner, Hoffmeyer & Luo, 2004) and this thinking is the starting point of our next subsections. For a better explanation of some of the already proposed works related to spectrum allocation, we have divided these works into two different domains: (1) spectrum allocation using game-theoretical approaches and (2) spectrum allocation using multiagent systems. Both approaches match precisely the dynamic and distributed nature of CR devices and can model their spectrum sharing behaviors, considering the competitive and cooperative environments. The other approaches such as auctions, MAC-based solutions are out of the scope of our work. In fact, the rich available literature and several interpretations of various authors related to game-theory suggest that the auctions could fall under the category of game-theoretical solutions.

1.4.1. Game-Theoretical Spectrum Sharing

Game-theory provides the mathematical and statistical basis for the analysis of interactive decision-making processes with the prediction of what will happen when players with conflicting interests interact (Myerson, 1984)(Saad, Han, Debbah, Hjørungnes & Basar, 2009) . Basically, a game consists of three main components: a set of players, a set of actions, and a set of preferences. In each game, two important assumptions are made, including the rationality assumption, in which, the players choose strategies that maximize their individual expected payoffs (or utilities) and common knowledge assumption, with all the players having the knowledge of other players joining and leaving the game, their action sets, and definitions of their preference relationship. When the players act, the whole outcome (possible utility of each player) for the game can be derived by their preference relationship. The most famous and best known property that each player must satisfy is called *Nash Equilibrium (NE)*, which is a solution concept of a game involving two or more players. In *NE*, each player is assumed to know the equilibrium strategies of the other players, and no player has anything to gain by changing his or her own strategy. If a player has chosen a strategy which remains unchanged and no other player can benefit by this, then the current set of strategy choices and the corresponding payoffs constitute a *Nash equilibrium*.

Broadly, game-theoretical concepts have been exploited for spectrum allocations in CR networks (Hosseinabadi, Manshaei & Hubaux, 2008)(Niyato & Hossain, 2008), where each CR user has one goal i.e. to maximize its spectrum usage and the *NE* is considered to be the optimal solution for the whole network. The primary and CR users participating in a game, behave rationally to choose strategies that maximize their individual payoffs. The desired payoffs can be in the form of

spectrum utilization for the respected time duration, the associated price, SNR, bit error rate (BER) and delay. To understand precisely the relationship between CR networks and game-theoretical environments, a comparison is depicted in Table 5. To understand Table 5, consider an example of CR network as a game where the CR users are the players. The rational action for a CR user is to sense the outside radio environment and get the spectrum portion which maximizes its throughput for longer time durations. Finally, the CR users follow an order to perform their functions (such as sensing, learning, adapting and sharing) as the players make their moves in a game. The other main reasons to use these two domains together are given below:

- Both the CR networks and game-theoretic approaches are distributed in nature.
- Game-theory models CR users' behaviors to the modest details including their actions, preferences and outcomes.
- Game-theory describes the conflicts, competition, agreements and disagreements for spectrum sharing between CR users.
- Like players, CR users have common goals i.e. to maximize their spectrum usage and the *Nash equilibrium* is considered to be the optimal network state for the participating users.

In the existing literature, game-theory is widely used for spectrum sharing, in a variety of formats according to game models and author prefer-

Table 5. Similarities between game-theory and cognitive radio networks (O'Neel, 2006)

Game	Cognitive radio network
Players	Cognitive radio users
Actions	Actions
Utility function	Throughput (delay, price, spectrum usage)
Outcome space	Outside world (amount of spectrum, SNR)
Order of play	Adaptation/timing

ences. These existing works aim to provide the solutions for dynamic and opportunistic spectrum sharing in a variety of ways and they constitute a rich literature for spectrum allocations. Thus, for the purpose of simplicity and on the basis of players' behaviors in a game, we have classified the already proposed works into three domains: (1) Stackelberg games, (2) Cooperative games and (3) Repeated games. These game-theoretical domains are interlinked i.e. few Stackelberg games can fall under the categories of both cooperative and repeated games and similar is the case for the other two domains.

Stackelberg Games

If in a game, a player's desired outcomes depend not only on its own actions, but on the actions of other neighboring players, then we say that the game is Stakelberg game (He, Prasad, Sethi & Gutierrez, 2007). In computer science literature, Stakelberg games are generally used for distributed resource allocation in different network domains including telecommunication, mobile and wireless networks (Wang, Han & Liu, 2007). Likewise, in CR networks, Stakelberg games have caught the attraction of few researchers for the purpose of dynamic spectrum sharing. In most cases, to efficiently utilize the scarce spectrum resource, the primary users adopt the roles of the leaders, by selecting a subset of neighboring CR users and granting them spectrum access. In return, the CR users work as the followers, by paying primary users (or the leaders) the relative price for spectrum utilization and maximizing their utilities in terms of spectrum access for a specific time period. Different scenarios have been addressed such as base station and mobile users configuration (Lai & El Gamal, 2008), power allocation between selfish nodes (Su & Schaar, 2009), etc.

The above mentioned works on Stackelberg games are based on two different hypotheses. The first hypothesis assumes that the primary users do not have the knowledge about their neighborhood.

In other words, the primary users are unaware of the presence of CR users, and CR users are only allowed to access the spectrum bands without causing collisions to the primary users' transmissions. The second hypothesis is based on the assumption that primary users are aware of the neighboring CR users and they have higher priority on accessing the corresponding spectrum bands. They work like market based *sellers* by charging CR users (or *buyers*) for their spectrum access. As mentioned in (Zhang & Zhang, 2009), even the primary and CR users can sometimes work by having knowledge about each other, still the primary users cannot charge CR users to improve their transmissions. In simple words, the aforementioned solutions do not consider the situations where CR users can work as *relaying nodes* to benefit the neighboring primary user transmissions.

Based on the above limitation, the work presented in (Zhang & Zhang, 2009) proposes a framework, where primary users select some appropriate CR users and use them as *relays* to improve their transmissions. In return, the CR users are rewarded with more chances to access the available spectrum bands. To achieve spectrum access, the CR users pay the related price to the primary users which is proportional to the total time they have utilized the corresponding band. For primary users, their utility is maximized in terms of both the transmission rate and the payment obtained from CR users. The proposed relaying approach can also fall under the category of cooperative games but still it considers the traditional perfect neighborhood knowledge assumption, where the CR users have to continuously monitor the primary users' moves. This assumption may sometimes lead CR users towards serious drawbacks of imperfect information.

Cooperative Games

As discussed in (Etkin, Parekh & Tse, 2007), in non-cooperative game-theoretical settings the players lack the necessary cooperation between themselves that may affect the whole performance of a game. Consequently, in many cases, the results obtained from non-cooperative approaches may be poor. Besides, in CR networks several users can coexist on the same band and if there is no inter-user cooperation, then this factor will lead us to an increase value of mutual interference and the effects of hidden and exposed terminal problems are much higher.

To mitigate the mentioned shortcomings, a very small number of game-theoretical researchers have drawn their focus towards using cooperative games for efficient spectrum allocations (Fujii & Suzuki, 2005)(Hamdi & Letaief, 2007)(Menon, Mackenzie, Buehrer & Reed, 2004). Considering these works, the distinction between cooperative and non-cooperative game-theory is simple to understand. For example, playing chess is clearly competitive as each player makes a move in its own benefit. While, gathering rock samples is an example of a cooperative game, where each robot gathers a rock sample as well as helps others for the maximization of a global utility.

In continuation to the above discussion, the cooperative games have not been widely applied to CR networks for spectrum sharing, because on contrary, the non-cooperative games are easy to deploy and they can even model the spectrum sharing situations to the precise details, producing accurate results. However, in (Menon, Mackenzie, Buehrer & Reed, 2004) and (Hamdi & Letaief, 2007), the authors apply the cooperative game-theory for spectrum sharing, both in centralized and decentralized settings. The former addresses the spectrum allocation problem in client-server setting, where the CR users sense the empty spectrum portions and send this information to the base station. In downlink transmission, the base station rationally decides which user should access the spectrum. In later work, spectrum sharing problem is modeled as a potential game and each CR user chooses the strategy which is best for itself. Another important element of these approaches is the amount of knowledge that each CR user has

about the others. For example, a CR user may not know the coexistence of the neighboring players on the same band, their utility functions, their transmit power. Therefore, the above solutions assume that the CR users' utilities, transmission powers and spectrum usage are common knowledge. Moreover, their utility functions are chosen in order to maximize the global utility. Yet, still the cooperative approaches require a feedback from each player to be sent to the centralized player (or server) about its utility function, which increases their algorithmic complexity.

Repeated Games

Repeated or static "Cournot" game is a type of competitive game, where the players compete for resources and products, by assuming their actions will not affect the decisions of their rivaling players. Applying repeated games to CR networks (Tian, Yang & Xu, 2007), the authors formulate the spectrum sharing problem as an iterative process, under some decision rules and constraints. These decision rules choose the next possible rational action for a CR user and the related constraints impose a punishment mechanism for selfish CR users. Under these constrains, the CR users which announce their true strategy are awarded with highest share of spectrum. Furthermore, the players (primary or CR users) repeat their games, so that they can make decisions based on the past moves of the neighboring players. This process can help them imposing threats and punishments for the selfish users (Wang, Wu, Ji, Liu, & Clancy, 2008).

One important reason to use competitive repeated games is the fact that in competitive scenarios sometimes the players may deviate from their loyal behaviors in order to maximize their individual profits. This deviation could provide higher profits to the deviating users but at the same time lowering the profits for the non-deviating (or loyal) users. Thus, some punishment mechanisms must be restored and if by repeating a game one player knows the past punishments of the other player due to deviation, collusion among the users can be maintained to choose the solution which results in highest profits for the loyal users.

A related solution to the above discussion is presented in (Niyato & Hossain, 2008) which is based on the concept of competitive pricing. The primary users sell their spectrum to the CR users. Related to each successfully shared spectrum portion, primary user receives the associated price. The CR users are considered to have the ability of moving from one spectrum portion to another. Both the cases are considered where a primary user can monitor the past strategies adopted by other users, and the case where a primary user can observe the spectrum demands from the CR users. The CR users' utility is the function of their transmission on the acquired band along with the price charged by the primary users. The users repeat their game multiple times and the previous outcomes of the other users can be observed. The game is divided into three action phases including *maintaining collusions*, *deviating from collusions*, and *punishment actions*. At the deviating phase all the players choose the strategy from which none of them wants to deviate. Though, the approach seems to be interesting, the authors of (Ji & Liu, 2008) argue that forming collusions among competitive users may seriously deteriorate the efficiency of dynamic spectrum sharing, causing interferences. To combat this limitation, they propose a pricing-based collusion-resistant dynamic spectrum allocation approach. The collection of the available spectrums from primary users is considered as a "pool" and the CR users accessing this spectrum pool have to pay the associated price for their spectrum usage. The authors follow the assumption where all the users are selfish and rational (i.e. their objectives are to maximize their own utilities) and the users are allowed to cheat or deviate from loyal behaviors whenever they believe these behaviors can help them to increase their utilities. Nevertheless, in these games usually establishing trust amongst the players is quiet a difficult task and most of

the players can carry on their selfish behaviors until the end of the whole game.

The above game-theoretical approaches seem promising for spectrum sharing; however, they inherit the fundamental limitation of being non-cooperative. Obviously, solutions based on cooperative game-theory can establish some amount of cooperation between the competitive players; still the researchers are hesitant to develop cooperative solutions considering the difficulty to create players who can work selflessly in order to maximize the global utility of a network. On contrary, multiagent system has been known as a way to overcome the mentioned problems. In recent works, some initiatives of using agents over CR devices has been taken into account by allowing CR devices to work together for dynamic spectrum sharing, Thus, our next section focuses on detailing the approaches using multiagent systems for dynamic spectrum allocation.

1.4.2. Spectrum Sharing Using Multiagent Systems

To move forward in today's communications network domains, the devices' functionalities should tend towards more autonomous algorithms, with the ability to respond to different network situations and conditions dynamically. In the future, these devices will also learn and adapt to their environment. Particularly, current network architectures are distributed, autonomous and unpredictable and the most suitable way to share the resources is to deploy a number of software agents that are able to share these scarce resources efficiently. When problems arrive where resources are interdependent, agents can also cooperate with one another to ensure that the interdependencies are properly managed. Especially, when the networks are highly dynamic and the devices can appear or leave the network at any time, the agents forming multiagent systems can perform information gathering and they can interact with each other in order to share the resources based on their gathered information.

Several researchers have applied multiagent systems for resource allocation and sharing in different contexts and it is been realized that to be successful in dynamic environments, research attentions should be given to the deployment of multiagent systems over present-day applications (Sycara, 1998). One of the novel contributions towards this step is the utilization of multiagent systems in CR networks (Mir, Merghem-Boulahia & Gaiti, 2009). Table 6 compares the similarities between an agent and a CR. It is clearly envisaged that both the agents and CR devices are aware of their surrounding environments through interactions, sensing, monitoring and they have autonomy and control over their current actions and states. They can work together (with their neighbors) to solve the assigned tasks as well as to share information about their goals and utility functions.

Preceding the above discussion, a related approach is presented in (Jiang, Ivan & Anita, 2007), where an MAS is used for information sharing and decision distribution amongst CR networks. The main focus of the article is on *distributed constraint optimization problem (DCOP)* which is concerned with efficient assignment of spectrum resources using agents' coordination. Multiple wireless LANs (WLANs) are collocated in a geographical area with agents deployed at each of the access points (APs). All the AP agents form an interactive MAS, which is responsible for managing radio resources across collocated WLANs. Further, the authors have presented each

agent's architecture (Figure 6), having two main parts including *predictive parameter estimation* (responsible for generating parameters estimates using the signal characteristics received from WLAN environments) and *resource management optimization* (makes the main decisions of AP including the requests to be accepted from mobile stations, and less interfered channel selection). This approach has been explained conceptually for both centralized and decentralized environments, but none of the simulation results are presented.

Unlike the DCOP approach, the works presented in (Kloeck & Jondra, 2006) (Tonmukayakul & Weiss, 2005) are based on the deployment of market-based multiagent systems for spectrum sharing. In (Kloeck & Jondra, 2006), a distributed and dynamic billing, pricing and resource allocation mechanism is examined. The protocol used for radio resource allocation between the CR devices and operators is termed as *multi-unit sealed-bid auction* protocol that is based on the concept of bidding and assigning goods. The behavior of each CR user is represented by a *radio resource good allocation agent (RAA)* that generates the bids to get the desired spectrum. An *auctioneer agent* represents the behavior of the operator, having the capabilities of announcing auctions (for spectrum sharing) and calculating the spectrum price. The whole environment architecture consists of several parts including:

Table 6. Possible similarities between an agent and a CR node

Agent	Cognitive radio
Environment awareness via past observations	Sensing empty spectrum portions, primary user signals, etc.
Acting through actuators	Deciding the bands/channels to be selected
Interaction via cooperation	Interaction via beaconing
Autonomy	Autonomy
Working together to achieve shared goals	Working together for efficient spectrum sharing
Contains a knowledge base with local and neighboring agents' information	Maintains certain models of neighboring primary users' spectrum usage

Figure 6. Block diagram showing an agent's operation (Jiang, Ivan & Anita, 2007)

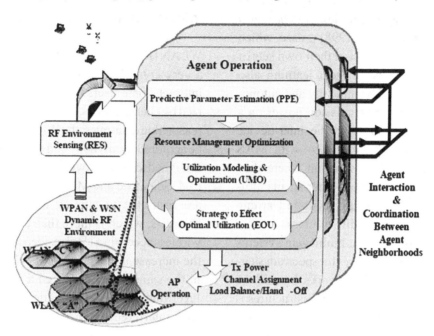

- *QoS buffer management (QoS-BM)*, determines the data to be sent first,
- *User profile manager (UPM)*, identifies the QoS requirements and spectrum preferences for the CR users, and
- *Bidding strategy (BIS)*, gets its input from *QoS-BM* to make a resource requesting bid.

All the above parts work together to make an input message (or a bid) and this message is then sent to the *auctioneer agent*. On the reception of a bid, the *auctioneer agent* decides (based on the user requirements) the part of the spectrum to be allocated to the CR user. Correspondingly, in the second approach (Tonmukayakul & Weiss, 2005), the CR users are represented as *consumer agents* and primary users are working as the *provider agents* to lease their spectrum to the requesting *consumer agents*. A *secondary agent* announces spectrum access bid (on behalf of *consumer agents*) to the neighboring *provider agents* along with the information including the part of spectrum

needed, degree of control over the spectrum and the price it is willing to pay. In return, the corresponding *provider agents* reply with their bids. If there is an agreement, then the spectrum sharing is started, otherwise requirements from both the agents go into a competitive scenario and the best agent wins the deal. However (as mentioned in Section 1.4.1), in competitive approaches, the agents can sometimes send false bids, requiring the necessity of complex schemes to be developed for managing and maintaining inter-agent trust mechanisms.

According to *Weib et al* (Weib & Sen, 1996), to improve a system's performance, an MAS should have the ability to learn from its past actions while adapting to the new ones. In vicinity, approaches based on MAS learning (i.e. delay sensitive and Q-learning) are presented in (Li, 2009)(Shiang & Van der Schaar, 2008). In these works, the CR users periodically exchange the information about the spectrum channels they are likely to be using, with their neighboring devices. They also provide the information of the relative traffic on a sensed channel. Based on the exchanged information, a multiagent learning approach similar to *fictitious play*[1] (Fudenberg & Levine, 1998) is used, which helps CR users to build a list of their own sets of appropriate channels. Multiagent learning also allows the CR users to dynamically and autonomously optimize their transmission power on a selected channel and to avoid the inter-device interferences. Using *fictitious play* with MAS can bring the agents to a situation where they have weak assumptions about other agents' utility functions and thus getting accurate learning information can become a difficult task.

To conclude this section, multiagent systems can be used in a variety of ways for spectrum sharing and allocation over CR networks, but still the deployment of MAS over these infrastructures is relatively a new concept. It is also obvious that a bundle of CR nodes serving together through MAS cooperation can efficiently utilize the available spectrum. Thus, our next section will focus on various (possible) spectrum allocation scenarios and the deployment of our cooperative multiagent approach in one of these scenarios.

1.5. SOME SPECTRUM SHARING SCENARIOS

The preceding sections gave a brief state of the art review of spectrum sharing using game-theoretical and multiagent system approaches for CR networks. This section provides some of the possible spectrum sharing scenarios[2], for which the techniques mentioned in Section 1.2 may be applied. For the convenience of the readers, we have divided the scenarios into four different domains as follows: (1) Spectrum Sharing via Interference Avoidance in ISM Bands, (2) Administrated Commons, (3) Opportunistic Utilization of TV Bands, and (4) Spectrum Allocation under "Ad-hoc" Terrains.

1.5.1. Spectrum Sharing via Interference Avoidance in ISM Bands

WLAN (Ruggeri, Iera & Polito 2005) has become a very common technology largely adopted by internet home users and companies. Characterized by cheap devices, autonomous behaviors and reasonable data-rates, the WLANs are available to be acquired by anybody and employed anywhere. Designed to operate over license-free ISM (Industrial, Scientific and Medical) bands, the WLANs are restricted to employ only few orthogonal channels, which is more than enough to provide wireless access in a local residence area. However, the increase in the number of WLANs operating in the same area introduced a new interference level that could not be anticipated. Nowadays, such interference represents the main limitation of the WLANs performance. Furthermore, this level of interference introduces new challenges to all the other technologies that operate in the ISM bands (Sawan, Yamu & Coulombe, 2005). Similar issues could happen with the development of LTE femto-cells (Mobile Dev & Design, n.d.). These small cells, located at a home or a private area, can provide better coverage and higher capacity in indoor environments. They however suffer from interference caused by other neighboring femto-cells. The common point of introducing these two cases is that the interference could sometimes be anarchic and any kind of alternative is required.

To be able to overcome the interference problem, we foresee a cooperative environment where the WLAN/LTE devices having CR capabilities are able to optimize the frequency reuse and can select an alternative spectrum portion, in case of interferences. Then, they can send the newly searched spectrum portion information to the neighboring devices in such a way that the possible collisions could be avoided.

1.5.2. Administrated Commons

This scenario is based on addressing the spectrum usage issues in mobile networks with devices having WiMAX connections (Shamsan & Rahman, 2008). Mainly, the area is administrated by a central entity (such as an ISP) which is able to impose basic rules (or spectrum etiquettes (Raychaudhuri & Jing, 2003)) to the users. Mobile stations using CR capabilities are supposed to perform signal measurements and apply etiquettes in order to contribute to an efficient use of the spectrum. This includes optimized frequency reuse (in ISM bands) and secondary usage of UHF (ultra high frequency) bands (GSM World, n.d.). Etiquette may be a combination of several behavioral rules, including: using correct MAC address, switching to a convenient access point and transmitting measurement reports. In such a context, distributed and autonomous operational modes will be privileged and different overlay functions may be implemented such as rendezvous facilities (Romdhani, Mounir Kellil, Lach, Bouabdallah & Bettahar, 2004).

An application example of this scenario is a hospital. In this application, many Wi-XX technologies can be used at the same time and the number of mobile users cannot be determined in a precise way. With the CR capability, a given terminal (a doctor's PDA) might be able to choose the best spectrum band. This choice is made by cooperating with the agents embarked on the other CR devices and also taking into account the number of current users and their priorities.

1.5.3. Opportunistic Utilization of TV Bands

The European countries are planning to improve TV services by stopping the broadcast of PAL (phase alternative line) signals and using DVB-T (digital video broadcasting- transmitter) standards instead (http://www.dvb.org/, n.d.). This improvement process will leave a sufficient amount of unutilized spectral resources (Figure 7) especially in the case of the famous digital dividend (European Commision Information Society, n.d.). To understand this scenario, let us describe the exploitation of the UHF bands to understand more precisely what the numerical dividend is. UHF bands are split in channels, and the channels 21 to 69 were originally assigned to TV services. These channels are 8 MHz width, consecutives, and the channel 21 corresponds to the bands 470-478 MHz. A DVB-T covers a city and its neighboring sectors, and uses 6 UHF channels to broadcast almost 36 TV programs, e.g. in France, nearly 100 DVB-transmitters are used for broadcasting (http://www.dvb.org/about_dvb/dvb_worldwide/france/, n.d.). In a given place, we can hence expect that the TV services utilize 6 among 49 UHF channels, leaving 43 channels free. The fact of good propagation properties and an ample amount of empty spaces, justify the world interest for these bands.

Discussions about the exploitation of the digital dividend have already been started in WRC'07 (World Radiocommunication Conference) (International Telecommunication Union, n.d.), where the researchers have decided to assign the UHF channels 60 to 69 to IMT (International mobile telecommunication) services. Nevertheless, still a large set of free spectral resources remains unutilized. In Europe, these remaining sets of resources could be used in an opportunistic manner. For this purpose, the first initiative was the creation of the task group 4 (TG4) (http://www.ero.dk/TG4, n.d.) by the European countries. TG4 is responsible for measuring the performance of DVB-transmitters and receivers in order to utilize the unused TV bands opportunistically and to compare these performances with the results obtained from mobile devices working in GSM or WiMAX.

To summarize, for the opportunistic utilization of spectral resources in digital dividend, firstly, efficient signal processing techniques must be developed, for the characterization of TV-bands,

Figure 7. TV bands utilization example (Corderio, Challapali, Birru & Shankar, 2006)

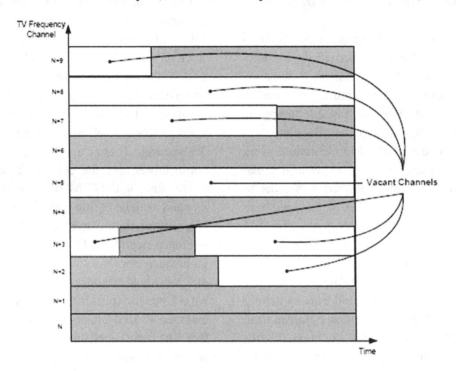

with the DVB-transmitters having CR function-alities. Secondly, because DVB-transmitters normally share their spectral resources with the radio microphones, hence more precise spectrum sharing techniques may be deployed (European Radiocommunications Committee Report, 2000). Finally, some mechanisms must be explored in order to differentiate between a DVB-T and a microphone signal.

1.5.4. Spectrum Allocation under "Ad-hoc" Terrains

To understand this "ad-hoc" terrain scenario consider an emergency case (during a trip or an accident in a very remote situation), where the user is in a non-covered zone (i.e. the radio resources at this moment are not available) or the radio access technology requires an energy that the terminal (a mobile, a laptop, or a PDA, etc.) does not own. In this case, the terminal 1 (as shown in Figure 8) having CR functionality,

observe the nearby terminals (or the rescue parties) and communicates with them using MAS cooperation (Steps 1 and 2). This cooperation will enable the corresponding terminal to use the other terminal's band and its access technology that takes into account the emergency priority (step 3). Thus, the CR plays the role of interoperability, such that the terminal can receive the information on the available operators on its neighboring zone with their radio access technology. Likewise, the role of the deployed agent is to cooperate and modify the terminal's software configuration by loading the necessary algorithms that fit the best to the current terminal state (step 4). Regarding this hot new area of research (Akyildiz, Lee, & Chowdhury, 2009), our proposed cooperative MAS approach is designed for ad-hoc networks, where the agents are deployed over each of the CR and primary user devices. These agents then cooperate within each other for spectrum sharing. The following subsection explains our proposed approach in detail.

1.5.5. A Cooperative Spectrum Sharing Framework

Since we have described a set of scenarios in which spectrum sharing can be possible in different ways, thus, in this section we propose the deployment of a cooperative MAS for opportunistic and dynamic spectrum sharing. We start our proposition by assuming an ad-hoc environment, with a number of primary and CR user devices, as shown in Figure 9. An agent is embarked over each device for the purpose of cooperation and performing main decision i.e. the selection of best spectrum sharing agreement. The primary and CR user agents cooperate using the message passing mechanism of contract net protocol. The CR users have established spectrum sharing agreements with the neighboring primary users using MAS cooperation. A CR user is not restricted to use only one spectrum portion at an instance of time, rather it can be the part of several spectrum sharing agreements simultaneously.

In the remainder of this section, we will focus on our design model shown in Figure 10, along with the behaviors of primary and CR users in Figures 11 and 12. Obviously, the primary user does not contain the cognitive radio module, while the agent module is common in both the primary and CR users. Basically, our design is based on five different interlinked parts that embody the working of our cooperative approach:

- Dynamic spectrum sensor;
- Spectrum characterizer;
- Secondary user interface;
- Agent's knowledge module; and
- Agent's cooperation module.

Dynamic Spectrum Sensor

The function of dynamic spectrum sensor (DSS) is the detection (or sensing) of radio *spectrum holes* or *white spaces* (Ghozzi, Zayen & Hayar, 2009). In other words, DSS is used to sense the empty

Figure 8. CR users in ad-hoc situations (Akyildiz, Lee, & Chowdhury, 2009)

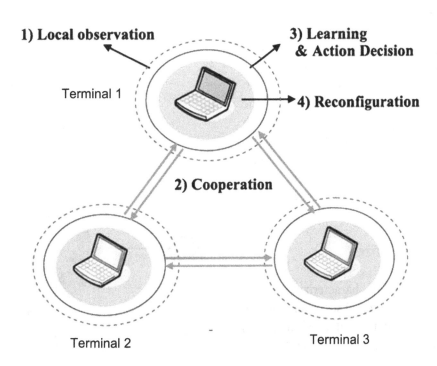

Figure 9. A cooperative ad-hoc CR network

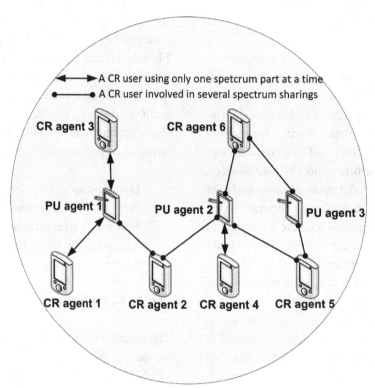

Figure 10. Working of CR and agent modules

spectrum portions. In essence, spectrum sensing is not within the scope of our work, however, any of the techniques mentioned in Section 1.2.1 could be deployed for spectrum sensing. For DSS, it is also necessary that the sensing is performed by considering a real-time dynamic environment, because it is not obvious at what time a spectrum band is occupied or when it is free. Thus, all the factors such as primary user's signal power with the respected noise, spectrum traffic (by calculating the number of current users and taking into account the application type (Fudenberg & Levine, 1998)), sampling time and intervals must be kept in consideration.

Spectrum Characterizer

Fundamentally, spectrum characterizing is considered to be a sub-function of spectrum sensing. In this regard, our spectrum characterizer (SC) module functions as to arrange/divide the spec-

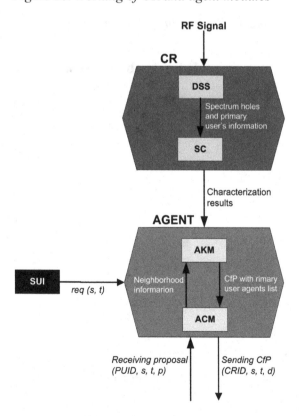

Figure 11. Working of a CR user

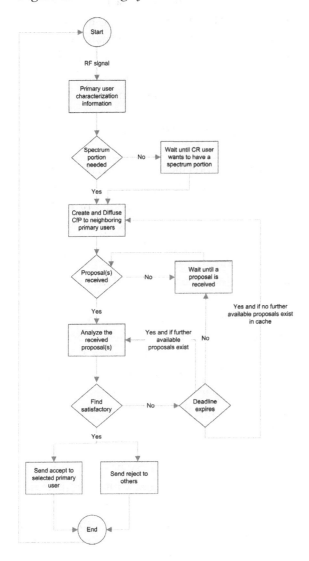

Figure 12. Working of a primary user

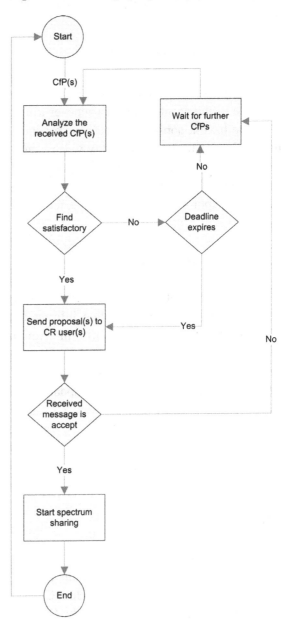

trum holes information (received through DSS) according to some specific criteria, i.e. capacity, primary user's signal power, etc. In a simple way, to create a capacity based descending ordered list of neighboring primary users (i.e. the users with available spectrum), the Shannon Theorem (Shannon, 1949) as formulated in (Clancy, 2006) is used:

$$C = B\log_2(1+SNR)$$

Where C is the capacity in *bits per second*, B is the bandwidth measured in *hetrz* and SNR is the respected signal-to-noise ratio in *watts*. For more details, the complete derivation and formulation of the above equation is found in (Clancy, 2006). In addition, research is in progress for characterization of sensed spectrum holes, based on other important factors like holding time, delay, and path loss.

Secondary User Interface

Secondary user interface (SUI) sends a *request* message to the agent module, whenever a user wants to have a portion of spectrum (for internet surfing, watching high quality videos, etc.). The message is of the form *req (s,t)*, where *s* is the amount of spectrum needed by the CR user depending upon its application in use, for a time duration *t*.

Agent's Knowledge Module

The fourth part, agent's knowledge module (AKM) gets primary user characterization information from SC module which serves as a motivation for agents that subsets of primary users having unutilized spectrum portions are available. This list is not permanent rather it is updated and maintained on regular time intervals. CR user's AKM (or CR-AKM) also gets the *req* message from SUI module and based on the inputs from both the modules, it prepares a *call for proposal (CfP)* message:

CfP (CRID, s, t, d)

where *CRID* is the CR user ID (or its agent's identification) and it is used to help primary user to reply back to the corresponding CR, *s* is the amount of spectrum needed by the CR user, *t* is the desired time limit (or holding time) for the spectrum utilization and *d* is the deadline to receive the primary users' responses (proposals). Parallel to *CfP* creation, CR-AKM maintains the neighboring CR users' information that is received via frequent interactions between the agents, along with a list of previously received proposals (if there exist any). This information includes the leaving and joining of neighboring nodes in a network and their current spectrum status and it helps a

CR user to create a more precise *CfP*. Uniformly, the PU-AKM module functions almost in the same manner by maintaining the neighboring CR users' information, the statistics of their arrivals and departures from the neighborhood and a list of their previous spectrum demands.

Agent's Cooperation Module

Agent cooperation module (ACM) is responsible for managing the cooperation between primary and CR users. After the reception of *CfP* message from CR-AKM, the CR-ACM sends the received *CfP* to the neighboring and currently available primary user agents. The primary users are considered to be available, if they still exist in the corresponding CR user's neighborhood with their unused spectrum portions. Besides, CR-ACM performs the main decision of selecting the appropriate *proposal* for a CR user. In much the same way, PU-ACM chooses the most suitable *CfP* for a primary user and sends the *proposal* in response. Finally, the appropriate agreements for both the primary and CR users is the one which is profitable and maximizes their utility values.

On average, the utility for primary user is the price paid by CR user agents for their spectrum utilization divided by the amount of spectrum a primary user has shared for the respected time period. The CR user agent's utility is represented as its spectrum usage for the required time divided by the corresponding price paid to the primary users. Thus, by assigning priorities (or weights) to each of the mentioned parameters, the desired utility values can be calculated.

In relation to the above description, Figures 11 and 12 delineate the behavioral working of CR and primary users respectively. The behaviors follow the same *sensing*, *characterizing* and *cooperating* steps mentioned before. For a CR user, the spectrum sharing process starts by getting the characterization results and the user requirements. This process continues until the sending of *CfPs*, receiving of *proposals* and ends either by accepting or rejecting a proposal and then going back to the start state. The primary user follows the same pattern by first analyzing the received *CfPs*, sending the *proposals* as responses and finally ending the process either by having an agreement or disagreement with the conforming CR user.

Behavioral Modeling using Petri Nets

Petri Net (PN) (Lyle, 1981) is a graphical and formal tool for the modeling of activity flows in a complex system. PN represents the interactions between devices and nodes in a system. Its distributed nature makes it highly suitable to model the interactions between the agents. Generally, it contains a set of places $P = \{p_1, p_2, ... p_m\}$, transitions $T = \{t_1, t_2, ... t_m\}$, inputs I, outputs O and markings M. Places (or circles) depict several states of a system and transitions (or boxes)

represent various phases the system has to pass through before ending. The marking of a PN is a vector, the components of which are positive integer values. The dimension of this vector is equal to the number of places. A *token* (represented by a small filled circle) is moved from one place to another when a transition is fired.

In Figure 13, a spectrum sharing process is drawn to capture the behavior of a cognitive radio user (CR_i) when it has to handle two proposals from primary users PU_j and PU_k. The process goes through several states and transitions (Tables 7 and 8) such as sending CfPs, receiving proposals, waiting, accepting and rejecting proposals, sharing and utilizing spectrum and finally paying the price. Moreover, CR_i has accepted the offer of PU_j due to its satisfactory proposal and at the same time it has rejected PU_k offer. The movements of tokens from one state to another delineate the message

Figure 13. A PN model for spectrum sharing (Mir, Merghem-Boulahia & Gaiti, 2010)

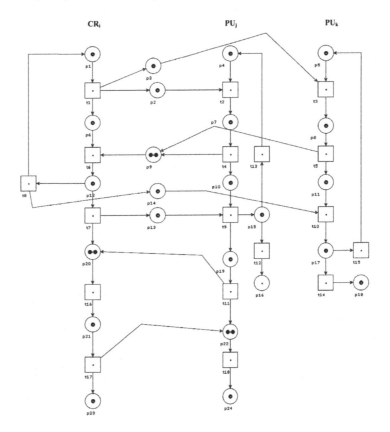

exchanges between cognitive radio and primary users, the transferring of spectrum usage from PU_j to CR_i and the payment of respected price from CR_i to PU_j. Likewise, Table 9 depicts the initial and final markings (M_O and M_f) of tokens after firing all the transitions and it verifies that the M_f becomes '3', only when a resource is been shared and the price is been paid.

Tables 7, 8 and 9 allow us to conclude following basic definitions related to spectrum sharing process.

Definition 1: The PN is said to be bounded free if the number of tokens in its places do not exceed k such that $k > 0$ and it is an integer.

A PN is bounded when it is k-bounded.

For a system, its bounded behavior is very important in order to verify the internal errors. Sometimes, tokens may stay permanently in a place for a longer time period, creating the possibility of deadlock. In Figure 13, the tokens are bounded to move from one place to another after firing the subsequent transitions, therefore the deadlock situation never occurs.

Definition 2: A Petri net $N_s = \{P_s, T_s, I_s, O_s, M_s\}$ for an empty part of the spectrum s, is said to be unsuccessful if moving from M_{os} to M_{fs}, results in no change in the utility functions of both the participating secondary and primary users such that:

$$U_{CRi} = 0 \ and \ U_{puj} = 0, \forall \ \{CR_i, PU_j\} \in \{CR, PU\} \tag{1}$$

where $\{U_{CRi}, U_{puj}\} \in R$

In Figure 13, the spectrum sharing process between CR_i and PU_k results in no change in their utility functions, proving to be unsuccessful.

Table 7. States

p_1	CR_i: ready to send CfP
p_2	PU_j: PU agent's cache (CfP arrives)
p_3	PU_k: PU agent's cache (CfP arrives)
p_4	PU_j: ready to receive CfP
p_5	PU_k: ready to receive CfP
p_6	CR_i: CfP sent and wait for proposals
p_7	PU_j: CfP received
p_8	PU_k: CfP received
p_9	CR_i: CR agent's cache (proposals arrive)
p_{10}	PU_j: proposal sent and wait for the final response
p_{11}	PU_k: proposal sent and wait for the final response
p_{12}	CR_i: proposal received
p_{13}	PU_j: PU agent's cache (accept arrives)
p_{14}	PU_k: PU agent's cache (reject arrives)
p_{15}	PU_j: temporary waiting phase
p_{16}	PU_j: further CfP receiving stopped
p_{17}	PU_k: reject received and temporary waiting phase
p_{18}	PU_k: further CfP receiving stopped
p_{19}	PU_j: ready to share the acquired spectrum
p_{20}	CR_i: ready to utilize spectrum
p_{21}	CR_i: spectrum utilized and ready to pay price
p_{22}	PU_j: spectrum shared and ready to receive price
p_{23}	CR_i: price paid
p_{24}	PU_j: price received

Table 8. Transitions

t_1	CR_i: send CfP
t_2	PU_j: receive CfP
t_3	PU_k: receive CfP
t_4	PU_j: send proposal
t_5	PU_k: send proposal
t_6	CR_i: receive proposal
t_7	CR_i: send accept
t_8	CR_i: send reject
t_9	PU_j: receive response (accept)
t_{10}	PU_k: receive response (reject)
t_{11}	PU_j: start sharing the spectrum
t_{12}	PU_j: continue receiving further CfPs
t_{13}	PU_j: stop receiving further CfPs
t_{14}	PU_k: stop receiving further CfPs
t_{15}	PU_k: continue receiving further CfPs
t_{16}	CR_i: start utilizing the acquired spectrum
t_{17}	CR_i: pay price
t_{18}	PU_j: receive price

Table 9. Initial and final markings

	M_o	t_1	t_2	t_3	t_4	t_5	t_6	t_7	t_8	t_9	t_{10}	t_{11}	t_{12}	t_{13}	t_{14}	t_{15}	t_{16}	t_{17}	t_{18}	M_f
p_1	1	-1							+1											1
p_2	1	+1	-1																	1
p_3	1	+1		-1																1
p_4	1		-1											+1						1
p_5	1			-1												+1				1
p_6	1	+1				-1														1
p_7	1		+1		-1															1
p_8	1			+1	-1															1
p_9	2			+1	-1	-2														2
p_{10}	1			+1					-1											1
p_{11}	1				+1					-1										1
p_{12}	1						+1	-1	-1											0
p_{13}	1							+1		-1										1
p_{14}	1								+1	-1										1
p_{15}	1								+1			-1	-1							0
p_{16}	1													+1						2
p_{17}	1											+1		-1	-1					0
p_{18}	1														+1					2
p_{19}	1									+1	-1									1
p_{20}	2						+1					+1				-1				3
p_{21}	1																+1	-1		1
p_{22}	2											+1					+1	-1		3
p_{23}	1																	+1		2
p_{24}	1																		+1	2

Definition 3: The Petri net $N_i = \{P_i, T_i, I_i, O_i, M_i\}$ is said to be successful for a $CR_i \in CR$, if the movement from initial marking M_{osi} to final marking M_{fsi}, maximizes its utility function U_{CRi}. And similar is the case for a primary user.

Definition 4: Let M_d be a desired markings set. The final marking set M_f is acceptable if and only if it represents the combination of both M_o and M_d i.e.

$$M_f = M_o + M_d \qquad (2)$$

Figure 13 is not restricted to the initial marking M_o, since it is possible to increase M_o of several places (such as $p_{16}, p_{18}, p_{20}, p_{22}, p_{23}$ and p_{24}) to M_f.

Some Results

To show the simulated working of our proposed approach, some results conducted in Java Application Development Environment (JADE) (http://jade.tilab.com/, n.d.) are depicted in this sub-section. For experiments, we have considered an ad-hoc scenario with multiple primary and CR user agents. We randomly place a number of primary and CR users in a specified area where each of the devices contains an agent deployed over it for cooperation purposes. For simplicity, two different fixed values of times (such as T1 and T2) are assumed, where Time 1 (T1) represents the short-term case and Time 2 (T2) is the longer period. When T1 is considered, the SU agents can ask for the amount of spectrum within one hour limit (i.e. $0 \leq T1 \leq 60$ Minutes) and similarly this limit is within two hours as in case of T2 (i.e. $0 \leq T2 \leq 120$ Minutes). Our simulation starts with the total number of 6 CR and 4 primary users, and for each next round there is an addition of 10 agents (i.e. 6 CR and 4 primary user agents). The simulation is conducted for 10 subsequent rounds, with a total of 20 hours per day, for both T1 and T2 respectively and the average values of parameters are taken to draw the graphs. The primary user agent's utility is represented as the price paid by CR user agents for spectrum utilization divided by the amount of spectrum it has shared for the respected time period (holding time) as required by the CR users. The CR user agent's utility is represented as its spectrum usage for the required time divided by the corresponding price paid to the primary users.

In Figure 14, we compare the average utility of primary and CR users at T1 with those at T2 for different numbers of users (10, 20, 30...). The figure shows that when the time limit is T2, the utilities are a bit less compared to the results obtained at T1. This is because the environment is partially mobile and some of the users are slightly hesitant to share their spectrum for longer periods. We observe that the average utility values show the linear behavior even with the increased number of agents.

Figure 15 illustrates the percentage resource utilization of CR users over time periods T1 and T2. The beginning of the graph indicates that all the required resources are completely shared; whereas when the number of CR users reaches the middle values (30 to 40), approximately 90% of resources are shared. This spectrum sharing trend continues following the same pattern reaching higher values with achieved percentage of resources is between 75 to 85%. Thus, the performance degradation in terms of spectrum sharing is not high, even with large resource requirements.

The above two graphs are presented just to understand the CR and primary user agents'

Figure 14. Average utility of each agent

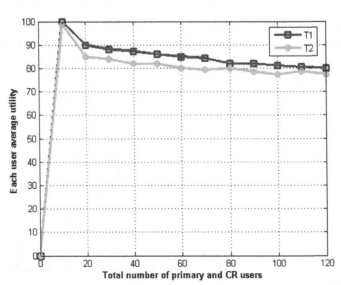

Figure 15. Total spectrum usage

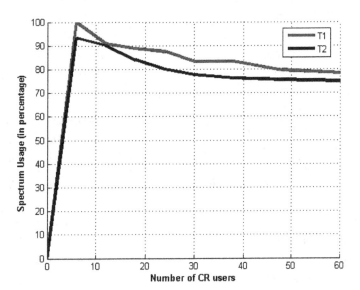

spectrum utilizations in terms of their achieved values of utilities. The proposed approach seems to converge well in a sense that it can find good utility based solutions using a small bilateral exchange of messages. Further results are in progress to monitor the agents' behaviors in various other simulation settings.

To sum up this section, we have stated four different scenarios concerning the spectrum sharing issues. Each one has its own relevance and importance for modern day communication networks. Therefore, we briefly detailed the areas and bands over which spectrum sharing techniques can be opportunistically deployed. Both the game-theoretical approaches and multiagent systems can be applied to these scenarios due to the dynamic and distributed nature of present wireless technologies. Applying these two approaches over wireless networks would allow us to design and implement systems which can give the detailed low-level behavioral representation of each wireless device up to the highest level representation of their collective behaviors. Important properties of collective systems such as autonomy, cooperation, competition could also be examined. Finally, to elaborate one of many possible examples of us-

ing MAS and game-theoretical approaches over the mentioned scenarios, we have applied our MAS approach to one of them. Our proposed approach can be summarized as a cooperative MAS architecture deployed over ad-hoc CR networks for dynamic spectrum sharing. The proposed MAS brings the primary and CR users into relative sharing agreements, thereby improving the overall spectrum utilization. The deployed agents can continue making parallel spectrum sharing agreements in a cooperative and distributed way, taking into account their utility functions. This type of cooperative spectrum sharing can also be applied to establish cooperation between the CR users for more effective spectrum usage.

1.6. CONCLUSION

This chapter is an effort to provide an overview of using multiagent systems over cognitive radio networks for dynamic spectrum sharing. Concisely, in this work, we have explained that avoiding unnecessary spectrum wastage problem requires performing the sharing and allocation functions opportunistically. Currently, many authors prefer the use of game-theoretical solutions for spectrum sharing, due to their distributed and fast behaving natures. Thus, by keeping in mind the frequent use of game-theory over cognitive radio network, we have presented a brief state of the art review of various spectrum sharing solutions using these approaches. Traditionally, game-theory lacks the basic inter-user cooperation where the nodes do not work together to maximize a global utility function. Therefore, in accordance to developing spectrum sharing solutions where the cognitive radio nodes can work collectively, a comprehensive study of utilizing multiagent systems over cognitive radio networks is presented.

Besides existing approaches, four increasingly different spectrum sharing scenarios are proposed for the ISM and UHF bands, the mobile and WiMAX networks, the digital dividend bands, and emergency ad-hoc networks. Each scenario introduces new issues and challenges for dynamic spectrum allocations. To prove the necessity of developing efficient spectrum sharing solutions in these scenarios, we have applied our cooperative multiagent system approach under ad-hoc conditions. In contrast, we argue when the environment is competitive, game-theory can produce good results. Finally, our current work can be extended to compare the proposed cooperative approach with the existing competitive solutions.

REFERENCES

Adomavicius, G., & Gupta, A. (2005). Toward comprehensive real-time bidder support in iterative combinational auctions. *Information Systems Research*, *16*(2), 169–185. doi:10.1287/isre.1050.0052

Aknine, S., Pinson, S., & Shakun, M. F. (2004). An extended multi-agent negotiation protocol. *International Journal of Autonomous Agents and Multi-Agent Systems*, *8*, 5–45. doi:10.1023/B:AGNT.0000009409.19387.f8

Akyildiz, F., Lee, W.-Y., Vuran, M. C., & Mohanty, S. (2006). NeXt generation/dynamic spectrum access/cognitive radio wireless networks: A survey. *International Journal of Computer and Telecommunications Networking*, *50*(13), 2127–2159.

Akyildiz, I. F., Lee, W.-Y., & Chowdhury, K. R. (2009). CRAHNs: Cognitive radio ad hoc networks. *International Journal of Ad Hoc Networks*, *7*, 810–836. doi:10.1016/j.adhoc.2009.01.001

Akyildiz, I. F., Lee, W.-Y., Vuran, M. C., & Mohanty, S. (2008). A survey on spectrum management in cognitive radio networks. *IEEE Communications Magazine*, *46*, 40–48. doi:10.1109/MCOM.2008.4481339

Annicchiarico, R., Cortés, U., & Urdiales, C. (2008). Agent technology and e-health. In Annicchiarico, R., Cortés, U., & Urdiales, C. (Eds.), *Whitestein series in software agent technologies and autonomic computing*. Babel, Switzerland: Birkhäuser Verlag.

Bennis, M., Lara, J., Wijting, C., & Thilakawardana, S. (2009). WINNER spectrum sharing with fixed satellite services. *VTC 2009: Proceedings of IEEE Vehicular Technology Conference*.

Bixio, L., Oliveri, G., Ottonello, M., & Regazzoni, C. S. (2009). OFDM recognition based on cyclostationary analysis in an Open Spectrum scenario. VTC 2009. *Proceedings of 69th IEEE Vehicular Technology Conference*.

Bouzegzi, A., Ciblat, P., & Jallon, P. (2008). Matched filter based algorithm for blind recognition of OFDM systems. *VTC 2002: Proceedings of 68ᵗʰ IEEE Vehicular Technology Conference*, (pp. 1-5).

Bui, T., Gachet, A., & Sebastian, H. J. (2006). Web services for negotiation and bargaining in electronic markets: Design requirements. *HICSS 2005: Proceedings of the 38th Annual Hawaii International Conference on System Sciences*, (p. 38).

Cabric, D., Mishra, S. M., & Brodersen, R. W. (2004). Implementation issues in spectrum sensing for cognitive radios. *Proceedings of 38ᵗʰ Annual Asilomar Conference on Signals, Systems and Computers*, (pp. 772-776).

Cao, L., & Zheng, H. (2005). Distributed spectrum allocation via local bargaining. SECON 2005. *Proceedings of 2ⁿᵈ Annual IEEE Conference on Sensor and Ad Hoc Communications and Networks*, (pp. 475-486).

Cao, L., & Zheng, H. (2008). Distributed rule-regulated spectrum sharing. *IEEE Journal on Selected Areas in Communications, 26*(1), 130–145. doi:10.1109/JSAC.2008.080112

Chen, B., Cheng, H., & Palenc, J. (2009). Integrating mobile agent technology with multi-agent systems for distributed traffic detection and management systems. *Journal of Transportation Research Part C. Emerging Technologies, 17*, 1–10. doi:10.1016/j.trc.2008.04.003

Chen, J., Sheu, S., & Yang, C. (2003). A new multichannel access protocol for IEEE 802.11 ad hoc Wireless LANs. *PIMRC 2003: Proceedings of 14th IEEE International Symposium on Personal Indoor, Mobile Radio Communications*, (pp. 2291-2296).

Clancy, T. C. (2006). *Dynamic spectrum access in cognitive radio networks*. Ph. D. dissertation, University of Maryland, MD, USA.

Corderio, C., Challapali, K., Birru, D., & Shankar, S. (2006). IEEE 802.22: An introduction to the first wireless standard based on cognitive radios. *The Journal of Communication, 1*, 38–47.

Dana, P. H. (1996). *The Geographer's Craft Project*. Boulder, USA: Department of Geography, University of Colorado.

Davies, J., Lytras, M., & Sheth, A. (2007). Semantic-web-based knowledge management. *IEEE Internet Computing Journal, 11*, 14–16. doi:10.1109/MIC.2007.109

De Wolf, T., & Holvoet, T. (2003). Towards autonomic computing: agent based modelling, dynamical systems analysis, and decentralised control. *INDIN 2003: Proceedings of IEEE International Conference on Industrial Informatics*, (pp. 470- 479).

Denning, P. J., & Martell, C. (1998). *Coordination*. USA: Springer Verlag.

Digham, F. F., Alouni, M.-S., & Simon, M. K. (2007). On the energy detection of unknown signals over fading channels. *IEEE Transactions on Communications, 55*(1), 21–24. doi:10.1109/TCOMM.2006.887483

Dimitrakopoulos, G., Demestichas, P., Grandblaise, D., Mößner, K., Hoffmeyer, J., & Luo, J. (2004). *Cognitive radio, spectrum and radio resource management. Wireless World Research Forum*. United Kingdom: WWRF.

Durfee, E. H., & Lesser, V. (1989). Negotiating task decomposition and allocation using partial global planning. In Gasser, L., & Huhns, M. (Eds.), *Distributed artificial intelligence* (*Vol. II*, pp. 229–244). USA.

DVB. (n.d.). *France*. Retrieved from http://www.dvb.org/about_dvb/dvb_worldwide/france/

Etkin, R., Parekh, A., & Tse, D. (2007). Spectrum sharing for unlicensed bands. *IEEE Journal on Selected Areas in Communications, 25*, 517–528. doi:10.1109/JSAC.2007.070402

European Commision. (2009). *Information society*. Retrieved from http://ec.europa.eu/information_society/policy/ecomm/radio_spectrum/topics/reorg/pubcons_digdiv_200907/index_en.htm

European Radiocommunications Committee. (2000). *Report (ERC Report 88) for the compatibility and sharing analysis between dvb–t and radio microphones in bands iv and v*. European Conference of Postal and Telecommunications Administrations (CEPT), Naples, February, 2000.

Fudenberg, D., & Levine, D. K. (1998). *The theory of learning in games*. Cambridge, MA: MIT Press.

Fujii, T., & Suzuki, Y. 2005. Ad-hoc cognitive radio-development to frequency sharing system by using multi-hop network. *DySPAN 2005: Proceedings of IEEE Symposium on New Frontiers in Dynamic Access Networks,* (pp. 589-592).

Gaurav, S. Kasbekar, & Sarkar, S. (2009). Spectrum auction framework for access allocation in cognitive radio networks. *Proceedings of the 10th ACM International Symposium on Mobile Ad hoc Networking and Computing,* (pp. 13-22).

Ghasemi, A., & Sousa, E. S. (2005). Collaborative spectrum sensing for opportunistic access in fading environment. *DySPAN 2005: Proceedings of IEEE Symposium on New Frontiers in Dynamic Access Networks,* (pp. 131–136).

Ghozzi, M., Zayen, B., & Hayar, A. (2009). Experimental study of spectrum sensing based on distribution analysis. *ICT-MobileSummit 2009: Proceedings of 18th ICT Mobile and Wireless Communications Summit,* June 10-12.

Gummadi, R., Balakrishnan, H., & Seshan, S. M. (2009). Coordinating spectrum sharing in heterogeneous wireless networks. *COMSNETS 2009: Proceedings of IEEE Communication Systems and Networks and Workshops,* (pp. 1-10).

Guo, H., Gao, J., Zhu, P., & Zhang, F. (2006). A self-organized model of agent-enabling autonomic computing for grid environment. *Proceedings of the 6th World Congress on Intelligent Control and Automation,* (pp. 2623–2627).

Hamdi, K., & Letaief, K. B. (2007). Cooperative communications for cognitive radio networks. *Proceedings of the 8th Annual Postgraduate Symposium, The Convergence of Telecommunications, Networking and Broadcasting,* (pp. 878-893).

Hamidi, H., & Mohammadi, K. (2006). Modeling fault tolerant and secure mobile agent execution in distributed systems. *International Journal of Intelligent Information Technologies, 2*, 21–36. doi:10.4018/jiit.2006010102

Haykin, S. (2006). Cognitive dynamic systems. *IEEE Journal on Selected Areas in Communications, 94*, 1910–1911.

He, X., Prasad, A., Sethi, S. P., & Gutierrez, G. (2007). A survey of Stackelberg differential game models in supply and marketing channels. [JSSSE]. *Journal of Systems Science and Systems Engineering, 16*, 385–413. doi:10.1007/s11518-007-5058-2

Hentea, M. (2007). Intelligent system for information security management: Architecture and design issues. *Journal of Issues in Informing Science and Information Technology, 4*, 29–43.

Hosseinabadi, G., Manshaei, H., & Hubaux, J.-P. (2008). *Spectrum sharing games of infrastructure-based cognitive radio networks*. (Technical report LCA-REPORT-08-027). France, 2008.

Huang, K.-C., Jing, X., & Raychaudhuri, D. (2009). MAC protocol adaptation in cognitive radio networks: an experimental study. *ICCCN 2009: Proceedings of 18th International Conference on Computer Communications and Networks,* (pp. 1-6).

International Telecommunication Union. (2007). *World Radio Communications Conference*. Retrieved from http://www.itu.int/ITU-R/index.asp?category=conferences&rlink=wrc-07&lang=en

Ioannis, N., Athanasiadis, & Pericles, A., & Mitkas. (2004). An agent-based intelligent environmental monitoring system. *Management of Environmental Quality International Journal, 15*, 238–249. doi:10.1108/14777830410531216

JADE. (2011). *Home page.* Retrieved from http://jade.tilab.com/

Jennings, N. R., Sycara, K., & Wooldridge, M. (1998). A roadmap of agents research and development. *AAMAS 1998: Proceedings of Autonomous Agents and Multi-agent Systems,* (pp. 7-38).

Ji, Z., & Liu, K. J. R. (2008). Multi-stage pricing game for collusion-resistant dynamic spectrum allocation. *IEEE Journal on Selected Areas in Communications, 26*, 182–191. doi:10.1109/JSAC.2008.080116

Jiang, X., Ivan, H., & Anita, R. (2007). Cognitive radio resource management using multi-agent systems. *CCNC 2007: Proceedings of Consumer Communications and Networking Conference,* (pp. 1123-1127).

Kloeck, H. J., & Jondra, F. (2006). Multi-agent radio resource allocation. *MONET 2006: Proceedings of ACM Mobile Networks and Applications,* (pp. 813-824).

Kumar, S., Raghavan, V. S., & Deng, J. (2006). Medium access control protocols for ad-hoc wireless networks: A survey. *International Journal of Ad-hoc Networks, 4*(3), 326–358. doi:10.1016/j.adhoc.2004.10.001

Lai, L., & El Gamal, H. (2008). The water-filling game in fading multiple-access channels. *IEEE Transactions on Information Theory, 54*, 2110–2122. doi:10.1109/TIT.2008.920340

Laleci, G. B., Dogac, A., Olduz, M., Tasyurt, I., Yuksel, M., & Okcan, A. (2008). SAPHIRE: A multi-agent system for remote healthcare monitoring through computerized clinical guidelines. In Annicchiarico, R., Cortés, U., & Urdiales, C. (Eds.), *Whitestein series in software agent technologies and autonomic computing* (pp. 25–44). Babel, Switzerland: Birkhäuser Verlag.

Li, H. (2009). Multi-agent Q-Learning of channel selection in multi-user cognitive radio systems: A two by two case. *SMC 2009: Proceedings of IEEE International Conference on Systems, Man and Cybernetics,* (pp. 1395-1422).

Li, Z., & Rudder, M. P. (2004). A rule-based multi-agent infrastructure for supporting autonomic grid applications. ICAC *2004: Proceedings of the 1st International Conference on Autonomic Computing,* (pp. 278–279).

Lunden, J., Koivunen, V., Huttunen, A., & Poor, H. V. (2009). Collaborative cyclostationary spectrum sensing for cognitive radio systems. *IEEE Transactions on Signal Processing, 57*(11), 4182–4195. doi:10.1109/TSP.2009.2025152

Lyle, J. (1981). *Petri net theory and the modeling of systems.* USA: Prentice Hall PTR.

Ma, L., Han, X., & Shen, C.-C. (2005). Dynamic open spectrum sharing MAC protocol for wireless ad hoc networks. *DySPAN 2005: Proceedings of New frontiers Dynamic Spectrum Access Networks,* (pp. 203-213).

Mailler, R., & Lesser, V. (2003). *Cooperative negotiation for optimized distributed resource allocation in soft real-time.* UMass Computer Science Technical Report, USA.

Menon, R., MacKenzie, A. B., Buehrer, R. M., & Reed, J. H. (2004). Game theory and interference avoidance in decentralized networks. *SDR 2004: Proceedings of Technical Conference and Product Exposition.*

Mir, U., Merghem-Boulahia, L., & Gaïti, D. (2009). Utilization of a cooperative multiagent system in the context of cognitive radio networks. *MANWEEK 2009: Proceedings of 5th International Week on Management of Networks and Services,* (pp. 100-104).

Mir, U., Merghem-Boulahia, L., & Gaiti, D. (2010). Multiagent based spectrum sharing using Petri nets. *AI&DS: Proceedings of 8th International Conference on Practical Applications of Agents and Multiagent Systems,* (pp. 537-546).

Mishra, S. M., Sahai, A., & Brodersen, R. (2006). Cooperative sensing among cognitive radios. *ICC 2006: IEEE International Conference on Communications*, (pp. 1658-1663).

Mitola, J. (2000). *Cognitive radio: An integrated agent architecture for software defined radio.* Ph.D Thesis, KTH Royal Institute of Technology, Sweden, 2000.

Mitola, J., & Maguire, G. Q. Jr. (1999). Cognitive radio: Making software radios more personal. *IEEE Personal Communications, 6*, 13–18. doi:10.1109/98.788210

Mo, J., Wilson, H.-S., & Walrand, J. (2005). Comparison of multi-channel MAC protocols. *Proceedings of the 8th ACM International Symposium on Modeling, Analysis and Simulation of Wireless and Mobile Systems*, (pp. 209-218).

Mobile Dev & Design. (2009). *LTE and Femtocells – An essential symbiosis.* Retrieved from http://mobiledevdesign.com/tutorials/lte-femtocells-0603/

Mokhtar, R. A., Khatun, S., Ali, B. M., & Ramli, A. (2009). Cooperative sensing in cognitive radio networks-avoid non-perfect reporting channel. *American Journal of Engineering and Applied Sciences, 2*(2), 471–475. doi:10.3844/ajeassp.2009.471.475

Myerson, R. B. (1984). *An introduction to game theory.* Northwestern University, Center for Mathematical Studies in Economics and Management Science, Discussion Papers 623, Sept. 1984.

Nilsson, J. N., Russell, S. J., & Norvig, P. (1996). *Artificial intelligence: A modern approach.* USA: Artificial Intelligence.

Niyato, D., & Hossain, E. (2008). Competitive pricing for spectrum sharing in cognitive radio networks: Dynamic game, inefficiency of Nash equilibrium, and collusion. *IEEE Journal on Selected Areas in Communications, 26*, 192–202. doi:10.1109/JSAC.2008.080117

O'Neel, J. (2006). *Analysis and design of cognitive radio networks and distributed radio resource management algorithms.* PhD Dissertation, Virginia Tech, Sep, 2006.

Peng, H., Zheng, H., & Zhao, B. Y. (2006). Utilization and fairness in spectrum assignment for opportunistic spectrum access. *ACM Mobile Networks and Applications, 11*(4), 555–576. doi:10.1007/s11036-006-7322-y

Pour, G. (2006). Multi-agent autonomic architectures for quality control systems. *ICIS-COMSAR 2006: Proceedings of IEEE/ACIS International Workshop on Component-Based Software Engineering, Software Architecture and Reuse*, (pp. 168-173).

Qureshi, F., & Terzopoulos, D. (2008). A simulation framework for camera sensor networks research. *CNS 2008: Proceedings of 11th Communications and Networking Simulation Symposium*, (pp. 41-48).

Ramanujan, S., & Capretez, M. A. M. (2005). ADAM: A multi-agent system for autonomous database administration and maintenance. *International Journal of Intelligent Information Technologies, 1*, 14–33. doi:10.4018/jiit.2005070102

Raychaudhuri, D., & Jing, X. (2003). A spectrum etiquette protocol for efficient coordination of radio devices in unlicensed bands. *PIMRC2003: Proceedings of 14th IEEE International Symposium on Personal Indoor, Mobile Radio Communications*, (pp. 172–176).

Ren, L.-H., Ding, Y.-S., Shen, Y.-Z., & Zhang, X.-F. (2008). Multi-agent-based bio-network for systems biology: Protein–protein interaction network as an example. *Journal of Amino Acids, 35*, 565–572. doi:10.1007/s00726-008-0081-2

Roman-Ballesteros, I., & Pfeiffer, C. F. (2007). *Multi-robot surveillance system for indoors fire detection: A case of study cost effective automation.* IFAC Conference on Cost Effective Automation in Networked Product Development and Manufacturing.

Romdhani, I., Mounir Kellil, M., Lach, H.-Y., Bouabdallah, A., & Bettahar, H. (2004). Mobility-aware rendezvous point for mobile multicast sources. *WWIC 2004. Proceedings of the 2nd International Wired/Wireless Internet Communications Conference*, (pp. 62-73).

Ruggeri, G., Iera, A., & Polito, S. (2005). 802.11-based wireless-LAN and UMTS interworking: Requirements, proposed solutions and open issue. *Computer Networks Journal*, *47*, 151–166. doi:10.1016/j.comnet.2004.07.002

Saad, W., Han, Z., Debbah, M., Hjørungnes, A., & Basar, T. (2009). Coalitional game theory for communication networks: A tutorial. *IEEE Signal Processing Magazine*, *26*, 77–97. doi:10.1109/MSP.2009.000000

Sahai, A., & Cabric, D. (2005). Spectrum sensing: Fundamental limits and practical challenges. *DySPAN 2005: Proceedings of New frontiers Dynamic Spectrum Access Networks*.

Sahai, A., Hoven, N., Mishra, S. M., & Tandra, R. (2006). *Fundamental tradeoffs in robust spectrum sensing for opportunistic frequency reuse*. Technical Report, March 2006. Retrieved from http://www.eecs.berkeley.edu/»sahai/Papers/CognitiveTechReport06.pdf

Sahai, A., Hoven, N., & Tandra, R. (2004). Some fundamental limits in cognitive radio. *Proceedings of 42nd Allerton Conference on Common, Control and Computing*.

Sahin, M. E., Guvenc, I., & Arslan, H. (2009). Uplink user signal separation for OFDMA-based cognitive radios. *EURASIP Journal on Advances in Signal Processing*, *61*(101), 290.

Sandholm, T., & Lesser, V. R. (1995). Issues in automated negotiation and electronic commerce: Extending the contract net framework. *ICMAS 1995: Proceedings of the 1st International Conference on Multiagent Systems*, (pp. 328-335).

Sawan, M., Yamu, H., & Coulombe, J. (2005). Wireless smart implants dedicated to multichannel monitoring and microstimulation. *IEEE Circuits and Systems Magazine*, *5*, 21–39. doi:10.1109/MCAS.2005.1405898

Schmid, S., Eggert, L., Brunner, M., & Quit, J. (2005). Towards autonomous network domains. *INFOCOM 2005: Proceedings of 24th Annual Joint Conference of the IEEE Computer and Communications Societies*, (pp. 847- 2852).

Shamsan, Z. A., & Rahman, T. A. (2008). Spectrum sharing studies of IMT-advanced and FWA services under different clutter loss and channel bandwidths effects. *Progress in Electromagnetic Research*, *87*, 331–344. doi:10.2528/PIER08102404

Shannon, C. (1949). Communication in the presence of noise. *Proceedings of the Institute for Radio Engineers*.

Shiang, H.-P., & Van der Schaar, M. (2008). Delay-sensitive resource management in multi-hop cognitive radio networks. *DySPAN 2008: Proceedings of New frontiers Dynamic Spectrum Access Networks*, (pp. 14-17).

Smith, R. G. (1980). The contract net protocol: High-level communication and control in a distributed problem solver. *IEEE Transactions on Computers*, *C29*, 1104–1113. doi:10.1109/TC.1980.1675516

Smith, R. G., & Davis, R. (1981). Frameworks for cooperation in distributed problem solving. *IEEE Transactions on Systems, Man, and Cybernetics*, *11*, 61–70. doi:10.1109/TSMC.1981.4308579

So, H. W., & Walrand, J. (2005). *McMAC: A multi-channel MAC proposal for ad-hoc wireless networks*. Technical Report, April 2005. Retrieved from http://www.cs.berkeley.edu/~so/pubs/mcmac_desc.pdf

Su, Y., & Schaar, M. (2009). A new perspective on multi-user power control games in interference channels. *IEEE Transactions on Wireless Communications, 8,* 2910–2919. doi:10.1109/TWC.2009.071058

Sugawara, T., Hirotsu, T., Kurihara, S., & Fukuda, K. (2008). Effects of fluctuation in manager-side controls on contract net protocol in massively multi-agent systems. *HMS 2008: Proceedings of IEEE International Conference on Distributed Human-Machine Systems.*

Sycara, K. P. (1998). Multiagent systems. *Artificial Intelligence Magazine, 19,* 79–92.

TG4. (2010). *Digital dividend.* Retrieved from http://www.ero.dk/TG4

TEROPP. (n.d.). *Website.* Retrieved from http://era.utt.fr/fr/projets_de_recherche/carnot_teropp.html

Tian, F., Yang, Z., & Xu, S. (2007). Spectrum sharing based on iterated prisoner's dilemma in cognitive radio. *Proceedings of International Symposium on Intelligent Signal Processing and Communication Systems,* (pp. 232–235).

Tianfield, H. (2003). Multi-agent autonomic architecture and its application in e-medicine. *IAT 2004: Proceedings of the IEEE/WIC International Conference on Intelligent Agent Technology,* (pp. 601–604).

Tonmukayakul, & Weiss, M. B. H. (2005). An agent-based model for secondary use of radio spectrum. *DySPAN 2005: Proceedings of New frontiers Dynamic Spectrum Access Networks,* (pp. 467–475).

Unnikrishnan, J., & Veeravalli, V. V. (2008). Dynamic spectrum access policies for cognitive radio. *CDC 2008: Proceedings of 47th IEEE Conference on Decision and Control,* (pp. 5545-5550).

Wang, B., Han, Z., & Liu, K. J. R. 2007. Stackelberg game for distributed resource allocation over multiuser cooperative communication networks. *INFOCOM 2007: Proceedings of 23rd Annual Joint Conference of the IEEE Computer and Communications Societies.*

Wang, B., Wu, Y., Ji, Z., Liu, K. J. R., & Clancy, T. C. (2008). Game theoretical mechanism design for cognitive radio network with selfish users. *IEEE Signal Processing Magazine, 25,* 74–84. doi:10.1109/MSP.2008.929552

Wang, S., & Song, H. (2008). A multi-agent based combinational auction model for collaborative e-procurement. *IEEM 2008: Proceedings of IEEE International Conference on Industrial Engineering and Engineering Management,* (pp. 1108-1112).

Weib, G., & Sen, S. (1996). *Adaptation and learning in multiagent systems.* Berlin, Germany: Springer Verlag.

Weiss, G. (2000). *A modern approach to distributed artificial intelligence.* USA: MIT Press.

Weyns, D., Holvoet, T., & Helleboogh, A. (2007). Anticipatory vehicle routing using delegate multiagent systems. *ITSC 2007: Proceedings of The 10th International IEEE Conference on Intelligent Transportation Systems,* (pp. 87-93).

Wooldridge. M. (2002). *An introduction to multiagent systems.* John Wiley & Sons Press, England.

World, G. S. M. (n.d.). *UHF bands for mobile.* Retrieved from http://www.gsmworld.com/our-work/public-policy/spectrum/digital-dividend/uhf_bands_for_mobile.htm

Xu, N. (2002). A survey of sensor network applications. *IEEE Communications Magazine, 8,* 102–114.

Yongle, W., Wang, B., Liu, K. J. R., & Clancy, T. C. (2008). Collusion-resistant multi-winner spectrum auction for cognitive radio networks. *GLOBECOM 2008. Proceedings of IEEE Global Telecommunications Conference*, (pp. 1-5).

Yucek, T., & Arslan, H. (2007). OFDM signal identification and transmission parameter estimation for cognitive radio applications. *GLOBECOM 2007: Proceedings of IEEE Global Telecommunications Conference*, (pp. 4056-4060).

Zhang, C., Lesser, V., & Shenoy, P. (2009). A multi-agent learning approach to online distributed resource allocation. *IJCAI 2009: Proceedings of International Joint Conference on Artificial Intelligence*, (pp. 361-366).

Zhang, J., & Zhang, Q. 2009. Stackelberg game for utility-based cooperative cognitive radio networks. *MobiHoc 2009: Proceedings of ACM 10th ACM International Symposium on Mobile Ad Hoc Networking and Computing*, (pp. 23-32).

Zhang, W., Deng, Z., Wang, G., Wittenburg, L., & Xing, Z. (2002). Distributed problem solving in sensor networks. *AAMAS 2002: Proceedings of the 1st International Conference on Autonomous Agents and Multiagent Systems*, (pp. 988–989).

ENDNOTES

[1] Fictitious play refers to a situation where each user presumes that its opponents are using stationary strategies. In the context of CR networks, it means that the CR users are not hesitant to share their information with other users and based on the information exchange they build the models about the spectrum utilization strategies of the neighboring users.

[2] These scenarios are addressed as a part of our on-going project named as TEROPP [110]. TEROPP is a Franco-German project based on deploying efficient solutions related to the various aspects of CR networks. Our contribution to the project is the development of a cooperative approach for opportunistic spectrum allocation.

About the Contributors

Phan Cong-Vinh received a PhD in computer science from London South Bank University (LSBU) in UK, a BS in mathematics and an MS in computer science from Vietnam National University (VNU) in Ho Chi Minh City, and a BA in English from Hanoi University of Foreign Languages Studies in Vietnam. He finished his PhD dissertation with the title of *Formal Aspects of Dynamic Reconfigurability in Reconfigurable Computing Systems* supervised by Prof. Jonathan P. Bowen at LSBU where he was affiliated with Centre for Applied Formal Methods (CAFM), Institute for Computing Research (ICR). From 1983 to 2000, he was a lecturer in mathematics and computer science at VNU, Posts and Telecommunications Institute of Technology (PTIT) and several other universities in Vietnam before he joined research with Dr. Tomasz Janowski at International Institute for Software Technology (IIST) in Macao SAR, China, as a fellow in 2000. From 2001 to 2010 he did research together with Prof. Jonathan P. Bowen as a research scholar and then collaborative research scientist at CAFM. From January 2011 to May 2011 he worked for FPT - Greenwich collaborative program at FPT University (FU) in Vietnam as a visiting lecturer. From June 2011 to present he has become a member of NTT University (NTTU) to take on the responsibilities of an IT Department's Deputy Dean. Regarding academic publications, he has been author or co- author of many refereed contributions published in prestigious journals, conference proceedings or edited books. He is the author of a book on computing science titled *Dynamic Reconfigurability in Reconfigurable Computing Systems: Formal Aspects of Computing* (2009) and editor of two titles besides the present work, *Autonomic Networking-On-Chip: Bio-Inspired Specification, Development, and Verification* (CRC Press) and *Advances in Autonomic Computing: Formal Engineering Methods for Nature-Inspired Computing Systems* (Springer), to be published in 2011 and 2012, respectively. He is also an IEEE member. His research interests center on all aspects of formal methods, autonomic computing and networking, reconfigurable computing, ubiquitous computing, and applied categorical structures in computer science.

* * *

Ahmad Al-Shishtawy is a PhD student at the Royal Institute of Technology (KTH), Stockholm, Sweden, and a Researcher at the Computer Systems Laboratory at the Swedish Institute of Computer Science (SICS), Stockholm Sweden. He received the B.Sc. and M.Sc. degrees in Computer Science from the Ain Shams University, Cairo, Egypt, in 2000 and 2006, respectively, and the Ph.Lic. degree in Electronic and Computer Systems from the Royal Institute of Technology, Stockholm, Sweden, in 2009. His research interests include large-scale distributed systems, peer-to-peer systems, autonomic computing, and control theory.

Christos B. Anagnostopoulos has received his B.Sc. in Computer Science from the Department of Informatics and Telecommunications at the National & Kapodistrian University of Athens (NKUA), Greece, in 2001 and his M.Sc. in Computer Science, Advanced Information Systems from the same department in 2003. He holds a Ph.D. in Modeling Mobile Computing Systems (2008) from NKUA. His research interest is focused on mobile and distributed computing computing systems, context- aware computing, information and approximate reasoning, Semantic Web, and ontological engineering. He had also participated in projects realized in the context of European Union Programs.

Josephina Antoniou received her B.A. (summa cum laude) in Computer Science and Mathematics from Wartburg College, IA, USA in May 2002, her MSc in Advanced Computer Technologies in June 2004, and her Ph.D. in Computer Science, in June 2010, both from the University of Cyprus. She is a Research Associate for the University of Cyprus since June 2002, for the, IST/ICT funded projects: SEACORN, B-BONE, C-MOBILE, and CCAST, dealing with enhanced UMTS, MBMS over UMTS, enhanced MBMS over converged networks, and currently, context-aware multicasting over converged, next generation networks. Her research interests include resource and session management in mobile networks.

Per Brand is Senior Researcher at the Swedish Institute of Computer Science (SICS) in Stockholm, Sweden. He is currently involved in research in the areas of cloud computing, overlays, middleware, and distributed programming systems. He led WP4 in the Peer-to-Peer EU PEPITO project (http://www. sics.se/pepito), where he and his group developed the DSS (a Peer-to-Peer enabled) language-oriented middleware system (http://dss.sics.se). He led WP1 in the recently concluded European project Grid4All and was the chief designer of the Niche platform (http://niche.sics.se) developed in the project and described in the chapter. He was the chief designer of the distribution support system of Mozart (see http://www.mozart-oz.org). He will lead two work-packages dealing with computational storage in the upcoming EU IP-project VISIONcloud.

Nermin Brgulja received his B.Sc. and M.Sc. degrees in Electrical Engineering from the University of Kassel, Germany, in 2003 and 2005, respectively. Since April 2005 he is working as Researcher (Ph.D. candidate) with the Department for Communication Technology at the University of Kassel. He has many years of experience in European research projects: CASCADAS, MobiLife, and mCDN. His research interests include autonomic and bio-inspired computing and communications, mobile computing and context awareness; in particular issues related to assessing the context data validity and distributed data self-organization. He is author of several articles and papers presented in international conferences and journals and has co-authored two chapters in The MobiLife Book: Enabling Technologies for Mobile Services.

Radu Calinescu is a Lecturer in Computing at Aston University, UK, and a part-time Lecturer on the Software Engineering Programme at the University of Oxford. He was previously a Senior Researcher on the Formal Verification research theme at the University of Oxford. He holds an award-winning DPhil in Computation from the University of Oxford, and has over ten years of academic and industrial research experience in developing complex software systems in areas including self-managing systems, model-driven architectures, and information systems for cancer research. His recent research on self-managing

IT systems and systems of systems won best paper awards at international conferences, and the generic development methods and general-purpose software tools he devised as part of this work are currently used by external researchers and practitioners involved in the development of self-managing systems. He has chaired or has been on the program committees of multiple international conferences on autonomic, self-managing and complex systems. He is a senior member of the IEEE and a member of the Editorial Advisory Board for the *International Journal on Advances in Intelligent Systems*.

Ranganai Chaparadza is a Researcher in the field of Internet and telecommunications networks, currently working for Fraunhofer-FOKUS Institute in Berlin, Germany. Current activities include: Technical-Manager and Researcher for the EC-funded FP7-EFIPSANS project, and Chairman of the growing ETSI-AFI-ISG, called "Autonomic network engineering for the self-managing Future Internet," He has plenty of peer-reviewed scientific publications in international conferences/journals/workshops, and implementation experience in the areas: formal-description-techniques (ITU-T SDL/ASN.1 languages) in protocol specifications and validations; OMG's MDE-techniques for advanced systems development/testing for complex systems; protocol verifications for gprs/umts networks; network management; measurements and monitoring in IP-based networks; QoS and traffic engineering in IP-based networks (IntServ/RSVP, DiffServ, MPLS); self-healing in ATM networks, and ATM traffic monitoring analysis. He recently worked in ETSI-STF-276(Specialist Task Force) that produced ETSI-standardized-interoperability-test-specifications for IPv6 protocols, and EC-funded-FP6-ANA (Autonomic Network Architecture)-project. Past-projects include: Siemens-ICN & BMBF KING Project: KING = Key components for the mobile Internet of the Next Generation.

Omar Cherkaoui received the PhD degree in Computer Science from Université de Montréal in 1988. He is a Professor in the Department of Computer Science at Université du Québec à Montréal, which he joined in 1984. He has been involved in numerous research partnerships with the industry, including the CANARIE Consortium and Cisco Systems. He has co-authored more than 50 peer-reviewed technical publications and books, and two patent disclosures. His research interests include network management and optical networks. He is a member of the IEEE and the IEEE Communications Society. Dr. Cherkaoui is a member of the technical program committees of a dozen conferences, including IM 2003, DSOM 2005, ACON 2006, and AICT 2007 and 2008.

Christophoros Christophorou has completed his undergraduate and graduate studies at the University of Cyprus (B.Sc. in Computer Science and M.Sc. in Advanced Computer Technologies, 2002 and 2005, respectively). He is currently working towards his Ph.D. also at the University of Cyprus in the area of mobile networks. He is a Research Associate at the University of Cyprus since April 2004, for the IST/ICT funded B-BONE, MOTIVE, C-MOBILE, and C-CAST projects. His research interests include radio resource management in 3G and beyond mobile cellular networks, specifically capacity and performance enhancements through dynamic and adaptive radio resource allocation and handover algorithms.

Mariusz A. Fecko is currently Director & Senior Scientist at Applied Research, Telcordia Technologies, Inc., USA. Mariusz received M.S. degrees in both Electronics and Computer Science from AGH University of Science and Technology, Poland; and M.S. and Ph.D. in Computer and Information Sciences from the University of Delaware. He has served as Principal Investigator in the ARL CTA Program on Distributed Survivable Resource Control for Tactical Networks (DSRC-T), PEO STRI iNET Management and Operations with Policy Controls (iMANPOL), and ONR Dynamic Tactical Communications Networks (DTCN). Mariusz has led Telcordia team in developing Domain Area Planning Utility (DAPU) for mission network-level planning and supported DAPU transition to WIN-TNMS. He published 14 journal and over 40 conference papers and co-chaired the 18th IFIP Int'l Conf. Testing Communicating Systems (TestCom'06). Mariusz's main interests are in the optimization, diagnostics, autoconfiguration, service discovery, and automated planning for wireless networks.

Lavinia Ferariu is an Associate Professor with the Department of Automatic Control and Applied Informatics, of the "Gheorghe Asachi" Technical University of Iaşi, Romania. She obtained her M.Sc. in Computer and Control Engineering (1991) and Ph. D. in Automatic Control (2004) from the same university. She performed two doctoral research internships at the University of Duisburg - Essen and the University of Sheffield. She (co-)authored 27 journal papers, 36 conference papers, and 2 books. Her research activity includes sub-symbolic artificial intelligence, nonlinear identification, and intelligent control. Last results refer to multiobjective genetic programming for nonlinear system identification, genetic design of neural networks, and multiobjective evolutionary feature selection for image recognition.

Stathes Hadjiefthymiades received his B.Sc. (with honours) in Computer Science from the Department of Informatics at the University of Athens, Athens - Greece in 1993 and his M.Sc. (with honours) in Computer Science (Advanced Information Systems) from the same department in 1996. In 1999 he received his Ph.D. from the University of Athens (Department of Informatics and Telecommunications). In June 2002 he received a Joint Engineering-Economics M.Sc. degree from the National Technical University of Athens. Since 1992, he was with the Greek consulting firm Advanced Services Group, Ltd. (ASG, Ltd.), where he was extensively involved in the analysis and specification of information systems as well as the design and implementation of telematic applications. Since 1995, he has been a member of the Communication Networks Laboratory of the University of Athens. He has participated in numerous projects realised in the context of EU Programs (ACTS, ORA, TAP, INFO2000, IST) as well as National Initiatives (Telematique, RETEX, Mentor). During the period Sept.2001-Jul.2002 he served at the University of Aegean, Dept. of Information and Communication Systems Engineering as a visiting Assistant Professor. He joined the faculty of Hellenic Open University (Patras, Greece) on the summer of 2002 as an Assistant Professor (on Telecommunications and Computer Networks). Since December 2003 he belongs to the Faculty of the Department of Informatics and Telecommunications, University of Athens, where he is presently an Assistant Professor (on Large Scale Software Systems). His research interests are in the area of wireless/mobile/pervasive computing and networked multimedia applications. He is the author of over 100 publications, in international scientific journals, conferences, and books in the above areas.

Sylvain Hallé received the BS degree in mathematics from Université Laval in 2002 and the MSc in mathematics and PhD in computer science from Université du Québec à Montréal in 2004 and 2008, respectively. He is currently a postdoctoral Research Fellow at University of California, Santa Barbara. He received fellowships from the Natural Sciences and Engineering Research Council of Canada (NSERC) in 2005 and Quebec's Research Fund on Nature and Technologies (FQRNT) in 2008. His major research interests include Web applications and formal verification. He is a member of the ACM, the Association for Symbolic Logic, the IEEE, and the IEEE Computer Society. He was co-chair of DDBP 2008, TIME 2008, and DDBP 2009.

Ibrahim Hokelek is a Senior Research Scientist at Telcordia Technologies, Inc. He has over 10 years of R&D experience in wireless communication and computer networking. He holds a Ph.D. degree in Electrical Engineering from the Graduate Center, the City University of New York (CUNY), and M.Sc. and B.Sc. degrees in Electrical and Electronics Engineering from Bilkent University, Turkey. He received full scholarships during his undergraduate and M.S. studies at Bilkent. At CUNY, he worked as a Research Assistant at U.S. Army and National Science Foundation funded projects on mobile ad hoc networks (MANETs). At Telcordia, he has been working on unicast and multicast routing, wireless network emulation, and heterogeneous intelligent content-based filtering projects for CERDEC PILSNER, dynamic survivable resource pooling and data dissemination for ARL CTA, seamless soft handoff in MANETs and prediction techniques for CERDEC, and Dynamic Tactical Communication Network for Navy. Dr. Hokelek's research interests include multicast and unicast routing protocols for MANETs, distributed mobile robotics systems, content-based data dissemination, modeling and analysis of wireless MANETs, and traffic engineering and QoS in IP networks. He has over 30 publications in peer-reviewed networking journals and conferences and has been active in IETF standards activities in the Routing area WG.

Shinji Kikuchi is a Researcher at Fujitsu Laboratories Limited, Japan. Prior to this, he received an MS degree in Information Technologies from Nagoya University. His current research themes are autonomic computing and cloud computing management based on mathematical approaches such as formal verification methods and process mining. He is a member of the IEEE Communication Society and has been on the program committees of multiple international conferences on autonomic computing and complex information systems.

Marta Kwiatkowska is Professor of Computing Systems and Fellow of Trinity College, University of Oxford. Prior to this she held appointments at the Universities of Birmingham, Leicester and the Jagiellonian University in Cracow, Poland. Marta Kwiatkowska spearheaded the development of probabilistic and quantitative methods in verification on the international scene. The PRISM model checker (www.prismmodelchecker.org) developed under her leadership is the leading software tool in the area, cited 2000 times, and is widely used for research and teaching. Applications of probabilistic model checking have spanned communication and security protocols, dependability analysis, nanotechnology designs, power management, and systems biology. Kwiatkowska has been invited to speak at a number of leading conferences and summer schools, including the LICS 2003, ESEC/FSE 2007, and FASE/ETAPS 2011 conferences, and the ESSLLI 2010 and Marktoberdorf 2011 summer schools. Her research is currently supported by £3.7m of grant funding from EPSRC, EU, and ERC, including the recently awarded ERC Advanced Grant VERIWARE "From software verification to everyware verification."

Antonio Manzalini received his M.Sc. degree in Electronic Engineering at Politecnico of Torino. In 1990 he joined Telecom Italia Lab (formerly CSELT) starting with research activities on technologies and architectures for advanced transport (SDH, DWDM) and networking (IP, GMPL). In 1997-2000 he was Rapporteur in ITU-T. In 2000-2002, he was Project Leader the FP5 IST Project LION. In 2002-2004 he was Project Leader of the FP6 IST Integrated Project NOBEL. In 2003 he was appointed as member of the Scientific Committee of CTTC (Centre Tecnològic de Telecomunicacions de Catalunya). From 2006-2008 he was Project Leader of the FP6 Future Emerging Technology Project CASCADAS whose main goal is developing and demonstrating an architectural vision for autonomic ecosystems. In 2008 he was awarded with the International Certification of Project Manager by PMI. He has been awarded 5 patents on networking and services systems and methods. Currently he is joining the long term research activities of the Future Centre of Telecom Italia.

Roberto Minerva, Manager, was focal point for Long Term Research within the Future Center & Technical Communication Department of Telecom Italia. He held many responsibilities within Telecom Italia Lab, including: Network Intelligence, Wireless Architecture and Business Services Area Manager. Roberto has a Master's Degree in Computer Science. Since 1987 he has been involved in the development of Service Architectures for Telecom (TINA, OSA/Parlay and SIP), in activities related to IMS, and in the definition of services for the business market (context-awareness, ambient intelligence and automotive). He is author of several articles and has presented papers in international conferences and journals.

Corrado Moiso received his M.Sc degree "cum laude" in Computer Science at University of Torino in 1984; in the same year he joined Telecom Italia Lab (formerly CSELT). From 1984-1991, he studied parallel logic and functional languages. From 1990-1991, he investigated the applicability of constraint programming to traffic management. From 1990-1994, he investigated object-oriented distributed platforms and their application to TMN. Since 1994, he has been investigating the introduction of IT in network intelligence: he designed and experimented service platforms based on TINA, investigated Telco/Internet convergence, contributed to Parlay standardization for service exposure, and analysed SOA-based SDP platforms. Currently, in the context of the long term research activities of Telecom Italia Future Centre, he is studying the adoption in Telco infrastructures of decentralised architectures and autonomic technologies. He joined projects founded by EC and Eurescom. He is author of several papers, and he has been awarded 7 patents on services systems and methods.

Felicián Németh received his M.Sc degree in Computer Science from the Budapest University of Technology and Economics in 2000. Since then he is at the Department of Telecommunications and Media Informatics of the same university. His research interests include performance evaluation of traffic schedulers and congestion control methods.

Nikos Parlavantzas is an Associate Professor at INSA Rennes, France, and member of the INRIA Myriads research team since 2009. Before joining INSA Rennes, he was a Research Engineer in the INRIA Sardes team in Grenoble, France, where he contributed to the FP6 project Grid4All. His research interests include autonomic systems, cloud computing, peer-to-peer systems, and configurable, component-based middleware. He has a Diploma in Computer Engineering and Informatics from the University of Patras, Greece, and a Ph.D. and M.Sc. from Lancaster University, UK.

421

Alina Patelli is a Ph. D. student with the "Gheorghe Asachi" Technical University of Iaşi, Romania. She received her Bachelor's in Applied Informatics from the same university in 2008. She was granted with doctoral research internships at the Department of Automatic Control and Systems Engineering of the University of Sheffield. Her thesis is devoted to nonlinear system identification based on genetic programming techniques, using nonlinear linear in parameters formalism. She (co-)authored 4 journal papers and 7 conference papers. She was awarded second prize in the International Doctoral Consortium organized by IEEE International Conference on Networking, Sensing and Control, Chicago, USA, 2010.

Andreas Pitsillides, Computer Science Professor, University of Cyprus (UCY), Chairman of the Cyprus Research and Academic Network, heads the UCY Networks Research Lab. Research interests include fixed, mobile/wireless networks, control theory, nature inspired techniques, and computational intelligence. He has published over 200 refereed journal, conference papers, and book chapters. He is the co-editor with Petros Ioannou of the book Modelling and Control of Complex Systems, participated in over 20 European Commission and locally funded research projects (principal/co-principal investigator), serves on the editorial board of the *Journal of Computer Networks*, and served on executive committees of international conferences (e.g. INFOCOM, WiOpt, ISYC, MCCS, ICT).

Arun Prakash received his Bachelor's in Electronics and Communications Engineering from the University of Madras in 2004, and his Master's in Automation and Robotics from the Technische Universität Dortmund in 2008. During his studies he focused on telecommunications, networking, distributed systems, computer systems, optimization, and artificial intelligence. In addition, he worked as a Software Engineer at Caritor (Keane), India and at Nokia, Germany. Arun Prakash did his Bachelor thesis in the field of speech compression, and his Master thesis in the field of evolutionary algorithms. He currently works as a researcher at FOKUS Fraunhofer, Berlin and is pursuing his PhD from Technische Universität Berlin. His main research interests include modeling, routing and autonomicity of the future Internet, and the use of the formal description techniques in the design of the future Internet and its components.

Gábor Rétvári received the M.Sc. and Ph.D. degrees in electrical engineering from the Budapest University of Technology and Economics (BME), Budapest, Hungary in 1999 and 2007, respectively. He is now a Research Assistant at the Department of Telecommunications and Media Informatics, BME. His research interests include routing, traffic engineering, and the networking applications of computational geometry and network flow theory. He is an avid Perl hacker, maintaining numerous open source scientific tools written in Perl, C, and Haskell.

K. Chandra Sekaran is currently working as Professor in the department of Computer Engineering, NITK Surathkal, India. He has 23 years of teaching and research experience at NITK (formerly:KREC). He was the Head of the department of Computer Engineering and, also the Dept. of Information Technology. His areas of interest include: distributed computing, cloud computing, bio-inspired computing, and business computing. He has more than 100 publications in reputed, peer-reviewed journals and conferences of international repute.

Cem Safak Sahin received his B.S. degree from Gazi University, Turkey in 1996 and his M.S. degree from Middle East Technical University, Turkey in 2000, both in electrical engineering. He is currently a Ph.D. candidate at the City College and the Graduate Center of the City University of New York. His research interests include wireless ad hoc networks, genetic algorithms, bio-inspired computation, optimization, machine learning, autonomous systems, mathematical modeling and simulation, and electronic warfare systems. He was a Senior Software Engineer at Elanti Systems, a New Jersey based intelligent software applications company, until 2010. Prior to this, he was a Principal Engineer in Systems Design at Mikes, a Turkish defense contractor, from 2004 to 2008, and a Research and Development Engineer at Roketsan, a Turkish defense contractor, until 2004.

Jose Simoes graduated with distinction in Telecommunications and Computer Engineering in 2006 at Instituto Superior das Ciencias do Trabalho e da Empresa (ISCTE), Portugal. He also studied at Universidade Federal de Santa Catarina in Brazil. He has worked for Netcall (1st VoIP Provider in Portugal) as Network Engineer and Business Consultant. He is a Ph.D student at Technical University of Berlin and a research fellow at Fraunhofer Institute FOKUS for next generation network infrastructures. His current interests are user Quality of Experience (QoE) (personalization, contextualization, adaptation, mobility and interactivity) and advertising, focusing on architectures for next generation heterogeneous networks.

Elkin Urrea received his B.S. degree in Electronics Engineering from Santo Tomas University, Bogota, Colombia in 1998, and M.Sc. degree in Electrical Engineering from City College of New York, The City University of New York (CUNY) in 2002. He is currently a Ph.D. candidate at the Graduate Center, CUNY. His interests include wireless mobile ad hoc networks, distributed mobile robotics, and communication networks.

M. Umit Uyar is a Professor in the Electrical Engineering Department at the City College of New York, and at the Computer Science Department of the Graduate Center at the City University of New York. Prior to joining to CCNY, he was a Distinguished Member of Technical Staff at AT&T Bell Labs. He holds Ph.D. and M.S. degrees from Cornell University, and a B.S. degree from Istanbul Technical University, all in Electrical Engineering. Prof. Uyar's research interests include design and implementation of bio-inspired algorithms for robotics applications, telecommunication network protocols design, testing and verification, mobile ad hoc networks design, VoIP (SIP, H.323) applications specification, design, verification, hardware and software verification tool development in C++, C#, VB.Net, and JAVA. In academia, Prof. Uyar received grants from the US Army for research on interoperability and survivability of mobile combat networks and from the National Science Foundation for building robotic controllers. He is author/co-author of more than 100 reviewed technical articles, holds three US patents, received three AT&T Bell Labs Vice Presidential Research Appreciation Awards, and a AT&T Bell Labs Vice Presidential Quality Award.

Emil Vassev received his M.Sc. in Computer Science (2005) and his Ph.D. in Computer Science (2008) from Concordia University, Montreal, Canada. His current research focus is ASSL (Autonomic System Specification Language), a framework dedicated to autonomic computing development that addresses the problem of formal specification and code generation of autonomic systems. In 2008, to continue his research on ASSL, Dr. Vassev was awarded a highly competitive IRCSET Postdoctoral

Fellowship at UCD (University College Dublin), Ireland. A part from the main research, Dr. Vassev's research interests include engineering autonomic systems, distributed computing, formal methods, software engineering, programming languages, operating systems, and compilers. He published 2 theses, each inspiring a book (both published by Lap Lambert Publishing, Germany in 2009). In addition, Dr. Vassev has published over 60 internationally peer-reviewed publications including: journal papers, book chapters, and conference and workshop papers. Dr. Vassev holds a US Patent on *Method of Improving System Performance and Survivability through Self-sacrifice* filed with NASA. Dr. Vassev has been a member of IEEE since 2008. He holds a few software engineering certifications including MCSD (Microsoft Certified Solution Developer - 2001).

Harish S. Venkatarama is currently working as Reader in the department of Computer Science & Engineering, Manipal Institute of Technology, Manipal, India. He has total of 20 years teaching experience, which includes 9 years at JNN College of Engineering, Shimoga, India and 11 years at MIT, Manipal. He is working toward his PhD in the field of Autonomic Computing. He is a research scholar in the Dept. of Computer Engineering, National Institute of Technology – Karnataka, Surathkal, India. He has a number of publications in international journals, as well as International and National conferences.

Bruno Vidalenc received his Engineering diploma from the Telecom SudParis in 2007 after a B.Sc degree in Computer Science from the University Paris-Sud XI in 2004. Since 2008, he is a PhD student at Institute Telecom SudParis working full time in the Networking and Networks domain at Alcatel-Lucent Bell Labs France. His PhD focuses on proactive mechanisms to help fault-management systems to anticipate failure. His research interests are on autonomic networking, fault-management, self-healing techniques, and failure prediction. He is currently involved in the FP7 EFIPSANS project working with proactive fault-management.

Roger Villemaire received the PhD degree from the University of Tübingen in 1988. He was a postdoctoral Fellow at McGill University and later at Université du Québec à Montréal (UQAM). He is a Professor in the Department of Computer Science at UQAM, which he joined in 1993. His research interests include applications of logic in computer science, in particular formalisms, methods, and algorithms which can help to realize reliable computing systems. He was co-chair of TIME 2008 and served on its program committee in 2009. He is a member of the ACM, the Association for Symbolic Logic, and the IEEE Computer Society.

Vladimir Vlassov is an Associate Professor in Computer Systems at the Royal Institute of Technology (KTH), Stockholm, Sweden. He received the Ph.D. in Computer Science from the St. Petersburg's Electrotechnical University (LETI), Russia, in 1984. Prior coming to KTH, he was an Assistant and Associate Professor at LETI (1985-1993). He was a visiting scientist at the University of Massachusetts Amherst (2004) and at Massachusetts Institute of Technology (MIT), USA (1998). His current research interests include autonomic computing, distributed and parallel computing (including Peer-2-Peer, Grid and Cloud computing), programming environments, performance modeling, and evaluation. He participates and has participated in a number of European research projects such as ENCORE (FP7), Grid4All (FP6), SELFMAN (FP6), CoreGRID (FP6), and PEPITO (FP5), and in a number of projects funded by Swedish funding agencies and NSF USA.

Michał Wódczak is a Senior Research Scientist and Program Manager at Telcordia Poland. He obtained M.Sc. degree in Telecommunications and Ph.D. degree in Wireless Communications Systems from Poznan University of Technology, Poland in 2001 and 2006 respectively. Currently Michal Wodczak participates in standardization activities as a Vice Chairman of the ETSI Industry Specification Group on autonomic network engineering for self-managing future Internet (ETSI ISG AFI). He is also involved in the area of autonomic networking in INFSO-ICT-215549 project EFIPSANS. Prior to that, he was with a telecommunications company where he was responsible for the technology for optical fiber termination and then he became a Research Expert at Poznan University of Technology where he worked in IST-2003-507581 WINNER and IST-4-027756 WINNER II projects on the topic of cooperative relaying in 4G systems. Michal Wodczak was also the Editor-in-Chief of the NEWCOM Newsletter in IST-2004-507325 Network of Excellence in Wireless Communications (NEWCOM(, and he has published in conference and journal papers, as well as in book chapters.

426

Index